HENRY RAEBURN

HENRY RAEBURN

Context, Reception and Reputation

EDITED BY

VICCY COLTMAN AND STEPHEN LLOYD

EDINBURGH
University Press

Edinburgh University Press is one of the leading university presses in the UK. We publish academic books and journals in our selected subject areas across the humanities and social sciences, combining cutting-edge scholarship with high editorial and production values to produce academic works of lasting importance. For more information visit our website: edinburghuniversitypress.com

Edinburgh University Press Ltd
The Tun – Holyrood Road
12(2f) Jackson's Entry
Edinburgh EH8 8PJ

Typeset in 11/13.5 Goudy Oldstyle by
Servis Filmsetting Ltd, Stockport, Cheshire, and
printed and bound by CPI Group (UK) Ltd, Croydon, CR0 4YY

A CIP record for this book is available from the British Library

ISBN 978 0 7486 5483 3 (paperback)

Published with the support of the Edinburgh University
Scholarly Publishing Initiatives Fund.

Contents

PART II   RECEPTION

PART III   REPUTATION

Figures

Abbreviations

BM   British Museum, London
BOD   Bodleian Library, University of Oxford
HA   Hamilton Archive, Lennoxlove, East Lothian
HTHL   Hamilton Town House Library, Hamilton, Lanarkshire
NA   National Archives, Kew, London
NAS   National Archives of Scotland, Edinburgh
NGS   National Galleries of Scotland
NLS   National Library of Scotland, Edinburgh
NMS   National Museums Scotland
NPG   National Portrait Gallery, London
NRAS   National Register of Archives of Scotland
NRS   National Records of Scotland, Edinburgh
NT   National Trust for England, Wales and Northern Ireland
NTS   National Trust for Scotland
NYPL   New York Public Library
RA   Royal Academy of Arts, London
RSA   Royal Scottish Academy, Edinburgh
SNG   Scottish National Gallery, Edinburgh
SNPG   Scottish National Portrait Gallery, Edinburgh
VAM   Victoria and Albert Museum, London

Foreword

Viccy Coltman and Stephen Lloyd

Outside Scotland Raeburn rarely makes more than an episodic appearance in survey exhibitions and has an uneven presence in books about portraiture. In spite of Sir Henry Raeburn being currently thought of as the 'in-house' portrait painter to members of the Scottish Enlightenment, a review in *The Burlington Magazine* of the most recent major Raeburn exhibition, held in Edinburgh and London during 1997–8, noted that 'it wears the aspect of closure rather than a new dawn' in Raeburn studies, with the artist being shown in 'solitary splendour'. However, interest in Raeburn was highlighted again in 2005 when *The Burlington Magazine* published Stephen Lloyd's article, '"Elegant and graceful attitudes": the painter of the "Skating Minister"', which argued the case for a change of attribution of the famous sporting picture of *The Revd Robert Walker ('The Skating Minister')* from Raeburn, Edinburgh's foremost portrait painter, to the versatile but little-known French émigré artist, Henri-Pierre Danloux. The ensuing controversy became a *cause célèbre*, which shed much light on the current reception and reputation of Raeburn. The question of the attribution of this unusual painting, which for better or worse has become an icon of the National Galleries of Scotland, remains in play. It will be instructive to see how this debate is able to be resolved – probably through consensus via archival discovery or technical analysis – and to what degree this discussion affects our understanding of Raeburn's artistic reputation. By finally removing this atypical cabinet picture from Raeburn's *oeuvre*, there is no doubt that much greater clarity – and less confusion – will be placed on his achievement as a painter and portraitist.

This volume seeks to recover Raeburn from his artistic isolation, by looking at his contexts in Scotland, Britain, and abroad, notably in France and the United States. It also analyses his critical reception and international legacy, both in his lifetime and posthumously. It focuses as much on

Edinburgh and London as on metropolitan markets and cosmopolitan contexts. Previously unpublished archival material is brought to light especially from the Innes of Stow papers and the archives of the dukes of Hamilton. The contributors, many of them writing on Raeburn for the first time, examine different aspects of the artist's career and legacy, through interdisciplinary perspectives, and in doing so, it is hoped that a new agenda for studies on the painter will be set. Traditional modes of art historical analysis are integrated with cultural, social, political and economic history.

The volume has a strong historiographical bent, due to the whole series of publications and exhibitions that were published and organised about the artist in Edinburgh, London and Paris between the 1870s and the 1930s, notably with monographs by Sir Walter Armstrong, *Sir Henry Raeburn* (1901), James L. Caw, *Raeburn* (1909) and James Greig, *Sir Henry Raeburn, R.A., his life and works, with a catalogue of his pictures* (1911). History of art as a discipline has advanced considerably since the early twentieth century as witnessed in these monographic publications. While recognising the excellent historiographical tradition of monographs devoted to Raeburn's life and art, this volume does not focus on stylistic discussion but on a rigorous examination of histories of art, society, politics, leisure and taste.

Nor will this book seek to engage with traditional art historical issues, such as the chronological dating of Raeburn's canvases – the so-called early, middle, and later years – which is notoriously difficult to do for Raeburn in light of the absence of the artist's sitters' and account books; it will deal with his visit to Rome only in passing, since this is barely documented. A complete catalogue of Raeburn's portraits is being prepared for publication by the Paul Mellon Centre for Studies in British Art and Yale University Press, so contributors here have avoided catalogue-type discussions and judgments of connoisseurship in favour of a more robust, critical volume.

This book draws on a conference, 'Henry Raeburn: critical reception and international reputation', held on 10 and 11 November 2006 to mark the 250th anniversary of the artist's birth in Edinburgh, which was co-organised by the editors of this volume. However new essays have been commissioned from the historian Stana Nenadic, established art historians Robyn Asleson, Matthew Craske and Nicholas Tromans, as well as from the emerging scholar Jordan Mearns. Also in 2006 the editors co-curated an exhibition, *Henry Raeburn and his Printmakers*, held at the Talbot Rice Art Gallery, University of Edinburgh, which was a partnership project between the National Galleries of Scotland and Edinburgh University. An exhibition catalogue was published with an introductory essay by the editors, 'Henry Raeburn: "Portrait painter in Edinburgh"', and a principal essay by David Alexander, 'Henry Raeburn and his printmakers'.

The 2006 conference was organised by the Scottish National Portrait Gallery and the Department of History of Art at the University of Edinburgh, and held at the Hawthornden Lecture Theatre in the Weston Link below the National Gallery of Scotland. The symposium was kindly supported by the Paul Mellon Centre for Studies in British Art, London, together with logistical support from the School of Arts, Culture, and Environment at the University of Edinburgh. The keynote lecture and the two main conference sessions were chaired by John Leighton, Professor Duncan Macmillan and Professor Murdo Macdonald respectively. The distinguished late art historian Robert Rosenblum, Professor at the Institute of Fine Arts, University of New York, had agreed to give the keynote address to open the conference with a lecture on 'Raeburn's portraiture: an international perspective'. However, due to what was to prove to be his final illness, he was not able to give his paper as planned. Fortunately, Dr Duncan Thomson, former Keeper of the Scottish National Portrait Gallery, and organiser of the major exhibition on Raeburn held in Edinburgh and London during 1997–8, presented a stimulating keynote address at very short notice on 'Raeburn: a decade of experiment', discussing the artist's pictorial style, in terms of his original use of light and shadow, during the 1790s.

Acknowledgements

The publication of this volume, and in particular the defraying of the costs for the colour illustrations and reproductions, has been most generously supported by grants from the Paul Mellon Centre for Studies in British Art, the John R. Murray Charitable Trust, the Marc Fitch Fund, the Binks Trust and the Carnegie Trust for the Universities of Scotland, to all of whom the editors are immensely grateful. We would also like to thank the various public institutions and private collections that have either generously waived their normal illustration fees or have reduced them substantially for reproducing images of artworks held by them, on account of the academic nature of this volume. The editors are also grateful to John Watson, Commissioning Editor at Edinburgh University Press for agreeing to recommend the publication of this book, and also to the two anonymous readers, whose comments helped in the final shaping of the volume. Sincere thanks for their assistance in many ways are also due to Brian Allen, Alan Bell, Dave Brown, Jenny Brown, Christopher Catling, John Dick, Sir Gerald Elliot, Jackie Gray, Philip Hunt, Murdo Macdonald, Duncan Macmillan, David Mannings, John Murray, Virginia Murray, the late Elaine Paintin, Mary Peskett-Smith, Martin Postle, David Solkin, Christine Thompson and Brenda Woods. John Watson and his colleagues at EUP have shepherded this volume through the production process to publication. Stephen Lloyd would like to thank Alice Thompson for her sage advice, patience and per-spective during the gestation of this book. Viccy Coltman would like to thank Stanley Wynd for his kindness, good humour and wise counsel, which she promises to listen to next time!

I

Introduction
'Indiscriminate praise is little better than censure': Critical Contexts for Understanding Raeburn's Portraiture

Stephen Lloyd

Raeburn's sudden death on 8 July 1823 at his home, St Bernard's in Stockbridge on the edge of Edinburgh's New Town, was marked by a number of obituaries (Fig. 1.1). Typical among them was a tribute by an anonymous author, assessing Raeburn's generous character as a man and pre-eminence as an artist, which was published during November that year in *The European Magazine and London Review*.[1] Initially, the writer delivered the customary eulogy for the recently deceased artist and his portraits, noting:

> The first impression made on the spectator of his pictures was by the striking effect of his head. They were drawn and painted in a style original, and exclusively his own; broad, square, firm; clear and brilliant in colour; surprisingly powerful in light and shade, and chiaro-scuro. He appeared to possess the rare, and in a portrait painter, the inestimable faculty of pourtraying intellectual expression, and dignity of demeanour, whenever they appeared in his subjects; and in fact he often approached in his portraits to the elevation of historical painting.

The anonymous obituarist concluded this opening passage by observing that 'indiscriminate praise is little better than censure'. The writer then proceeded to refer to various earlier criticisms of Raeburn's exhibited work at the Royal Academy and how in the final display of them there earlier that

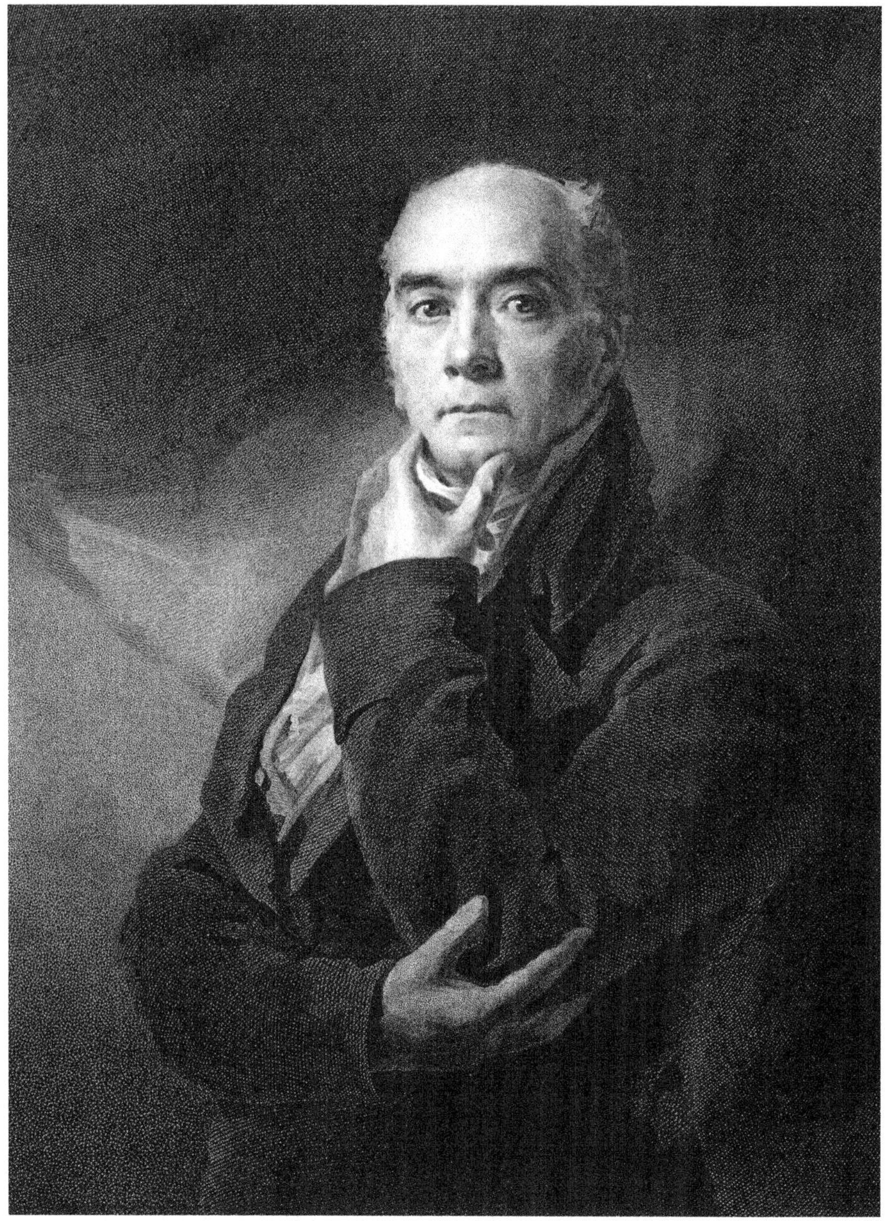

Figure 1.1 William Walker after Henry Raeburn, *Sir Henry Raeburn R.A., Painter to His Majesty for Scotland, Fellow of the Royal Society of Edinburgh*, 1826, stipple, published by the engraver in Edinburgh and London, 37.8×27.4cm, Scottish National Portrait Gallery, Edinburgh

summer, his paintings had 'evinced more harmony of colour, more scientific display, and a better arrangement of the whole'. The critic then continued by re-stating the strengths of the British school – 'the variety of our styles' – in advantageous contrast to that of France, owing 'in a great measure, to that boldness, and independence of national character resulting from the free and liberal institutions of our country'. The author confirmed this point about the variety of British artists as analogous to a painter's palette, but where Raeburn's had an occasional predominance of black and green. The writer then concluded by listing the portraitist's most significant honours, not just as a Royal Academician, his knighthood and appointment as 'Portrait Painter in Scotland to his Majesty'; but also his membership of the Royal Society of Edinburgh, the Academy at Florence and the recently founded Academy of New York. This introduction sets out the themes of the various essays that elaborate on various points made in Raeburn's obituary: providing critical contexts for the artist within Scottish society and the British art world, alongside key elements of his reception and legacy, both national and international.

The context, reception and reputation of Henry Raeburn can be understood, not just through an analysis of the artist and his studio with the prolific production of around 1,000 canvases, alongside the patchy documentary and archival record of the portraitist's life and career, but also though the critical contemporary literature and later historiography on the artist. Raeburn's reception and reputation have simultaneously been defined by the availability and performance of his paintings when presented on the international art market, predominantly through the auction houses and art dealers centred in London, and to a lesser degree via those businesses based in Scotland, Paris and New York. This context encompasses a number of key phases. Firstly, there are the critical responses to Raeburn in Edinburgh and London during his lifetime. This was followed by a fifty-year-long period immediately after his death, when a number of tributes and reminiscences were published but also when the market lowered its value of the artist's paintings. There was a revival of the art market for Raeburn's work and a closely linked resurgence of interest in the artist from art historians after the spectacular exhibition on the artist held in Edinburgh and London during 1876–7 and also in 1877 with the London auction of the Raeburn family's collection of pictures. There followed an explosion of market worth for the artist's pictures and new reproductive engravings between 1890 and 1930, alongside the appearance of numerous monographic publications. Raeburn's paintings became a key element in the international art trade, the so-called 'Duveen' taste, between Britain, France and North America. This peak of interest in the artist's work can be witnessed in the monographic exhibition of thirty pictures, organised by The French Gallery of Pall Mall in London, for which an accompanying catalogue was printed with enthusiastic reviews from across the British Press together with installation shots of the symmetrical displays of the paintings hung under draped fabric (Fig. 1.2).[2] The economic depression that followed the Great Crash of 1929 hit the British sector of the transatlantic art market severely, and the prices for Raeburn's portraits and prints declined substantially. The early post-World War II period witnessed a low ebb of the market value for the artist's works, alongside a reformulation of Raeburn's reputation, which was focused on the re-emergence of the small cabinet picture depicting *The Revd Robert Walker ('The Skating Minister')*, acquired by the National Gallery of Scotland at a London auction in 1949, and whose attribution to Edinburgh's foremost portrait painter was questioned controversially by Lloyd in 2005.

The last twenty-five years has witnessed the paradox of the continual de-accessioning, usually at auction, by American museums of Raeburn's lesser works. At the same time this period has seen the acquisition of a number of Raeburn's most important works by key international public collections. These include the bequest by Sir Alfred Lane Beit to the National Gallery of Ireland, Dublin, of the 1792 masterpiece, *Sir John and Lady Clerk of Penicuik* (Fig. 7.4); the purchase by the Musée du Louvre of the late full-length *Major James Lee Harvey* (Fig. 13.6); the Kimbell Art Museum in Forth Worth, Texas, buying *The Allen Brothers*, painted in the early 1790s; and the National Gallery, London, acquiring under the Acceptance-in-lieu procedure *The Ferguson Brothers ('The Archers')*, executed in c. 1789–90 (Fig. 2.2).

Raeburn's finest portraiture has not only been appreciated again by the international art market and acquired by some of the world's leading art museums, but it has been included in recent scholarly exhibitions. Again over the last quarter century, Raeburn's work has been discussed regularly in surveys of British art and portraiture of the period, and his paintings have been included in a number of major survey exhibitions, with a resultant set of mixed emphases. In his study of the meaning and purpose of British portraiture, *The Georgians: Portraiture and Society* (London, 1990), Desmond Shawe-Taylor discussed six of Raeburn's pictures, with an emphasis on his portraits of women and children. John Wilson in his survey of 'The Romantics 1790–1830', a chapter in *The British Portrait, 1660–1960* (Woodbridge, 1991), paid relatively little attention to Raeburn, when compared to the greater emphasis he placed on his English contemporaries, John Hoppner, William Beechey and Thomas Lawrence. However, in the Tate Gallery's exhibition *The Swagger Portrait: Grand Manner Portraiture in Britain from Van Dyck to Augustus John, 1630–1930* (London, 1992–3), Raeburn was given a strong focus in the selection of pictures, almost equal to that of Joshua Reynolds,

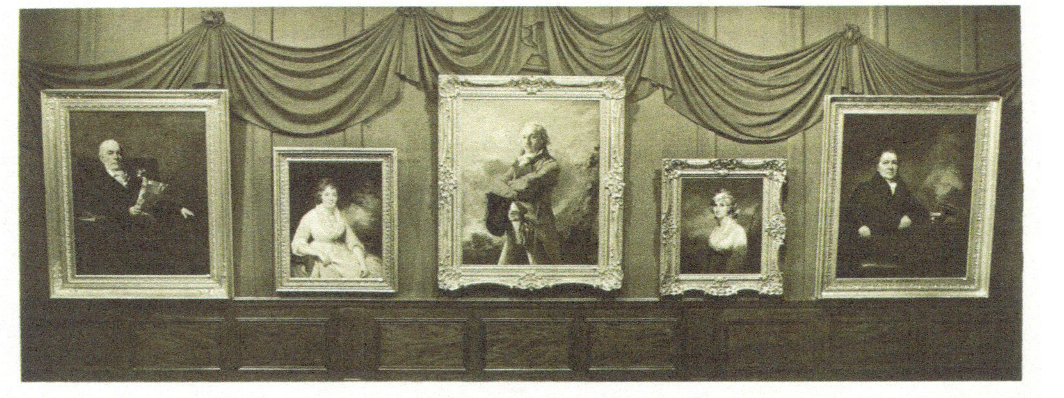
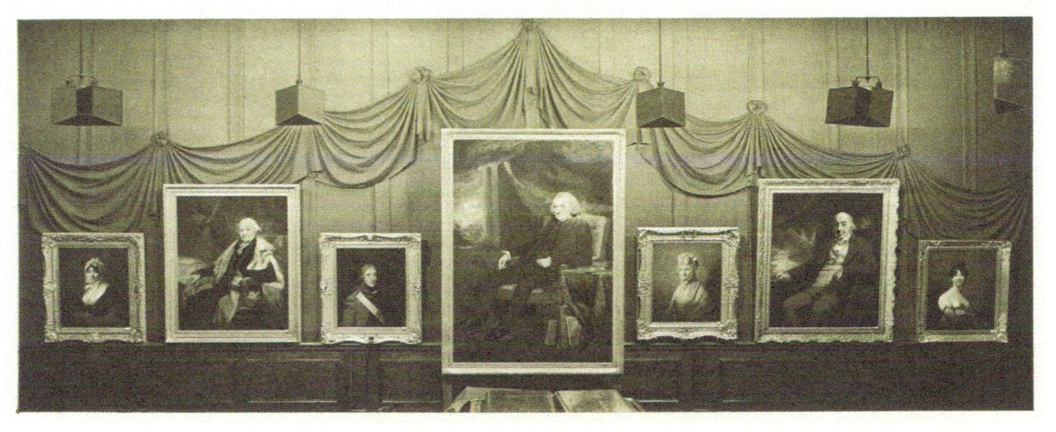

Figure 1.2 Unknown photographer, 'The Raeburn Exhibition', from James Greig, *Pictures by Sir Henry Raeburn, R.A.: the one hundredth exhibition at The French Gallery, 120 Pall Mall*, London 1911 (courtesy of Edinburgh City Libraries)

Thomas Gainsborough and Lawrence. In the exhibition and catalogue *The New Child: British Art and the Origins of Modern Childhood, 1730–1830* (University Art Museum, Berkeley, 1995), two of Raeburn's paintings were selected and discussed: his sentimental Royal Academy diploma piece, *Henry Raeburn Inglis ('Boy and Rabbit')* (RA, London) (Fig. 7.6) and the affectionate *John Tait and his Grandson* (National Gallery of Art, Washington, DC). In 2007 *Henry Raeburn Inglis ('Boy and Rabbit')* and the *Allen Brothers* were key loans to another more contextual exhibition on the portrayal of youth: *The Changing Face of Childhood: British Children's Portraits and their Influence in Europe*, organised by the Dulwich Picture Gallery in London and the Städel Museum in Frankfurt.

In 2001, the seminal exhibition *Art on the Line: The Royal Academy Exhibitions at Somerset House 1780–1836* attempted to recreate the crowded hang of pictures in the top-lit Great Room of the Royal Academy at Somerset House in London. Rather surprisingly, given how regularly Raeburn exhibited at the Academy every year from 1809 until his death in 1823, only two of his paintings were displayed: *Walter Scott* (Buccleuch Collection) (Fig. 7.1), which had originally been exhibited at the Academy in 1810, and the artist's diploma piece *Henry Raeburn Inglis ('Boy and Rabbit')* (RA, London), which had been shown there first in 1816. It was unfortunate that the selectors were not able to include one of the artist's full-length tartan portraits, such as *Francis MacNab* (Diageo plc) (Fig. 7.2), that had made such an impact when exhibited originally. As Thomas Lawrence noted admiringly, 'his portrait of Highlander MacNab, is the best representation of a human being that I ever saw. Mr Raeburn's style is freedom itself'.[3] In the 2001 exhibition at Somerset House, far greater attention was paid by the selectors, in the number of works shown, to other London-based artists of the period, namely Reynolds, Gainsborough, De Loutherbourg, Fuseli, Lawrence, Wilkie and Turner. The relatively modest impact made by Raeburn in the 2001 exhibition placed him alongside his lesser English contemporaries: Hoppner, Beechey, Owen and Phillips.

In 2005 Raeburn was seen, for once outside a narrowly Scottish or exclusively British context, when three of finest works – *James Hutton* (SNPG, Edinburgh), *Sir John and Lady Clerk of Penicuik* (National Gallery of Ireland, Dublin) and the late equestrian full-length *Major William Clunes* (SNG, Edinburgh) – were included in the exhibition *Citizens and Kings: Portraits in the Age of Revolution 1760–1830*, curated by Robert Rosenblum and held at the Grand Palais, Paris, and the Royal Academy, London, in 2006–7. There, Raeburn's portraits held their own among the greatest of his British, European and American peers, including Reynolds, Gilbert Stuart, David, Goya and Lawrence.

The last quarter-century has also seen the publication by American museums of a number of significant groups of Raeburn portraits that have added greatly to our knowledge of his work now in the United States. Notable among these critical and systematic museum catalogues have been Richard Dorment's *British Painting in the Philadelphia Museum of Art: from the seventeenth through the nineteenth century* (Philadelphia, 1986); John Hayes's editing of the catalogue of *British Paintings in the National Gallery of Art* (Washington DC, 1993); the publication by various curators of *French and British Paintings from 1600 to 1800 in the Art Institute of Chicago: a catalogue of the collection* (Chicago, 1996); Robyn Asleson and Shelley M. Bennett, *British Paintings at The Huntington* (San Marino, 2001); and Katharine Baetjer, *British Paintings in The Metropolitan Museum of Art, 1575–1875* (New York, 2009).

As to the surprisingly little-known holdings of Raeburn's portraiture in Scottish public collections, colour images are increasingly being made available on the 'Your Paintings' section of the BBC's website, which has been organised since 2003 by the Public Catalogue Foundation (PCF), as part of their admirable UK-wide photographic campaign to make available on their website images of all paintings in public collections. Already the collection of Raeburn portraits belonging to Glasgow Museums – hitherto mostly in storage – and those belonging to Aberdeen Art Gallery are available for consultation on-line. The photography and preparation of the collections of oil paintings belonging to the National Trust for Scotland – notably the thirteen portraits by Raeburn at Fyvie Castle in Aberdeenshire – are well under way, and also for the Edinburgh collections at the City Art Centre and in other civic and educational bodies such as the University of Edinburgh, where in the 'Raeburn Room' of Old College six of the artist's portraits of seated academics have been displayed together since the 1880s (Fig. 1.3).[4] The substantial collections of paintings by Raeburn belonging to the National Galleries of Scotland at the Scottish National Gallery (around 35 works) and the recently refurbished Scottish National Portrait Gallery (around 30 works) – many of which are on long-term loan to Duff House in Aberdeenshire and Paxton House in the Scottish Borders – are also about to be prepared for inclusion on the PCF and 'Your Paintings' websites. This application of new technology to the photography of works by Raeburn will greatly increase access to and awareness of the artist's production. However, there is still a need for Scotland's public museums to research, write and publish – whether in print or online – critical and systematic catalogues of their paintings, including those by Raeburn. A major critical catalogue of British paintings in the collection of the Scottish National Gallery is well under way and its future publication is greatly to be welcomed. Likewise, it is very much to be hoped that a much-needed systematic catalogue of the

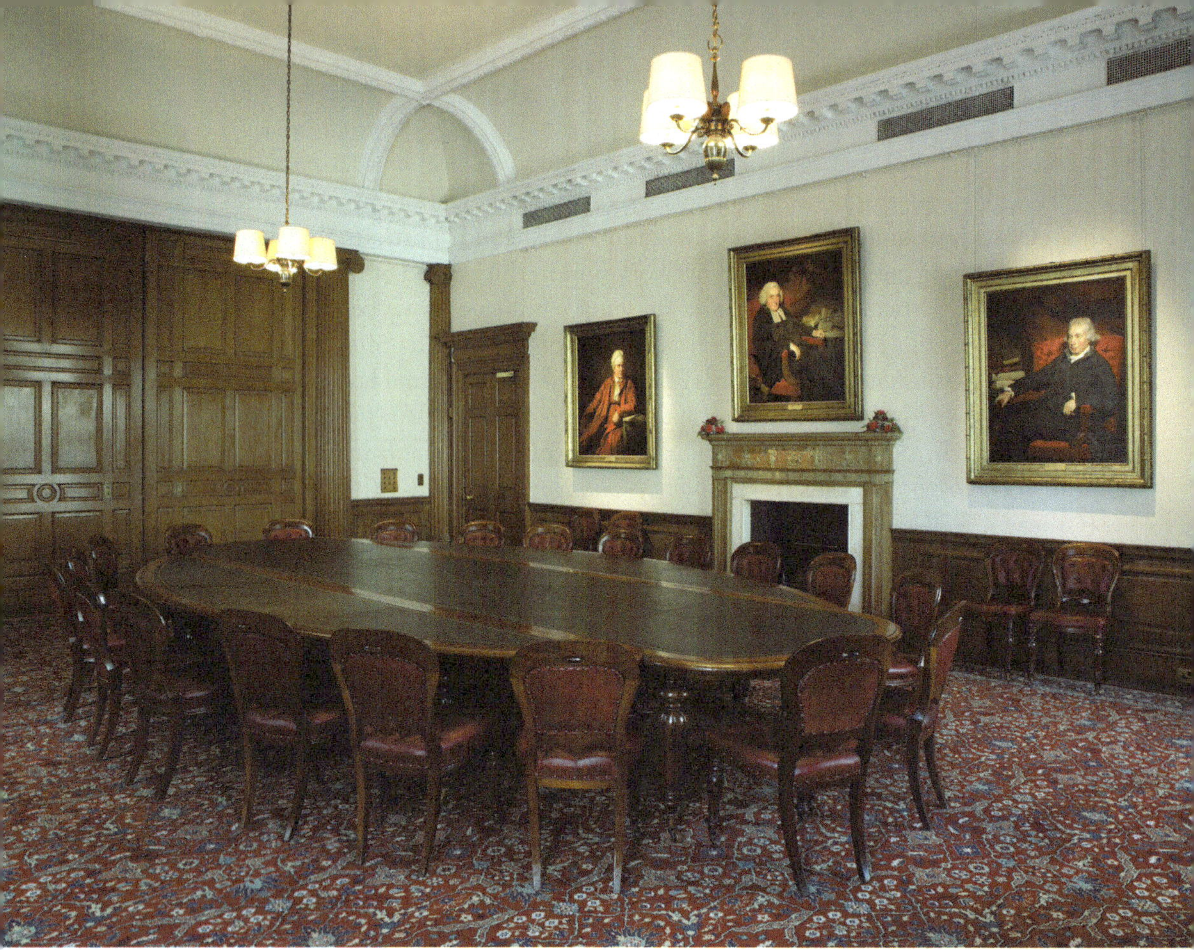

Figure 1.3 The Raeburn Room, Old College, University of Edinburgh, 2006
(courtesy of the University of Edinburgh)

collections in the Scottish National Portrait Gallery will be commissioned
in the near future. At the moment the whole group of paintings by Raeburn
in Scotland's two national collections remains relatively under-researched,
inadequately published and thus of limited public and scholarly accessibility.

Within the interwoven contextual narrative of reception, criticism, reputation, taste, collecting and the art market, this introduction presents the
volume's sequence of chapters that are signified by the interests and arguments of the contributors. This international group of art historians – from
Scotland, England, France and the USA – is drawn from both the academic
and curatorial worlds, and includes interventions from established scholars
– and an early career scholar – working on the late eighteenth and early
nineteenth-century European and North American art world but who have
often not written specifically on Raeburn before.

The first five chapters examine issues arising from the matrix of contemporary contexts within which Raeburn operated. In his opening chapter 'I

cannot coin money for them': Raeburn in the Nexus of Patronage, the Art Market and Global Trade, Stephen Lloyd sheds light on Henry Raeburn's career as a portrait painter and businessman in Edinburgh. His portrait practice was operational for nearly forty years around 1800, when the city was the hub of a highly developed culture and society, and simultaneously when the nearby port of Leith was a nodal point of global trade: with ships sailing to North America with timber, to the West Indies for sugar and rum, to the ports based around the North Sea and in the Baltic, and also to the recently founded settlements in Australia. By examining newly discovered letters among the papers of the powerful banker Gilbert Innes of Stow (1751–1832), as well as investigating the archives of the two principal Scottish banks, Raeburn's activities as a businessman – and those of his family concern, Henry Raeburn & Co. – can be seen within the nexus of the art market and patterns of patronage that promoted an exceptionally talented and sociable artist in Edinburgh. The Innes papers shed light for the first time on Raeburn's collecting of a small group of Old Master paintings and reveal he was prepared to restore them himself and offer them as gifts to close friends in times of his own need. Raeburn's career as an artist was promoted and sustained by the support of a number of influential Edinburgh figures, such as the banker Innes and the physician Andrew Duncan senior (1744–1828), whose relationship with the painter was vital both as a friend and as a go-between or fixer for portrait commissions. This chapter also considers the role of Edinburgh institutions, such as the University, the Royal Company of Archers and one of the two main Edinburgh-based banks, in maintaining Raeburn's career as a painter and businessman. This dual activity can also be seen as exemplary of the risky economic opportunities and vicissitudes that initially brought prosperity to, but then destroyed his own family's Leith-based business in shipping and the West India trade, a situation that led directly to the collapse of the Henry Raeburn & Co. in 1807 and the ensuing bankruptcy of the artist himself in the following year.

In 1997, the National Galleries of Scotland mounted the first major exhibition on Raeburn since 1956. Among the exhibits drawn from the Galleries' unparalleled holdings was his definitive self-portrait of c. 1815, intended as his diploma piece for the Royal Academy; and an exquisite marble bust of Raeburn – *all' antico* – that was completed by the Scottish neoclassical figure and portrait sculptor Thomas Campbell (1791–1858) in Rome in 1822. Previously undocumented, although one of Campbell's most accomplished early works, this bust has always been described as a derivative likeness dependent upon Raeburn's own self-portrait. In her chapter Scotland's Canova and the Immortal Raeburn, Helen E. Smailes presents new research based on Campbell's correspondence with his most committed and visionary patron – Gilbert Innes, Depute Governor of the Royal Bank of Scotland and the richest commoner in Scotland. This research has revealed that the bust was actually modelled from life in Edinburgh in 1818 as a commission from the sitter. Innes himself, who was acquainted with Raeburn by 1808, probably brokered his protégé's introduction to Scotland's premier portrait painter, who was well known for his exemplary generosity towards younger artists. While apprenticed as an Edinburgh monumental mason, Campbell secured Innes's patronage in or about 1815 and within two years became the beneficiary of a loan scheme facilitating study at the Royal Academy Schools in London and, from 1819, a ten-year sojourn in Rome. The presence of *modelli* of busts of Campbell's celebrity sitters Raeburn and Innes in his Roman studio, awaiting translation to statuary marble, was integral to the aspiring sculptor's stratagem for self-advancement. Discussion of the Raeburn bust is contextualised in a wider review of the critical importance of this Roman interlude in developing Campbell's ambition to challenge the prevailing English hegemony in public sculpture in Scotland and to become the sculptural heir-presumptive to Canova through the patronage of the 6th Duke of Devonshire.

Based on unpublished archival research, Godfrey Evans's chapter In the Shadow of Jacques-Louis David's *Napoleon*: The 10th Duke of Hamilton and Raeburn provides a novel account of the artist's full-length portrait of the aristocratic collector Alexander, 10th Duke of Hamilton (1767–1852). Placing the commission in the context of the major spending spree associated with the then Marquis of Douglas and Clydesdale's marriage to Susan Euphemia Beckford, the daughter of the celebrated collector William Beckford, in 1810, he proceeds to connect it with the completion of a tapestry of the Empress Catherine the Great by the Imperial Tapestry Factory in St Petersburg in May 1811 and the ordering and execution of Jacques-Louis David's great full-length portrait of *The Emperor Napoleon in his Study at the Tuileries* (now in the National Gallery of Art, Washington, DC) between August 1811 and September 1812.

Evans's discussion reveals that the premier peer of Scotland refused to attend the necessary later sittings for the Raeburn portrait and regarded Scotland's leading portrait-painter's broad-brush treatment as much inferior to David's very carefully composed, detailed and meticulously finished, brilliant propaganda portrait of Napoleon. He establishes that Raeburn almost managed to complete the portrait of the Duke, on his own initiative and without any help from the sitter, in the spring of 1823, and that the 10th Duke contested Raeburn's son's charge of 350 guineas and did not agree to Raeburn junior's well-written and flattering request for permission to display the portrait in the posthumous Raeburn exhibition, which was held in Edinburgh during March 1824. Evans concludes by showing that the Raeburn portrait was superseded by Henry William Pickersgill's embarrassingly florid full-length portrait of the 10th Duke after he became a Knight of the Garter in 1836. It was this portrait that was displayed in the 120-foot-long Gallery of Hamilton Palace, while Raeburn's painting was effectively hidden away in the Old Dining Room and finally demoted to the lobby and passage leading to the Duchess's Rooms.

In her chapter Raeburn's *John Hope, 4th Earl of Hopetoun*: The 'Knotty' Business of Portrait Painting in London and Edinburgh in the 1810s, Viccy Coltman uses Raeburn's under-studied portrait of John Hope in the County Hall at Cupar, Fife, as a case study to focus on the economics of portrait painting in the period of the later 1810s, during the stereotypically rakish, but historically opaque Regency. At the same time as being about prices, Coltman's chapter is also about the cultural and social politics in the business of portrait painting. It examines the negotiations and machinations involved in the commissioning of a portrait of John Hope, the 4th Earl of Hopetoun by a group of Fife landowners. This corporate commission resulted in internal politicking when the Earl of Leven, one of the committee, petitioned Thomas Lawrence, the leading portrait painter in the London market, in preference to his Edinburgh counterpart, Raeburn, who had already been approached by the chair of the committee, the Earl of Kellie.

Rather than focusing on Raeburn's artistry, as so many existing studies of the artist have done to date, Coltman's narrative seeks to investigate the commercial and competitive business culture of portrait painting that resulted in the Hopetoun portrait commission being envisaged for Lawrence and subsequently awarded to Raeburn. While Raeburn and Lawrence were the two main contenders for the Hopetoun portrait, a third artist was involved in a consultative capacity. The Fife-born David Wilkie was one of the Scottish diaspora who, unlike Raeburn, relocated to London to pursue his career. Wilkie maintained a correspondence with his patron, the Earl of Leven, who was one of the committee, navigating Leven's son, Leslie Melville, through the unfamiliar territory of London portrait painters. In sum, the paper examines the sequential stages of the 'knotty' business of portrait painting, from the awarding of the commission, to the execution of the portrait, its Edinburgh-made frame, its installation in the County Hall at Cupar and its reproduction in engravings by William Walker.

In her chapter Raeburn and the Print Culture of Edinburgh c. 1790–1830: Constructing Enlightened and National Identities, Stana Nenadic begins with an overview of the character of engraved portrait production and collecting in Edinburgh during the long eighteenth century. This provides a context for understanding the local print culture c. 1790 to 1830, when over fifty singly-issued prints based on Raeburn portraits were made available – some for sale through print shops or frame-makers, some through private subscription – and when the social, political and visual culture of the Scottish capital helped to shape a distinctly Scottish 'enlightened' and national identity. The different categories of Raeburn's prints are explored – lawyers, academics, churchmen, medical men, political leaders and national celebrities – along with the different reasons for producing a print, which included the obituary celebration of a great life. All of the singly-issued engravings based on Raeburn's portraits were of men and the discussion argues that most can be associated with a carefully articulated elite public sphere of civic and professional institutions.

The following four chapters elaborate aspects of Raeburn's reception in London, in France, in America, and by comparison with his contemporary Goya and the impact of the two painters' work on later nineteenth-century artists. Nicholas Tromans in his chapter A Portrait of the Artist in London: The Critical Reception of Raeburn's Royal Academy Exhibits, 1792–1823, examines the artist's relationship with London, which may seem to have turned on a brief and embarrassing flirtation which gave satisfaction to neither party. In 1810 Raeburn went south to investigate the opportunities suggested by the death in that year of the leading English portraitist John Hoppner. The English painters feted him, toasted his genius, and waved him off back to Scotland – a result, suggested by Duncan Thomson, which 'from a national point of view . . . now seems just as well'. Thomson meant that Raeburn had unfinished business in Scotland in terms of documenting the twilight of Edinburgh's golden age. But the idea that Raeburn may have been ready to abandon that project unsettles our understanding of it. Did Scotland really mean so little to him that a promotion, in British terms, would have lured him away? And as for the London artists who greeted him as a visiting dignitary, rather than a potential senior colleague, did they not behave meanly in failing properly to see what he had achieved?

This contribution to the book returns to a familiar episode in Raeburn's career and uses it to open up arguments about the artist's place in British visual culture, and to better understand the relationships between the London and Edinburgh art worlds of the early nineteenth century. The chapter maps out clearly the opportunities for viewing Raeburn's work in London during his lifetime, and presents for the first time a careful analysis of its reception there. It argues that the commercial nature of art criticism in London has been underestimated in recent art-historical literature – that critics understood their role as participating in the formation of a healthy English school of artists, and did not see it as their business to pass judgement in any detail on artists from abroad (or upon the Old Masters when their work began to be shown at loan exhibitions from the 1810s). Hence Raeburn's presence in criticism is relatively modest, as were the numbers of major works to enter London collections during his life.

Perceived as something of a patrician figure, Raeburn may have been too far removed from the melee of London professional politics to generate substantial critical debate there. Yet his importance for the larger British art world can still be traced. First, his position as a sort of honorary Scottish Royal Academician in the last years of his life raises interesting questions regarding the identities and remits of the London and Edinburgh art institutions. The chapter goes on to examine Raeburn's Academy diploma piece, *Henry Raeburn Inglis ('Boy and Rabbit')*, which was clearly an attempt to cater to a perceived English model of the painting of sentiment. Secondly, Raeburn's imagery can after all be identified at the centre of the London art scene, if we are willing to look for it in the work of another painter – David Wilkie, a younger fellow Scot whose London career had been so extraordinarily successful and who had been Raeburn's cicerone there in 1810. Wilkie was of course a consummate assimilator of the work of the Old Masters, through whose formats and techniques he expressed his modern life subjects. But Wilkie was also a skilled assimilator of the work of his Scottish contemporaries, whose careers, at least in London, never took off as his had done. Wilkie evidently borrowed Scottish subject matter from Alexander Carse, and turned it to great metropolitan profit. From Raeburn he borrowed the forms of specific individuals – Niel Gow and David Baird for example – but also the format of the heroic highlander, as in Wilkie's portraits of George IV and the Duke of Sussex in Highland dress. Through such pictures, the English came to consume more of Raeburn than they were aware of. By examining Raeburn's relations with the English, and particularly by asking in what ways his art was filtered, blocked or reformatted in London, this chapter enables us to chart more clearly the structures of Scottish art in a period during which that category was largely defined by him.

In his chapter The Critique of the Modern French School from Reynolds to Constable, Philippe Bordes notes – from Joshua Reynolds's *Discourses* in the 1770s down through remarks made by Henry Raeburn in the 1820s and John Constable in the 1830s – that the negative construction of contemporary French painting was a recurrent means to consolidate a sense of identity and confidence among artists in Britain. But because of the Revolutionary war between England and France, there was little awareness of the new classical manner adopted by Jacques-Louis David and his contemporaries in the 1780s. Until the year long Peace of Amiens in 1802–3, when British artists flocked to Paris to discover a nation transformed by the Revolution, appreciation of the French School was based on a superficially decorative style that had ceased to be dominant after the death of François Boucher in 1770. In spite of a hostile environment due to economic rivalry and political tensions, French painters were eager to exhibit their works across the Channel, lured by the prospect of financial rewards and private commissions. British discovery of the younger generation at the forefront of the French School, as manifest in exhibitions in London of paintings by Boze, David, Géricault, Robert-Lefèvre, Dubost, Guillon-Lethière and Isabey (Fig. 8.1), provoked revealing discussions. Issues of finish and truthfulness to nature were central both for British painters, who stood fast in their opposition to the Continental trend, and for French painters who were increasingly fascinated by the relatively freer handling that distinguished the British School. Constable denounced the 'stern and heartless petrifactions of men and women' that characterised French painting, while Barbier-Walbonne, a pupil of David, admitted that 'the painting of our school looks pedantic and dull next to theirs'.

Scotland's influence on American culture has been documented across a wide range of academic disciplines. Yet remarkably few scholars have turned their attention to the fine arts and examined Scotland's role in the development of early American art and artistic institutions. The chapter by Robyn Asleson, Raeburn in America: Scottish–American Art Networks, 1791–1845, redresses this oversight by examining the reception of Henry Raeburn's portraiture in the United States during the Early National period. It shows how a handful of artists and patrons in New York, Philadelphia, and Charleston promoted Raeburn's career in the United States, being motivated not only by a commitment to establishing fine art on a sound footing but also by deep personal affinities with Scotland. The chapter tracks Raeburn's interactions with artists, patrons, and art academies in the United States as well as the circumstances that brought a number of his paintings to the new nation.

Particular attention is devoted to Raeburn's portraits of *Peter Van Brugh Livingston* and *Dugald Stewart*, which became highly influential once transplanted to the United States. Placed in art academies where they were on perennial display to students and the general public, these paintings were endlessly copied and imitated, providing the foundation for much American art education and matters of taste. Exhibition data, published reviews, and private commentary on Raeburn – including documentation of his working methods by amateur and professional American artists – shed light on his growing reputation across the Atlantic and his frequent use as a foil to the far more famous Thomas Lawrence. Enjoying a degree of prestige and influence in the United States that was equalled only in Scotland itself, Raeburn emerges as a highly influential figure during a formative period in American art.

The chapter by Sarah Symmons, Raeburn and Goya: The Redefinition of Artistic Personality, asks what is it that links Raeburn and Goya together as portrait painters? Was it their admiration for the portraits of Velázquez, their bold and original strategies for portraying their sitters, their love of dramatic lighting, strange new poses and powerful expressions which made their work seem disconcerting to contemporary spectators? Working in Edinburgh and Madrid respectively, they attracted a cross section of contemporary society to their studios, and offered striking new solutions, which changed the conventions of European portraiture. Yet it was not until the end of the nineteenth century that the true value of their achievements became clear. There are striking parallels in their careers as portrait painters. Both experimented with miniature painting, explored similar influences and developed specific and striking personalities as portraitists, often to the detriment of their careers. This essay examines their influences on the later nineteenth century, their strategies for creating new directions in their portraits, particularly the full-length, as well as their images of women, which reveal their profound knowledge of contemporary fashion. Both artists display a daring stylistic inventiveness which makes them major forerunners of early modern portraiture, inviting comparisons with Whistler, Manet, Sargent, Augustus John, Kilimnik and Hambling. Essentially, Raeburn and Goya emerge as stylistic outsiders in a demanding artistic tradition. This chapter also contains previously unpublished material from the writings of Mary Graham, a Scottish aristocratic female traveller in Madrid, and her reaction to Spanish painting, from the Golden Age to the art of Goya.

The final section of this volume investigates four aspects located in the formation of Raeburn's posthumous reputation and legacy, focusing on Allan Cunningham's life of the artist, the reputation of the artist's portraits of women and, in the decades on either side of 1900, the impact of the artist's work in France as well as the print revival in Britain. In his chapter Raeburn's First Biography: Allan Cunningham's Presentation of the Artist as a Model Scottish Gentleman, Matthew Craske reassesses the most important early account of Raeburn's 'life', published in the fifth volume of the influential art critic's *The Lives of the most Eminent British Painters, Sculptors and Architects* (1829–33). The chapter is essentially concerned with an exploration of the personal prejudices of Allan Cunningham as a biographer of artists. It aims to show how Cunningham's established social values influenced his account of Raeburn. This refers largely to Cunningham's conception of an admirable Scottish gentleman: his idea of a patriot, a manly Scot, and of what it was to pursue a profession in the arts in an honourable manner. The main point here is that this biography, whilst a foundation stone of all studies of the artist, is as much a portrait of Cunningham as of Raeburn. This realisation does not,

Craske argues, nullify the value of the biography as a primary source, for it cannot be assumed that the biographer and artist did not actually share many similar values. The main question here is historiographic: that of whether a very opinionated biography can be a useful route into the historical comprehension of an artist. The argument here is that we cannot be sure of any stance on this question, in this particular case, because Cunningham is such an important primary source that it is difficult to see a 'real' Raeburn behind his legend. In essence, the conclusion is that, for all the obvious bias of the biography, it is far from irrelevant. On the contrary, it is suggested that twentieth-century accounts did not make good use of the text and that in the twenty-first century we need to find ways of using this anecdotal material more effectively. Cunningham's biography remains, it is argued, closer to Raeburn's world, and therefore more enlightening, than most attempts to place a 'context' around him in the last thirty years. Cunningham was not overtly concerned with the key concepts of recent secondary literature such as 'the Edinburgh Enlightenment'. We can, perhaps, consider this a prompt to reconsider recent interpretations of Raeburn's social forum, rather than to dismiss Cunningham's vision as a mere paean to clubbable masculinity.

In his chapter 'Synonymous with manly portraits': Re-evaluating Raeburn's Women, Jordan Mearns seeks to address the prevailing focus in the existing literature on Raeburn's male portraits – particularly those that depict Scottish Enlightenment figures – by suggesting a historiographical root for this phenomenon. Instead of subjecting Raeburn's portraits of women to extensive formal analysis it explores the continuity between late nineteenth- and early twentieth-century writings on Raeburn, which routinely suggest that his male portraits more readily convey a sense of the intellectual attributes and character of their sitter as well as a clearer sense of Scottish national identity. This essay discusses female portraiture to argue that Raeburn drew significant inspiration from his metropolitan contemporaries in a way that is often underplayed in existing accounts of his output.

In comparison with Joshua Reynolds, Thomas Gainsborough and Thomas Lawrence, Raeburn's reputation in France started late, as is revealed by Olivier Meslay in his essay Raeburn and France. The first printed mention of the artist occurs in 1816, in a book published by Louis Simond about his travels in Britain during 1810–11, in which he gives a report of Edinburgh's annual exhibition. Raeburn is described as a painter of the first rank. However, the crucial moment for Raeburn's reputation among French art-lovers has to be the great Manchester exhibition of art treasures in 1857. It was then, with portraits like *Francis MacNab* or *Henry Raeburn Inglis* (*'Boy and Rabbit'*) from the Royal Academy, that his reputation was built. At this period the most important printed reference to Raeburn's reputation was made in 1871 by the influential critic Théophile Thoré, who published a long entry on the artist in his *Histoire de Peintres de toutes les écoles, Ecole anglaise*. Since the later nineteenth century, Raeburn's fame in France has never diminished. It was so prevalent that it took only a year to see Armstrong and Caw's 1902 catalogue on Raeburn translated into French and published in France.

Arguably the most spectacular aspect of Raeburn's reputation and reception across the Channel is the sheer number of the portraits bought and sold at this period. Some collectors like Camille Groult, the most important collector of British art in France around 1900, had at least two portraits, among them that of *Major James Lee Harvey* now in the collection of the Musée du Louvre. Another collector, Maurice Kahn, owned eight portraits. His collection was later dispersed by the dealers Duveen and Gimpel, and one of them, the portrait of *James Cruikshank*, was acquired by the Frick in 1908 to complete their noted pair of the Cruikshanks. More than forty portraits by Raeburn were acquired by French collectors and institutions during the first part of the twentieth century; making France pre-eminent for his work outside Britain. Some of his best portraits remain in French public collections, such as the Musée du Louvre with its *Captain Hay of Lawfield and Spott* or *Nancy Graham ('Innocence')*.

At the end of nineteenth century there was renewed interest in British portraiture, which was given publicity by the sale of aristocrats' paintings by Reynolds, Gainsborough, Romney and Hoppner, to American millionaires. As a result more attention was paid to the mezzotint reproductions of such paintings, which had been made in these artists' lifetimes, and John Chaloner Smith's catalogue of these appeared in the 1880s. Subsequently the grandest of these prints were enthusiastically collected. The high prices that these engravings, particularly those of young women and literary figures, were sold for, made it economic for the printmakers of the late nineteenth and early twentieth century to make new reproductions.

One of the painters most copied between 1890 and 1930 – when the Depression all but destroyed the print market – was Raeburn. This can partly be explained because none of his female portraits had been engraved in his own day. Engravers in the early twentieth century felt more comfortable when there was no earlier print of a painting to which their productions might be unfavourably compared. In his chapter Raeburn and the Mezzotint Revival, 1890–1930, David Alexander discusses the importance of artist's pictures in the print market of this later period, and the varied reputations of the engravers concerned, including a few women printmakers. Among other topics explored are the popularity of colour printed mezzotint, and the way in which prints were marketed through advertisements in periodicals such as the *Connoisseur*, which had sales on both sides of the Atlantic.

It is to be hoped that this multi-authored volume will re-invigorate critical research into Raeburn's life, art and career alongside further investigations into the contexts and environments within which he operated and also with respect to how his reputation and legacy is continually being transformed and re-evaluated. As a case study for the need for ongoing research on paintings by Raeburn – or formerly attributed to him – the suspension of the elegant, problematic and atypical sporting picture of *The Revd Robert Walker* (*'The Skating Minister'*) (Fig. 1.4) from Raeburn's *oeuvre* will not only permit a more dispassionate understanding of this graceful but enigmatic work but also focus attention on the impact of Raeburn's own highly individual pictorial style. *The Burlington Magazine*'s publication in July 2005 of Stephen Lloyd's article, '"Elegant and graceful attitudes": the painter of the "Skating Minister"', reassessed the twentieth-century history of the painting and the long-expressed doubts by some of the curators at the Scottish National Gallery since that institution's acquisition of the work in 1949. Lloyd made the case – on stylistic and iconographical grounds – for the removal of the painting from Raeburn's *oeuvre* and put forward a new attribution to the French émigré painter Henri-Pierre Danloux (1753–1809), who – together with his wife – made various visits to Edinburgh and its vicinity between 1796 and 1800.[5] The only scholar to date who has publicly defended the case for the retention of the traditional family attribution of the painting to Raeburn – still clung to by the Scottish National Gallery despite reservations expressed in the label – has been Duncan Thomson, the former Keeper of the Scottish National Portrait Gallery and organising curator of the 1997–8 exhibition on Raeburn held in Edinburgh and London.[6] He marshalled the arguments for the Raeburn attribution – based mainly on connoisseurship and stylistic analysis in a shorter notice, 'Raeburn revisited: the "Skating Minister"', published in the March 2007 issue of *The Burlington Magazine*.[7]

Since the publication of the original article by Lloyd in July 2005, no new archival or documentary evidence has emerged concerning the commissioning or painting of the picture. Meanwhile, more manuscript and printed contemporary materials have been discovered, concerning the personal and social life of the Revd Robert Walker and also on the artistic activities of Danloux in Scotland, notably his patronage from Henry, 3rd Duke of Buccleuch and his wife Elizabeth Montagu, Duchess of Buccleuch.[8] However, two related pieces of evidence can now be brought to light, that confirm the damaged state and restored condition of *The Skating Minister*, when the picture was purchased cheaply at auction by the Scottish National Gallery in 1949. Four years later, in an issue of the *The Scottish Art Review* mainly devoted to the public galleries of Edinburgh, Glasgow and Aberdeen, David Baxandall, the recently appointed Director of the National Galleries of Scotland, while

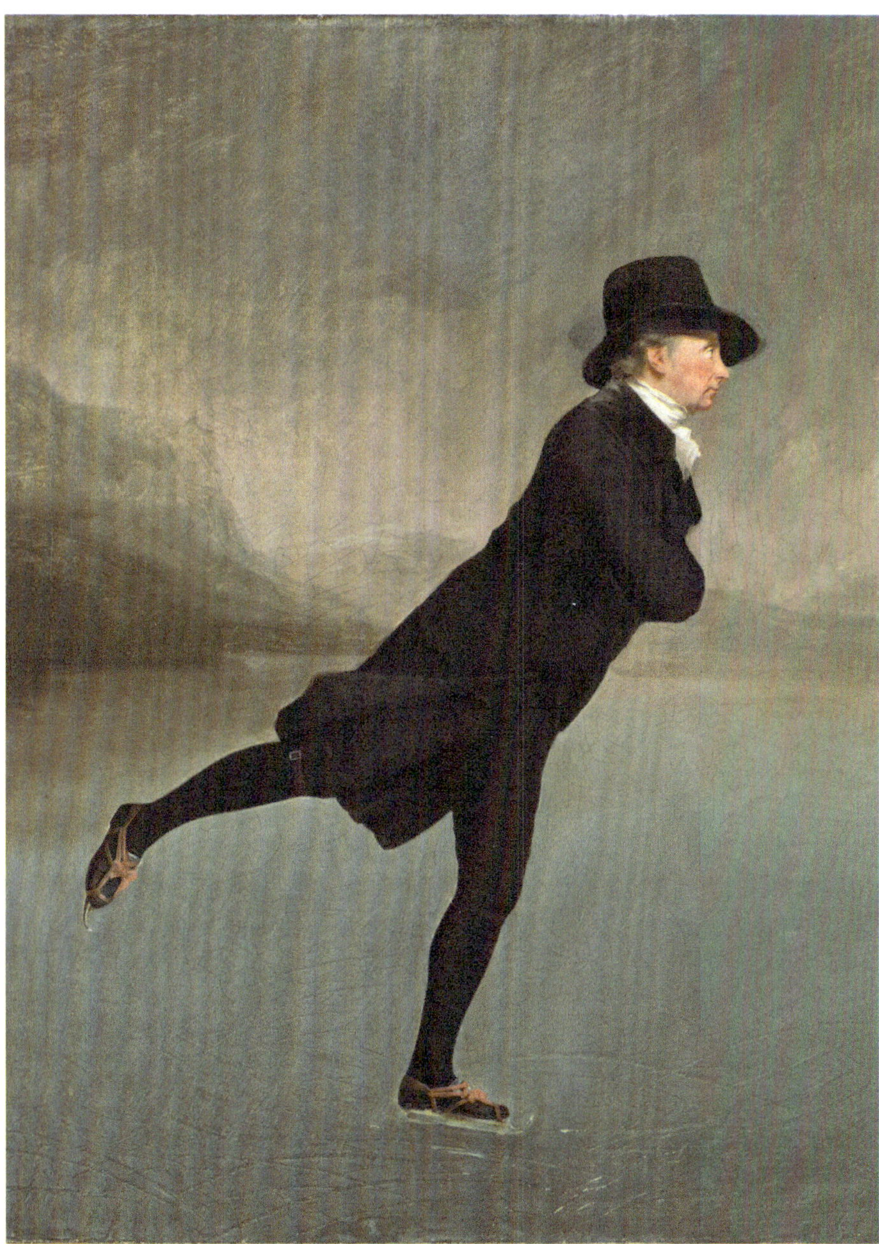

Figure 1.4 Here attributed to Henri-Pierre Danloux, *The Revd Robert Walker ('The Skating Minister')*, c. 1798–9, oil on canvas, 76.1×63.5cm, Scottish National Gallery, Edinburgh

discussing new acquisitions at the National Gallery of Scotland, described the recent conservation treatment of *The Skating Minister*:

> When this picture was bought it was disfigured by dirty varnish, the paint was beginning to leave the canvas, and there was a great deal of later repainting; to restore it to a condition its painter would have recognized was a considerable task.[9]

The painting was in fact conserved and restored in Edinburgh in 1949 by Harry Woolford, as can be seen from the recent re-discovery of the conservation ledger-books compiled by this first Keeper of Conservation at the National Galleries of Scotland from c. 1930 to the mid-1960s; in the volume for work done for NGS between 1947 and 1966, he noted that the painting was damaged in various places, had been repainted in the sky and in the figure, while the varnish was very discoloured.[10]

Further light is shed in this publication for the first time on the physical history of *The Skating Minister* thanks to an infrared reflectogram scan and X-radiograph, even though these two images were assembled in 2005.[11] In the infrared reflectogram scan (Fig. 1.5), the complete earlier version of the hat, with its lower crown, is clearly presented and similarly the earlier altered profile of the crossed arms on the sitter are visible. The X-radiograph of the painting (Fig. 1.6), in which the lead-white pigment comes up as white, as the X-rays are unable to penetrate it, is clearly present in the impasto of the white neckerchief, and can also be seen in the painting of the ice, landscape and sky. However, lead-white pigment is hardly visible in the figure and is most particularly absent in the face. This lack of lead-white is utterly alien to the typically rough and expressive application of this key pigment in the underpainting of the faces in Raeburn's portraits. This technique can be witnessed in many examples of his pictures at the National Galleries Scotland that have had X-radiographs taken of them, as well as in a major painting of *The Johnstone Family* group at the National Gallery of Art, Washington, DC.[12] This evidence from the X-radiograph of *The Skating Minister* of complete lack of lead-white in the face of the skating figure is a compelling demonstration that this painting cannot be from the hand of Raeburn. However, until technical examination is made of Danloux's similarly dated cabinet paintings, this data is not enough to make one certain of a definitive re-attribution to the French artist, although he still remains the prime candidate for the authorship and execution of the composition.[13]

Returning to the chapters in this volume on Raeburn, it is the editors' hope that the new evidence and fresh lines of approach discussed will provide a stimulus to forthcoming historical and critical research on the painter and

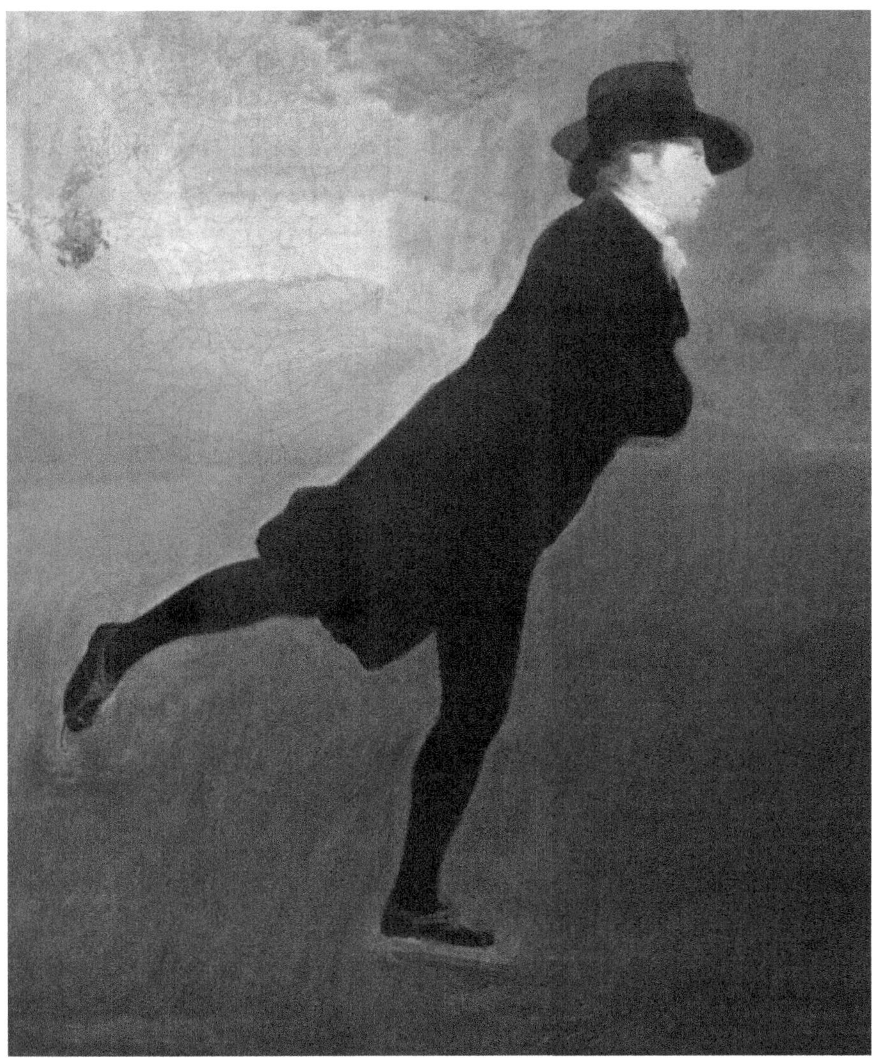

Figure 1.5 Infrared reflectogram scan of the detail of the figure of *The Revd Robert Walker ('The Skating Minister')*, assembled in 2005, reproduced courtesy of the Conservation Department, National Galleries of Scotland

his substantial body of portraiture, which made such an impact on his own society and his artistic contemporaries in Scotland and London, and later on in France and North America.[14] Further research and analysis could be undertaken on a variety of social and artistic contexts within which the painter operated; a better understanding of his social and artistic milieu will enrich our comprehension of how his portraits were received, viewed and

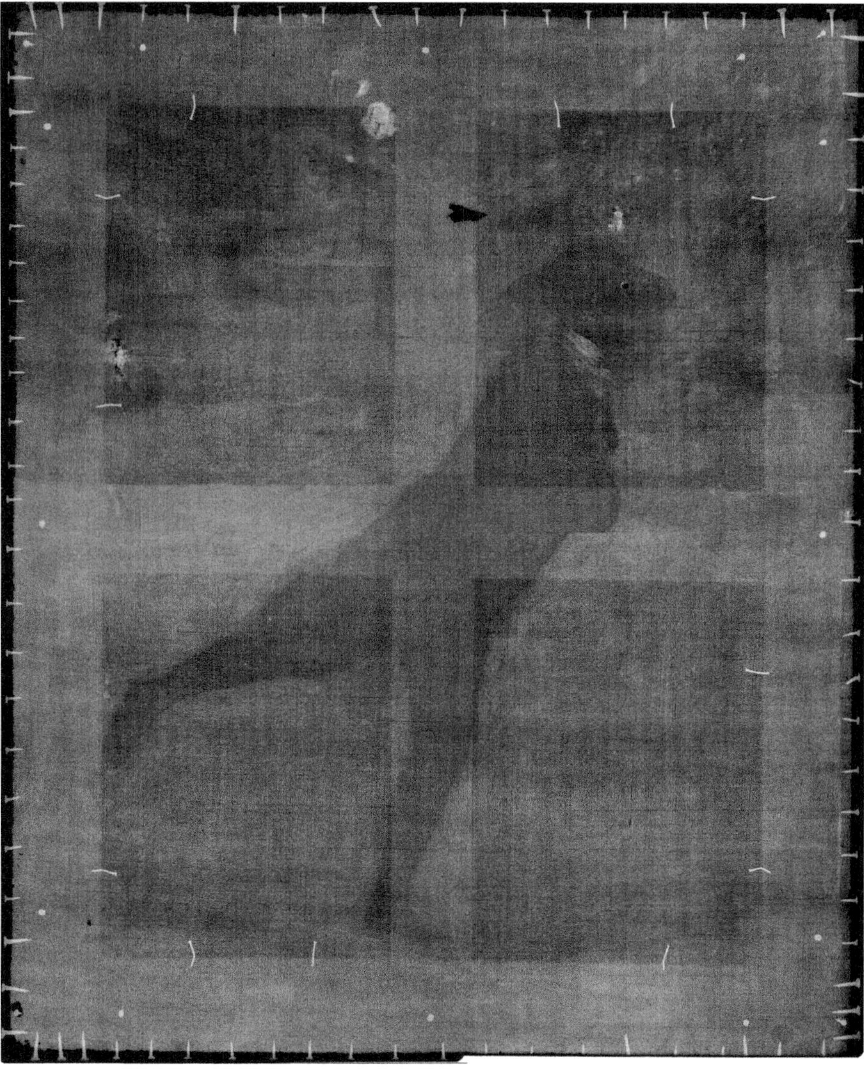

Figure 1.6 X-radiograph of *The Revd Robert Walker* (*'The Skating Minister'*),
assembled in 2005, reproduced courtesy of the Conservation Department,
National Galleries of Scotland

displayed. Areas for further research within Raeburn's immediate Scottish context might include for his early life and career a deeper understanding of his upbringing within the textile-businesses and mills of the Water of Leith; what kind of education he received at George Heriot's Hospital; the silver he designed and engraved during his apprenticeship to the goldsmith James Gilliland; the influence of his friendship with the lapidary, etcher and antiquarian, David Deuchar; his work as a portrait miniaturist in the 1770s;[15] his activity as a portrait draughtsman and the influence of older fellow portraitists – a John Brown, working in pencil and Archibald Skirving, painting in crayons;[16] and the nature of his response to the paintings by the leading portraitist in oils, David Martin. After 1780, further topics for analysis might include Raeburn's social advancement enabled by his marriage; the business practice of portraiture at his studio in Edinburgh; and the development of his experimental style of paint, light and shadow during the late 1780s and 1790s with respect to current intellectual ideas of perception and optics. After 1800 further research needs to be done on the artist's business affairs and his family firm's bankruptcy in 1808, leading to strained relations with his step-children;[17] his central role in the founding of the Associated Society of Artists in Edinburgh that held exhibitions in the gallery above his studio in York Place from 1808 to 1816; and his activity as a property developer on his and his wife's estate in Stockbridge as 'Raeburnville', an elegant suburban extension to the north-west of Edinburgh's New Town.[18] Other issues concerning Raeburn's career that need exploring include the role of the artist (or his assistants) in making versions or repetitions of his own portraits and copies of works by other artists; his portrayal of families and of children; his relationship with his critics in Edinburgh and Scotland; how the artist reacted to his younger contemporaries in Scotland, such as George Watson, John Watson (Gordon), Colvin Smith and John Syme, who for three years completed Raeburn's unfinished portraits left in his studio at his death;[19] and the retention by Raeburn of a collection of prime versions of portraits of some of his famous – and mostly male – contemporaries, in effect a collection that was one of the forerunners of the Scottish National Portrait Gallery, which was founded in 1882.[20]

In terms of Raeburn's activities outside Scotland, much research still needs to be undertaken on the exact nature of the impact made on the artist, during his Roman sojourn, by James Byres, one of the leading dealers and ciceroni resident in the city; Raeburn's response to seeing portraits in London by Reynolds and by other English artists in their studios and at the Royal Academy; the artist's relationship with the London critics, the politics of the Royal Academy and with his fellow academicians, notably his friends and allies David Wilkie and Francis Chantrey, and his competitors, John Hoppner, William Beechey, Thomas Phillips and most importantly Thomas Lawrence.

After Raeburn's death, the artist's reputation and legacy were initially sustained through a series of monographic exhibitions in Edinburgh in 1824, 1850 and 1876, all of which were important events that need further study and scrutiny. The afterlife of Raeburn's studio in York Place as a working studio for other artists during the 19th and 20th centuries also needs further examination.[21] The reasons for the exceptional art-market boom in Raeburn's work from the 1870s and its sudden decline after 1929, especially in France and North America, will merit further study based on the pioneering chapters by Olivier Meslay and David Alexander in this volume, alongside the detailed entries on Raeburn's paintings in the recent British paintings' catalogues published by American art museums.[22] The most extensive collections of Raeburn's portraits are preserved in the National Galleries of Scotland, both in the Scottish National Gallery and in the Scottish National Portrait Gallery.[23] The full cataloguing of these core collections is yet to be completed and published, but of equal interest would be the publication of research into the formation of these two parallel groups of portraits, which effectively represent the national collection of Scotland's greatest portraitist. Since the building and opening of the underground New Wing of the Scottish National Gallery in the 1970s – used as a rather unsatisfactory display space for the finest paintings in the national collection of Scottish art – the smaller paintings by Raeburn have been hung there disadvantageously. The split nature of the Raeburn collection is confirmed by the hanging of a selection of his grandest full-lengths in the octagonal bay at the north-western end of the main floor of the Gallery. By contrast the revived Scottish National Portrait Gallery has moved its central collection of Raeburn portraits from the central gallery – formerly known as the 'Raeburn Room' – on the top floor, where they had been shown to great effect. They are now displayed to less effect in the north-western gallery on the top floor of the building, which is devoted to the theme of 'The Age of Improvement'. Significant groups of paintings by Raeburn have been placed on long-term loan since the 1990s at the National Galleries of Scotland's two country house partner galleries at Paxton House in the Borders and at Duff House in northern Aberdeenshire. Currently, it could be argued that the National Galleries of Scotland's outstanding collection of paintings by Raeburn – both in terms of quality and numbers – is disconnected and needs rethinking to show the artist to better advantage at both the Scottish National Gallery and the Scottish National Portrait Gallery, not just within traditional tropes of 'Enlightenment and 'Improvement' but reflective of empire, trade and business, the Scottish elites the artist depicted so intuitively and in which he was so deeply embedded.[24]

There is no doubt that our deeper understanding of Raeburn has the potential to act as a useful critical component in cultural debates around an emerging and reflexive Scottish identity within shifting national and global paradigms.[25] One example of the endurance of Raeburn's legacy to contemporary definitions of 'Scottishness' and its potent manipulation by the pen

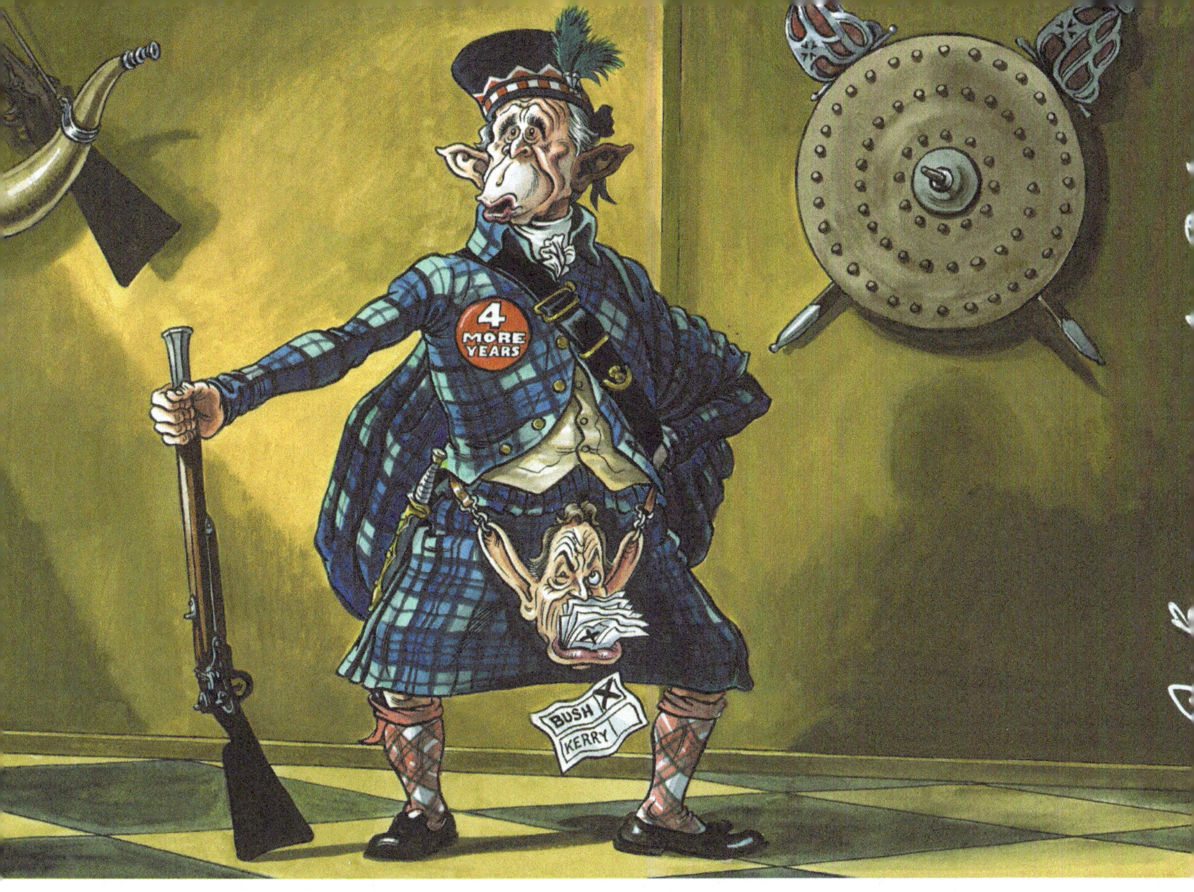

Figure 1.7 Dave Brown after Henry Raeburn, *Rogues Gallery: MacDubya of Glenballot*, cartoon, published in *The Independent*, London, 23 October 2004

of the visual satirist is Dave Brown's *MacDubya of Glenballot* cartoon, published in *The Independent*, London, on 23 October 2004 (Fig. 1.7). Brown reproduces Raeburn's iconic portrait of *Colonel Alastair Ranaldson Macdonell of Glengarry*, 1812 (Fig. 1.8) recasting the Highland Chief as MacDubya of Glenballot – a simian George W. Bush. Making an uncompromising comment on Anglo-American relations and, specifically, on the relationship between President Bush, then seeking re-election for a second term and the subservient British Prime Minister, Tony Blair, Blair's disembodied head and his famously protruding ears hang below MacDubya's waist employed as his anthropomorphic sporran. Crammed in Bush's mouth are a series of ballot papers, marked with a cross by Bush's name, rather than his Democratic opponent, John Kerry. One paper falls to the floor as Blair strains to retain the remaining papers in his gaping mouth. Brown dresses MacDubya in recognisable Black Watch tartan – making reference to Blair's recent acquiescence to a US request that six hundred troops from the Black Watch (The Royal Highland Regiment) be redeployed to an American-controlled area of Iraq. In the countdown to the November election, this action was widely

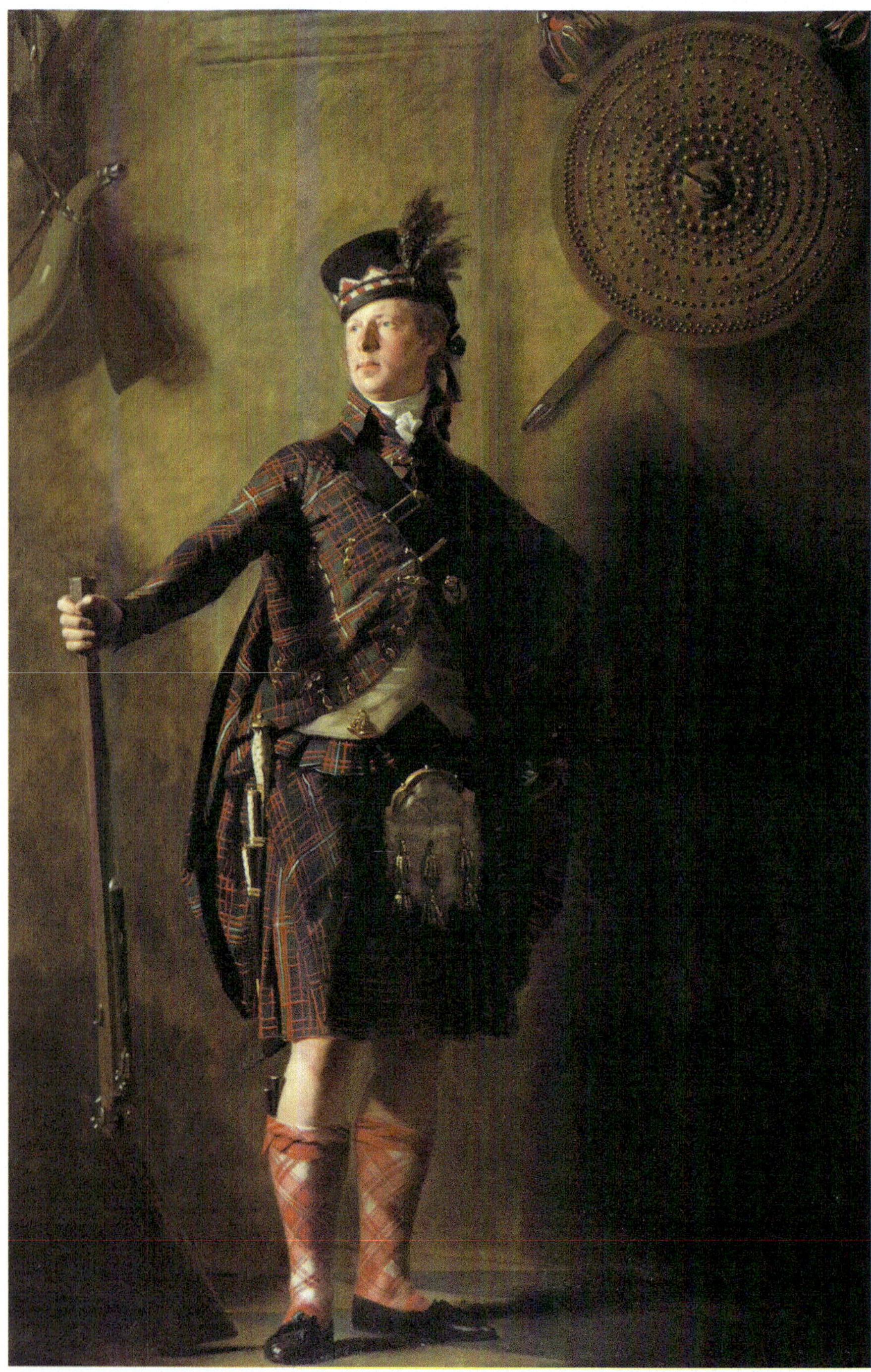

Figure 1.8 Henry Raeburn, *Colonel Alastair Ranaldson Macdonell of Glengarry*, 1812, oil on canvas, 241 × 150cm, Scottish National Gallery, Edinburgh

seen as an attempt by Bush to convince voters that he had a strong coalition of countries supporting the war. This satirical image of Blair's Premiership – as a literal and metaphorical sporran to Bush's war-mongering chieftain – enjoyed wide currency in the centre-left British public's assessment of Blair's legacy.[26] Raeburn's portraits as a conduit for contemporary artists might help us to redress the supposed conservatism of the genre of portraiture in his own historical period and today.

It is sincerely hoped that this volume of essays will refocus attention towards the highly original body of paintings produced by Edinburgh's outstanding portraitist, whose life and *oeuvre*, social context and critical environment, reception and reputation, are revealed by the contributors to form a surprisingly complex prism in the making of Raeburn's art and legacy.

Notes

1. *The European Magazine* 1823, pp. 435–7. Also for an obituary that compared Raeburn's portraits to those by Reynolds and ranked the Scot as 'either the first, second, or third in the English School', cf. 'Character of Sir Henry Raeburn as a Painter', unsourced press cutting, July 1823, V, p. 1384, bound volume of press cuttings from English newspapers, National Art Library, Victoria and Albert Museum, London. I am grateful to Helen E. Smailes for drawing these two published obituaries to my attention.

2. London 1911, unpaginated, but the illustrations occur after the text of the catalogue. The portraits by Raeburn illustrated in the top register from left to right are titled *Robert Allan (1740–1818)* [now at the Laing Art Gallery, Newcastle-upon-Tyne]; *Miss Janet Law*; *Captain David Birrell* [now at University of North Carolina at Chapel Hill]; *Mrs MacLeod (1767–84)*; *Professor John Playfair* [loaned to the exhibition by the Marquess of Lansdowne]. The bottom register from left to right are titled: *Mrs Patrick White (b. 1752)*; *Provost Elder, of Forneth (1727–99)* [now at the University of Edinburgh]; *General Sir James Stevenson Barnes (1773–1850)*; *James Veitch, Lord Eliock (1712–93)*; *Mrs Malcolm* [now at the Courtauld Gallery, London]; and *John Francis, Earl of Mar (m. 1770)*.

3. Morrison 1844, p. 17, quoted in Lloyd 2003, p. 113.

4. Edinburgh 2006, p. 7, fig.4

5. Cf. James Fenton, 'Ice follies: Danloux or Raeburn? A Franco-Scottish puzzle', *The Guardian*, 7 May 2005, p. 24; also see Stephen Lloyd, 'Edinburgh's "Skating Minister": a sporting picture or a cultural icon?', *York Georgian Society*, Annual Report, 2010, pp. 27–9; and Richard Wendorf, 'Skating around Raeburn', *After Sir Joshua: Essays on British Art and Cultural History*, New Haven and London 2005, pp. 109–33, which considers how the painting has been attributed to Raeburn and then raises questions about evidence in art history.

6. Stephen Lloyd and Duncan Thomson were interviewed extensively by the writer and journalist Alan Taylor in a TV documentary, 'Who painted the Skating Minister?', directed by Jan Leman, and made by Leman Productions for broadcast on BBC2 Scotland on 30 August 2006. In the course of his research for this programme Lloyd drew attention to a painting by Raeburn, 'A Portrait of the late Dr Walker' (34×24 1/2in), which was lot 91 in an auction *Catalogue of a valuable collection of Modern Pictures . . . and interesting works by Ancient Masters . . .*, Dowell's, 18 George Street, Edinburgh, 14 November 1896. By examining the roup rolls for Dowell's auctioneers, Jan Leman established that this painting, as well as a 'Portrait of a Gentleman' (29 1/2×24 1/2in) by Raeburn (lot 92) and five cabinet or head-and-shoulder oils by Sir John Watson Gordon PRSA, depicting members of that artist's family (lots 93–97), had been offered for sale by a descendant of the Revd Robert Walker D.D. Lot 91, the 'Portrait of the late Dr Walker' is therefore very likely to be Raeburn's untraced portrait of the Senior Minister of the Canongate, the canvas of which is four inches higher than that used in the painting of *The Skating Minister*. Assuming that Raeburn painted a portrait of Walker, it is likely to be in the half-length seated format, showing ministers wearing white bands at the neck over clerical robes or dark grey coats. Compare Raeburn's half-length portrait of *The Revd Walter Buchanan, D.D. (d. 1832)*, appointed by the City of Edinburgh in 1789 as the minister of the second charge to the Canongate kirk, Important English Pictures, Christie's, London, 27 March 1981, lot 137, 75.5×63.5cm, sold for £850, also illustrated in The Very Revd Dr Ronald Selby Wright, *A Short Guide to the Canongate Kirk (The Kirk of Holyroodhouse), Edinburgh*, Edinburgh, 1974, pl. 9. I am grateful to the Revd Charles Robertson, former Minister of the Canongate, for discussing Raeburn's portrait of Buchanan with me.

7. The publication of Thomson's shorter notice drew an emailed response to Lloyd, dated 26 March 2007, from Dr Gerrit Walczak, a scholar of French émigré artists active during the 1790s: 'I am rather puzzled by the lack of understanding of émigré art in general: nobody could be more likely to experiment than a French painter desperately trying to make his living among clients proud of their national school of painting, a school more or less defined by its opposition to French art . . .'.

8. This archival material on Danloux commissions for the Buccleuch family will be published by the author in the near future.

9. David Baxandall, 'Some recent accessions at the National Gallery of Scotland', *Scottish Art Review*, IV, no. 3, 1953, pp. 1–6.

10. 'Sir Henry Raeburn – Rev. Robert Walker skating on Duddingston Loch' <u>Condition</u> Ptd. On canvas, relined, with glue of crossbar stretcher, size of ptd surface 29 1/2×24 3/4. Damages & repainting in sky & figure, varnish very discoloured.

<u>Treatment</u> Taken off relining canvas and glue removed. Four damages to canvas and the remains of a linen stamp – the crown. Laid on to another canvas with wax. At this stage the discoloured varnish was removed and the damages photo by Annan.
Markings on stretcher 758JJ 67CE
In chalk 80
In chalk Feb 25 – 49
In chalk Feb 6 – 14
In chalk Feb 89
Paper label. The Rev. Robert Walker D.D. <u>of Cramond</u> / died 1808 / (Skating on Duddingston, Loch, Edinburgh) / by Raeburn
In blue pencil L.I. Hume
Bourlet label E5961
obliterated paper label
Acetone 50 white spirit 50. Continually stronger mixture with which to remove repaints'. cf, MS note-book, labelled S.O. Book 129, Paintings treated at NGS 1947–66, fol. 8r, Woolford Archive, National Galleries of Scotland (Archive donated to NGS by Cooper Hay in February 2012); also see 'Obituary of Harry Russell Halkerston Woolford (1905–99)', *The Scotsman*, 11 September 1999. I am grateful to current NGS Keeper of Conservation Jacqueline Ridge for her assistance.

11. These images were kindly taken and assembled in 2005 by the late Donald Forbes and by Lesley Stevenson, Senior Paintings' Conservators in the NGS Conservation Department in 2005, under the auspices of the former NGS Keeper of Conservation, Michael Gallagher. I am grateful to them all for their comments on these technical images.

12. Cf. John Dick in Edinburgh and London 1997–8, pp. 39–45, esp. p. 41; and cf. Stevenson 1998.

13. For an endorsement of the importance of the X-radiography for the understanding and attribution of *The Skating Minister*, as discussed by John Dick, former NGS Keeper of Conservation, in the BBC2 Scotland TV documentary, 'Who painted the Skating Minister?', broadcast on 30 August 2006, cf. John Leighton, 'Caring and sharing: Conservation and Cultural Politics in Scotland', The 9th annual Harold Plenderleith memorial lecture, given at the Hawthornden Lecture Theatre in the National Galleries of Scotland on 30 November 2006, *ICON News: The Magazine of the Institute of Conservation*, Issue 9, March 2007, pp. 18–21. Among the many art historians, supportive of – or sympathetic to – the proposed Danloux re-attribution of *The Skating Minister*, who corresponded to this effect with Lloyd at the SNPG between 2005 and 2009, were Dr Colin B. Bailey, Dr Carrie Rebora Barratt, Professor Philippe Bordes, Colin Harrison, the late Professor David Irwin and Dr Francina Irwin, Alex Kidson, Alastair Laing,

Neil MacGregor, Professor David Mannings, Olivier Meslay, Dr Patrick Noon, Professor William Pressly, Dr Gerrit Walczak and Dr Humphrey Wine.

14. Stephen Lloyd, 'Raeburn: a new portrait', *Scottish Review of Books*, II, no.1, February 2006, pp. 17–18.

15. Irwin 1973; Stephen Lloyd, *Portrait Miniatures from the National Galleries of Scotland*, exh. cat., SNPG, Edinburgh, 2004, pp. 50–1, no. 33, pl. 10; Lloyd, *Portrait Miniatures from Scottish Private Collections*, SNPG, Edinburgh, 2006, pp. 46–7, no. 55, pl. 13 and pp. 89–90, nos. 56–58. Raeburn's portrait miniatures will be the subject of a forthcoming article by Lloyd for *The Burlington Magazine*.

16. For three of Raeburn's drawn studies for portrait miniatures at the SNG, cf. Stephen Lloyd and Kim Sloan, *The Intimate Portrait: Drawings, Miniatures and Pastels from Ramsay to Lawrence*, ex. cat., SNPG and the British Museum, 2008–9, pp. 50–1, nos. 10–11; and for a set of around 100 drawn copies, water-marked c. 1800–10, made after Van Dycks' *Iconographia* and compositions by Michelangelo, cf. *Sir Henry Raeburn (1756–1823) R.A., Studies, "Journey to Italy"*, exh. cat., BADA 90th Anniversary Exhibition, The Titian Gallery, Stow-on-the-Wold, Glos, 2008. I am grateful to Ilona Johnson-Gibbs for showing me these copies.

17. London 1997 (now Raeburn MSS, NLS, Acc. 11479).

18. Kerr 1982 and Byrom 2005.

19. Also cf. Stephen Lloyd, *Raeburn's Rival: Archibald Skirving 1749–1819*, exh. cat., SNPG, Edinburgh, 1999.

20. For the artist's studio, cf. Soden 2006; for the collection of portraits, cf. Macmillan 1996–7

21. Raeburn's York Place studio was purchased by Colvin Smith and used by him as his own studio until his death in 1875. It was also leased to the Royal Scottish Academy for academicians, such as Stanley Cursiter, Robert Heriot Westwater and Alberto Morocco to use as a portrait studio from 1962 to 1975, cf. Soden 2006.

22. The activities of James Greig, the Raeburn expert, who worked for the London art trade before the First World War, and whose papers for an uncompleted catalogue raisonné on Raeburn, are now deposited in the archive of the SNPG, Edinburgh, would merit closer study. For a useful list of 132 paintings by Raeburn known to be in 55 American and Canadian art museums, cf. John D. Morse, *Old Master Paintings in North America*, New York, 1979, pp. 219–22.

23. NGS 1997; Smailes 1990.

24. Another area of research that is likely to bear fruit is Raeburn's close connection with clients and patrons among the mercantile elites of Glasgow and the sugar economy of the river Clyde, notably the transatlantic trading port of Greenock, cf. George Fairfull-Smith, *The Wealth of a City: a 'glance' at the Fine Arts in Glasgow – Volume One: 1641–1830*, privately published with the imprint of

the Glasgow Art Index, Glasgow, 2010; also cf. Emma Rothschild, *The Inner Life of Empires: an eighteenth-century history*, Princeton and Oxford 2011. This important volume examines the complex lives of the Johnstone family, originally from Westerkirk in Dumfriesshire, who made their careers in the burgeoning markets of empire in the Subcontinent with the East India Company and across the Atlantic in North America and the West Indies. Raeburn painted portraits of various members of the family, most notably in c. 1795 the group of *John Johnstone of Alva, his sister Elizabeth Johnstone and their great-niece Miss Wedderburn* (National Gallery of Art, Washington, DC), which is illustrated on the book's dust-jacket. Viccy Coltman's most recent work on Raeburn (under consideration) looks at an exceptional group of seven half-length portraits of members of the Fraser of Reelig family, whose commission between 1800 and 1816, inserts a hitherto understudied imperial accent into his practice.

25. Forbes 1998.

26. Viccy Coltman would like to thank Helen E. Smailes for bringing this image to her attention and Dave Brown, for his commentary on it.

Part I

Context

2

'I cannot coin money for them': Raeburn in the Nexus of Patronage, the Art Market and Global Trade

Stephen Lloyd

Raeburn's career as a portrait painter and businessman in Edinburgh during the transformative years – of Revolution and war, Romanticism and reform – from 1786 until his death in 1823 occurred when the city's New Town was developing into the hub of a highly developed bourgeois culture or polite society. Simultaneously, Edinburgh's nearby port of Leith had been established as a nodal point of local and global mercantile activity, communicating regularly with leading English ports, trading raw materials and manufactured goods throughout the North Sea to mercantile hubs such as Rotterdam and Hamburg, and across the Atlantic servicing the former North American colonies and plantations in the Caribbean. Raeburn, who was born into a family of manufacturers, can be situated within the nexus of Scottish establishment patronage from friends, families and institutions and also as a feature of a British art market that promoted a talented, clubbable and business-like artist. Raeburn's career as an artist and man of business can now be more fully understood within the vortex of economic opportunities and vicissitudes that were to destroy Henry Raeburn & Co., the artist's family venture in shipping and the West India trade.[1]

That cataclysm directly caused Raeburn's own bankruptcy in 1808 and necessitated his becoming a property developer while operating as an even more commercially minded portraitist in London as well as in Edinburgh. This chapter reveals for the first time the causes in 1807 of the collapse of the Raeburn family business together with the artist's ensuing financial collapse and it illuminates the nature of key friendships with two influential members of the Edinburgh establishment who assisted him in his predicament and helped to protect his reputation.

On Saturday, 7 June 1823, just four weeks before Raeburn's unexpected death, one of his oldest friends, Andrew Duncan senior, an eminent physician in Edinburgh then in his eightieth year, paid a visit to the artist at his studio in York Place. He later recounted in a memorial address to his friend: 'I called at his painting rooms, after concluding the business I had allotted for the day. After he had finished his business, we walked together to Leith Links. There removed from the smoke of the city of Edinburgh we conjoined with pleasing conversation, a trial of skill at a salutary and interesting exercise, to which we had both a strong attachment'.[2] After their round of golf, the two friends enjoyed a 'temperate meal' at the hall of the Honourable Company of Golfers of Edinburgh where both men were long-standing members, and in whose dining-room were displayed at least two portraits of fellow golfers – William Inglis and Alexander Wood – both painted by Raeburn.

A few months later Andrew Duncan recalled with great warmth and affection that summer day of 'healthful and manly exercise' as he composed a memorial to his recently deceased friend. He delivered this as the address at the annual dinner of the Harveian Society of Edinburgh, of which Duncan was the founder and Raeburn had been an associate member for many years. This society, which still meets to this day, celebrates the achievement of the renowned English seventeenth-century physician William Harvey, who discovered the circulation of the blood. Duncan's address was published in Edinburgh and London during April 1824 as *A Tribute of Regard to the Memory of Sir Henry Raeburn, R.A. Portrait Painter to the King for Scotland.* On the title-page Duncan listed his own achievements, including his position as 'First Physician to the King of Scotland' and as 'Father of the Royal College of Physicians' of Edinburgh. Raeburn's great friend, who was professor of medicine at the University of Edinburgh, was a leading figure in Scottish medical circles. He was a pioneer of psychiatry in Scotland by establishing an Asylum for the Insane in Edinburgh, remembered to this day in the Andrew Duncan clinic at the Royal Edinburgh Hospital. He also pioneered free medicine for the poor through his foundation of the Royal Dispensary in Edinburgh, which can be seen in the framed painting that is shown hanging in the background of Raeburn's portrait of Duncan, which was painted around 1818 (Fig. 2.1).

In this tribute of regard to his late friend Henry Raeburn, Duncan effectively made the case for himself as a key patron or supporter in both the artist's early career and as it developed later. He recalled that – over forty-five

Figure 2.1 Henry Raeburn, *Andrew Duncan senior*, c. 1819, oil on canvas,
127×101.6cm, Royal College of Physicians, Edinburgh

years earlier – in 1778 he had commissioned from Raeburn, who was then
apprenticed to the Old Town goldsmith James Gilliland, a memorial brooch
set with a lock of hair from the head of Charles Darwin, a brilliant young
medical student of Duncan's, who had died suddenly. On the front of the
trinket Duncan recalled that Raeburn had made a tiny picture of *A Muse
weeping over an Urn*, which is since untraced.[3] Duncan also stated that he had
been instrumental in commissioning three oil portraits from Raeburn at the
beginning of his career as an oil painter. These represented the golfer William
Inglis, the surgeon Alexander Wood and Andrew Duncan himself. Already
one can see the importance of the support network of male Edinburgh society
for the development of Raeburn's artistic career. In this closely knit world of
men, the professions such as medicine – and later law and academia – merge
within the highly convivial social and sporting milieus that were so active
across Edinburgh during the late eighteenth and early nineteenth centuries.
Further on in his tribute to the artist Duncan claimed to have played an
important role in securing the commissions for Raeburn to paint three of

the leading personalities in the building of the University of Edinburgh's Old College, designed by Robert Adam. These men were Thomas Elder, the city's Lord Provost; Adam Ferguson, the famous moral philosopher; as well as the Revd Dr William Robertson, the eminent historian and Principal of the University.[4] Duncan then went on to describe the remarkable visual impact of these and other portraits by the artist:

> For Raeburn was not more successful in taking a striking likeness, than in giving to it the most flattering aspect, with all the spirit of the original. And it has been justly said of his pictures, that they were the men themselves, starting from the canvass.

Clearly in his memorial address Duncan gave himself a prominent role in celebrating Raeburn's portraiture for its ability to capture 'the look' and essence of the sitter, but he additionally wished to present himself as a true friend and supporter of the artist, who had assisted him in a crucial group of commissions at the outset of his career as an apprentice goldsmith, then for the Honourable Company of Golfers of Edinburgh and later for the University of Edinburgh.

However, when discussing Raeburn's career it would be misleading to think of his relationship within Scottish artistic patronage in terms of a single rich patron or one family or a royal court controlling his artistic development and production, as it was understood in terms of artists' careers across continental Europe during the seventeenth and eighteenth centuries. By contrast the art world in Britain during the eighteenth and early nineteenth century was dominated by the output of portraiture by artists, who were mostly based in the metropolis of London, although other regional administrative, business and leisure centres, such as Edinburgh, Dublin, York, Liverpool and Bath, could sustain busy studio practices. Portraitists ran competitive businesses within developing social milieus and economic markets constantly prone to the forces of changing taste and fashion.[5] After Raeburn's return to Edinburgh in late 1786 from his two-year stay in Rome, he rapidly established himself in a New Town studio as the leading young portraitist in the Scottish capital. Over the next thirty-seven years the artist painted over one thousand portraits: a prolific business that at his death was worth around three thousand pounds a year.[6] Raeburn's clientele was to a very large extent composed of the Scottish professional classes and their families: the legal, academic, medical, religious, military and mercantile elites, combined with the landed gentry, highland lairds and some elements of the aristocracy.[7] A number of Scottish families remained especially loyal to Raeburn over the decades around 1800. For example the families of Dundas, Erskine,

Ferguson of Raith, Forbes of Pitsligo, Fraser of Reelig, Hay, Inglis, Johnstone of Westerkirk, Kennedy of Dunure, Stewart of Ardgowan and Wauchope of Edmonstoune, among others, provided considerable work for the artist at various stages of his career. Families such as these may be described both as key clients and as fundamental networks of patronage.

Of special significance for the launch of Raeburn's career as a portrait-ist in oils after his return from Italy was the sustained number of commissions over the following decade from one particular family, the Fergusons of Raith. The series he produced for them of at least ten painted portraits included some of the artist's boldest and most immediate compositions of the late 1780s and early 1790s. William Ferguson (formerly William Berry) had recently inherited from his uncle, Robert Ferguson of Raith, a substantial fortune and an estate in Fife, an event celebrated in the conversation piece by Johan Zoffany painted in 1769.[8] Nearly two decades later in around 1787 William Ferguson commissioned Raeburn to portray him in an informal three-quarter length seated portrait together with his youngest son William as a child (private collection). In probably the same year William Ferguson senior commissioned the artist to paint an ambitious full-length seated por-trait of his wife Jean Craufurd of Restalrig – the sister-in-law of the 6th Earl of Dumfries – together with two of her youngest children, William and Beatrice (private collection).[9] That particular portrait and others painted within the following decade, such as *Sir John and Lady Clerk of Penicuik* (Fig. 7.4), bear the strong pictorial and compositional influence of Sir Joshua Reynolds's paintings, which Raeburn is likely to have seen when in London in 1784, as Andrew Duncan stated in his posthumous tribute of 1824.[10]

In the tribute to his late friend Duncan placed emphasis on the leading British portraitist, Reynolds, as the other key artistic influence on Raeburn during the early part of his career. Duncan stated that Raeburn went to London, en route to Italy in 1784, to spend time in Reynolds's studio. Duncan continued that '[Raeburn] had sufficient ambition to think that, as a portrait-painter in oil colours, he might imitate the noble example of Sir Joshua Reynolds'. The President of the Royal Academy may also have pro-vided further encouragement to Raeburn to use his visit to Rome to further his artistic studies. Duncan continued in his tribute to draw parallels between the careers of Reynolds and Raeburn, noting their similar genius and talents, their enjoyment of literary company in London and Edinburgh respectively, and of course the royal approbation of their knighthoods. While this linking together by Duncan of the two pre-eminent portraitists working in England and Scotland may be interpreted as flattering the memory of Raeburn in this typical memorial eulogy, the close artistic respect by Raeburn for Reynolds may be considered as more than likely in light of the close friendship between

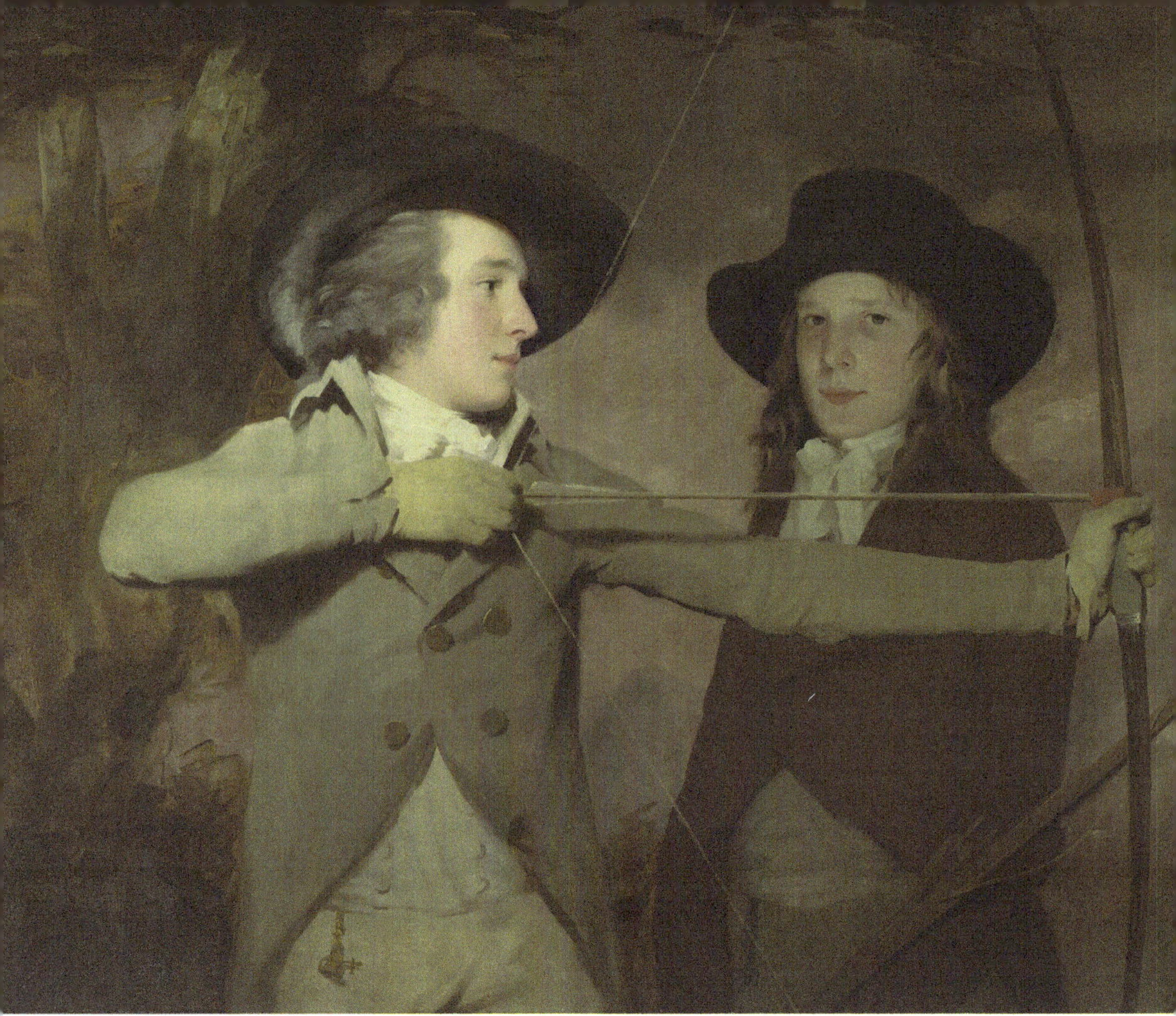

Figure 2.2 Henry Raeburn, *Robert Ferguson of Raith and his younger brother General Sir Ronald Ferguson ('The Archers')*, c. 1789–90, oil on canvas, 101.6×127cm, National Gallery, London

Duncan and Raeburn, enabling the transmission of the artist's thoughts and opinions.

During the late 1780s and early 1790s William Ferguson's intensive patronage of Raeburn continued when he commissioned the artist to paint two portraits of his eldest son Robert. In the painting known as *'The Archers'* of c. 1789–90 (Fig. 2.2), Raeburn produced one of his most radical and original compositions, in which the principal subject, Robert Ferguson of Raith, is shown in profile, extending the bow, while his younger brother, General Sir Ronald Ferguson, is represented in shadow behind the bow. The full-length portrait of the older brother, Robert Ferguson of c. 1792 (private collection) is painted with dynamic energy and economy, to create a fresh portrait exuding vitality and alertness, as epitomised in the rapidly painted hunting dog in the foreground. Around two years later in c. 1794–5 William Ferguson commissioned Raeburn to paint an ambitious full-length portrait of his second son Ronald Ferguson (private collection) standing in a landscape beside his horse, within a dramatically lit composition. The covert martial aspect of this portrait may reflect that the subject was an ambitious soldier; this work was most probably painted to mark Ronald Ferguson's recent appointment as lieutenant-colonel of the 84th Regiment and just before he was due to travel out to India with his regiment.

Another highly significant quasi-military portrait commission for Raeburn at this period came from the Royal Company of Archers, based in Edinburgh, which was arguably the leading sporting association for men in elite Scottish society, with its members drawn from the aristocracy, landed gentry, professional and mercantile classes. Raeburn was himself a member, alongside the Ferguson brothers, the older portraitist David Martin, who was a keen collector of bows and arrows, and what were to be many of Raeburn's future clients.[11] In April 1791 the Company commissioned two full-length portraits in oils to adorn the recently built Archers Hall in Edinburgh. The President, Sir James Pringle of Stichill, was painted by the senior artist, David Martin, at a cost of fifty pounds; while for a similar sum Raeburn was invited to portray the eminent surgeon and noted archer, Dr Nathaniel Spens of Craigsanquhar (Fig. 2.3).[12] Raeburn created a spectacular and strongly-lit portrait of Spens, shown about to loose an arrow, that can be seen as the artist's first great masterpiece in the demanding format of the full-length. This portrait, after it was unveiled in 1795, can be said to have established the artist's dominance of the market for portraiture in Edinburgh, and this was confirmed when Martin died two years later. The renown of the portrait – and Raeburn's reputation – was further established when the line-engraver John Beugo was invited by the Company to reproduce the full-length portrait firstly in a monochrome wash and china ink drawing that was preparatory for a line engraving to be paid for by a subscription raised among the Archers (Fig. 2.4).[13] Beugo printed 150 impressions of the engraving for the subscribers, who mostly paid for and received their prints in 1795 and 1796 (Fig. 2.5).[14]

The patterns of Raeburn's patronage from certain families in Scotland can be contrasted with the activities of two other contemporary artists, who were active in Edinburgh during the second half of the 1790s, one of whom shunned conventions and another who stuck closely to an exiled royal court and one powerful but sympathetic aristocratic family. Archibald Skirving (1749–1819) was an outstanding pastellist who was much admired as an artist by Raeburn; the younger painter exhibited his oil portrait of Skirving at the Royal Academy in 1812 (private collection).[15] Eccentric by nature

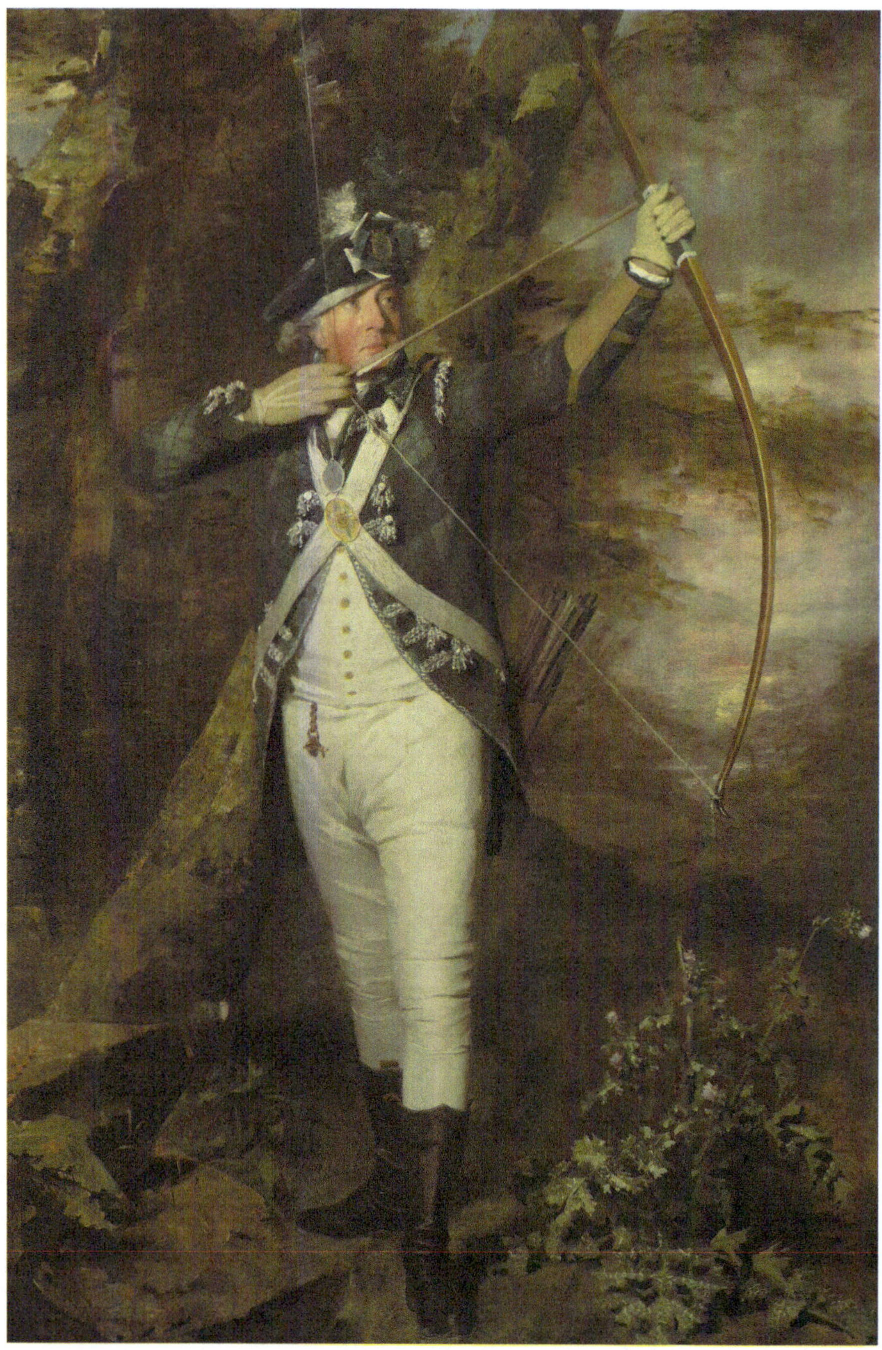

Figure 2.3　Henry Raeburn, *Dr Nathaniel Spens of Craigsanquhar*, 1791–3, oil on canvas, 236.9 × 149.2cm, The Queen's Body Guard for Scotland (The Royal Company of Archers), Edinburgh (on loan to the Scottish National Portrait Gallery, Edinburgh)

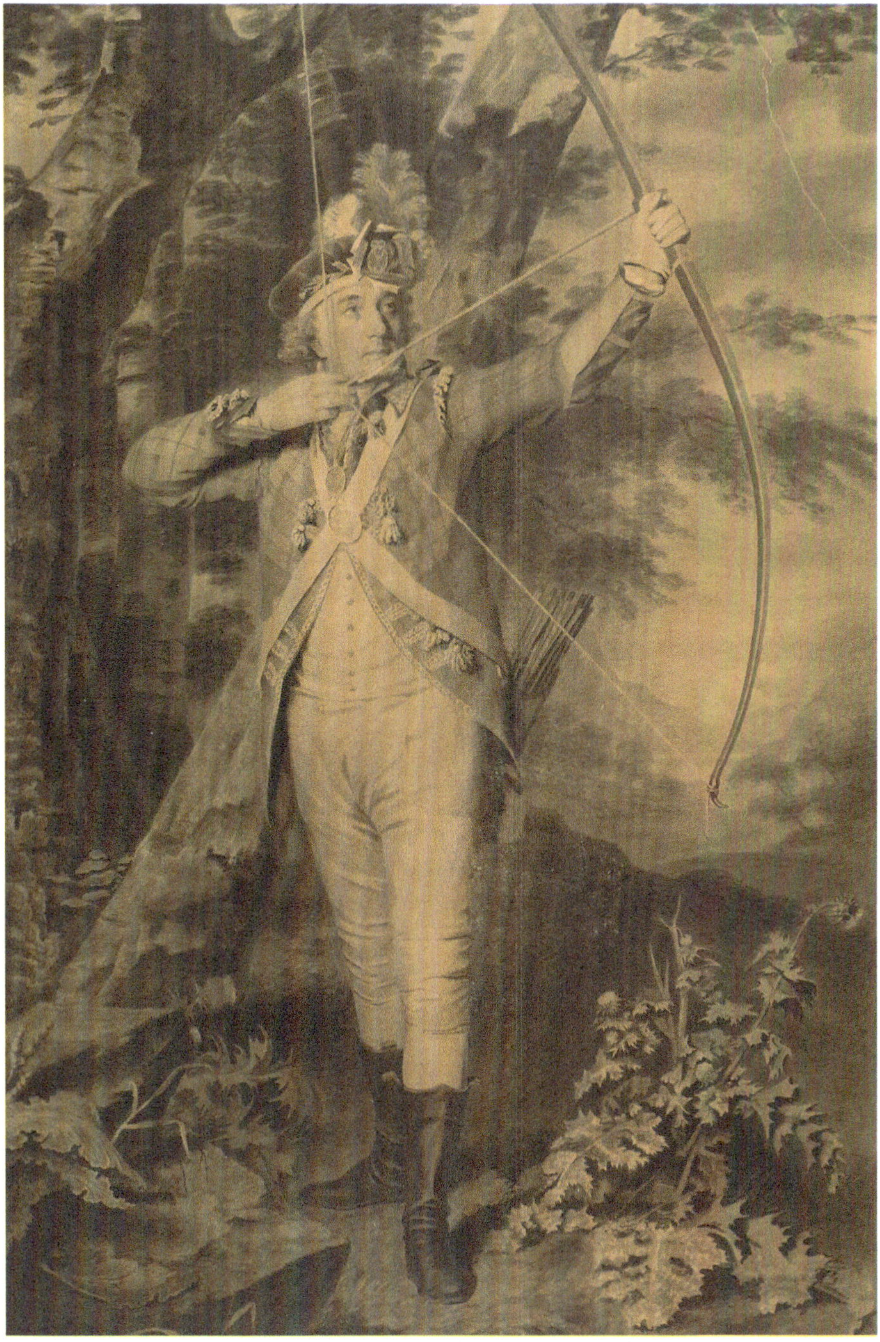

Figure 2.4 John Beugo after Henry Raeburn, *Dr Nathaniel Spens of Craigsanquhar*, 1794, monochrome wash and graphite on paper, 81.4×52.4cm, Royal Scottish Academy, Edinburgh

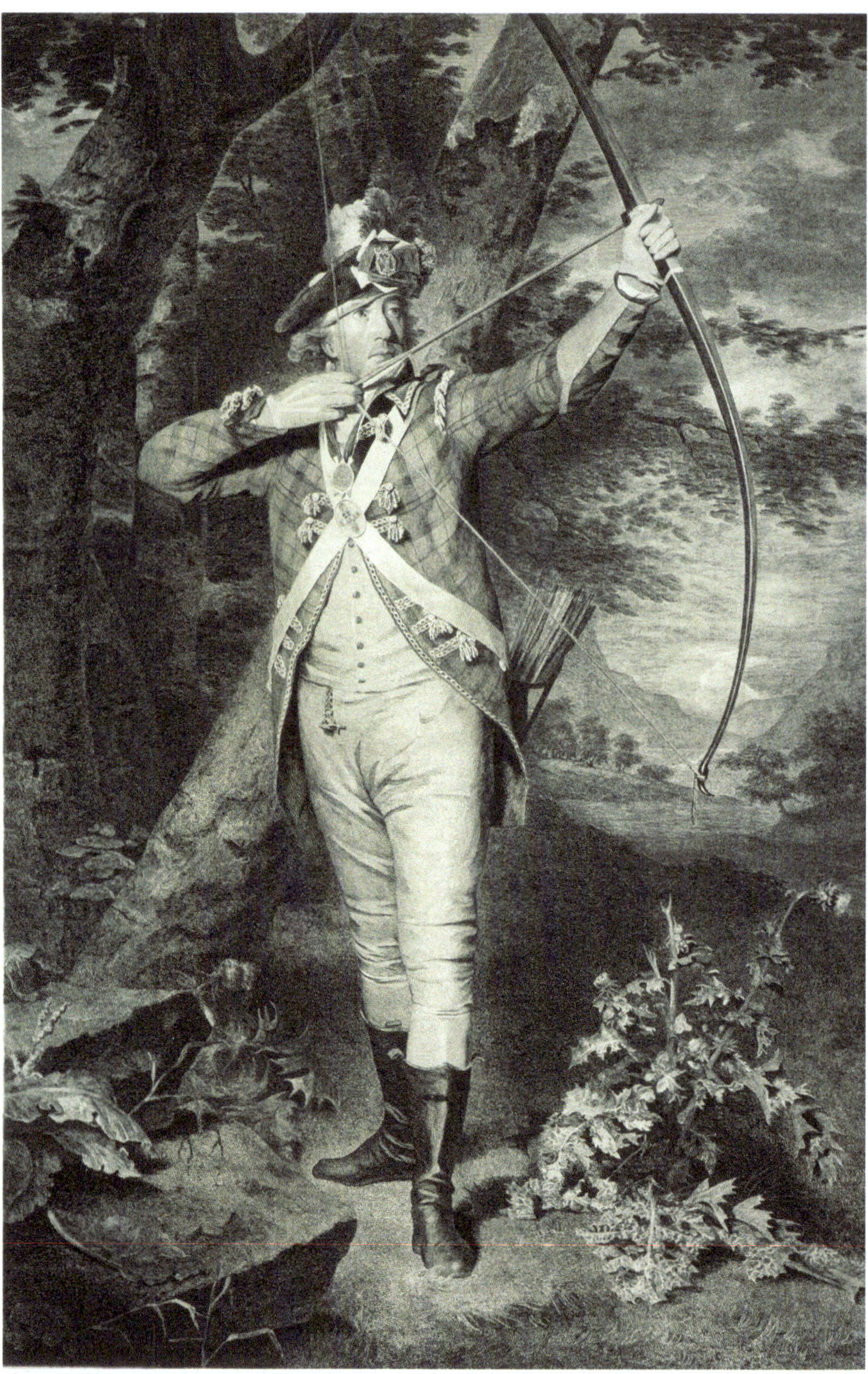

Figure 2.5 John Beugo after Henry Raeburn, *Dr Nathaniel Spens of Craigsanquhar*, 1796, line engraving, 67.8×46.2cm, Scottish National Portrait Gallery, Edinburgh

and unconventional in his working practices, most unusually for a portrait-ist Skirving declined to have a show-room next to his painting-room in his Edinburgh studio, and he was known to demand up to fifty sittings from sitters. The artist produced arresting portraits of painstaking verism, while he was notorious for his unpredictability and short temper. On one occasion he ordered the society beauty, Lady Caroline Campbell – daughter of the 5th Duke of Argyll – out of his studio, on account of her continually bringing her husband and her lapdog to the studio, and thus disrupting the artist's concentration. In a similar episode, one of Scotland's leading aristocrats and artistic patrons, Henry, 3rd Duke of Buccleuch, was turned away from the artist's studio on account of his arriving late for an appointment. Not sur-prisingly Skirving only attracted a small clientele of dedicated patrons, and it is thought that he may have produced as little as fifty portraits in pastels throughout his professional career from the early 1780s up until his retire-ment in 1803, the year in which he created his last masterpiece in pastels, *An Unknown Elderly Lady* (private collection on loan to the SNPG), one of the most moving and uncompromising depictions of old age from this period.[16]

In contrast to the eccentric and socially awkward Skirving was the French émigré artist, Henri-Pierre Danloux, who by force of circumstance and neces-sity worked hard to gain commissions and who frequently adapted the degree and level of the painterly finish to his canvases to suit different clients and patrons. During the course of a number of extended visits to Edinburgh from his main studio in London during the second half of the 1790s, he used his aristocratic connections with the exiled French court of the comte d'Artois (later Charles X), based at the Palace of Holyroodhouse, to gain a series of major portrait commissions from Henry Scott, 3rd Duke of Buccleuch and his wife, the duchess, Elizabeth Montagu. The central portrait commission in this group is the highly finished conversation piece of the duke and duchess surrounded by eight members of their family grouped together in the park at Dalkeith House near Edinburgh. As the surviving letters and bills indicate, the Buccleuch family clearly acted as the major patron of Danloux, princi-pally in Scotland, but also in London, where they were well connected at court. At least fifteen oil portraits of the Duke and Duchess, their family and retainers were commissioned and painted within the space of five years.[17]

The Buccleuch family's patronage of Danloux can be seen in the context of further portrait commissions dispensed to other leading English portrait-ists such as Reynolds, Gainsborough and Beechey. By contrast Raeburn, the pre-eminent Scottish portraitist, was not favoured with patronage from this leading Scottish family on account of their antipathy towards what was perceived as the shortcomings of Raeburn's 'sketchy' style of painting and the 'unfinished' nature of his portraits. This aversion was revealed in correspondence of 1819 from Charles, 4th Duke of Buccleuch, to his kinsman Sir Walter Scott about Raeburn and plans to commission a portrait of the poet and novelist for the new library at Bowhill:

> Raeburn should be warned that I am well acquainted with my friend's hands and arms as with his nose – and Vandyke was of my opinion. Many of his works are shamefully finished – the face is studied, but everything else is neglected . . . Besides Raeburn has really a fair opportunity of producing something worthy of his skill & talents.

Despite this criticism Buccleuch did agree to Scott sitting to Raeburn, but after the fourth duke's death the eventual sittings took place a few years later in 1822–3, with the principal version of *Scott* remaining in the artist's family after his death in 1823 (now SNPG) and a studio replica, commissioned by Henry, Lord Montagu (private collection). Scott himself had strong reservations about Raeburn's painting style as he relayed in a letter of 7 February 1822 to Lord Montagu: 'I was to charge Raeburn to paint the hands &c with the sure accuracy with the face instead of his usual sketchy way of disposing of the person as to accessories'.[18]

While the artistic relations between Raeburn and the influential Buccleuch family were troubled, resulting in minimal patronage and commissions from the artist, he did receive far greater support from the influential Scottish banker Gilbert Innes of Stow (1751–1832), who was a colleague of Henry, 3rd Duke of Buccleuch, in the governance of the Royal Bank of Scotland. Innes also knew the leading medical figure Andrew Duncan. In his memorial address about Raeburn to the 1824 meeting of the Harveian Society in Edinburgh, it is significant that Duncan dedicated its publication to Innes. All three men were keen golfers and members of the Royal Company of Archers, the King's Bodyguard in Scotland. Innes was not only an extremely important friend to Raeburn, but he was a key financial supporter and adviser of the artist over the last two decades of his life, including during times of great financial difficulty, especially around 1808, the year of Raeburn's declaration of bankruptcy.[19]

As Helen E. Smailes's research has demonstrated, Gilbert Innes of Stow was a well-known banker in his lifetime but hitherto obscure, despite the preservation of much of his personal and business archive in the National Archives of Scotland. However, he has now been revealed as one of the most culturally significant figures active in Edinburgh during the late Georgian and Regency period. His father, George Innes, was second and then first cashier of the Royal Bank of Scotland between 1745 and 1780. Having made his wealth from managing sequestered Jacobite estates as Depute-Receiver

General of Scotland, George Innes himself purchased an estate at Stow in Peeblesshire. Gilbert Innes later became a Deputy Lieutenant of Midlothian (the Lord Lieutenant was Henry, 3rd Duke of Buccleuch). Like his father, Gilbert worked for the Royal Bank of Scotland, becoming a Director in 1787, and seven years later being appointed as Depute-Governor, a post he held until his death (the Governor of the Royal Bank until his death in 1812 was the 3rd Duke of Buccleuch). In 1793, with the onset of a national financial crisis caused by the declaration of war by revolutionary France, Innes distinguished himself by travelling to London to plead successfully with the government led by William Pitt for a loan of four million pounds to the Scottish banks to save Scotland's economy. Innes himself died intestate, and is said to have left over one million pounds in cash (worth over 40 million pounds today); he also died unmarried but leaving at least sixty-seven illegitimate children by various women. Innes, whose Edinburgh townhouse was on St Andrew Square, adjacent to the Royal Bank of Scotland's headquarters, was not only a friend and consistent client of artists such as Raeburn, but he was the committed patron of the talented Scottish neoclassical sculptor Thomas Campbell. He was deeply involved in the elite networks of patronage that promoted and controlled Edinburgh's social, economic and cultural life, and he was closely involved in the building of Edinburgh's so-called Second New Town in the Regency period. Among other roles, Innes was a key personality in the Highland and Agricultural Society as its Treasurer; he was a major financial supporter of Edinburgh's Musical Society, based at St Cecilia's Hall in the Old Town, which brought leading professional singers and musicians from London to perform with the music-playing amateurs of Edinburgh's polite society. Thus Innes can be seen to have used his influence and money to support a wide variety of cultural and social activities in Edinburgh and among Scottish society at a period when the city was expanding its prestigious New Town development.

Raeburn's connections with Innes were to be significant in terms of financial support, portrait commissions and through gifts of Old Master paintings. Innes himself was an avid collector of the fine and decorative arts for his various houses both in and around Edinburgh; and as a frequent visitor to London, he would have known the London art world well. An instance of this first-hand knowledge of a masterpiece of contemporary art, which would have made an impact on artists in Edinburgh including Raeburn, is the banker's housing in central Edinburgh of one of the outstanding portraits from the 1780s: *The Skater* (Fig. 2.6). A celebrated and highly naturalistic full-length portrayal, it was painted by the gifted young American artist Gilbert Stuart in 1782. It represented Innes's close friend, William Grant of Congalton, from East Lothian but then working as a lawyer in London. The picture

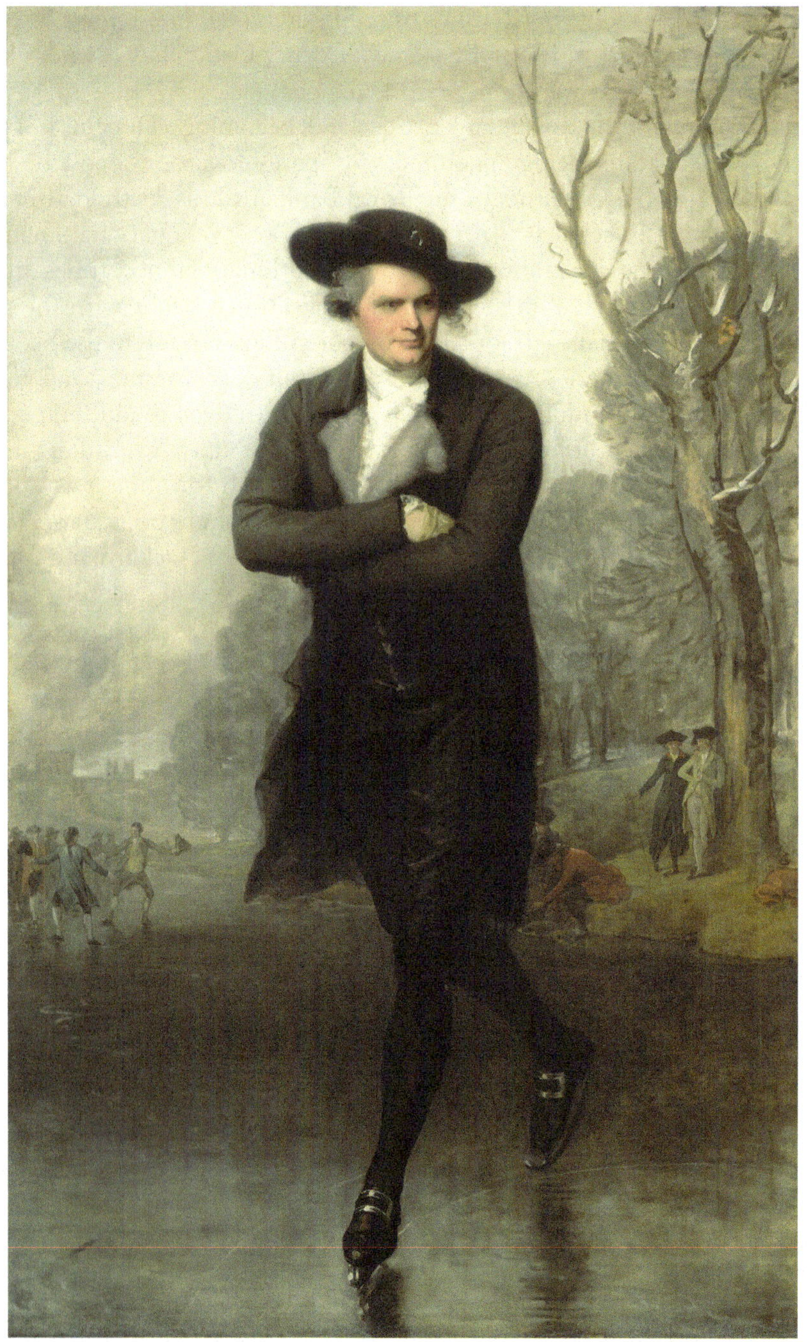

Figure 2.6　Gilbert Stuart, *William Grant of Congalton ('The Skater')*, 1782, oil on canvas, 244.5×147.4cm, Andrew W. Mellon Collection, National Gallery of Art, Washington, DC

was exhibited at the Royal Academy that year, where it caused a sensation on account of the novelty of its animated subject and lively composition. After the painting had remained in Stuart's studio for five years, a financial misfortune compelled the artist to leave London for Dublin. Grant, who was in London, wrote a letter on 1 December 1787 to Innes in Edinburgh, stating that the large picture of him as 'the skating figure' would be packed up and shipped to the banker's house ('of a modest man such as you are') in St Andrew Square at the heart of the New Town. Grant concluded his letter by requesting, perhaps ironically, to Innes that he: 'will not make me a public Exhibition but lodge me the most retired corner of your house allowing me only a little light & air for the benefit of my complexion – If you find me of the least incumbrance I assure you of an early removal'.[20]

If Raeburn had seen this radical portrayal of *The Skater* in Stuart's studio, either when visiting London en route to and from Italy in 1784 and 1786, or when it was lodged in Innes's grand townhouse in Edinburgh after it had arrived there in 1788, there is no doubt that this highly original and naturalistic work would have made a great impact on the Scottish artist, having just returned from Rome, in terms of how a young artist could make his mark though vitality of brushstroke and inventiveness of pose.[21]

The relationship between Raeburn and Innes is recorded in unpublished letters preserved in the Innes manuscripts held at the National Archives of Scotland as well as in the Royal Bank of Scotland, and they constitute an important addition to our knowledge of Raeburn's financial affairs and dependence on Innes. The first documented connection between Raeburn and Innes occurred in a letter from the artist to the banker, written at the studio in York Place on 18 November 1803. Raeburn writes: 'I have got back the head again by Rembrandt, which I had given to Mr Fletcher, and beg you will accept of it from me as a small token of my Esteem and regard'.[22] While it is not clear what the subject of this painting was, or indeed whether it was by Rembrandt, let alone who Mr Fletcher was, this letter is of significance in that it reveals for the first time Raeburn to have been a collector of Old Master paintings, if only on a modest scale. The fact that he was prepared to give a painting by such a revered Old Master to Innes, indicates that he already knew the banker well. Raeburn may have wanted to make an addition to Innes's art collection with a timely gift, and this may have been done in gratitude for a piece of financial advice or for a loan from the banker. This gift may also have been a speculative donation for the artist to curry favour with Innes to smooth the way for possible future financial assistance. Certainly it is worth noting that Raeburn was prepared to relinquish an important Old Master painting rather than retain it for the purposes of artistic study or the prestige of the artist-connoisseur.

In contrast to Raeburn in Edinburgh, many successful artists based in London during the eighteenth and early nineteenth century formed important collections of Old Master paintings, prints and drawings, as well as of sculpture and *objets d'art*. One might cite artists such as Jonathan Richardson, Thomas Hudson, Sir Joshua Reynolds, Sir Robert Strange, Benjamin West, Nathaniel Hone, Paul Sandby, Richard Cosway, Sir John Soane and Sir Thomas Lawrence. These artists used their collections both as a study resource for understanding pictorial composition in addition to painting and drawing techniques, which occasionally involved investigative restoration as in the instances of Reynolds and Cosway. Their art collections also acted as a suitable decoration for their owners' fashionable studios, and for projecting an image of artists as gentlemen and connoisseurs. Paintings by Old Masters could also be sold by these artists to some of their key patrons and clients, while leading painters were considered by art dealers to be the best connoisseurs, useful for their authoritative critical judgements on the attributions of paintings and for the access they brought to leading patrons and collectors. Raeburn and Skirving were known as the pre-eminent artists and experts in Scotland for the connoisseurship of Old Master paintings as they had both studied art in Italy. They were therefore much valued by their fellow Scot, William Buchanan, who was arguably the outstanding art dealer and speculator based in Regency London.[23]

Further light on Raeburn's collecting habits and attitude to Old Master paintings is found four years later in a letter from the artist to Innes, sent from his studio in York Place on 11 December 1807, announcing that he is sending to the banker as a gift the painting he owned of the *Martyrdom of St Bartholomew* by Guido Reni. He wishes that the gruesome subject matter had been more pleasing but considers the picture to be 'one of the best specimens of the Master and one of the best pictures in Scotland'. He continued to describe the content and condition of the painting, as well as his two alternative proposed restorations of the damaged arm of one of the figures, in some detail:

I have taken the liberty of sending you a Picture by Guido – which I beg you will do me the honor to accept of. – I wish the subject had been more pleasing. – with respect to its merit, I stake my credit as an artist, on its being one the best pictures in Scotland, – The vulgar and rude form of the executioner, with the atrocity of his expression and action, having put the bloody knife with which he was flaying the saint, into his mouth, while he stops to tye him up a little faster, – is admirably contrasted with the elegant form and calm resignation of the martyr. – I think it is a picture of the first rate, but I shall never be able to form a collection myself, and one solitary picture in my possession is not worth keeping.

– you have already two or three very good pictures and this will add to your collection, and speak from the heart when I say I do not think it can be so well bestowed – and therefore[e] I flatter myself you will not hurt me by refusing it.–

I could have wished to have shown my gratitude for what is already past, under circumstances less equivocal, that time I hope is yet coming. But I call heaven to witness it has been my intention to send you this picture for a long time past, but I hesitated whether I should send it as it is or cover up the arm. I now think it better to let you have it as it came from the hand of the master – and after you have had it for some time in this state if you wish it, afterwards, I will paint the arm as like the other one as I can, or paint it as covered with a cloth, and do it with some paint that will wash of[f] again if desired.[24]

Raeburn's motives in offering Innes this Old Master painting – as a sweetener or as a strategic present – to enhance Innes's own small collection were revealed as the artist continued his letter to the banker by referring to the looming financial crisis about to overwhelm his family's mercantile business in Leith: Henry Raeburn & Co., which was involved in shipping and the West India trade. This entailed importing sugar and other raw materials in their own ships from plantations in the Caribbean, many of which were owned and run by Scots, and then in the same boats exporting from Leith various cargoes of manufactured and luxury goods to service the plantations and communities in the colonies. The two directors of the company were Henry Raeburn's stepson-in-law James Philip Inglis and his own son, Henry Raeburn junior, but Raeburn himself was a guarantor of the company and was liable for the debts if it collapsed.

Further light on the exact nature of Henry Raeburn & Co.'s shipping business and West India trade can be found in published shipping records and in advertisements placed in Edinburgh newspapers. The company owned a brand new ship the *Isabella Simpson*, which was built for the West India trade, sailing from Leith, often via the Thames estuary or Portsmouth, out to Madeira, then across the Atlantic to plantations in Jamaica and Trinidad. According to a description of the *Isabella Simpson* in *Lloyd's Register* of 1809, she had been built in Leith in 1807, sheathed in copper in 1808, and was a three-master square-rigged ship of 307 tons, single deck with beams, fifteen foot draught when loaded, and built of the first quality materials.[25] An advertisement placed in the Edinburgh newspaper, *The Caledonian Mercury*, and published on 2 July 1807, gave notice of the vessel's forthcoming sailing across the Atlantic to Jamaica the following month on 1 August:

FOR MADEIRA & JAMAICA, To sail with LICENCE, The SHIP ISABELLA SIMPSON, THO. IRVING Commander, Will be ready to receive good about

the 15th proximo, and sail on the 1st August, for Madeira, Port Morant, Morant
Bay, and Kingston on the south, and Port Antonio and Arunatto Bay on the
north side of Jamaica.
The Isabella Simpson is a fine new ship, mounting 16 guns, copper sheathed,
and has excellent accommodation for passengers.
Apply to HENRY RAEBURN & CO.
Leith, June 26, 1807.
Several CLERKS and MECHANICS WANTED for the island of Jamaica –
Apply as above.[26]

This ship, a Westindiaman, like others owned by the Raeburn family
company, was directly involved in the West India trade of sugar produced by
slaves on plantations in the British colonies of the Caribbean.[27] These vessels
would then re-cross the Atlantic from Leith, as well as from other British
ports, loaded with general goods, provisions and luxuries for the colonies,
such as: ale, barley, books, candles, china, cloth, coal, cotton, haberdashery,
hardware, herrings, iron, lead, linen, machinery, musical instruments, painters colour, saddlery, shoes, snuff, stationery, stoneware, tallow, tar, umbrellas
and wine.[28]

During 1807 a financial crisis – centred in the Caribbean that was then
beset by economic difficulties due to the ongoing war between Britain and
France for trading and colonial superiority – began to unfold around the business interests of Henry Raeburn & Co. This collapse is detailed in three newly
discovered and increasingly anxious letters written by Raeburn that revealed
his family's exposure to a series of calamitous events effecting the Jamaican
sugar economy and in particular his ships in the West India trade, which
were caught up in hostile action by French forces during the Napoleonic
Wars. These letters were written by the painter to his principal financial
advisers at the Royal Bank of Scotland, with the first two missives sent on
29 April and 20 July to William Simpson, Chief Cashier of the Bank, which
were followed by a more desperate one to the Depute Governor, Gilbert
Innes himself, on 5 October.[29]

Raeburn's letter of April 1807 sent to Simpson referred to the predicament that his son and his stepson-in-law, John Philip Inglis, found themselves in that year, due to investing all of their funds in ships that had been
purchased for the West India trade but without leaving enough money to pay
for the basic business costs and cargo duties owed in Leith or other British
ports. Raeburn informed Simpson he was confident that the owners of Henry
Raeburn & Co. would, if necessary, take the drastic action of selling one of
their ships. Yet Raeburn continued by reassuring Simpson that he had confidence in the two partners and their plans, which he asserted with further

financial support could help the family firm recover its economic health. Raeburn concludes by letting Simpson know that he had warned his son and stepson-in-law that 'I cannot coin money for them' and that they need to be patient:

> I have had a long and serious conversation with my son and Mr Inglis on the subject of your advice of last night, the propriety and the value of which they are perfectly sensible of and determined to follow.
>
> Hitherto they have not advanced a single shill[ing] to any West Indian, except tempory advances after the goods were in their possession – they have got into a good business without it – and it is their fixed purpose to persevere in this system of not advancing money. –
>
> But they see they have committed an error in vesting almost the whole of their capital in ships, without leaving themselves a sufficiency for conducting their business at home, they are therefore determined, to retrench in that department of their business that they may apply more of their capital to the other but they hope that you will allow them to do it by degrees, and that you will have the goodness as you have hitherto done – to assist them with part of the duties on the cargos of their two ships which are to sail from Ja[mai]:ca in the beginning of May and are expected here early in July
>
> After the sales of these cargos are over they will see how they stand and if they find they have not a sufficient sum of money to enable them to go on without encroaching so much on your goodness, – they will rather sell one of their ships – and be satisfied with doing less, till their capital by degrees shall enable them to extend it with propriety – these resolutions I approve of and have confirmed them in –
>
> I see however that their business is an excellent one and with the command of more funds could be made both a sure and a profitable concern – but I cannot coin money for them and they must have patience.

However less than three months later, on 20 July 1807, the financial position had clearly not improved as Raeburn needed to write again to Simpson at the bank, on behalf of his son and stepson-in-law, requesting the loan of urgent funds to cover the costs of Custom House duties on cargo in one of the family company's ships, which had arrived from Jamaica and was due to dock imminently in Leith:

> My young friends hearing that you are just setting off to the country are very uneasy less they should be deprived of that friendly assistance which you have hitherto so liberally afforded them, having a ship in that fleet which is now arrived on the Downs, and which they hourly expect to see in Leith. They have

requested me to write to you and to entreat that before you go, you would enable them to pay some duties at the Custom House and also to beg that you would leave some directions with the person who will have the charge in your absence to accommodate them as far as possible the arrangements they are making will not make it necessary to be so heavy upon you in future occasions. –

I would have done myself the honour of calling upon you – but conceive you may be much occupied previous to your going away.

The lack of ready cash and further forthcoming loans continued to cause problems for Henry Raeburn & Co., as well as for Raeburn himself, since two and a half months later on 5 October 1807 the artist was compelled to write a desperate letter to Innes, the Depute Governor at the Bank, recounting the series of unfortunate economic events in the Caribbean – and notably the effect of the Napoleonic War on the company's ships – that had brought the firm close to collapse (Fig. 2.7):

My son whose business for a time was doing remarkably well has in the course of this last year, met with so many disasters, by one ship being lost – another long delayed by capture, recapture, and afterwards captured outright, and a third after being long delayed in Ja[mai]:ca from the shortness of this crop (which has disappointed many ships altogether and obliged others to come home with little more than ballast) has been obliged after all to go to London without a sale of cargo, – thus for more than a twelve months past his capital and credit has been on the stretch, not only without benefit to himself but with loss, – and to all this may be added, that there is no demand for West India produce nor likely to be, – all these things put together have so vext, disappointed, and disgusted him with ships, and with the West India trade in general, that he has come to the final resolution of relinquishing it altogether, being persuaded that he could make much more of his capital in any other line, and with the hundredth part of trouble and anxiety, that he has undergone for some time past. – and I finding that this business would not be carried on without my frequently applying to the Bank for aid – a circumstance extremely painful to me, and which I could not bring myself to do much longer, have agreed to his proposal with much pleasure, – accordingly the ship, which by the last accounts was in the Downs, and I suppose is now in London, – is already consigned to a House there, with orders to sell her, as soon as the cargo is out of her, – and it is also resolved that a new ship, which they had got for the trade, shall likewise be sold immedi-ately, – when these are done my mind will be relieved. – I have only to request and I think it will be the last time I shall have occasion to ask any thing of the kind that in case any of the bills, for which I am bound and which are all at your Bank, should fall due befor[e] the freight of that ship which is now arrived

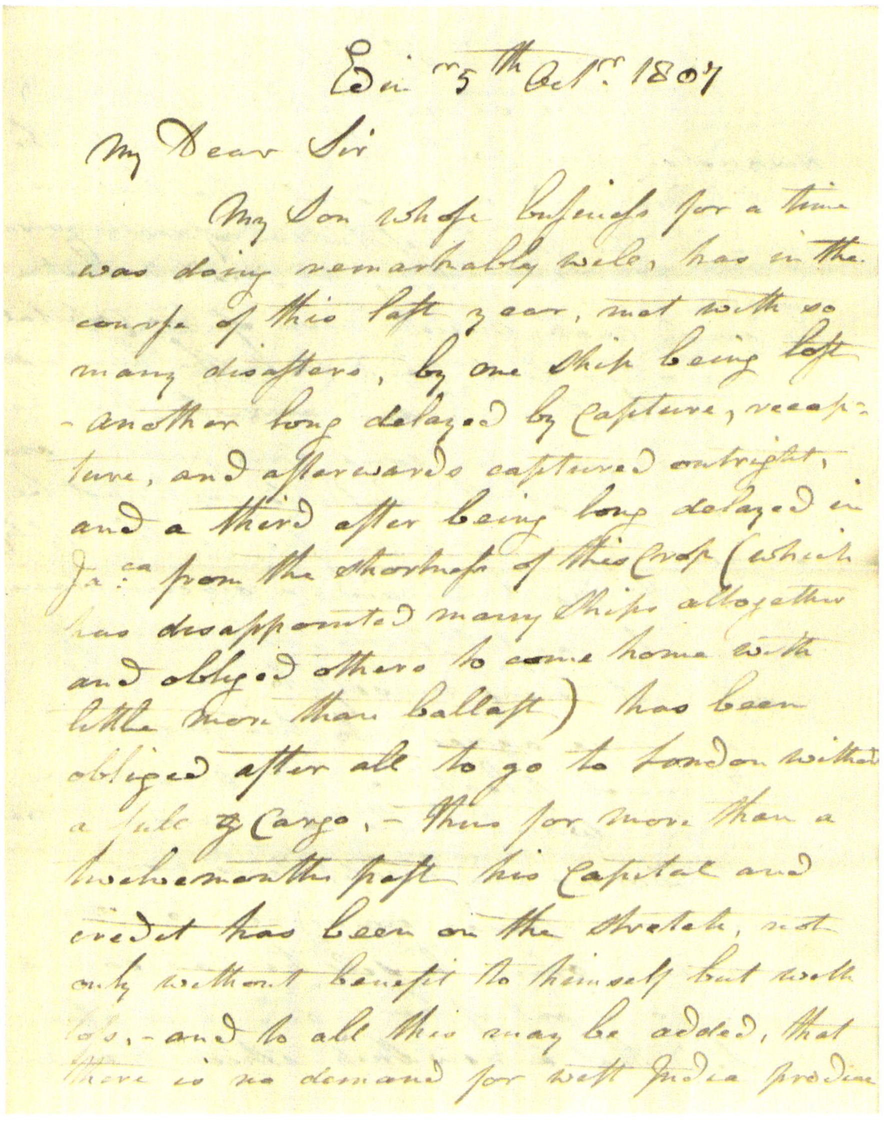

Figure 2.7 Letter from Henry Raeburn to Gilbert Innes, 5 October 1807, RBS Archives, RB/837/1743, fol 1r (reproduced by permission of the Royal Bank of Scotland Group plc)

can be collected, that you will have the goodness to renew them in part, – and my friend Mr Vere [Raeburn's stepson-in-law, Daniel Vere of Stonebyres], who knows and approves of my son's retiring from this business – and who has a large estate unencumbered and entailed, will join me in such as may be renewed if it be thought necessary. – on looking [at] my book I find the first one will fall due on the 24th of this month. I hope they will be in funds by that time, but in case they should not I take the liberty of making this early application that I may not be obliged to come upon you abruptly. When all this business is over, which I hope will soon be now – I shall have the pleasure of waiting on you to thank you for all your favors, and also Mr Simpson who has behaved to me in the kindest and most liberal manner, till then I confess I do not wish to see you. –

I had scroled this letter for you on Saturday – and was just done finishing it – when Mr Inglis called – and told me that Mr Simpson would not discount two bills that I had agreed to put my name to unless I first called upon you I hope what I have said above will make my calling unnecessary. – as you are in possession of every thing I can say upon the subject, and of what is already in train for being soon accomplished.

The impending crisis enveloping Henry Raeburn & Co. had reaching breaking point by the end of 1807, when – as has been discussed above – Raeburn in his letter written to Innes on 11 December offered his friend the banker a significant gift of a slightly imperfect Old Master painting of the *Martyrdom of St Bartholomew* by Guido Reni. The letter continued immediately on to the subject of Raeburn's exposure to liabilities on his son's and stepson-in-law's business and an urgent request for a personal loan:

My Dear Sir, my circumstances compell me to commit violence, on every sentiment of delicacy, and every feeling I have of propriety by thus accompanying what is in fact, the spontaneous effect of gratitude, with a request that will give you it all the delicate air of a vulgar bargain. –

I beg you will read the enclosed letter from my son, by which you will see that the ship [the *Isabella Simpson*] is not yet sold – and the uncertainty of her being sold in time to answer some demands that are coming on, keeps me in that state of anxiety that I have no peace or comfort. I wish to have it in my power to raise £1200, or 1300, by discounting a bill if I should require it, and renewable for some little time, and befor[e] I asked it. I would give a disposition to my house in town [York Place] as a security and which I am informed is worth more than £2,000, – As to the house I have long come to the resolution of selling it any rate, as I sit at by far too high a rent. – I therfor[e] pledge myself of my own accord to sell the house and repay the money – in the course of eighteenth months or two years at farthest. If not payed long befor[e] that which I have little doubt of, and by that time I shall have another place proposed that will answer my purpose equally well. –

I do not ask you to apply to the Bank – for that believe would be in vain, but perhaps it may be in your power to help me to it in some other way – I wish I could depend on some sort of it by 23 and the rest by the 28th of this month –.[30]

In another letter written six weeks earlier by Raeburn to Innes, the artist had listed the value of his property assets in Edinburgh with respect to his financial exposure of his son's firm, and in particular to his two closest financial supporters, his stepson-in-law Daniel Vere of Stonebyres and Gilbert Innes. This list of Raeburn's property assets had been drawn up by the valuer John Campbell, and they were listed as follows: his home, 'a property at St Bernard's' in Stockbridge at £10,000; 'another property at Stockbridge besides St Bernard's, a separate purchase' at £2,000; his house in town at York Place 'which builders reckon worth £2,000 and upwards even to them to sell over again'; and property in Leith 'which Mr Campbell considers as valuable'.[31] Raeburn continued in his letter: 'I will also endeavour instantly to raise some money upon some other part of my property – and if I am susceptible it will principally go to lessen my engagements with the Bank'. Raeburn then asked Innes to renew his current loans with the Bank, before signing off: 'believe me with a full sense of the obligations I am under to you'. The extent of Raeburn's problem with his family were also revealed in a letter sent the previous month (12 October 1807) from Raeburn to Innes, in which the artist had reacted to Innes's concerns over the fact that Raeburn's stepson-in-law Daniel Vere was guaranteeing the transactions of the family firm of Henry Raeburn & Co. to the Bank to the extent of £20,000.[32]

Despite the best efforts of Raeburn's family and friends, loans from the Bank and support from his friend Innes, the pressure on Henry Raeburn & Co. and on the artist's liability, became intolerable. The company went bust and a notice declaring its bankruptcy was placed in the *Edinburgh Gazette* on 12 January 1808.[33] The debts were over £36,000, against credits of just under £30,000, leaving, after adjustments, an outstanding debt of just over £14,000.[34] Innes himself was appointed one of the commissioners upon the estate of Henry Raeburn & Co., who assisted in the offer of a composition to satisfy the artist's creditors. To raise capital, the artist sold his studio in York Place, but retained a life-long lease. The company's new ship, the *Isabella Simpson*, was finally sold in 1808.[35] Meanwhile, a notice was placed in the Edinburgh newspapers announcing the sale – 'for behoof of creditors' – by public roup or auction at Mr Grinly's salerooms in Leith on 21 May 1808 of part of the sequestrated estate of Henry Raeburn & Co. All the articles of the roup and the inventory of the vessel were in the hands of Mr W. Scott Moncrieff, trustee on the sequestrated estate or John Ross, W.S.'.[36] This roup or sale by auction comprised of the good ship or lugger, called *The Harlequin*, 'with her Furniture and Apparrelling', as well as nine hogsheads 'of scale sugars on bond and six dozen of sherry wine'. Later that day in the warehouses of Henry Raeburn & Co. in North Leith, it was announced that there were to be sold 271 baskets or hampers, and 248 covers to them; about 20,000 fire bricks, three brass-barrelled blunderbusses; and an 'excellent six-seated writing-desk' and other articles belonging to the counting-house. Despite this financial catastrophe for Henry Raeburn and his family, it was not long before their entrepreneurial streak manifested itself again as property developers. From 1811 onwards the painter and his son, Henry Raeburn junior, began feuing the family's land on the St Bernard's estate in Stockbridge, with the intention of turning it into a fashionable property development – initially named Raeburnville – situated on the west side of the Water of Leith, just to the north-west of Edinburgh's New Town, and to this day known as Stockbridge.[37]

The full impact of the bankruptcy of Henry Raeburn & Co. and that of Raeburn himself was considerable, as is revealed in the important group of Raeburn documents and letters that emerged at auction in London in 1997 and were purchased by the National Library of Scotland. There were considerable tensions within the extended Raeburn family, notably between the artist and his two step-daughters Anne and Jacobina by his wife Anne Edgar, who had firstly married James Leslie. Jacobina – or Bina as she was known to her family – had married Daniel Vere of Stonebyres, who was one of the chief creditors of the failed company. Vere was owed substantial sums of around £8,000 by Raeburn, of which just over half had been repaid to Vere by the end of the artist's life. In an impassioned letter to Vere of 8 March 1813 Raeburn attempted to explain his financial predicament and his resorting to property development on the family estate by the Water of Leith, which created a suburb to Edinburgh's New Town:

> I am now fifty-seven years of age, and I foresaw and felt, that unless I could make something out of the ground – my payments from my own labor alone, tho I wore my life out in the struggle would never be worth the naming, not to say that if I fell sick I could neither pay nor live, for while I thus continued to labor with the hopeless and dispiriting prospect before me of never being out of debt, and still paid every farthing as I made it, it would never be in my power to make the smallest provision, even for my own existence in old age, if my unhappy situation suffered me to reach it much less for paying my debts, – It behoved me then in my humble opinion to make some effort, and try whether I could not establish an income that would with the assistance of my own business afford me facilities of paying my debts, that without such assistance, I could never expect to accomplish, tho I exhausted both my health and spirits and shortened my days in the hopeless attempt, and I saw none so likely to succeed, as going into that scheme of encouraging Builders to feu, by aiding them with a sum on the security of their Houses, and that would be safe both from the smallness of the

sums compared with the value of the Houses, and by following the advice of an eminent lawyer . . .[38]

Alongside the forced entrepreneurial development of the Raeburn family land by the Water of Leith, Raeburn continued to develop his critical relationship with the banker Gilbert Innes, who had assisted in the composition of the artist's massive debt, which was paid off gradually partially through his continuing portrait practice. Innes himself sat to Raeburn for an unidentifiable portrait, which after the banker's death was presented in 1834 by his surviving sister Miss Jane Innes (1748–1839) to the Society of Antiquaries of Scotland. Another three-quarter length portrait of Innes by Raeburn was passed down through collateral descendants of Innes and survives in a private collection, while a different half-length portrait by Raeburn of Innes is in the collection of the Royal Bank of Scotland. In October 1809, the year after the bankruptcy, Innes also paid Raeburn thirty guineas for his portrait of William Simpson of Parson's Green (d. 1808), who was Cashier to the Royal Bank of Scotland, and which remains in the bank's collection.[39]

Twelve years later Innes was involved in a plan to secure a highly prestigious commission for Raeburn. In July 1821 Andrew Duncan senior, the doctor and close friend of the artist, approached Innes to contribute to an association which was being formed to commemorate the reign of George III. Duncan suggested that a portrait of the late king by Raeburn should be hung in the public library of the University of Edinburgh 'to which he [the late King] had been a most liberal benefactor', the portrait costing £300.[40] It is not clear whether this commission ever went ahead, as the painting is not known to have been commenced or completed. However, the letter would appear to be evidence of Raeburn's old friends attempting to support him by engineering a royal portrait commission at the University of Edinburgh, to which he had contributed a number of portraits of some of its most distinguished members.[41] Nonetheless, shortly afterwards, during what was to be the last fifteen months of his life, Raeburn did receive royal approbation for his artistic achievements from the recently crowned George IV. On 10 May 1822, he received a letter from Sir Robert Peel informing him that he was appointed to the office of Painter to his Majesty in Scotland. Later that year, Raeburn received another letter from Peel stating that 'it is his Majesty's intention to confer on you the honour of knighthood, as a mark of approbation of your distinguished merit as a painter', and on 29 August 1822, during the last day of George IV's visit to Scotland, Raeburn was knighted by the king at Hopetoun House.[42]

These royal honours conferred on Raeburn by the king and the British state, even though granted at the end of his life, must have been immensely gratifying to the artist. He had dominated the Scottish art market and patronage for portraits, painting over one thousand likenesses since his return from studying in Italy over thirty-five years earlier. In the process Raeburn had created a new vision for the representation of Scotland's local and global elites, whether from the landed, mercantile or professional classes, whether from lowland or highland families, Glaswegian businessmen or Edinburgh lawyers, and whether from the East India Company or the West India Trade. The reasons for Raeburn's success can be located in his artistic talent, prodigious work-rate and gentlemanly, sociable demeanour. His network of friends and supporters such as Andrew Duncan and Gilbert Innes brought him key commissions and protected him as much as they could against the fallout from the disaster that overwhelmed his family's trade and shipping business venture to and from the Caribbean, for which he was the major guarantor. Although from a modest manufacturing background, Raeburn became part of – and indeed a nexus of – the Scottish establishment that he knew so well and which he depicted so intuitively.

For parallels to Raeburn's close connection with the West India trade and the resultant bankruptcy, it is instructive to compare key episodes from the lives of two other leading Scottish cultural figures of the period. In 1786 Robert Burns had almost taken ship for employment in the sugar plantations of Jamaica, a venture that was only curtailed on the success of the Kilmarnock Edition of his poetry, which had been published that year. Likewise, in 1826 the bankruptcy of Sir Walter Scott was caused by the unlimited liability he was responsible for when the publishing firm of James Bannatyne collapsed. Scott spent the last six years of his life keeping up a punishing schedule of writing in an attempt to pay back his creditors. He died prematurely in 1832 aged 62 with his health ruined, just as Raeburn's death in 1823 aged 67 was unexpected and his health had been adversely effected by his need to paint for money to keep his creditors at bay after his family firm's bankruptcy. As Scott put it in a letter of 15 April 1819 to Charles, 4th Duke of Buccleuch, when discussing whether to sit for a portrait by Raeburn as a commission for the duke's new library at Bowhill: 'I hesitate a little about Raeburn, unless your Grace is quite determined. He has very much to do; works just now chiefly for cash, poor fellow, as he can have but a few more years to make money'.[43]

Notes

1. I am much indebted to the following colleagues for their generous assistance and help in sourcing and providing me with access to the new archival and printed matter presented here: Richard Callander, Iain Milne, Ann Nix, Michael Nix,

Ruth Reed, Helen E. Smailes and Joanna Soden. For a recent contextual and thematic survey of Scots active in the British empire, see T. M. Devine, *To the Ends of the Earth: Scotland's Global Diaspora*, London, 2011; for Scots involved in business in London, with focal points on members of three families, Dalrymple of North Berwick, Sutherland of Rearquhar and Campbell of Barcaldine, see Stana Nenadic, 'Military Men, Businessmen and the "Business" of Patronage in Eighteenth-Century London', in Nenadic 2010, pp. 229–52; for the global interests of the Johnstone family of Westerkirk, see Emma Rothschild, *The Inner Life of Empires: an eighteenth-century history*, Princeton and Oxford, 2011. The dust jacket of the latter volume is illustrated with a reproduction of a rare family group portrait by Raeburn depicting adults: *John Johnstone, his sister Betty Johnstone and their great-niece Miss Wedderburn*, c. 1790–95, National Gallery of Art, Washington, DC.

2. Duncan 1824, p. 21; and John Chalmers (ed.), 'Duncan and Sir Henry Raeburn', *Andrew Duncan Senior: Physician of the Enlightenment*, Edinburgh, 2010, pp. 212–19. I am grateful to Iain Milne, the Librarian of the Royal College of Physicians of Edinburgh, for showing me Duncan's presentation copy to the library of his memorial address to Raeburn as well as the college's portrait of Duncan by Raeburn.

3. Mackie in Edinburgh and London 1997–8, p. 202 (for the year 1778).

4. All three portraits still belong to the University of Edinburgh and are still displayed in rooms in Old College, cf. Coltman and Lloyd in Edinburgh 2006, pp. 6–7.

5. See for instance: Marcia Pointon, *Hanging the Head: Portraiture and Social Formation in Eighteenth-Century England*, New Haven and London, 1993, esp. pp. 36–52; Stephen Lloyd et al., *Richard and Maria Cosway: Regency Artists of Taste and Fashion*, exh. cat., SNPG, Edinburgh and NPG, London, 1995–6; David H. Solkin (ed.), *Art on the Line: The Royal Academy Exhibitions at Somerset House, 1780–1836*, exh. cat., Courtauld Gallery, London, 2001 (New Haven and London, 2001); and A. Cassandra Albinson, Peter Funnell and Lucy Peltz (eds), *Thomas Lawrence: Regency Power and Brilliance*, exh. cat., NPG, London and Yale Center for British Art, New Haven, 2010–11.

6. For a catalogue of Raeburn's portraits, see Mackie 1994. After Raeburn's death there was a considerable backlog of unfinished portraits in his studio that needed completing. Duncan noted in his tribute to the Harveian Society: 'I have been informed by an ingenious young artist, Mr John Syme, who has been employed to finish Sir Henry's pictures, that he does not expect to be able to accomplish that undertaking in less than three or four years'. cf. Duncan 1824, p. 25. For Raeburn's portrait business being worth £3,000 per annum and the prospect (unfulfilled) of the London-based portraitist Thomas Phillips taking it over, see *The European Magazine* 1823, p. 436.

7. See chapters in this volume by Nenadic on Edinburgh's male professional elites and by Coltman and Evans on Raeburn's complex relationships with the Scottish aristocracy.

8. Cf. Mary Webster, *Johan Zoffany 1733–1810*, New Haven and London, 2011, pp. 152–4, and *Johan Zoffany RA: Society Observed*, Martin Postle (ed.), ex. cat., Yale Center for British Art, New Haven and Royal Academy of Arts, London 2011–12, p. 110, fig. 102 and p. 250, no. 79.

9. For Raeburn's portraits of the Fergusons of Raith, cf. Edinburgh and London 1997–8, pp. 70–3, nos. 11 and 12, and pp. 86–7, no. 18.

10. For Raeburn's response to Reynolds's work, cf. Irwin 1973, pp. 239–44. As David Mannings has noted, Raeburn's well-known double portrait of Sir John and Lady Clerk of Penicuik is closely based on the composition of Reynolds's painting of *The 2nd Earl of Egmont and his first wife Catherine Cecil* (Cartwright Hall Art Gallery, Bradford), which was engraved in 1756. Also see an interesting but anonymous critique of Raeburn's painting style, which was compared favourably to that of Reynolds, published after the artist's death in a unknown London newspaper; cf. 'Character of Sir Henry Raeburn RA as a Painter', Volumes of Press Cuttings from English Newspapers, July 1823, V, p. 1384, National Art Library, VAM.

11. James Balfour Paul, *The History of the Royal Company of Archers: The Queen's Body-guard for Scotland*, Edinburgh and London, 1875; *The Royal Company of Archers 1676–1951*, Edinburgh and London, 1951; *Archery in Scotland: an elegant and manly amusement*, by Margaret Buchanan, exh. cat., Glasgow Art Gallery and Museum, 1979; and John Burnett, *Riot, Revelry and Rout: Sport in Lowland Scotland before 1860*, East Linton, 2000, pp. 188–9.

12. Edinburgh and London 1997–8, pp. 83–5, no. 17. The portrait is currently on loan from The Queen's Body Guard for Scotland (Royal Company of Archers) to the SNPG, Edinburgh.

13. Bequeathed in 1874 by Beugo's daughter Agnes, Mrs John Scott, to the Royal Scottish Academy, Edinburgh, acc. no. 1993.199, cf. *Art Property in the Possession of the Royal Scottish Academy*, Edinburgh, 1883, p. 14.

14. Edinburgh 2006, pp. 29, and p. 27, ill.; the subscription and payment for the print is extensively documented in the archive of the Royal Company of Archers, Edinburgh.

15. Stephen Lloyd, *Raeburn's Rival: Archibald Skirving (1749–1819)*, exh. cat., SNPG, Edinburgh, 1999, p. 29, fig. 27 and p. 76, no. 155.

16. Ibid., pp. 24–5, fig. 18 and p. 67. no. 98; for *An Unknown Lady*, cf. ibid., pp. 67–8, no. 99, p. 18 and Stephen Lloyd and Kim Sloan (eds), *The Intimate Portrait: Drawings, Miniatures and Pastels from Ramsay to Lawrence*, exh. cat., SNPG, Edinburgh and BM, London, 2008–9, p. 93, no. 49.

17. For Danloux in Edinburgh, see Helen E. Smailes, 'A French painter in exile:

Henri-Pierre Danloux (1753–1809)', exh. cat., SNPG, Edinburgh, 1985, in *France and the National Galleries of Scotland*, Edinburgh, 1985, pp. 31–54; A. J. Mackenzie-Stuart, *A French King at Holyrood*, Edinburgh, 1985; and Lloyd 2005.

18. Lloyd 2003, p. 108.

19. Correspondence between Innes and the Scottish neoclassical sculptor Thomas Campbell, which refers to Raeburn on various occasions over the period from 1817 to 1823 is published in full in Smailes 2009; also see the chapter by Helen E. Samiles in this volume.

20. Innes MSS, NRS, GD 113/1/158/188.

21. *Gilbert Stuart*, by Carrie Rebora Barratt and Ellen G. Miles, exh. cat., The Metropolitan Museum of Art, New York and National Gallery of Art, Washington, DC, 2004–5, pp. 34–8, no. 6; and Andrea G. Pearson, 'Gilbert Stuart's *The Skater (Portrait of William Grant)* and Henry Raeburn's *The Reverend Robert Walker, D.D., Skating on Duddingston Loch*: a study of sources', *Rutgers Art Review*, VIII, 1987, pp. 55–70. Pearson concludes that there is no formal or stylistic link between the two paintings. However, if Stuart's painting of *The Skater*, remained viewable by artists either in Edinburgh or in East Lothian, Henri-Pierre Danloux may have had access to it, when painting *The Skating Minister*, although he went on to create a very different type of composition, emphasising the elegant and graceful forms created by Walker in full profile. Like William Grant and the Revd Robert Walker, Gilbert Innes was a keen skater, being President of the Edinburgh Skating Club for many years at this period, having joined the club in 1778, the same year as Grant and two years before Walker.

22. Innes MSS, NRS, GD 113/5/452/34.

23. See above n. 4, Lloyd (ed.), 1995–6, pp. 73–88 and pp. 130–3; and also Stephen Lloyd, 'The Cosway Inventory of 1820: listing unpaid commissions and the contents of 20 Stratford Place, Oxford Street, London', *The Walpole Society*, LXVI, 2004, pp. 163–217. For Raeburn and Skirving as art advisers in Scotland for Buchanan, cf. Hugh Brigstocke (ed.), *William Buchanan and the 19th century Art Trade: his Letters to his Agents in London and Italy*, Paul Mellon Centre for Studies in British Art, London, 1982. Also see William Buchanan, *Memoirs of Painting, with a Chronological History of the Importation of Pictures by the Great Masters into England since the French Revolution*, 2 vols, London, 1824.

24. Innes MSS, NRS, GD 113//5/457/167. This painting is untraced. However, Guido Reni is known to have painted at least one canvas of this subject, which formerly belonged to Queen Christina of Sweden in Rome and the ducs d'Orléans in Paris before the latter collection was exported to London during the 1790s and sold there by a consortium and through public exhibition. It is possible that this painting is the one that was owned by Raeburn, although it is more likely to be a variant by Guido Reni or from his studio.

25   These advertisements, which are from the series of microfilmed Edinburgh newspapers held in the Edinburgh Room of the Edinburgh Central Library, were drawn to my attention by Michael Nix. Ann Nix also informed me of the description of the ship in *Lloyd's Register* for 1809, when she was later owned by Sibbald & Co. and captained by master Gourlay. It was stated that the vessel was defended with '2×6 pounder guns' and '8×18 p[oun]d[e]r carronades'.

26.   In addition a Henry Raeburn & Co advertisement from earlier that year, placed in *The Caledonian Mercury* on 30 January 1807, referred to another ship, the *Addington*, which announced: 'AT LEITH FOR TRINIDAD, The Coppered Ship ADDINGTON, Capt. –, Is now ready to receive goods, and will sail from this early in February to join the first convoy at Portsmouth. For freight or passage apply to HENRY RAEBURN & CO. Leith, Jan. 24, 1807. TWO BLACKSMITHS WANTED, to whom liberal encouragement will be given.'

27.   See Ralph Davis, *The Rise of the English Shipping Industry in the 17th and 18th Centuries*, Newton Abbot 1972. For an overview of the deep Scottish involvement in the Caribbean sugar trade and plantations worked by African slaves, cf. T. M. Devine, *Scotland's Empire 1600–1815*, London, 2003, pp. 221–49, and T. M. Devine, *To the Ends of the Earth Scotland's Global Diaspora*, London, 2011, pp. 32–55.

28.   These items are a selection drawn from a typical inventory of goods exported from Leith to Jamaica in 1820, which has been extracted from the *Leith Commercial List*, and which was drawn to my attention by Michael Nix.

29.   These letters (RB/837/1613; RB/837/1683; and RB/837/1743) were brought to my attention by Ruth Reed, Senior Archivist at The Royal Bank of Scotland Group plc, Edinburgh. Extracts from the three letters are published here for the first time by permission of The Royal Bank of Scotland Group plc.

30.   Innes MSS, NRS, GD 113/5/457/107.

31.   Innes MSS, NRS, GD 113/5/457/148.

32.   Innes MSS, NRS, GD113/5/147/175.

33.   Mackie in Edinburgh and London 1997–8, p. 205.

34.   Raeburn's predicament in early 1808 was described in a letter of 16 February written by his friend Alexander Cunningham and sent to John Morrison at Auchincruive House, Ayrshire: 'I had a walk with my worthy friend, Raeburn. He had realised £17,000, which is all gone. He has offered a small composition, which he is in hopes will be accepted. He quits this to try his fate in London, which I trust in God will be successful. While I write this I feel the tears start'. The original letter is untraced, but was published in the *Glasgow Herald*, 28 November 1908, and quoted in Greig 1911, pp. xl–xli and Mackie in Edinburgh and London 1997–8, p. 205.

35.   Between 1808 and 1826 the *Isabella Simpson* was owned by the established Leith and Edinburgh mercantile firm of William Sibbald and Co., who traded West

India sugar and rum. The firm of Henry Raeburn & Co. owned another ship, *The Ann*, which may have been named after Raeburn's wife. A Westindiaman bearing this name is depicted in a painting – in effect a standard triple portrait of the ship – titled *The Ann off Birkenhead*, painted by Robert Salmon (1775– c. 1845), c. 1810, oil on canvas, 85.1×135.9cm, National Maritime Museums, Greenwich, acc. no. 1928–47.

36. Advertisement, [Edinburgh Newspapers] before 21 May 1808, microfilm in the Edinburgh Room, Edinburgh Central Library.

37. For the Raeburn family's development of their land as Raeburnville (Stockbridge), see Kerr 1982; John Gifford, Colin McWilliam and David Walker, *The Buildings of Scotland: Edinburgh*, Harmondsworth, 1991 (1st edn, 1984), pp. 404–10, for 'The Raeburn Estate', Stockbridge; and Connie Byrom, *The Edinburgh New Town Gardens: 'Blessings as well as Beauties'*, Edinburgh, 2005, pp. 363–6.

38. The previously unknown collection of Raeburn manuscripts was sold at Phillips, London, 13 November 1997, lot 350; they were purchased by NLS, acc. 11479. They include the letter from Raeburn to his stepson-in-law Daniel Vere of Stonebyres, which was sent from the artist's studio in York Place, Edinburgh, on 8 March 1813. Despite repayments made by Raeburn and his family, a claim of £17,816.8s.4d was still outstanding against Henry Raeburn & Co. as late as 1885.

39. Information about the portrait of Innes by Raeburn in a private collection has been provided kindly by Helen E. Smailes. See Innes MSS, NRS, GD 113/5/368, for the receipt for 30 guineas, signed by Henry Raeburn in October 1809, and paid by Gilbert Innes of Stow, for a portrait of the late William Simpson.

40. See Innes MSS, NRS, GD 113/5/478/134, for the letter from Duncan to Innes of 16 July 1821.

41. Coltman and Lloyd in Edinburgh 2006, pp. 3–7.

42. Thomson in Edinburgh and London 1997–8, p. 28 and Mackie in Edinburgh and London 1997–8, p. 211.

43. For Burns see Eric J. Graham, *Burns & the Sugar Plantocracy of Ayrshire*, Ayrshire Archaeological and Natural History Society, Ayrshire Monographs XXXVI, Ayr, 2009, esp. pp. 7–13, 59–61 and 93–7. For Scott see Iain G. Brown, 'Scot, Literature and Abbotsford', *Abbotsford and Sir Walter Scott: the image and the influence*, Iain G. Brown (ed.), Society of Antiquaries of Scotland, Edinburgh, 2003, pp. 4–36; and ibid. '"Consigned with indifference to the chance of an auction": the lives and meanings of Sir Walter Scott's "Writing-Cabinet"', *Bulletin of the Edinburgh Sir Walter Scott Club*, 2010, pp. 10–20. For Scott's quotation about Raeburn and money, see Lloyd 2003, p. 103.

3

Scotland's Canova and the Immortal Raeburn

Helen E. Smailes

'The first day I called he asked if I was an Artist and where from I told him I had the Misfortune to be a Scotchman'. With this cryptically loaded statement, the Edinburgh monumental mason and novice figure sculptor Thomas Campbell (1791–1858) described in a letter to his first known and most influential patron Gilbert Innes of Stow, Depute-Governor of the Royal Bank of Scotland, his initial encounter with Thomas Lawrence in London in the autumn of 1817. Painter-in-Ordinary to the King and a leading Royal Academician recently knighted by the Prince Regent, Lawrence had courteously 'asked very kindly after Mr. Raeburn.' The circumstances of Lawrence's solicitousness towards Raeburn require some explanation, likewise Campbell's perception of his ethnically defined 'Misfortune'.[1]

In March 1810 David Wilkie had noted in his private journal that Raeburn had leased the late John Hoppner's house in London with a view to settling there permanently. Throughout May 1810 Wilkie brokered introductions for Raeburn to a number of prominent London artists, culminating in a meal on 4 June at the Crown and Anchor in the company of the Royal Academy President Benjamin West. Raeburn was much fêted. Two years earlier he had petitioned for sequestration following the catastrophic failure of the firm in which his son Henry and his stepson-in-law were business partners. This declaration of bankruptcy and the redemption of Raeburn's own related debts had obliged him to sell his Edinburgh tenement on the north side of York Place, which incorporated a gallery for the public display of portraits and a studio built to his own specifications. The eventual outcome of Raeburn's London reconnoitre was a decision not to transfer his portrait practice to the south. But, as the doyen of Scottish portrait painters and, from 1810, a regular exhibitor at the Royal Academy, he had continued to aspire to the status of Academician – an ambition finally realised in 1815. Stylistically and conceptually, especially in its heightened romanticism, Raeburn's finest portraiture of this period reveals his intense awareness, if not emulation, of Lawrence (one of the best known examples is the half-length of *Margaret Macdonald, Mrs Robert Scott Moncrieff* in the Scottish National Gallery, painted about 1814; Fig. 12.1). And on 18 June 1818, being equally mindful of Lawrence's metropolitan pre-eminence and European reputation, Raeburn was to pen a letter of recommendation to Sir Thomas on behalf of their shared protégé Thomas Campbell.[2]

Born in Edinburgh in 1791, the son of a local 'gentleman servant', Campbell had served an apprenticeship as a monumental mason with John Marshall, marble cutter of Leith Walk. About 1813, Campbell received his first recorded independent commission as a figure sculptor, executing two freestone (sandstone) heads for the portico of St Mary's Chapel (the present St Mary's Metropolitan (Roman Catholic) Cathedral) in Edinburgh. By 1815, when he modelled a bust of Professor Robert Blair of the University of Edinburgh, he had attracted the attention of Gilbert Innes of Stow (1751–1832) while employed in fitting out Innes's lavish townhouse at 24 St Andrew Square. As late as 1858 the *Art Journal*'s obituary of Campbell, which is clearly redolent of first-hand knowledge, was to revive the memory of Innes's early patronage as a paradigm of enlightened capitalism.[3]

By the time he embarked on his sustained patronage of Campbell, Innes had already received the freedom of the City of Edinburgh in 1814 for his exceptional contribution to the improvement of the public amenities and the cultural life of the Scottish capital. And he was well on the way towards becoming the richest commoner and self-made magnate in Scotland: at his death in 1832, his assets exceeded £41,000,000 in modern terms.[4] Gilbert's own progress towards such unprecedented ascendancy over a period of fifty years had been initiated by the entrepreneurship of his father George (1703–80), the second son of Gilbert Innes of Rora and a scion of the Aberdeenshire gentry. George Innes had inaugurated a powerful and prolonged dynastic association between the Royal Bank of Scotland, the Inneses and their close kinsmen the Simpsons and the Mitchells. This was to be perpetuated through the Bank's directorate into the 1880s. Serving as second cashier from 1745 to 1777 and then as cashier from 1777 to his death in 1780, George Innes – who was succeeded in the senior post by his nephew William Simpson – may also have benefited privately from his official administration of the Jacobite estates confiscated after the Forty-Five Rising. In 1758, when Deputy-Receiver General for Scotland, he purchased from Lord March the Borders barony of Stow near Galashiels. The Innes family's expansionist re-assimilation into the landowning classes and related spheres of influence was continued by Gilbert from the 1780s with comparable acumen and opportunism.[5]

After studying at Edinburgh University – but apparently without graduating – Gilbert inherited the Stow estates and all of his father's stocks and shares on the latter's death in 1780. That same year, Gilbert featured for the first time in the Edinburgh street directories as a resident of Mylne's Court near the Tron Kirk, then an exclusive locality frequented by the hereditary aristocracy and the senior judiciary. His occupation was given as 'writer', a generalised designation which may have signified 'man of business' rather than advocate as in common parlance.[6] In 1784, while still in his early thirties, Innes made a strategic move to 24 St Andrew Square in the heart of the socially exclusive commercial and banking quarter of the New Town. Boasting no fewer than forty windows and gardens at the back affording panoramic views across the Firth of Forth towards the hills of Fife, Innes's town mansion was eventually equipped with two four-wheeled carriages and three male servants.[7] Within three years of this move, he was appointed a director of the Royal Bank. His promotion to Depute-Governor in 1794 coincided with the escalation of the French Revolutionary turmoil, ensuing paranoia in Scotland about the prospect of an invasion of Britain, and fears of a commercial disaster in an era of greatly increased demand for money and a vast extension of credit. During a credit crisis in Glasgow with repercussions throughout Scotland, Innes excelled as a front line negotiator with the government of William Pitt the Younger. Partially devised by the Royal Bank's delegation, the rescue plan was still recalled in 1832 when the *Caledonian Mercury* published the most informative contemporary review of Innes's business career and profile in public life in its obituary of 1 March.

As the *Caledonian Mercury* observed in 1832, 'Mr Innes was connected with all the useful and fashionable institutions of the city of Edinburgh' through a combination of genuine philanthropy and self-serving commitment to his family's social advancement. At twenty-one he was already a member of the prestigious Edinburgh Musical Society, rising to Director in 1782 and assuming much of the Society's administration during its final phase in the 1790s. And from the 1780s he cultivated a phenomenally diverse range of other cultural pursuits through membership of societies whose constituency encompassed the professional, intellectual and social elites of Scotland: the Society of Antiquaries of Scotland (a fellow from 1784 and Vice-President at his death in 1832); the Royal Society of Edinburgh (elected an ordinary fellow in 1800); the (Royal) Highland and Agricultural Society of Scotland (admitted in 1799 and honorary treasurer from 1814 to 1832); the Wernerian Natural History Society; the Astronomical Institution; the Caledonian Horticultural Society; and the (Tory) Pitt Club, amongst others. Most significantly for his patronage of Thomas Campbell, Innes was appointed in 1808 a commissioner of the Board of Trustees for Manufactures in Scotland, the governing body of Edinburgh's pioneering school of applied design, the Trustees' Academy. He was to remain a commissioner until 1832, his death also occurring one month after his election as an ordinary director of the Royal Institution for the Encouragement of the Fine Arts in Scotland of which he had been a founding member in 1819.[8] Concurrently, Innes acted as a manager of the Royal Infirmary of Edinburgh, one of several quasi-public offices which earned him the freedom of the city in 1814.

Innes's prodigious energy in the public domain was matched by his personal life, a fact edited out of all contemporary press obituaries. The totality of his private as well as public enterprises was apparently not revealed until 1839 and then only as a direct consequence of the death of his similarly unmarried and only surviving legitimate sister, Jane Innes, his sole heir and executrix, in 1832. Jane herself having lived with extreme frugality in the interim, the inheritance of the substantially increased Innes fortune was vigorously contested by several kinsmen. Within a year the case was resolved in favour of William Mitchell of Parson's Green (1778–1860), second cousin of Gilbert and Jane Innes and, from 1841 to 1843, an ordinary director of the Royal Bank of Scotland. From 1840, as heir-at-law to the financial assets of his late second cousins, Mitchell assumed the additional surname and the arms of Innes. The remaining landed estates, including Stow, passed to Mitchell's grand-nephew Alexander Mitchell (1831–73), then a minor.

Both of the Mitchells were shortly to become involved with Thomas Campbell's final portrait commission for the extended Innes family.[9] In the meantime W. Strathearn, a 'law genealogist' embroiled in the litigation, pronounced that, 'Gilbert begat 67 Bastards . . . and the acts of his whoredom are written in the parish chronicles of Scotland'! Despite their problematic social status, several 'bastards' fathered by Gilbert Innes in the Burnet family made comfortable middle-class marriages (three of the Burnet daughters married Dr George Wood, Major Menzies, and the Madeira wine merchant Robert Wallace or Wallas respectively). Among Campbell's first sitters in Edinburgh were Euphemia Menzies, née Burnet, and Dr Wood whose busts were both ordered by Innes. Beginning in 1815, these commissions typified the combination of altruism and expediency which motivated Innes's extension of his existing patronage of the fledgling sculptor, almost invariably by investing inexpensively in portraits of close family members or kinsmen by marriage.[10]

However modest, these commissions played a crucial role in facilitating the sculptor's transition from craftsman to artist. Campbell's dilemma or 'Misfortune', as outlined to Sir Thomas Lawrence in 1817, was that of all contemporary indigenous Scottish artisans aspiring to the practice of sculpture as a fine art prior to about 1830. In 1837 Campbell's special pleading would be echoed in George Cleghorn's polemical review of the state of the arts in Scotland in which he opined that, since the Middle Ages, 'sculpture, with the exception of the mere trade of a marble cutter, was a dead letter, all our busts, statues and monuments being executed by English and foreign artists.' Cleghorn identified three fundamental problems which impeded the development of a resident rather than a partially expatriate Scottish school of sculpture: the relative inadequacy of localised educational provision; the as yet unchallenged hegemony of English sculptors, both in portrait and in monumental figure sculpture (most conspicuously exemplified by the award of the Edinburgh Burns Monument statue to John Flaxman in 1822 and the city's George IV Monument to Francis Chantrey in 1824); and the lack of guaranteed institutional facilities for exhibiting work publicly and attracting patronage.[11]

Formed in 1808 with the aim of establishing an annual exhibition in Edinburgh comparable to that of the Royal Academy, the Associated Artists had hoped to stem the relentless exodus of Scottish artists to London by intensifying the stimulus of internal competition and improving the prospects for local patronage. This was to be achieved by instituting a relatively autonomous academy regulated by artists for artists and under the presidency of the Edinburgh portraitist George Watson, a slightly younger competitor of Raeburn. Raeburn's motivation in subletting his private gallery at 16 (now 32) York Place to the newly constituted association was ideological as well as financial. But this market-oriented palliative measure was to prove short-lived and was sabotaged by factionalism, allegedly fuelled by Raeburn's interventionism and high-handed conduct.[12] Six years after the demise of the Associated Artists and two years after Campbell's introduction to Thomas Lawrence, the Institution for the Encouragement of the Fine Arts in Scotland was inaugurated – modelled, with correspondingly high expectations, upon the British Institution in London (Fig. 3.1). But although the Edinburgh Institution sought to address many of the issues highlighted by Cleghorn, including the education of public taste in Scotland, the exclusion of practising artists from the administration of the Institution's promotional exhibitions of modern Scottish art and their financial management, precipitated the schismatic formation of the (Royal) Scottish Academy in 1826.

Both of these crucial institutional developments, with their promise of a cultural renaissance in Scotland, nurturing and nurtured by indigenous practitioners, came too late for Campbell. In the meantime, the only viable local supplement to a traditional apprenticeship as a monumental mason was provided by the Trustees' Academy of which Gilbert Innes was a

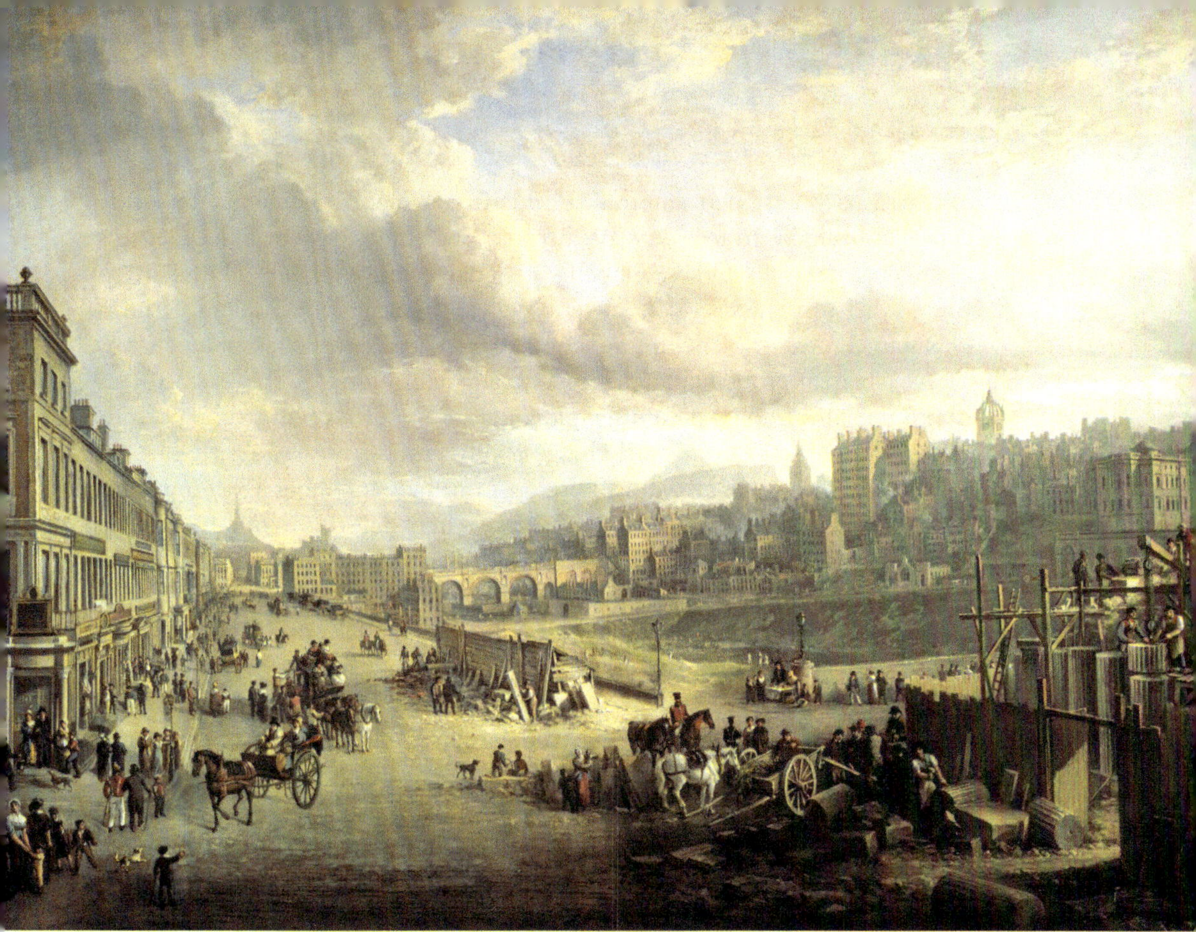

Figure 3.1 Alexander Nasmyth, *Princes Street with the Commencement of the Building of the Royal Institution*, c. 1825, oil on canvas, 122.5 × 165.5cm, Scottish National Gallery, Edinburgh

governor by virtue of his office as a commissioner of the Board of Trustees for Manufactures in Scotland. Established on strictly utilitarian principles as an elementary drawing school for the improvement of applied design in 1760, the Trustees' Academy had evolved organically into the only sustainable facility in Scotland for training artists as well as craftsmen. In 1798 the Trustees had resolved to broaden their founding remit by promoting advanced art education, citing as their paradigm the Royal Academy Schools in London. Almost twenty years later, the Edinburgh academy still lacked two vital resources which could have alleviated Campbell's 'Misfortune' – formal tuition in life drawing and a sizeable teaching collection of plaster casts after the canonical pieces of antique figure sculpture. However, *faute de mieux*, Campbell sought and was granted admission to the Trustees' Academy, *gratis*, in November 1815.[13]

From 1817, presumably on the conclusion of the usual two-year period of study at the Trustees' Academy, the novice sculptor became the beneficiary of a visionary although paternalistic loan repayment scheme, proposed by Innes and subject to five percent interest. Sustained for over a decade, this arrangement facilitated Campbell's otherwise unattainable admission to the Royal Academy Schools in January 1818 as a mature student of John Flaxman, Professor of Sculpture since 1810. Once enrolled, Campbell was able to benefit from Flaxman's recent augmentations of the cast collection while also finding gainful employment as a journeyman to the portrait and narrative sculptor Edward Hodges Baily (1788–1867), a newly elected Associate.[14] From his arrival in London in or by September 1817 until the mid-1820s, Campbell chronicled his progress in exhaustive detail in a prolific correspondence with Innes. The sculptor's own letters were motivated by a highly developed if rather erratic sense of accountability, a constant need for moral support, and a genuine personal regard, which was reciprocated by Innes with quasi-paternal affection despite Campbell's relative maturity. By the spring of 1818, according to his own testimony, Campbell was admitted to Flaxman's studio, had secured a similar entrée to the elderly Joseph Nollekens on a privileged basis and was receiving informal advice from 'Mr. Westmacott'. Campbell's mentor was probably Sir Richard Westmacott (1775–1856), a former student of Canova and, as Britain's premier official sculptor of public monumental statuary at this time, another role model for the ambitious younger Scot.[15]

In the course of 1818 Campbell persuaded Innes to extend their standing arrangement to an indeterminate period of study in Rome. This was to encompass the intensive practice of life drawing, immersion in the legacy of classical antiquity, expert instruction in carving and polishing statuary marble, and integration into the international community of sculptors in Rome then dominated by Antonio Canova and Bertel Thorvaldsen.[16] Peter Free of the Royal Bank of Scotland's London agents, Pole, Thornton, Free, Down & Scott, was authorised by Innes to bankroll Campbell on demand, remitting money via Messrs Torlonia of Rome. Free, who took an independent interest in the sculptor's progress and commissioned a bust of himself in 1817 or 1818, was additionally entrusted with the shipment of his unfinished portrait busts to Italy in the form of artist's plasters.[17]

En route to Italy, Campbell wintered in Paris where, over the New Year of 1819, he obtained an introduction to the Dowager Duchess of Devonshire, stepmother to the 6th Duke, the creator of the celebrated sculpture gallery at Chatsworth and one of Canova's most distinguished patrons.[18] On 17 March, Campbell reached Rome, where he took lodgings in a former convent at 18 via S. Isidoro: he was equipped with a wittily ambivalent testimonial to Canova from the Duchess. In limping Italian, she warmly commended the 'Sfortunato Scultore Scozzese' – again, the clichéd conjunction of Scottishness and misfortune, but from an English, cosmopolitan and aristocratic perspective! While Campbell's commitment to self-improvement and his zeal to meet Canova were exemplary, his inarticulacy in French or Italian and his unprepossessing demeanour were to be deplored. But, she maintained, he was no less deserving of Canova's protection.[19]

Within a week of arriving, Campbell wrote exultantly to Innes that Canova had 'received me very kindly and has thrown his studio entirely open to me I may go and do what I want at any convenience . . . The other artist Torwaltzden [sic] has made the same liberal promises.' Paradoxically, by the close of the year, Campbell reported that unnamed fellow sculptors had 'advised me to keep clear of Canova, which I do as much as possible, and to ground myself in the Greek style.'[20] But, following his permanent return to Britain in 1830, Campbell's complex adulation of Canova and Thorvaldsen and his implicit claim for recognition as an artistic heir of both sculptors were to be reflected in the furnishing of his London studio with plaster casts after their greatest works. Meanwhile, both Canova and Thorvaldsen were persuaded to collaborate in enterprises which served incidentally to enhance Campbell's independent professional standing both in Rome and in Edinburgh.

In 1816 the Board of Manufactures – of which Innes was then an experienced commissioner – had secured some highly desirable casts after the newly arrived Elgin Marbles. This initiative inspired a far-reaching although rather ad hoc programme of compensatory purchasing of casts for the Trustees' Academy. As a self-styled authority on the antique, Innes's protégé acted as the Board's accredited agent on the Continent from 1821 to 1826 or 1827. In 1821, following Canova's offer to the Trustees of a prime cast of any of his own works, Campbell negotiated the gift of a 'first cast' of Thomas Hope's *Venus*. By 1822 Campbell was able to ship from Leghorn a cast of Thorvaldsen's *Mercury* as another prize acquisition for the Edinburgh academy.[21]

Coincidentally, the *Scots Magazine*, which had long enjoyed an expatriate as well as resident Scottish readership, carried a feature on the two doyens of European sculpture in 1821 – testifying to the intense interest among the middle class as well as aristocratic Scottish connoisseurs and Grand Tourists. The extent to which Campbell himself stood to gain by cultivating this dual association was confirmed the same year by an unqualified eulogy in a review of the (Royal) Institution's exhibition of modern paintings in Edinburgh. The *Edinburgh Magazine and Literary Miscellany* opined as follows:

> We rejoice, for the honour of this country, however, that it has given birth to
> an artist, who, though he has furnished nothing to this Exhibition, is destined,

we are confident, to raise the celebrity of the island, in the art of sculpture, to an eminence which it has never yet attained. Those of our readers who have been in Italy, need not be informed that we allude to Mr. Campbell, who is now completing his education at Rome under the auspices of Canova and Thorvaldsen, whose productions have fully justified the sanguine expectations which his friends formed of his future eminence before leaving this country. These two great masters have already pronounced him to be the first young sculptor in Italy; and judging from his first essays, some of which are at present in this city, we have no hesitation in predicting that, if he continues to advance as he has hitherto done, he will be an ornament to his country, and give to the name which he bears the same distinction in sculpture, which it has already attained in the sister art of poetry.[22]

Among the consignment of Campbell's *modelli* shipped to Rome in 1819 by Peter Free was a bust of Innes himself begun in 1816 or 1817 and another of the above-mentioned Euphemia Menzies, one of Innes's sixty-seven 'bastards'. As already observed, while studying at the Royal Academy Schools, Campbell had closely monitored Chantrey's technical facility and working methods. In March 1818 Campbell sought permission to execute a second bust of his patron 'in Chantry's plan which requires only four sittings', and simultaneously announced his intention of leaving London briefly for Scotland following a family bereavement in Edinburgh. On 18 June 1818 Raeburn penned his letter of introduction to Lawrence on behalf of Campbell. This was either posted to London or, more credibly, handed to the sculptor in person. Six months later, Free was asked to ship the *modello* of Campbell's new bust of Raeburn from London to Rome.[23]

Gilbert Innes himself was acquainted with Raeburn by or before 1808, conceivably as a result of the latter's sequestration that year, or, in the light of fresh evidence, as a result of a series of commissions to Raeburn from close kinsmen of the Innes family. Either way, Campbell probably owed his entrée to the painter to this pre-existing business connection with Innes. In its posthumous appreciation of Raeburn in November 1823, the *European Magazine* extolled his generosity towards younger artists. His empathy with Campbell's challenging professional circumstances at the outset of his career – his determination to achieve the transition from artisan to sculptor despite the inherent social disadvantages of his humble origins – seems very plausible.[24]

The precise degree of Sir Henry's wider intellectual and aesthetic engagement with the practice of sculpture is still open to speculation. In 1792 as his ascendancy over David Martin, the previous doyen of Edinburgh portraitists, began to pay dividends, Raeburn had modelled a profile self-portrait in red wax to be cast in vitreous paste in collaboration with James Tassie (Fig. 3.2).

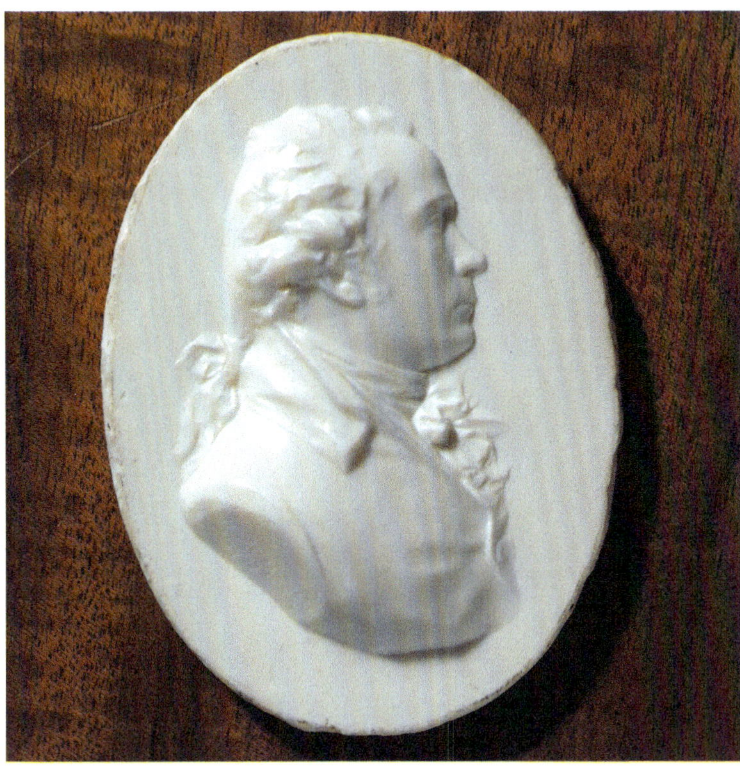

Figure 3.2 Henry Raeburn and James Tassie, *Henry Raeburn*, 1792, paste medallion, height 7.6cm, Scottish National Portrait Gallery, Edinburgh

The artistic lineage of this supposedly unique experiment is surely to be sought in Raeburn's formative association with the goldsmithing profession and his early independent practice as a miniature painter. But his subsequent connections with and regard for Francis Chantrey are arguably far more suggestive. During the late 1980s, the status of two remarkable companion portrait drawings of and by Raeburn and Chantrey in the Scottish National Portrait Gallery was investigated by the present writer with the assistance of the American photographic historian Larry J. Schaaf. Later inscriptions on both drawings – apparently in the hand of Wilkie Collins, the novelist and son of the painter William Collins – explain that they were executed in Princes Street, Edinburgh, on the same occasion in 1818 when Chantrey allegedly returned to the Scottish capital on account of his Viscount Melville monument for Parliament House. Both drawings have been recognised since the 1980s as productions of the camera lucida, an optical instrument invented by William Hyde Wollaston in 1807 and, in a slightly different form, much

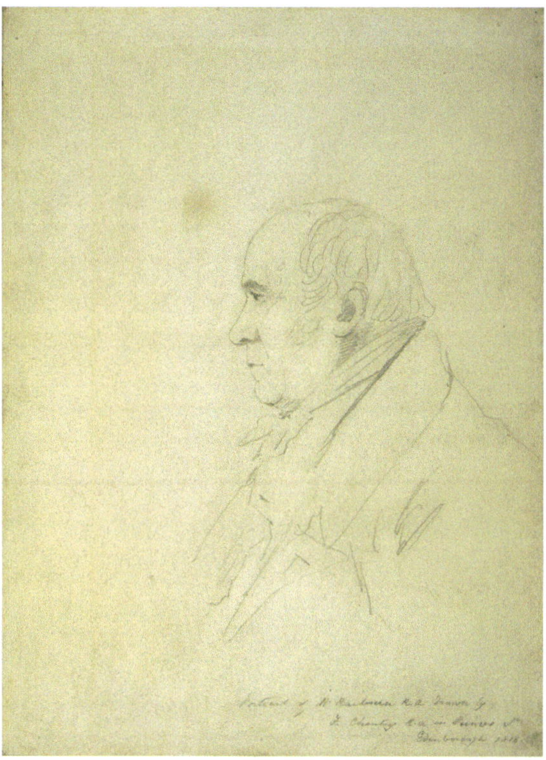

Figure 3.3 Francis Legatt Chantrey, *Henry Raeburn*, 1818, camera lucida pencil drawing, 29.3×21.4cm, Scottish National Portrait Gallery, Edinburgh

favoured by Chantrey as an expedient for preparatory portrait studies. His expertise in manipulating this popular but recalcitrant device is revealed by the assured handling of his profile of Raeburn (Fig. 3.3). Raeburn's handling, by comparison, is markedly tentative.[25] But both drawings testify to a valued acquaintance since at least 1814 when Chantrey sat for one of two known oil portraits by Raeburn and of which one was gifted by the painter to his sitter. Furthermore, as David Mackie has observed, the parameters of this relationship extended to occasional reciprocal facilitation of portrait commissions.[26]

Campbell's own eloquent posthumous tribute to Raeburn adds a further dimension to existing speculation about Sir Henry's reported fascination with sculpture. On 4 October 1823 Campbell wrote to Innes from Rome, as follows:

I am exceedingly sorry to hear of the death of my worthy friend Mr. Raeburn his advice to me on art I esteem more than even Canova or Thorwalsden he had such an Idea of breadth in sculpture and so very free from affectation or French style which is so much the rage of the present day. If there is a Monument to be Erected I hope they will allow me to send a Design for it as I think I have an Idea that might perhaps suit.

This revealing letter of condolence was drafted just over a year after the translation to marble of Campbell's unique bust of Raeburn, once in the possession of his great-grandson William Raeburn Andrew and, since 1926, in the Scottish National Portrait Gallery. This bust bears an incised inscription on the back: THO:S CAMPBELL ROMA. 1822.

At his most accomplished, as T. L. Donaldson commented in the *Art Journal* in 1858, Campbell 'possessed the peculiar felicity of seizing the individual likeness of his sitters and giving them a sentiment and expression highly characteristic'.[27] Yet the bust of Raeburn is invested with a visionary intensity and senatorial gravitas that transcends particularity and is redolent of apotheosis. In this respect, it is certainly analogous with Raeburn's own self-portrait as a summation of artistic achievement. Now in the Scottish National Gallery, this *Self-portrait* (Fig. 3.4) was submitted to but declined by the Royal Academy upon Raeburn's election as an Academician, self-portraits being ineligible for the Diploma collection. The portrait therefore reverted to the artist. Although an archetypal image and a powerful symbol of Raeburn's metropolitan renown, his self-portrait was, however, neither the immediate prototype for nor the direct antecedent of Campbell's bust *all'antico*, as has previously been assumed. Nor was William Nicholson's etching after the self-portrait, executed in 1818 for the serially published *Etched Portraits of Distinguished Scotsmen* and accompanied by an interesting biographical account of Raeburn and critique of his style.[28]

In March 1818 the bust of Raeburn was still an unrealised project, the deadline for its inception being Campbell's anticipated departure for Italy in May – actually deferred until November. But, in the New Year of 1819, the original plaster was shipped to Rome in time for the sculptor's arrival in March. On 1 November 1821 Campbell wrote to Innes from Rome, as follows:

Mr. Raeburn's Bust will be finished [ie in marble] on the fourth of Novr., when I shall take the liberty of drawing upon you for the Amount of fifty pounds, in favour of Messrs. Torlonia & Co payable at Messrs. Down, Thornton & Free . . . when I had just finished the Model at Mr. Raeburn's house he insisted on me taking five pounds to Account. So that there will be still five pounds remaining, which I shd. wish to be paid to Mrs. Hogarth My Aunt [ie in Edinburgh] whom

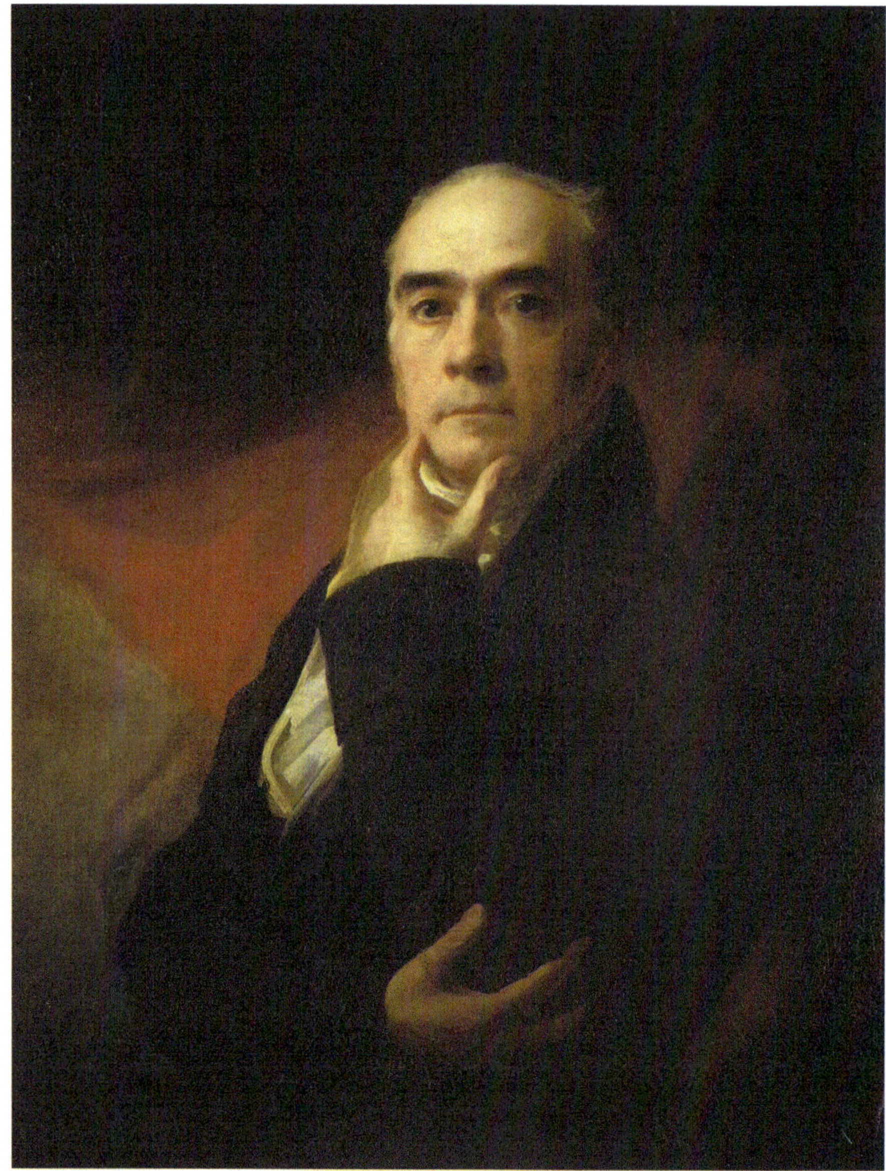

Figure 3.4 Henry Raeburn, *Self-portrait*, 1815, oil on canvas, 89×69.5cm,
Scottish National Gallery, Edinburgh

I have commissioned to purchase some necessaries for me. The Bust will cost
Sixty Pounds. Therefore I will need a receipt for the five pounds making in full
fifty five pounds, and write immediately to Mr. Raeburn that I have drawn upon
you for that Amount.

Campbell's statement, corroborated by Innes's meticulous record keeping, seems quite clear. Raeburn commissioned his own bust (Fig. 3.5), almost certainly as a means of furthering the sculptor's career. Interim payment was then channelled through Gilbert Innes as their mutual benefactor. And the timing of Raeburn's letter to Lawrence – June 1818 – is surely indicative of the period of Raeburn's sittings to Campbell in Edinburgh. Further corroboration is provided by Innes's exhaustive chronicling of Campbell's circumstances on the eve of his departure for London in the summer of 1818. The entry for 22 June 1818 in Innes's private memorandum book included the following observation:

> Thos Campbell goes for London tomorrow . . . he also carries a new Clay Bust lately made for me one of Mr Raeburn & [one] of Mr Gilchrist [Ebenezer Gilchrist of the British Linen Bank] along with him these with Peter Frees & Mrs Menzies are all to be cut in Statuary Marble.[29]

It may or may not have been fortuitous that Campbell's bust was completed in marble in Rome and delivered to Edinburgh in 1822, the year in which Raeburn was knighted during George IV's visit to Edinburgh. In 1824 the secretary of the Board of Manufactures congratulated Campbell belatedly on his achievement, recalling Sir Henry's own gratification.[30] One possible reading of the sculptor's self-promoting letter of condolence to Innes, as cited above, is that he envisaged a potential public monument to Raeburn as the most convincing stratagem for launching his own career as Scotland's indigenous counterpart to Chantrey and / or Samuel Joseph in monumental sculpture. If that was indeed the case, Campbell's genuine expression of grief and regret was here combined with an opportunistic and rather ill-judged bid to canvass Innes's support. In the event, Campbell was to make his monumental debut a year later by securing the commission for the Edinburgh memorial to the 4th Earl of Hopetoun – a coup in which, as will become apparent, the backing of Innes, Sir James Gibson Craig of Riccarton and Lord Gray of Kinfauns was to prove decisive.

In the meantime Campbell was patently unaware that his own opportunism had been anticipated by his exact contemporary, the expatriate London sculptor Samuel Joseph (1791–1850). In 1821 Joseph had become the first notable English sculptor to set up a studio in Edinburgh, developing a lucrative business in portrait busts on the basis of the Scottish patronage which he had obtained since 1815. Such was his success in integrating himself into the Edinburgh intelligentsia that, in 1826, he was to become a founder-member of the (Royal) Scottish Academy. But in 1829 he was to return to London after failing to secure any major public commission in competition with, amongst others, Chantrey and Campbell.[31]

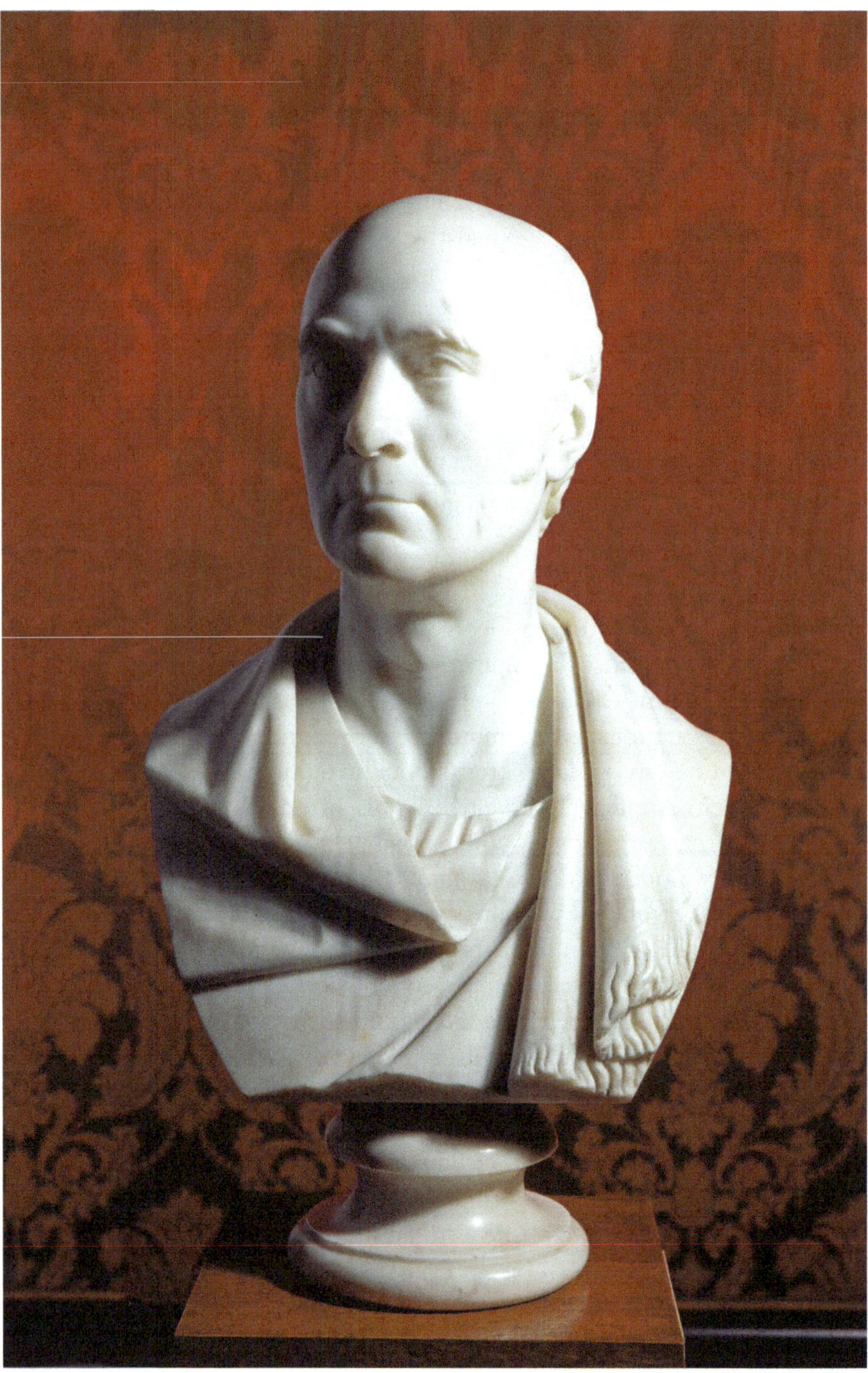

Figure 3.5 Thomas Campbell, *Henry Raeburn*, 1822, marble bust, height 64.4cm, Scottish National Portrait Gallery, Edinburgh

Immediately after Raeburn's death on 8 July 1823, Joseph had been invited by Henry Raeburn junior to make a death-mask despite his profound distress over his late father's changed appearance. When approached by the Edinburgh phrenologist George Combe in a letter written on the day of Raeburn's death, Raeburn junior demurred, expressing his repugnance at the prospective use of any cast in a public exposition of phrenology. Moreover, it was only in response to a more sensitive intervention from Lord Chief Commissioner William Adam of Blair Adam, a sitter and patron of Sir Henry, that the younger Raeburn had overcome his reluctance to have any deathbed likeness taken. In his delayed reply to Combe, Henry Raeburn emphasised the strictly private nature of this undertaking by Joseph. But in replying to Adam on 18 July, Henry Raeburn was already consoling himself with the idea of a public monument which might be erected in his father's native Edinburgh through the influence of the Lord Chief Commissioner. For the likeness he envisaged three potential sources: Raeburn's own *Self-portrait* (Fig. 3.4) which, as already explained, had remained in the artist's own possession; the death-mask by Joseph; and Campbell's bust.

By October 1823 news of the death-mask, a supposedly private memorial, had reached the directorate of the Institution for the Encouragement of the Fine Arts in Scotland. The existence of the mask was probably leaked by Joseph himself who was then reputedly working on a commemorative medal of Raeburn and whom the Institution contemplated approaching for a marble bust of him as the nucleus of a projected (national) collection of modern Scottish art.[32] Ultimately, however, it was not until 1900 that Raeburn would be appropriately honoured through the Board of Manufactures's commission to James Pittendrigh Macgillivray, the Queen's Sculptor for Scotland, for a full-length statue for the façade of the Scottish National Portrait Gallery.

In commissioning his own likeness as an act of friendship and patronage, Raeburn conferred the highest accolade upon Campbell's aptitude for portrait busts, already recognised by Gilbert Innes in advance of the sculptor's admission to the Trustees' Academy. Within a year of his Roman debut in 1819, the rapid expansion of Campbell's clientele for this genre necessitated a strategic move to a larger studio in the basement of 12 Piazza Mignanelli and one with especially rich associations. In 1770 the same premises had been occupied by Thomas Banks and his collaborator the Scottish sculptor James Durno. Campbell's new studio was adjacent to the Piazza di Spagna which, since the seventeenth century, had been the epicentre of Roman artistic and literary life: it was here that the itinerant Grand Tourist colony preferred to reside and congregate. Furthermore, Campbell's chosen locality was close to the Via Babuino and another sculptural enclave, clustered around one of Canova's former studios.[33] In 1824, two years after the death of Canova, the up-and-coming English neo-classical sculptor John Gibson noted that, 'the Cavr. Thorwalsten is now the prince of sculptors. Among the English a <u>Mr Campbell</u> [illegible] of edinbourg has the most to do <u>but it is in busts</u>.' Campbell had finished Gilbert Innes's bust in July 1820, Canova himself having volunteered to procure a flawless block of Carrara marble – a luxury which was effectively financed by the sitter and would doubtless have been unaffordable without his sustained sponsorship.[34]

Canova's collaboration was the ultimate tribute Campbell could offer his patron. In March 1821 the sculptor ingratiatingly rationalised the delayed despatch of his portrait bust to Scotland:

> I was persuaded by my friends to keep it beside me while the English travellers and families of distinction remained in Rome . . . and I am sure from expierience that you will feel pleasure in thinking that your Bust has proved the means of my professional success . . . I am at present engaged with the Busts of the Duke of Hamilton, Sir Wm. Drummond, Sir James Erskine, and Mr. Hamilton, under Secretary of State.

Flattery aside, Innes's multifarious social and business network, which encompassed both the professional middle class and the hereditary aristocracy in Scotland, endowed this bust with the magnetism to attract yet further high profile patronage. And a similar level of expectation may well have attached to the presence in Campbell's Roman studio of his definitive bust of Raeburn, both with regard to Scottish Grand Tourists and to their London-oriented English counterparts. Of the works in progress itemised by Campbell, his marble bust of Sir James Erskine of Torrie, 3rd Bart (1772–1825), a kinsman of the Earls of Mar, a former Major-General in the Peninsular War and connoisseur-collector of Dutch Old Master painting, was completed in 1823 and is currently on loan to the National Galleries of Scotland from a Scottish private collection. In 1823 the last baronet, Sir John Drummond Erskine, was to renew his late brother's patronage of Campbell with a similar commission following the latter's return to Britain.[35]

Increasingly, Campbell viewed patronage for bust portraiture as a means to an alternative end. Portraiture was a corollary to monumental and / or ideal sculpture, a genre in which the proximity of Canova and Thorvaldsen fired him into emulation. The roll-call of Campbell's sitters in 1821, as he revealed in the letter cited above, was headed by the premier peer of Scotland, the 10th Duke of Hamilton. Hamilton's first order – for his own bust – initiated an extremely prestigious sequel of commissions which could well have launched Campbell as a monumental sculptor. In November he risked the Duke's confidentiality and his promised remuneration of £400 through disclosure to Innes:

> I continue to study on as extensive a scale as my means will permit. My having been kept in suspense almost the whole summer by the Princess Borghese who was to have sat to me for her Bust, I have not been able to execute a very extensive Order with which the Duke of Hamilton honored me. Not only a Bust but a Statue of the Princess Borghese to be done in Marble and sent to Scotland, but the death of her Brother has postponed it for a time The Duke wished this to be kept secret therefore I would not wish it to go much further.[36]

When Hamilton's scheme foundered, a virtually identical commission was offered to Campbell by another *cavaliere servente* of Pauline Borghese, the 6th Duke of Devonshire. Devonshire likewise began by sitting for his own bust in Rome in 1823 before resolving upon a bust and a monumental figure of Napoleon's celebrated sister. Despite the sculptor's disclaimers, the finished statue was conceived from the outset as a pendant to Canova's *Madame Mère*, as purchased for Chatsworth in 1818. For the privilege of doing 'ample justice to Your Grace' and executing a work 'that shall be able to stand beside the high finishing of Canova', Campbell ventured a (disputed) price of £500 sterling and cited in justification similar estimates quoted to Lord Kinnaird and the Duke of Leeds for ideal groups then in progress. But if Campbell indeed aspired to become the British sculptural heir-presumptive to Canova courtesy of ducal patronage, he forfeited his chances by failing to deliver the Borghese group until 1840 – eighteen years after the Marchese's death and ten years after his own return to Britain.[37]

By the mid-1820s Campbell's landed patrons included a strong group in central Scotland: Lord Gray of Kinfauns near Perth (also a patron of John Gibson), Lord and Lady Ruthven, Lord Balgonie (later Earl of Leven and Melville), and the 8th Baron Kinnaird of Rossie Priory. A connoisseur-collector of Italian Old Master painting and Graeco-Roman antiquities, Lord Kinnaird was the older brother of Byron's friend, banker and executor, Douglas Kinnaird. Kinnaird patronage, including busts of both brothers and of Lady Olivia Kinnaird, was to produce Campbell's consummate achievement in ideal statuary and his most focused attempt to test the problematic market for this genre in his native Scotland. Currently on loan to the Scottish National Gallery, his exquisite group of Arthur Fitzgerald Kinnaird as *The Young Ascanius* (the son of Aeneas of Troy) (Fig. 3.6) was executed in Rome at Byron's suggestion after an exclusive costume ball in 1822 at which the young Lord Conyers Osborne appeared in comparable undress as *The Young Hannibal* and was also sculpted by Campbell for his father the Duke

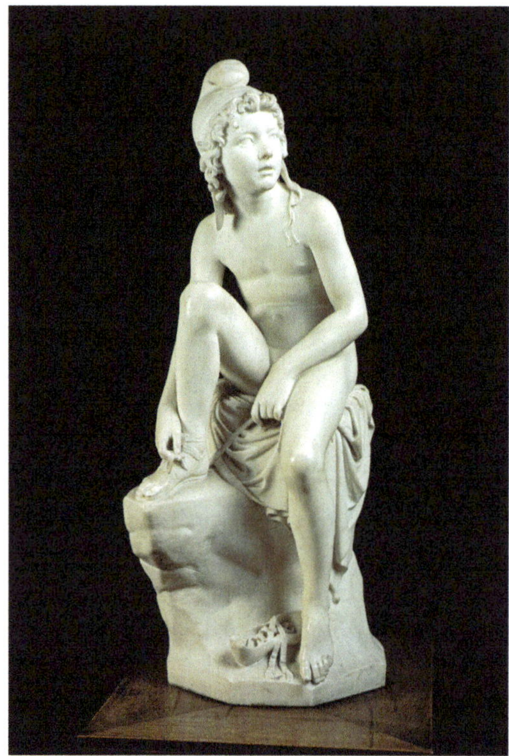

Figure 3.6 Thomas Campbell, *The Young Ascanius*, 1822, marble statue, height 117cm, private collection (on loan to the Scottish National Gallery, Edinburgh)

of Leeds. Despite their exceptional quality, these examples of a hybrid genre uniting the attributes of portraiture and ideal statuary had no known succession in Campbell's work.[38]

In 1858 Campbell's obituarist T. L. Donaldson censured him for his failure to integrate into the British expatriate artistic community in Rome, while admitting that, 'he, however, associated much with Thorvaldsen and the German artists [Nazarenes] and occasionally with the French, by whom he was highly esteemed.' In a rare overview of the fine arts in Rome in 1829, *The Scotsman* likewise rehearsed received opinion about Campbell's unpopularity among his British peers, but patriotically conceded his excellence in busts and figures. Predictably, this same review lionised Thorvaldsen and, in particular, his *Shepherd in Repose* or *Shepherd Boy* of 1817. Such was the renown of this group that, during the mid-1820s, a fourth version was under execution in Thorvaldsen's Roman studio – later acquired by the Hope family and now in Manchester City Art Gallery. Canova having died in

1822 and contemporary connoisseurship having pronounced this group to be a masterpiece, there seems little doubt of Campbell's intention of measuring himself against the surviving doyen of European neo-classical sculpture in designing *The Young Ascanius*.

In addition *The Scotsman* of 1829 highlighted Campbell's most ambitious, expensive and controversial commission to date and the one upon which he was now depending for the launch of his career as a monumental sculptor, the eagerly anticipated monument to Raeburn having come to nothing. By April 1829 Campbell was engaged in refining in his Rome studio the colossal model for the Edinburgh monument to the 4th Earl of Hopetoun (1765–1823). General Sir John Hope had been a distinguished combatant in the Peninsular War, notably at Corunna. Latterly, in civilian life, he proved a discerning picture collector and restructured the Old Master collections at Hopetoun with the self-interested agency of Andrew Wilson (1780–1848), the Scottish landscape painter, dealer and, from 1818 to 1826, Master of the Trustees' Academy.[39] From 1820 until his death in 1823 Hopetoun served as Governor of the Royal Bank of Scotland, his tenure thus coinciding with that of Gilbert Innes as Depute-Governor (1794–1832).

Constituted in 1824, the high-powered subscription committee for the Hopetoun Monument was dominated by Innes as honorary treasurer and by the prominent Whig lawyer, Sir James Gibson-Craig of Riccarton (1765–1840), a friend of Innes and another dedicated Campbell patron. In September 1824 Campbell was one of a restricted number of candidates invited to submit designs in quasi-open competition. His principal rival was Samuel Joseph. Shortly after arriving in Edinburgh in 1821, Joseph had secured the backing of William Trotter of Ballindean, head of the premier Scottish dynasty of cabinetmakers, subsequently Lord Provost of Edinburgh in 1824–5 and an ex-officio member of the Monument committee. Despite this powerful alliance and to Joseph's utter mortification, the commission was awarded to Campbell on Christmas Day 1824. He owed this victory to the combined advocacy of Innes, Gibson-Craig and, reputedly, Lord Gray of Kinfauns.

Having thus broken the English monopoly of public sculpture in Scotland, from Flaxman to Chantrey, Campbell was hyped by the *Edinburgh Magazine and Literary Miscellany* as the 'vigorous genius' who 'may probably originate the sculptural fame of his country.'[40] Triumphalist expectations of the regeneration of Scottish sculpture as a longer-term consequence of this breakthrough were surely intensified by the re-siting of the Monument from Charlotte Square at the west end of the city to a prime position symbolic of the Royal Bank's strategic role within the Scottish national economy. In 1819 the Bank had expanded into new premises in St Andrew Square. Six years later the Bank relocated again to Dundas House, the former Excise Office which had originally been built by Sir Laurence Dundas as the most imposing private residence in the New Town. Campbell's monument, costing 6000 guineas, was to be erected on this key site in the mansion's gardens, fronting the east side of the square and, fortuitously, within direct sight-line of Gilbert Innes's house at number 24.

As already noted, Innes was a founding director of the Institution and a long-serving commissioner of the Board of Manufactures, the proprietors of the Institution building on Princes Street which was designed by William Henry Playfair and opened in 1826. In 1829 Campbell was allowed to display his colossal model of the Earl of Hopetoun in Playfair's new temple to the arts. This promotional exhibition coincided with that of Laurence Macdonald's equally colossal ideal group of *Ajax and Patroclus*, then in plaster and shown at the same venue. This exceptional privilege, extended simultaneously to Campbell and Macdonald, epitomised public and institutional aspirations then focused on the Hopetoun Monument. And the Board and the Institution shared a wider vision of the actual building (Fig. 3.1) as a cultural powerhouse for Scotland, providing stylish accommodation for the Trustees' Academy, and rented facilities for the Institution's exhibitions, and for the Society of Antiquaries of Scotland and the Royal Society of Edinburgh.

Disastrously for Campbell, the Hopetoun project was jeopardised by ongoing cash-flow problems arising from non-payment or deferred payment for other private commissions and compounded by conceptual difficulties. The installation of the Monument was delayed until 1834, a decade after its inception. As evidenced by the report in *The Scotsman*,[41] the public response was ambivalent – especially in relation to the unresolved 'awkwardness' of the whole composition and, by implication, Campbell's unorthodox choice of a dismounted, standing figure in Roman consular pose (Fig. 3.7). Despite his immersion in the antique, he had eschewed predictable sculptural compositional precedents for the representation of a military hero and in particular the celebrated bronze group of Marcus Aurelius on the Piazza del Campidoglio in Rome. Although the genesis of the Monument was so protracted, Campbell's eventual sources of inspiration were probably far more localised and contemporary: the late equestrian full-length portraits by Raeburn which are monumental in scale and conception and deeply indebted to the work of Reynolds. Raeburn's own portrait of the *4th Earl of Hopetoun* (Fig. 4.8) had been completed about 1817 and in 1822 the Edinburgh engraver William Walker had published a fine reproductive stipple print (Fig. 4.9).

In the meantime Innes, whose relationship with his protégé had been undermined by the debacle over the Hopetoun Monument, had died in February 1832. In September the sculptor's surviving Edinburgh ally Gibson-

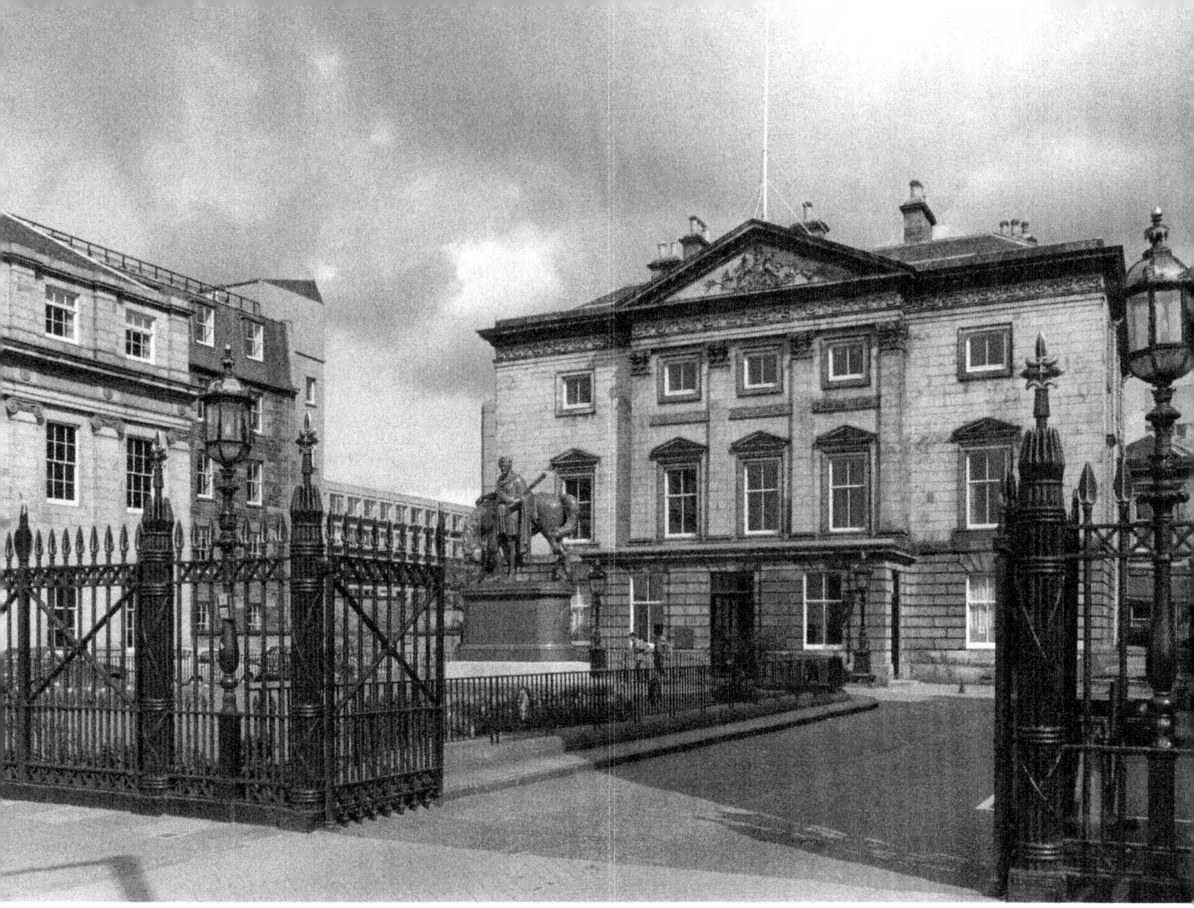

Figure 3.7 *The Hopetoun Monument and Dundas House (Royal Bank of Scotland)*, reproduced courtesy of the Royal Commission on the Ancient and Historical Monuments of Scotland, Edinburgh (photograph © Joe Rock)

Craig warned him that his unconscionable dilatoriness would cost him an even more prestigious public commission for the Scott Monument, to be financed by international public subscription and erected on Princes Street. Although Campbell disregarded this prediction and submitted a design for a standing figure of Sir Walter Scott in cast iron, the contract went to the young John Steell who, like Campbell himself, had had to make the transition from artisan to sculptor. Thereafter Steell was to assume, in lieu of Campbell, the primacy in Scottish monumental sculpture. In 1830, as the *Art Journal* recalled in 1858, he returned permanently to Britain from Rome with commissions worth £30,000. But he settled in London and his later British patrons, apart from the 10th Duke of Hamilton, were predominantly English.

Following Innes's death, intestate, in 1832, his unmarried sister Jane became his sole heir and executrix and prey to a bombardment of charitable requests as well as begging letters from her late brother's illegitimate offspring. Just prior to her own death in 1839 Jane Innes agreed to commission a memorial bust of Gilbert for the Royal Highland and Agricultural Society of Scotland of which he had been a member since 1799 and honorary treasurer from 1814 to 1832. This idea was first mooted in 1838. The instigator was apparently Sir John Forbes of the Royal Bank, Innes's successor as the Society's honorary treasurer and who recalled Innes's own unrealised offer of presenting a bust of himself for the Society's hall. An approach having been made to Jane Innes, the renewed proposal was promptly frustrated by her death and that of the nominated sculptor Francis Chantrey. In 1842, however, Jane Innes's principal heir-at-law William Mitchell of Parson's Green took up the project after assuming the additional surname and arms of Innes in 1840. The Society's directorate now favoured John Steell as the resident and rising star of Scottish bust portraiture and monumental public sculpture. But Mitchell-Innes, whose young co-heir-at-law and grand-nephew Alexander had inherited Campbell's original marble bust of Gilbert Innes, decided upon Campbell.[42]

Based in London since 1830, Campbell was then completing the Aberdeen monument to the Duke of Gordon, his only Scottish commission of this type since the ill-starred Hopetoun Monument mediated by Innes, Gibson-Craig and Lord Gray back in 1824. With unusual promptitude, Campbell executed this replica (Fig. 3.8) of his original bust as Mitchell-Innes's gift to the Society. It was delivered within four months in April 1843. The donor himself had been invited to become honorary treasurer to the Society, thus perpetuating the Innes family connection, but had declined on health grounds. It is nonetheless tempting to speculate that his altruism was not unrelated to the public legitimisation of his recently contested claims to the Innes fortune.[43]

Campbell himself, perhaps mindful of having alienated Gilbert Innes's good opinion through his conduct over the Hopetoun Monument, had condoled with Jane Innes in March 1832 over the loss of 'one who was my first & best Patron.' The sculptor was also mortified by the realisation that the delayed despatch of his bust of Dr Wood, husband of Innes's illegitimate daughter Marion Burnet, must have coincided with Gilbert's death. In concluding his letter to Jane Innes, Campbell attempted to set the record straight with regard to his own indebtedness to Innes:

> A few years since I was so anxious to have a likeness of my respected Patron, that I had a portrait painted by Mr Watson Gordon, which was left in St Andrews Square, until I should have a house of my own fit to receive it. Perhaps you will do me the favour of taking charge of it, until I am so circumstanced.[44]

But the last word on the Scottish Canova, his relationship with Innes and the latter's probable involvement in the sculptural immortalisation of Raeburn,

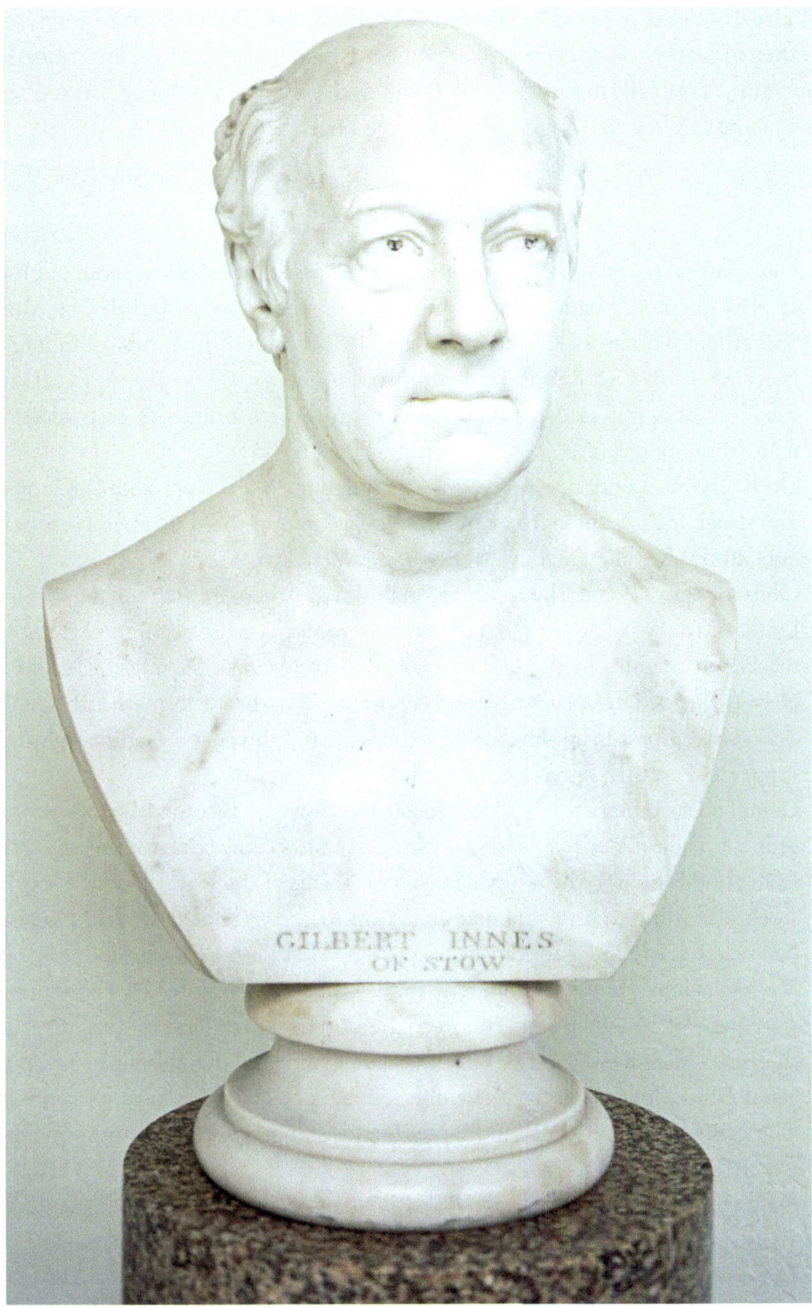

Figure 3.8 Thomas Campbell, *Gilbert Innes of Stow*, 1843 (autograph replica of the original marble bust of 1821) marble bust, height 49.5cm, reproduced by kind permission of the Royal Highland and Agricultural Society of Scotland (photograph by AIC Photographic Services for the Scottish National Gallery, Edinburgh)

had already been penned by Peter Free, the Royal Bank's London agent, in an effusive letter to his co-adjutor Gilbert Innes in 1819: 'You are indeed his Maecenas. You talk about Scotch pride and Poverty. As far as I have seen, the warmest hearts & longest Purses have been Scotchmen.'[45]

Notes

1. I am grateful to the following people for their assistance with research published in this chapter: Hugh Honour, Willie Johnston, Paolo Marini, Jim Murray and Adele Thomson. Letter from Campbell, London, to Innes, Edinburgh, 6 November 1817 (NRS, Innes of Stow Muniments, GD113/4/163(357)). See Smailes 2009, pp. 242–3, which is based on these Muniments with additional contextual material.

2. On Raeburn's London venture, see Cunningham 1843, I, pp. 280, 296, 297 and 299. Raeburn's letter of recommendation is among the Lawrence correspondence in the Royal Academy Archives, LAW/2/288.

3. Obituary by Thomas Leverton Donaldson in the *Art Journal*, New Series, London, 1858, IV, pp. 107–8. For the most recent concise account of Campbell, see Helen Smailes in the *Oxford Dictionary of National Biography*, Oxford and New York, 2004, IX, pp. 866–7; and Robin Lee Woodward, 'Nineteenth-Century Scottish Sculpture', unpublished doctoral thesis, University of Edinburgh, 1977, I, pp. 56–9 and III, pp. 41–5.

4. Campbell's obituarist T. L. Donaldson (see note 3) recorded Innes's personal estate at the time of his death as being over £1,000,000 (in sterling, as distinct from pounds Scots), the equivalent of two-thirds of the Royal Bank of Scotland stock according to an estimated valuation in 1829. This figure had previously been quoted in *A Series of Original Portrait and Caricature Etchings by the late John Kay, Miniature Painter*, Edinburgh, 1838, I, p. 307 (footnote). A contemporary statement of Innes's assets, countersigned by his sister Jane as executrix, is in the Innes Muniments (NRS, GD113/5/122); and a related inventory of his personal estate, lodged on 23 November 1832, is NRS, SC70/1/47, pp. 798–807. The NRS curatorial staff kindly provided the modern computation of Innes's fortune.

5. Neil Munro, *The History of the Royal Bank of Scotland 1727–1927*, Edinburgh, 1928, lists the Bank's successive governors, directors and cashiers. The purchase of the Stow estate in 1758 began the process of gentrification (NRS, GD113/3/513(20)). Gilbert Innes's independent investments as a landed proprietor continued until at least 1820 with the purchase of The Drum at Gilmerton from a judicial sale.

6. This interpretation was volunteered by Gillian Peebles: Gilbert Innes is not recorded as a member of the Faculty of Advocates. For George Innes's testa-

ment, see NRS, CC8/8/125, fols. 205ff; other lands inherited by Gilbert from his father are inventoried in *Ledger for the Rent of Lands & Houses belonging to Gilbert Innes of Stow . . . (1780–1809)*, NRS, GD113/1/339.

7. Ruth Reed, Archives Manager of the Royal Bank of Scotland Group, has confirmed that the present 24 St Andrew Square, was indeed Innes's town residence. The building was partially remodelled in 1970.

8. Innes's appointment to the Board was noted in the Trustees' minute books on 16 November 1808, NRS, NG1/1/31, p. 10. The extent of the surviving documentation in the Innes Muniments suggests that he was probably proactively involved with the Musical Society. See J. L. Cranmer, 'Concert Life and the Music Trade in Edinburgh c. 1780–1830', unpublished doctoral thesis, University of Edinburgh, 1991; and Philippa Godfrey, 'Gilbert Innes, Esq, of Stow: Banker, Musician and Patron of Music in Eighteenth-Century, Edinburgh', unpublished Masters dissertation, University of Edinburgh, 1992.

9. An obituary of Jane Innes was published by *The Scotsman*, 7 December 1839, reiterating previous accounts of Gilbert: 'The great bulk of the fortune which is the largest, we believe, ever gained by one individual in Scotland, was the acquisition of Mr. Innes himself, and was due to his industry and skill as a banker.' The legitimisation of the contested Mitchell claims depended upon their direct descent from Elspet Simpson, niece of George Innes of Stow, first cousin of Gilbert and Jane, and wife of Alexander Mitchell (d. 1822). See *Burke's Landed Gentry of Great Britain* under Mitchell-Innes of Whitehall.

10. References to Innes's illegitimate daughters occur throughout Campbell's extant correspondence in GD113. The inventory of Gilbert's 'bastards' is MS 624 among numerous papers concerning the 1839–40 litigation, NLS, MS 623–632.

11. George Cleghorn, *Remarks on Ancient and Modern Art, in a Series of Etchings by an Amateur*, Edinburgh, 1837, pp. 241ff.

12. On the Associated Artists (or Society of Incorporated Artists), see Irwin and Irwin 1975, ch. II, pp. 186–7 and Duncan Forbes, 'Art and Anxiety in Enlightenment Scotland: The Society of Incorporated Artists 1808–1813', *Scotia: Interdisciplinary Journal of Scottish Studies*, Norfolk, VA, 1997, XXI, pp. 1–17. Allegations about the negative effects of Raeburn's conduct were aired by the Edinburgh drawing-master John Brooks in 1842, Royal Institution papers, NRS, NG3/6/18/6(2).

13. Campbell's admission was recorded by the Trustees on 22 November 1815, Board Minutes, NRS, NG1/1/33, pp. 291–2. There is as yet no comprehensive account of the Trustees' Academy (also known successively as the Drawing Academy, School of Design and School of Art), the direct predecessor of the present Edinburgh College of Art. For the Academy's history in the eighteenth century and the first half of the nineteenth century, see J. Mason, 'The Edinburgh School of Design', *Book of the Old Edinburgh Club*, XXVII, 1949, pp.

67–96, and Patricia Brookes, The Trustees' Academy, Edinburgh 1760–1801: The public patronage of art and design in the Scottish Enlightenment, doctoral thesis, Syracuse University, 1989; UMI reprint, Ann Arbor, 1989.

14. Rhodri Winsor Liscombe, 'The "Diffusion of Knowledge and Taste": John Flaxman and the Improvement of Study Facilities at the Royal Academy', *Walpole Society*, 1987, LIII, pp. 226–38. By 1813 Wilkie was a member of the Academy's Council, a factor which may have influenced the admission of his younger compatriot to the Schools. Campbell's debut was recorded in the Council Minutes (1813–18), vol. 5, pp. 427–8, Royal Academy Archives. See also Sidney C. Hutchison, 'The Royal Academy Schools, 1768–1830', *Walpole Society*, 1962, XXXVIII, pp. 123ff: Campbell's admission is noted on p. 171.

15. Westmacott's unofficial advisory role to the British Museum trustees in connection with the arrangement of the Elgin Marbles and occasional unrelated purchases of sculpture would have impressed Campbell. See Marie Busco, *Sir Richard Westmacott Sculptor*, Cambridge, 1994. In 1830 Campbell competed unsuccessfully against Westmacott for the commission for the Duke of York Column in Carlton House Terrace, London. For Campbell's dealings with Baily, Flaxman, Nollekens, Westmacott and Chantrey, see especially his letters to Innes of 2 September and 28 November 1817, 15 March and 4 July 1818, NRS, GD113/4/163(42), GD113/4/163(336), GD 113/4/163(621) and GD113/4/163(559). Chantrey's participation in the resented hegemony of English sculptors in Scotland is substantiated by the edition of the Chantrey ledger in *Walpole Society*, 1991–2, LVI (entire volume).

16. While in Rome, Campbell distanced himself from his British peers, preferring to fraternise with the Nazarenes and the French artists. See his obituary (note 3) by the architect and future President of the RIBA, Thomas Leverton Donaldson (1795–1885). This emphasises Campbell's association with Thorvaldsen. On 25 April 1829 *The Scotsman* carried a similar report on Campbell in a feature about the arts in Rome.

17. Munro, ibid. (note 5), pp. 191–2. The London banking consortium Down, Thornton & Free, had become the Royal Bank's agents in 1790. By 1815, after several changes of personnel, the group became Pole, Thornton, Free, Down & Scott. After this bank failed in 1825, it was superseded as the Royal Bank's agents by Coutts and Company of the Strand. Campbell's bust of Free was completed in London, presumably in plaster, in March 1818, letter of 15 March to Innes, NRS, GD113/4/163(621).

18. Campbell referred to the Duchess in letters to Innes from Paris 8 December 1818 and 9 January 1819, NRS, GD113/5/472(15) and GD113/5/473(23).

19. The Duchess's original letter, dated 19 February 1819, is in Epistolare comune (IV/334/3084) in the archives of the Museo Civico, Bassano del Grappa. See Smailes 2009, p. 292.

20. Letters to Innes from Rome 23 March 1819 and 9 December 1819, NRS, GD113/5/474(47) and GD113/5/475(3). In the first letter Campbell gossiped about Thorvaldsen's unlikely engagement to the Honourable Frances Mackenzie, daughter of Lord Seaforth.

21. For the later furnishing of Campbell's London studio, see the 1858 obituary (note 3), p. 107. A preliminary account of his dealings with the Board is Helen E. Smailes, 'A History of the Statue Gallery at the Trustees' Academy in Edinburgh and the acquisition of the Albacini casts in 1838', *Journal of the History of Collections*, 1991, III, no. 2, pp. 25–43.

22. The *Scots Magazine*, VIII, 1821, pp. 361–6 (extracted from *Rome in the Nineteenth Century*, recently reviewed in the magazine); the *Edinburgh Magazine and Literary Miscellany*, 1821, VIII, pp. 411–12, in a review of the exhibition of Modern Paintings at the Institution for the Encouragement of the Fine Arts in Scotland. The sculptor's namesake was the well-known English poet and critic (1797–1844).

23. Letters to Innes (first mention of the projected bust of Raeburn) and 16 March 1818 under a single cover; 12 August 1818; 9 January and 9 December 1819, NRS, GD113/4/163(621); GD113/5/471(11); GD113/5/473(23); and GD113/4/475(3).

24. On Innes family patronage of Raeburn, see Stephen Lloyd's chapter in this volume. For an appreciation of Raeburn, see *European Magazine* 1823.

25. Edinburgh and London 1997–8, cat. no. 65, pp. 196–7. This commentary does not credit Schaaf's assessment on which subsequent literature has depended. Chantrey's former studio assistant Allan Cunningham recalled his master's presence in Edinburgh in 1818 in an important anonymous 'puff' in *Blackwood's Edinburgh Magazine*, 1820, VII, p. 8. Chantrey's use of the camera lucida is described in Alex Potts, *Sir Francis Chantrey 1781–1841. Sculptor of the Great*, London, 1980, p. 8, and Richard Walker, *National Portrait Gallery: Regency Portraits*, London, 1985, I, pp. 624–5.

26. Cunningham 1829–1833, V, 1832, p .227; Mackie 1994, II, cat. nos. 148, 149b, and III, pp. 541–2 (concerning the Raeburn and Chantrey collaborations). One Raeburn portrait of Chantrey was sold at Christie's, London, 12 April 1991, lot 22. A further instance of Raeburn's interest in sculpture is his subscription in 1822 to the projected monument to Canova to which Thomas Lawrence also subscribed.

27. See note 3.

28. Campbell informed Innes on 1 November 1821 of the imminent completion of Raeburn's bust (NRS, GD113/5/480(42)). For Campbell's letter of condolence, also describing Euphemia Menzies's bust with the attributes of Flora, see NRS, GD113/5/485(50). Now considered to be ad vivum, the bust of Raeburn was previously considered to be a derivative likeness and is discussed in those

terms by Duncan Thomson in Edinburgh and London 1997–8, cat. no .66, pp. 198–9. An incomplete copy of Nicholson's extremely rare publication is held by the Fine Art Library of Edinburgh Central Public Library. The biographical account of Raeburn mentions his friendship with and mentoring by the Scottish draughtsman John Brown (1749–1787) as a key factor in Raeburn's espousal of easel painting.

29. Letter to Innes 1 November 1821 from 12 Piazza Mignanelli, Rome (Campbell's studio address from 1820), as note 28. The surviving related account (November 1821) and references to Innes's own bust and that of Euphemia Menzies (October 1824) are in NRS, GD113/5/359 (discharged accounts of Gilbert Innes 1824). Innes's private memorandum book (November 1816–February 1832) is in a private collection, by descent. See also Smailes 2009, pp. 224 and 235.

30. Letter from the Board Secretary to Campbell, Rome, 16 February 1824, Board Letterbook, NRS, NG1/3/23.

31. Terry Friedman, 'Samuel Joseph and the Sculpture of Feeling', ed. Fiona Pearson, *Virtue and Vision. Sculpture and Scotland 1540–1990*, National Galleries of Scotland, Edinburgh, 1991, pp. 59–62, with bibliography.

32. Raeburn junior replied to Combe on 7 August 1823, NLS, MS 7122, fols. 25r–26v. The politician and advocate William Adam of Blair Adam (1751–1839), son of John Adam and nephew of the architects Robert and James Adam, had sponsored Sir Henry's election to the Royal Society of Edinburgh in 1820 and journeyed with him and Sir Walter Scott in Fife a few days before the artist's death. See Mackie 1994, II, pp. 148–9. Henry Raeburn's important letter to Adam is in the National Register of Archives of Scotland survey of the Adam of Blair Adam papers (NRAS, 1454/2/649). A summary of this letter is in the survey repertory and is cited with the kind permission of the owner. The potential commission to Joseph was aired by James Skene of Rubislaw in a letter of 18 October 1823 to the Institution's secretary Francis Cameron, NRS, NG3/4/5(3).

33. James Hamilton has researched the successive occupancy of 12 Piazza Mignanelli, in relation to J. M. W. Turner's stay there with Charles Eastlake in 1828 and kindly shared much information. Campbell himself installed Joseph Severn in Eastlake's studio during the latter's absence in 1821. See Grant F. Scott, *Joseph Severn Letters and Memoirs*, Aldershot 2005, p. 65.

34. In 1824 Campbell informed Innes that a block of fine statuary marble suitable for a bust cost twenty to thirty shillings in Rome (entry for 10 September 1824 in Innes's Memorandum Book (1816–32), Private Collection by descent). Martin Greenwood generously drew my attention to the Gibson letter, addressed to John Bernard Crouchley from Carrara on 27 August 1824, John Gibson Papers, MS 4914D, p. 30 (cited by permission of Llyfrgell Genedlaethol Cymru / The

National Library of Wales). Canova's involvement was relayed to Innes on 9 December 1819, NRS, GD113/5/475(3).

35. Letter to Innes 31 March 1821, NRS, GD113/5/30f(4). Both of the Erskine of Torrie busts are on loan to the National Galleries of Scotland and are displayed at Duff House, Banff. See Stephen Lloyd, *Catalogue of Paintings and Sculpture at Duff House*, Edinburgh, 1999, p. 33. Related letters (1832–7) to Sir John Drummond Erskine are among the unpublished Thomas Campbell correspondence, General Collection, MS 226, Beinecke Rare Book and Manuscript Library, Yale University. Of Lanarkshire descent, the antiquary and diplomat William Richard Hamilton (1777–1859), a former private secretary and longstanding associate of the Earl of Elgin, had several dealings with Campbell.

36. Letter to Innes 1 November 1821, NRS, GD113/5/480(42). Hamilton's sustained patronage of Campbell, including later commissions, is explored in Godfrey Evans, Alexander, 10th Duke of Hamilton (1767–1852) as Patron and Collector, unpublished doctoral thesis, University of Edinburgh, 2008.

37. J. Kenworthy-Browne, 'Pauline and the Bachelor Duke', *Country Life*, 28 January 1971, pp. 208–21, and 'A Ducal Patron of Sculptors', *Apollo*, October 1972, XCVII, pp. 322–31; Helen Smailes, 'Thomas Campbell and Laurence Macdonald: the Roman Solution to the Scottish Sculptor's Dilemma', Fiona Pearson (ed.), ibid. (n. 31), pp. 65 and 69. Correspondence from Campbell is included in a bound volume of receipts and other documentation on the 6th Duke of Devonshire's sculptural commissions (Chatsworth Library and Archives).

38. Unfortunately, Campbell's correspondence with Innes in 1822 does not seem to have been preserved. His group *The Young Hannibal* (private collection, by descent) is mentioned in a letter to Innes from Rome 4 October 1823, NRS, GD113/5/485(50). Byron's involvement is discussed in the account of Rossie Priory and its collections in A. H. Millar, *The Historical Castles and Mansions of Scotland. Perthshire and Forfarshire*, Paisley and London, 1890, p. 24. In 1828 Campbell showed *The Young Ascanius* at the Royal Academy with the title *Cupid receiving the instructions of Venus to assume the form of Ascanius*, thus adding a further allusive complexity. Aeneas, the father of Ascanius, was himself the love-child of Venus and Anchises.

39. On the 4th Earl of Hopetoun, see Viccy Coltman's essay in this volume and Julia Lloyd Williams et al., *Dutch Art and Scotland. A Reflection of Taste*, National Galleries of Scotland, Edinburgh, 1992, including pp. 165–6. Wilson, who settled in Italy in 1826, succeeded Campbell as the Trustees' agent in developing their cast collection. His importance as a dealer in Old Masters from about 1808 approached that of William Buchanan and has yet to be fully researched and recognised. See: Basil Skinner, 'Andrew Wilson and the Hopetoun Collection', *Country Life*, 15 August 1968, XLIV, pp. 370–2; Helen Smailes et

al., *Andrew Geddes 1783–1844. Painter-Printmaker: 'A Man of Pure Taste'*, exh. cat., National Gallery of Scotland, Edinburgh, 2001, ch. 5; and Peter Humfrey, Timothy Clifford, Aidan Weston-Lewis and Michael Bury, *The Age of Titian. Venetian Renaissance Art from Scottish Collections*, exh. cat., National Galleries of Scotland, Edinburgh, 2004, especially pp. 417 and 420 (with bibliography).

40. On the complex history of the Hopetoun Monument, see W. M. Parker, 'A Note on the Hopetoun Monument', *The Book of the Old Edinburgh Club*, 1938, XXII, pp. 28–37; Robin Lee Woodward, ibid. (note 3), I, pp. 30–53; and Smailes 2009, pp. 231–3 and 236–7.

41. *The Scotsman*, 17 September 1834 (unpaginated).

42. Campbell's original marble bust, completed in 1820, is still unlocated.

43. The final choice of Campbell was partially justified by the 'excellent like-ness' of the original bust. See the *Sederunt Book of the Highland and Agricultural Society*, 1842–3, 6 April 1843, XVIII, p. 480; and *Letterbook of the Highland and Agricultural Society*, 1842–4, pp. 113, 228 and 234 (letters to William Mitchell-Innes of Parson's Green, 15 December 1842, 1 and 10 April 1843). See Smailes 2009, Appendix VI, pp. 312–16.

44. Letter of condolence from Campbell, 28 Leicester Square, London, to Miss Innes, Edinburgh, 10 March 1832 (NRS, GD113/5/86c(12)), transcribed in Smailes 2009, p. 283. The half-length Watson Gordon portrait was apparently never reclaimed by Campbell and passed through the sale of the collection of A. H. Mitchell-Innes of Whitehall (son of Alexander Mitchell-Innes of Stow, Jane Innes's second co-heir-at-law) at Dowell's of Edinburgh on 11 April 1896, lot 115. The portrait was then bought back by another member of the family and has passed by descent to a private collection. Campbell himself and his Edinburgh-based aunt Mrs Hogarth also sat to Watson Gordon. Both of their portraits were offered to but declined by the Board of Manufactures in 1898, Board Minutes 2 June 1898, NRS, NG1/1/53. That of the sculptor was recently with the Carroll Gallery, London, before being sold online by Waddington's of Toronto on 19 October 2009, lot 40. I am grateful to Margaret Stewart of Edinburgh College of Art for bringing this to my attention.

45. Free's letter of 20 July 1819 to Innes (NRS, GD113/5/474(59)) is transcribed in Smailes 2009, p. 283.

4

Raeburn's *John Hope, 4th Earl of Hopetoun:* The 'Knotty' Business of Portrait Painting in London and Edinburgh in the 1810s

Viccy Coltman

He [Raeburn] ought to be richer than I can be; for he can paint three pictures for my one. His prices are much too small. His portrait of the Highlander McNab [Fig. 7.2] is the best representation of a human being that I ever saw. Mr. Raeburn's style is freedom in itself.[1]

Sir Thomas Lawrence's double-edged critique of Raeburn has become an intrinsic part of the latter's biography.[2] Published in *Tait's Edinburgh Magazine* for 1843 as one of the random reminiscences of Sir Walter Scott and Raeburn by the surveyor, topographical draughtsman and painter, John Morrison, the quotation from Lawrence is frequently cited as historical fact, rather than being considered as anecdotal evidence.[3] Duncan Thomson, the leading Raeburn scholar, assumed that Lawrence would have viewed the autochthonous MacNab portrait at the 1819 Royal Academy exhibition.[4] Yet Lawrence spent that entire year in Vienna and Rome, executing portraits of the allied rulers and commanders who had defeated Napoleon four years previously, in a serial portrait commission – or royal mission, as it has recently been dubbed – from the Prince Regent for the Waterloo Chamber at Windsor Castle.[5] Although the historical veracity of Lawrence's statement remains in play, as does the precise nature of his encounter with the MacNab portrait, Lawrence's well-known comment forms the starting point for a narrative that focuses on Raeburn and Lawrence. It is not so much about their differing painterly styles – Raeburn's intuitive practice that involved him painting immediately onto canvas, versus the studied layers of drawing with chalk overlaid with oils that produced Lawrence's painterly perfectionism – as it is about Lawrence's reported comment that Raeburn's prices were 'much too small'. This chapter is concerned with the economics of portrait painting in the period of the 1810s, during the stereotypically rakish, but largely historically opaque Regency.

At the same time as being about prices, the chapter is also about the cultural and social politics in the business of portrait painting. It examines the negotiations and machinations involved in the commissioning of a portrait of John Hope, 4th Earl of Hopetoun, by a group of Fife landowners. This corporate commission resulted in internal politicking when the Earl of Leven, a member of the committee, petitioned Lawrence, the leading portrait painter in the London market, in preference to his Edinburgh counterpart, Raeburn, who had already been approached by the chair of the committee, the Earl of Kellie. As Marcia Pointon has noted in her groundbreaking study of portrait painting as a business enterprise in 1780s London, the metropolis was the portrait capital of Britain and her entire global empire.[6] Lawrence's position as premier resident portraitist was secure by the 1810s: appointed Painter to the King in 1792, aged twenty-three, and knighted in 1815. The relationship between Raeburn and Lawrence, between the two leading portrait painters in their respective urban centres has been defined to date in terms of complementarity. For instance, in the compositional correspondences between Raeburn's *Lady Gordon Cumming* (location unknown; Fig. 7.8) and Lawrence's *Mrs Jens Wolff* (Art Institute of Chicago; Fig. 12.3), and between Lawrence's double portrait of *Mr and Mrs John Julius Angerstein*, 1792 (Musée du Louvre) with Raeburn's *Sir John and Lady Clerk of Penicuik* (Fig. 7.4), which was exhibited in London at Boydell's Shakespeare Gallery in 1792 (National Gallery of Ireland).[7] Rather than such compositional correspondences, striking as they are, this narrative seeks to extend Pointon's discussion into the Regency period of the 1810s – to investigate the commercial and competitive business culture of portrait painting that resulted in the Hopetoun portrait commission being envisaged for Lawrence and subsequently awarded to Raeburn.

The chapter utilises a cache of documents among the Leven and Melville papers in the National Archives of Scotland, which were first published by Hamish Miles in the early 1970s, in an article which has inexplicably failed to register in the Raeburn literature since publication.[8] A close re-reading of this material reveals how the political, social and economic dynamics in the business of portraiture were intertwined in the Hopetoun commission with issues of identity. Identity refers here in part to an artist's native extraction, as Scottish or English, and also to his reputation in the commercial and competitive urban marketplace. At the same time, it concerns a sense of burgeoning civic identity in the portrait commissions initiated by the counties of Fife, Linlithgow, Perth and the city of Norwich. This narrative exposes how the social dimension of a portrait commission involved a precarious balancing act between the three parties: in the case of Hopetoun's portrait, between the artist, the sitter and the patrons. One of the most contentious aspects of these transactions was that while there was one sitter, the multiple patrons that constituted this commission by committee were unable to agree on their preferred artist – until external economic constraints decided on their behalf.

While Raeburn and Lawrence were the two main contenders for the Hopetoun portrait, a third artist was involved in a consultative capacity. The Fife-born David Wilkie was one of the Scottish diaspora who, unlike Raeburn, relocated to London to pursue his career. Wilkie maintained a correspondence with his long-standing patron, the Earl of Leven, who was one of the committee, navigating Leven's son, Leslie Melville, through the unfamiliar territory of London portrait painters in the Spring of 1817, as he had done for Raeburn seven years earlier in 1810.[9] Wilkie later painted Kellie, the newly appointed Lord Lieutenant of the County of Fife, in a full-length portrait, measuring 243×171cm, signed and dated 1828.[10] This commission, which according to one of his contemporaries was, 'quite out of the way of his profession' was Wilkie's first official portrait as King's Limner for Scotland, a post he was awarded following Raeburn's death in 1823.[11] Wilkie's portrait represents Kellie sitting with his legs crossed swathed in his peer's robes 'transacting business' (in the artist's phrase), with an open folio, a tasselled seal case and a candlestick with a shade on the table beside him. The penetrating frontal gaze of the sedentary, elderly sitter is contrasted by the alert greyhound in the right foreground looking to the left off canvas. This portrait of Kellie was commissioned to accompany that of the Earl of Hopetoun by Raeburn in the County Hall at Cupar in Fife, where both portraits are still displayed today. The narrative juxtaposes the professional competitive rivalry between Raeburn and Lawrence, with the collegiate relationship between fellow Scots Wilkie and Raeburn at the intersection of their artistic careers, where Wilkie is also the intermediary between Raeburn and Lawrence, Edinburgh and London, individual portrait practice and the institutionalisation of the arts that was the Royal Academy. As Pointon has written, 'Between the artist and the Academy lay a gulf that had to be bridged by personal contact, nepotism, patronage and determination' – Wilkie helped Raeburn navigate this precarious gulf, which was further compounded by the geographical distance from London to Edinburgh.[12] In due course, the narrative also engages with the business practices of sub-contraction and collaboration, looking at the framing and display of Raeburn's portrait of Hopetoun, along with its later reproduction. In other words, by using Raeburn's portrait of Hopetoun as a case-study, this piece will survey the totality of the commercial and competitive business culture of early nineteenth-century portrait painting. By examining the sequential stages of the business, from the awarding of the commission, to the execution of the portrait, its installation in the County Hall at Cupar in Fife and its reproduction in mezzotint engravings.

The incentive for commissioning the portrait of John Hope, or Lord Niddry, as he had recently been ennobled (in 1814), was brought about by an event of European significance, a martial victory – a pyrrhic victory as it turned out after he escaped from Elba and landed in France – that was the 1814 defeat of Napoleon. The corporate committee that comprised the noblemen and gentlemen freeholders of the County of Fife wished to send, so its minutes for a meeting on 19 May record, a congratulatory address to the Prince Regent celebrating the annihilation of tyranny and the restoration of peace, 'which promise a happy termination to the troubles of Europe'.[13] Hot on the heels of this national self-congratulation, is a specific, local reference in the minutes to 'our countryman' Lord Niddry, who was one of the generals who had fought under Wellington against the French in Spain and Portugal. The chairman of the committee proposed that this British military hero be invited to sit for his full-length portrait as a visual record of his memory, to 'perpetuate the remembrance of this great and universally beloved character'. The portrait should be executed by 'the first Artist in London', 'finished in the most complete and Elegant stile' and be placed in the County Hall at Cupar. Even at this preliminary stage of initiating the commission, the prestige of the artist in the metropolitan capital, the size and finish of the portrait and its intended location, were stipulated. The first of these requirements was to impede the progress of the commission as the decade progressed.

Two weeks after the committee launched the portrait initiative, the sum of 285 guineas had been collected by subscription. A 'List of subscribers to the Earl of Hopetons Picture' dated 1816, records the total sum collected as being £409.10s with the names of some forty-four subscribers, who were contributing one of three staggered rates of £15.15s, £10.10s or £5.5s (Fig. 4.1).[14] In a sign of the partisan social politics of a portrait commission, two contributions were returned on the grounds that their 'Names would not be agreeable to his Lordship' (a Mr Thomson of Kinloch and a Mr Pitcairn of Kinnaird). Despite the brimming coffers, a year later, the portrait remained unexecuted. What followed was an exchange of letters between key members of the committee and the portrait sitter. Lord Leven wrote to the 4th Earl of Hopetoun, as Niddry had become in 1816, who replied that he had thought

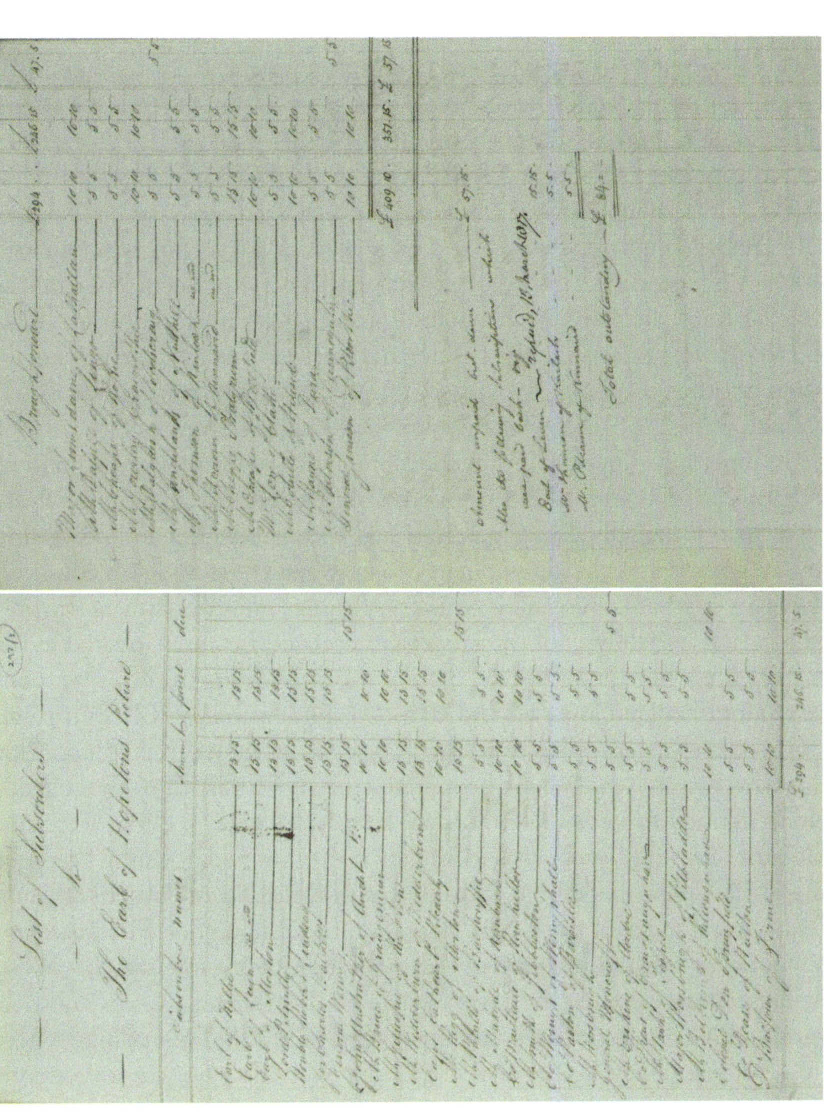

Figure 4.1 'List of subscribers to the Earl of Hopetons Picture', GD26/13/297/3, National Archives of Scotland, Edinburgh

the committee members had preferred Raeburn, but that he would 'cheerfully attend any other artist in Edinburgh or in London' to 'do whatever is most agreeable'.[15] In this we see the social niceties or the polite face of the portrait business, where the sitter defers to the patrons who commissioned his portrait in determining the choice of the artist. This was not always the case and when in 1802, the Directors of the Bank of Scotland wanted a portrait of Henry Dundas, 1st Viscount Melville, it was the sitter who chose Raeburn.[16]

Leven then wrote to Kellie on 30 January 1817, citing the minutes of the 1814 May meeting, that the first London artist be employed to paint Lord Hopetoun's picture.[17] Reading between the lines, it becomes apparent that Leven had already applied to Sir Thomas Lawrence for his terms. His letter to Kellie refers to Lawrence as the premier portrait painter in London, and pre-empts his European reputation by envisaging the projected portrait as 'one of the finest in Scotland if not in Europe'. Notwithstanding his 'high respect for the merits and talents of Raeburn as a man and as an artist', Leven describes another corporate commission from a Scottish county that would satisfy him: 'Lithgow Shire' wanted a duplicate of the County of Fife portrait of Lord Hopetoun. Implicit in Leven's comments is an inferior estimation of both the artist Raeburn and the corporate patron, the County of West Lothian, who would respectively be satisfied with producing and possessing a copy. In addition to the one-upmanship between these Scottish counties, another part of what Leven called 'this knotty affair', was the issue of the preferred location and display of the Hopetoun portrait. Leven wondered in his letter to Kellie where precisely the picture was to be hung in the great room in the County Hall at Cupar and asked for the dimensions of the court room and the book room in order that 'the very best station [be] fixed upon for hanging the Picture which must be manufactured of a very fit to the space.'

Kellie replied to Leven's letter a week later, 'that my feelings were not a little hurt' and that Raeburn had already been solicited at Kellie's request by one of the subscribers, Lord Pitmilly (4th on the list of subscribers, Fig. 4.1), who was a judge of the Court of Session in Edinburgh.[18] The justiciary of the Court of Session was one of the many Edinburgh institutions whose members sat for Raeburn; the professoriate of the University was another. Raeburn's chief competitor for the Fife commission, Sir Thomas Lawrence, had also been solicited by Leven's son, Leslie Melville who was in London. Melville wrote to his father on 24 February 1817, that Lawrence was 'hardly come-at-able'; of how he had failed to procure an audience with the artist, despite having called at his house at 65 Russell Square, in the fashionable district of Bloomsbury, every day for the last seven days.[19] Though the artist himself was not in residence, these visits had enabled Melville to come face-to-face with examples of his work, whether in the studio or the showroom, is unclear. He writes of having viewed 'his paintings at his House in numbers & I know not w^h most to admire the stile of the painting or the very admirable likenesses of the portraits of some whose faces were familiar to me'. Melville here identifies two of the dominant critiques of painted portraiture: the style of painting and the protean issue of likeness.

But critical information was to follow in Leslie Melville's letter to his father that excluded Lawrence as the painter of Hopetoun's portrait for Fife on account of his exorbitant prices and his dilatory working practices. One of Lawrence's 'sort of assistant[s]' had informed Melville of the artist's terms, that a full-length portrait of full size would cost 500 guineas without the frame. The Hopetoun portrait is now classified as equestrian for the first time. With Hopetoun represented on horseback, the cost would be 'an immense deal more' on account of the size of the enlarged painted canvas – 13 or 14 feet high and 9 or 10 feet wide without the frame – and the additional labour incurred. The standardisation of prices according to portrait sizes will be addressed in due course. Melville's other concern was the open-ended timeframe. Lawrence's assistant he writes, 'would not tell me how many years Sir Thos would require to paint it – He is famous for keeping his performances long on hand which he does not so much mind as he has half the money paid down, & when he is hurried to finish a picture report says he occasionally employs an inferior painter for the ground work &c as soon as he has painted the figure.' The division of labour in Lawrence's studio among his pupils and assistants is currently under-researched. An advance payment of half the portrait fee appears to have been a standard transaction between artist and patron in the metropolitan centre; the outstanding half being paid on the completion of the commission. The Edinburgh market operated differently, with Raeburn being paid on completion of a portrait. In one extreme case, which interestingly was another corporate commission, he waited six years to be remunerated for a portrait of William Law (Fig. 4.2), the former Sheriff of East Lothian, and charged interest accordingly, making the total fee twenty-seven pounds and six shillings.[20] On this occasion, Raeburn produced a Kit Kat-sized copy from his existing portrait of Law in judicial wig and robes, which was predestined to be hung in the Sheriff's Court Room in Haddington, East Lothian.

With Sir Thomas Lawrence fully committed and his 500 guineas fee beyond the collected subscriptions of the county of Fife, Leven sought advice on other portrait painters working in the metropolitan centre from his protégé, the émigré Scottish artist, David Wilkie. In a letter of 8 March 1817, Wilkie proposed William Owen, the principal portrait painter to the Prince Regent, to Leven as 'the next best [after Lawrence] . . . who I am sure both in point of high talent as a portrait painter and correctness in fulfilling his engagements would give satisfaction'.[21] In other words, Wilkie's

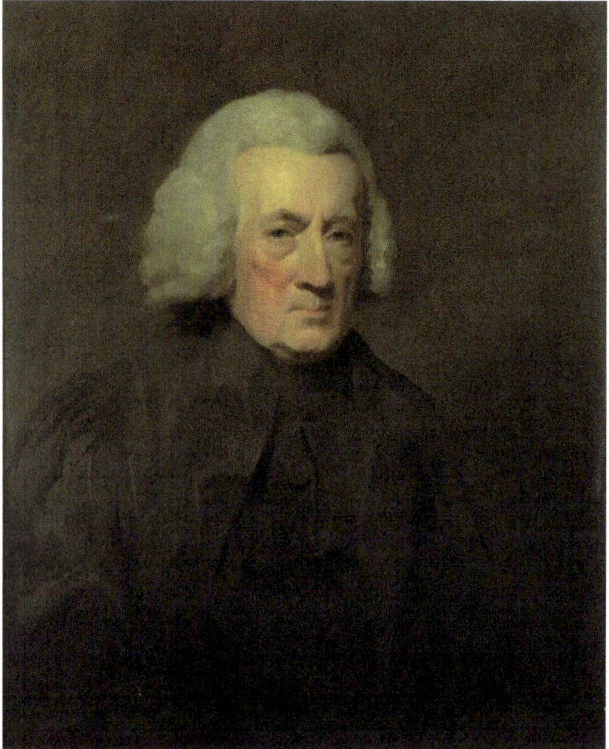

Figure 4.2　Henry Raeburn, *William Law*, c. 1804, oil on canvas, 93.7×83cm,
East Lothian Council Museums Service

recommendation of Owen assured that he was not only technically accomplished, but also professionally accountable. Owen's terms would be secured, along with those of Lawrence, which would be ascertained 'exactly', rather than vaguely via his assistant by word of mouth. Wilkie's letter continues by saying that if Raeburn is to be passed over, it must be for an artist of first-rate excellence and 'then there is no one so capable in this respect as Sir Thos. Lawrence.' He also suggests that Lawrence might complete the canvas on account of its being 'a commission of such importance as this would be to Lawrence himself', so reminding us of the traffic of esteem in the business of portrait painting that was multi-directional, between artist, patron and sitter, rather than being entirely artist-centred.

Wilkie's letter to Leven of March 1817 had been prompted by a visit to his terraced house in Kensington High Street from Leven's son, Leslie Melville. The latter communicates the essential points of their discussion in a letter to his father. According to Melville, Wilkie had confirmed Lawrence's 'idleness in finishing off a picture', but had invoked the cachet of the sitter and the 'eclat of being employed for such a work' as reasons for pursuing his services. Wilkie's professional opinion of Owen, 'for colouring he reckons him superior to Lawrence, but not for the tout ensemble, or elegance of style' had apparently been confirmed by a visit to Owen's house, where Wilkie and Melville 'examined his works, but voted them very inferior to Lawrence. His likenesses are good, but there is a sort of want of grace, & he paints the most frightful, stiff <u>hands</u> I ever saw.'

Such access to artists' studios and private galleries in their London residences was actively encouraged, as it was one of the means by which they procured commissions; lists of the principal painters were published annually in popular guidebooks like *The Picture of London*, where the artists' names are organised alphabetically and their addresses listed according to the genre in which they worked.[22] There was no prescribed entry fee as such, although a shilling to the artist's servant was recommended by *The Picture of London* as a 'general compliment'.[23] Another urban venue for viewing portraits where the entrance fee was also a shilling was the Royal Academy's annual Spring exhibition. The artists whose works were represented at Somerset House did not orchestrate the most advantageous display of their productions as they could in their own properties.

Recent research has mapped the migration of artists across the urban expanse of London from the eighteenth to the twentieth centuries and their colonisation of particular districts.[24] The Royal Academy President, Benjamin West, bought 14 Newman Street, Marylebone in 1774 and resided there until his death in 1820. During this half century, Marylebone became a highly populated artists' colony. In just one year, in 1810, there were six Royal Academicians residing in Newman Street alone: Henry Howard, James Ward, John Jackson, Henry Thomson, George Dawe and Thomas Stothard.[25] West made a number of alterations to the property that he purchased with ground to the rear by Rathbone Place, in order to display his work to its advantage. A ground plan of the house when it was sold in 1829 shows how it consisted of a long gallery leading to a great room that is recorded as being top-lit.[26] Beyond the great room was an inner room and beyond that, the studio, 22 × 29 feet, to the left of which were two colour rooms.

The study of the demarcation of the interiors of houses belonging to artists and the designated spaces for domestic accommodation, artistic production (the studio) and viewing (the show room or gallery) is ongoing. The contents of James Barry's house at 36 Castle Street East, London, where he lived and worked as an artist and printmaker from 1788 to 1806, for instance, has been tirelessly reconstructed from an inventory made on his death and from a catalogue of its contents that were auctioned a year later.[27] Another manuscript inventory documenting the contents of Richard and Maria Cosway's

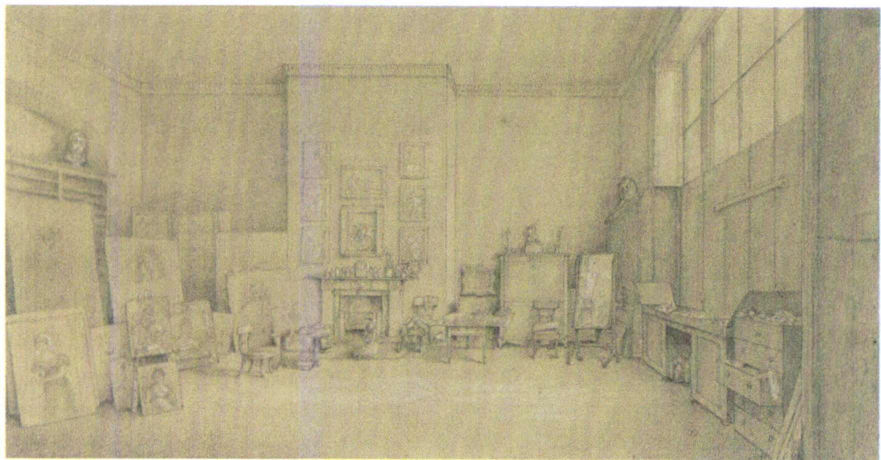

Figure 4.3 Emily Greenwood Calmady, *Thomas Lawrence's painting room*, 1824, graphite heightened with white gouache, 22.9×43.5cm, Paul Mellon Fund, Yale Center for British Art, New Haven

residence at 20 Stratford Place, Oxford Street, London, has recently been transcribed and published in full.[28] Compiled in 1820, the 229-page inventory includes lists of the contents of the Cosways' possessions and collections room-by-room, starting with the ground floor, followed by the second floor, first floor and finally the attic area. The Saloon or Richard Cosway's painting room was on the ground floor and according to the inventory it contained twenty-three paintings by Old Masters and Cosway himself as well as fifty-eight pieces of furniture and sculpture. Following a visit to Stratford Place in 1811, when Cosway was not at home, Sir Thomas Lawrence described it in a letter to his close friend Joseph Farington as 'an <u>Artist's House</u>' with 'such a Mass of <u>fit Materials</u>' that it made his own house and collections seem impoverished – that of an amateur, woefully lacking the 'proper Character of an artistic dwelling'.[29] A pencil drawing by the amateur artist, Emily Greenwood Calmady, provides a tantalising view of Lawrence's painting studio at 65 Russell Square, Bloomsbury, in 1824, which was the property visited by Leslie Melville in February 1817 (Fig. 4.3).[30] Calmady's daughters were sitting for a double portrait to Lawrence, who is partially reflected holding a palette in the full-length mirror in the right-hand corner. An assortment of painted faces on canvas in varying sizes and at varying stages of completion is collected opposite the large, south-facing shuttered window. The drawing was engraved by C. G. Lewis as a private plate in about 1830. In an anonymous engraving of the same year, the viewer is invited into Lawrence's private sitting room, which is crammed with objects from

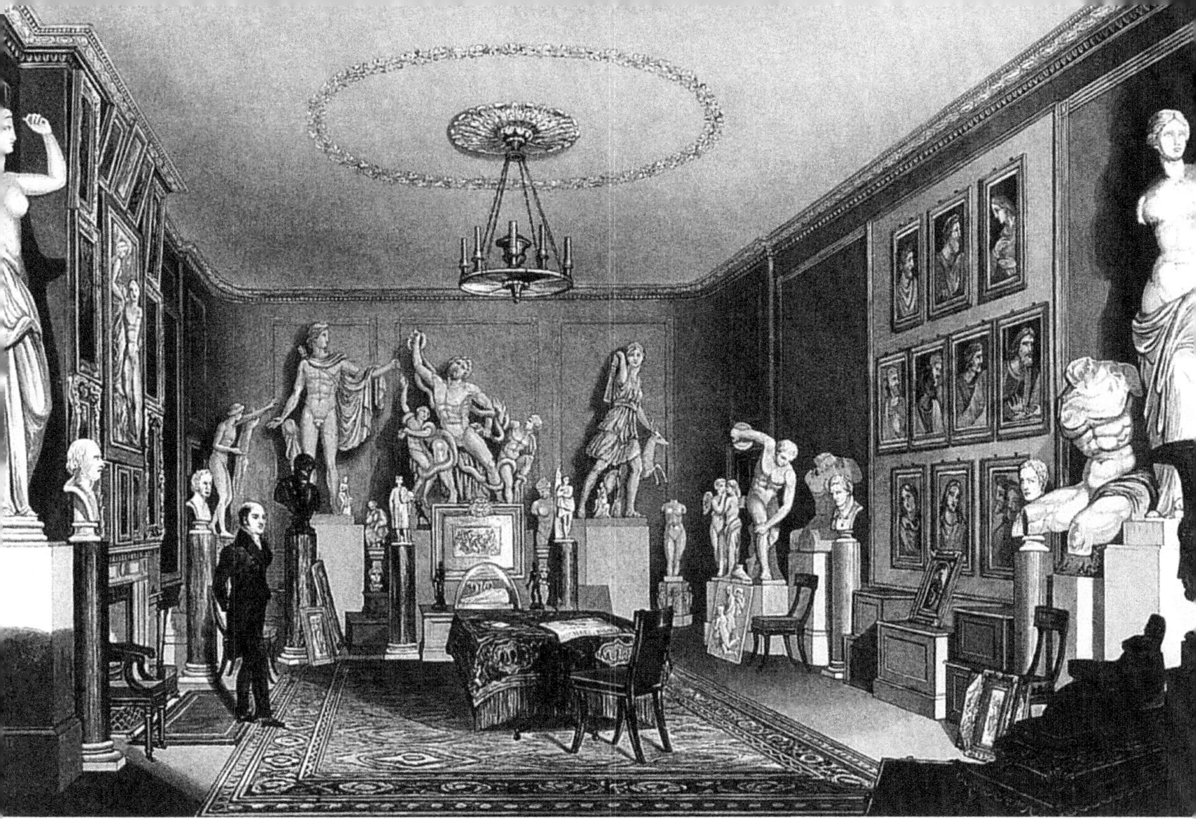

Figure 4.4 Anon., *The private sitting-room of Sir Thos. Lawrence*, 1830, aquatint and etching, 30×42cm, Department of Prints and Drawings, The British Museum, London (© The Trustees of the British Museum, London)

his expanding collections (Fig. 4.4).[31] The far wall is lined with plaster casts of classical sculptures including the *Laocoön*, the *Apollo Belvedere* and the *Diana Chasseresse*. These reduced-size copies are displayed on pedestals, in the company of Lawrence's friends and fellow artists, who are themselves represented as art objects – with portrait busts of Flaxman, Stothart, Fuseli and Smirke by the sculptor Edward Hodges Baily and statuettes of Raphael and Michelangelo by Flaxman to either side of the *Laocoön*. The right-hand wall contains a sea of ten framed faces after the apostles in Leonardo's *Last Supper* – the collected contents making the sitting room less of a space for sedentary social intercourse as a domestic academy of masterpieces for aesthetic study.[32] The Scottish sculptor Thomas Campbell recounts a visit to Lawrence's house in November 1817 when the painter 'asked very kindly for Mr. Raeburn' and brought a portrait of the deceased Princess Charlotte out of his study specifically for Campbell to view. 'My acquaintance with him [Lawrence] is very slight,' Campbell wrote to one of his Scottish patrons, 'the first day I calld he asked if I was an artist and whence from I told him I had the misfortune to be a Scotchman'.[33] Campbell's visit to 65 Russell Square demonstrates that access to artists' properties was not confined to visits from potential patrons or portrait sitters, since it included fellow artists. In May and June 1810, David Wilkie accompanied Raeburn on visits to the houses of William Beechey and Thomas Stothard at Newman Street.

Like Stothard's Newman Street neighbour Benjamin West, Henry Raeburn's property at 32 York Place in Edinburgh was similarly modified by the resident artist. Its interior consisted of a painting room on the first floor with a top-lit exhibition gallery 55 feet long×35 feet wide×40 high on the storey above.[34] The dominant feature of the painting room was a greatly-enlarged, north-facing window that was fitted with a complex set of adjustable shutters at the sides and top by which the artist could control the flow of light into the room.[35] This calculated illumination is one innovative aspect of Raeburn's portraiture that has dazzled sitters and viewers alike. Given the extent to which the exterior and interior features of properties were adapted in this manner, it is not surprising to find that they were occupied by successive artists. In November 1775, for instance, George Romney moved into Francis Cotes' former studio at 24 Cavendish Square in the newly-fashionable district of London to the west of Oxford Circus.[36] Cavendish Square was superseded in the early nineteenth century by Newman Street as the artists' preferred district. In March 1810, Raeburn was reputed to be moving into John Hoppner's former London house at Charles Street, St James's Square, in a transfer of his practice that would have certainly affected the history of early nineteenth century Scottish, not to mention British, art.[37] Raeburn could no longer be entrenched as the in-house portrait painter of members of the Scottish Enlightenment.

Leslie Melville's 1817 letter to his father concerning Hopetoun's portrait continues by citing the similar scenario that the experienced portrait sitter, one William Smith, had found himself in earlier in the decade. In another example of a corporate commission, the City of Norwich wanted a portrait of Smith who was their Member of Parliament. On finding Lawrence unlikely to execute the portrait within two years, Smith chose the now obscure Regency portrait painter Henry Thomson, one of the residents of Newman Street. Thomson's full-length (241×149.5cm) image of Smith holding the Bill for the Abolition of the Slave Trade locates him unambiguously within his Norwich constituency, with views of the Castle and the tower of St Peter Mancroft church in the left and right background (Fig. 4.5).[38] Thomson's portrait of Smith was exhibited at the Royal Academy three years earlier in 1814. Melville's letter proceeds to paint an image of the urban London market as one thick with portrait painters; as far as Melville could ascertain from their discussions, Wilkie thought Raeburn equal to William Beechey, who was then portrait painter to the Duke of Gloucester, citing a third possible contender, Thomas Phillips.[39] Though William Smith had rated

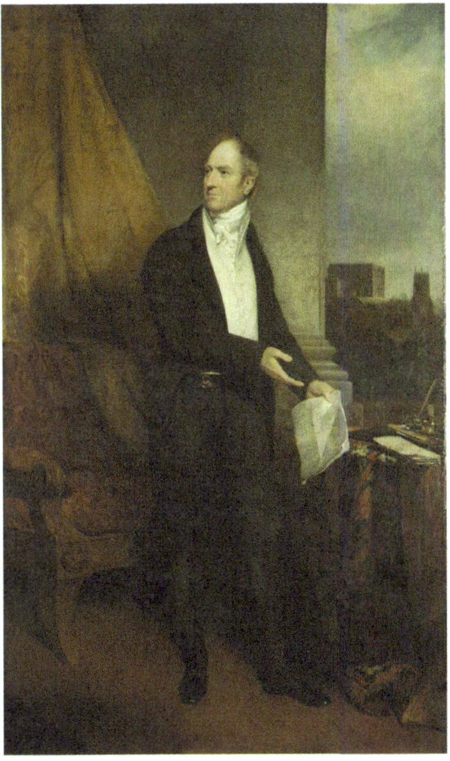

Figure 4.5 Henry Thomson, *William Smith*, c. 1814, oil on canvas, 241 × 149cm, Norfolk Museums and Archaeology Service (Norwich Castle Museum and Art Gallery)

Phillips as 'a very rising Painter', Melville describes his head and shoulders (58.5 × 46cm) portrait of Samuel Thornton which had been exhibited at the Royal Academy in 1815 as doing 'him no credit in my opinion, & indeed I have heard few favourable remarks made upon it by any one'.[40]

Thus, the politics of patronage in the precarious and competitive business of portrait painting in 1818 London was related to Melville and in an epistolary turn, to his father, Leven, from a variety of different perspectives: from the experiences of a recent sitter, William Smith; from one of the portraitists' fellow artists (who was himself not yet a portraitist), David Wilkie; as informed by Melville's own first-hand opinion in consultation with Wilkie and, in the case of Phillips' portrait of Thornton, by unsubstantiated criticism. These different constituents had vested levels of interest in the execution of the Hopetoun portrait. For instance, Melville's letter ends with Wilkie's desire that the picture should do credit to his native county of Fife, as well as to the still undecided artist.

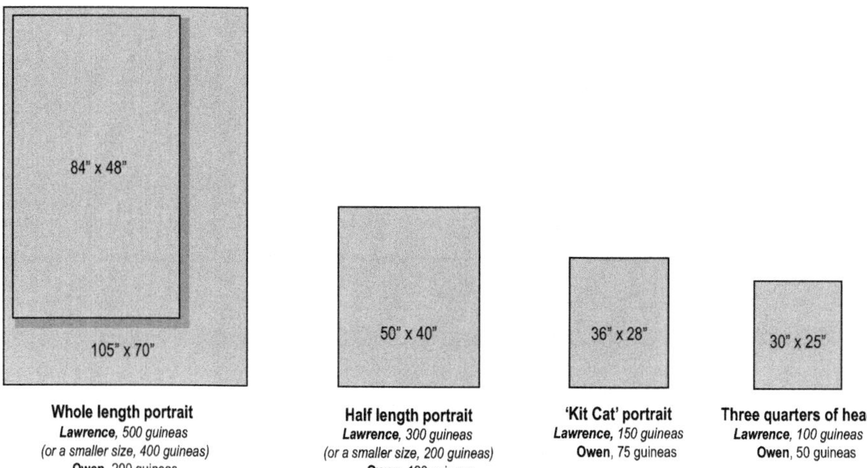

Figure 4.6 Charges for the portraits from Thomas Lawrence and William Owen in March 1817

Notes of the respective portrait prices charged by Lawrence and Owen were enclosed by Melville in his letter to his father (Fig. 4.6).[41] Both artists required half the fee to be paid at the first sitting, which as we have seen, was metropolitan practice. Though their prices were fixed according to standardised portrait sizes, Owen's prices were, in most cases, half those of Lawrence. Owen's fees were also listed starting with the least expensive; Lawrence's fees, started with the most costly. So while Lawrence charged between 400 and 500 guineas for a whole length, Owen wanted 200. Lawrence further differentiated between large and small whole lengths and half lengths, charging 300 guineas for a large half length, while Owen, 120 guineas. For a Kit Cat portrait as popularised by Kneller in the 1730s measuring 91.5×71cm and depicting the sitter the size of life including one hand, Lawrence charged 150 guineas; Owen, 75. A head size portrait, or three-quarters of a yard, was 100 guineas from Lawrence, 50 from Owen.[42] Lawrence's prices had been increasing throughout his career, rising steadily at first, from 160 guineas for a whole length in 1793, to 200 guineas by 1807.[43] Lawrence's prices rose again in 1810 on the death of his chief London competitor, John Hoppner. His 1817 fee of 500 guineas for a large whole length would double in 1820 after his return from Europe to a substantial 1000 guineas. Writing from Rome in June 1819, the sculptor Thomas Campbell, who Raeburn had directed to Lawrence via a letter of introduction written the previous year, invoked Lawrence's European and global reputation in a single sentence: 'the Romans and French think him inspired one said to me alors c'est fini sans doute il est le premier Peintre dan la monde'.[44]

Leslie Melville's letter to his father refers to the date of its composition, 8 March 1817, as being 'the last day on which such information can be of use to you'. This sense of urgency was dictated by a committee meeting in Cupar five days later which had been called to quell anxiety among the subscribers as to the lack of progress in the execution of Hopetoun's portrait. The minutes confirm the absence of Lord Kellie from the meeting, while recording his earlier communications with Henry Raeburn whose terms he has ascertained as being £105 for a full-length portrait of Hopetoun without a horse and 150 guineas with a horse – making Raeburn fifty guineas cheaper than the second-ranked portraitist in the London market.[45] The frame would cost £40 or £50, so bringing the total for a full-length equestrian portrait complete with its frame to about £200, which would leave sufficient outstanding monies to commission a print for each of the subscribers.

In the meantime, the pro-Lawrence faction as championed by Lord Leven had not been idle. Having followed to the letter the committee's 1814 consensus regarding the first artist in London, Leven had solicited the services of Sir Thomas Lawrence, whom he describes as 'the present Raphael of Britain if not of Europe'. Lawrence's letter to Melville was read to the committee. In it, the price for a whole length portrait of standard size (7 feet 10 inches×4 feet 10 inches or 84×48 inches) is confirmed as 400 guineas. With a horse, the dimensions of the canvas would increase by a foot in height and width, to 8 feet 10 inches×5 feet 10 inches. As the canvas expanded, so the price would rise accordingly. Lawrence's letter conveys his fear of completing the picture in the required time on account of pressure to exhibit a still unfinished portrait that had been ordered two years previously at the forthcoming Royal Academy's Spring exhibition.

The image in question had been commissioned by another Scottish borough. The County of Perth wanted a full-length portrait of the British military hero, Thomas Graham, Lord Lynedoch of Balgowan, who had been second in command to the Duke of Wellington during the Peninsula Wars.[46] Lawrence's portrait of Lynedoch is the largest of the full-length portraits discussed here (105×70in) and provides an example of one of the artist's so-called half-history portraits, where the portrait has an edifying historical resonance (Fig. 4.7).[47] It was commissioned from Lawrence for the sum of £420 collected by Perth Council from individual subscriptions not exceeding three guineas – making it a genuinely more democratic commission than its Cupar counterpart, whose staggered rates began at £5.5s. Lynedoch is shown 'in the height of his career of military renown', according to the *Perth Courier* for 1829, standing full-length in military uniform wearing the Gold Peninsula

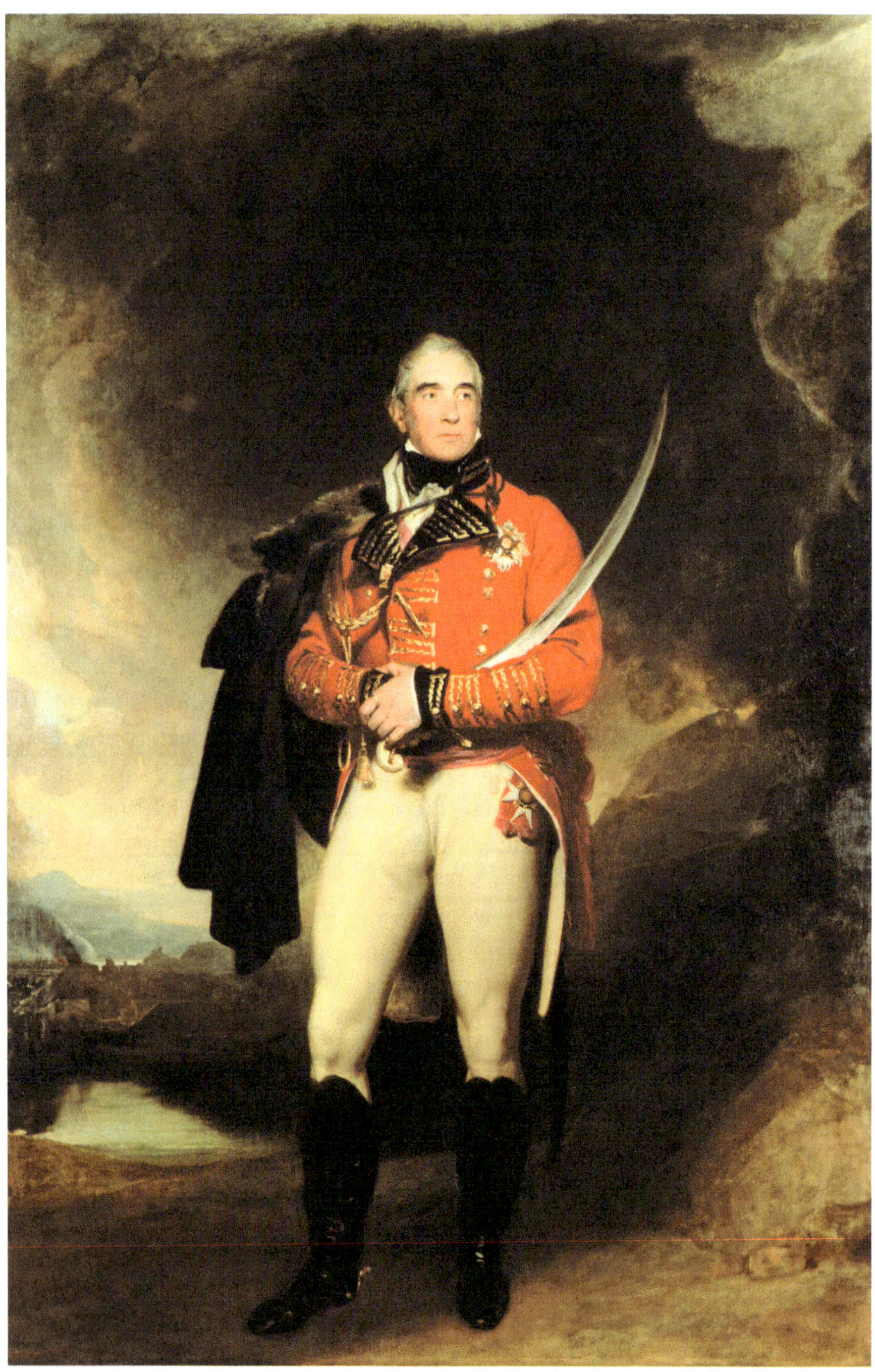

Figure 4.7 Thomas Lawrence, *Thomas Graham, Lord Lynedoch of Balgowan,* 1815–19, oil on canvas, 266.7×175cm, Perth Museum and Art Gallery

star on his chest, as well as the badge, star and sash of the Order of the Bath and cradling an upraised shamshir in his arms. The expanse of dark, billowing clouds filling the sky and reflected behind him, with the smoking ruins on the left, evokes the battlefield at Barossa in Spain in 1811, while simultaneously throwing into relief the outline silhouette of Lynedoch's massive physique with the dramatic red and white colour palette of his uniform. In terms of iconographical strategy, this portrait is a fitting close relation to those in the series of portraits of the allied rulers and commanders that the Prince Regent commissioned from Lawrence for the Waterloo Chamber at Windsor Castle; that of the leader of the Prussian forces, Field Marshall Gebhardt von Blücher, 1814–15, bears many points of compositional mirroring and is similarly colossal in sitter's stature and canvas size.[48] An earlier portrait by Lawrence of the Scottish aristocrat, John, Lord Mountstuart, was exhibited at the Royal Academy in 1795. Art historian Lucy Peltz's comment invitingly suggests that 'Lawrence entices viewers to run their eyes over the forms, surfaces and bulges of Mountstuart's imposing body' in a head-to-toe visual caress and back up again, that is equally applicable to Lynedoch, with his skin-tight pantaloons and the deep, almost sculptural folds of his military cloak.[49]

Like the as yet unexecuted portrait of Hopetoun for neighbouring Fife, the Lynedoch portrait by Lawrence was of a British military hero in a European conflict with a local Scottish connection. It was also commissioned for a predetermined location, for the Assembly Room of the Public Hall in Perth, Sir Robert Smirke's new County building on the west bank of the River Tay. Mezzotint engravings by Thomas Hodgetts were available by 1829 in three options and for three staggered prices: as proofs to the subscribers for £2.2s; as prints at £1.1s and in a de luxe limited edition of fifty proofs on India paper at £3.3s.

Back at the meeting in Cupar, one of the original subscribers to Lord Hopetoun's portrait, Henry Wedderburn, encouraged his fellows via letter 'that no time ought to be lost in employing Mr Raeburn, an Artist of our own Country, of distinguished merits, of which there is at present sufficient proof from the Picture he made of his Lordship [Hopetoun] for West Lothian.' This was the portrait Lord Leven had already referred to in a letter to Kellie for Lithgowshire. Hopetoun is depicted by Raeburn in dress uniform, dismounted, with one arm resting on the saddle of his chestnut horse whose head is raised, the other holding a sabre. In the version for Fife that Raeburn eventually executed the following year, in 1818, the horse is grey with its head lowered (Fig. 4.8). The size of the Fife portrait was less than Lawrence had estimated, at about 7 feet 6 inches × 5 feet 7 inches. It was, as Leven had cautioned, 'manufactured of a very fit to the space' for £200 including the cost of the frame.

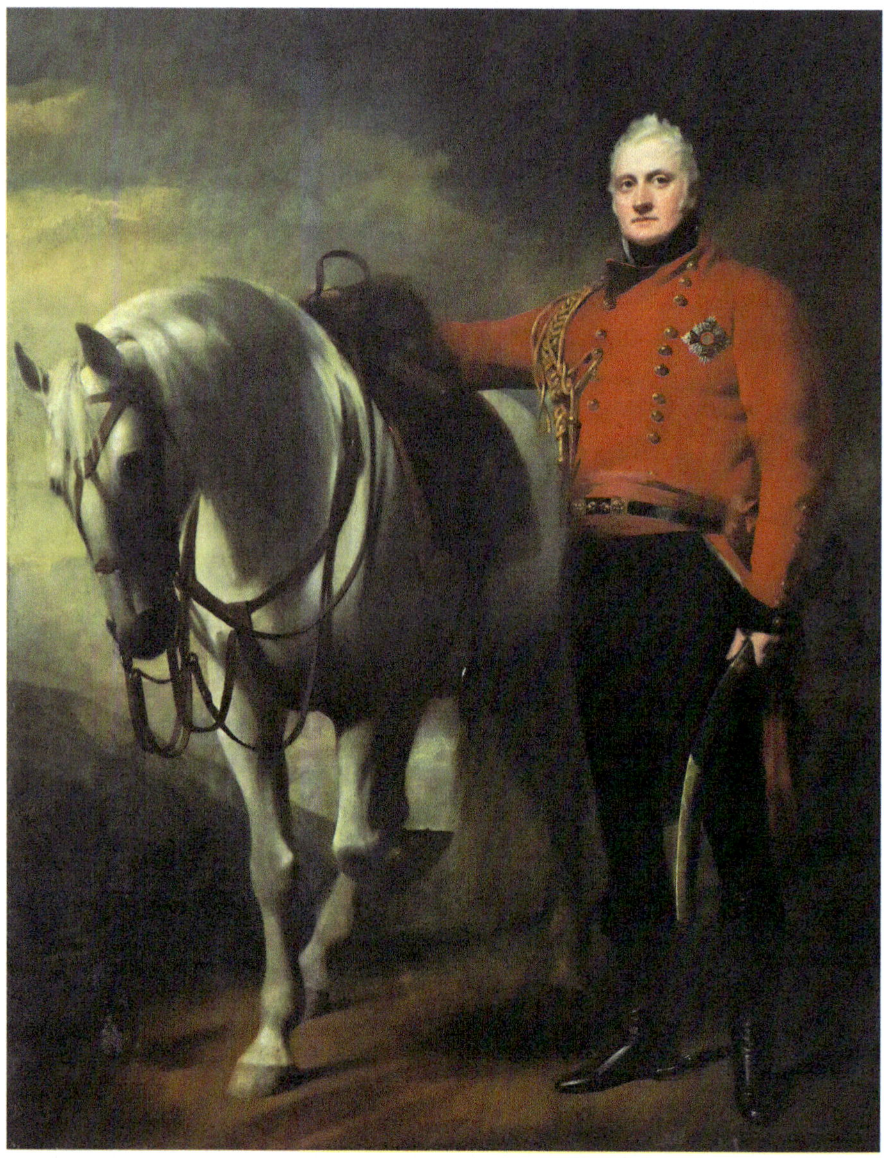

Figure 4.8 Henry Raeburn, *John Hope, 4th Earl of Hopetoun*, 1817, oil on canvas, 233.7×175cm, Cupar Town Hall, Fife Council

Mention of the frame introduces other luxury trades in the specialist urban marketplaces that formed an essential component of the art and business of portrait painting: framemaking and engraving. The craftsmen who made picture frames were generally known as carvers and guilders rather than picture framemakers hence their works offer an interface between the business of painting with that of furniture making.[50] The elaborate gilt frame that still surrounds Raeburn's portrait of Hopetoun is surmounted with the Hopetoun arms, which are crowded to either side by the symbols of martial victory – cannons, cannon balls, flags, swords, guns and other militaria. Hopetoun is referred to in an inscription below the coat of arms by his many titles, which records the portrait as being a commission from the County of Fife. A letter of David Wilkie's reveals that this ornate trophy frame was manufactured in Edinburgh, although the identity of its maker is unknown.[51] Based on the evidence of surviving receipts and still-attached labels, Raeburn is known to have used a succession of framemakers throughout his career, including at least five in Edinburgh. One Archibald Howison made the fluted frames in 1788 for the pair of Raeburn portraits of Sir William Forbes and his wife at Craigievar Castle. A decade later in 1798, James Liddle based at Teviot Row framed Raeburn's full-length portrait of the entrepreneur *William Forbes of Callendar* (Capt. W. F. E. Forbes loan to the SNPG, Edinburgh). On into the early nineteenth century one Alexander Thomson, Raeburn's neighbour at York Place, is known to have produced the frames for his portraits. Beyond Edinburgh, the sub-contracting and collaboration between portrait painter and framemakers is documented in a letter of Raeburn's to one of his other Scottish patrons, the Lord Chief Commissioner, Sir William Adam. Referring to his portrait of Lord William Russell, Raeburn recommends one Michael Tijou, of 17 Greek Street, Soho, London, as a framemaker who apparently 'works to Sir Tho Lawrence and a great many of the first nobility and to whose care I commonly address all the pictures to London and whom I have always found to be remarkably attentive'.[52] On this occasion, Raeburn invokes the social cachet of Lawrence and his aristocratic clientele. Actually his information is out of date; by the early 1820s, Tijou is known to have been superseded by one George Morant of New Bond Street, London, as Lawrence's framer of choice.[53] Morant is most likely responsible for the gilded frame that surrounds Lawrence's portrait of Lynedoch, with its inner frieze of stylised leaves and acorns and its outer scrolling leaves, which have been identified by Jacob Simon as a Lawrentian innovation.

Some framemakers, like Alexander Thomson in Edinburgh and William Crib and Thomas Macdonald in London, were also print publishers, drawn into printselling by the increased demand for framed prints.[54] Even before the contentious commission for Lord Hopetoun's portrait had been awarded to a painter in 1817, the Earl of Kellie envisaged engravings as presentation copies to the original subscribers as a means of spending the surplus funds. Five years later, in 1822, Raeburn's portrait of Hopetoun was engraved and published by William Walker with a dedicatory inscription to the noblemen

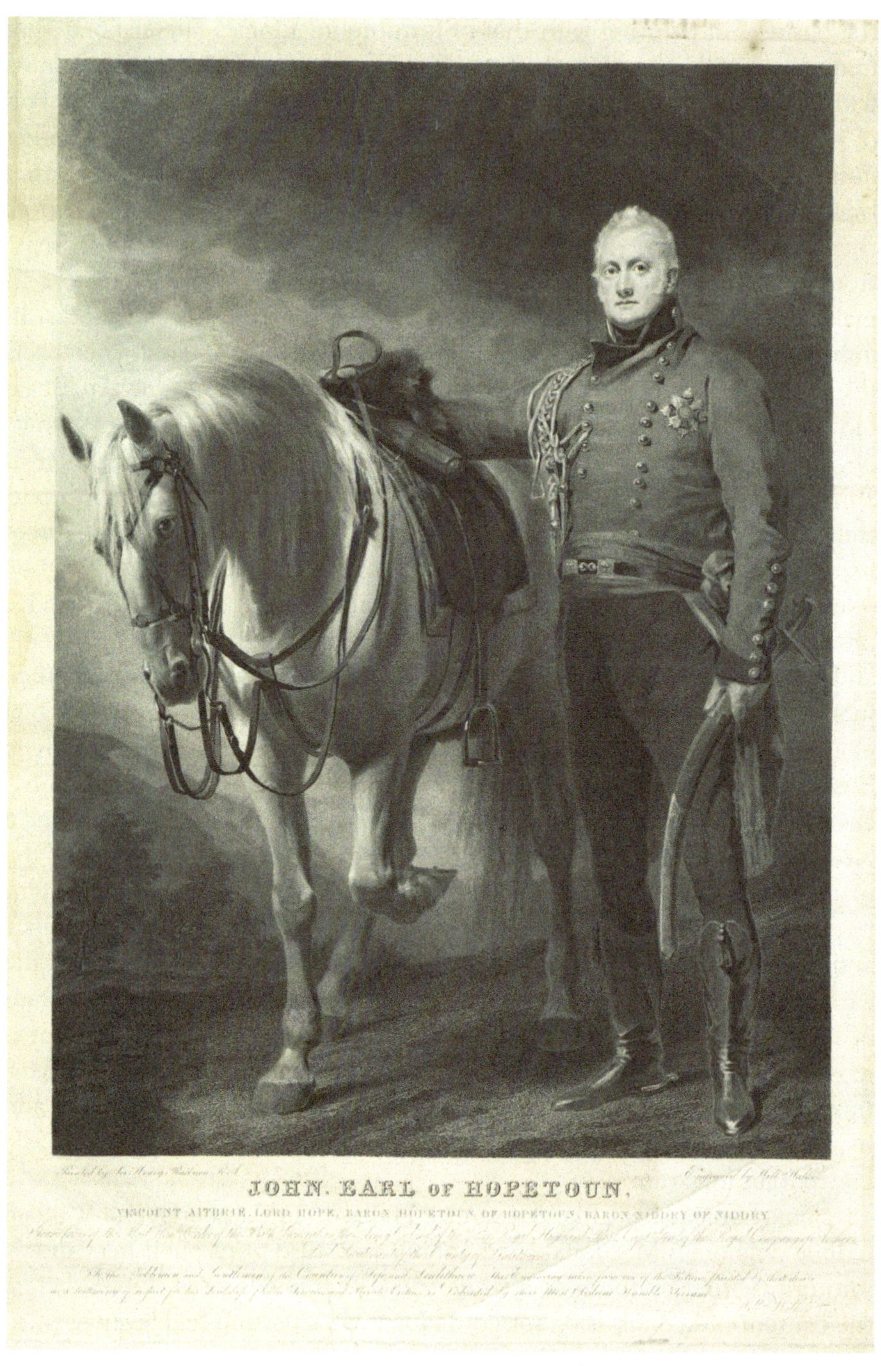

Figure 4.9 William Walker after Henry Raeburn, *John, Earl of Hopetoun*, 1822, line engraving, published by the engraver, 75.6×50.5cm, Scottish National Portrait Gallery, Edinburgh

and gentlemen of the Counties of Fife and Linlithgow (Fig. 4.9). Even though the Linlithgow canvas was the primary version in terms of chronological output, the Fife portrait seems to have superseded it in reputation. Walker is thought to have engraved at least nine of Raeburn's portraits including, most famously, the artist's own self portrait, produced as his diploma piece on his election to the Royal Academy in 1815 – and refused on the grounds that self-portraits were not acceptable for this purpose (Fig. 3.4).[55] Though Walker and Raeburn were acquainted and the latter seems to have supervised the production of his plates, Raeburn's business transactions with Walker were far from exclusive. As with the framemakers he used in both Edinburgh and London, so a cluster of engravers produced works after Raeburn.[56] In a letter to Wilkie of 1823, Raeburn bemoans that 'the Engravers have not been so liberal to me as I understand they generally are to others. I have seldom got above one or two impressions – but . . . I will take care in future that you shall have a proof of every after Print'.[57] The projected proofs offer another form of evidence or material testimony of the personal and professional esteem between Raeburn and Wilkie.

In conclusion, for all its polite façades or painted faces, the business of portrait painting in London and Edinburgh in the 1810s has been shown to be a commercial and competitive enterprise; as much of an industry as an art, that involved painters, corporate patrons and Scottish-born sitters who were military heroes in the pantheon of British worthies. We have seen how a portrait commission was dictated by local politics, economic constraints and social niceties; facilitated by collaboration with a cohort of framemakers and engravers. Having demonstrated its multi-faceted characteristics and constituents, the narrative concludes with an often-cited letter dated 12 September 1819, from Raeburn to David Wilkie. Entreating Wilkie to write at least annually to him in Edinburgh with news of the London art scene, Raeburn's letter evocatively conveys a sense of his isolation from the metropolitan centre and its cultural institutions in the form of exhibitions and newspaper reviews.[58] Employing a familiar trope, Raeburn professes to know as little about London artists 'as if I were living at the Cape of Good Hope'.

The most telling part of the letter for our purposes is that which refers, implicitly rather than explicitly, to the economic circumstances that resulted in the Fife commission for Lord Hopetoun's portrait being awarded to Raeburn rather than his London rival, Sir Thomas Lawrence. Asking,

> Are the Portrait Painters as well employed as ever: Sir Tho⁵ Laurence they tell me has refused to commence any more pictures till he gets done those that are on hand and that he has raised his prices to some enormous sum. is that true and will you do me the favour to tell me what his prices realy are and what Sir

W. Beachy or Philips and Mr Owen have for their pictures it will be a particular favour if you will take the trouble to ascertain these for me properly for I am raising my prices too, and it would be a guide to me, not that I intend to rise mine so high as your famous London Artist.

Raeburn's letter names the same four London portrait painters who figured in the discussions between the Fife committee members: Lawrence, Beechey, Phillips and Owen. His request to Wilkie to properly ascertain their prices suggests the knotty business, or an edited version, concerning the portrait of Lord Hopetoun that had been recounted to him in much the same way as it has been discussed here.

Notes

1. Thanks to Maria Devaney, Anne Dulau, John Getley, Imogen Gibbon, Gavin Grant, Erika Ingham, Stephen Lloyd, Hamish Miles, Lucy Peltz, Mark Pomeroy, Craig Statham and Sarah Vince, for their assistance with aspects of the research for this paper. Jacob Simon generously supplied me with a copy of his unpublished article 'Raeburn and picture frames'. Versions were given as lectures in 2006 at the Raeburn conference in Edinburgh and in 2010 at the conference accompanying the National Portrait Gallery, London and Yale Center for British Art, New Haven, exhibition on Sir Thomas Lawrence at the Paul Mellon Centre for Studies in British Art, London.
2. Irwin and Irwin 1975, p. 147, rightly note the implied criticism as well as the admiration in Lawrence's critique of Raeburn.
3. Morrison 1843, p. 17. See my remark 'Anecdote is a constituent of life writing with its own distinct conventions that have yet to be systematically discussed by scholars': Viccy Coltman, 'The "peculiar colouring of the mind": Character and painted portraiture in the Scottish Enlightenment', Susan Manning and Thomas Ahnert (eds), *Character, Self and Sociability in the Scottish Enlightenment*, Basingstoke, 2011, p. 165.
4. Edinburgh and London 1997–8, p. 150.
5. A. Cassandra Albinson, Peter Funnell and Lucy Peltz (eds), *Thomas Lawrence: Regency Power and Brilliance*, exh. cat., Yale Center for British Art, New Haven and National Portrait Gallery, London, 2010, p. 217.
6. Marcia Pointon, 'Portrait-painting as a business enterprise in London in the 1780s', *Art History*, VII, 1984, p. 187. See the essays by Peter Funnell, 'The London art world and its institutions', pp. 154–66 and Andrew Wilton, 'Painting in London in the early nineteenth century', pp. 167–86 in Celina Fox (ed.), *London – World City, 1800–1840*, exh. cat., Villa Hugel, Essen; New Haven and London, 1992.

7. Edinburgh and London 1997–8 p. 27; Michael Levey, *Sir Thomas Lawrence*, New Haven and London, 2005, p. 120, p. 113.

8. Miles 1973–4.

9. Cunningham 1843, I. p. 296, p. 297, p. 299. On the relationship between Wilkie and Leven, see the important letter dated 28 November 1816 (GD26/13/301, NAS) in which Wilkie refers to 'the obligations not only my father & myself but almost every branch of my family have received from your Lordship'. His letter later describes a painting in progress for a friend of Leven's, the Marquis of Stafford (*The Breakfast*), which 'affords me the means of conveying an idea . . . of the most complete English comfort.'

10. H. A. D. Miles, 'Wilkie as a Portraitist: Observations on "A National Misfortune",' *Sir David Wilkie of Scotland, 1785–1841*, Raleigh, 1987, pp. 52–3, no. 29.

11. 23 August 1824, J. Steuart to James Gillespie. Steuart wrongly thought Wilkie would decline the commission and encouraged Gillespie to use his influence to promote John Watson; GD314/580/11, NAS.

12. Pointon, 1984, p. 41.

13. GD26/13/297/1, NAS. The Earl of Kellie sent a copy of the minutes to the Earl of Morton with a letter dated 3 June 1814, asking him if he wanted to subscribe and, on his return to England, if he would recommend an artist to execute the commission; GD150/3509/37, NAS.

14. GD26/13/297/3, NAS.

15. 28 January 1817, GD26/13/297/5, NAS.

16. C. A. Malcolm, *The Bank of Scotland, 1695–1945*, Edinburgh, 1948, p. 230.

17. 30 January 1817, GD26/13/297/6, NAS.

18. 7 February 1817, GD26/13/297/7, NAS.

19. 24 February 1817, GD26/13/297/8, NAS. Lawrence moved to 65 Russell Square in 1813. For his version of the events, see his letter dated 26 April 1817, GD364/1/1276/15, NAS.

20. 30 October 1810, GD302/12/13, NAS. Law had died four years previously.

21. GD26/13/303, NAS.

22. Kit Wedd, *Creative Quarters: The art world in London, 1700–2000*, London, 2001, p. 70.

23. *The Picture of London*, 17th edn, London, 1816, p. 138.

24. Giles Waterfield (ed.), *The Artist's Studio*, Compton Verney, 2009; Kit Wedd, *Creative Quarters: The art world in London, 1700–2000*, London, 2001; Giles Walkley, *Artists' Houses in London, 1764–1914*, Aldershot, 1994.

25. Wedd, ibid. (note 22), p. 72.

26. Giles Walkley, *Artists' Houses in London, 1764–1914*, Aldershot, 1994, p. 15.

27. Michael Phillips, 'No. 36 Castle Street East: A reconstruction of James Barry's

house, painting and printmaking studio and the making of *The Birth of Pandora*',
British Art Journal, IX, no.1, 2008, pp. 15–27.

28. Stephen Lloyd, 'The Cosway Inventory of 1820: Listing unpaid commissions and the contents of 20 Stratford Place, Oxford Street, London', *Walpole Society*, LXVI, 2004, pp. 163–217.

29. Quoted op. cit., p. 167.

30. Albinson, ibid. (note 5), no. 27.

31. Op. cit., no. 28.

32. Kenneth Garlick, *Sir Thomas Lawrence*, Oxford, 1989, fig. 4.

33. 6 November 1817, GD113/4/163/357, NAS. Smailes, 2009, no. 2, p. 243. Helen Smailes' chapter in this volume offers a detailed account of Raeburn and Campbell.

34. The dimensions of the gallery are given in Cunningham 1829–33, V, p. 223.

35. Thomson 1994, p. 13.

36. Alex Kidson, *George Romney, 1734–1802*, London, 2002, pp. 22–3.

37. Cunningham 1843, I, p. 280.

38. Andrew Moore and Charlotte Crawley, *Family and Friends: A regional survey of British Portraiture*, London, 1992, no. 88.

39. These now obscure Regency portrait painters are crying out for an art historian to resuscitate them. There is an M.A. thesis in the Courtauld Institute on Phillips by Charlotte Miller, 1977.

40. Christie's, London, 4 March 2004, lot 354.

41. GD26/13/297/12/1, NAS (Lawrence's terms); GD26/13/297/12, NAS (Owen's).

42. My understanding of the terminology of portrait sizes has been greatly assisted by David Mannings, 'Notes on some eighteenth-century portrait prices in Britain', *British Journal for eighteenth-century studies*, VI, no. 2, 1983, pp. 185–96.

43. Kenneth Garlick, *Sir Thomas Lawrence*, Oxford, 1989, p. 20.

44. 18 June 1818, LAW/2/288, Royal Academy of Arts Archive; 19 June 1819; GD113/5/474/48, NAS; Smailes, no. 16, p. 261.

45. GD26/13/297/13, NAS.

46. Garlick, ibid. (note 32), no. 521; Hugh Belsey, *Gainsborough's Beautiful Mrs. Graham*, Edinburgh, 2003, plate 15 and Hugh Belsey, 'Sir Thomas Lawrence's portraits for the County Building, Perth', *The Burlington Magazine*, CXLIX, 2007, pp. 158–64.

47. Shearer West, 'Thomas Lawrence's Half-History portraits and the politics of theatre', *Art History*, XIV, 1991, esp. p. 225 and p. 245.

48. Albinson, ibid. (note 5), no. 39.

49. Op. cit., p. 124.

50. My discussion is based on Laura Houliston, 'Frame Making in Edinburgh, 1790–1830', *Regional Furniture*, XIII, 1999, pp. 58–77 and on Jacob Simon's unpublished paper 'Raeburn and picture frames'.

51. 21 August 1828, GD26/13/310/6, NAS.

52. 3 May 1823, 1454/2/bundle 290, NRAS.

53. Jacob Simon, *The Art of the Picture Frame: Artists, Patrons and the framing of portraits in Britain*, London, 1996, p. 88 and p. 100.

54. David Alexander, 'Kauffman and the print market in eighteenth-century England', W. W. Roworth (ed.), *Angelica Kauffman: A Continental artist in Georgian England*, London, 1992, p. 163.

55. F. C. Daniell, 'William Walker and his family, 1791–1867', *Print Collector's Quarterly*, XIX, 1932, pp. 320–40.

56. Sanderson 1925.

57. 12 March 1823, MS 9835, ff. 162–163, NLS.

58. MS 1003, ff. 74–75, NLS.

5

In the Shadow of Jacques-Louis David's *Napoleon*: The 10th Duke of Hamilton and Raeburn

Godfrey Evans

The full-length portrait of Alexander, Marquis of Douglas and Clydesdale, who succeeded as the 10th Duke of Hamilton in 1819 (Fig. 5.1), was one of the most important commissions awarded to Sir Henry Raeburn. It should have been a relatively easy, quick and very satisfying undertaking, but the artist's son, Henry Raeburn junior, wrote in 1824:

> That the Portrait was not finished 9 or 10 years ago, was not owing to my Father, he did not touch it for many years in expectation of his Grace sitting again, but seeing no likelihood of that, he at length determined to finish it, & accordingly [. . .] in the Course of last Spring, brought it to its present state [. . .].[1]

The portrait had been ordered by a proud but insecure man, who knew that he would become the premier peer of Scotland and had every intention of becoming a great patron and collector. Unfortunately, Douglas's intense ambition and his failure to brief Raeburn properly soon turned this highly prestigious commission into over a decade of frustration and heartache for Scotland's leading portrait painter and also worsened his financial plight. Douglas did not like the portrait that was taking shape in 1812–13, and the work that is now at Lennoxlove is the result of a remarkably successful salvage operation, which Raeburn almost completely finished, without the 10th Duke's help, in the spring of 1823 – shortly before his death on 8 July 1823.

In order to understand the extraordinary, troubled history of this

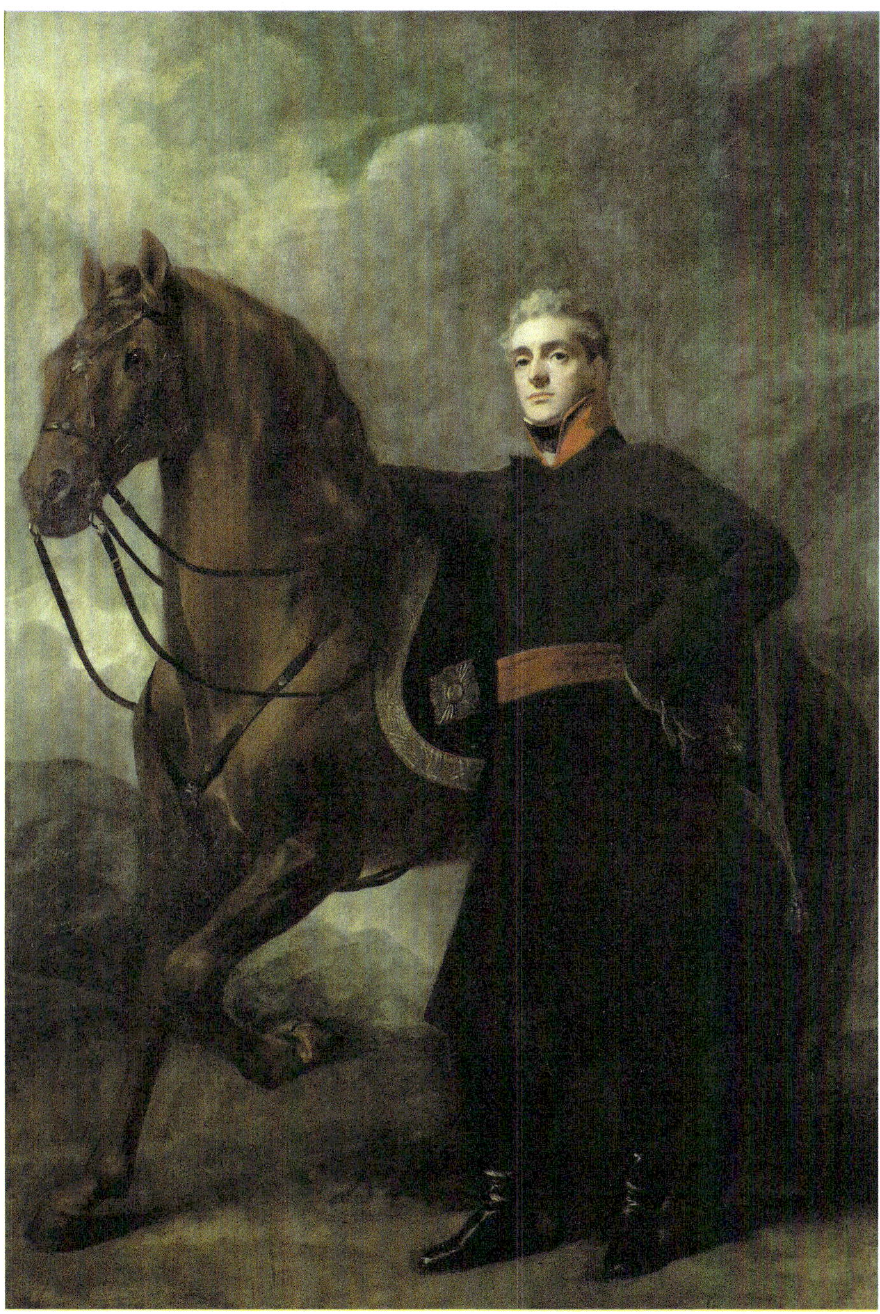

Figure 5.1 Henry Raeburn, *Alexander, 10th Duke of Hamilton*, c. 1812–23, oil on canvas, 245.1 × 179cm, acquired by the 16th Duke of Hamilton in 2011 and now at Lennoxlove, East Lothian (photograph courtesy of the Trustees of National Museums Scotland)

impressive swagger portrait we need to know a good deal about the early life, aspirations and difficulties of the patron. Alexander, 10th Duke of Hamilton (1767–1852), only started to become a significant figure when Douglas, 8th Duke of Hamilton, died without legitimate issue in 1799, and his father, Lord Archibald Hamilton – the second son of the 5th Duke of Hamilton and uncle of the 8th Duke – became the 9th Duke. Overnight, Mr Alexander Hamilton was transformed into the Marquis of Douglas and Clydesdale (the courtesy titles used by the elder sons and heirs of the Dukes of Hamilton and Brandon). At this time, Douglas was living in Italy, following his father's earlier example, and he began to collect in earnest. Among his earliest major trophies were the colossal altarpiece of the *Madonna and Child with Saints* by Girolamo dai Libri, of about 1520, that now dominates the early Renaissance gallery in the Metropolitan Museum of Art, New York, and the so-called *Golden Gospels*, written in gold on purple-stained vellum in the tenth century, which were believed to have been presented to Henry VIII by Pope Leo X when he made the king 'defender of the faith' in 1521, now in the Pierpont Morgan Library, New York.[2]

The 9th Duke, who suffered badly from gout and depression, declined to play a leading role in Whig politics, and it was therefore left to his sons to represent the family in local and national politics. Douglas stood for and won his father's old seat of Lancaster at the 1802 General Election, while his younger brother, Lord Archibald Hamilton, was elected MP for Lanarkshire (the 'home county' of the Dukes of Hamilton). In the wake of his sons' successes, the 9th Duke decided to give up the bother and responsibility of running the Scottish estates and 'retir'd'[3] (to use his own word), to live out his last years at his old home, Ashton Hall, near Lancaster. He authorised Douglas to run the Hamilton estates in Scotland as his 'Commissioner'. The immediate consequence was that Douglas soon found himself working hard as Lord Lieutenant of Lanarkshire and Colonel of the Royal Lanarkshire Militia, training auxiliary forces and protecting Britain against invasion by Napoleon. This obviously affected his collecting, but by the end of 1806 he had amassed at least 120 medieval and renaissance manuscripts and probably also Signorelli's altarpiece of *The Circumcision of Christ*, of about 1491, which is now in the National Gallery, London.

After the Whig 'Ministry of All the Talents' came to power in 1806, Douglas and his brother were rewarded with Douglas's appointment as Ambassador to St Petersburg. It was not a successful period in office, partly because Douglas was inexperienced and naïve, but also because the Whig administration was unwilling to provide Tsar Alexander I with all the military and financial support he wanted to oppose Napoleon. Consequently Douglas was criticised by both the British and the Russians as ineffective.[4]

Nevertheless, the posting provided him with the opportunity to order three important works: bronze busts of *Peter the Great* and *Catherine the Great*, after the original bronze and marble busts by Bartolomeo Carlo Rastrelli and Jean-Antoine Houdon, of 1723–29 and about 1773 respectively, and a full-length tapestry portrait of *Catherine the Great* by the Imperial Tapestry Factory, based on the official oil portrait of the Empress by Fyodor Stepanovich Rokotov.

In a complete departure from normal protocol, Douglas stayed on in Russia after the 'Ministry of All the Talents' fell in March 1807 and he was replaced by his cousin, Lord Granville Leveson Gower. Douglas seems to have remained in Russia primarily to try to marry the Countess Zophia Potocka (1760–1822), a former courtesan who had become the third wife of Count Stanislaw Szczesny Potocki, the richest Polish aristocrat and landowner in the Ukraine. The Count had died in 1805 and his widow had moved to St Petersburg to combat the claims of his divorced wife and get a better education for her children. As Leveson Gower anticipated in a letter to Lady Bessborough,[5] Douglas followed the Countess from the Russian capital to her extensive estates – mini-kingdom is a more accurate description – at Tulczyn, but marriage and enormous wealth eluded him.

Douglas returned to Britain in October 1808 inspired by the patronage and collecting of the Empress Catherine the Great and leading Russian and Polish aristocrats and the proud owner of dozens of newly acquired items, including many made of lapis lazuli, agate and other semi-precious stones. But he also came back with very substantial debts that Alexander Young, one of his Edinburgh lawyers and 'men of business', arranged under three headings: debts that would 'be paid in full whenever funds could be Commanded for the purpose', debts for which 'partial payments might be promised at stated periods', and those that would 'lye over, bearing Interest if demanded'.[6]

Having failed to win the heart and fortune of the Countess, Douglas needed to marry another rich woman or heiress without delay. He did not have to look far, because Susan Euphemia Beckford was almost served up to him on a platter by her father, the immensely wealthy collector William Beckford (who was related to Douglas and had known him since childhood) and Susan's carer, Douglas's own sister, Lady Anne Hamilton. It was unquestionably an arranged marriage, with Douglas, at forty-two, gaining funds, and Susan, at only twenty-three, becoming a Marchioness and prospective Duchess (and Beckford himself acquiring enhanced status). It was agreed that, after the wedding ceremony, Douglas would gain possession of Susan's investments of £6,100 of bank annuities and get £10,000 from Beckford 'for his own use'. In addition, he would also receive 'a perpetual annual Sum or yearly rent charge of £2000 Sterling' from Beckford's plantations and estates in Jamaica.[7] Despite his debts, and before the marriage settlement was even finalized, Douglas began spending large sums of money recklessly. Like the spendthrift Prince of Wales (later King George IV), he began to order very expensive items from the royal goldsmiths Rundell, Bridge and Rundell, who had supplied the government-issue, official ambassadorial service of almost 7,000 ounces of white silver and silver-gilt of 1806 and Douglas's own private order for many additional pieces. In September 1809, Douglas purchased a 'very fine Pearl Necklace' with fifty-five large pearls from Rundell's for £808.10s, and in December he was charged £998.10s.4d for three silver candelabra, weighing over 1,138 ounces.[8]

In March 1810 – a month before his wedding – Douglas went on an even bigger spending spree. On 14 March Rundell's provided him with 'a remarkably fine Brilliant Comb' (a hair ornament set with diamonds), a 'large Brilliant Drop to play over the Centre', and a 'pair of very curious India Cut drops to play on each side of' the comb, for £3,964.[9] At the same time Douglas also acquired a 'remarkably fine' 22-grain emerald costing £150, apparently for himself. On 26 March he was charged £277.5s.6d for another pair of candelabra.[10] These purchases were not Douglas's only extravagances prior to his wedding. At Christie's on 31 March he bought Rubens's celebrated oil painting of *The Loves of the Centaurs*, of about 1630, now in the Gulbenkian Museum, Lisbon, which had been owned by Sir William Hamilton, for 610 guineas.[11] The same day, Mease Sutton and Son of Wilton invoiced him £436.1s for three crimson Brussels carpets and borders.[12]

Marriage to Susan Beckford on 26 April 1810 did not calm Douglas down, but fuelled his desire to demonstrate his taste and status. On 6 June he acquired a Koran and two other manuscripts at Christie's sale of the important collection of Oriental manuscripts assembled by Captain Archibald Swinton, while Beckford's friend and agent Gregorio Franchi was buying other manuscripts for his father-in-law. About a fortnight or so later, Douglas made a 'very liberal offer' to purchase the Portland Vase – the finest and most prestigious surviving example of ancient Roman cameo glass – from the Duke of Portland.[13] This had also passed through the hands of his revered relative Sir William Hamilton, and it seems that Douglas was wanting to show that he had the taste and the resources to restore major Hamiltonian items to family ownership and was therefore, emphatically and unequivocally, the dynamic, effective head of the House of Hamilton.

In March 1811 Rundell's supplied Douglas with 'A very fine Emerald' costing £630, which appears to have been an 'upgrade' of the £150 emerald purchased the month before his wedding.[14] It was followed, in May, by 'A very curious opal Brilliant' worth £63, which was set 'in plain gold for a Ring' for another £1.18s; and in June Rundell's furnished him with an even more

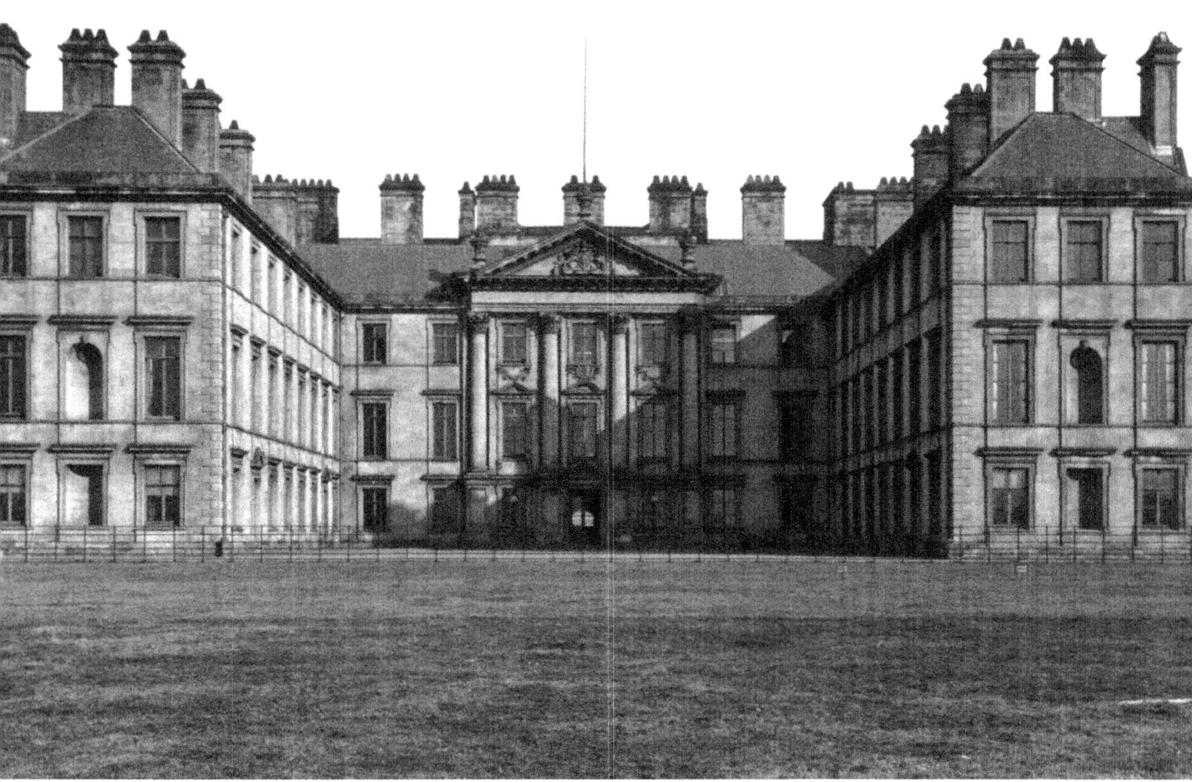

Figure 5.2 *The southern façade and the west and east wings of Hamilton Palace,* designed by James Smith and built between c. 1693 and 1701, photograph taken in 1919 (courtesy of Country Life Picture Library)

obvious status symbol: a massive silver inkstand weighing over 48 ounces, with gadrooned decoration, costing £33.[15]

While all this was going on in England, Douglas was also spending thousands of pounds on improving Hamilton Palace (Fig. 5.2) and the adjacent policies, around Hamilton in Lanarkshire, and the Hamilton estates in central Scotland and on the Isle of Arran. Improvements were made to the exterior and interior of the palace involving the architect James Gillespie Graham, and an extensive restoration and refurbishment of many rooms was carried out by the wrights Gavin and John Rowat and other craftsmen. A lot of new fittings, furnishings, furniture and other goods were acquired and installed,[16] and Douglas began the systematic introduction of black marble into Hamilton Palace. In 1810 he ordered four black marble chimneypieces for a 'Dining Room', a 'Drawing Room' and two bedrooms and six black marble tables for the Long Gallery from the Glasgow architect David Hamilton.[17] These ten pieces cost over £200 and provided both the foundation and the springboard for the decision to order two colossal black marble chimneypieces and an enormous black marble door surround for the Long Gallery from David Hamilton in 1829. These, in turn, would lead to the commissioning of two more colossal black marble chimneypieces and door surrounds for the first-floor Grand Entrance Hall in the mid-1830s and the great black marble double staircase, which was begun in 1840 and cost over £10,000. The final result, supplemented by many other orders, would be a quite extraordinary use of black marble, both as a demonstration of power and wealth and as a visual unifier of the old and new parts of the palace, on the south-north axis.

It is also extremely revealing to find that between at least January 1809 and November / December 1810 Douglas was keeping an eagle (which had obvious royal and imperial associations) and a wolf (an animal that had almost certainly become extinct in Scotland in the seventeenth century and, in this case, had probably been imported from Russia or Sweden).[18] Moreover, he is also documented as owning a 'Spanish Horse' in February–March 1809 and a 'Grey Arabian horse' in March–April of the same year. It is a moot point whether these references relate to one or two horses, but Douglas was definitely sending at least one of his finest stallions to Colonel Leatham in Edinburgh for breeding purposes in March–April 1810; and the following spring he was having his 'mares covered by the Arabian'.[19]

All this highlights Douglas's desire and determination to project and emphasise his status, wealth, knowledge, taste and all-round abilities. Surviving bills for repairs and refurbishment in Hamilton Palace indicate it would have been necessary to re-display the collection of paintings once most, if not all, of the work had been completed, and the taking of an inventory in 1811 confirms that a re-hang did take place. The 1811 inventory and two earlier inventories reveal that Douglas had a very large collection of important and interesting Italian and Flemish Old Master paintings and did not need to buy pre-1800 pictures as a priority.[20] What emerges from a careful reading of the 1811 inventory is the dearth of recent and contemporary art. Indeed, only two such works – a 'Landscape [by] Gainsborough' and a sketch of 'Hercules' by Sir Joshua Reynolds – are listed among the 9th Duke's and Douglas's paintings on the 1811 Hamilton Palace inventory.[21] There were other 'modern' paintings, notably Gavin Hamilton's huge canvas of *Hector's Farewell to Andromache*, commissioned by the 8th Duke of Hamilton during his 'Grand Tour' in the mid-1770s, and Anne Forbes's life-size portrait of the 8th Duke, which were both displayed in the Long Gallery in Hamilton Palace in 1811;[22] but these – and probably other portraits of the 8th Duke by Gavin Hamilton, George Garrard and other artists elsewhere in the palace and in other Hamilton residences – would only have underscored the pressing need for Douglas to commission and acquire contemporary portraits and other pictures.

The full-length portrait of Susan Euphemia Beckford that Thomas Phillips executed for Beckford in 1810 probably prompted Douglas to think seriously about a full-length portrait of himself, but he evidently decided against a single commission and a solitary portrait. Douglas seems to have reflected on the full-length portraits of his predecessors in the 120-foot-long Long Gallery and noted that the portraits of the early Dukes were displayed with full-length portraits of *King Charles I on Horseback* after Van Dyck and *King Gustavus Adolphus of Sweden*.[23] The inclusion of these two portraits showed his ancestors honouring Charles I for creating the dukedom of Hamilton and Gustavus of Sweden for championing the Protestant cause, and gave explicit visual expression to the sympathies and allegiances of the seventeenth-century Hamiltons.

Douglas may already have owned the state portraits of *King George III* and *Queen Charlotte* by Allan Ramsay, now in the British Government Art Collection and the Musée du Louvre respectively, which would later be displayed either side of his ambassadorial throne in the Long Gallery, but, more importantly, he had a real interest in the Empress Catherine the Great.[24] Two small portraits of the Empress were already on display in Hamilton Palace in 1811; the bronze bust of the Empress after Houdon was awaiting shipment from St Petersburg, and in May 1811 it was announced that the Imperial Tapestry Factory had completed the full-length tapestry of the Empress (Fig. 5.3).[25]

Catherine the Great was unquestionably one of the outstanding rulers during Douglas's early life. Over the course of her enlightened reign of thirty-four years, Catherine introduced many economic, legal, administrative and educational reforms and expanded the Russian empire into eastern Poland, the Crimea and other lands surrounding the Black Sea. She was a patron of Falconet, Quarenghi, Cameron and many other artists and architects, transformed St Petersburg and the Imperial residences around the capital, and acquired thousands of paintings, cameos and other items by buying over twenty major French, German and British collections, either *en bloc* or as selected assemblages.[26] Douglas evidently fully accepted Catherine's importance and decided to partner or pair the tapestry portrait of the Empress with a portrait of the Emperor Napoleon, the acknowledged 'Colossus of the Age'. That Douglas should have acquired a portrait of Napoleon is not really surprising. He was a Whig: Francophile, in agreement with many of the ideals of the French Revolution, determined to see Napoleon as their saviour and continuator, and keen to institute a *rapprochement* between Britain and France. Moreover, the commissioning and ownership of a large portrait of Napoleon in the early 1810s had the added attractions for Douglas that they proclaimed and trumpeted his full commitment to the Whig cause and his defiant opposition to the Tories.

The key point here is that Douglas was acting very unwisely and rashly. He was laying himself open to charges of disloyalty and treason and,

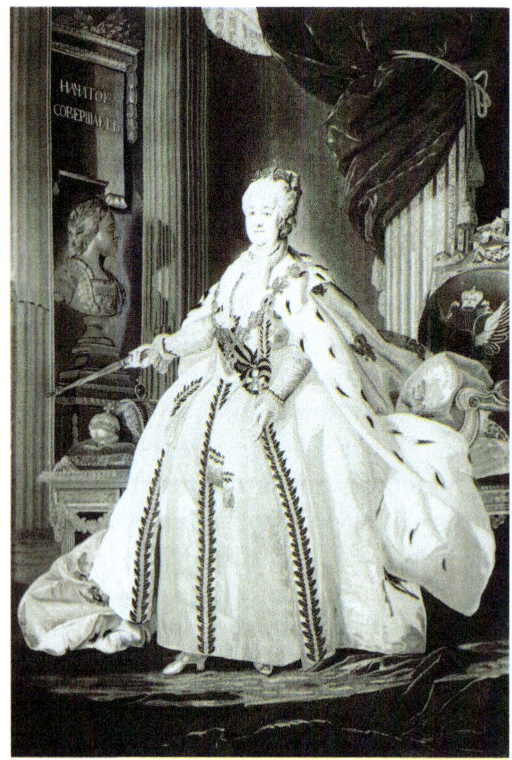

Figure 5.3 *The Empress Catherine the Great*, tapestry by the Imperial Tapestry Factory, St Petersburg, commissioned by the Marquis of Douglas and completed in 1811. The tapestry was included in the 1882 Hamilton Palace sale, lot 1941, and was with French and Company, New York, from 1918 to 1940 (photograph courtesy of the French and Company Archive, Getty Research Institute, Los Angeles)

potentially, to very harmful criticism, ostracism, and even physical violence against himself, his family and Hamilton property. Britain was at war with France, Napoleon's control over Europe was at its zenith, and the birth of the King of Rome (on 20 March 1811) looked likely to ensure the continuation of the Napoleonic dynasty and its domination of the Continent. It was definitely not the moment to place an important commission for a portrait of Napoleon, yet Douglas went ahead. He could have purchased James Northcote's 'as large as life' portrait of the young Napoleon mounted on a rearing white horse, with sword on shoulder, of 1801 (Fig. 5.4), which would have complemented *King Charles I on Horseback* and the portrait of himself with his horse by Raeburn. Northcote's *Napoleon* was on sale by private

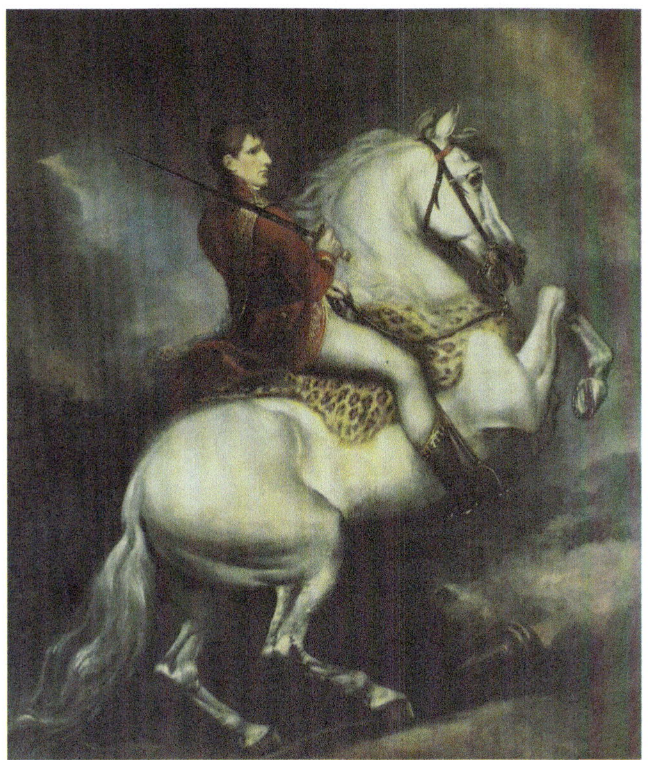

Figure 5.4 James Northcote, *Napoleon Bonaparte on a White Horse*, signed and dated 1801, oil on canvas, 272×239cm, location unknown (photograph courtesy of Sotheby's)

treaty from the European Museum, in London, from 1808 and was offered at Christie's on 18 February 1809 and by Farebrother on 24 May 1811.[27]

Douglas probably rejected Northcote's painting as too out of date, mediocre and militaristic, but he presumably also knew that it had been exhibited by the London print-seller John Jeffryes, the European Museum and the auction houses and was a very over-exposed, stale work that would have brought little glory to its owner. Instead, Douglas decided to commission a portrait of Napoleon by Jacques-Louis David, the Emperor's own painter, which would 'match' the official tapestry of the Empress Catherine woven by the Imperial (Russian) Tapestry Factory. The tapestry of the Empress only cost 2,000 roubles (less than £200), but by the time Douglas came to commission David, in August 1811, he was prepared to pay a great deal more – in the end, 1,000 guineas – and to give David *carte blanche* to produce what became *The Emperor Napoleon in his Study at the Tuileries*, which is now in the National Gallery of Art, Washington, DC (Fig. 5.5).[28]

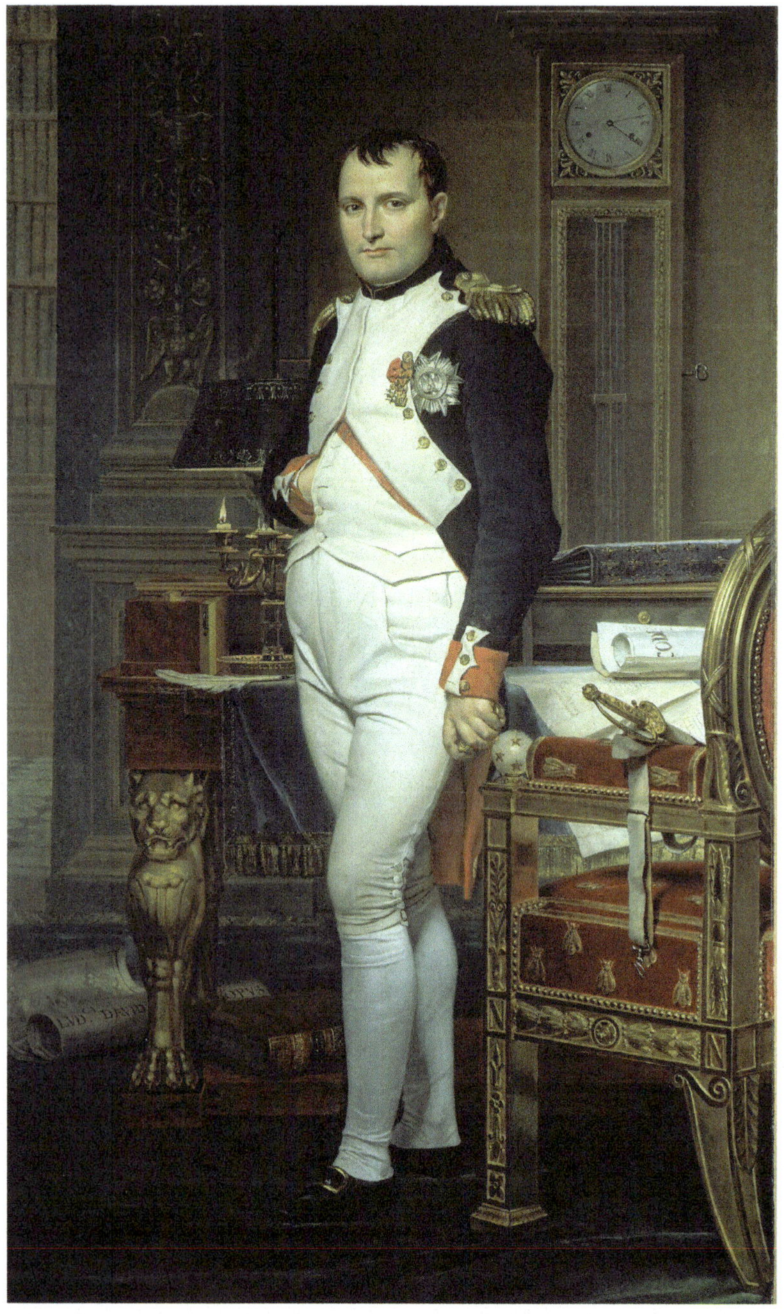

Figure 5.5 Jacques-Louis David, *The Emperor Napoleon in his Study at the Tuileries*, commissioned by the Marquis of Douglas in 1811, signed and dated 1812, oil on canvas, 203.9×125.1cm, Samuel H Kress Collection, National Gallery of Art, Washington, DC

Around this time, Douglas must have commissioned Raeburn to paint a full-length portrait of himself, with his favourite or best horse, which seems to allude to his own participation in the Napoleonic Wars and great events. On 8 September 1812 Raeburn informed Alexander Young that the 'portrait of the Marquisses Horse is not yet finished' and went on to explain that this was due to the lack of instructions about the composition from Douglas: 'As I somehow understood that the Marquis himself was to have been painted either on him or standing beside him.'[29] Raeburn was evidently irritated by the delay, but it is impossible to gauge how many months he had been kept in limbo. Interestingly, the second part of the letter refers to Raeburn's willingness to undertake a portrait of the Marchioness and her son, and the citation of his current charge of 100 guineas for a full-length portrait implies that it was a full-length picture that was under discussion.

Unfortunately, Douglas's lavish patronage, collecting and 'improvements' increased his financial problems. An *aide-memoire*, written in his own hand, reveals that his gross income in 1810 came to only £34,189 and that over £18,000 of this disappeared in annuities to his brother, sisters and the Marchioness of Exeter, the divorced wife of the 8th Duke (£6,000), and the payment of interest (£2,500), taxes (£4,500), factors and agents (£3,000) and stipends (£2,100). A further £9,857 was swallowed up on 'Improvements' to the estate, while £3,835 was 'spent at Hamilton'. Once 'Sundries' of £600 had been deducted, only £1,797 was 'clear'.[30] By 1812 the situation had worsened considerably and was being exacerbated by Douglas's decision to buy more old houses and properties in the vicinity of Hamilton Palace. By this date, Douglas's debts apparently came to around £90,000, and even Douglas seems to have recognised that he could not continue in such a profligate manner.[31] During a meeting prior to September 1812, he had given Alexander Young 'such a picture of the state of his finances' that even the highly critical lawyer 'could not avoid sending him any money which I had at my command' and had sent him an order for £800.[32]

Douglas did not stop buying items, but his most extravagant purchasing seems to have halted, at least for a few years. He had already returned the emerald and pair of candelabra acquired from Rundell's in March 1810 and been credited with £130 for the ring on 15 February 1812 and £256.10s.6d for the candelabra on 6 March 1812. His major acquisitions from the goldsmiths end with the purchase of 'An Enamelled foot of a very richly chased gold Custodia', weighing over 38 ounces and costing £241.18s.6d, on 17 July 1812. From then on, money that would previously have been spent on new purchases was used, instead, to reduce Rundell's bill, which stood at almost £7,500 in August 1812.[33]

Before we move on, however, we should focus on the enamelled gold

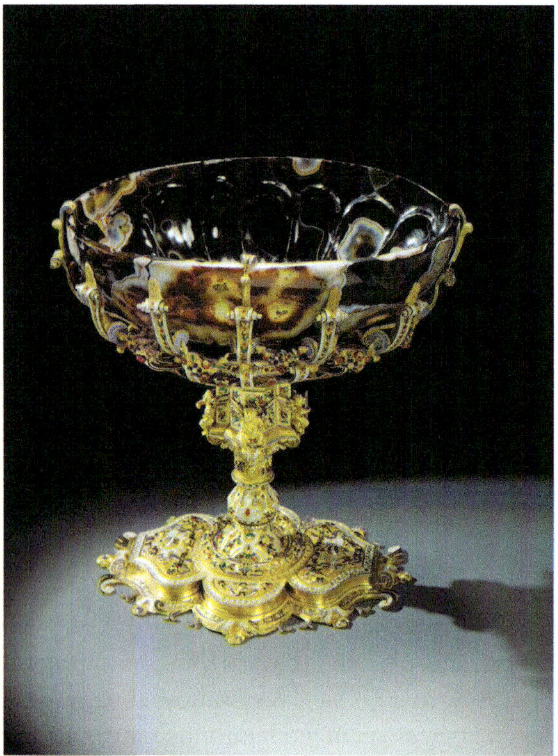

Figure 5.6 *Late Roman or Byzantine sardonyx or agate bowl mounted on an enamelled gold foot from a gold monstrance*, the two parts united by the 10th Duke of Hamilton between 1812 and 1825, 26.7×26.6×18cm, National Museums Scotland, Edinburgh (photograph courtesy of Sotheby's)

foot or stand (Fig. 5.6), because it sheds further light on Douglas's view of his extremely exalted status and his ambitious collecting, which was certainly orientated towards imperial subjects and items with imperial associations. The foot or stand was part of a massive gold monstrance that had been looted from the Monastery of the Escorial and auctioned in London the previous year. Today, we know that this extremely rare and important example of Mannerist gold had been given to the Monastery by Philip II of Spain between 1563 and 1571. On the stand, Douglas mounted his most expensive Russian acquisition, an exceptionally large, carved sardonyx or agate bowl, which he believed was the 'Bénitier de Charlemagne': the holy water stoup of the Emperor Charlemagne, the founder of the Holy Roman Empire. Both Douglas's children, William, the future 11th Duke, and Susan, were apparently baptised using this bowl, in 1811 and 1814. The finished two-part 'Vase' or 'Cup' was valued at £1,500 in the 1825 and 1835 Hamilton Palace inventories, and was by far the most highly insured item in the Hamilton collection during the first half of the nineteenth century.

Regrettably we do not know exactly why the Raeburn commission foundered, but the difficulty definitely lay with Douglas. Douglas was willing to give David a free hand over the portrait of Napoleon, and was deftly handled by the former regicide, who fed him gracious compliments and information about the work.[34] Raeburn, though, was not given this artistic independence and was stymied by Douglas's proximity, at Hamilton and, on occasions, in Edinburgh itself. His letter to Young of 8 September 1812 refers directly to the lack of a clear brief and to a patron who had spoken about two very different compositions but failed to come to a decision: 'My portrait of the Marquisses Horse is not yet finished. As I somehow understood that the Marquis himself was to have been painted either on him or standing beside him.'

The 10th Duke of Hamilton took a long time to develop most of his major projects and frequently changed his mind. The paramount example is the new addition to Hamilton Palace (Fig. 5.7), which saw the Edinburgh architect James Gillespie Graham dropped in 1822 in favour of the Glasgow architect, and the Duke's 'kith and kin', David Hamilton. In June 1822 David Hamilton was sufficiently confident with the planning of the new north block that he felt able to calculate 'the expense of the whole Masonry' at £7,900 and the finishing of the interiors at £9,900 – a total of £17,800.[35] However, the Duke wanted to review and revise the plans and this delayed things almost another two years. In November 1824, David Hamilton was plainly embarrassed when he came to present his bill to the Duke's principal factor, Robert Brown, and explained the high charge with the comment: 'You will see that the amount, is considerable being £492 „ 16 „ 6, but you will also see that the time spent on the Duke's business is 178 days of myself and 183 of my clerk, which was owing to the frequent change of the plans and frequent attendance upon His Grace'.[36]

Other examples of poor command and control include the Duke's desire, in 1827, to change the planned heights of some of the first-floor rooms in the new north block, and the employment of no fewer than five Continental and Scottish architects on the Hamilton Mausoleum. In the later period, there is also the project for the Scottish sculptor Thomas Campbell to produce a full-size bronze copy of the Roman equestrian statue of the Emperor Marcus Aurelius, fitted with a colossal bronze head of the Duke, which limped, on and off, for almost a decade before being finally abandoned in 1848.

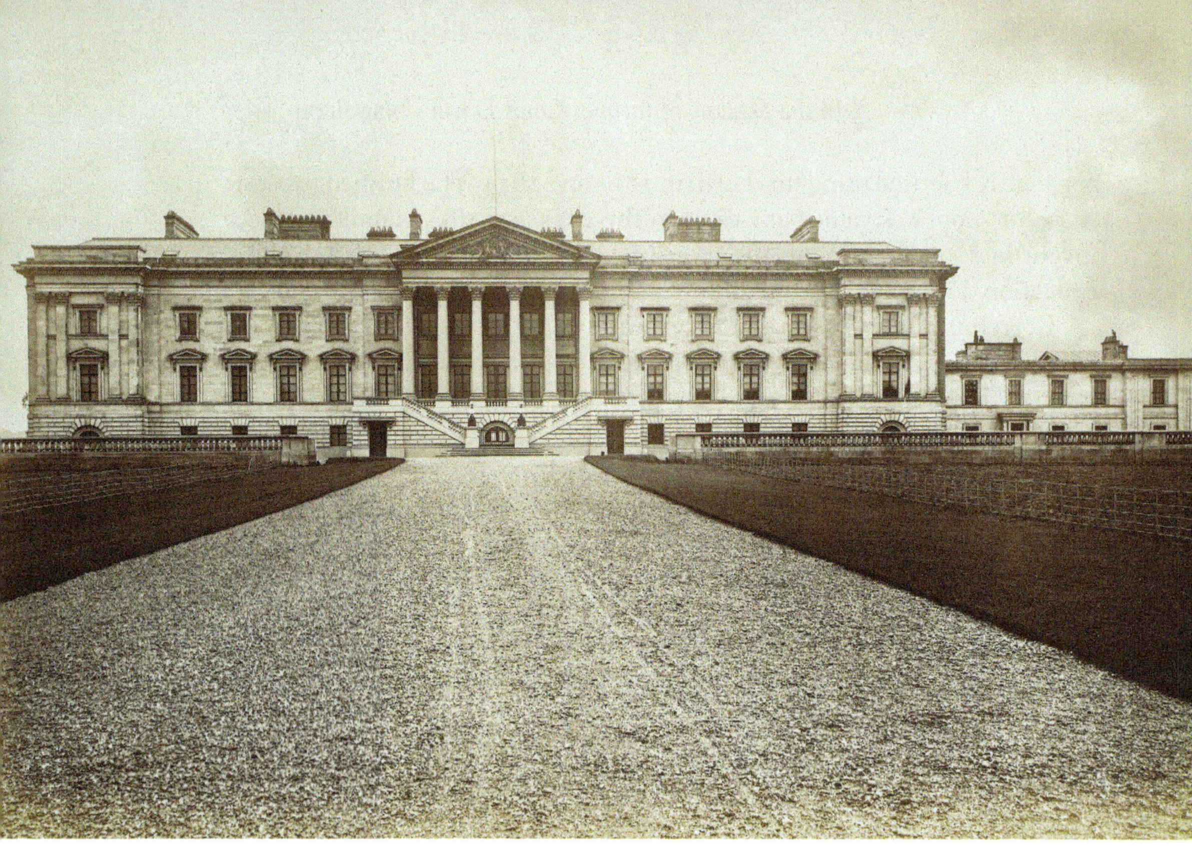

Figure 5.7 Thomas Annan, *The north-facing addition to Hamilton Palace*, late 1870s or early 1880s, photograph, Hamilton Town House Library, Hamilton (courtesy of South Lanarkshire Leisure and Culture Ltd and the Trustees of National Museums Scotland)

One can therefore legitimately focus on Raeburn's letter to Young of 1812. It is also probably fair to say that Douglas would have been distracted in 1812–13 by the state of his finances and by his wife's poor health following the birth of their son. That said, the problem with the Raeburn portrait was almost certainly compounded after the delivery of David's portrait of Napoleon in 1813. Douglas was delighted with this brilliant piece of propaganda, which shows a modest man working early into the morning on the *Code Napoléon* and non-military matters for the benefit of France and Western civilization. In an unpublished draft letter in French, preserved inside one of David's multiple letters of 30 April 1813, he informed the painter:

I must tell you of my arrival in London and the pleasure I felt in finding there the portrait you had the kindness to make for me of your Emperor. ~~I am extremely pleased with it~~ It arrived in the best possible condition, not a stain or a scratch – It seems just out of the artist's hands, without having suffered the perils of the sea and long journey. I have great pleasure and pride in showing it to our

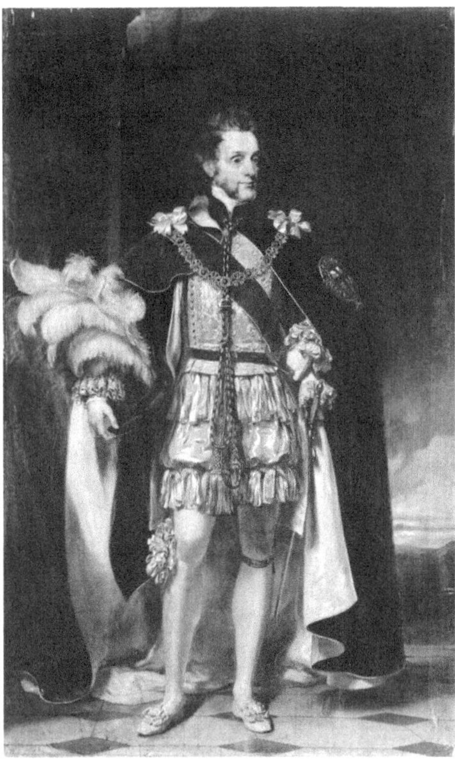

Figure 5.8 Henry William Pickersgill, *Alexander, 10th Duke of Hamilton, wearing the robes of a Knight of the Garter*, 1836–8, oil on canvas, c. 237.5×146cm, location unknown (photograph courtesy of the National Portrait Gallery, London, and AC Cooper (Colour) Ltd)

English artists, especially Mr West [Benjamin West, the President of the Royal Academy].

If you could have heard their observations you would have been very pleased.[37]

The David portrait seems to have been regarded as such a high-profile success, and such a credit to Douglas, that it was kept in London. Douglas's letter establishes that it was definitely on display in London – presumably in the Grosvenor Place house – in 1813, and it seems likely that it is the first entry – 'My N – picture' – on the list of items that he left in the 'Church room' in early August 1816, before departing from London to Italy with his family.[38]

David's meticulous, polished treatment was at variance with Raeburn's atmospheric, 'broad brush' approach to painting. The quality of the David and the clash of styles must have left Douglas worried and wanting a similar treatment of himself in his portrait, especially if he still had doubts over the basic composition of the Raeburn portrait and planned to display the two portraits in close proximity. Around 1813–14 Douglas seems to have taken an aversion to his own portrait and stopped sitting for it. This must have been a conscious decision, rather than simply difficulty finding time for sittings, because Raeburn was painting the portrait of his son, William (now at Lennoxlove) around this period. It might be thought that Douglas withdrew his cooperation when his own portrait was still in its very early stages, but a letter from Young to Brown dated 19 November 1816 suggests it must have been quite far advanced when the first phase came to an end:

> M[r]. Raeburn the Painter has been urging me frequently for payment of 45. Guineas as the price of Lord Angus' Portrait and a much larger sum for that of the Marquis and his Spanish Horse, I could have wished to parry him at this time, but as he seemed to be in despair and unable to get a shilling from any of his Customers I this day give him the 45. Guineas for the young Lord's Portrait, leaving the Marquis's to be settled at a more convenient opportunity.[39]

A letter from the artist's son, Henry Raeburn junior, to Brown dated 16 January 1824 states categorically that Douglas failed to attend any more sittings after 1814 or 1815:

> That the Portrait was not finished 9 or 10 years ago, was not owing to my Father, he did not touch it for many years in expectation of his Grace sitting again, but seeing no likelihood of that, he at length determined to finish it, & accordingly [. . .] in the Course of last Spring, brought it to its present state [. . .][40]

Douglas's failure to sit from the summer of 1816 to the autumn of 1819 is explained by his absence in Italy. The family left London in August 1816 and, although Douglas returned to England in July 1818 (when it was believed that his father was dying) and was in the country about five weeks, he would have been unable to attend sittings in either Hamilton or Edinburgh before early October 1819 when he was back in Scotland.[41]

The portrait could have been revived between October 1819 and the winter of 1820, but all the indications suggest it was a dead commission that stood little chance of resurrection. In February 1819, Douglas had become the 10th Duke of Hamilton and the premier peer of Scotland and was now a very elevated man, who was deeply conscious of his status. As far as the Duke was concerned, the portrait would have been associated with debt, retrenchment, withdrawal from expensive collecting, criticism and failure. The degree of failure should not be underestimated. The Raeburn portrait was not a single, isolated, distasteful episode, but one of a number of highly upsetting setbacks that had occurred between 1811 and 1815. In August 1812, the Russian banker Baron Rall had written Douglas a stinging letter, criticising him for trying to delay payments on a loan of 58,000 roubles and casting aspersions on his honour.[42] This sullied the tapestry portrait of the Empress Catherine that Rall sent to Britain the following year.[43] In 1813 Douglas also learnt that the large mirrors commissioned from the Imperial Glass Factory in St Petersburg in 1807 had been broken during transportation from Russia in 1812–13.[44] Things had not worked out well and Douglas had been deprived of the opportunity to show a cluster of major new acquisitions together, to visual and personal advantage. In irritation and perhaps even despair, he had ended up placing both the tapestry of the Empress Catherine and a specially ordered Russian parquetry floor, which had been acquired in 1811 and sent from St Petersburg in 1812, into long-term storage.[45]

Looking back, the Duke would have seen the Raeburn portrait as a work mired in failure and would have been loath to return to it. Moreover, the Duke had undergone considerable personal change and development over the past three years in Italy. He was now the ardent admirer of Napoleon's notorious sister, Princess Pauline Borghese, and the friend and helper of Napoleon's mother, Madame Mère, and uncle, Cardinal Fesch. Even more significantly, he was also beginning to make the transition into a great collector who could rival the Prince of Wales (shortly to become George IV) and his own father-in-law, the maniacal collector William Beckford. Over the past three years he had concentrated on acquiring examples of porphyry, coloured marbles and *pietre dure* – arguably the most expensive and high-status forms of collecting in the early nineteenth century. In 1817 he had bought two huge porphyry slabs from the church of San Pancrazio fuori le Mura in Rome, and was now planning to mount them on magnificent gilt bronze stands specially commissioned from the Parisian founder Jean-François Denière, all now in the Art Gallery of Ontario, Toronto. Furthermore, he had already handed over some of his acquisitions of *pietre dure* to the London furniture-maker Robert Hume and commissioned the extremely impressive clock cabinet, which is now in the Gilbert Collection, in the Victoria and Albert Museum, London.[46]

The Duke was now a much more 'international' and ambitious man. He planned to return to Rome, to resume life with Princess Pauline and her family and to continue collecting marble and *pietre dure*. Even more crucially, he had already employed the Neapolitan architect Francesco Saponieri to produce designs for a major addition to Hamilton Palace and was embarking upon the process of creating the most intimidating powerhouse and treasure house in the history of Scotland.[47] From the Duke's standpoint, the Raeburn portrait represented the past and failure. He was looking forward, not back, and the portrait had become a bitter and avoidable irrelevance.

For his part, Raeburn must have hoped that the Duke would resume sittings, if only to show his backing for Scottish painters and craftsmen. However, any approach after November 1820 would have been unwelcome because the Duke's debts had risen again to their 1812 level of around £90,000 – following the much delayed decision to settle with the illegitimate daughter of the 8th Duke and pay her £60,000 plus interest over the next decade.[48] During the first half of 1821 the Duke was back in Italy, and therefore unavailable for sittings. In October 1821, not long after his return, he issued instructions to Roger Aytoun, another of his Edinburgh lawyers and 'men of business', on the need 'to introduce the most rigid economy into every branch of my expenditure'.[49] If Raeburn had spoken to Young, Aytoun or Brown about the Duke's portrait in 1822, he would probably have been advised to delay approaching the Duke, as all three men would have been all too well aware that the Duke had been asked to bail William Beckford out of his financial embarrassment, to prevent the sale of Fonthill Abbey and his collection. To complicate matters even more, the discovery of the parlous state of the north wall of Hamilton Palace necessitated its rebuilding and advanced, rather than delayed, the construction of the very expensive new north-facing addition to the palace.[50]

Nevertheless, Raeburn could not simply leave the portrait of the Duke unfinished. His need to complete the portrait of the premier peer of Scotland increased in August 1822 when George IV visited Edinburgh and was received at Holyroodhouse by the Duke as hereditary keeper of the royal palace. At the dinner given by the City of Edinburgh to the sovereign, the Duke made a widely reported speech, which expressed his Whig independence, and went on, three days later, to lead the Freemasons of Scotland in laying the foundation stone for the monument to the dead of the Napoleonic Wars, in the form of a reduced copy of the Parthenon, on Calton Hill.[51] The 10th Duke was therefore not only the pre-eminent Scottish aristocrat in 1822–3, but a very high-profile, topical figure, who looked as though he would provide much greater leadership to the Whigs in Scotland in the years to come.

Viewed from this perspective, it is perfectly understandable that Scotland's leading portrait painter should have wanted to complete the portrait as soon as possible after August 1822. According to his son, Raeburn 'finished' the Duke's portrait in the spring of 1823, 'with the trifling exception' explained in a previous letter to the Duke, dated 8 December 1823.[52] This earlier letter has still to be found, but the 'trifling exception' is clarified in a letter from H. D. Dickie to the Duke, dated 28 October 1823, which clearly states that the portrait 'was finished by Sir Henry, with the exception of the Buttons, on the Coat' (i.e. the Duke's coat).[53]

The Duke was distinctly underwhelmed by the completion of his portrait, and was soon querying the charge being levied and refusing to lend the portrait to the retrospective exhibition that was being organised to celebrate Raeburn's life and achievements. Only a few of the relevant letters have been tracked down to date and it is therefore worth laying out the sequence as it exists at present. The series currently commences with a letter from the lawyer William Young Herries to Brown, dated 11 October 1823, which begins by noting that, as 'His Grace's Picture was fortunately very nearly completed before the death of Sir Henry Raeburn', he (Herries) will 'therefore pack up and return you the Saddle &ᶜ by whatever conveyance you think best, as there is no farther occasion for it here.'[54] Herries goes on to inform Brown that Sir Henry's executors had appointed a 'promising artist', John Syme (1795–1861), 'to complete any of the unfinished Portraits, which I believe he has done well', and passes on Syme's request 'to beg from the Duke the favor of being allowed to take a Copy of Sir Henry's Portrait of His Grace, of which he has had the care (along with all the others) since Sir H Raeburn died.'

Herries's letter is followed by H. D. Dickie's letter to the Duke of 28 October, which was his second letter to the Duke and written in reply to a letter of 23 October from the Duke. Dickie's letter starts with the matter of the unfinished buttons, mentioned earlier, 'for which your instructions were required; and which will now be executed agreeably to the Directions you may be pleased to give'. The point to concentrate on here is that neither before Sir Henry's death nor during this exchange of correspondence had the Duke bothered to provide the necessary 'instructions' or specifications. The remainder of the letter is Dickie's response to a passage in the Duke's missing letter of 23 October which evidently queried or objected to the charge for the portrait:

> With regard to the Price, I beg leave to explain that no Sum is filled up in Sir Henry's Books – But his regular charge for a full length & horse was 250 Gui[neas]. The Portrait of Your Grace however is of an unusually large Size, such as he Seldom did, and on this Ground the Charge of 350 Guineas was made.
>
> I am however instructed by Mr. Raeburn to say that as the Portrait is out of the usual Course, he is willing to withdraw the Charge which has been made, and if agreeable to your Grace to allow Sir Thomas Lawrence to fix what the Price should be.[55]

The next communication we have is Henry Raeburn junior's very well written letter to the Duke of 2 December 1823, requesting permission to include the Duke's portrait in the retrospective exhibition of his father's paintings. Raeburn cleverly sets the request in the context of the 'earnest desire' of '[s]ome of the most distinguished individuals' of the City of Edinburgh 'to have an Exhibition of the latter works of my lamented Father' and of his 'anxious' desire 'to gratify their wishes'. Writing with consummate skill, Raeburn alleges that, as he began to identify the exhibits,

> your Graces splendid Portrait, with the beautiful Arabian Horse, at once occurred to me, as one of the most desirable, not only on acc[ount] of the distinguished original, but because it is one of the very happiest of my Fathers productions – It was esteemed as such by himself, & is universally admired by all who have seen it as a most exquisite painting – I therefore take the liberty of requesting your Graces permission to retain the Portrait & place it in the Gallery during the approaching Exhibition.[56]

Raeburn goes on to 'solicit' the loan of the portrait of the Duke's son – 'it being one on which my Father set a high value' – and to assure the Duke that he would send a 'proper person to pack & bring in the Picture, & would be answerable for its being safely returned to the Palace'.

It was an excellent 'loan letter' to an owner and potential lender, but it failed to win over the Duke. In a draft letter, with untidy revisions, to Raeburn junior, dated 6 December, the Duke appears to have intended to declare that he was 'ready to testify to the high estimation in which [he] held S[ir] H Raeburn's talents as an artist', but that he could not give 'any consent or to withhold it in regard to placing the picture alluded [to] in the exhibition'.[57] The Duke states that Sir Henry was to have been paid £200 for the picture, and that he had given instructions 'that no body [i.e. Syme] should venture to touch it under the idea of finishing' it. However, he had objected to Mr Dickie's demand for £350, 'instead of £200', '& therefore it is that I cannot at present assume any right whatever over the picture'.

Given the dispute over the cost, the Duke was fully entitled to state his objection in trenchant language, but he could then have moved on – as a great and munificent patron and lover of the arts – to accede charitably and graciously to Raeburn junior's request to display the portrait. His lack of enthusiasm for the painting and support for the exhibition is further reflected in his curt closing lines: 'I am sorry not to be able to send you the portrait of my son to be exhibited with the other works of S[ir] H Reaburn I sh[ould] do it with pleasure but The Duchess is not to be persuaded to let it [i.e. the portrait of her son] go out of room'.

The artist's son was naturally disappointed and irritated at this complete lack of support from the premier peer of Scotland and Keeper of Holyroodhouse. He apparently wrote to the Duke on 8 December to explain the price of the portrait, but his explanation proved unsatisfactory. Brown evidently sent him a letter to this effect on 14 January. Writing to the factor two days later, Raeburn found himself 'at a loss how to reply to your letter, without recapitulating what is already before his Grace'.

As the Duke was failing both to pay and to back the exhibition, Raeburn felt that some straightforward speaking was called for and immediately went on:

> There is a question put however which demands a pointed answer – you say "He [the Duke] now puts the question whiether you really Consider it fair to encrease the price beyond the original agreement merely because it was not finished, as it should have been, 9 or 10 years ago – To this I reply, that were this the Ground, on which the demand for the encreased price, rests, it would be idle indeed for me to make it, & certainly would not have deserved an answer from his Grace – I do Certainly Consider the demand I have made perfectly fair, otherwise I should not have made it, but it is not made on the Ground stated in the question.'[58]

It is at this point that Raeburn told Brown, in no uncertain terms, that the portrait was not finished nine or ten years ago because the Duke stopped sitting for it, and that it had been completed, independently, without the Duke's help, during the spring of 1823. Raeburn's annoyance and exasperation becomes even more obvious in his final sentences:

> I understand there is not now time to get a suitable Frame made, so that however much it is to be regretted, that such a Portrait should not appear in the Exhibition, there is now I fear no help for it – this is a disappointment which will be felt not be [i.e. by] me only, but by all who value the art –
>
> I shall now be glad to be favoured with his Graces determination respecting the pay[ment] of the price [. . .]

Exactly what happened in the wake of this is unclear. The portrait is listed as exhibit 47 – 'His Grace the Duke of Hamilton and Brandon, with his favourite Arabian Horse' – in the catalogue of the Raeburn exhibition.[59] As the exhibition did not open until 3 March, there would have been time for some sort of change of mind and possibly time for a simple frame to have been made, but there is no mention of the portrait in the review of the exhibition in *The Scotsman* of 6 March.[60] The nearest potential corroboration that we have at present is Andrew Duncan's sentence, in his tribute to the memory of Raeburn published in 1824, that 'The Duke of Hamilton, the Earl of Hopeton, Sir David Baird, Sir Walter Scott, Principal Hill, Dr Hunter, Mr Dugald Stewart, and many other justly distinguished Scotsmen, will long live on canvass by his exertions'.[61] However, this is definitely not a simple selection of portraits in the retrospective exhibition. The 1824 catalogue includes entries for portraits of Scott, Hopetoun and Stewart, but not of Baird, Hill and Hunter, so one cannot use Duncan's lines to securely 'place' the portrait of the 10th Duke in the exhibition. We can divine that there must have been some movement between January and June 1824 because the portrait of the 'Duke of Hamilton' appears with a charge of £315 – not £350 – against it on the inventory of Sir Henry's estate submitted on 9 June 1824.[62] Nonetheless, this lesser sum was still outstanding on 9 June 1824.

After all the problems and unpleasantness, one would not expect to find the Raeburn hanging in a position of honour in Hamilton Palace, and so it proves. David's portrait of *The Emperor Napoleon in his Study at the Tuileries* ended up in the New Dining Room or Saloon, with the stupendous silver-gilt tea service commissioned in connection with Napoleon's marriage to Marie-Louise of Austria (purchased in 1830) sometimes on the table and the colossal marble bust of *Napoleon Apotheosized* by Thorvaldsen (bought in 1846) outside in the Tribune, while the tapestry of the *Empress Catherine the Great* was shown with other particularly prized treasures in the Boudoir, in the last of the New State or Tapestry Rooms.

In 1836 the 10th Duke became a Knight of the Garter and seized the opportunity to be depicted in his Garter Robes by Henry William Pickersgill (1782–1875), Sir Thomas Lawrence's former pupil and acknowledged successor (Fig. 5.8). The Duke was successfully elected and invested at a Chapter of the Most Noble Order of the Garter held at St James's Palace on 5 February 1836,[63] and wasted no time in commissioning and sitting for a portrait of himself, resplendent in his Garter Robes. Less than two months later, on 21 March 1836, he paid Pickersgill £150.[64] The Duke gave Pickersgill a further £150 on 15 March 1838,[65] which would seem to be the final settlement on a work costing £300, and the evidently satisfactory and approved portrait was shown at the Royal Academy's annual exhibition a few weeks later.[66] Needless to say, it was Pickersgill's florid costume-piece that joined the full-length paintings of previous Dukes of Hamilton in the famous Long Gallery.[67]

In 1852–3 the Raeburn portrait was apparently slumbering with other less highly regarded works in the Old Dining Room on the ground floor of the north block.[68] By 1876, following the closure of Hamilton House in London, it had become one of twenty works hanging in the 'Lobby and Passage leading to [the] Duchess's Rooms' on the first floor of the east wing of the old baroque palace.[69] It was a sad fate for a work that had been commissioned during an extraordinary and truly exceptional bout of patronage and collecting, to demonstrate and project status, leadership and political interests, and which was directly related to a full-length tapestry of *Catherine the Great* and David's universally acclaimed, classic image of Napoleon as a modest man and a benevolent ruler.

Thankfully, this was not the end of the story. After the great 1882 Hamilton Palace sale, Raeburn's portrait was moved into the Tribune. This was the principal 'hub' on the main route through the palace on the first floor, which gave access to the Hamilton Library, New Dining Room, Long Gallery, and the west and east wings of the old baroque palace. Here the portrait of the *10th Duke of Hamilton* was displayed in a suitably grand space, along with Winterhalter's huge full-length portrait of *Princess Marie of Baden*, the wife of the 11th Duke and cousin of Napoleon III, and marble busts of *Princess Pauline Borghese, Napoleon III* and the *Empress Eugénie*.[70]

Hamilton Palace was little used after the 12th Duke's death in 1895, and the portraits of the 10th Duke by Raeburn and Pickersgill were both included in the November 1919 Hamilton Palace sales, along with most of the remaining good works of art and other items, prior to the demolition of the palace.[71] Raeburn's portrait was bought by Thomas Agnew and Sons for 3,300 guineas (£3,465) – a very respectable sum when one sees that Pickersgill's portrait only fetched £22.3s.[72] It passed to Viscount Cowdray and Cowdray Park, Midhurst, West Sussex, where it was hung above the main staircase.

After the Second World War, Douglas, 14th Duke of Hamilton (1903–73), acquired Lennoxlove, near Haddington, in East Lothian, as the main seat of the Hamilton family. The 14th Duke appreciated the significance of the 10th Duke and subsequently wrote to the 3rd Viscount Cowdray to let him know that he would like to acquire Raeburn's portrait of the 10th Duke if ever Lord Cowdray was minded to sell it. Sadly, it transpired that Lord Cowdray liked the painting and wanted to retain it, and the 14th Duke's enterprising initiative failed.[73]

However, all was not lost. A splendid opportunity arose half a century later when the 4th Viscount Cowdray decided to sell Cowdray Park and much of its content. Through decisive action, and with great good luck, Alexander, 16th Duke of Hamilton, was able to secure the portrait of his ancestor on the first day of Christie's Cowdray sale, on 13 September 2011, for the relatively small sum of £67,250.[74]

Raeburn's portrait of the 10th Duke is now on display at Lennoxlove. Back amongst other representations of the premier peers of Scotland, it stands out as a very successful full-length painting in its own right, whilst at the same time complementing Raeburn's much smaller portraits of the

8th and 11th Dukes. Looking up at Raeburn's dramatic representation of the 10th Duke, few would guess that the sitter had withdrawn his cooperation and that Raeburn had been forced to use a very considerable amount of imaginative dexterity to complete the work. It is one of the clearest demonstrations of his genius that he was able to turn the stalled, unfinished portrait of 1812 into this magnificent painting, with unified bravura brushwork, after a gap of around eight or nine years, in 1823.

Notes

1. I would like to record my deep gratitude to the late Angus, 15th Duke of Hamilton, for permitting me to study and transcribe papers in the Hamilton family archive at Lennoxlove and on deposit at Hamilton Town House Library for my Ph.D. thesis on 'Alexander, 10th Duke of Hamilton, as patron and collector', University of Edinburgh, 2008, and also thank his son, Alexander, 16th Duke of Hamilton, for his on-going assistance and for allowing me to publish my findings here. I am also very much obliged to the following for their help with my research and the preparation of this particular paper: David Caldwell, Amber Green, Nick Holmes, Odile and David Hughson, Stephen Lloyd, Fraser Niven, Clare Rider, Lord Selkirk of Douglas, Joyce Smith, Lyndsay Stuart and Richard Thomson. This contribution is based on chapter three and appendix eight of my thesis, but also draws on another three chapters and some of the other appendices. For the quotation, see HA, M4/55, Henry Raeburn junior to Robert Brown, 16 January 1824.

2. For these works and Douglas's early collecting, see Godfrey Evans, 'The Hamilton Collection and the 10th Duke of Hamilton', *Journal of the Scottish Society for Art History*, VIII, 2003, pp. 54–9.

3. See HA, C4/557, draft letter 9th Duke of Hamilton to Lord Archibald Hamilton, 16 November 1805.

4. Douglas's problems with Lord Grenville and Viscount Howick (the future Earl Grey) and the Russians are recorded in HA, Volumes 1604–1606, and NA, FO 95/227 and FO 342/8. Non-governmental criticism of his performance is contained in the diaries of the artist Joseph Farington and Martha Wilmot: see Kathryn Cave (ed.), *The Diary of Joseph Farington*, VIII (July 1806–December 1807), New Haven and London, 1982, p. 3023, and the Marchioness of Londonderry and Harford Montgomery Hyde (eds), *The Russian Journals of Martha and Catherine Wilmot*, London, 1934, p. 291.

5. Castalia, Countess Granville (ed.), *Lord Granville Leveson Gower, First Earl Granville: Private Correspondence 1781 to 1821*, London, 1917, II, p. 278.

6. HA, Bundle 1602, Young to Douglas, 26 October 1813.

7. See BOD, MS. Beckford c. 89/1 and c. 89/2, draft indentures between William

Beckford, Alexander Hamilton and Susan Euphemia Beckford, dated 23 December 1809 and March 1810.

8. HA, F2/1030, invoice from Rundell, Bridge and Rundell to the Marquis of Douglas and Clydesdale for 1809–10, and HA, M12/5/18, invoice from Rundell, Bridge and Rundell to the Marquis of Douglas and Clydesdale for 1808–11.

9. HA, F2/1030.

10. HA, M12/5/18.

11. *Catalogue [. . .] of the Pictures, Original Drawings and Articles of Ancient Sculpture of the late Hon. C. F. Greville*, Christie's, London, 31 March 1810, lot 95. Christie's clerk's copy of the catalogue is annotated '95 ~ 640. 10 Marq. Douglas. [tick with line through it]'.

12. HA, Bundle 679, copy of bill from Mease Sutton and Son, dated 31 March 1810.

13. See HA, Bundle 956, 'Scott Portland' to Douglas, 3 July 1810.

14. HA, M12/5/18.

15. Ibid. and HA, M12/5/19, copy of invoice from Rundell, Bridge and Rundell to the Marquis of Douglas and Clydesdale for 1808–18.

16. For further information, see HTHL, Hamilton Estate Vouchers and Accounts, Bundles 20/6 and 23.

17. HTHL, Bundle 20/6, bill from David Hamilton and Company to the Marquis of Douglas and Clydesdale, dated 1 August 1810, and Bundle 23, bill from Gavin and John Rowat to the 9th Duke of Hamilton for work carried out at Hamilton Palace in 1810.

18. For the bills and receipts for the 'Sheep Plucks [. . .] for His Lordships Eagle at Hamilton Palace' from 9 January 1809 to 28 November 1810 and 'Butcher Meat [. . .] for His Lordships Wolf at Hamilton Palace' from 6 January 1809 to 1 December 1810, see HTHL, Bundle 20/6. On the extinction of wolves in Scotland, see http://www.wolftrust.org.uk/a-lastwolves.html (last accessed 14 June 2009), quoting from Robert Sibbald's *Scotia Illustrata*, published in 1684, that the species had been exterminated by this date, and dismissing the story of a man called MacQueen killing a wolf in Scotland in 1743. It is possible that Douglas also owned a big cat of some sort around this time, but the only dated documentation discovered up to now relates to J. W. and G. Fairley 'putting up Den at Whamb [i.e. Chatelherault, to the south of Hamilton Palace] for Leopard' in December 1832, at a cost of £8.11s.3d (HTHL, Hamilton Estate Ledger, 1829–36, p. 336).

19. For all these references to horses, see HTHL, Bundle 20/5, account of 'John Bradley Groom at Hamilton Palace for the Expence of taking His Lordship's Spanish Horse' to Edinburgh, 28 February to 4 March 1809, and account of 'Walter Colquhoun Groom for expences of Carrying his Lordship's Grey Arabian horse to Coll. Leatham at Edin[burgh] and remaining with him to shew the

Colonel's Servants how to use him', March and April 1809, and Bundle 22/1, bill relating to getting the Marquis of Douglas's mares covered by the Arabian in Edinburgh, May and June 1810.

20. The 1811 Hamilton Palace inventory of pictures, entitled 'Pictures. Hamilton Palace. 1811.' (HA, M4/67) has 190 entries. It includes references to Mantegna's *The Vestal Virgin Tuccia with Sieve* and *Sophonisba drinking Poison* (National Gallery, London), Tintoretto's *Resurrection of Christ* (Ashmolean Museum, University of Oxford) and *Moses striking the Rock* (Städelsches Kunstinstitut, Frankfurt), *St Jerome as Cardinal* attributed to El Greco (National Gallery, London), Van Dyck's *Henrietta, Princess of Pfalzburg and Lorraine* (Kenwood House, London) and Rubens's *Birth of Venus* (National Gallery, London). The entries are discussed briefly in Godfrey Evans, '"Vaulting ambition, which o'erleaps itself": The Dukes of Hamilton and Titian' in *The Reception of Titian in Britain from Reynolds to Ruskin*, ed. Peter Humfrey, forthcoming Turnhout 2012.

21. HA, M4/67, entries 96 and 126.

22. Ibid., entries 30 and 33. Gavin Hamilton's *Hector's Farewell to Andromache* is now in the Hunterian Art Gallery, University of Glasgow; Ann Forbes's portrait of the 8th Duke is at Lennoxlove.

23. Ibid., entries 17 and 24.

24. Douglas's keen interest in Catherine the Great is strikingly demonstrated early in 1809, when he placed 'A sable muff belonging to Catherine II Empress of Russia' in the Charter Room of Hamilton Palace, along with 'My full powers as Ambassador to the Court of Russia'. The muff was obviously a highly regarded item and Douglas recorded what he had done in a memo dated 10 January 1809, HA, M10/179.

25. In 1811 a portrait of 'Catharine 2d· of Russia' was hanging in the Breakfast Room (the first room in the Old State Rooms in the west wing), while a portrait of 'Catharine 2,ᵈ· Empress of Russia' was in a 'Drawing Room', apparently in the east wing: see HA, M4/67, entries 44 and 130. The two bronze busts of Peter the Great and Catherine the Great were awaiting shipment with four crates of mirrors and two other crates of Douglas's belongings: see C. Zecalewsky to Douglas, 15 / 28 October 1812. On 3 May 1811 Richard Riga informed Douglas: 'The Tapestry Work (H:I:M Catharines Picture) I understand is quite ready'. Both letters are in HA, Bundle 698.

26. For further background, see Isabel De Madariaga, *Catherine the Great: A Short History*, New York and London, 2002, and Nathalie Bondil (ed.), *Catherine the Great: Art for Empire*, Ghent, 2005.

27. The European Museum, in King Street, St James's Square, tried to sell the painting between 1808 and 1816. It was offered at Christie's on 18 February 1809 as 'Northcote [. . .] Portrait of Napoleon Bonaparte on Horseback, as large as life, universally allowed to be the best painted, as well as the most striking likeness,

of this extraordinary character' (*A Catalogue of a Valuable Collection of Original Pictures [. . .] lately exhibited and so much admired at the European Museum*, 17–18 February 1809, lot 93). Farebrother's described the work in more or less the same terms – 'Northcote .... Napoleon Bonaparte on Horseback, as large as life, in the Consular Uniform; allowed to be the most striking Likeness of that extraordinary Character' (*A Catalogue of the Splendid Collection of Original Pictures [. . .] lately forming the Grand Exhibition at the European Museum*, 23–24 May 1811, lot 117) – but, once again, it failed to sell and was bought in at £157.10s. Northcote's *Napoleon* was subsequently included in Stanley's sale on 3 July 1816, as lot 93, with unknown result. It was apparently purchased by a London dealer and had passed to James Burt in Exeter by April 1829 (see Josephine Gear, *Masters or Servants? A Study of Selected English Painters and Their Patrons of the Late Eighteenth and Early Nineteenth Centuries*, New York and London, 1977, pp. 225–8). Northcote's *Napoleon* resurfaced at Sotheby's sale of British paintings held in London on 16 November 1983, as lot 82.

28. The tapestry itself cost 2,000 roubles and Douglas was also charged 1,500 roubles 'Pour la Glasse' and 200 roubles for 'L'Embaillage': HA, Bundle 1006, bill from the Imperial Tapestry Factory, 6 June 1811. David asked for and was given 1,000 guineas, but only received 18,650 francs, instead of the expected 25,000 francs, because of the poor exchange rate: see HA, Bundle 768, David to Douglas, 22 June, 15 August, and 20 October 1812.

29. Young's letter is published in *The Book of the Old Edinburgh Club*, XXXI, 1962, p. 173.

30. HA, F2/1042/27, note about income in 1810 written by Douglas.

31. In 1820 Brown recalled 'In the year 1812 The Dukes debts were about £90,000': see his draft letter to Young, dated 26 November 1820, in HA, Bundle 1767.

32. HA, Bundle 1581, Young to Brown, 6 September 1812.

33. HA, M12/5/19.

34. David's letters to Douglas are included as an appendix to Alan Andrew Tait's article on 'The Duke of Hamilton's Palace' in *The Burlington Magazine*, CXXV, July 1983, pp. 401–2. The freedom that Douglas gave the artist and David's willingness to take charge of the subject matter and treatment are clearly evident in his first letter to Douglas, dated 20 September 1811 (HA, Bundle 768), on p. 401.

35. HA, Bundle 606, Hamilton to Duke, 28 June 1822.

36. HA, C4/706/1, Hamilton to Brown, 15 November 1824.

37. HA, Bundle 1129, draft letter Douglas to David, undated. This appears to be a draft of the letter Douglas sent to David on 31 March 1813, because the first paragraph of David's letter of 30 April is a natural response to it: 'The letter Your Lordship honoured me with on the 31st of last month fulfilled all my wishes, telling me of the delivery of the portrait of the man of the century and that my

work has met with your approval and, you add, is admired by all. These praises, from as distinguished a friend of the arts as Your Lordship, flatter me infinitely and make me wish to obtain new ones, which I shall always try to be worthy of' (HA, Bundle 1129). According to David's letter to Douglas of 13 April 1813, the portrait had been shipped from Ostend on 21 November 1812, but David had still not heard if it had arrived safely when he sent off this letter (HA, Bundle 1001).

38. HA, F2/1040, notebook used by Douglas in 1816, unpaginated. The list is dated 7 August 1816.

39. HA, Bundle 1673, Young to Brown, 19 November 1816.

40. HA, M4/55, Henry Raeburn junior to Brown, 16 January 1824.

41. Douglas's movements can be tracked using his notes about his banking transactions between 1816 and 1819 (HA, F2/1036).

42. HA, Bundle 1006, Rall to Douglas, 16 August 1812.

43. HA, Bundle 1129, Matthew Anderson to Douglas, 16 / 28 May 1813.

44. On the breakages, see Matthew Anderson's letter to Douglas of 22 April / 4 May 1814 in HA, Bundle 706.

45. The 1825 Hamilton Palace inventory records the 'Russian Tapestry', valued at £60, and the 'Russian Flooring' in the 'Room above Back Kitchen': HA, M4/70, p. 137.

46. For the resulting pieces, see Ronald Freyberger, 'The Duke of Hamilton's Porphyry Tables', *Antiques*, September 1993, pp. 348–55, and 'The Duke of Hamilton's Clock Cabinet', *Christie's International Magazine*, June 1991, pp. 10–13.

47. Saponieri's design of a new north front for Hamilton Palace, signed and dated 1819, is preserved in the Hamilton archive as drawing 165, along with a very closely related, unsigned design, drawing 166.

48. See HA, Bundle 1767, draft letter Brown to Young, 26 November 1820.

49. HA, Bundle 680, Duke's draft of orders to Aytoun, 26 October 1821.

50. For further information, see Godfrey Evans, 'The Restoration and Enlargement of Hamilton Palace by the 10th Duke of Hamilton, 1806–32', *Review of Scottish Culture*, XXI, 2009, pp. 35–66.

51. See *The Scotsman*, 31 August 1822, pp. 271 and 275–6.

52. HA, M4/55, Raeburn junior to Brown, 16 January 1824.

53. Ibid., Dickie to Duke, 28 October 1823.

54. HA, C4/52, Herries to Brown, 11 October 1823.

55. HA, M4/55, Dickie to Duke, 28 October 1823.

56. Ibid., Raeburn junior to Duke, 2 December 1823.

57. The Duke's draft is written on Raeburn junior's letter.

58. HA, M4/55, Raeburn junior to Brown, 16 January 1824.

59. Edinburgh 1824, p. 6.

60. *The Scotsman*, 6 March 1824, p. 6 (on line at http://archive.scotsman.com, last accessed 14 July 2007). None of the exhibits are singled out for comment in the review of the exhibition in *The Caledonian Mercury*, 13 March 1824, p. 3.

61. Duncan 1824, pp. 18–19.

62. NRS, SC70/1/31, Record of Inventories, Inventory of Sir Henry Raeburn presented 9 June 1824, p. 249 (on line at http://www.scotlandspeople.gov.uk, last accessed 12 July 2007).

63. St George's Chapel Archives and Chapter Library, Windsor Castle, SGC G.6, Register of the Order of the Garter, VIth William IV, chapter X.

64. HA, Bundle 924, notebook of the 10th Duke of Hamilton's account with Hoare's bank, 1829–39, unpaginated.

65. Ibid.

66. Pickersgill's portrait was exhibited at the Royal Academy in 1838 as number 184. It was included in Christie, Manson and Woods's sale of *Fine Historical Portraits and Ancient and Modern Pictures, the Property of the Trustees of His Grace the late Duke of Hamilton*, London, 6 November 1919, as lot 42, with measurements of 93½×57½in (237.5×146cm), and is recorded passing through a Robinson, Fisher and Harding sale on 6 March 1930 in the files of the National Portrait Gallery, London. An oil study measuring 50×30cm was auctioned at Sotheby's, London, on 11 April 1973, as lot 110, and was bought by Crawshaw for £70.

67. HA, Volume 1228, p. 137 ('Alexander 10.th Duke of Hamilton [by] Pickersgill').

68. Ibid., p. 156: as 'Alexander the 10th. Duke of Hamilton', with an added attribution in pencil, in a shaky hand, which looks like 'Madmea', and a valuation of £50. The relatively high valuation, in comparison to other added valuations, suggests that this was the Raeburn portrait. However, it is possible that it was a portrait of the 10th Duke by Willes Maddox and that the artist's surname had been garbled.

69. HTHL, 1876 Hamilton Palace Inventory, p. 32 ('Full Length Portrait of Alexander 10th Duke of Hamilton [by] Sir Henry Raeburn').

70. HTHL, Copy of the Inventory and Valuation of Pictures, Decorative Objects, Furniture and Effects at Hamilton Palace, Holyrood and Dungavel made by Mr. Tom Cox, 1915, inventory and valuation of pictures at Hamilton Palace, p. 7, and valuation of decorative objects, furniture and effects at Hamilton Palace, p. 15. Cox described the painting as 'Sir Henry Raeburn', 'Portrait of Alexander, 10th Duke of Hamilton, full length, standing by his charger, in a landscape', with measurements of 96×72in (243.8×182.9cm), and valued it at £4,000. A 'List of Pictures and Engravings in Hamilton Palace', which belonged to the Trustees of the late 12th Duke of Hamilton, records that during the late nineteenth to early twentieth centuries Raeburn's and Winterhalter's very grand, aristocratic portraits were displayed with: a huge marine view with seagulls on a

rock by T. Gudin, measuring 105×142in; an 'Interior of a Chinese Joss House' by G. Caneva, dated 1861, with dimensions of 40×55in (which had been in the Tribune when the 1876 inventory was taken); a 'Landscape with Cattle and Sheep'; '3 Pointers in Landscape'; and a 'Mastiff in Landscape' (HA, Volume 1986, p. 35). The last two were almost certainly the two works attributed to B. Killingbeck and said to be dated 1777 – the 'Portraits of Three Pointers, in a wood', and 'A Mastiff, in a landscape', measuring 42½×60in and 32½×43in respectively – that were included in Christie, Manson and Woods' sale of Hamilton Palace paintings on 7 November 1919, as lots 147 and 149. These five works reflected the less elevated tastes of the 12th Duke and his preoccupation with sport.

71. Christie, Manson and Woods, *Catalogue of Family Portraits, Works by Old Masters and Modern Pictures, The Property of The Trustees of His Grace the late Duke of Hamilton*, London, 6–7 November 1919, lot 45. The catalogue entry gives the measurements of the portrait as 98×72in (248.9×182.8cm) and states that it was 'Exhibited at the Raeburn Exhibition, 1824'.

72. Ibid., lot 42.

73. I am most grateful to Fraser Niven, the Chief Executive of the Hamilton and Kinneil Estates, and Lord Selkirk of Douglas, the second son of the 14th Duke of Hamilton, for alerting me to the 14th Duke's approach to Lord Cowdray. I am also much obliged to Lyndsay Stuart, the present Duke's private secretary, for trying to find the two letters in the Lennoxlove archive.

74. Christie's, *The Cowdray Sale: Works of Art from Cowdray Park and Dunecht House*, Cowdray Park, 13–15 September 2011, lot 368. Christie's gave the portrait's measurements as 96½×70½in (245.1×179cm) and the estimate as £40,000–£60,000.

6

Raeburn and the Print Culture of Edinburgh, c. 1790–1830: Constructing Enlightened and National Identities

Stana Nenadic

Raeburn's celebrity was based on a long and successful career in which he painted as many as a thousand portraits of men, women and children, mainly Scots from the middling and upper layers of society.[1] His best works and his many portraits of prominent contemporary personalities were exhibited in public places in both Edinburgh and London and he thereby commanded a wide popular audience. And, in common with most artists of note, his audience was extended through the reproduction of some of his portraits in the form of engraved prints.[2] This essay is about those prints and the social and business world that called them into existence during Raeburn's lifetime and immediately after his death. It considers the distinct character of Edinburgh's professions and civic institutions that were responsible for the production of most of the prints. Focused on the 1820s, a time of vibrant demand for engravings, but also of considerable business volatility, the essay also looks at some of the economics of print publication, including the frequent bankruptcies of businessmen who engaged in this area of costly luxury production. Finally, the essay explores the prints engraved after Raeburn as social documents, displayed in Edinburgh houses, offices and club rooms, that offer a privileged perspective on Scottish culture and cultural identities in the late eighteenth and early nineteenth centuries.

There was a massive commercial and private production of engraved British portraits during the eighteenth and nineteenth centuries, and the uses to which engraved portraits were employed were complex and changing.[3]

Some portraits were kept in portfolios along with other types of prints, both modern and antique, and were accumulated in large numbers by wealthy collectors whose interests lay either in acquiring specimens of high quality and value, or in collecting around a specialised subject that reflected a personal passion or complemented a collection of original pictures. Significant print collections were occasionally sold, usually by auction in London, and the catalogues for such auctions provide an insight to this most exclusive end of the market for engraved portraits.[4] However, most engravings were not destined for the portfolios of rich gentleman, but rather were put to more popular and practical uses. Through much of the eighteenth century there was a demand for printed portraits of contemporary or historical figures to be used by more modest collectors to 'extra-illustrate' published volumes of history. The creation of these so-called 'grangerised texts', a term that was derived from the Revd James Granger, the individual who first made the practice well known, was often a family hobby with wives and daughters involved in the cutting and pasting of pictures interleaved with text.[5] The extra-illustration of published histories reflected a popular desire to have a visual record of prominent men and women alongside a written account of their deeds, but the hobby had gone out of fashion by the early nineteenth century when this demand was mostly satisfied by book publishers using new production technologies to produce lavishly illustrated volumes at affordable prices. Indeed, illustrated volumes of collective biography, sometimes issued in parts or in the form of magazines, and with such titles such as 'Eminent Men of Our Time', were a staple of the nineteenth-century publishing industry.[6]

The commonest use of engraved portraits, and the use for which most of the engraved output based on Raeburn originals was probably put, was as framed pictures for hanging on walls for decorative purposes – what is usually termed the 'furniture print'. Through most of the eighteenth century the engraved portrait, mainly of men in public life or of historical importance, was the dominant type of framed picture to be found in the houses of the middle ranks and above. Maps were framed and were popular among merchants, printed views of towns and cities were framed, as were religious, satirical or moral subjects, the latter dominated by the works of William Hogarth, but the commonest type of print that was likely to be owned by men and women above the ranks of the labouring poor was the mass produced portrait in a simple black and gilt frame of about 16×12 inches. A popular subject of mid-eighteenth-century Edinburgh was that of Hew Dalrymple, Lord Drummore, prominent local judge and leading light of the Edinburgh Musical Society, who died in 1754 and whose image was engraved for commercial sale in an iconographically dense mezzotint based on a portrait in oils of a few years earlier by Allan Ramsay.[7] Engravings of celebrity figures were a standard element in printsellers' catalogues and many prominent Scotsmen throughout the eighteenth century – including Allan Ramsay the poet, John 3rd Duke of Argyll (the subject most commonly collected in Scotland in the mid-eighteenth century), James Beattie the celebrated Aberdeen poet and philosopher, and William Hunter, the medical man, were widely collected and were themselves also collectors of prints. Allan Ramsay the poet also sold prints from his Edinburgh bookshop. Indeed, if the 3rd Duke of Argyll was the most commonly owned print in the modest domestic print collections of middle ranking Scots in mid-eighteenth-century Scotland, the most commonly cited 'eminent' Scotsman to be listed in the major print collections that came to auction in London in the second half of the eighteenth century was almost certainly the anatomist Dr William Hunter.[8]

Framed portraits were usually hung in the dining room, which was the principal room in a house or Scottish flat and the room that was mostly likely to be used for hospitality, particularly by male householders entertaining other men.[9] By the end of the eighteenth century middle class domestic space was more complex and more likely to reflect a feminised aesthetic agenda through furniture prints showing children and animals, sentimental themes or romantic landscapes, but portraits remained popular and on display in those parts of the house or associated business premises that were exclusive to men, such as the study, library or office. Portraits of men were also to be found in those new and increasingly opulent semi-public spaces such as club, society and committee rooms that were associated with the burgeoning masculine world of elite urban sociability and the growth of professional and commercial organisations. Not surprisingly, many of these bodies, including the University, the High School and the Company of Archers in Edinburgh, commissioned original portraits and engravings after portraits from celebrated local artists such as Raeburn or from his near contemporary David Martin, both of whom were members of the archers' club. Indeed throughout the nineteenth century the Company of Archers, in common with other organisations populated by the rising breed of professionals, were also gifted portraits of past and present members to decorate their buildings and public rooms, which were often modelled on the public rooms and picture galleries of aristocratic country houses.[10]

There was a popular and growing demand to see portraits of eminent individuals, either as originals on display in public spaces, as illustrations in books, or of a type that could be used for decorating homes, clubs or business premises. However, the circumstances that gave rise to an engraving being produced in the first place could vary widely, as could the numbers of prints produced, the manner of distribution, the quality, which was normally a product of the engraving technique, and the price.[11] Not surprisingly it was the fame of the individual or a connection with famous events that gave rise to the most commercially successful engravings. Two individuals, both Scottish and both the subject of many portraits, serve as an illustration: one, Walter Scott, was painted by Raeburn and that portrait was engraved, while the other, Admiral Adam Duncan, was also painted by Raeburn but there were no engravings based on this original, though many other commercial images of the naval hero were available for purchase by his admiring public.

Raeburn twice painted Walter Scott, in 1808 and again in 1823, the final year of the artist's life.[12] Another commission was sought from Raeburn by the 4th Duke of Buccleuch at about the same time as the last picture, destined for the duke's house in the Scottish Borders, Bowhill, not far from Abbotsford, but the artist died before it could be undertaken (Fig. 6.1).[13] The 1808 portrait was commissioned by Scott's publisher, Archibald Constable, and shows the poet (the Waverley novels were still some years in the future) seated by a ruin in a romantic landscape with a dog at his feet. It was always intended for public display. Having been exhibited in Edinburgh to popular acclaim in 1809, it became the most famous and iconic image of the great literary man; so much so, that it was reproduced as a furniture print by five separate publishers between 1810 and 1838 and there were half a dozen or more derivative prints produced during the same period, mostly as book-plates.[14] There was a relentless demand for images of Walter Scott at home and abroad, and Constable, who kept the original in his office premises, used these images as a marketing device to promote Scott as a literary celebrity and enhance the sale of his books. But like many entrepreneurs in the volatile 1820s, Archibald Constable's business eventually failed and he took his star author down with him. In 1826 the 5th Duke of Buccleuch, determined like his father before him to acquire a portrait of his celebrated neighbour and kinsman, purchased the 1808 Raeburn original from the wreck of the Constable bankruptcy, and it still hangs at Bowhill today.

The second eminent Scotsman whose portrait was widely produced and sold was Admiral Adam Duncan. The celebrity enjoyed by Admiral Duncan was more fleeting than that of Scott. He was the naval hero of the Battle of Camperdown in 1797 during the French Revolutionary Wars, ennobled as Viscount Camperdown, whose fame was soon eclipsed by Nelson's tragic heroism at Trafalgar in 1805. There was a flurry of patriotic print publishing activity at the time of Camperdown, mostly orchestrated from London. As a Scotsman with a Dundee family home and Edinburgh professional connections, there were several Scottish initiatives to celebrate the local hero, then in his sixties, through portrait commissions and associated engravings. One of these came from the county proprietors of the recently-completed Town and County Hall of Forfar, in the County of Angus, not far from

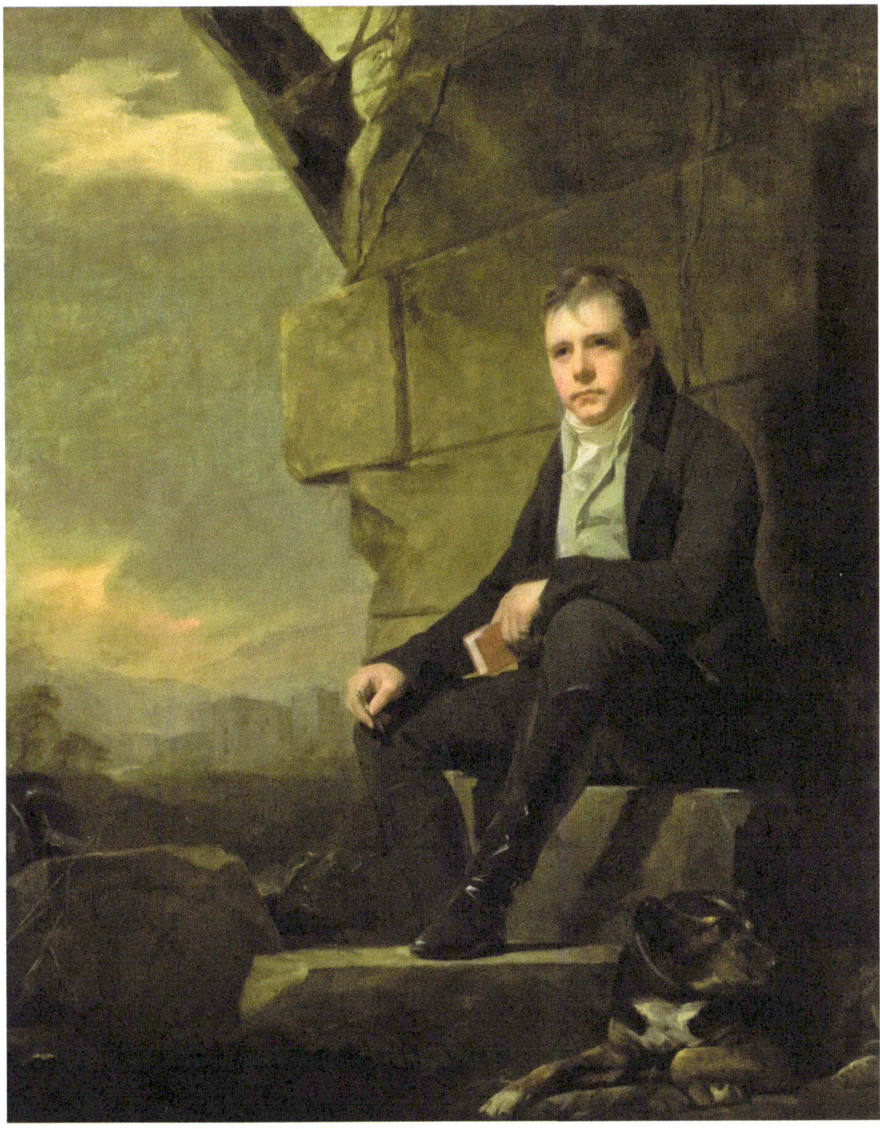

Figure 6.1 Henry Raeburn, *Sir Walter Scott*, 1808–9, oil on canvas, 182.9×147.3cm, Buccleuch Collection (photography by Todd-Whyte)

Dundee. They ordered a superb piece of London-made silver tableware to be presented to Duncan as a token of their esteem, and also commissioned a portrait from the London artist John Hoppner, to be hung in the Town and County Hall alongside portraits of politicians Henry Dundas and David Scott MP. The portrait was first exhibited at the Royal Academy before travelling north to Scotland and was accompanied by a commercial engraving from the famed London print publisher, John Boydell. In the following year, the Masters and Assistants of Trinity House in Leith also commissioned a portrait of Duncan, this time from Raeburn, which was exhibited for the public at Trinity House. An engraving was proposed and a subscription was advertised in the *Edinburgh Evening Courant*, but the project collapsed, probably because the market was already saturated with commercial images and Duncan souvenirs, including engraved portraits, Wedgwood cameo medallions and even Carron-made cast iron fire surrounds that incorporated the profiles of military and naval heroes.[15]

Individuals with national fame, such as Admiral Duncan or Walter Scott, dominated the printsellers catalogues and their images were reproduced by the thousand. Yet commercial engravings of celebrities were not always successful ventures for their publishers. Another printed depiction of a Scottish war hero, General Thomas Graham, Lord Lynedoch, based on an original portrait by Thomas Lawrence, which was commissioned in 1817 for the County Building in Perth, was repeatedly advertised by the publisher, Alexander Hill of Princes Street in Edinburgh, many years after the plate had been engraved and costs incurred, signifying a very slow rate of return on a significant investment.[16] But most of the engravings based on Raeburn portraits were not of this commercial-celebrity type; rather they were of individuals who were notable only in narrowly defined circles, their modest fame giving rise to only a limited local demand. This privileged the 'subscription' system of publishing, which was also used for expensive and specialised books, whereby the production costs were raised in advance of engraving and printing with no risk to the publisher, unless, of course, 'promised' subscriptions failed to materialise. In some cases Raeburn's engraved portraits were not commercial ventures at all, but were done at the behest of a small group or family for 'private' circulation. So why were portraits of people of modest or little fame, worthies rather than celebrities, reproduced in prints? Sometimes it was at the instigation of the subject himself, who used the portrait as a device for promoting his own career.[17] This may have been the motive behind the production in 1791 of an Edinburgh-published engraved portrait based on a Raeburn original of Robert Dundas of Arniston, who was in his early thirties and, through family patronage (he was married to his cousin, the daughter of Henry Dundas), was recently appointed both Lord Advocate and MP for Edinburghshire. Robert Dundas was a young man embarking on public life and keen to be noticed. His more celebrated father, Lord Arniston, with a long and more distinguished legal career, had died in 1787 aged seventy-four, and his portrait was engraved in London in 1790 from a Raeburn original painted just before his death (Fig. 10.2).[18]

The advanced age of Lord Arniston at the time his portrait was painted and the subsequent engraving was typical of men who though locally distinguished were neither aristocrats nor celebrities. And often it was the immediate family and friends of the sitter who had instigated the engraving in order to celebrate the life and achievements of one who was loved and esteemed as he neared the end of his career. Teachers, medical men, lawyers and clergymen were all marked out in this way, with the initiative usually channelled through some organisation with which they were associated and where an original portrait could be displayed. They included the Revd Dr Robert Dickson, a popular clergyman in his sixties who had long officiated at the South Leith Parish Church. Members of the Church Session sought an original portrait from Raeburn in 1822, to be hung permanently in the Session House 'to preserve a memorial of their affectionate attachment and regard.' They raised a voluntary subscription for the purchase and an engraving by Charles Turner of London was published in the same year.[19] The mezzotint allowed the congregation at large, including women who were not part of the Kirk Session, access to an image of their popular pastor who died just two years later (Fig. 6.2). Sales of the print might also have helped to defray the costs of the original.

Another local Edinburgh figure who was celebrated through an original portrait by Raeburn and a print reproduction was Alexander Adam, Rector of the High School in Edinburgh (Fig. 6.3). Adam's engraved portrait of 1808, just a year before he died aged almost seventy, was published in Edinburgh by Alexander Thompson, Carver of Caltonhill, with a dedication 'to the Gentlemen who have placed his [original] Portrait in the High School.'[20] Adam was a much-admired and innovative teacher in his day and it is easy to understand why his former pupils, mostly men associated with the Edinburgh professions, might wish to commission a portrait for their old school and also own an engraved copy for display at home or in the office. The Raeburn portrait was engraved again in 1835 for inclusion in Robert Chambers' *Biographical Dictionary of Eminent Scotsmen*. The continued interest in the old Rector many decades after his death is explained by his associations with the early life and education of Walter Scott, for it was said that 'with Adam's encouragement, the young Scott translated Horace and Virgil into English verse and made his first attempts at original composition.'[21]

The commercial production of an engraving many years after the death of the subject was by no means unusual. Niel Gow, the Scottish fiddler and writer of traditional music, was painted by Raeburn c. 1796 but an engraving was not produced until 1814, seven years after Gow's death (Fig. 6.4). The reason for the print at that time was a new edition of Gow's tunes published

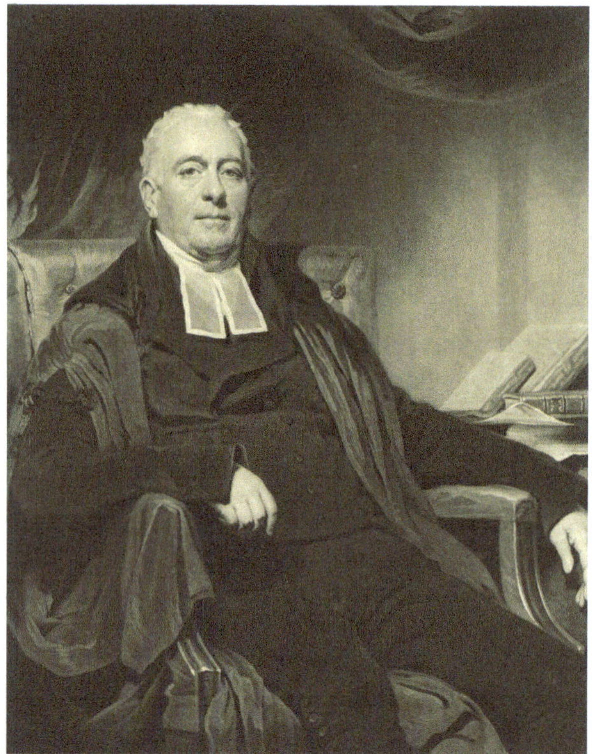

Figure 6.2 Charles Turner after Henry Raeburn, *Robert Dickson D.D., First Minister of South Leith*, 1822, mezzotint, published in London by the engraver, 46.2×33.7cm, Scottish National Portrait Gallery, Edinburgh

by his son Nathaniel, a successful dance-band impresario and sheet music entrepreneur, with retail premises in both Edinburgh and London. He also presented a set of engraver's plates and proofs to the British Museum in celebration of his father's musical achievement and memory.[22] Memorial or obituary prints could be highly commercial, as in the Niel Gow case, which was even sold in a coloured version for the popular market – seemingly the only Raeburn print to be distinguished in this way during Raeburn's lifetime. Other memorial engravings, though produced in large numbers and often at high cost, were circulated privately. This was seen in 1817 when William Cuthill, secretary to the Duke of Buccleuch at Bowhill, arranged for a payment of £276.8s to Henry Meyer for engraving an unidentified portrait of the late Duchess and the supply of two hundred impressions 'on French paper'. Cuthill also took instruction from his employer as to the subsequent distribution of the prints in the form of gifts within a network of family, friends and estate workers.[23]

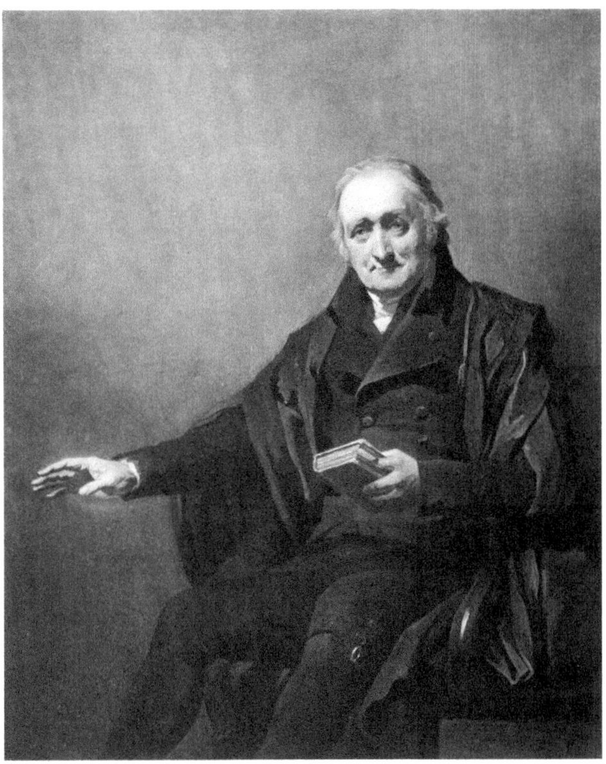

Figure 6.3 Charles Turner after Henry Raeburn, *Alexander Adam, LL.D., Rector of the High School of Edinburgh, Author of Roman Antiquities*, 1808, mezzotint, published in Edinburgh by Alexander Thompson, 50.6×35.2cm, Scottish National Portrait Gallery, Edinburgh

The production of images of a loved one after death could be a complex and multi-formed process and sometimes private grief could be turned into business profit where the deceased had held a public reputation. An illustration is furnished by one of Raeburn's successful English contemporaries, Thomas Lawrence, and the memorial engraving of Dr Matthew Baillie, a Scottish physician, nephew of William Hunter and heir to Hunter's London medical practice, who enjoyed great professional patronage among the British aristocracy and royalty. Baillie had been portrayed many times during his lifetime, and there were several images in public and medical society collections, though an unsanctioned commercial engraving, based on an original by John Hoppner, had been withdrawn from the market following threatened legal action by Dr Baillie. When the doctor died in 1823, his widow asked Lawrence to produce a drawing of her husband based on a portrait bust

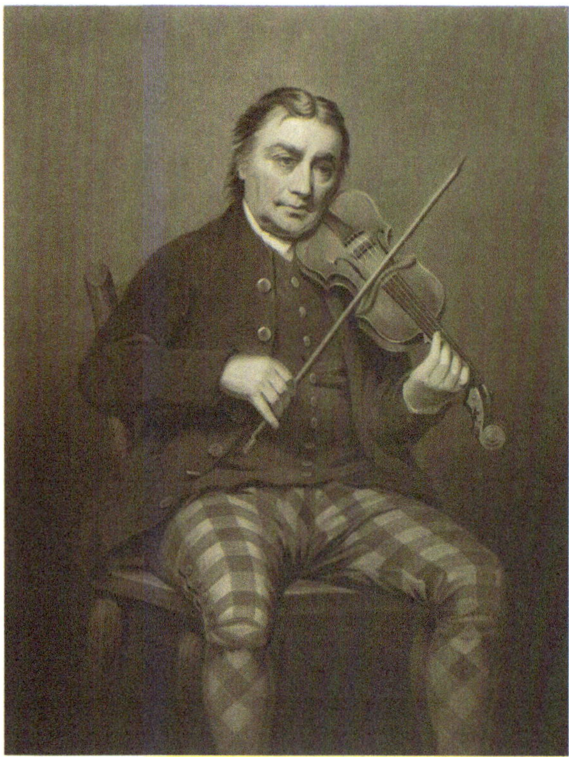

Figure 6.4 William Say after Henry Raeburn, *Niel Gow*, 1816, mezzotint,
published in London by Thomas Macdonald, 50.6×35.2cm,
Scottish National Portrait Gallery, Edinburgh

by the sculptor Joseph Nollekens that she thought a good likeness, and also
requested that the drawing be engraved and a small number of prints be made
for private distribution. She further requested that Lawrence organise the
commission of a miniature portrait of her husband for her own personal use.
Neither Lawrence nor Miss Jones, the miniaturist, had met Matthew Baillie.
It was Lawrence who first suggested a commercial publication, offering his
own publisher for the enterprise. Mrs Baillie, who did much to promote her
husband's posthumous reputation, agreed to the commercialisation of her
husband's image, which doubtless generated a profit for Lawrence, and in
the following year the engraving was published.[24] Famous artists, including Raeburn, often painted copies of portraits done by others, having never
met the sitter. Indeed, on 11 February 1826, the *Edinburgh Evening Courant*
advertised the publication of an engraved portrait of Charles James Fox, the
famous Whig politician, long dead but still revered, painted by Raeburn from
an original portrait by John Opie.

Like Thomas Lawrence and the Baillie commission, many portrait painters were closely involved in the business of producing engravings from their original portraits and thereby marketed their own portrait practices as well as generating additional income if the reproduction venture proved a commercial success. This was particularly true of artists with a permanent base in London, where most engravers and print publishers were located.[25] Raeburn, however, took only a passing interest in or profit from the engravings market. He had a portrait output of about one thousand canvasses, but only about fifty singly-issued subjects were engraved during a career of almost forty years and few of these at Raeburn's own instigation.[26] Raeburn had limited dealings with print publishers and supervised only a few of his engravers, who were mainly based in London while he lived in Edinburgh.[27] Raeburn did, of course, have complex family business interests unrelated to art production, and, in the wake of his bankruptcy of 1808 (the consequence of failure in his other enterprises) he did enter into an arrangement with the London publisher Cadell and Davies to supply ten portraits to be 'engraved in the crayon manner' for their *British Gallery of Contemporary Portraits*, which was a serial publication issued between 1809 and 1816.[28] But other entrepreneurs, as detailed in this essay, instigated most of the single-issue commercial prints based on Raeburn originals that were published during his lifetime.

Just as the circumstances that gave rise to the publication of an engraving were complex, as we have seen, so the world of the print engravers, publishers and sellers was complex and multi-layered. In addition to specialised engravers acting on their own account, there were a variety of trades and retailers who sub-contracted to the engravers, including booksellers, frame-makers and carvers and gilders, for whom print publication and selling represented just one aspect of their business. These were businessmen in the luxury trades, where an eye for fashion and a good understanding of elite markets, along with a prestigious shop front on one of the high-status shopping streets and a well-appointed shop interior, were all essential for success. Commercial print publishers often raised the capital for the initial engraving through a system of pre-payment (or promised payment) via a subscription list of notable individuals. Newspaper advertisements, or printed circulars sent through the post to potential customers, were used to elicit initial subscriptions, and once a subscription was launched, the list itself was also made public both to advertise the status of the enterprise and attract further subscribers. Publishers of books as well as prints repeatedly petitioned their prospective subscribers to give support in name as well as cash, and those individuals who were known to be patrons of the arts were bombarded with such requests.[29] Contributions to charities and to a vast array of voluntary organisations were similarly organised through the published subscription list.

At the start of Raeburn's career, Edinburgh's print publishers and sellers were a relatively small group and much of what was available for sale in Scotland was selected from London printsellers' catalogues. At the time of the Admiral Duncan case around 1800, when Raeburn was mid-career, there were several instances of local print proposals being advertised in the Scottish press that were never translated into an actual product because of the market dominance and economies of scale enjoyed by London publishers. By the 1820s, however, there had been a massive increase in the provincial middle class demand for commercially produced art on local themes or subjects and, in an age of burgeoning romantic nationalism and landscape tourism, 'Scottishness' now carried a high social cachet.[30] The rise of the art unions and semi-commercial devices for exhibiting art to a wide public, along with a revolution in other areas of print culture such as illustrated book and magazine production, meant that Edinburgh now supported a wide array of businesses in the field of engraved picture publication and selling. Several successful engravers such as William Walker, who as a young man in the 1820s was responsible for some of the finest outputs based on Raeburn originals, including the famous self-portrait, were co-located in both London and Edinburgh and also acted as publishers. Indeed, in his later career William Walker, from his base in London, commissioned original pictures specifically with the intention of producing engravings for sale. The most famous of these was the 'Distinguished Men of Science' engraving of 1862, based on an original drawing by John Gilbert, J. L. Skill and Walker himself, which comprised fifty-one portraits, many of them famous Scots, in an imagined setting in the Royal Society.[31]

Publishing a print could be an expensive and speculative business, even when a subscription had been raised in advance. The cost of engraving commonly exceeded the price paid to the artist for the original and the process could be so lengthy that the market interest in a notable individual might have peaked and passed before the print was commercially available. An indication of the complexity of the business undertakings of one of Edinburgh's notable print publishers and sellers is provided in a lengthy advertisement in *The Scotsman* newspaper of 3 April 1830 by Alexander Hill, 'Bookseller and Artists' Colourman' of 50 Princes Street. Hill announced that he 'has received from that spirited publisher Mr M. COLNAGHI [of London], impressions of the following spirited engravings.' The first two listed were of religious subjects, 'THE OPENING of the SIXTH SEAL . . . from the celebrated Picture by Mr Danby, engraved by Mr G. H. Phillips' and 'THE PASSAGE of the RED SEA' by the same artists. The third item was a

PORTRAIT of his MAJESTY the KING, in the Robes of the Garter, executed
in mezzotinto, on steel, by Mr Hodgetts, from the magnificent Picture painted
by Sir Thos. Lawrence, and presented by his Majesty to the city of Dublin. Prints
£2,12s.6d, Proofs, £4,4s; India Proofs, £5.5s. This chef-d'oeuvre of Engraving is
now exhibiting in the rooms of the Scottish Academy.

The royal portrait was followed by one of Miss Croker, a celebrated London
society beauty and another of the Duke of Wellington, both based on original portraits by Lawrence. Alexander Hill then went on to list the prints that
he was publishing himself, headed by a portrait of General Sir David Baird,
'from the celebrated full-length Picture, in military uniform, with horse,
painted by Sir Henry Raeburn, R. A., and engraved in the finest style of
mezzotinto by Mr Hodgetts. Price to subscribers – Prints, 21s, Proofs, £3,3s.
First Proofs before the Letters, £4,4s.' This was a print that Hill had first
published in 1822 and was now reissuing following the recent death of the
distinguished military man. The very successful 1832 biography of Sir David,
written by a popular novelist at the request of his widow, resulted in another
surge of advertising for the picture a few years later.[32]

Alexander Hill's *Scotsman* advertisement of 1830 went on to list a portrait of William Murray, Esq. of Polmaise, Lieutenant Colonel Commander
of the Stirlingshire Yeomanry Cavalry, from a full-length picture with horse,
painted by John Watson Gordon, and engraved by Hodgetts, a London-
based practitioner with whom he seemingly had a close association and who
also engraved Raeburn portraits for other publishers.[33] There was a print of
'The COVENANTERS, from the Picture now exhibiting in the Scottish
Academy, painted by George Harvey, esq. S. A.' There was also the engraved
Lawrence portrait of Lord Lynedoch from the County Hall at Perth, mentioned above, and several books of landscape and marine prints along with
'VIEWS OF THE HIGHLANDS OF SCOTLAND'. This array of notable
individuals, religious scenes and landscapes – several based on originals
that were then on public display in Edinburgh – was the stock trade of most
printsellers by the 1820s and 1830s, when a surge in middle class evangelical
Christianity was matched by popular romanticism. Hill ended his advertisement with a reminder to his customers of the core elements of his retail
business – 'A. H. has always for sale a most complete assortment of Artists'
Painting Materials of first rate quality, of which a fresh supply is received
every month'.[34]

Another *Scotsman* advertisement for 1 July 1826 offers an insight into the
shop contents of a publisher and retailer of prints, Adam Elder, carver and
gilder, who had published the engraving of Raeburn's portrait of Dr James
Hamilton, Physician to the Royal Infirmary in 1813, when he had premises

on North Bridge and also the engraving after Raeburn of John Clerk, Lord Eldin in 1814, when his business premises were nearby at Greenside Place. Both prints were of living subjects associated with major Edinburgh institutions and London-based Charles Turner, who worked on many Raeburn portraits, engraved both.[35] Adam Elder's publishing activity embraced other artists in Edinburgh and London. For instance, in 1818 he published a portrait of the celebrated novelist, Henry Mackenzie, now an elderly man, painted by Andrew Geddes and engraved by Rhodes of London. The impressive list of subscribers for this print included the Earl of Seaforth.[36] The business was well established in a seemingly flourishing condition, but the circumstances that gave rise to the *Scotsman* advertisement of 1826 was a business failure, for the contents of the shop were then being advertised for sale 'for behoof of creditors'. Over five days, and supported with a full catalogue of the 'sequestrated estate', Adam Elder saw his valuable stock-in-trade fall under the hammer at auction. On the first day, one hundred and fifty frames 'of various descriptions', convex mirror ornaments, moulds, four hundred feet of moulding, varnish 'and other articles connected with the trade' were all sold to the highest bidders. On the next two days there were large quantities of glass plate, dressing glasses, 'Large Pier, Chimney and Convex Glasses, richly framed', some valued as high as forty guineas each, and also 'a number of large and beautiful Landscapes and some Paintings, most richly framed.' Day four saw the sale of more dressing and other framed glasses, with more framed pictures and also framed prints. And the final day, which also saw the sale of the shop furnishings, was devoted to '11 writing desks, Drawing Materials, Fancy Articles of every description, 100 Portrait and other Frames; Portfolio, containing 200 old and new Prints, Views, Landscapes, Hunting Pieces, Caricatures, Coloured Prints, &c; Desks, Counters, Glass Cases, &c'.[37]

Adam Elder's bankruptcy was not unique and others involved in the publication of engraved portraits after Raeburn also saw their businesses fail.[38] These included John Marnoch, carver and gilder, who was responsible for the memorial portrait of Andrew Hunter, Professor of Divinity at the University, and the portrait of Revd David Johnston, Minister of North Leith and founder of the Edinburgh Blind Asylum, both issued in 1810. Three years later he published Lord Blair, President of the College of Justice, and there was Sir Charles Hay, Lord Newton, another judge, in 1814. Both of these were memorial portraits and the Blair was co-published with the famous London firm of Boydell. Marnoch, in common with many in the business, had extended his commercial interests way beyond the original trade of carving and gilding decorative frames for pictures and mirrors. At his bankruptcy in 1816 – a time of post-war market uncertainty which saw the demise of many small firms in the consumer goods sector – he had prestigious retail premises in Princes Street containing the usual stock of frames, mirrors, prints and plates, but he also owned a set of original Old Master paintings, allegedly by Raphael and Rembrandt, which were sent to London for sale. His creditors were scattered throughout Britain, including Birmingham and London and one of his business associates was a Mr Howe, partner in an enterprise to exhibit a panoramic painting of the Battle of Waterloo.[39]

Just a few years later in 1819, John Steele, 'gilder and dealer in prints' also saw his business go under. A lesser undertaking than that of Marnoch or Elder, Steele, who was based in Leith Street at the time, had published a print in 1812 after a Raeburn portrait of the Revd Sir Henry Moncrieff Wellwood, Chaplain to King George. Earlier in his career, in 1806, when trading jointly with David Hatton, Steele had also published a memorial portrait of Henry David Inglis, Advocate. While Hatton, with premises on Princes Street, flourished to become the largest single Edinburgh-based publisher of Raeburn prints and was still trading in the 1820s when he styled himself 'Print Seller to His Majesty', Steele floundered and ended in the bankruptcy courts. His sequestered stock included engraved plates, picture frames, utensils and materials. He had creditors in both Birmingham and London. But his main debts were owed to the Society of Incorporated Trades of Calton, who may have given him loans to try to stabilise the business.[40]

Though, as we have seen, it was sometimes a risky business for the publisher, the engraved portrait was popular and purchased because the subject meant something to the owner who put it on display in a house or office. Within a domestic or commercial spatial context such pictures conveyed subtle cultural messages.[41] They can also be read as social documents in their own right irrespective of context, since in most cases the image was embellished with accompanying text in the form of names, qualifications and dedications. They sometimes included coats of arms and iconographical objects or scenes depicted in the portrait itself or in decorative borders. Early and mid-eighteenth-century engravings were most likely to be heavily embellished and even included symbolic visual detail that did not figure in the original picture, which allowed the observer of the print to read and interpret the life of the sitter as a prominent individual worthy of close study. Such images were often dressed in the robes of state or professional office, which again reinforced an entitlement to public regard. Later engraved portraits, including those after Raeburn, were more likely to express the life of the individual devoid of iconographical visual embellishment and without the distinguishing dress of high office. But the public positioning of the subject's status was enhanced through growing levels of written information provided at the foot of the image, and also through the parallel publication of text biographies illustrated with portrait images as in the General Sir David Baird case described above.

As a social document, Raeburn's fifty or so singly-issued engraved portraits offer an interesting commentary on a period that witnessed the late enlightenment and a cultural flowering of early romantic nationalism.[42] Unlike the original portrait output, which included large numbers of the landed gentry from across Scotland, the published engravings should be read as a peculiarly Edinburgh phenomenon. They are a fascinating subset of the portraits for being entirely male and mostly elderly and they were also predominantly professional men who were closely linked to the organisations of Scottish civil society in the church, the law, education and medicine. It was men who were prominent in Edinburgh's institutions, not celebrities, who were mainly recorded in prints after Raeburn. There were no women among the engravings, although Raeburn painted many fine portraits of women, young and old, and pictures of famous beauties and distinguished bluestockings were sold in Edinburgh's print shops. During an age of war and popular militarism, when disproportionate numbers of Scots entered the army, some of the officers painted by Raeburn, there was a distinct shortage of military men among the Raeburn engravings, other than David Baird. But again the local print-sellers supplied this demand through the works of other artists. Raeburn's published engraved portraits included only one hereditary peer, John Hope, 4th Earl of Hopetoun – not surprising, really, since he was Edinburgh's own local aristocrat as well as being a distinguished military man. But both John Hope and David Baird were engraved because of their post-war contributions to Scottish civil society and deep involvement in public and charitable affairs in Edinburgh in the early 1820s, rather than the noble birth of one or the wartime military achievement of the other.[43]

By far the largest group, representing about a third of the total output of engravings after Raeburn portraits, comprised the lawyers and judges, with about a half of their portraits published following the death of these mostly elderly men. The next largest group was Edinburgh University professors, again about a half of them published as memorial portraits. Edinburgh's civic leaders and town council members were another prominent cohort, as were ministers of the Church of Scotland who were mostly associated with Edinburgh parishes. A smaller but still significant group comprised the medical men, some attached to the University and some connected with other Edinburgh institutions, such as Dr James Hamilton of the Royal Infirmary of Edinburgh, who was also physician to George Watson's School for Boys.[44] The institutional character of these men was echoed in subscriptions and dedications, with the following organisations recorded in text on the prints – Writers to the Signet, Court of Session, Edinburgh Town Council,

Edinburgh High School, Edinburgh Institution for the Encouragement of Fine Arts, the Edinburgh Company of Golfers and the Edinburgh Company of Archers. The latter two were organisations with a distinct Scottish identity to which large numbers of Edinburgh's elites belonged, including many lawyers and doctors and also John Hope, 4th Earl of Hopetoun, who was Captain-General of the Archers at the time of George IV's Edinburgh visit of 1822 – the same year that Hope's engraved portrait was published – and involved in much of the ceremony that attended the King.[45]

Perhaps not surprisingly given the national attention that was generated by the royal visit, along with the heightened sense of pride in Scottishness – albeit a fabricated, myth-laden, Highland version of Scottishness – 1822 was a significant year for engraved Raeburn portraits.[46] One of these was of Alastair Ranaldson Macdonell of Glengarry, an old-style laird and clan leader who was a well-known Edinburgh personality and had played a prominent role in the tartan processions that attended the King to Holyrood. Glengarry promoted a theatrical version of clanship that inspired Walter Scott's highland novels and had been captured by Raeburn in perhaps his most famous tartan portrait – the one that was now engraved – which was first exhibited at the Royal Academy in 1812 (Fig. 6.5).[47] David Hatton of Princes Street published the engraving and the laird carried the title of 'Colonel', which linked him to the local volunteers. Unusual for an engraved Raeburn portrait, it was dedicated to a nobleman, Alexander Gordon, 4th Duke of Gordon.[48] Read in context, this popular print was a powerful evocation of loyalty, romantic military highlandism and aristocratic prestige that clearly reflected one aspect of Scottish and, indeed, Edinburgh cultural identity. Similar ideas were conveyed through some of the other 'celebrity' engravings, including those of Scott, Neil Gow the composer and fiddler, and John Home the Scottish dramatist and author of *Douglas*, the celebrated 'Scottish' play.[49] But this was really a minor theme in the corpus of engraved Raeburn portraits, though it reflected a major popular preoccupation of the day.

Coming towards the end of the 'age of enlightenment', in a context where portraits and prints had long been employed to articulate an ideal 'enlightened' personality, the main theme that emerges from the engraved Raeburn portraits is that of a late-enlightenment culture of masculine, meritocratic, knowledge-based, institutional authority. This was an enlightened public sphere dominated by the distinctly Scottish knowledge professions of law, church, education and medicine, that was to evolve throughout the nineteenth century in parallel with romantic military highlandism and offered an alternative, albeit less obviously flashy and popular, manifestation of pride in the nation. In Edinburgh, a capital city without a court society, unlike London or the capitals of Europe, the Enlightenment was

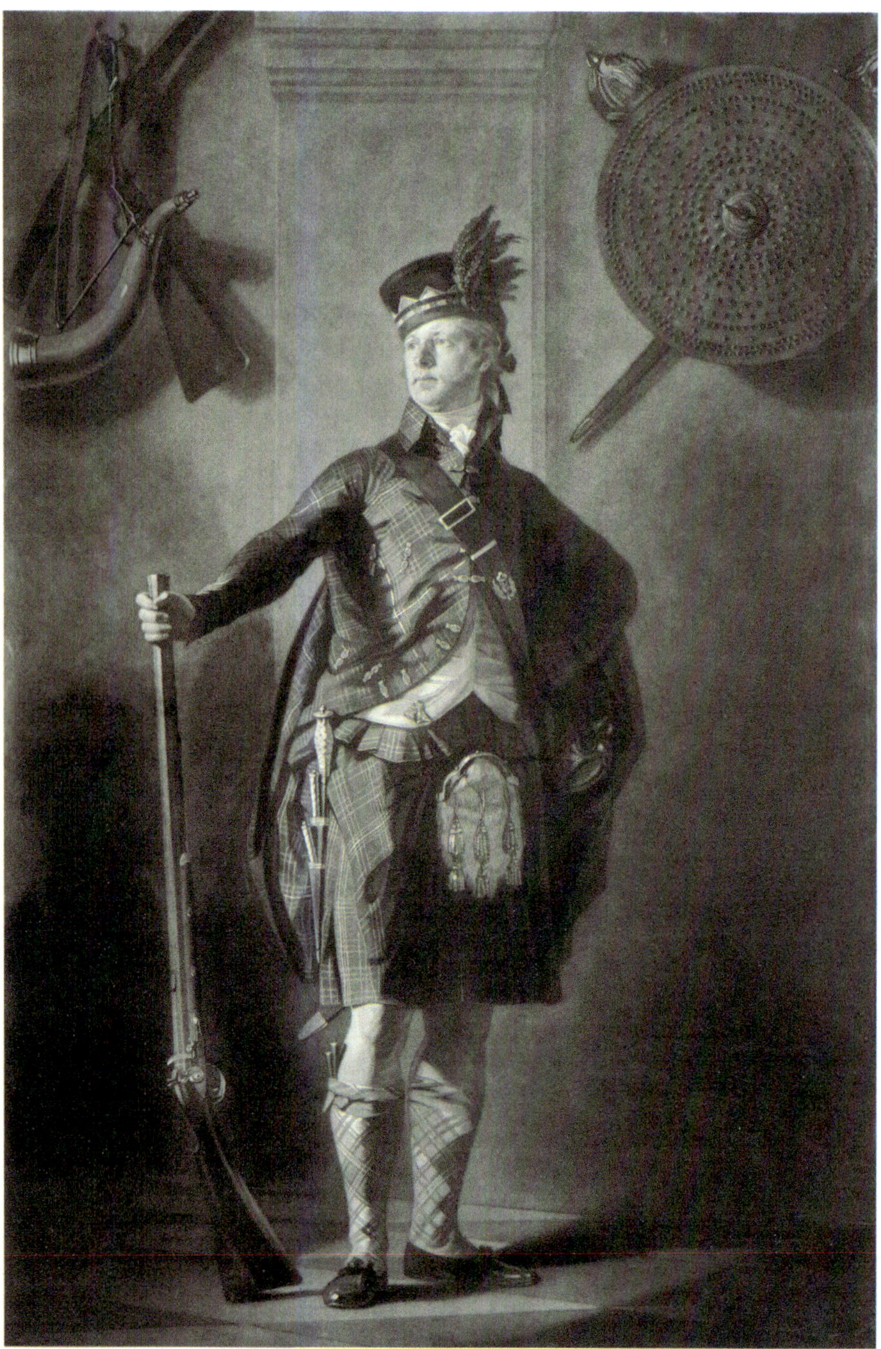

Figure 6.5 Thomas Hodgetts after Henry Raeburn, *Colonel Ranaldson Macdonell of Glengarry*, c. 1822, mezzotint, published in Edinburgh by David Hatton, 68.8×40.2cm, Scottish National Portrait Gallery, Edinburgh

always fundamentally a male and institutional affair and increasingly it was defined by a severe, intellectually robust and reformist, but materially plain aesthetic associated with hard working, practicing professionals. This is symbolised very strikingly in the clothing that appeared in Raeburn's engraved portraits during the years of greatest output, from around 1800 to 1823, when most subjects were dressed in an austere 'uniform' of simple black suit, white shirt and cravat and short-cut natural hair that gives no hint of occupation or status. Indeed, when Edinburgh printseller David Hatton published an engraved portrait of King George IV in 1822 based on a portrait by Raeburn of Professor Thomas Charles Hope, with the King's head superimposed on the original, the monarch was also represented in the day clothes of the working professional gentleman.[50]

This late enlightenment identity was a far cry from the more humane and inclusive Scottish Enlightenment of the early or mid-eighteenth century. It was exclusive, forbidding, humourless and even self-important. It was technical, statistical and knowledge-based. It gave rise to the cold science of political economy and was defined by the institutional authority of an increasingly powerful professional elite represented by increasingly large and wealthy institutions. Though this elite looked backwards to the glory days of their own formation, which they celebrated in engravings of the mostly elderly or dead men who made them and their representative organisations what they were, they were fundamentally progressive and modernising. This was a confident and assured vision of Scotland, particular to Edinburgh, but it was a vision that also echoed an evolving identity for successful Scotsmen in London, where large numbers had migrated over the course of the eighteenth century to make their careers, particularly in the professions.[51] Like the highland myths version of Scottish national identity – so powerfully paraded in 1822 during the royal visit to Edinburgh and so popular in England – this enlightened civil society version of Scottishness was consistent with a parallel sense of Britishness, since most of the men depicted were in one way or another upholders of the ideals of the British state through the Scottish institutions that were enshrined in the Act of Union, and they celebrated the same ideals in such national publications as the influential *Edinburgh Review*, first published in 1802 by Edinburgh lawyer and reforming intellectual, Francis Jeffrey. 'Scotch knowledge' and learning, which was satirised in London-produced caricature magazines by the 1820s, became associated in very particular ways with a form of Scottish identity that was distinct but was also seen as a positive good for Britain as a whole.[52] Scottish institutions enjoyed a high reputation in England as well as in Scotland, and the products of those institutions, be they doctors or lawyers or any number of other types of educated men were celebrated nationally. Indeed, such was the prominence of all things Scottish, including learned and professional Scotsmen, that one English commentator of the early 1820s, William Hazlitt, the essayist and sometimes portrait artist, was moved to remark:

> Scotch magazines, Scotch airs, Scotch bravery, Scotch hospitality, Scotch novels, Scotch logic. What a blessing that the Duke of Wellington was not a Scotchman, or we should never have heard the last of him.[53]

It was a backhanded compliment, to be sure, but Raeburn and his Edinburgh contemporaries, with their portrait collections of Edinburgh worthies arranged along the walls of comfortable offices and opulent club and committee rooms, will no doubt have been quietly pleased with themselves.

Notes

1. I am grateful to the Carnegie Trust for the Universities of Scotland for a grant that allowed me to undertake research for this essay in London archives.
2. The prints are listed in Edinburgh 2006.
3. See, *Catalogue of Engraved British Portraits Preserved in the Department of Prints and Drawings in the British Museum*, London, 1908, 2 vols.
4. British Museum, Department of Prints and Drawings, Index of Print Sales Catalogues, 1716–1812.
5. Lucy Peltz, 'Engraved portrait heads and the rise of extra-illustration: The Eton correspondence of the Rev. James Granger and Richard Bull, 1769–1774', *Walpole Society*, LXVI, 2004, pp. 1–161.
6. For an example, see Robert Chambers, *A Biographical Dictionary of Eminent Scotsmen*, Glasgow, 1835. See also, Stana Nenadic, 'Writing medical lives: creating posthumous reputations. Dr Matthew Baillie and his family in the nineteenth century', *Social History of Medicine*, XXIII, 2010. pp. 509–27.
7. Stana Nenadic, 'Print collecting and popular culture in eighteenth century Scotland', *History*, LXXXII, 1997, pp. 203–22. Stana Nenadic, 'Portraits of Scottish professional men in London c. 1760–1830. Careers, connections and reputations', *Journal for Eighteenth Century Studies*, XXXIV, 2011. pp. 1–17.
8. Survey of auction catalogues as detailed in footnote 4.
9. See, Nenadic, 'Print collecting', Stana Nenadic, *Lairds and Luxury: The Highland Gentry in Eighteenth Century Scotland*, Edinburgh, 2007, pp. xi–xiv.
10. See, for example, Ian Hay, *The Royal Company of Archers 1676–1951*, Edinburgh and London, 1951, Appendix J, pp. 268–92.
11. Details are given in Edinburgh 2006.
12. Lloyd 2003.
13. Edinburgh, and London 1997–8, p. 194.

14. Francis Russell, *Portraits of Sir Walter Scott: A Study of Romantic Portraiture*, London, 1987.

15. Helen Smailes, 'Prints and propaganda: the artist's victory', pp. 51–67 in Janice Murray (ed.), *Glorious Victory: Admiral Duncan and the Battle of Camperdown, 1797*, Dundee, 1997.

16. Hugh Belsey, 'Sir Thomas Lawrence's portrait for the County Building, Perth', *The Burlington Magazine*, CXLIX, 2007, pp. 158–64.

17. Robert Mylne, the London-based Scottish architect did this in the 1780s. Stana Nenadic, 'Patronage and professional identities: Scottish architects in eighteenth-century London', unpublished paper given to the 'Fruits of Exchange' conference, Paul Mellon Centre for Studies in British Art, London, 5 October 2007.

18. 'Robert Dundas, Lord Arniston.' *Oxford Dictionary of National Biography*, Oxford, 2004. Details of the life of the son are sketched in the biography of his more notable father.

19. NRS, S CH2/716/31. Letter from South Leith Church Session to Henry Raeburn, 9 August 1822.

20. Mezzotint by Charles Turner, published 14 November 1818, see Edinburgh 2006, p. 23.

21. Chambers, *Biographical Dictionary*.

22. Mary Anne Alburger, 'Musical Scots and Scottish music patrons in London and Edinburgh', in Stana Nenadic (ed.), *Scots in London in the Eighteenth Century*, Lewisburg, 2010; Edinburgh 2006, p. 24.

23. NAS, GD224/669/34. Vouchers of William Cuthill, Secretary to the Duke of Buccleuch, 1817; GD224/628/5/10, 'Memorandum as to the distribution of prints', 1818.

24. Nenadic, 'Writing medical lives.' Nenadic, 'Portraits of Scottish professional men.' Royal College of Surgeons of London: Hunter Baillie Papers: H-B iii 80. Letters from Thomas Lawrence to Mrs Baillie, 1823–4.

25. See, Martin Postle, *Joshua Reynolds: The Creation of Celebrity*, London, 2005.

26. While Alexander (Edinburgh 2006) has fully catalogued about fifty singly-issued prints made after Raeburn's portrait during his lifetime, an earlier authority, Kenneth Sanderson, in a manuscript file titled 'Engravings after Raeburn' suggests there were seventy-one contemporary and posthumous engravings (53 mezzotints, 10 stipple and 8 line) and a further 50 portraits that were engraved for book illustrations; see, SNPG, Sir Henry Raeburn Files: Folder 23:no. 22, and also see Sanderson 1925.

27. David Mackie, 'Documentation', in Edinburgh and London 1997–8, pp. 201–13. For Raeburn's relationship with William Walker in Edinburgh and London, see essay by Coltman in this collection.

28. SNPG, Sir Henry Raeburn Files: Folder 23/ 22.

29. See, for instance, the correspondence of the Duke of Buccleuch in NAS. GD224.

30. Janet Wolff and John Seed, *The Culture of Capital: Art, Power and the Nineteenth-Century Middle Class*, Manchester, 1988.

31. Edinburgh 2006, p. 19. F. M. O'Donoghue, 'William Walker, 1791–1867', *ODNB*.

32. Theodore Hook, *The Life of the Right Honourable Sir David Baird*, London, 1832.

33. Edinburgh 2006, pp. 13–14.

34. *The Scotsman*, 3 April 1830, p. 5.

35. Gillian Forrester, 'Charles Turner, 1774–1857', *ODNB*.

36. NAS, GD46//17/49. Letters and papers of the Mackenzie family, Earls of Seaforth.

37. *The Scotsman*, 1 July 1826, p. 5.

38. The average life expectancy of nineteenth-century small firms was just seven years. Stana Nenadic, 'The small family firm in Victorian Britain', *Business History*, XXXV, 1993, pp. 86–114.

39. NAS, CS96/3072, 3073. Sequestration of John Marnoch, carver and gilder, Edinburgh, Sederunt Books, 1816.

40. NAS, CS96/415/1. Sequestration of John Steele, gilder and dealer in prints, Edinburgh, Sederunt books 1819–25.

41. Nenadic, 'Print collecting.'

42. For a perspective on this subject, see, for example: Roger L. Emerson, Essays on *David Hume, medical men and the Scottish Enlightenment: Industry, knowledge and humanity*, Farnham, 2009; David Allan, *Making British Culture: English readers and the Scottish Enlightenment*, New York, 2008; David Duff and Catherine Jones (eds), *Scotland, Ireland and the Romantic Aesthetic*, Lewisburg, 2007; Colin Kidd, *Subverting Scotland's Past: Scottish Whig Historians and the Creation of an Anglo-British Identity, 1689 to c. 1830*, Cambridge, 1993.

43. The post-war public activities of both men in Edinburgh can be traced through newspaper reports. See, for example, *The Scotsman*, 6 December 1823, p. 4, which details 'A very numerous Meeting of Noblemen and Gentlemen' called by 'requisition in the Edinburgh newspapers' for 'transmitting to posterity a permanent record of respect for the distinguished professional talents, as well as the private virtues, of the late General the Earl of Hopetoun.' The meeting was held in the Waterloo Tavern on 3 December and was chaired by Sir David Baird. A subscription followed.

44. Published by Adam Elder in 1813.

45. Hay, *Royal Company of Archers*, pp. 22–3.

46. A vivid description of the visit from the letters of the Grant family of Rothiemurchus, is given in B. C. Skinner, 'A contemporary account of the

royal visit to Edinburgh, 1822', *The Book of the Old Edinburgh Club*, XXXI, 1962, pp. 65–167.

47. Edinburgh and London 1997–8, p. 152.
48. Edinburgh 2006, p. 25.
49. Home, a minister by profession, who first produced *Douglas* on the Edinburgh stage in 1757 and took the London stage by storm in the 1760s, remained popular for many decades. His portrait in old age was published in 1797 by Birrell of London, see Edinburgh 2006, p. 22.
50. Edinburgh 2006, p. 28.
51. Nenadic, *Scots in London*.
52. Detailed in, Stana Nenadic, 'Introduction.' in Nenadic, *Scots in London*.
53. Quoted in Paul Langford 'South Britons' reception of North Briton', T. C. Smout (ed.), *Anglo-Scottish Relations from 1603 to 1900: Proceedings of the British Academy*, CXXVII, Oxford, 2005, p. 165.

Part II

Reception

7

A Portrait of the Artist in London: The Critical Reception of Raeburn's Royal Academy Exhibits, 1792–1823

Nicholas Tromans

In 1801 the English topographical artist and epic diarist Joseph Farington visited Scotland and made a point of assessing the state of the art of painting in the capital. Farington sought out Raeburn's York Place house with its painting room and 'Show Room', and finding the proprietor absent, had the opportunity carefully to study his portraits:

> Some of Mr. Raeburn's portraits have an uncommonly true appearance of Nature and are painted with much firmness, but there is great inequality in his works. That which strikes the eye is a kind of Camera Obscura effect, and from those pictures which seem to be his best, I should conclude he has looked very much at Nature, reflected in a Camera.

Farington was greatly impressed with Raeburn's apparent wealth, noting his large house at Stockbridge and his aloofness from the company of other artists.[1] Already in these brief comments, the visitor has provided us succinctly with the fundamental themes in the English interpretation of Raeburn: the physical absence of the painter himself; the anonymity of his sitters; the isolation of the artist from his professional colleagues; the power and weakness found simultaneously in his work; and the supposed relationship of his images to mechanistic models of perception. This essay will expand upon these themes in the specific context of press criticism of Raeburn's exhibits at the Royal Academy in London, to which he sent pictures from 1792 down to the year of his death in 1823. It will begin by considering Raeburn's exhibiting strategy and his status among Royal Academicians. Then it will summarise the London critics' responses to his Academy exhibits. Some of the key concerns, emphases and anxieties expressed in this body of criticism will then be interpreted in pursuit of a fuller understanding of the reception of Raeburn in London as a dynamic process in which the refraction of his images through the visual culture of his English contemporaries generated a particular cluster of ideas around the artist. These ideas do not necessarily add up to a coherent interpretation of the artist's work, let alone a convincing portrait of the man himself. Rather, the intention here is to trace some of the complex and unpredictable routes through which images are translated from one place to another.

Raeburn visited London on several occasions, but so far as we know his only residence there of any significant duration was in 1810 when, aged 54, as a potential solution to his financial troubles, he had considered removing permanently to the metropolis. His friend in this aborted venture was fellow Scot David Wilkie, thirty years Raeburn's junior but already a star of the London scene where he had found overnight fame in 1806 with his *Village Politicians*, a picture mocking Scottish radical politics of the 1790s. Wilkie attempted to introduce Raeburn to some of the leading London painters but found them (actually or tactically) not at home.[2] The London artists deflected Raeburn's ambition by declining personal encouragement but offering instead a corporate homage. His visit lasted long enough for him to attend the Royal Academy's annual Royal Birthday dinner in early June, at which Raeburn was flatteringly positioned at table, and where his presence prompted a toast to the Fine Arts (and by implication the Academy's leadership of them) throughout the United Kingdom.[3] This encounter marked the beginning of the Academy's adoption of Raeburn as their Scottish representative, a position formalised once he was elected first as an Associate and then a full member of the Academy in November 1812 and February 1815 respectively.

Scots had been only minimally connected with the Royal Academy since its foundation in 1768 (even the well-connected portraitist Allan Ramsay was never an academician), and Raeburn was the first member to be resident in Scotland. This novelty signified the confident extension of the Academy's writ north of the border, and its embrace of Scottish painting as an element of the British school, a dual process which took place during and, especially, immediately following the French Wars which ended in 1815. Cut off from the Continent during the Napoleonic period, the English embraced Scottish tourism and the poetry of Walter Scott (Fig. 7.1), while the contribution of Scottish regiments to the war effort created a newly prestigious place for the

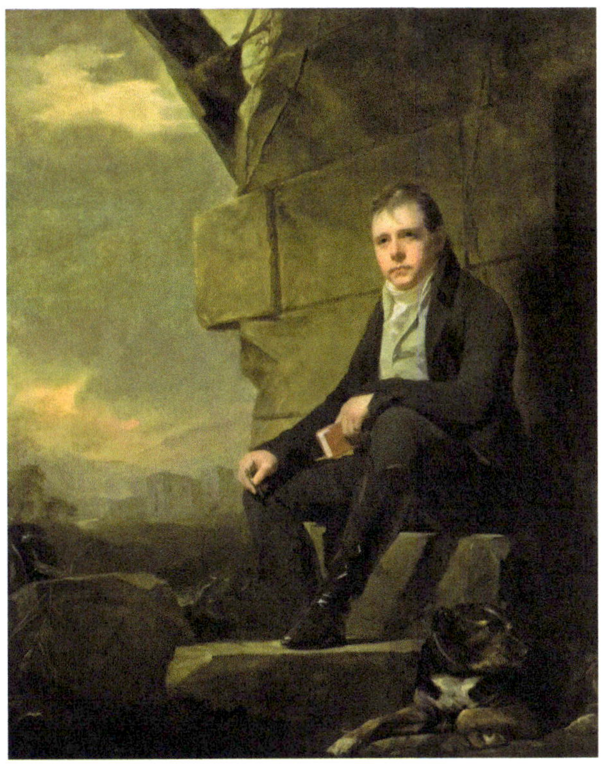

Figure 7.1 Henry Raeburn, *Sir Walter Scott*, exh. RA 1810, 182.9×147.3cm,
Buccleuch Collection (photography by Todd-Whyte)

idea of Scotland within the British Empire. In these years, Scottish themes
were especially prominent on the walls of the annual Academy exhibition,
from the hands of both Scottish and English artists. For example, in 1810
Samuel Drummond's scenes from *Ossian* were widely reviewed, although he
was far from being the first to use that source for Academy pictures. Of the
1811 exhibition, the *Repository of Arts* complained that 'The rooms, as we
expected, are overcharged with trash from Walter Scott's last poem [*The
Lady of the Lake*]. You meet with the *representatives* of *Rhoderic Dhu*, *Fair Ellen*,
and *Allan Bane*, at every step'.[4] And in 1816 there was felt to be an especially
strong Scottish presence at the Academy when William Allan's *Circassian
Slaves at Constantinople* and Alexander Nasmyth's *Culzean Castle* were both
among the favourite pictures of the year. From this point, London began to
think in terms of an identifiable Scottish body of painting, but again always
one contained within the British, or even English school of art. Wilkie, who
in 1817 resolved to make his pictures 'more Scottish in future', thought in

terms of Northern and Southern branches of an English school.[5] There were those who became convinced this influx of Scots would lead to a takeover by the more ambitious northerners, turning the Academy into another East India Company (where Scots were perceived to dominate), and when in 1821 Andrew Geddes' vast painting of *The Discovery of the Regalia of Scotland* was hung prominently at Somerset House (the Academy's premises on the Strand), there were dark mutterings about Scottish influence somewhere behind the scenes.[6]

The point that concerns us here is that during the years in which Raeburn exhibited regularly at the London Academy, that is between 1810 and 1823, Scottish art was very far from being a novelty there, and indeed 'Scottishness' formed very little part in the critics' explicit terms of reference when discussing Raeburn. (Although, as will be argued below, there were some interpretations of his work, especially those involving a perceived mechanistic visuality, which have to be understood in terms of certain English assumptions regarding Scottish culture.) It has often been supposed that Raeburn's magisterial Highland chieftains – particularly *Glengarry* (exh. RA 1812; Fig. 10.4) and *MacNab* (probably exh. RA 1819; Fig. 7.2) – must have bemused or shocked their London audience, but there is no evidence of this.[7] Nor should this surprise us, as English artists were themselves already regularly in the habit of showing dramatic Highland portraits, and were indeed seen to outdo Raeburn on this territory. Thus William Beechey drew plaudits for his *Duke of Sussex as Earl of Inverness in Highland Costume* in 1816 while Thomas Lawrence's 1797 portrait of *Lord Seaforth* represented Highland romance fully recruited to the glory of the British army (Raeburn showed his portrait of the same sitter at the Academy in 1814). Most convincing, however, as evidence for the relative unimportance of Highlandism for Raeburn's reception in London, were the two MacNabs who both appeared at the Academy in 1819. Raeburn's great *Francis MacNab*, it seems probable, was the *Highland Chief* shown that year, but this familiar masterpiece (as it now is to us), while receiving some praise, was entirely eclipsed by Martin Archer Shee's portrait of *James Munro Macnabb* in full Highland costume who, according to press accounts, 'attracted universal attention' with his dirk, pistols, filibeg, plaid, red-barred stockings and sword (Fig. 7.3).[8]

Raeburn first showed at the Royal Academy in 1792, exhibiting portraits of John Home (who controversially combined the professions of clergyman and playwright) and an unidentified lady. Apparently he also intended to exhibit his ambitious portrait of *Sir John and Lady Clerk of Penicuik* but somehow that picture arrived too late to be hung and was placed instead in the publisher John Boydell's Shakespeare Gallery on Pall Mall (Fig. 7.4).[9] Single male portraits were exhibited in 1798 (*Sir Walter Farquhar*), 1799

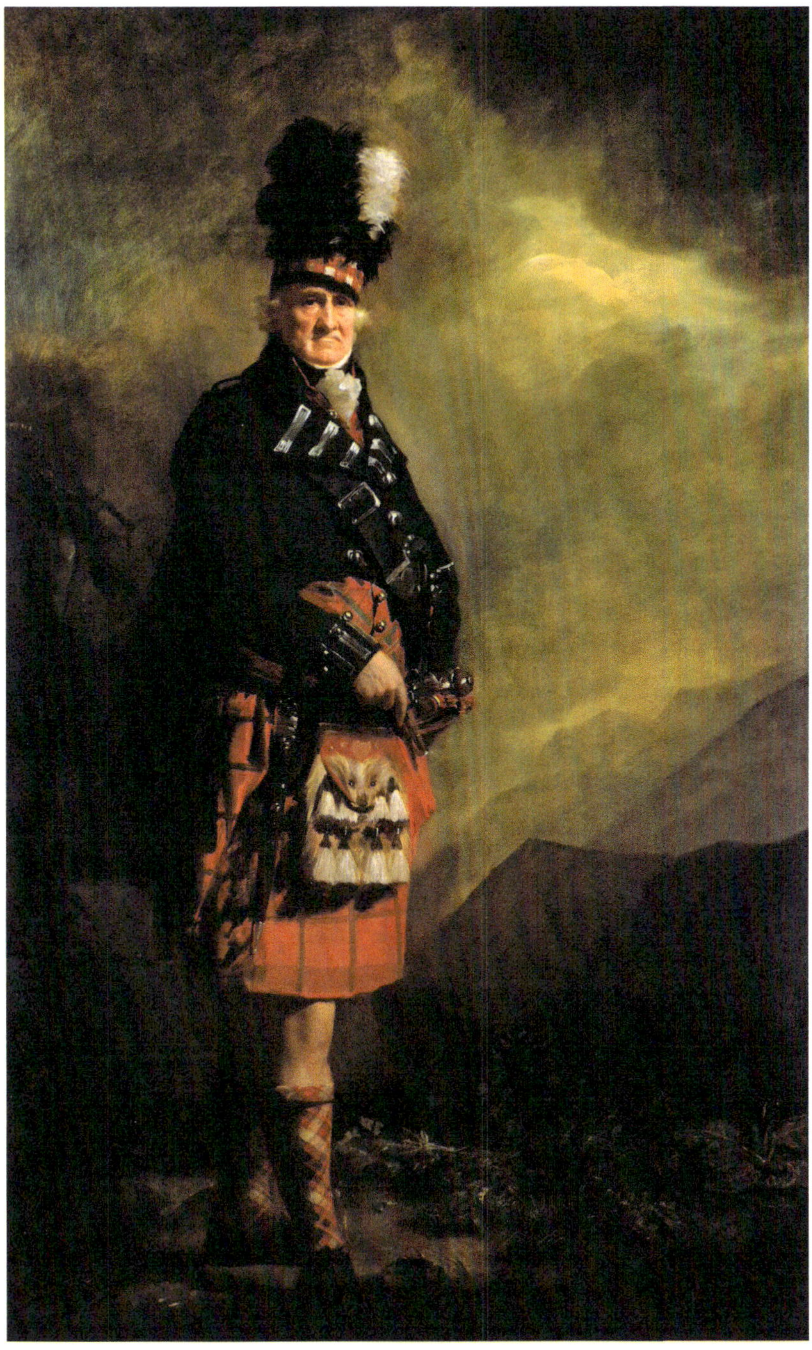

Figure 7.2 Henry Raeburn, *Francis MacNab ('The MacNab')*, probably exh. RA 1819, oil on canvas, 241.3×152.4cm, Diageo plc (on loan to Kelvingrove Art Gallery and Museum, Glasgow Museums)

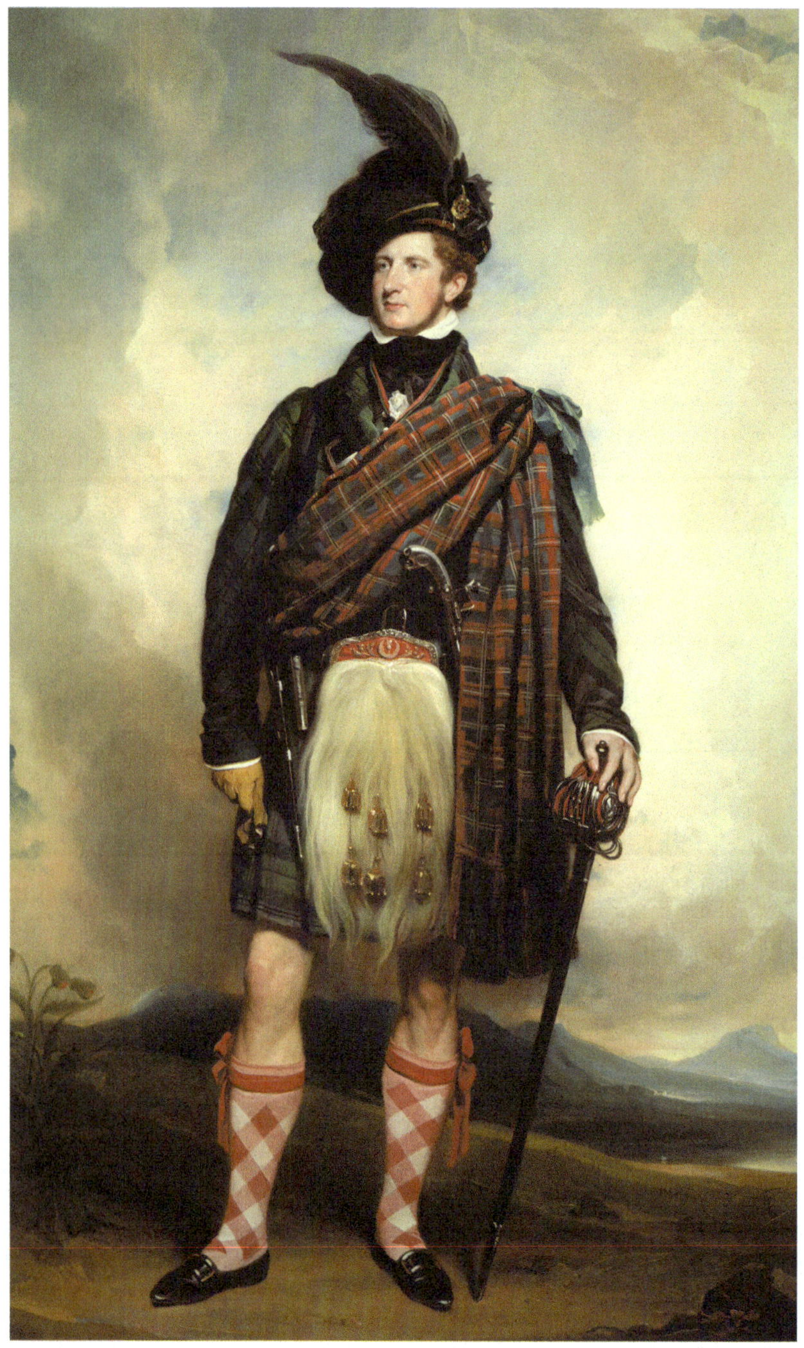

Figure 7.3 Martin Archer Shee, *James Munro Macnabb*, exh. RA 1819, 233.5×142.5cm, private collection

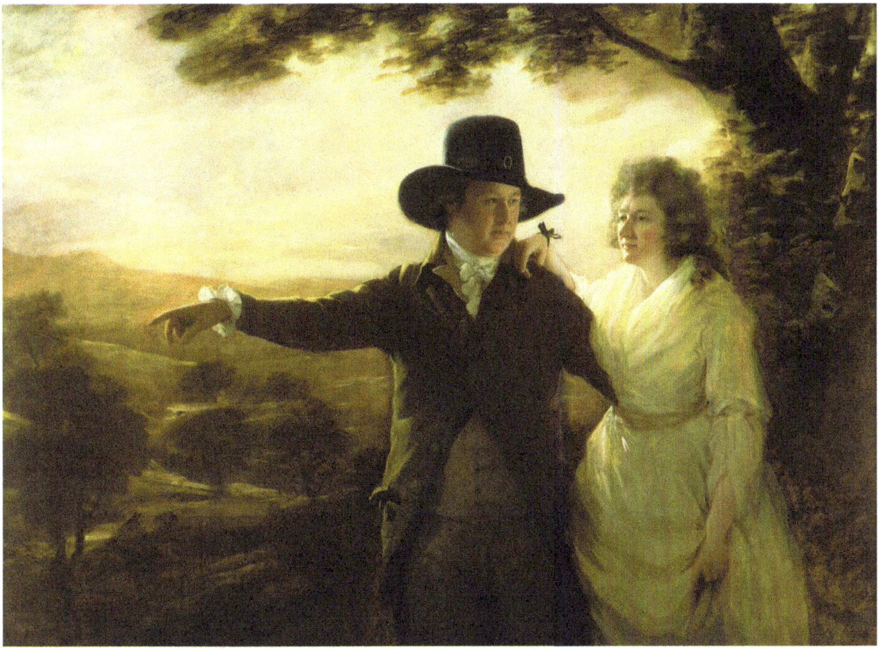

Figure 7.4　Henry Raeburn, *Sir John and Lady Clerk of Penicuik*, exh. Boydell's
Shakespeare Gallery, London 1792, oil on canvas, 144.8×204.5cm,
National Gallery of Ireland, Dublin

(unidentified *Gentleman*), 1802 (*Professor Daniel Rutherford*), 1810 (*Walter
Scott*; Fig. 7.1) and 1811 (*Revd Sir Henry Moncrieff Wellwood*) before Raeburn
went up a gear in 1812, the year of his election to Associateship. From now
on he showed every year, generally sending in several portraits (up to a
maximum of five). In total Raeburn exhibited 53 paintings at the Academy
of which only six were of women. While there must have been occasions
when the client particularly requested their picture be shown in London (as
seems to have been the case with the portrait of *Admiral Milne* commissioned
by George Home of Paxton[10]), and others where simple logistics suggested
the choice (for example the *Scott* portrait shown in 1810 may have been
in London immediately beforehand being engraved), it seems clear that in
selecting works to show at Somerset House, Raeburn intended to demonstrate the widest range of his art. The exception, as we have noted, was his
practice in female portraiture. Possibly this under-representation reflected
a lack of confidence in this department of his art, but more likely it should
be explained by an assumption on the part of the artist that his male clients
would be embarrassed by being asked to lend the portraits of their wives and

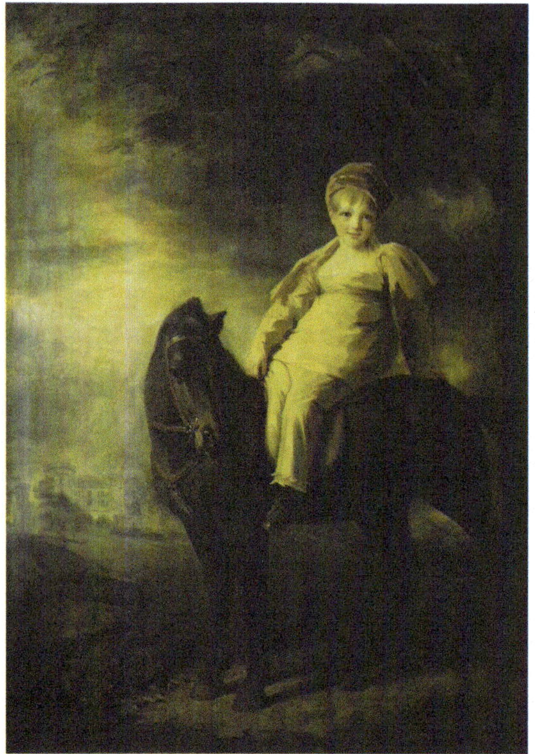

Figure 7.5 Henry Raeburn, *Archibald William, Lord Montgomerie, later 13th Earl of Eglinton*, exh. RA 1818, oil on canvas, 212×151cm, Bearsted Collection, Upton House, The National Trust

daughters to such a public metropolitan event. How much disappointment this may have caused the sitters themselves is not possible to say.

Thus, between 1812 and 1823, Raeburn showed members of the Edinburgh social and professional elites, Highland chieftains, English aristocrats, naval and army officers, fellow artists (Archibald Skirving and Francis Chantrey), an aristocratic child on a pony (the Earl of Eglinton; Fig. 7.5), the glamorous young polymath Lady Eliza Gordon-Cumming, and even a sort of genre picture – the portrait of the gamekeeper of the Earl of Kintore.[11] Fifteen portraits were exhibited with the title given only as *Portrait of a Gentleman* (or of a *Young Gentleman*), and it seems that the only occasions on which the London press was able to supply the missing names for exhibition visitors were in 1812 when the *Morning Post* identified Skirving and 1823 when the *Literary Chronicle* recognised Archibald Constable.[12] As Raeburn himself observed, along with many of the critics, he had no way of knowing how his pictures compared with the latest fashions and so, removed from the London scene as he was, he could perhaps have followed no other course than to seek to represent the breadth of his practice – perhaps rather weighted towards the grander male sitters.

Before turning to the question of how these exhibited portraits were received in London, we should consider how Raeburn himself was professionally positioned within the Academy as an institution. After his 1810 foray into the London art world Raeburn rarely returned, dedicated as he was to working out in Edinburgh the massive losses incurred as a result of his bankruptcy in 1808.[13] Although he retained fond memories of some of those artists who had treated him so royally in 1810, such as his fellow portraitist Beechey, and was on occasion visited in Edinburgh by a touring academician, Raeburn felt obliged to press Wilkie to write at least once a year to keep him informed of London news.[14] Wilkie was nothing if not a conscientious correspondent, but even his missives could not prevent Raeburn's notorious lament of 1819 that he felt he might as well be 'living at the Cape of Good Hope' for all he knew of the metropolitan scene.[15] Raeburn's novel status as the Academy's member for Scotland certainly caused awkwardness on both sides on account of the artist having little opportunity to learn the intricacies of the organisation's regulations and traditions. In 1810 for example Raeburn was ticked off by a critic for not observing the unwritten rule that it was bad form to exhibit a portrait (the *Walter Scott*) of which a print had already been published.[16] When by 1817 Raeburn had still not managed to collect the academician's diploma he had been awarded on his election as a full RA in 1815, his absence from London caused procedural ambiguities over whether or not he had vacated his position as Associate.[17] But the most embarrassing of these misunderstandings occurred over Raeburn's diploma painting, the picture each new academician was required to donate to the Academy as a specimen of their work.

After his election as Associate in 1812 Raeburn had continued to play for the London artists the role that it seemed they expected from him, of a lonely patrician beyond the competitive field. Thus although he was clearly determined to upgrade to full membership of the Academy and was in London for the opening of the 1813 exhibition, when an opportunity arose in 1814 to stand for election as an academician Raeburn claimed to feel unable to canvass for votes.[18] Nevertheless, with the encouragement of Wilkie and the support of influential networkers including Farington and the latter's close friend, the leading portraitist Lawrence, Raeburn stood again, this time successfully, early the next year. Informing Farington of the result, Lawrence boasted that the RA had matched Raeburn's Scottish high-mindedness in its impartiality: 'The Academy has certainly given a very signal proof of disinterestedness in electing Persons for whom there was no canvassing, an Example even for Scotland itself'.[19] Wilkie wrote with the good news to Raeburn who replied asking to know the names of those who had voted for him so as to be able to thank them. He also requested advice regarding his diploma work: 'I am much at a loss to know what sort of picture I am to paint for the approbation of the [Academy] Council – what do you think on that subject?'[20] But Wilkie either failed to reply or gave incomplete information for Raeburn submitted his self-portrait only to be told self-portraits were not admissible.[21] In fact portraits generally were considered inappropriate as diploma pieces at this period, and so several portraitists had turned to genre versions of their general practice for this purpose. Thus in 1794 Lawrence submitted a gipsy girl holding a chicken she has just poached and in 1807 another leading portraitist, William Owen, offered a picture of a boy feeding a kitten.[22] So when Raeburn sent, as a replacement for his self-portrait, a picture of his step-son with a pet rabbit, he was following an established trend which encouraged portraitists to represent themselves to their new Academic colleagues in the guise of the slightly more elevated role of producer of 'fancy pictures' in the mould of Thomas Gainsborough or the Academy's founder, Sir Joshua Reynolds. In tone, Raeburn's picture is entirely in keeping with such eighteenth-century English precedents, the emotional novelty of which, based on a reconfigured and 'naturalised' notion of children and the nuclear family, seemed so distant by the twentieth century that *Henry Raeburn Inglis* (*'Boy and Rabbit'*) merely appeared 'cloyingly sentimental' (Fig. 7.6).[23] Recent scholarship has however done much to recover the ethical content of such imagery, which in Raeburn's case was of course not confined to this formal Diploma work: from a similar period dates, for example, his portrait of *William Scott–Elliot of Arkleton* (Metropolitan Museum of Art, New York), showing a little boy collecting flowers from a grassy bank.[24]

If the *Boy and Rabbit* can be connected with other Diploma works by earlier Academy artists, its appearance at exhibition provided a further relationship between Raeburn and the London-based painters. Both the *Boy and Rabbit* and Raeburn's self-portrait were shown at the Academy exhibition of 1816, as was Wilkie's piece of comic Caravaggism, *The Rabbit on the Wall* (Fig. 7.7), in which a father entertains his family with hand shadows. It is tempting to see in these rabbits something more than a coincidence given that we know that on other occasions Wilkie more explicitly referenced Raeburn's pictures in his own. Raeburn's portrait of the fiddler *Niel Gow* is recycled in Wilkie's *Penny Wedding*, a picture which when shown at the Academy in 1819 seemed a sort of cumulative statement of Scottish art's recent achievements. Then twenty years later Raeburn's equestrian portrait of *General Sir David Baird* (exh. RA 1814) was the source for the hero's posthumous appear-

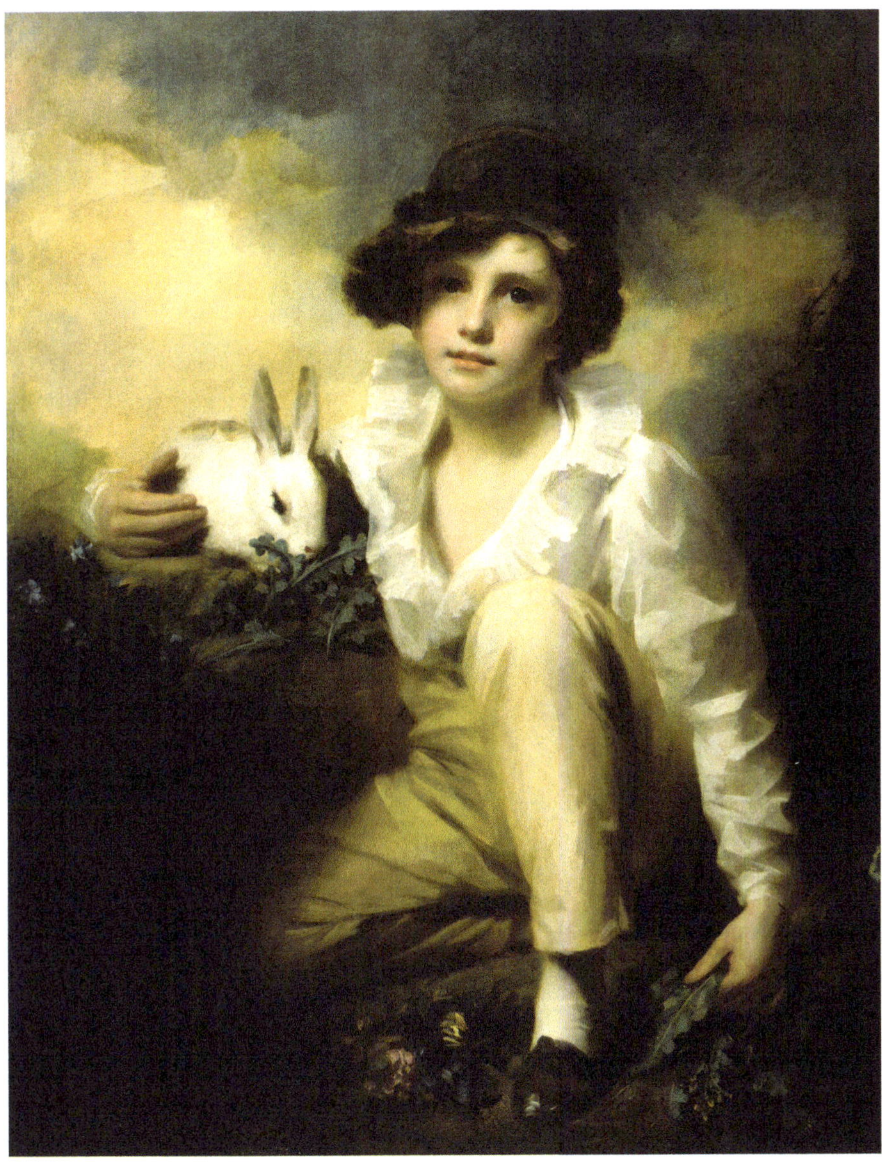

Figure 7.6 Henry Raeburn, *Henry Raeburn Inglis ('Boy and Rabbit')*, exh. RA 1816, oil on canvas, 101.6×78.8cm, Royal Academy of Arts, London

ance in Wilkie's painting of the storming of Seringapatam. Wilkie seems to have subsumed Raeburn into his ever-expanding archive of sources, finding in his portraits a Scottish contribution to the amalgamated style by which Wilkie was recognised as the consummate modern Old Master.

Turning now to the reception of Raeburn's Academy exhibits, anyone

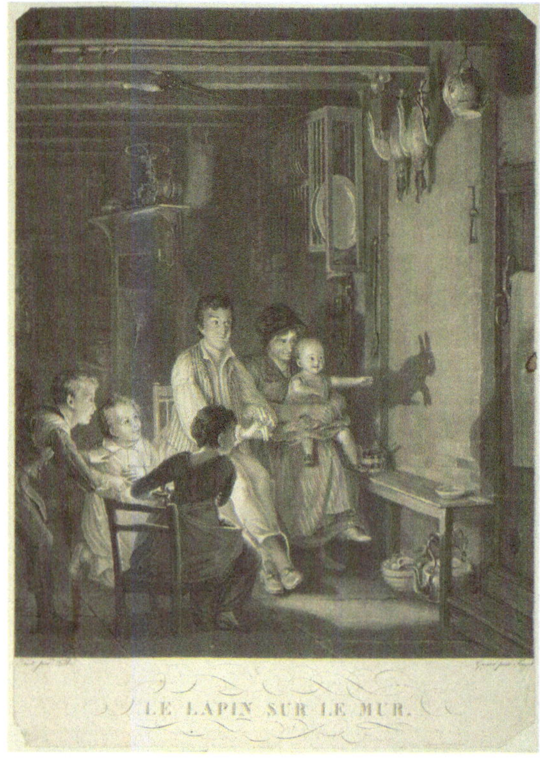

Figure 7.7 Jean-Pierre Jazet after David Wilkie, *The Rabbit on the Wall*, c. 1821, aquatint, Scottish National Gallery, Edinburgh (painting exh. RA 1816, current location unknown)

trawling through early nineteenth-century art criticism in the daily and weekly London papers will probably end having some sympathy with the compilers of the catalogue of the pictures of Benjamin West, the Academy's President from 1792 to 1820, who concluded that this corpus of writing 'is remarkable chiefly for its vacuity'.[25] Certainly the kind of sensitive, detailed pictorial analysis that we conventionally associate with the idea of the aesthete art critic was in short supply, and judgments were typically passed without any supporting evidence or argument. Often this was a reflection of the limited space made available to exhibition reviews, especially in the dailies where listing the good, the bad and the ugly was all the reporter had the opportunity to do. Nevertheless on many occasions the very absence of a precise critical vocabulary with which to describe the works of art on show led writers to make wider associations and comparisons which allow us insights into the broader visual culture of the age.[26]

Raeburn was never a major presence in the columns devoted to the Fine Arts in the London periodicals of his day, even if from time to time some hyperbolic praise was bestowed upon his pictures. To make sense of the critics' perspectives we need to bear in mind that many of them saw it as their job simply to let their readers know where, within the exhibition rooms, to find the pictures of the most famous artists (in Raeburn's time this meant Wilkie, Lawrence, Turner and West). Other, more serious critics were concerned to help direct the development of modern British art, but such writers often saw Raeburn as not relevant to their concerns: not because he was not excellent, or not properly British, but because his distance from London and perceived independence and aloofness marked him *hors concours*, beyond the reach of the critics' influence, rather in the same way that the London critics took a long time to get used to the idea of offering critiques of exhibitions of Old Master paintings after these began to be regularly mounted from the 1810s (at the British Institution which had taken over the Shakespeare Gallery). We can in fact trace a particular interest in Raeburn on the part of a couple of the more distinguished critics of the day, but first I will try to give a general sense of the response to his Academy exhibits in the London press.

On the positive side, Raeburn's portraits (which we have noted were overwhelmingly male) were perceived as 'manly', full of confident handling and assertive execution.[27] Often they were said to be lifelike, especially the heads, and the countenances of the sitters felt to be intelligent.[28] It was central to the London critics' interpretation of Raeburn that, in almost all cases, they knew little or nothing about the sitters and had never seen them. This meant that occasionally some offensive personal remarks were passed on their portraits, comments which would be unthinkable were the sitter an English lord whom the writer might one day encounter (thus in 1822 Lord Douglas was described as 'an odd-looking little man').[29] It certainly meant that the critics responded to Raeburn's work in a much more formalist mode than was common in their dealings with other major portraitists: his pictures' properties of light and especially colour were unusually carefully described. It was often said of portraits at the Academy that although the sitter was unknown to the writer the likeness was nevertheless convincing.[30] But this notion of likeness as an idea, rather than verifiable fact, was applied to Raeburn with particular self-consciousness by the critics, who emphasised that his portraits might be preferable precisely because of their anonymity, allowing them to be enjoyed essentially as pictures. Two of the best-received works by Raeburn to be shown at the Academy were the (still) completely anonymous portraits of gentlemen exhibited in 1814 and 1823. Of the first, a critic concluded 'Perhaps we admire it the more because it is an anonymous likeness', while of the second another wrote: 'From the strength and clearness of its character, we should take it for granted that this portrait is faithful to its original'.[31] It was however, at the same time, the consideration of Raeburn's portraits *as pictures* that gave rise to some of the most negative comments upon them.

The Royal Academy had clear rules on what was and what was not a picture, and central to their definition was the notion of background. A painting or drawing could, at least in theory, not be exhibited without a background that provided the subject with a setting, and therefore suggested a perspectival space through which to generate the 'relief' that was such a concern of contemporary critical discourse.[32] Raeburn's first Academy exhibit to make any critical impact was his portrait of Scott shown in 1810 (Fig. 7.1). The genteel *Repository of Arts* did not hide its disappointment that the romantic bard (he was not yet the 'Author of Waverley') had been shown to be so unromantic in personal appearance: 'never was a more unpoetical physiognomy delineated on canvas: we might take him for an auctioneer or a land-surveyor, a travelling dealer and chapman; in short, for any character but a bard'.[33] But the background of the painting was praised elsewhere in the press for its success in evoking a suitable setting in a Scottish landscape of melancholy ruins.[34] However, thereafter, Raeburn's backgrounds came to be a real sticking point for the critics. They were simply too flat, dark and incomplete. They gave no sense of place, threatening the geographic status and hence significance of the sitter, and potentially even the status of the portrait itself as a picture. The handling in the backgrounds was sometimes so sketchy as to suggest carelessness; they were distressingly cold – a vacuum of grey-green offering no assurance of life; and their lack of variation was a mannerism: 'The backgrounds of all his pictures have the same sky, and it is a sky which never existed since the creation except in the unpoetical fancy of Mr Raeburn'.[35] In the 1840s an acquaintance of the artist's recalled a conversation in which Raeburn had declared his belief that a background 'ought to be nothing more than the shadow of a landscape' aspiring to the character of Death as described in Milton's *Paradise Lost*, a black form existing somewhere between substance and shadow.[36] It seems just as likely that here the writer was expressing the perception of Raeburn's backgrounds as melancholy black holes as much as recording any fixed philosophy of the artist himself.

The art critics writing regular Academy reviews in the early nineteenth century typically published them anonymously. There were essayists such as William Hazlitt and Thomas Griffiths Wainewright who wrote occasional longer pieces on the exhibitions but among the jobbing reviewers very few names are known today. Two exceptions are Robert Hunt and William Paulet Carey, both of whom were, at least for much of the time, champions of Raeburn. Hunt was one of the three brothers associated with the left-wing

Examiner newspaper established in 1808. Leigh Hunt was the editor and John Hunt the publisher, while Robert, who had been apprenticed to an engraver, wrote on art. True to the rule that art history tends only to remember art critics in order to scoff at their blindness, Robert Hunt is today best known for his uncompromising denigration of William Blake. But this attack was of a part with Hunt's stated principles, which turned on the ethical role of art in improving modern society, and he could see no place for Blake's visions in that project. Hunt even once printed a paragraph from Kames's *Elements of Criticism* (first published in 1762) at the head of one of his columns to support his own view of the moral seriousness of art, and possibly his familiarity with Scottish philosophy inclined him to look closely at Raeburn (he had certainly taken a serious interest in Wilkie's genre painting).[37]

Hunt declared his discovery of Raeburn in 1812, devoting a stand-alone paragraph on the Royal Academy to the portrait of *Glengarry*.[38] The next year Hunt seems to have surprised himself with his enthusiasm: 'Mr. Raeburn's portraits are – I was going to say – almost faultless, so well are they drawn, so broad and so forcible in their masses, and so easy and so natural in their attitudes'.[39] But if Hunt took his art criticism seriously, then this meant a reciprocal arrangement whereby artists needed to take as much notice of him as he did of them, and here Raeburn defaulted. Gradually Hunt seems to have become exasperated at his own lack of purchase upon the Scottish painter whom he admired, and he began to join in the attacks upon Raeburn's palette. His unnatural green skies were 'rather too original appendages', the critic was lamenting by 1818, and in 1819 Hunt gave the notion of Raeburn's melancholy palette an explicitly humoural twist, courtesy of Shakespeare:

> In spite of the bright carnations in his figures, they appear as if some storm of fate was ready to burst over their devoted heads, from the unnaturally 'green and yellow melancholy' clouds and back-grounds.[40]

By the time of the artist's last appearance at the Academy, Hunt declared him to be 'in the unprogressive class', unable for all his talent to overcome his faults which 'are and have long been great'.[41]

Hunt's frustration seems to express something of the larger sense of despondency that overtook politically progressive writers in the acutely reactionary post-Waterloo years. As Wilkie (easily alarmed by expressions of Radicalism) wrote in 1818: 'The opinions of the Examiner Hunts upon Pictures as well as in Politics are in their influence decidedly upon the decline'.[42] But Hunt's frustration with Raeburn's unchanging colour schemes was also shared by many critics who could not understand why he seemed unwilling to accommodate his art to the competitive arena of the metropolitan exhibition, to join in the professional mêlée of modern art. In 1823 the *European Magazine* complained:

> But why will this otherwise highly-accomplished artist adhere so tenaciously to the crude tones, which he delights to introduce into his back-grounds? We fear that he does not avail himself of the principal advantages of the Exhibition, that of enabling painters to compare themselves with one another.[43]

That Scottish artists in particular should take advantage of the grander stage of the Academy to improve themselves was assumed, for example in the praise offered to Patrick Nasmyth's *Loch Katrine* in 1811: 'the present performance is a striking proof of the benefit he has derived from an association with our London artists'.[44] Raeburn himself was made to feel acutely conscious of this supposed failing, telling Wilkie in a letter of 1819 that his Academy exhibits were now

> merely an advertisement that I am still in the land of the living, but in other respects it does me no good, for I get no notice from anyone, nor have I the least conception how they look beside others.[45]

Considering the *Examiner*'s early support for Raeburn, and recalling the dissatisfaction expressed at his rough style by Scottish Tories such as Walter Scott, we may be tempted to see, with Duncan Macmillan, a whiggish bluntness dividing his viewers along political lines.[46] But perhaps the London paper that reviewed Raeburn's Academy exhibits with the most consistent enthusiasm was the staunchly Tory (indeed partly Government-directed) *Sun*. Some of the impetus for this coverage may have been due to the paper's Scottish editor between 1813 and 1817, William Jerdan, but the *Sun* announced its special interest in Raeburn when he first sent an important work to the Academy, in 1810. Devoting a whole paragraph to the portrait of Scott, the *Sun* declared 'We have here an excellent specimen of the state of painting in Scotland', which 'may be considered as the offspring of genius, matured by judgment and experience'.[47] The *Sun* went on to pronounce Raeburn 'One of the best portrait painters of the time', yet always with the usual caveats that 'His manner is very peculiar', with its want of finish, its darkness and lack of relief.[48]

When Jerdan left the *Sun* in 1817 it was to become founding editor of the *Literary Gazette*, which he succeeded in turning into one of the leading reviews of the Regency period. His principal art critic was the Irishman William Paulet Carey, an intriguing figure who sometimes brought to his art journalism the same flair for controversy he had shown in Ireland where, in the 1790s, he had been a radical member of the United Irishmen, only to fall out with them so completely as to have received Government funding for the newspapers he subsequently set up, and to have moved to England after the 1798 uprising supposedly in fear of attack from his former comrades.[49] In his English journalism Carey was a vocal supporter of initiatives to establish art institutions beyond London, reporting for example in 1819 on Edinburgh's art scene in a piece for the *New Monthly Magazine* in which he included a sketch of Raeburn's practice.[50] He had already made a point of introducing Raeburn to the readers of the *Gazette* in 1817 when he gave a close description of *Lady Gordon-Cumming* (Fig. 7.8) and a *Young Gentleman* (no. 91: 'seated under a tree, and holding a large spotted dog'), and concluded that: 'his portraits betray *no trace of imitation.* His style is *altogether original,* and founded upon his own warm feeling of nature'.[51] Carey went on regularly to draw his readers' attention to Raeburn, offering restrained praise without ever becoming entirely enthusiastic. The kind of pictures that really inspired him were the huge, bombastic scenes of biblical devastation by the likes of West and William Etty. He recognised something exceptional in Raeburn and was as always keen to advertise the achievements of an artist based outside London. But ultimately perhaps Raeburn simply appeared too comfortably settled for Carey, whose regularly published pamphlets depended on the kind of controversy that the portraitist never seemed ready to supply.[52]

As was noted above, many exhibition reviewers of this period struggled to put into words the precise visual effect of the pictures they had seen, but this deflection or confusion of language before images generated comments which instead – consciously but also it seems partly unconsciously – address issues which the writers perceived as connected with the picture being viewed. In the case of Raeburn we can begin by noticing the parallel between his perceived lack of ambition within the metropolitan professional arena and the perceived flatness of his pictures. The critics typically both lamented the competitive strategies resorted to by artists desperate to stand out among the hundreds of canvases on display at the Academy, but also celebrated the achievements of those, such as Wilkie and Lawrence, who managed to succeed best in this struggle. The domination of the annual exhibition by portraiture was habitually complained of because of the consequent detriment to more high-minded historical subjects and also because of the fatiguing impression of so many sitters squabbling for attention. 'We cannot avoid repeating' announced the *Morning Herald* in 1810, 'how much we are disgusted with the innumerable portraits which are thrusting themselves, as it were, so impertinently upon our notice, in every direction'.[53] But it was exactly the sense of projection, of dynamic relief, which propelled Lawrence's sitters to the foreground. Take for instance his *John Kemble as Coriolanus*, a

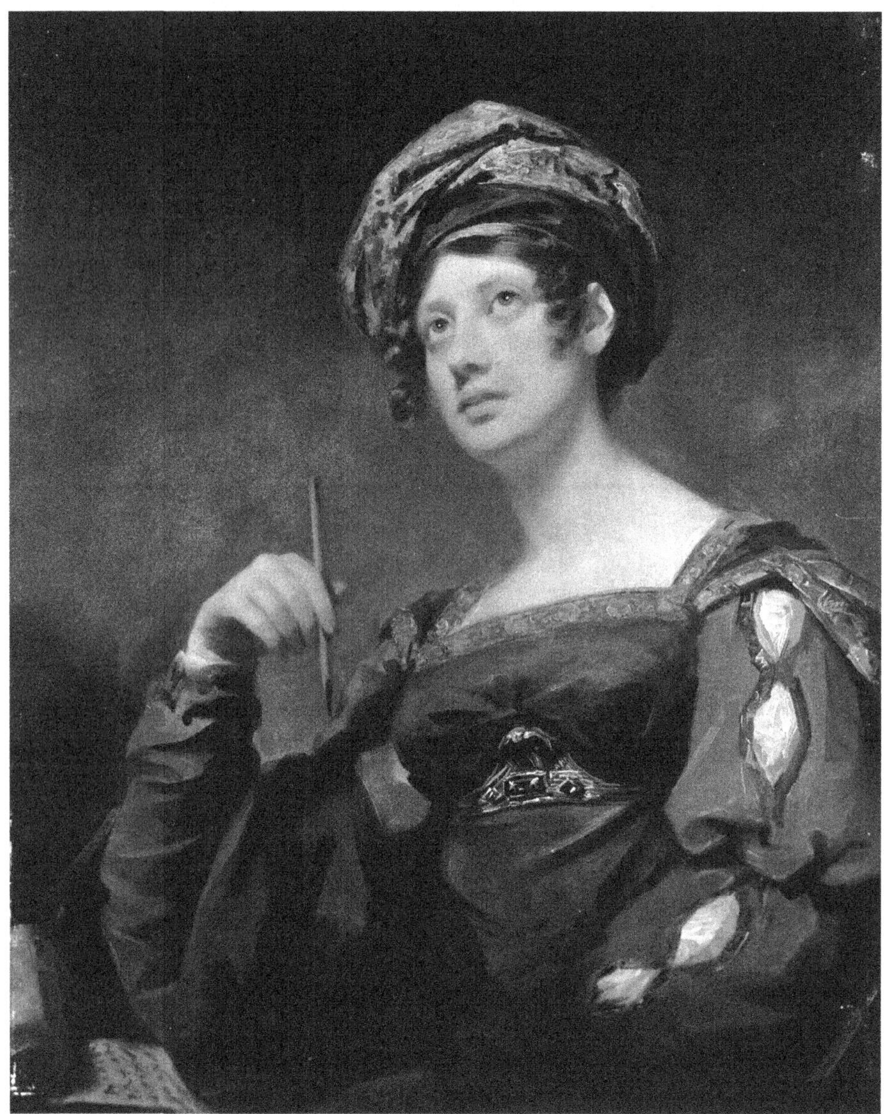

Figure 7.8 Henry Raeburn, *Eliza Mary Campbell, Lady Gordon-Cumming*, exh. RA 1817, oil on canvas, 76.2×63.5cm, formerly in the collection of Sir Felix Cassel in 1951, current location unknown (photograph courtesy of the Witt Library, Courtauld Institute of Art, London)

great success at the Academy in 1798, showing the actor stepping out of the picture frame towards the viewer. Once hung 'on the line' at Somerset House – lifted above the heads of the audience and tilted slightly forward – Kemble's towering figure would have really appeared to be making a grand entrance into the Great Room. Duncan Thomson has compared the arm-folded posture of this portrait to Raeburn's *Lord Compton* (later Marquess of Northampton) shown in London in 1821, but in that picture there is nothing of Lawrence's projection of the figure.[54] The background is indeed virtually non-existent and the portrait, although of an English aristocrat, was more or less entirely overlooked at the Academy. To take a parallel case, when in 1819 Raeburn and Shee exhibited their rival *MacNabs*, the limbs of Shee's portrait were said to have been 'wrought with such exquisite skill, that they actually appear to stand out from the canvas', while Carey said of Raeburn's that although 'a capital work', it was missing 'the slightest relief' with which 'to throw out its massive and broad forms'.[55] Indeed even such dramatic and romantic compositions of Raeburn's as the *Marquess of Huntly* (later Duke of Gordon; exh. RA 1820) work essentially across the plane of the picture rather than in relief. The nearest thing Raeburn showed in London to this desired model of projected figures was his Diploma picture in 1816, in which the boy's knee is thrust outwards towards the viewer in the manner of one of Lawrence's centrifugal toddlers. Raeburn's empty backgrounds, then, appeared to have absorbed their occupants – to have held them back – reflecting the artist's own apparent reluctance to come forward and join the fray.

The comparison between Raeburn and Lawrence was a common trope among the critics, and has remained a crucial point of interpretation. Thomson has identified, and regretted, the influence of the London artist on Raeburn's later period, when 'a highly strung mannerism infused many of his works, mostly, it seems, due to the influence of Sir Thomas Lawrence'.[56] Specifically he cites the portrait of *Lady Gordon-Cumming*, comparing it convincingly to Lawrence's *Mrs. Jens Wolff* (exh. RA 1815), and quoting, it seems with disappointment, Raeburn's own verdict that the Gordon-Cumming portrait was 'by much the best and handsomest female picture I have yet painted'.[57] The implication is that Raeburn was led astray from his true manner by a misplaced sense of inferiority to the leading London portraitist.[58] The Scottish artist's close interest in Lawrence's progress suggests there is some truth in this, but if the press were partly to blame, the Edinburgh critics were as much if not more at fault than their London colleagues. In 1815 the *Scots Magazine* ran a very negative article on Raeburn's pictures at the Edinburgh Exhibition Society, and a correspondent wrote in with purportedly supporting evidence from London where he had seen Raeburn's Earls of *Fife* and *Kinnoull* very well placed at the Academy yet made to seem 'black and dingy . . . by a comparison, which it was impossible to avoid making, with Lawrence's magnificent portrait of the Regent'.[59] The same journal, even when disposed to admire Scotland's greatest portraitist, could join in London's lament at his lack of ambition:

> In looking at such a picture [*Lady Innes-Kerr* at the Associated Society of Artists'
> Edinburgh exhibition of 1812], we regret the small field of action offered to
> such an artist in our city, and believe that had he commenced his career in the
> metropolis, instead of this place, he would ere now have ranked with any master
> of the present age.[60]

But Raeburn was not one for open competition, even on so secure a ground
as his native Edinburgh, and by the time the *Scots Magazine* published this
opinion Raeburn had resigned from the Associated Artists in resentment
at his pictures being poorly placed there in comparison with those of his
younger rival George Watson, confessing that 'he cannot prevail upon
himself to act a second part in the eye of the public to any man in his own
line'.[61] Of course he realised this would have been his fate in London, and
Raeburn and Lawrence each kept to their separate spheres, no doubt to the
better peace of mind of both.

A tidy separation is always possible to construe in terms of complementarity as well as mere difference: 'Lawrence made all his men courtiers;
Raeburn made all his philosophers' was for example a fairly common opinion
by the 1820s, with Lawrence as the prince of painters and Raeburn as 'the
Apelles of Scotland'.[62] At the Academy this complementary characterisation
was developed on quasi-physiological axes of colour and eroticism. In 1816
Robert Hunt wrote that although

> [t]he green, blue and dark hues in Mr Raeburn's pictures are certainly less har-
> monious and rich than the brighter ones of Lawrence, Beechey, &c., ... they
> recommend themselves by their originality of effect, and by being well amalga-
> mated with each other. A picture or two of this Artist among portraits of the
> usual warmer cast would materially improve their effect by the contrast.[63]

So Raeburn's very chromatic difference had the potential to bring greater
harmony to Somerset House where, as the Radical paper the *Champion*
expressed it, the conglomerated mass of portraiture appeared to the bewil-
dered visitor like some appalling meta-human monster 'worked up, in desperate competition among its individual parts, to the tone of a nosegay of
artificial flowers'.[64] Specifically, Raeburn's greens offered the complementary
hues to Lawrence's ruddy tones and, beyond this, developing the metaphor of
the assembled Academy pictures as the body of British art, Raeburn supplied
the melancholy balance to the sanguine humour of Lawrence's much more
fleshly portraiture. Raeburn's perceived mode of modest retirement, and the
flatness of his images, soothed the sensual excess of the English artist's pictures to which non-optical epithets were often applied, especially 'tasty', and

in which mouths were represented as veritable orifices, not just patterns on the face.[65] Robert Louis Stevenson, reviewing the Raeburn retrospective held in Edinburgh in 1876, wrote bluntly that in his portraits 'you miss sex', and there seems to have been, in the London critics' constant harping on the excessive green of Raeburn's palette (which is not always obvious today), a distinct echo of the association of that colour with sexlessness.[66] Green Sickness, or Chlorosis, was supposed to be an illness, causing greenness of the skin, occurring particularly in unmarried young women suffering from the lack of a sex life.[67] In Raeburn, the perceived excess of green was it seems partly suggested by the apparent erotic deficit which his pictures presented in comparison with the sexier portraits of his English contemporaries, a deficit in turn associated with the artist's imagined own weak libido evident in his retirement from Academic competition (most obviously in his declining to canvass for votes in the RA elections). As we have noted, his female portraits, in their anonymity, implied a perhaps excessive modesty, while the only named female sitter, the romantically distracted *Lady Gordon-Cumming*, wore a dress, Carey tells us, of 'dark olive'.[68]

In summary, it seems clear that in their comments on Raeburn the London critics were interpreting his pictures as a necessary complement to the English works on show at the Academy exhibitions. This effectively incorporated him, and by extension Scotland, into the British school of art and the Royal Academy's leadership of it. Further, one of Raeburn's special contributions to the newly extended British school was to provide a retiring modesty compensating for Lawrence's excessive corporal projection. This latter role took place, it seems, to some degree on a subliminal register, the supposed greenness of Raeburn appearing as a kind of after-image consequent on a partially suppressed anxiety over the full-blooded bodies of Lawrence.

The apparent flatness of Raeburn's pictures, and the imagined passive persona of the artist himself, helped generate another layer of interpretation, turning now on contemporary theories of perception and image-making, an interpretation which was again not brought to explicit statement but which is suggested in some scattered references. In this implied line of interpretation, Raeburn's art again played foil to the leading English artists, pointing up the modernity of their style by holding on to a model of representation – the passive mode of receiving images through a camera obscura – which had been superseded by more dynamic models of generating pictures.

Since the later nineteenth century Raeburn has been recruited as a recent ancestor of Impressionism, a member of a select band of artists – foremost among them being Diego Velázquez and Frans Hals – able to see with a transparency of vision unavailable to more 'classical' or academic artists.[69] His naturalism – which as we have been stressing was often denied by his English contemporaries – was thus a timeless quality, one Raeburn managed somehow to tune into perhaps by virtue of his stoic independence from the art-worlds of his own day. But in the twentieth century, Raeburn's transparency was recruited as an aspect of his Scottishness. During the 1980s in particular this quality of Raeburn's was represented as a fundamental link with the Scottish Enlightenment's investigations of psychology and epistemology, entrenching the artist thoroughly in a Scottish cultural tradition. By the time of the 1997 Raeburn exhibition mounted in Edinburgh and London (in the year of the referendum which led to the re-establishment of a Scottish Parliament) a contributor to the catalogue stated, as if it were generally accepted, that Raeburn was 'the visual philosopher and moralist of the Scottish Enlightenment'.[70] The same writer even went so far as to make the improbable claim that 'Raeburn shared the [Scottish] moralists' distrust of genius and high rank'.[71] There are plenty of worthwhile debates to be joined around such essentialising of a democratic Scottish culture. One might easily kick off such a conversation by noting how the artist's apparent readiness to abandon Edinburgh for London in 1810 suggests a less than absolute commitment to the former: a cheap shot perhaps. Or we might point out that it was several times observed how often the viewer is required literally to *look up to* Raeburn's sitters, whom he was said to have positioned on a platform in his painting room.[72] But here I would like to pursue what I take to be the essential point urged in favour of the 'Enlightenment Raeburn', that is, his pictures' supposed affinity with the Common Sense school of Scottish philosophy.

In his 1986 survey, *Painting in Scotland: The Golden Age*, Duncan Macmillan argued that there was in Raeburn a realism, a rejection of idealism, that corresponded with the philosopher Thomas Reid's refutation of the epistemological scepticism of Locke and Hume, for whom knowledge of the world can only ever be through *ideas* (sense impressions) of what *appear* to be objects. For Reid such scepticism led directly to religious doubt and he insisted that, as common sense inclines us to believe, it is indeed possible to infer that objects we perceive really have an independent existence (using intuitions or suggestions generated by an in-built facility for interpreting the language of sensation). Now surely if we are to characterise, with Macmillan, Raeburn as a kind of Impressionist *avant le mot* ('We are given a surface pattern in which structure is left to look after itself'[73]) then the Common Sense school is precisely the wrong affiliation to suggest, given its insistence upon the actuality of the world, and given Impressionism's being predicated upon optical sensation. It seems clear that in fact Raeburn's substance-less forms, demolished by light and expressed on the canvas without relief, fit much better the older model, famously adopted by Locke, of the mind as a camera obscura into which images are projected, the ultimate source of which we cannot ever be completely certain of. It is true that Reid makes a distinction between perceiving light and perceiving objects, and that he assumes the former is of little concern to anyone but the painter (that is, the perception of light *per se* is of little everyday practical use for finding our way in the world but artists need to learn to isolate its appearance in order to paint convincingly).[74] But that Reid makes this assumption about painters generally in a book written in the early 1760s makes it hard to see how it can be of peculiar relevance to Raeburn. Once we reverse Macmillan's account of Raeburn's relationship to the Locke / Reid argument, this will help us understand the last layer of English interpretation of the artist referred to above.

In the year after Raeburn's death Hazlitt asked this rhetorical question: 'What has the dry, husky, economic eye of Scotland to do with the florid hues and luxuriant extravagance of Rubens? Nothing'.[75] The contrast Hazlitt insists upon echoes the characterisation we have offered of the London critics' view of Raeburn as sexless, and places it in a larger context of English suspicion of Scottish philosophy, associated as it was understood to be – by the early nineteenth century – with 'economic man' and godlessness. Looking again at Farington's comparison between Raeburn's pictures and images thrown into a camera obscura, with which this essay began, the association appears flattering from the conventional perspective of Art History. Photography was only years away, destined to be pioneered in Edinburgh, and we may feel that somehow Raeburn manages, as if through some special local optical insight, to be proto-photographic.[76] But at bottom, the problem of Raeburn in London was that he was perceived there from a *post*-photographic point of view, that is he was seen as working within a redundant, essentially monocular and mechanistic model of perception.[77]

Farington's comparison was made at a moment when the Lockean camera obscura model of perception was, according to Jonathan Crary's influential re-reading of the history of visuality, on the point of being superseded.[78] New physiological models, emphasising the body's own capacity to generate colours and indeed images, replaced the more passive model of the mind as an empty camera. The new understanding of vision embraced the binocular viewer, and therefore the stereoscopic, three-dimensional images which supplanted the model of the image projected upon a flat surface (the wall of the camera, or the canvas). In London, and archetypically at the Royal Academy exhibitions, the modern viewer was mobile, unlike the static camera, in search of figures in relief with which to match their own sense of the active physicality of looking. Blake's image of *Newton* (1795) was, *pace* Robert Hunt, in keeping with its times in deriding the monocular and mechanistic legacy of the Scientific Revolution. We can find a less explicit, but still comparable, satire in the gentle humour of Wilkie's *Letter of Introduction* (exh. RA 1814) in which a bust of Locke helps set the scene in the study of an Enlightenment *philosophe* now finding himself disconcertingly out of kilter with the nineteenth century.[79] Wilkie's *Rabbit on the Wall* – a picture about projected images, which, so to speak, ran against Raeburn's own rabbit – should also be seen as a moment where a philosophy of perception became a joke.

Raeburn's flattened images registered in London as relics of an antiquated mode of picture-making, one reliant upon the passive camera model of the Enlightenment and thereby associated with the 'dry' scientism supposedly characterising that tradition, especially in Scotland. His paintings' flavour of the camera obscura suggested a monocular flatness entailing the absence of the objective world, while their lack of background removed them from actual spaces and their melancholy figures wanted relief. Raeburn's images had the aura of having been *processed* in some way, and therefore some kind of optical device seemed to be needed to reactivate these representations – to turn them back into proper pictures. In 1809 an English traveller in Scotland signing themselves only 'R. T.' published their impression of Raeburn's *Clerk* double-portrait (the one shown in London in 1792), now encountered at Penicuik, a picture which came to life only once re-processed through a monocular optical instrument:

> The lady leans her beautiful naked arm and hand on the Baronet's shoulder; and, seen with a perspective, or what is commonly called an opera-glass, the illusion is so great from the skill with which the light and shade are managed, that one might almost fancy the persons represented were living.[80]

Raeburn's pictures were thus perceived by Farington and 'R. T.' as having a special relationship with monocular technology which by the early nineteenth century seemed, to the visual culture of the period, a hangover from a more mechanistic age. Later generations, after the successes of photography and of Impressionism, were able retrospectively to adopt Raeburn as a precursor of late nineteenth-century visual culture, and thereby to anoint him as in some sense 'modern' or even avant-garde in having been ahead of the game. This essay has argued that the artist's own London contemporaries saw him very differently, as the assimilated 'other' of the English school of painting, the crowd-pleasing novelties of which both enthused and troubled the critics. Cast as the alternative to the uncompromisingly competitive and explicitly erotic Lawrence, Raeburn in his London guise was something of a phantom. This image of the aloof, independent, cerebral, mechanistic

Scottish portrait painter was conjured up in the eyes of metropolitan viewers thrilled by, and yet apprehensive about, their own modernity.

Notes

1. Joseph Farington, *Diary*, Kathryn Cave, Kenneth Garlick and Angus Macintyre (eds), 16 vols, with index volume by Evelyn Newby, New Haven and London, 1978–98, V, pp. 1631, 1641, entries for 23 and 30 September 1801.
2. Cunningham 1843, I, pp. 296–9.
3. Holger Hoock, *The King's Artists: The Royal Academy of Arts and the Politics of British Culture 1760–1840*, Oxford, 2003, p. 107.
4. *Repository of Arts*, June 1811, p. 344.
5. Nicholas Tromans, *David Wilkie: The People's Painter*, Edinburgh, 2007, pp. 220, 247.
6. William Carey, 'Edinburgh Artists and Amateurs', *New Monthly Magazine*, October 1819, p. 340; *Literary Chronicle*, 16 June 1821, p. 382.
7. For instance see Duncan Thomson, 'Henry Raeburn', *Oxford Dictionary of National Biography*, Oxford, 2004, http://www.oxforddnb.com/index/101023007/ Henry-Raeburn (last accessed 29 May 2012).
8. *Literary Chronicle*, 29 May 1819, p. 29; *New Monthly Magazine*, June 1819, p. 455. The Macnabbs of Arthurstone assumed the clan chiefdom from the family of Raeburn's sitter in the twentieth century.
9. *Morning Chronicle*, 31 May 1792.
10. Exh. RA 1818: see Greig 1911, pp. xliv–xlv.
11. For details of the scientific interests of Lady Gordon-Cumming (c. 1798–1842) see M. R. S. Creese, 'Fossil hunters, a cave explorer and a rock analyst: notes on some early women contributors to geology' in C. V. Burek and B. Higgs (eds), *The Role of Women in the History of Geology*, London, 2007, pp. 40–1.
12. For Skirving see Mackie in Edinburgh and London 1997–8, p. 208 (cf. Stephen Lloyd, *Raeburn's Rival: Archibald Skirving*, exh. cat., SNPG, Edinburgh, 1999, no. 155); for Constable see *Literary Chronicle*, 17 May 1823, p. 317.
13. Edinburgh and London 1997–8, p. 26, following W. T. Whitley, *Art in England 1800–1820*, Cambridge, 1928, p. 199, counts five documented or inferable visits to London: 1784, 1786 (i.e. en route to and from Rome), 1810, 1812 and 1813. While there may have been further visits, it is thus possible that Raeburn was never in London as a Royal Academician.
14. Farington, *Diary*, XII, p. 4268, entry for 19 December 1812; Cunningham 1829–33, V, p. 231.
15. Greig 1911, p. xlvi.
16. *Public Ledger*, 7 May 1810.
17. Farington, *Diary*, XIV, p. 5043, entry for 30 June 1817. Eventually Raeburn

was allowed to sign the Roll of Academicians *in absentia* from London (Royal Academy Council Minutes, RA Library, London, RAA/PC/1/5, p. 413, 29 August 1817).

18. Cunningham 1829–33, V, p. 231.

19. Lawrence to Farington, 17 February 1815 (RA Library, LAW/2/98). The genre specialist Edward Bird was elected on the same evening. For Lawrence's portraiture see now A. Cassandra Albinson, Peter Funnell and Lucy Peltz (eds), *Thomas Lawrence: Rregency Power and Brilliance*, exh. cat., Yale Center for British Art, New Haven and National Portrait Gallery, London, 2010, p. 217.

20. 20 February 1815 (Fondation Custodia, Institut Néerlandais, Paris).

21. RA Council Minutes, RA Library, RAA/PC/1/5, p. 226, 10 November 1815.

22. However the portraitist John Hoppner, whose death in 1810 had encouraged Raeburn to visit London, was represented in the Diploma Collection by a self-portrait. See Sidney C. Hutchison, *The History of the Royal Academy, 1768–1986*, London, 1986, p. 74.

23. Phillipson in Edinburgh and London 1997–8, p. 37.

24. On the iconography of children in British art of this period, among a now substantial literature see most recently Marcia Pointon, '"Charming Little Brats": Sir Thomas Lawrence's Portraits of Children' in Albinson, ibid. (note 19), pp. 55–83.

25. Helmut von Erffa and Allen Staley, *The Paintings of Benjamin West*, New Haven and London, 1986, p. 163.

26. On art criticism in this period see J. D. O'Hara, 'Hazlitt and Romantic Criticism of the Arts', *Journal of Aesthetics and Art Criticism*, XXVII, no. 1, 1968, pp. 73–85; Maura Barnett, 'The Contemporary Response to British Art before Ruskin's *Modern Painters*', unpublished Ph.D. thesis, University of Warwick, 1993; and Mark Hallett, '"The Business of Criticism": The Press and the Royal Academy Exhibition in Eighteenth-Century London', in D. H. Solkin (ed.), *Art on the Line: The Royal Academy Exhibitions at Somerset House 1780–1836*, exh. cat., Courtauld Gallery, London; New Haven and London, 2001, pp. 65–75.

27. For instance see the *Examiner*, 4 July 1819, p. 430. Jordan Mearns' chapter in this volume pursues the theme of Raeburn's 'manly' portraits.

28. For instance see the *Sun*, 11 May 1818, apparently confusing nos. 32 and 268.

29. *Literary Gazette*, 22 June 1822, p. 393.

30. Marcia Pointon, '"Portrait! Portrait!! Portrait!!!"' in Solkin, ibid. (note 26), p. 105.

31. Press Cuttings from English Newspapers, National Art Library, London, vol. 3, p. 886; *Literary Register*, 7 June 1823, p. 365.

32. Hutchison 1986, p. 82.

33. *Repository of Arts*, June 1810, p. 367.

34. *Public Ledger*, 7 May 1810; *St. James's Chronicle*, 8 May 1810, p. 4.

35. National Art Library cuttings, vol. 5, p. 1210 (unidentified).

36. Morrison 1844, p. 17; cf. John Milton, *Paradise Lost*, Book 2, ll. 666 ff.

37. *Examiner*, 5 May 1811, p. 283 (for Kames).

38. *Examiner*, 5 July 1812, p. 428.

39. *Examiner*, 13 June 1813, p. 378.

40. *Examiner*, 31 May 1818, p. 347; 4 July 1819, p. 430: cf. *Twelfth Night*, II. iv, 99.

41. *Examiner*, 22 June 1823, p. 411.

42. Tromans 2007, p. 24.

43. *European Magazine*, May 1823, p. 443.

44. *Repository of Arts*, June 1811, p. 342. Nasmyth, son of the Edinburgh landscape painter and teacher Alexander Nasmyth, had recently relocated to London from Scotland.

45. Greig 1911, p. xlvi.

46. Duncan Macmillan, 'Raeburn' in David Bindman (ed.), *The Thames and Hudson Encyclopaedia of British Art*, London, 1985, p. 200. For Scott's view of Raeburn see Stephen Lloyd, '"A Very Chowder Headed Person": Raeburn's Portraits of Scott', in Iain Gordon Brown (ed.), *Abbotsford and Sir Walter Scott. The Image and the Influence*, Edinburgh, 2003, pp. 98–114.

47. *Sun*, 8 June 1810.

48. *Sun*, 6 June 1816; 23 May 1815. The *Sun* was especially approving, on patriotic grounds, of Raeburn's *Admiral Milne* (23 May 1818).

49. See Michael Durey, 'The Dublin Society of United Irishmen and the Politics of the Carey-Drennan Dispute, 1792–1794', *Historical Journal*, XXXVI, no. 1, 1994, pp. 89–111.

50. Carey 1819, p. 341.

51. *Literary Gazette*, 21 June 1817, p. 347.

52. By the time of Raeburn's death Carey evidently considered himself something of an authority on his work among London art critics and suggested to the artist's son that he should write, or at least revise, his 'official' obituary: Henry Raeburn junior to Carey, 15 March 1824 (transcription in Whitley Notebooks, Department of Prints and Drawings, BM, London, vol. 10, fol. 1223; the *Annual Biography* for 1823, London 1824, contained an anonymous account of Raeburn usually attributed to Walter Scott and Hugh Murray).

53. *Morning Herald*, 1 May 1810.

54. Edinburgh and London 1997–8, no. 61.

55. *Literary Chronicle*, 29 May 1819, p. 29; *Literary Gazette*, 19 June 1819, p. 394.

56. Edinburgh and London 1997–8, p. 186.

57. Letter to sitter's husband, Sir William Gordon-Cumming, December 1818; so the judgment is in the way of flattery, and the sentence continues: 'I may thank the subject for that [the portrait's beauty] you will say' (photograph of letter in

Witt Library, London; cited without source in Edinburgh and London 1997–8, p. 27).

58. Cunningham (1829–33, V, pp. 236–7) suggested Raeburn did change his backgrounds to placate London critics.

59. *Scots Magazine*, June 1815, p. 413 (letter from 'U. F.'); cf. same journal, May 1815, p. 329.

60. *Scots Magazine*, May 1812, p. 350; see Edinburgh and London 1997–8, no. 48 for the portrait mentioned.

61. Edinburgh and London 1997–8, pp. 26, 208.

62. *Arnold's Library of the Fine Arts*, December 1832, p. 143; *Morning Post*, 3 October 1822. A less flattering epithet for Raeburn was 'the Lawrence of Scotland', *Literary Chronicle*, 17 May 1823, p. 317.

63. *Examiner*, 16 June 1816, pp. 380–1.

64. *Champion*, 7 May 1814, p. 149.

65. For 'tasty' as applied to Lawrence, see for instance *Belle Assemblée*, June 1811, p. 316 (*Mrs Stratton*) and *London Magazine*, June 1820, p. 701 (*Selina Meade*).

66. Stevenson 1992, p. 36.

67. Forming part of new discourses of adolescence, Chlorosis 'was marked by a-sexuality'; see Karl Figlio, 'Chlorosis and Chronic Disease in Nineteenth-Century Britain: The Social Constitution of Somatic Illness in a Capitalist Society', *Social History*, III, no. 2, 1978, p. 178.

68. *Literary Gazette*, 21 June 1817, p. 346. According to Alexander Fraser ('Sir Henry Raeburn', *Portfolio*, X, 1879, p. 202) 'The walls of his [Raeburn's] painting-room were a dark olive'.

69. See W. D. McKay, 'Raeburn's Technique: Its Affinities with Modern Painting', *Studio*, February 1908, pp. 3–22. Wilkie had compared Raeburn to Velázquez as early as the 1820s (Cunningham, 1843, II, pp. 504–5).

70. Phillipson in Edinburgh and London 1997–8, p. 29; see Forbes 1998, pp. 223–6, for interpretation of the exhibition's reception.

71. Edinburgh and London 1997–8, p. 35.

72. Cunningham 1829–33, V, p. 241.

73. Edinburgh and London 1986–7, p. 79.

74. Thomas Reid, *An Inquiry into the Human Mind, on the Principles of Common Sense* [1764], 4th edn, London, 1785, pp. 165–6.

75. William Hazlitt, *Sketches of the Principal Picture-Galleries in England*, London, 1824, p. 56.

76. Our concern here remains the interpretation of Raeburn; it is not important for the present argument to determine whether or not he did in fact experiment with a camera obscura. He certainly used a camera lucida: see Edinburgh and London 1997–8, no. 65.

77. See Geoffrey Batchen, *Burning with Desire: The Conception of Photography*,

Cambridge, MA, 1997, on the visual culture of photography in the decades prior to its official invention in 1839.

78. Jonathan Crary, *Techniques of the Observer: On Vision and Modernity in the Nineteenth Century*, Cambridge, MA, 1992, chapter 2.

79. *Inquirer*, II, 1814, p. 184.

80. R. T., 'Some Observations made in a five weeks' recent excursion from London to Edinburgh and back', *Belle Assemblée*, November 1809, p. 195. The instrument is defined in Alexander Jamieson, *A Dictionary of Mechanical Science, Arts, Manufactures, and Miscellaneous Knowledge*, 2 vols, London, 1829, II, pp. 740–1. Among the Scottish philosophers to discuss its significance for viewing paintings was Reid (*An Inquiry* . . ., 1785, pp. 400–1).

8

The Critique of the Modern French School of Painting from Reynolds to Constable

Philippe Bordes

Writing to David Wilkie (1785–1841), on 12 March 1823, Henry Raeburn (1756–1823) fully endorsed his criticism of the art of Jacques-Louis David, that the exhibition of the repetition of *The Coronation of Josephine* in London had prompted him to express:

> I have read portions of your last to gen[eral]ly very good judges who have seen David[']s works and who coincide most perfectly with your criticisms about him and which I think might be transferred to the whole of the French school – but this is too wide a field to enter upon at present.[1]

Wilkie's remarks are lost, but no doubt they echoed criticism voiced with increasing confidence since the outbreak of the French Revolution. By 1789, after several decades of enlightened moralising on cultural matters on both sides of the Channel, taking a stand on contemporary art practice and production had become impossible without bringing in broader social and political concerns. In Britain, evaluation of the modern French School of painting was over-determined by the reality of war with France, from 1792 to 1802 and again from 1803 to 1815, with only the year long Peace of Amiens interrupting these two long stretches of military conflict. This situation fostered a critical vision of the character and culture of the other country conditioned by nationalist bias and commercial imperatives. Perceptions however were rarely attuned to what was actually going on at a given moment, not only because of the sporadic nature of the direct contacts, but also due to the rapid pace of change in the Parisian art world after the Revolution. Even around the time of Raeburn's exchange with Wilkie, notwithstanding the climate of political appeasement introduced by the Restoration regime, at least one writer was still bitten by Napoleonic arrogance when he castigated the French nation as 'not inspired with genuine love of art: It is merely a love of display. In the composition of his piece, the artist is more solicitous to exhibit his own talents than to represent the simple truth; in purchasing it, the patron is equally desirous of displaying himself. Even their national gallery is display, where the noblest works are prized, not as triumphs of genius, but as trophies of conquest'.[2] This last remark is a reminder that the creation of the museum in Paris, by focusing attention on the Italian and Northern Schools, deflected confrontation between the French and English Schools and revived the earlier literary and cultural debate opposing *anciens et modernes*. The new institution modified the criteria of judgment, imposing on contemporary works more strongly than before the measure of the great masters, and further heightened the drama of art practice by offering artists only two options: the promise of immortality with the Old Masters or the cruel prospect of oblivion.

This chapter will explore the 'too wide a field' that Raeburn chose not to enter upon in his letter to Wilkie, in line with two pioneering studies of British art by William Vaughan published in 1990 and 1993.[3] Vaughan documents how the negative construction of contemporary French painting helped to consolidate a sense of identity and confidence among artists in Britain after the death of Joshua Reynolds (1723–92). His second study, focused on Jacques-Louis David (1748–1825), takes its cue from an aspersion – 'David's brickdust' – coined in his diary by Benjamin Robert Haydon (1786–1846) in 1841 when the older painter was embittered to see the decoration of the Houses of Parliament allotted to a younger generation influenced by German mural painters. For Haydon, Britain was falling under the spell of an imported style, with its roots in the French School. He writes: 'We escaped the contagion of David's brickdust which infected the continent, and the frescoes at Munich are but a branch of the same Upas tree'.[4] His metaphor is telling, for the sap of the Upas tree was a substance employed for poisoning arrowheads.

A temporal distortion between what was actually being painted in France and what was presumed to be painted is already evident in Reynolds's *Discourses*. The president of the Royal Academy, in his sixth discourse delivered in 1774, invoked as major figures of the 'modern' French School three deceased painters: Antoine Watteau (1684–1721), Coypel, either Antoine (1661–1722) or Charles-Antoine (1694–1752), and François Boucher (1703–1770).[5] Reynolds had spent time in Paris in 1752 on his way back from Italy, and again in 1768. When he spoke at the academy those French painters who most deserved credit for the revival of the historical genre, Charles-Joseph Natoire (1700–77), Carle Vanloo (1705–65), Joseph-Marie Vien (1716–1809) and Gabriel-François Doyen (1726–1806), were apparently unknown to him.

It was no longer ignorance, but bad faith which inspired a later declaration in his twelfth discourse of December 1784: 'Our neighbours, the French, are much in this practice of *extempore* invention, and their dexterity is such as to excite admiration, if not envy; but how rarely can this praise be given to their finished pictures!' He refers to Boucher as the 'late Director of their Academy', a misleading remark implying that the teaching institution was as he had left it at his death in 1770, a slur since he insists that he took pride in working without models. Reynolds manages to praise the 'recourse to nature' in Boucher's early work, but ends with a damning peremptory evaluation that engulfs the whole French School: 'his imitators are indeed abominable'.[6] In truth, Reynolds was making his argument just when David was in Rome painting the *Oath of the Horatii* (Paris, Musée du Louvre). It was too early for reports on the work in progress to reach London, but presumably some news filtered through regarding the group of young history painters that had entered the scene at the Paris Salons since 1779. David's showing in the 1781 and 1783 exhibitions had in particular created quite a stir in the press and society circles.

The change of direction in French painting was remarked upon by an anonymous reviewer of the Salon in 1785, who signed as '*le peintre anglais*' but who was probably a Frenchman passing himself off for a fashionable critic, since he offers not one comparative reference to the arts in England. Of interest though, while he censures the last flickers of the mannered French style, he characterises the new style as '*froid*' and warns repeatedly against an excess of '*sécheresse*'. The *Oath of the Horatii* merits his praise, but he scoffs at the partisanship it generates: '*Et on appelle génie ce qui est froid et raide*'.[7] A true Briton, possibly John Boydell, the enterprising print-publisher and art entrepreneur, did travel to Paris two years later to visit the Salon. The resulting 'Observations on the State of the Arts in Paris' appeared in the London society journal *The World* in October 1787.[8] The explicit aim of the critic was to dispel a prejudice concerning the 'present school of painting in France', too readily identified in Britain with 'the wretched productions of their last set of artists, which are cited proverbially as models of bad taste'; he goes so far as to invoke 'a new scene of emulation, and perhaps of imitation, well worthy the attention of our English students'. There follows an enthusiastic and detailed description of David's *Death of Socrates* (New York, The Metropolitan Museum of Art), 'the most exquisite and admirable effort of art which has appeared since the *Capella Sistina* and the *Stanze of Raffaelle*.' Reynolds no longer ignored the art of David after the publication of this article, for he had the flattering text translated and sent to the French painter with his compliments. Encouraged by this contact, David had Brooke Boothby ask Reynolds for permission to submit a picture to the Royal Academy exhibition in London in 1788. Boothby indicated to Reynolds that David did not fear making such a bold proposal for he 'knows enough of the liberality of your mind'. Indeed, when president of the Royal Academy Reynolds was most welcoming to foreign artists, and as late as 1791 he gave his support to the *émigré* portraitist Jean-Laurent Mosnier (1743–1808).[9]

By the time of Reynolds's last *Discourse*, delivered in December 1790, reaction to the violent sequence of events that shook monarchical authority in France had closed such cosmopolitan perspectives and reinforced isolationist sentiment. Burke's *Reflections on the Revolution in France* had appeared the previous month and even Reynolds was receptive to his critique of initiatives that purported to be rational, but were too abstract and contradicted by the complexities of human nature and society. The desire to distance Britain from the turmoil across the Channel prompted an about-turn with regard to the new style of the French School. Although Reynolds most likely had not seen pictures by David and his pupils, he was aware that their style could not be subsumed within the *manière française* of Boucher. In his last *Discourse*, he thus grafted what he negatively terms the 'newly-hatched unfledged opinions' – not clearly identified but presumably the antique style whose emergence in France and elsewhere he had witnessed – onto the classicising history paintings that had come out of the Roman artistic scene and which had always made him uncomfortable. He had in mind classicising compositions by Nathaniel Dance (1735–1811), Gavin Hamilton (1723–98), Anton Raphael Mengs (1728–79) and probably by association, those produced in London by Benjamin West (1738–1820). He could chart through prints the prestige, if not the popularity, of what appeared to be slavish imitations of antique bas-reliefs and works by Nicolas Poussin (1594–1665). His recent change of mind concerning the art of Thomas Gainsborough (1727–88) further exemplifies his mounting hostility toward the ideal beauty, smooth finish and taut draughtsmanship said to characterise the modern French School. Refusing to go along with the canonical lesson of Pliny's tale of Zeuxis and the maids of Crotona favoured by continental academies, he saw a dangerous course for young artists in the notion that a 'union of different excellencies would be the perfection of Art'.[10] Holding theorists in France led by André Félibien and Roger de Piles explicitly responsible for such unnatural abstractions, he found himself adopting an aesthetic position which paralleled the political critique of his friend Burke.

As for David in the meantime, sending a picture to London as he had intended was no longer his priority, for Revolutionary events prompted him to focus on reform of the Parisian academy. Descriptions of his works nonetheless reached Britain from Rome and Paris. Visiting David's studio in Paris in 1802, Joseph Farington, noted that he 'had in England heard much' of the *Horatii* and *Brutus* (Musée du Louvre, Paris) that finally he could contemplate. He wrote in his diary: 'Fuseli and Hoppner thought it [the *Horatii*] his best picture, and the latter that it was a good deal like the painting of N[athaniel] Dance. I had heard so much of it that it did not answer my expectation. I thought it poorly conceived and a dry picture, formally composed and unnatural throughout.' His remarks on *Brutus* were in a similar vein: 'As a composition, the whole is in my opinion unconnected and badly composed'.[11]

Between the publication of Burke's *Reflections* and the Peace of Amiens, the principal voice crediting David with the restoration of 'a higher and better order of things' in French art, was James Barry. In his *Letter to the Dilettanti Society* of 1799, he dared to write: 'With hands lift up to heaven, and a heart full of exultation, I then hail the generous exertion of David and his noble fellow-labourers in that glorious undertaking, wishing it a long and a prosperous carriere.' Regretting the lack of support for history painting in Britain, he added:

> How happy am I to think, that they have a public who will meet their work with correspondent feelings, who will give it the same generous, becoming patriotic reception, which has ever so peculiarly and so exemplarily characterised that gallant nation![12]

Barry's provocative vision, in a time of war with France, led to his expulsion from the Royal Academy, on the grounds of openly favouring a republican government and, according to Farington, because 'he has highly commended David', who continued to be rebuked, long after the Terror, as a former agent of Robespierre with blood on his hands.[13] With regard to artistic style, Barry had promoted a middle course, between over-scrupulous imitation of the antique – which he labels the *statuino* or stony manner – and disregard of such models:

> The grand style of art now pursuing in France does high honour to their choice who adopted it; [. . .] I sincerely hope they will now, in the close of the eighteenth century, and with the glorious collection of pictures which gives such brilliancy to the Louvre, be able wisely to keep the right channel between the Scylla and Charybdis on either side.[14]

For Barry, approval of David's example of artistic ambition and civic responsibility did not preclude caution against the dangers of a radically classical pictorial style. An Irish friend and patron of Barry from Cork, Cooper Penrose, a collector of antiques and old masters as well as an activist against the slave trade, sought out David during his visit to Paris in 1802 to commission his portrait. Like Barry he was probably as much attracted by the Frenchman's Revolutionary reputation as by his international renown as a painter.[15]

The contemporary painting that most attracted British visitors in Paris during the Peace of Amiens was the *Intervention of the Sabine Women* (1799; Musée du Louvre) by David, a spectacular canvas he was promoting in a permanent exhibition in the Louvre palace. It appeared to possess all the qualities and defects of the modern French School. Farington reported at length the observations of his fellow visitors to Paris, one of whom expressed the general opinion that 'French painters have a great deal of that knowledge which is wanting in England, careful drawing and finishing', but that their compositions were artificial. Farington recorded his own opinion: 'I never saw a composition in which the art of arranging was less concealed'.[16] Whereas in Britain painting had parted ways with sculpture – Canova's patrons had no qualms sitting to Lawrence for their portrait – in France until the advent of the romantic generation, the aesthetic dependence of painters on antique statuary remained strong. West, also in Paris during the Peace of Amiens, considered that 'the French paint statues', which, as William Vaughan has observed, was a remark also aimed at the lack of humanity that the violence of the Revolutionary years had revealed. This peculiarity of French pictorial style had become so distinctive by 1823 that a critic could posit a reverse flow of influence, from painting to sculpture, and qualify a *Dancer* by Canova to be 'of that fantastic French school, to which this celebrated artist belonged', a novel remark which would have surely horrified the recently deceased Italian sculptor.[17]

It is possible that Raeburn's hostility to the polished manner ascribed to David and his school was an indirect response to criticism of 'a want of finish' addressed to his portraits by London critics, as in 1815, or of being 'half-finished' according to a patron in 1819.[18] He was probably not aware that in France as well, after the Revolution, a heated debate prevailed regarding finish, a pictorial quality predicated on the relation of painting to sculpture. In texts written much earlier but only published in the 1790s, Diderot had railed against what he called '*léché*', literally 'licked', a cold and insipid overworking giving the unpleasant sensation that painting was toilsome.[19] By David's time, such technical proficiency had suffered much criticism, although the success of *Cupid and Psyche* (Salon of 1798; Musée du Louvre) by his pupil François Gérard (1770–1837) and the master's *Sabine Women* focused attention on polished execution, a manner which gained authority within the context of the museum's unequivocal homage to sixteenth-century Italian painting. Although no painters could ignore that many critics as early as 1795 were resolutely unhappy with the '*productions sèches et froides*' of this '*nouvelle méthode*' founded on the imitation of sculpture, the notion that a nacreous finish visually metaphorised the smooth forms of antique statues remained entrenched. It is paradoxical, in light of constant British projection of this concern onto David, to note that he criticised this mode and was determined to give greater painterliness to his manner and warm his palette after completing the *Sabine Women*. This led Farington to write that his portrait of Penrose had 'a sort of woolley appearance as if done in crayons', hardly a suggestion of high finish.[20]

Criticism of French predilection for finish was brutally voiced in 1805 by John Hoppner (1758–1810) in the preface to his *Oriental Tales*, with regard to portraits that Élisabeth Vigée-Lebrun (1755–1842) had painted two years earlier in London. After declaring that 'the works of the present French School' bore no relation to good art, 'whether they be painted by David or Madame Le Brun', he formulated more specific criticism with regard to her painting:

> Few things have tended to produce more error in judgement passed on pictures, than the imposing quality of smoothness, which is generally conceived to be the effect of successful labour, and close attention to finishing; and appears to have been spread over the work of the insipid, as a kind of snare for the ignorant. On the art of spreading these toils, and on a feeble, vulgar, and detailed imitation of articles of furniture and dress, rests the whole of Madame Le Brun's reputation.

Shedding all sense of restraint, he belittled 'the expensive trash of this lady' and concluded rhetorically: 'what English artist could be warmed with the frigid productions of French art?'[21]

However this hostile environment, with its roots both in traditional rivalry and in contemporary tensions, did not discourage a series of French painters from transporting their works across the Channel, lured by the prospect of sales, private commissions and, in the event of a successful exhibition, financial rewards along with the limelight of an international reputation. In June 1801, Joseph Boze (1745–1826) presented the topical double portrait, *Bonaparte accompanied by General Berthier, at the Battle of Marengo, the moment of Victory*.[22] Other French painters were similarly keen to address curiosity in Britain for the figure of Napoleon, which could manifest itself more freely once his downfall was imminent. In December 1814 a recent portrait of *Napoleon* by Robert Lefèvre (1755–1830) was ominously advertised as 'most probably the last that will ever be painted of him in Europe'. From

April to July 1815, during the months leading to Waterloo and after the victory, on show were three works by David, who had not made the trip to London: a version of *Bonaparte crossing the Alps* (1802–3, the face reworked at a later date; Musée national du Château, Versailles,), a variant of *Napoleon in his study* (1812; French Government with a usufructurary restriction), and *Pius VII and Cardinal Caprara* (about 1805; Philadelphia Museum of Art). It was Lefèvre's portrait that caught most of the public's attention and, unlike David's three pictures, it eventually found a buyer. When the following year, in 1816, the precocious Charles Eastlake (1793–1865) exhibited his *Napoleon Bonaparte on board the 'Bellerophon' in Plymouth Sound* (Greenwich, National Maritime Museum) in London, the critic of the *Annals of the Fine Arts* was deferential towards David, but made the usual distinction between the British and the French style of painting:

> Compared with David's celebrated whole length of Bonaparte in his cabinet, it has all the individuality of parts which belong to that excellent picture, but accompanied by a certain freedom from restraint and manner, which at once decides the former as belonging to the Modern French school, and the latter as being of no school but that of nature.[23]

A few French artists were bold enough to exhibit ambitious historical compositions in London. In July 1806 Antoine Dubost (1769–1825), a pupil of David, exhibited *The Sword of Damocles* (Chhatrapati Shivaji Maharaj Vastu Sangrahalaya, formerly the Prince of Wales Museum of Western India, Mumbai), which he had shown at the Paris Salon two years earlier. Benjamin West remarked on its characteristically French qualities – 'It is finished Oh! you can have no conception how much, every particular but no whole, it is in that respect like the modern French school' – but also on new inflections to which English artists might pay attention: 'more transparency and greater force'.[24] Ten years later, in 1816, the artistic entrepreneur William Bullock took the risk of exhibiting a huge composition Guillaume Guillon-Lethiere (1760–1832) had been working on since the late 1780s, *Brutus Condemning his Sons to Death* (1812; Musée du Louvre, Paris). That same year Jean-Baptiste Wicar (1762–1834) travelled from Rome with *The Raising of the Son of the Widow of Naim* (1816; Musée des Beaux-Arts, Lille), which he probably showed in the studio of Benjamin West, an appropriate venue since the latter had for several years been working on a series of large paintings from the life of Christ. In spite of their shared grandiloquence and dramatic appeal, the Christian miracle, unlike the Roman beheading, failed to draw a public or elicit commentary in the press.[25]

West's balanced regard for Dubost's *Damocles* and his support of Wicar hints at the fact that some observers had come to recognise an evolution in French painting. After the Terror, David's pupils were determined to explore subject matter and pictorial styles that ostensibly broke with the master's practice. But could their iconographic and stylistic innovations, leading to bold dramatic effects as in Dubost's picture, still make much of a difference and appease those British artists and critics most reluctant to hold a dialogue with their traditional enemies? Many indeed believed that the youthful English school had little to gain from commerce with an exhausted French school. New conditions favouring this dialogue existed however, although narratives of exclusive British nationalism understandably downplay them. There was a growing consensus regarding the respective merits of the two rival schools, as the commentary on the Royal Academy exhibition sent to Gérard in 1822 by Barbier-Walbonne, another former pupil of David, indicates:

> Ce qu'il y a de particulier, c'est que la peinture des Anglais est pleine de lumière, de force et de richesse dans les tons. [. . .] Leurs portraits ont des reliefs que nous sommes loin d'atteindre. Il y a des portraits de [Thomas] Lawrence, de [Thomas] Phil[l]ips, etc., qui ont l'air de faire partie du public qui les regarde. L'école anglaise suit toujours l'école de Reynolds, mais avec plus de mollesse. [. . .] Malgré tous leurs défauts, leurs tableaux écraseraient les nôtres. Ils se soutiennent bien dans les galeries à côté des maîtres. La peinture de notre école paraît pédante et terne à côté de la leur. Quant au genre élevé de l'histoire, ils y sont presque nuls. Je pense même qu'ils ne songent point à y atteindre. Ils en sont à ne pas savoir dessiner une rotule. [. . .] Dans les portraits, tout est sacrifié à la tête, et je suis forcé de trouver qu'ils ont raison. M. Wilkie a un tableau, à l'exposition, qui fait foule. Le sujet est un homme qui lit le bulletin de la bataille de Waterloo. Il faut que cette bataille de Waterloo leur ait tiré une fière épine du pied, car ils en parlent encore comme d'hier.[26]

An opportunity to mollify negative attitudes toward the French School was offered in 1820 by the one-man show held by Jean-Baptiste Isabey (1767–1855) (Fig. 8.1) and William Bullock's exhibition of *The Raft of the Medusa* by Théodore Géricault (1791–1824) the following year. On both occasions the critic of *The London Literary Gazette* insisted that artists from each nation might learn from one another. Isabey, described as 'the celebrated French artist', presented seventy-four works, for the most part drawings and miniatures. The review in the *Literary Gazette* attempted to transcend divisive national sensibilities:

> That there does exist very opposite feelings with regard to art, between France and England, is not to be denied; and if it were denied, this Exhibition would

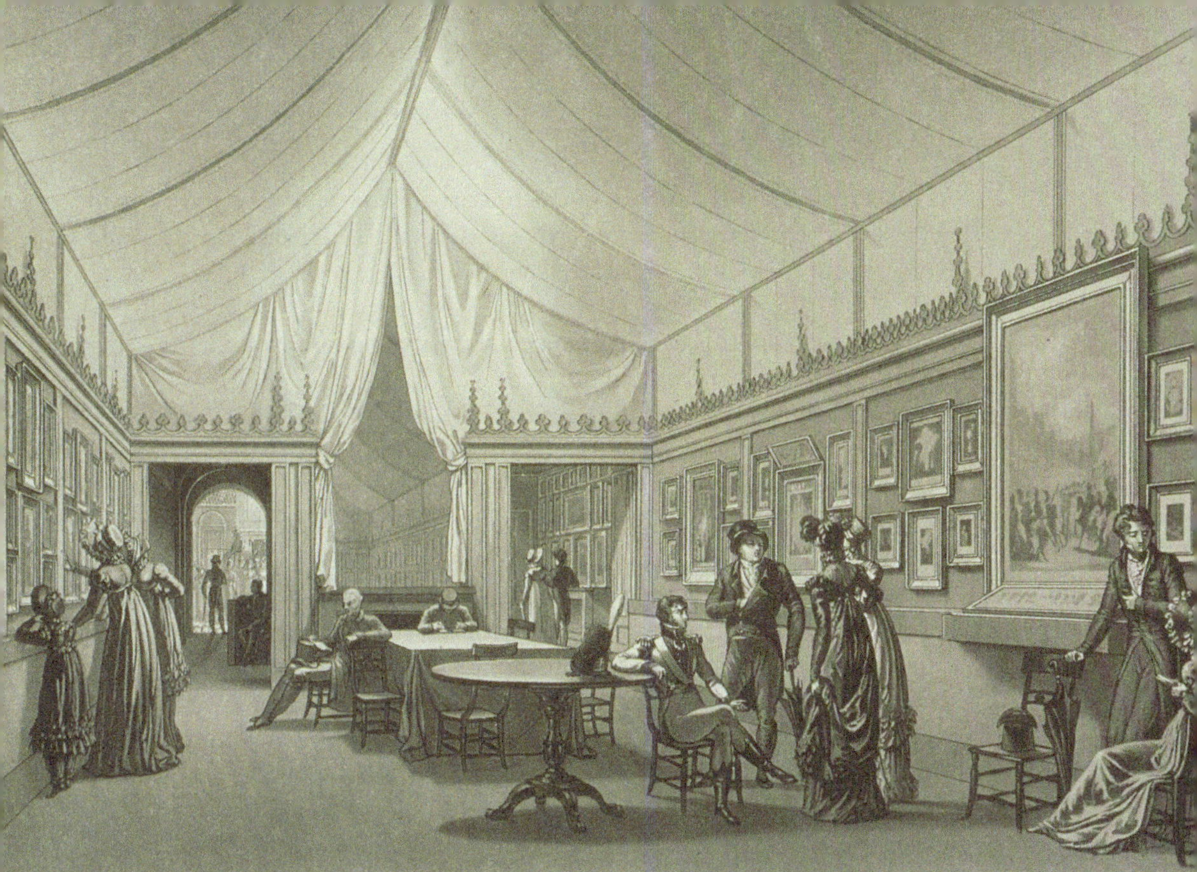

Figure 8.1 William Bennett after Jean-Baptiste Isabey, *Mons. J. Isabey's Exhibition Rooms, 61 Pall Mall / Salle d'Exhibition de J. Isabey à Londres* 1820, aquatint, 20.8×27.8cm, City of London, London Metropolitan Archives

disprove the allegation. The defects, as well as the qualities belonging to each, are distinct; and it may with justice be remarked, that relinquishing a portion of dogmatism would be extremely advantageous for either. For if there are errors to avoid, there are also beauties to imitate, on both sides; and in many instances a little of the French finish might be as beneficially bestowed upon our bolder sketches, as in others the spirit of our school might be admitted to elevate the precision of our continental competitors.[27]

This conciliatory attitude was adopted by some critics in front of Géricault's painting, which could not have been more different from Isabey's selection:

[. . .] taken all together, his work is [. . .] one of the finest specimens of the French school ever brought to this country. It cannot therefore fail to stimulate the exertions of the British talents to a further display of those powers which already have so happily and so honourably distinguished our artists and art. To Mr Bullock we think great praise is due for procuring such opportunities for examination and comparison of the two national schools. If he continues to bring over chefs-d'œuvre of French painters, he will do as good a thing as could be done to advance British art. Emulation is a noble teacher.[28]

Of course, such appeals to unprejudiced curiosity and mutual understanding would remain largely unheeded.

Unlike the French romantic artists, who constructed their identity in opposition to an earlier generation, their British contemporaries lauded their immediate forbearers with a sense of national pride. They were keen to endorse the exhibition of paintings by Reynolds, Hogarth, Gainsborough, Wilson and Zoffany that the British Institution, founded in 1805, organised on a regular basis. They also parted with their colleagues in France in their advocacy of the beauties of the art of Watteau. The sincerity of their taste is well documented and cannot be doubted, in particular in the case of Wilkie, but certainly the provocation with regard to the modern French school was relished.[29] It was more expedient to follow Reynolds's example and turn a blind eye to the diversity of the French artistic scene and the many signs of change. It was easier to simply continue to decry David and his epigones for the relatively dull range of colours they employed, for the impression of 'brickdust' as Haydon called it, and not register the richer palette and looser brushwork adopted by a number of prominent painters. In his later work David was clearly attentive to Flemish models, and even more boldly, Antoine-Jean Gros (1771–1835) revived the *Rubéniste* tradition in portraits and Napoleonic commissions that British artists and critics ignored completely.[30]

In 1835, John Constable (1776–1837) reacted harshly to works exhibited for sale in London by the family of David, deceased ten years earlier. These included *The Death of Marat* and *Mars and Venus*, the two pictures which presumably prompted this morally deprecatory remark: 'David seems to have formed his mind from three sources, *The Scaffold*, *The Hospital*, and a *bawdy house*.' The tone was far more acrimonious than his earlier comment in 1822 when, like Wilkie, he had been curious to visit the exhibition of David's *Coronation of Napoleon*. He found the French painting inferior to Veronese and Rubens, and criticised the execution, and yet seemed receptive to its modernity, adding: 'But I still much prefer it to West – only because it does not remind me of the *schools*'.[31]

Constable had made a more general point in the course of his *Lectures on Landscape Painting* in 1833. After berating '"French taste" (as opposed to good taste)', and in particular Boucher – 'Boucher is Watteau run mad – bereaved of his taste and his sense' – he attacked the successive stylistic reaction in France:

> It is remarkable how nearly, in all things, opposite extremes are allied, and how they succeed each other. The style I have been describing was followed by that which sprung out of the Revolution, when David and his contemporaries exhibited their stern and heartless petrifactions of men and women, – with tree, rocks, tables, and chairs, all equally bound to the ground by a relentless outline, and destitute of chiaroscuro, the soul and medium of art.[32]

Such a representation of the French as a profoundly perverse nation, always at odds with the order of nature, is all too familiar. The novelty in Constable's view of French painting is the sense of historical distance that inspires his vision of successive styles. But worth noting is his refusal to register the latest style, that of the artists who had acclaimed and were inspired by his own work when it had been on view at the Paris Salon in 1824. One suspects that this oversight was less tactical than during earlier decades, and more the expression of the belief that for several decades the British school had been on an independent course.[33]

Notes

1. For their help collecting material for this chapter, it is a pleasure to acknowledge the generosity of Bruno Chenique, Mehdi Korchane, Cyril Lécosse, Simon Lee, Stephen Lloyd, Olivier Meslay and Helen Smailes. Raeburn's letter (Edinburgh, NLS, MS 9835, fols. 162r–163v) is excerpted in Edinburgh and London 1997–8, p. 212 (transcript kindly provided by Stephen Lloyd). The dates and location of the exhibition of David's repetition of the *Coronation* in 1822–3 are furnished by Simon Lee, 'Napoleon amongst the Shopkeepers: David's 1815 Exhibition in London', in *David after David: Essays on the Later Work*, Mark Ledbury (ed.), Williamstown, 2007, p. 341, n. 53.
2. John S. Memes, *Memoirs of Antonio Canova with a Critical Analysis of His Works, and a Historical View of Modern Sculpture*, Edinburgh, 1825, pp. 393–4; cited by Christopher Johns, *Antonio Canova and the Politics of Patronage in Revolutionary and Napoleonic Europe*, Berkeley, 1998, p. 12.
3. William Vaughan, 'The Englishness of British Art', *Oxford Art Journal*, XIII, no. 2, 1990, pp. 11–23; and Vaughan, '"David's Brickdust" and the rise of the British school', in *Reflections of Revolution, Images of Romanticism*, Alison Yarrington and Kelvin Everest (eds), London and New York, 1993, pp. 134–58 (reprinted in *Polish and English Responses to French Art and Architecture: Contrasts and Similarities: Papers Delivered at the University of London, University of Warsaw History of Art Conference, January and September 1993*, Francis Ames-Lewis (ed.), London, 1995, pp. 95–111).
4. Quoted in ibid., 1993, p. 134. Haydon's view of the French School had been

more positive in the early 1810s, according to Frederick Cummings, 'Poussin, Haydon and *The Judgement of Solomon*', *The Burlington Magazine*, CIV, no. 709, pp. 146–52.

5. Joshua Reynolds, *Discourses on Art*, Robert R. Wark (ed.), New Haven and London, 1997, p. 108; see also pp. 51, 89 for further references to Watteau, p. 150 for Coypel, and pp. 224–5 for Boucher.

6. Ibid., 1997, pp. 224–5.

7. *Le Peintre anglais au Salon de Peintures, exposées au Louvre en l'année 1785* [Paris], 1785; *Supplément du Peintre anglais au Salon*, [Paris, 1785]. (Copies in the Bibliothèque Nationale de France, Département des Estampes et de la Photographie, Collection Deloynes, vol. 14, nos. 327–8.) The quote concerning David is from the *Supplément*, p. 3.

8. For full texts and details, see Philippe Bordes, 'Jacques-Louis David's anglophilia on the eve of the French Revolution', *The Burlington Magazine*, CXXXIV, no. 1073, August 1992, pp. 482–90.

9. For Reynolds's support of foreign artists, and in particular Mosnier, see Anne Puetz, 'Foreign Exhibitors and the British School at the Royal Academy, 1768–1823', in *Art on the Line: The Royal Academy Exhibitions at Somerset House 1780–1836*, David Solkin (ed.), New Haven and London, 2001, pp. 229–30, 236; Gerrit Walczak, 'Die Französische Revolution und der Kunstmarkt Englands: Jean-Laurent Mosnier in der Londoner Emigration', *Zeitschrift für Kunstgeschichte*, LXIX, no. 1, 2006, p. 43. Both authors note that xenophobic sentiment had become prevalent at the academy by 1790.

10. Reynolds, 1997 (as in note 5), p. 270 (*Discourse XV*, delivered on 10 December 1790).

11. Joseph Farington, *The Diary of Joseph Farington*, V (August 1801–March 1803), Kenneth Garlick and Angus Macintyre (eds), New Haven and London, 1979, p. 1862 (20 September 1802).

12. James Barry, A *Letter to the Dilettanti Society* [. . .], 2nd edn, London, 1799, p. 65.

13. On Farington's account, see William L. Pressly, *The Life and Art of James Barry*, New Haven and London, 1981, pp. 180, 222 n. 24.

14. Barry 1799 (as in note 12), p. 67. *Statuino* was a term employed by Malvasia, an author cited p. 69.

15. Philippe Bordes, *Portraiture in Paris Around 1800: Cooper Penrose by Jacques-Louis David*, exh. cat., Timken Museum of Art, San Diego, 2003, pp. 14–20.

16. Farington 1979 (as in note 11), pp. 1824–5 (3 September 1802).

17. For West's remark, see Vaughan, 1990 (as in note 3), p. 14. The reference to Canova is from *La Belle Assemblée*, new series, XXVII, 1823, p. 281; cited by Puetz, 2001 (as in note 9), p. 241. Farington voiced his fundamental criticism of French painters on several occasions, notably on 6 October 1802: 'Painting is limited by these Artists to execute only the Ideas of a Sculptor who is neces-

sitated to regulate his conceptions as to be within the powers & capacities of his Art. It seems surprising that with the examples of the great works which are now publickly placed before them, comprehending the whole extent of Art from the polished care of Leonardo da Vinci to the freedom & Splendor of Rubens, the French still continue insensible to the advantages of judicious light & shade and of Colour, and to that extent in Composition which Painting admits but which Sculpture does not allow' (Farington, 1979 [as in note 11], p. 1903).

18. Edinburgh and London 1997–8 (as in note 1), pp. 209–10. As Puetz has stressed, systematic criticism of the French school justified a manner like Raeburn's: 'Recast as an entirely mechanical achievement, as a triumph of the hand over the mind, the much-vaunted precision of French draughtsmanship provided a perfect foil for the broad and "free" brushwork of native artists' (2001 [as in note 9], p. 237).

19. Denis Diderot, *Essais sur la peinture. Salons de 1759, 1761, 1763*, Gita May and Jacques Chouillet (eds), Paris, 1984, p. 275 ('Lexique des termes d'art', pp. 257–88).

20. For an overview of the debates around 1800, see Bordes, 2003 (as in note 15); Farington is quoted on p. 18, and the critics of the Salon of 1795 on p. 39 n. 65. For the immediate posterity of these debates in the criticism of François Guizot in 1810, see the ample discussion by Jacqueline Lichtenstein, *La tache aveugle: Essai sur les relations de la peinture et de la sculpture à l'âge moderne*, Paris, 2003, pp. 121–40.

21. Hoppner's text is excerpted by Joseph Baillio in the appendix to *Élisabeth Louise Vigée Lebrun 1755–1842*, exh. cat., Kimbell Art Museum, Fort Worth, 1982, pp. 139–40. His attack notably darkens the tone of criticism that had been addressed to another society portraitist, Jean-Laurent Mosnier, active in London from 1791 to 1797; critical reactions to his paintings at the Royal Academy exhibitions are closely documented by Puetz, 2001 (as in note 9), pp. 236–8, and Walczak, 2006 (as in note 10).

22. Gérard Fabre, *Joseph Boze: Portraitiste de l'Ancien Régime à la Restauration 1745–1826*, exh. cat., Musée Ziem, Martigues, 2004–5, pp. 226–31. The title is that on the print by Anthony Cardon, published in London in 1802. In truth, the work had been painted in collaboration with Robert Lefèvre and Carle Vernet (1758–1836).

23. On the exhibitions by Lefèvre and David, see Lee 2007 (as in note 1); the quoted references to Lefèvre, p. 333, and to Eastlake, p. 338.

24. Richard E. Spear, 'Antoine Dubost's *Sword of Damocles* and Thomas Hope: An Anglo-French skirmish', *The Burlington Magazine*, CXLVIII, no. 1241, August 2006, pp. 520–7; West quoted p. 523.

25. On Lethière and Wicar in London, see Oskar Bätschmann, *The Artist in the Modern World: the Conflict between Market and Self-expression*, Cologne, 1997,

pp. 47–8; on the London exhibition of Lethière's *Death of Virginia* (1828; Paris, Musée du Louvre) in 1828, three years before its appearance at the Salon, see p. 52. For the fuller context of Bullock's initiative, see Susan Pearce, 'William Bullock: Collections and exhibitions at the Egyptian Hall, London, 1816–25', *Oxford Art Journal*, XX, no. 1, 2008, pp. 17–35.

26. *Lettres adressées au Baron François Gérard peintre d'histoire* [. . .], Henri Gérard (ed.), 3rd edn, Paris, 1888, I, pp. 231–2. Translation of text: 'So curious is how the paintings of the English seem so full of light and how the hues are strong and rich. [. . .] Their portraits have a relief that we are far from obtaining. There are portraits by [Thomas] Lawrence, by [Thomas] Phil[l]ips, etc., that seem to merge with the public looking at them. The English School still pursues in the footsteps of Reynolds, but with greater slovenliness. [. . .] In spite of all their faults, their pictures would crush ours. They stand well their ground in the galleries next to the Old Masters. The paintings of our School appear pedantic and dull next to theirs. When it come to practising the lofty genre of history, they are near null. I believe they don't even think of reaching so high. They are at the point of being unable to draw a kneecap. [. . .] The portraits sacrifice everything to make most of the head, and I must admit that they are right. Mr Wilkie has a picture in the exhibition that draws a crowd. The subject is a man reading the bulletin of the battle of Waterloo. That battle of Waterloo surely relieved them of a bad thorn in their side, for they still speak as if it happened yesterday.'

27. *The London Literary Gazette, and Journal of Belles Lettres, Arts, Sciences etc.*, no. 174, 20 May 1820, p. 333, 'Mr Isabey's Exhibition' (reference furnished by Cyril Lécosse).

28. *The Morning Post*, 13 June 1820; quoted by Lee Johnson, 'The "Raft of the Medusa" in Great Britain', *The Burlington Magazine*, XCVI, no. 617, August 1954, p. 251.

29. See Selby Whittingham, 'Watteaus and "Watteaus" in Britain c. 1780–1851, in *Antoine Watteau (1684–1721), le peintre, son temps et sa légende*, François Moureau and Margaret Morgan Grasselli (eds), Geneva and Paris, 1987, pp. 270–3, with further references. For Wilkie, see Francis Haskell, *Rediscoveries in Art: Some Aspects of Taste, Fashion and Collecting in England and France*, Ithaca, NY and London, 1976, p. 57: 'It is an exaggeration, but not a wholly distorting one, to say that in these decades [1800–1830] Watteau plays something of the same sort of role for these [Constable, Turner and Wilkie], the most adventurous English painters of the period, as did the early Flemish and Italian artists for the more extreme followers of David and Ingres – with the two outstanding differences that in England no revival of interest in Watteau was really necessary, as he had never lacked admirers, and that his influence was supported rather than combated by "official" opinion.'

30. The total lack of consideration for the art of Gros, not once mentioned by

Farington in his diary, remains a mystery. Although Gros's introverted personality, which kept him away from social gatherings where painters like Gérard and Isabey purposefully mingled with British visitors during the Peace of Amiens and which probably kept him from exhibiting abroad, may have been a factor, that his manner contradicted the British idea of the French school may have been the problem.

31. Charles Robert Leslie, *Memoirs of the Life of John Constable, R.A.* (1843), Andrew Shirley (ed.), London, 1937, pp. 135 (quote from 1822), 327 (quote from 1835). Vaughan, 1993 (as in note 3), pp. 136, 151–2.

32. Ibid., 1937, pp. 393 ('French taste'), 394 (David) and note 2 (Boucher).

33. Vaughan notes that around 1830 perception of the French school was increasingly idiosyncratic on account of the complexity of the British artistic scene, which played out against competing invocations of Reynolds and Hogarth and was intensified by moral and religious considerations (1993 [as in note 3], pp. 150–1).

9

Raeburn in America: Scottish–American Art Networks, 1791–1845

Robyn Asleson

It is well known that portraits by Raeburn commanded tremendous prestige in the United States during the heyday for collecting British art in the first decades of the twentieth century. The seemingly insatiable demand of wealthy American bankers and industrialists inflated Raeburn's prices to record levels, a phenomenon illustrated by the sale of *Mrs Anne Hart* for £6,930 in 1907 and for an unprecedented £31,000 in 1913, the highest auction price ever paid at an English auction. American dollars continued to fuel an overheated market for Raeburn's portraits until the stock market crash in 1929.

A subject that has hitherto remained unexplored is Raeburn's equally remarkable reception in America one hundred years earlier, over the six decades preceding the mid-nineteenth century. During that seminal era in the development of American art and art institutions, Raeburn's reputation and influence in the United States rose to a level unequalled outside of Scotland itself. As the following analysis will show, Raeburn owed his prominence to the advocacy of a few influential supporters in New York, Philadelphia, and Charleston who by birth, education, or ancestry identified closely with Scotland. Like other civic and cultural leaders in the United States, they actively promoted the appreciation and practice of fine art as a necessary prerequisite to their young nation's claims to civilization. However, whereas other proponents of the fine arts fell into one of two aesthetic camps – either conservative (promoting the emulation of European Old Masters and the luminaries of England's Royal Academy of Arts) or nationalistic (eschewing European models in favour of an unmediated and indigenous school of art) –

Raeburn's advocates appear to have shared no coherent aesthetic philosophy other than a deep and abiding affinity for Scottish culture. Their interventions on behalf of Raeburn brought him to the fore of America's nascent art culture, securing his high standing within recently founded art institutions and ensuring that his paintings were among the limited number of artistic models that influenced the country's fledgling painters and connoisseurs. Drawing on hitherto unpublished letters and other documents, this essay examines the Scottish–American connections that underpinned Raeburn's early reception in the United States, expanding the extensive literature on Scottish–American cultural exchange into the domain of the visual arts.

Raeburn was a familiar figure to the prime movers of New York's earliest art institutions. First-hand knowledge of his practice and personality emanated from two professional artists of the Robertson family who had transferred their practice from Aberdeen to New York in the late eighteenth century. The eldest brother of the family, Archibald Robertson (1765–1835), made Raeburn's acquaintance in about 1782 when they were both students at the Trustees' Academy School in Edinburgh. Robertson later told one of his New York colleagues, the painter and writer William Dunlap (1766–1839), that he and Raeburn had formed 'a school for mutual improvement' with two other young students, the portraitist George Watson (1767–1837) and the genre painter Walter Weir (d. 1816). Meeting in the green room of the Theatre-Royal in Princes Street on the three evenings a week that performances were not held, they made life drawings from the obliging theatre porter and studied plaster casts provided by Alexander Runciman (1736–85), master of the Trustees' Academy. According to Dunlap, the young men were compelled to organise the class because 'at that time there was no academy of fine arts in that city [Edinburgh]'.[1] Raeburn's sustained advocacy of art education and exhibition opportunities in Edinburgh ultimately contributed to the founding of the Incorporated Society of Artists in 1808 and, later, the Royal Scottish Academy, established in 1826.

Robertson's efforts came to fruition much earlier, thanks to the intervention of three civic-minded New York gentlemen eager to establish a school of art instruction in their city.[2] All three had personal or intellectual roots in Scotland: Robert R. Livingston (1746–1813), chancellor of New York, was descended from a family which had for centuries wielded great power in Scotland and now held sway in New York; Dr Samuel Bard (1742–1821), a patron of civic and cultural institutions, had studied medicine in Edinburgh and replicated Scottish practices at the medical school he helped found at King's College, New York (later Columbia College); and John Kemp (1763–1812), a professor at Columbia College, was born in Auchlossan and trained at Marischal College in Aberdeen. Scottish traditions and institutions had shaped each man's contributions to New York society, and it was in Scotland that they sought an artist to establish and run the city's first institution for fine arts training.

At their request Kemp's associate, Dr Thomas Gordon of King's College, Aberdeen, recruited Archibald Robertson, who had burnished his credentials with a stint at the Royal Academy Schools in London and was now operating the only independent drawing school in Aberdeen. In October 1791 Robertson opened the Columbian Academy of Painting in New York.[3] The following year his younger brother, Alexander (1772–1841), left Aberdeen for New York in order to help operate the Academy. A decade later, in 1802, Alexander established his own art school in the city, the Academy of Painting and Drawing, and in the same year Archibald published *Elements of the Graphic Arts*, one of America's earliest books of art instruction. Also in 1802, Archibald Robertson became a patron of the American Academy of Fine Arts, newly founded that year in New York by a coterie of wealthy gentlemen led by Robert R. Livingston and his brother Edward, the mayor of New York. Although art students were permitted to copy works displayed at the Academy, the institution's primary focus was providing the city's elite with opportunities to refine their taste and discernment through exposure to art. The membership was dominated by civic leaders and professionals, chiefly merchants, doctors, lawyers, and bankers. Archibald Robertson was initially one of only four practicing artists in the group – and the only one based in the United States. Indeed, for many years, Archibald and Alexander Robertson were the only professional artists residing permanently in New York. Together, they instructed a generation of amateur and professional American artists in the academic practices and aesthetic sensibilities they had absorbed in Edinburgh and London.

The Robertson brothers had a direct conduit to the artistic cultures of those two British cities through their younger brother, Andrew (1777–1845), a miniature painter active in both. Andrew had gone to Edinburgh around 1793 in order to study landscape and scene painting under Alexander Nasmyth (1758–1840), but he wasted no time in beating a path to Raeburn's door. In an undated memoir (published posthumously), Robertson recalled how the artist had answered his knock, 'palette and brushes in hand, each a yard long, for he painted at arm's length'.[4] On learning of the young student's desire to copy some of his paintings, Robertson claimed, Raeburn set up a small room adjoining his studio for Robertson's use, obtained permission for him to copy several portraits still in hand, and allowed the student to observe him at work. Raeburn had begun his career as a painter of portrait miniatures and his young protégé followed suit. In 1799 Andrew Robertson sent his miniature copy after Raeburn's *Niel Gow* to his brothers Archibald and

Alexander in New York, where it presumably took its place among the collection of model art works that students of the Columbian Academy studied and copied as part of their training.[5]

Andrew Robertson's letters from London (where he transferred his studies in 1801) teem with admiring references to Raeburn, whom he considered a personal patron. On 1 January 1802, he reported to his brothers in New York, 'Shee and Lawrence are rivals, and with Hoppner and Beechy carry all off – Raeburn is equal to any of them, and if he had any spur or opposition would do much better'.[6] Though Robertson viewed Raeburn's professional isolation in Edinburgh as an impediment to his artistic progress (affording little in the way of stimulating competition), it nevertheless crystallised his international reputation as an ethnically 'pure' artist and the head of a distinctive Scottish school of art. In the United States, he was invariably referred to as 'The Scottish painter Raeburn' or 'Raeburn of Edinburgh.' His staunch adherence to the country of his birth bore obvious relevance for American painters who, in an increasingly nationalistic climate, struggled with the dilemma of whether to pursue superior opportunities for training and patronage in the Old World, or preserve the clarity of their New World vision by remaining in the United States.

The contemporary British painters that Andrew Robertson named as stars of the London art scene in his letter of 1802 – Martin Archer Shee (1769–1850), Thomas Lawrence (1769–1830), John Hoppner (1759–1810), and William Beechey (1753–1839) – were known in the United States only through the pages of imported journals and the 'Foreign Intelligence' columns of local newspapers. Indeed, for much of the nineteenth century, original paintings by Shee, Hoppner, and Beechey remained rarities in American collections and public exhibitions. The situation was rather different for Lawrence. In April 1802, New Yorkers caught their first glimpse of his work when the art dealer Edward Savage exhibited *The Princess Amelia* at his Columbian Gallery.[7] Works by or purporting to be by Lawrence cropped up with increasing regularity at public exhibitions in the United States from the 1820s onwards. They were joined by numerous replicas of Lawrence's paintings by American artists and even, on occasion, by third-hand American copies of other American copies of his paintings.

Raeburn was the only British portraitist of his generation to approach Lawrence in terms of the exposure and influence of his paintings in America during the formative first few decades of the nineteenth century. The first of Raeburn's pictures to be exhibited publicly in the United States was an unidentified *Portrait of a Gentleman*, which was displayed in the second exhibition of the American Academy of Fine Arts in May 1817. Raeburn had been elected a Royal Academician two years earlier and his reputation had evidently crossed the Atlantic by the time of the exhibition. Readers of *The American Monthly Magazine* and *Critical Review* were informed that he was 'an English R.A. though a Scotchman and resident in Edinburgh', and that 'He is sometimes called the Scotch Reynolds'. The painting on display evidently failed to live up to that distinction, however, for the critic added, 'From this specimen, we should not think him deserving the title, unless Scotland is very barren of portrait painters, and the title is conferred by comparison'.[8]

The portrait by Raeburn had been loaned to the New York exhibition by James Renwick (1792–1863), a wealthy young Scottish-American scholar who would shortly be appointed professor of natural philosophy and experimental chemistry at Columbia College, a position vacated by his uncle and mentor, John Kemp. Kemp, it will be remembered, was the civic worthy whose contacts in Aberdeen had brought Archibald Robertson to New York in 1791. The identity of the Raeburn portrait exhibited by Renwick is unknown. However, Renwick had a clear opportunity to acquire it while visiting Great Britain from June 1815 to February 1816. On part of the trip he was accompanied by his close friend Washington Irving (1783–1859) – another American of Scottish descent – soon to achieve fame as the author of *The Legend of Sleepy Hollow* (1820) and other Gothic tales of Knickerbocker New York. Through Irving's letters we learn that Renwick (whom he dubbed 'the laird') spent a portion of the summer of 1815 in London, where Raeburn was exhibiting four portraits at the Royal Academy.

Renwick spent the autumn and winter in and around Edinburgh, where his uncle, the merchant John Jeffrey, resided. Irving's letters facetiously describe the professor throwing himself into Scottish life: 'figuring among the Caledonian Hunts,' 'playing the roaring blade,' and 'fleec[ing] all the old ladies in Dumfries at cards'.[9] Raeburn's studio evidently figured among Edinburgh's popular tourist attractions at that time. In his *Caledonian Sketches* of 1809, Sir John Carr commented on the 'distinguished and highly-merited celebrity' of both Raeburn and Alexander Nasmyth, adding that 'their galleries, which are open for the inspection of the public, well deserve the attention of tourists'.[10] A visit to Raeburn's studio would certainly have appealed to Renwick, himself an amateur artist and collector of contemporary painting.

Renwick had other reasons for bringing back to America a specimen of Scottish culture in the form of a portrait by Raeburn. He had grown up in a family environment steeped in loyalty to and affection for Scotland. His namesake and progenitor, the Revd James Renwick (1662–88) was the last of the prominent covenanting leaders to go to the scaffold. His mother, the former Jean Jeffrey of Lochmaben (1774–1850), was famous in New York social circles as the teenage muse who had inspired two songs by her family's intimate friend, the poet Robert Burns.[11] Possessed of 'a true Scottish heart', she was described by a friend as 'ardently loyal to her native land; its tones were music to her ears, its legends and auld-warld stories rife in her memory and often overflowing in her conversation'.[12] Her home overflowed with relics of Scotland, among them a silver casket containing a pair of gloves supposedly belonging to Mary, Queen of Scots, and a portrait of Walter Scott by the New York portraitist John Wesley Jarvis (1780–1840) – a copy after the well-known portrait of 1810 'painted by Sir Henry Raeburn of Edinburgh' – which she lent to the tenth exhibition of the American Academy of Fine Arts in 1824.[13] Jean Renwick was in fact devoted to Walter Scott. She requested a lock of his hair from a friend in Scotland and reportedly planted a shoot of Scott's favourite ivy from Melrose Abbey at Sunnyside, the New York home of their mutual friend Washington Irving.[14] This act of symbolic convergence, uniting three great Scottish writers (Scott, Irving, and Burns) became a New York legend, ultimately celebrated in verse by the Scottish-American poet Wallace Bruce (1844–1914).[15]

Raised in this hothouse of transplanted Scottish culture, James Renwick learned to take great pride in his Caledonian roots. Small wonder, then, that a picture by Edinburgh's leading portrait painter was one of the very first art acquisitions he made in his early twenties. By exhibiting Raeburn's painting at the American Academy, Renwick raised the flag of contemporary Scottish art (which no doubt pleased his mother), but he also acted as a patriotic American, doing his part to improve public taste and provide a worthy aesthetic model for the emerging class of professional American artists. Imitation of exemplary works of art formed the cornerstone of art education in America at the time. No other method was considered more effective in forming 'correct' taste and developing technical skill. Because the American Academy and its sister institutions lacked adequate funds to purchase art outright, they relied on loans and donations from collectors such as Renwick, who had been elected a director of the Academy on 5 May 1817. The rub was that these newly affluent members of the middle class – with their ready cash, limited knowledge of art, and upwardly mobile pretentions – had become notoriously easy marks for unscrupulous picture dealers. It was an open secret that most of New York's private art collections at that time were awash in spurious Old Masters and crude copies.

In the months following the American Academy's first public exhibition in 1816, the institution's directors arrived at a new scheme for acquiring indisputably authentic works of art while incurring no additional expense to the institution. The plan was to extend honorary memberships to leading artists who would be encouraged, in exchange, to contribute an example of their work to the institution's permanent collection. Benjamin West (1738–1820), John Trumbull (1756–1843), and Thomas Lawrence had already been invited to join the ranks of honorary members of the American Academy of Fine Arts without an explicit quid pro quo request. Rather more aggressive tactics were adopted following a meeting at the Academy on 1 February 1817, at which a committee was 'appointed to report the names of distinguished artists and others proper to become honorary members'. The committee consisted of two members: the merchant John R. Murray (vice-president of the Academy), who had studied drawing and painting with the Robertsons, and the painter and dramatist William Dunlap (keeper), who would devote a full ten pages to the Robertsons in his seminal book *A History of the Rise and Progress of the Arts of Design in the United States* (1834). On 5 July 1817, Murray and Dunlap provided their wish list:[16]

[Antonio] Canova	Statuary	Rome
Joseph Nollekens}	D	London
M[artin]. A[rcher]. Shee}		
D[avid]. Wilkie}	Painters	London
Andrew Robertson}		
Washington Allston}		
George Hatfield	Architect	Washington
Charles W. Peale	Painter	Philadelphia
Mr. [Carl Johan] Fahlcrantz}	Painters	Stockholm
Chevalier [Carl Fredrik von] Breda}		
Thomas Barrow		New York
Mr. H[enry]. Raeburn	Painter	Edinburgh

Strikingly, of the eight non-Americans on the list, three (Wilkie, Robertson, and Raeburn) were Scottish, an imbalance that reflects the Robertsons' influence as tastemakers at the Academy as well as the canny expectation that their personal connections would ensure a favourable response. Certainly, when compared with the preeminent Europeans on the list – such as Canova (president of the Academy of St Luke in Rome) or Von Breda (recently ennobled by Charles XIII for his contributions to Swedish art) – the Scots appear somewhat lacking in official honours and distinctions.

In any case, it was Alexander Robertson, in his capacity as Academy secretary, who ultimately wrote to Raeburn, inviting him to become an honorary member and delicately broaching the subject of a donation, as follows: 'The institution is in a flourishing condition, and the collection of paintings is rapidly increasing. The friendly donations of many of the honorary members will enable it to boast of specimens of most of the distinguished artists of the day'.[17] Two years passed before Raeburn replied to Robertson's letter. According to the artist, the donation had been the sticking point:

'The delay arose from a wish to send along with my acknowledgement some small specimen of my own painting,' he wrote on 10 August 1819. 'And that it might have an interest with you beyond any thing that I could give it, I wished it to be the portrait of some gent of your own country on whose own account it might be held in some estimation'.[18]

Raeburn found that gentleman in Peter Van Brugh Livingston (c. 1793–1868), 'who during the short time he was here [in Edinburgh] acquired the good will, esteem and respect of every person who had the honour of his acquaintance'.[19] Livingston hailed from the same noteworthy Scottish-American family as his cousin Robert R. Livingston, the New York patron of Archibald Robertson and founder of the American Academy of Arts. After graduating from Columbia College in 1811, Peter Van Brugh Livingston spent the years 1816–19 on a glittering Grand Tour of Europe, dancing with princesses in Paris and so dazzling Mme Jerome Bonaparte at a ball in Austria that she reportedly declared him 'the handsomest man she had ever seen'.[20] Livingston's tour culminated in a seven-month sojourn in Scotland. From late January to late June 1819, he lingered in Edinburgh, held up by a fractured arm suffered in a fall from a horse.

In a letter sent from Harrogate, Yorkshire, on 27 July 1819 to his mother in New York, Livingston recounted the circumstances in which he came to be painted by 'the celebrated artist Raeburn, who in point of professional merit is considered second only to the famous Lawrence'.[21] At a dinner party in Edinburgh he learned from the Revd Archibald Alison (1757–1839) that Raeburn had a particular reason for wishing to make his acquaintance. On being introduced, Raeburn explained that in gratitude for the honour bestowed by the American Academy of Fine Arts, 'he wished to present them with a specimen of his portrait painting' and asked Livingston whether, 'as I was a New York gentleman, I would do him the favor to give him a sitting for that purpose'.[22] It was possibly this sitting that Raeburn was trying to arrange in a letter of 9 March 1819, in which he urged Livingston to visit his studio that Friday at noon. Raeburn complained that he had been 'much vexed' on discovering that Livingston had been turned away by his servant during an earlier unscheduled visit to the studio, but he warned, 'I am so busy at present that if you were to call again without fixing the time, it would be a chance if I would see you above a minute or two'.[23] Raeburn's statement confirms the crushing pace of his work in 1819. The fact that he nevertheless took the time and effort to execute a portrait, gratis, for the American Academy in New York underscores the importance he attached to professional distinctions such as the honorary membership, as well as his eagerness to expand his reputation and relevance beyond Edinburgh. He would articulate this yearning quite clearly a few months later in a letter to

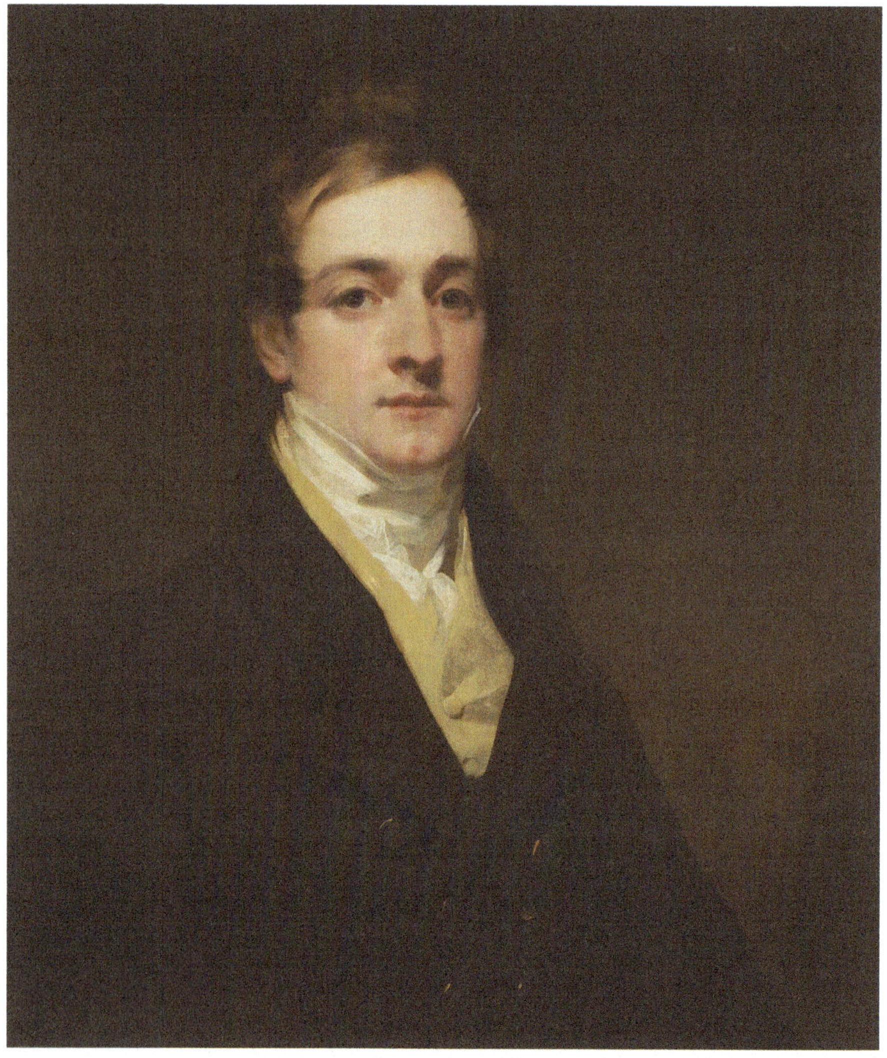

Figure 9.1 Henry Raeburn, *Peter Van Brugh Livingston*, 1819, oil on canvas, 75.6×63.2cm, purchased by subscription, Wadsworth Atheneum Museum of Art, Hartford

David Wilkie, pleading for news of the London art scene and the reception of his portraits there.[24]

Livingston informed his mother that Raeburn's portrait 'was considered by all who saw it an uncommonly striking likeness' (Fig. 9.1).[25] Encouraged by this result, he asked the artist to paint a replica, to which Raeburn reportedly replied, 'Oh no – not a copy, I will paint another view of your head'. Livingston duly sat for a second portrait (Fig. 9.2) – a gift for his mother,

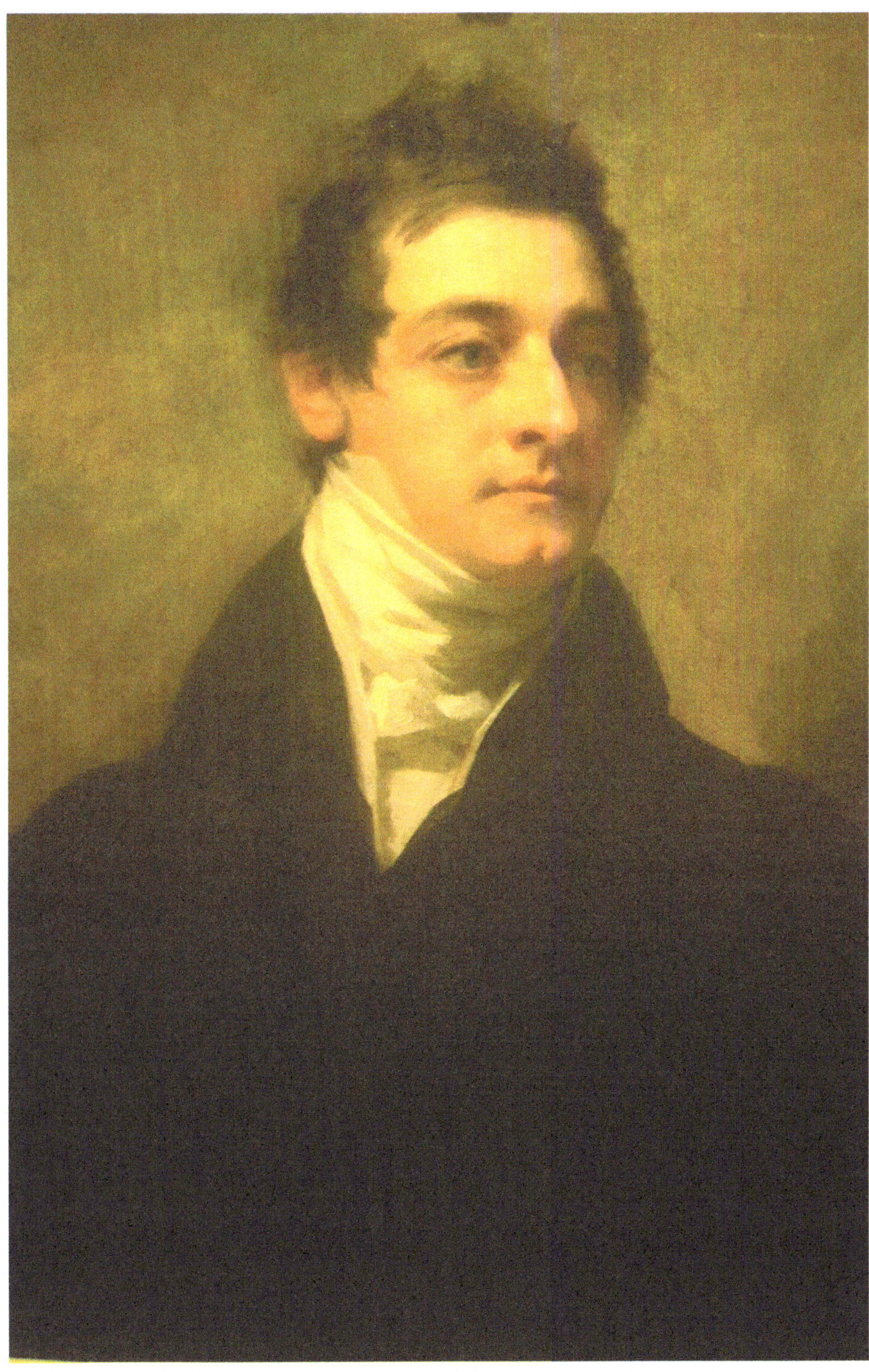

Figure 9.2 Henry Raeburn, *Peter Van Brugh Livingston*, 1819, oil on canvas, 76×63.5cm, New York Public Library

who had been dissatisfied with a succession of Grand Tourist portraits he had sent her in 1817 from Naples, Rome, and Paris.[26] When the two paintings were complete, however, Raeburn had second thoughts about the one he had intended for the Academy. According to Livingston, the portrait for his mother was 'considered as even better than the former, and Mr. R. was very desirous that I should make an exchange, but I would, by no means consent to it'.[27] The chagrined artist packed both paintings together in a case and sent them to Livingston, then at Liverpool, asking that he ship them on to the Academy in New York. Raeburn accounted for the two portraits in his letter of thanks for the honorary membership, explaining, 'The one without the frame which I like the best and wish it had been for you, was done for his [Livingston's] mother who resides at New York'.[28] Unable to give the portrait of his choice to the Academy, Raeburn at least ensured that his American peers had an opportunity to examine it before it disappeared into Mrs. Livingston's private collection.

It is instructive to compare Raeburn's two portraits of Livingston. Very different interpretations of the same man, painted over a brief span of time in the spring of 1819, they illustrate the potential for variety in Raeburn's response to his sitters. Despite the dazzling social successes of his recent continental tour, Livingston had introduced himself to Raeburn in the most self-effacing manner, insisting, 'I am not one of the famous Livingstons – only an unknown American merchant'.[29] It is precisely this modest and unassuming character that Raeburn captures in his first portrait of Livingston. The well-groomed gentleman meets our gaze politely and with a slightly tentative expression. The evenly diffused lighting, monochromatic colour scheme, and unobtrusive brown-toned background reinforce the impression of well-mannered reserve, as does Raeburn's rather staid mode of execution: restrained, undemonstrative, and smooth, with every button accounted for. This perfectly genteel and conservative image must have seemed eminently safe as an official 'specimen' of Raeburn's work destined for semi-public institutional display.

Raeburn took greater liberties in the second portrait, transforming the unknown American merchant into a dashing romantic hero. With a dramatic turn of his head, Livingston gazes into the distance, one side of his face catching the light while the other is subsumed in shadow. His hair has lost its smooth, elegant sheen. Instead, rapid brushstrokes summarily describe a hairstyle of tousled nonchalance – its spirited, windswept appearance creating an impression of barely contained vitality. The backdrop of swirling blue, grey, and green reinforces the theatricality of the presentation. Whereas in the previous picture, Raeburn had taken care to articulate the materials and construction of Livingston's three-piece suit, his later conception is literally less buttoned up. Livingston's head and neck rise from an indistinct black mass that betrays no sign of the tailor.

No longer a stranger, Livingston was by then on terms of some intimacy with his portraitist. In a letter written soon after the painting's completion, Raeburn addressed Livingston warmly, declaring himself 'much rejoiced' to hear of his recovery from his 'unfortunate accident' and assuring him 'That every thing that is good may attend you is my sincere wish'.[30] Freed from the constrained circumstances of the earlier commission, Raeburn allowed himself to paint with greater abandon in this private portrait for the family of a man he had come to know personally.

The two portraits may also document a metamorphosis in Livingston's self-fashioning. No longer the elegant Grand Tourist who had waltzed his way through Vienna, Paris, and Moscow, nor even the unknown American merchant who had presented himself to Raeburn, Livingston had, by the time of his second round of portrait sittings, assumed the weightier character of the wistful scion of a proud Caledonian ancestry. Livingston's letters reveal that his sojourn in Scotland initiated a somewhat obsessive fascination with the genealogy and historical circumstances of his illustrious Scottish forebears. Following a visit to the ruins of Livingston castle, he succumbed to an intensely romantic and melancholy nostalgia. 'The pensive eye imperceptibly moistened with the tear of gloomy sensibility,' he confessed, 'while my bosom heaved with many a sigh, at the sad contrast of the present with that of former days'.[31] At Linlithgow, Livingston toured another family castle, pored over genealogical charts and indulged in bittersweet ruminations on the past. Walter Scott bestowed the final romantic patina on Livingston's ancestral musings, assuring him of the great historic distinction of the Livingston family, exhuming a book of genealogy to demonstrate his own kinship with a maternal branch of Livingston's family, and inviting Livingston to stay at Abbotsford that summer.[32] On returning to New York in 1819, the Caledonian convert immediately renamed the 233-acre farm he had inherited from his father 'Callendar' after his ancestors' Scottish home, and began extensive compilations of his family's genealogy.[33]

Raeburn's preferred portrait of Livingston – the bravura picture destined for the sitter's mother – had a very limited audience during the nineteenth century. It remained with the Livingston family until the 1880s when the sitter's son sold it to the New York merchant and philanthropist Alexander Maitland (1846–1909) on the condition that he would ultimately place it in the Lenox Library, an institution founded in 1871 by Maitland's great uncle James Lenox (1800–80), a wealthy collector and philanthropist of Scottish Presbyterian descent.[34] Maitland presented the portrait to the library in

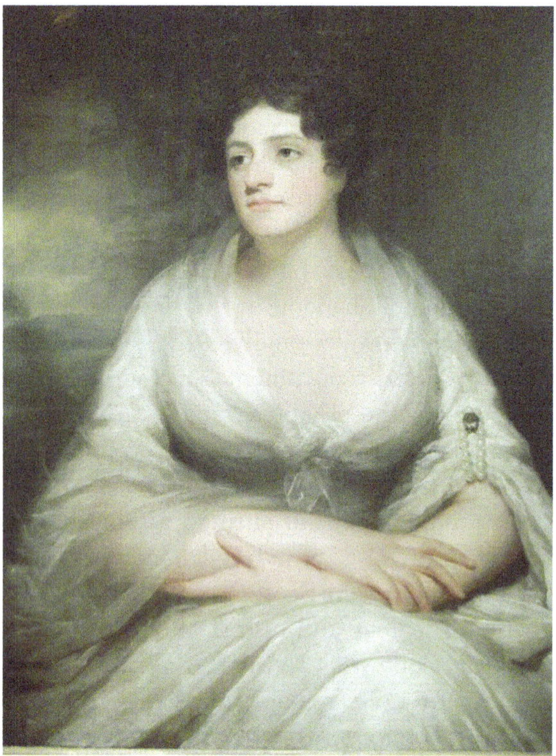

Figure 9.3 Henry Raeburn, *Penelope Macdonald Hamilton, Lady Belhaven and Stenton*, c. 1790, oil on canvas, 90.2×69.8cm, New York Public Library

1889, whereupon *Peter Van Brugh Livingston* joined another Raeburn portrait, *Lady Belhaven* (Fig. 9.3), which James Lenox had acquired some time earlier. It was only in the early twentieth century – after the dramatic surge in Raeburn's reputation (and prices) that his compelling second portrait of Livingston began to be studied and copied by American artists.[35]

The fate of Raeburn's first portrait of Livingston was altogether different. By 4 December 1819, this 'valuable & masterly portrait' was on display at the American Academy of Fine Arts.[36] On 9 May 1820 one of the Robertson brothers proposed a toast to 'Henry Raeburn, Esq. of Edingburg' [sic] at the 'elegant dinner' following the opening of the annual exhibition.[37] Among the works on display was the Academy's latest acquisition, *Peter Van Brugh Livingston*, whose conspicuous excellence made up for the lacklustre example of Raeburn's work displayed three years earlier. A writer for *The New-York Columbian* observed:

This is only the second picture we have seen in the country of this excellent
artist. A deep, broad manner, a freedom of execution, great strength of character
and harmony of colouring, immediately distinguish it from the other portraits
in the room. From the specimen here presented we have every reason to believe
that the talents of the painter have in no way been overrated, and we cordially
unite with his countrymen in ranking him a first rate artist.[38]

The portrait would re-appear in every subsequent annual exhibition of the
American Academy of Fine Arts until 1828. In March 1841 it appeared
in New York one last time at an exhibition of the recently formed Apollo
Association for the Promotion of the Fine Arts in the United States,
where a newspaper correspondent declared it 'a bold and striking picture,
worthy of this eminent Scottish artist, and of the study of our own painters'.[39] Later that year, the American Academy of Fine Arts was dissolved.
In February 1842, a group of trustees of the Wadsworth Gallery, founded
that year in Hartford, Connecticut, privately negotiated the purchase of
Peter Van Brugh Livingston and other works from the Academy's collection. From 1844 to 1850, Raeburn's painting appeared in four exhibitions
at the Wadsworth Gallery, which ultimately purchased the painting by
subscription in 1855.[40]

In his letter to Raeburn of 10 December 1819 acknowledging receipt
of Livingston's portrait, Alexander Robertson predicted the painting's
formative influence on the rising generation of American artists:

> In an infant institution like ours a few well selected specimens in the different
> departments of art is almost sufficient to form a school, & in that of portrait,
> we now feel we possess that which will enable our students to advance on firm
> ground and when I assure you that this standard specimen from your pencil is
> destined to form the manner of our artists, I am sensible it will be gratifying to
> you to know the value of the gift.[41]

Robertson's choice of words is telling. Because so few works of art were at
that time publicly accessible in the United States, care was required to ensure
that students saw only 'well selected specimens' providing 'firm ground' for
instruction. The New York Academicians valued Raeburn's painting so
highly because it was a 'standard specimen' – a relatively conservative and
solidly executed piece of work. Indeed, they may have heaved a collective
sigh of relief on discovering that it was the more staid version of *Peter Van
Brugh Livingston* that was intended for the Academy and not the second,
more virtuoso piece – a tough act for any novice painter to follow without the
years of study that informed its dramatic conception and dashing execution.

Concern that the first generation of artists trained in the United States might be misled by the wrong sort of artistic models recurs in discussions of art published during the early nineteenth century. For instance, a critic writing on the 1828 exhibition of the American Academy of Fine Arts recalled approvingly that 'Sir Henry Raeburn's presentation portrait was full of breadth and vigour'. He was less pleased with 'the colouring and chop-stick handling of Sir Thomas Lawrence,' whose portrait of Benjamin West he deemed 'a cold slaty affair, and much inferior to both his earlier and later works'.[42] The Lawrence painting had been commissioned by the American Academy in 1818 as a tribute to West, the American president of England's Royal Academy of Arts. Delivered in 1822, it was the first full-length portrait by the celebrated Lawrence to be exhibited publicly in the United States and was a favourite piece for students to copy – facts that the critic very much regretted. 'It is a pity it ever came to this country,' he observed. 'It has done much more hurt than good.'

Raeburn's *Peter Van Brugh Livingston* also became the object of close analysis and imitation by American art students, as Alexander Robertson had predicted. At a time when the predominant method of learning to paint was to copy pictures by accomplished European masters, Raeburn's portrait became a didactic touchstone. Not only was the painting acces-sible to members and associates of the Academy, but from 1820 to 1831 Alexander Robertson (then serving as keeper of the Academy) operated his own independent drawing and painting school in the same building, employing the Academy's collection of paintings, sculptures, and prints as teaching aids. Raeburn's portrait would undoubtedly have been among the models most favoured by Robertson, who had confessed to the artist his 'respect for your great professional acquirements, which I have known from my earliest youth, tho' not personally known to you'.[43] Numerous extant copies of Raeburn's portrait of Livingston attest to its careful study by artists of widely divergent degrees of expertise.[44] Obvious student pro-ductions include a copy that descended through the family of Frederick S. Agate (1807–44), who studied at the American Academy of Fine Arts in 1825.[45] Ironically, the indifference and obstructions Agate faced that year while trying to make copies at the Academy fuelled the disaffection of William Dunlap and other affiliated artists, leading them to abandon the American Academy and found the more artist-oriented National Academy of Design in New York in 1825.

At the opposite end of the spectrum from student work like Agate's was the masterly copy of *Livingston* by the eminent American portraitist Thomas Sully (1783–1872), begun on 19 August 1828 and completed that December.[46] Earlier in the year, on 20 February 1828, Sully had been elected an honorary member of the Royal Scottish Academy. In accepting that distinction, Sully declared his gratitude to 'a city endeared to me by my earliest recollections', referring to the childhood years he had spent in Edinburgh, where his parents, English actors, had a fixed engagement until 1792 when they immigrated to Virginia.[47] In 1824, perhaps seeing an opening created by Raeburn's death, the cash-strapped Sully had reportedly considered transferring his portrait practice to Scotland after receiving 'pressing invitations to come to Edinburgh, and there take up his permanent residence'.[48] He had narrowly missed crossing paths with Raeburn in London a decade earlier, having ended his eight-month visit there on 8 March 1810 – just days before Raeburn arrived in the city. While in London, Sully had sought advice from all the leading portraitists: West, Shee, Hoppner, Beechey, and Lawrence. The latter had the greatest impact on Sully, who came to be known as the 'American Lawrence'.

Nevertheless, Sully evidently felt Raeburn had something of value to teach him. According to William Dunlap, Sully copied Peter Van Brugh Livingston purely for his own edification. Sully recorded his observations on Raeburn's materials and techniques (along with those of other artists) in a notebook he began in London in 1809 and kept up till the end of his life. Dunlap quoted extensively from this manuscript in his *History of the Rise and Progress of the Arts of Design in the United States*, published in 1834. Of the pigments Raeburn used in glazing and his own efforts to replicate the artist's effects, Sully wrote:

> I found much use made of glazing colours of green, purple, asphaltum, and lake. The green made of prussian blue and asphaltum; the purple, of prussian blue and lake. After dead-colouring near life, I tinted the flesh, white drapery, and back-ground with yellow, red and blue tints: when dry, glazed and improved the shadows, and scumbled [added broken patches of pigment to] the lights, on which I improved the tinting and finished the picture.[49]

In his *History*, Dunlap emphasised the practical manner in which Sully went about refining his technique through study and replication of other painters' works. 'Mr. Sully was incessantly making experiments,' he observed, 'but not losing his time in search of nostrums and secrets. He made notes of the palettes of eminent men – he tried their practice.'

Sully instructed his students in the same way, and numerous extant copies of *Peter Van Brugh Livingston* dubiously attributed to Sully or (more plausibly) his students suggest that Raeburn's portrait (or, rather, Sully's imitation) was among his favourite teaching tools.[50] Sully exhibited his copy of *Livingston* at the Pennsylvania Academy of the Fine Arts in 1831, his fifteenth and final year as director of that institution, thereby furthering its stated mission 'to promote the cultivation of the Fine Arts in the United States of America, by introducing correct and elegant copies from works of the first masters in sculpture and painting'.[51]

Sully had replicated another Raeburn portrait, *Dugald Stewart* (1819–23), prior to making his copy of *Peter Van Brugh Livingston*. His careful analysis of Raeburn's pigments and their mode of application had enabled him to reconstruct the artist's principal palette as well as his finishing palette. Dunlap published both palettes in his *History*, along with Sully's observations on their use:

> It is a list of colours applicable to most complexions, varying, as occasion demands the tints No. 5 [Brown ochre and Indian red], 6 [no. 5 with additional white], and 7 [no. 6 with additional white]. In very florid complexions, as those of red-haired persons, or of very fair, a different scale is requisite; for such, perhaps, burnt terra de sienna and vermilion. Light red and Naples yellow, with vermilion and white tints would be better. In glazing, I found he had incidentally employed cobalt with the tint No. 12 (Indian red and black); cobalt with asphaltum; also asphaltum with No. 12.

He added: 'It is well to paint with daring boldness and strength in determining the head. In finishing with the different tints, more circumspection must be used'.[52] The lengthy notes on Raeburn's materials and methods, together with Sully's critique of them, provided a how-to guide for practicing artists, a virtual seminar in flesh-painting. It is significant that Dunlap – who, it will be remembered, had served on the committee that proposed Raeburn as an honorary American Academician – included this extensive technical section on a non-American painter in what was ostensibly a history of American art. In so doing, he further disseminated Raeburn's practice, which by 1834 had already contributed materially to the education of American artists.

A manuscript notebook of c. 1835–40 belonging to the New York banker and genre painter Francis William Edmonds (1806–63) documents a further stage in this dissemination of Raeburn's methods among American artists. Like Sully's notebook, Edmonds's served as a repository of technical information on painting, its examples drawn from the practice of Gilbert Stuart, Lawrence, Sully, Raeburn, and a handful of others. Edmonds's notes on Raeburn clearly derive from Dunlap's *History* and other published sources. He included, for example, a pen-and-ink drawing of Raeburn's palette (Fig. 9.4), labelled with the pigments as described by Sully, and he paraphrased some of Sully's comments on Raeburn as quoted in Dunlap's book.[53] Edmonds

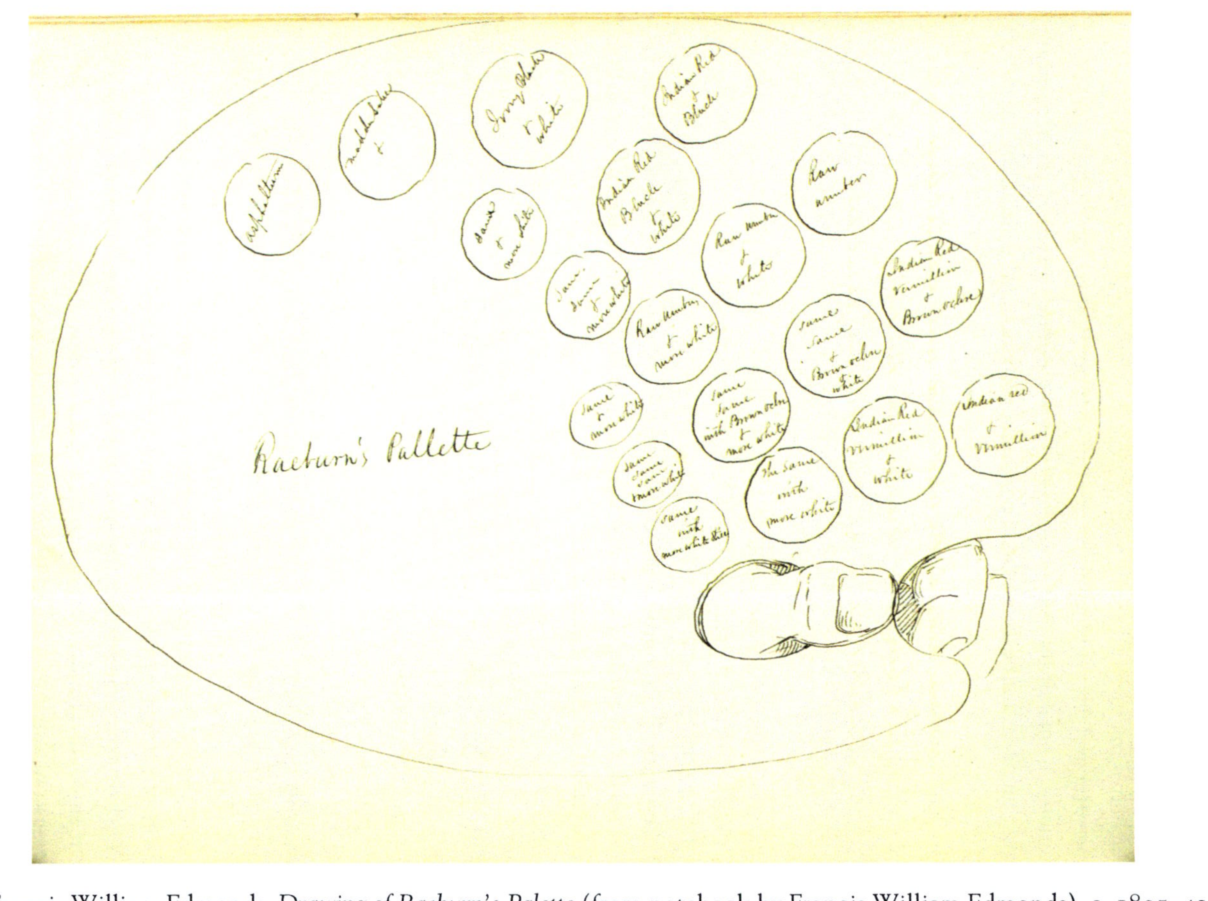

Figure 9.4 Francis William Edmonds, *Drawing of Raeburn's Palette* (from notebook by Francis William Edmonds), c. 1835–40, pen and ink on paper, 22.9×18.4cm, Collection of the New York Historical Society

also described Raeburn's unmediated approach to commencing work on his canvas – an account that echoes the well-known one published in Allan Cunningham's *Lives of the Most Eminent British Painters and Sculptors* (1829–33) but with subtle differences that suggest an alternative source:

> Raeburn's manner of beginning a portrait was by standing some 30 feet from the sitter and after surveying the general effect of his head attentively for some minutes, to march up to his easel with his eye intently fixed upon the canvass and then work in the whole head without raising his eyes again to the sitter.[54]

On the same page, Edmonds (like Cunningham) contrasted Raeburn's procedure with the more elaborate preparatory method of Thomas Lawrence. 'It is said of Sir Thomas Lawrence', Edmonds wrote, 'that on almost all occasions he made a finished drawing of his sitter in crayon on paper before he commenced painting.' Here again, Lawrence is invoked as Raeburn's foil. Though Edmonds offers no opinion as to which artist's practice is preferable, most American painters found Raeburn's direct method difficult to emulate, gravitating instead toward Lawrence's use of preliminary drawings. Sully, for example, in conscious emulation of Lawrence, executed a full-scale chalk drawing on canvas, which served as a model for the actual oil painting, carried out on a separate canvas.[55]

The circumstances surrounding Sully's copy after Raeburn's *Dugald Stewart* shed further light on the way in which individual and familial affinities with Scotland among American cultural leaders boosted Raeburn's reputation and influence in the United States. As chair of Moral Philosophy at the University of Edinburgh from 1785 until his retirement in 1809, Stewart had entranced a generation of scholars with his eloquence and urbanity. Around 1806, Raeburn had painted a head-and-shoulders portrait of the professor in his prime. He began an ambitious half-length in 1819, the same year he painted *Peter Van Brugh Livingston*, by which time both the artist and his sitter were in their sixties. According to Stewart's wife, Helen, the professor appears far younger in Raeburn's portrait. 'I sometimes think', she observed, 'that Raeburn who had known Mr. Stewart all his life & had the most enthusiastic admiration for him, painted from remembrance as well as present sight, tho he sat to him oftener, than almost anybody ever did'.[56] Her impression of Raeburn's indebtedness to a mental ideal of his sitter contrasts with the common-sense philosophy articulated by John Reid and Dugald Stewart, which insisted on the strictly empirical character of painting, concerned exclusively with 'the visible appearance of an object' rather than 'the notion of it'.[57]

Helen Stewart also reported that there was a long hiatus before Raeburn completed her husband's portrait shortly before the artist's death in 1823. When the following year the painting appeared in the Raeburn memorial exhibition in Edinburgh, it was evidently still not paid for; an outstanding payment of £105 is recorded in Raeburn's inventory of 9 June.[58] Shortly thereafter, a request to purchase the painting was advanced by Philip Tidyman (1776–1850), a former student of Dugald Stewart, now a distinguished physician and plantation owner in Charleston, South Carolina. Tidyman's maternal grandfather had emigrated from Scotland to Charleston and had sought to instill a fierce Scottish pride within his family.[59] Numerous relations remained in Aberdeen, where Tidyman was sent as a young boy following the death of his father, an English silversmith based in Charleston. Tidyman went on to pursue medical studies in Edinburgh and finally returned to the United States in 1801 after an absence of fifteen years.[60] On his return, he devoted himself to promoting cultural and scientific endeavours in Charleston, where he lived, and in Philadelphia, where he spent the summer months.[61] He never abandoned his attachment to Scotland, however.[62] Indeed, while hosting a dinner party on 3 March 1828, he bored his Scottish guest, Margaret Hunter Hall, by reminiscing at length about his former intimacy with 'Baron Hume, the Mackenzies, and many others' and his ongoing correspondence with Dugald Stewart's wife, Helen.[63]

For Tidyman and many other educated Americans, Dugald Stewart held a pre-eminent position as one of the great moral thinkers of the day. Through his lectures and publications, the charismatic professor had won over many American intellectuals and civic leaders to the anti-idealist philosophies that he associated with a distinctly Scottish school of moral thought.[64] It was this special bond with America, which, according to Helen Stewart, convinced Stewart and his family to allow the portrait by Raeburn to leave Scotland. Tidyman's ability to settle the debt with Raeburn's executors no doubt contributed to the decision as well. There was yet a further consideration, to which Helen Stewart alluded in a letter of 6 May 1825 to Tidyman:

> It is the only fine picture of Mr. Stewart in existence, but we all (I mean his family) felt, that considering the very kind and flattering way in which it was asked, we had no choice, if any was sent, this Original Picture by the best Artist Scotland ever produced, must go.[65]

The 'kind and flattering way' in which Tidyman had asked for the painting probably included his intention of presenting it to the Pennsylvania Academy of the Fine Arts in Philadelphia. The twenty-year-old Academy was in a thriving state, having recently augmented its premises with a new library and a gallery to accommodate its burgeoning collection of books and works of art, donated by benefactors at home and abroad. At that time, Philadelphia was still the most important city in the United States and the Pennsylvania Academy the closest thing to a national gallery of art. Tidyman could scarcely have found a more prestigious setting for Raeburn's *Dugald Stewart*, nor a more conspicuous means of bringing Scotland's twin achievements in intellectual and artistic endeavour before the eyes of a generation of American artists and amateurs.

Dugald Stewart left Edinburgh in May 1825. On 12 July Tidyman wrote to the president and directors of the Pennsylvania Academy, announcing his recent coup in acquiring the portrait and requesting that it be placed in the Academy 'for the gratification of the enlighten'd Citizens of Philadelphia'.[66] Thomas Sully, in his capacity as a director of the Pennsylvania Academy, responded to Tidyman in a letter of 13 August, assuring him:

> The picture will be highly appreciated by Artists & Amateurs of this Country as a Standard of fine style in Portrait Painting & at the same time it will be invaluable to the Community as a resemblance of the greatest moral writer of the age.[67]

Like *Peter Van Brugh Livingston*, Raeburn's *Dugald Stewart* was valued as a model – 'a Standard of fine style in Portrait Painting' – that could safely influence the practice of artists and public taste. Accordingly, the painting was given a high profile at the Pennsylvania Academy. The painting appeared in fifteen public exhibitions at the Academy between 1827 and 1845, leaving Philadelphia only once, in 1831, for an exhibition at the Boston Athenaeum.[68]

The arrival of Raeburn's painting in Philadelphia was publicised by a lengthy newspaper article (essentially a press release), which appeared in the *National Gazette* on 5 September 1825. Newspapers from Maine to Virginia republished the account, which notified readers that the portrait of Stewart 'by the late and celebrated artist Sir Henry Raeburn' had been purchased by Tidyman ('a former pupil and ardent friend and admirer of the illustrious professor') and bestowed 'on an institution wherein he thought it would be most suitably placed for the benefit of artists and the gratification of the largest number of Americans and strangers'.[69] Further dramatising the momentousness of Philadelphia's acquisition of Raeburn's *Dugald Stewart*, the author observed:

> The picture was brought to this city from Liverpool in the packet ship Delaware. Neither the owners nor captain of the vessel would consent to receive any compensation for the freight. We mention this trait of liberality on account of the enlightened spirit which it indicates.

The author, the American publicist and diplomat Robert Walsh (1785–1859), was well-suited to announce the arrival of *Dugald Stewart* in the United States. Walsh had joined the ranks of Stewart's American disciples after attending a series of the professor's lectures at Edinburgh in 1808. In 1811, as editor of the *American Review of History and Politics*, he offered a ringing endorsement of Stewart's *Philosophical Essays* (1810), referring to 'the excellence of this new and illustrious proof, of the unrivalled genius and learning' of the author.[70] Walsh went on to review other publications by Stewart and his own writings were so influenced by Stewart's ideas that they have been characterised as 'a monument to the influence of Scotch philosophy and aesthetics on the American mind'.[71] Walsh used his lengthy notice of Raeburn's portrait in the *National Gazette* as an opportunity to reinforce the notion of Stewart's seminal influence on American intellectual life, paralleling the effort to promote Raeburn as a 'sound' influence on American painting.

Within weeks of the picture's arrival, Thomas Sully had begun work on the copy already discussed, a replica that Tidyman had commissioned for the South Carolina Academy of Fine Arts in his native Charleston.[72] In the *National Gazette* article of 5 September 1825, Robert Walsh notified his readers that 'Mr. Sully has made satisfactory progress in his work and bears the most earnest testimonies to the high merits of Raeburn's pencil.' Raeburn had been elected an honorary member of the South Carolina Academy a few years earlier, in November 1821 – just months after the institution had been founded.[73] As at the American Academy in New York, Scottish loyalties very likely bolstered support for Raeburn within the South Carolina Academy. The tightly-knit enclave of Caledonian immigrants and descendents in Charleston is known to have sustained links with their homeland and promoted Scottish interests locally.[74] Raeburn's principal rival in Edinburgh, George Watson, evidently had ties to this vibrant Scots community, for in 1822 he gave his portrait of Benjamin West to the South Carolina Academy and, in gratitude, was elected an honorary member.[75] Watson's painting was exhibited at the Academy in 1823, along with two Scottish genre subjects by Alexander Fraser (1785–1865), the Edinburgh-trained colleague of David Wilkie. Paintings such as these provide evidence of an affinity for Scotland among the directors and members of the South Carolina Academy. Among them was the founding president, Joel Roberts Poinsett (1779–1851), who had studied medicine at Edinburgh in 1789–90, and one of the most active directors, the miniaturist Charles Fraser (1782–1860) whose South Carolina plantation, 'Wigton', was named after the family's ancestral home in Wigtownshire, Scotland.

Philip Tidyman was among the Scottish-American advocates of the

Academy in Charleston, ultimately replacing Poinsett as president. Lack of support and poor management caused the institution to languish and its last exhibition was held in 1829, with Sully's copy after Raeburn's *Dugald Stewart* among the featured works. The Academy disbanded soon thereafter.[76] In a letter of 2 March 1831 to the Philadelphia jurist John Kintzing Kane (1795–1898), a director of the Pennsylvania Academy, Tidyman wrote:

> You have applied just in time for a loan of Mr Shee's Kemble [a portrait of John Philip Kemble by Martin Archer Shee], & I have this Day rescued it from the neglected walls of our unfortunate Academy. I am sorry to say that I found this fine Picture cover'd with dust & cobwebs, & the Frame injured, but I trust to your politeness to interest our valued & amicable Friend Mr Sully in its behalf.

Sully's copy of *Dugald Stewart* was presumably also covered in dust and cobwebs when Tidyman rescued it from the defunct Academy and hung it in his house in Charleston. In the letter to J. K. Kane cited above, he closed with the request, 'Pray tell Mr Sully that his copy of Sir Henry Raeburn's *Dugald Stewart* is now in my Drawing Room in a high state of preservation, and much admired.'

Always a generous benefactor of cultural institutions, Tidyman began giving away his possessions in earnest in the 1840s as he approached his seventieth year. On 11 February 1842 he presented Sully's copy after Raeburn's *Dugald Stewart* to the St Andrew's Society of Charleston, a social and charitable organisation for men of Scottish ancestry, founded in 1729. The Society immediately elected Tidyman an honorary member and resolved that all correspondence and resolutions relating to his gift of *Dugald Stewart* be published in the daily newspapers.[77] The painting survived a fire at the St Andrew's Society in 1861, rescued from the flames and transported for safekeeping to a warehouse in the city of Columbia. That warehouse, too, went up in smoke four years later when Columbia was torched during the civil war.[78] Sully's painting was destroyed in the blaze.

Ironically, a similar fate had already befallen Raeburn's original portrait, which Tidyman had sanguinely imagined safely stowed at the Pennsylvania Academy of Fine Arts. In June 1845, it was destroyed along with many other works of art when the mentally-ill nephew of a janitor working for the Academy set a fire that demolished much of the building. Commentators struggled to articulate the enormity of this 'national calamity'. One writer mourned the fact that 'the torch of an incendiary has nearly destroyed the largest and best collection of the works of art [sic] in the United States and which has been the labor of near forty years in collecting. The loss is irreparable, and will be felt by a large number of artists and amateurs of painting and sculpture'.[79] Every newspaper account drew attention to Raeburn's *Dugald Stewart* among the most important works lost. A writer for the *North American* of Philadelphia reported, 'In the Directors' room there was sad – sad havoc, and we feel sick at heart at the bare task of reciting it.' After listing paintings by Titian, Guido Reni, and Kneller, the writer added: 'In the same room was Sir H. Raeburn's original portrait of Prof. Dugald Stewart, of Edinburgh – the only likeness of that eminent man extant. This was lost, and it will be felt most sensibly, for few pictures were more studied by artists'.[80]

Indeed, during its brief twenty-year existence, Raeburn's *Dugald Stewart* (like *Peter Van Brugh Livingston*) generated considerable interest among American artists and amateurs. One noteworthy patron of the arts in South Carolina, the naturalist and physician Robert Wilson Gibbes (1809–66), remarked in 1846, 'The finest portrait which it has been my good fortune to see, was that of Dugald Stuart by Raeburn'.[81] Numerous copies by students and associates of Sully provide further evidence of the admiration and esteem in which it was held and indicate that, like *Peter Van Brugh Livingston*, it was promoted by Sully as an object lesson for students.[82] The amateur poet John Houston Mifflin (1807–88) painted a copy of *Dugald Stewart* (Fig. 9.5) around 1835 while studying with Sully at the Pennsylvania Academy in preparation for his brief career as an itinerant portraitist.[83] Also at that time, Sully's student James Reid Lambdin (1807–89) painted a copy that was purchased by the Pennsylvania Academy in 1845, presumably to replace the original by Raeburn that had burned that year.[84] Raeburn's painting was also copied by the Philadelphia artist Alfred Newsam (1809–64), an associate of Sully and Lambdin, who was patronised by Tidyman. Newsam's drawing was published as a lithograph on 1 September 1830 by Cephas Grier Childs (1793–1871), also of Philadelphia (Fig. 9.6).[85] This lithograph, together with the copies in oil, now provide our only clues as to the appearance of a painting that played a seminal role in the aesthetic education of American artists and art amateurs during the second quarter of the nineteenth century.

In the 1830s and '40s, paintings by Raeburn (or copies after them) continued to trickle into the United States through Scottish–American channels. For example, Andrew Richardson (1799–1876), 'a young landscape-painter, recently from Scotland', informed a newspaper correspondent visiting his New York studio in May 1839 that he had purchased the previously mentioned version of Raeburn's *Lady Belhaven* (Fig. 9.3) in Edinburgh 'out of the effects left by the great painter'.[86] The correspondent's rhapsodic description of the painting went some way toward justifying the steep asking price of $1,000. The previous year Richardson had exhibited *Lady Belhaven* at

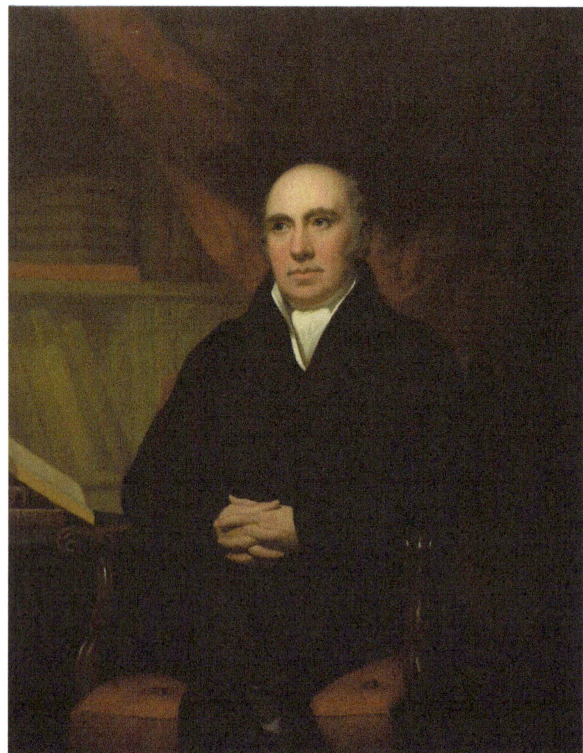

Figure 9.5 John Houston Mifflin after Henry Raeburn, *Dugald Stewart*, 1835, oil on canvas, 101.6 × 127cm, The State of Pennsylvania, Pennsylvania Historical and Museum Commission, Harrisburg

Richardson's Landscape Gallery in Washington, DC, along with a painting by Francis Danby and a handful of copies he had made at the Louvre after Claude, Bercham, Cuyp, and Ruysdael. A review published in the *Morning Herald* on 5 December 1838 extolled *Lady Belhaven* as being the best of the group. 'Last, but best, is the gem of the exhibition. "Portrait of a Lady" – an original by Raeburn. For harmony, grace, color, simplicity, tone, and fidelity to nature, this exquisite work of art was never excelled'.[87]

Around the same time that Richardson purchased Raeburn's *Lady Belhaven*, the aspirant portrait painter John Woodhouse Audubon (1812–62), son of the famous naturalist, made three successive visits to Edinburgh between October 1834 and July 1839. According to his daughter, he 'confined himself almost wholly to copying portraits . . . giving great attention to the beautiful work of Sir Henry Raeburn'.[88] He may have gained access to the artist's works (or, perhaps, studio versions) through Raeburn's erstwhile assist-

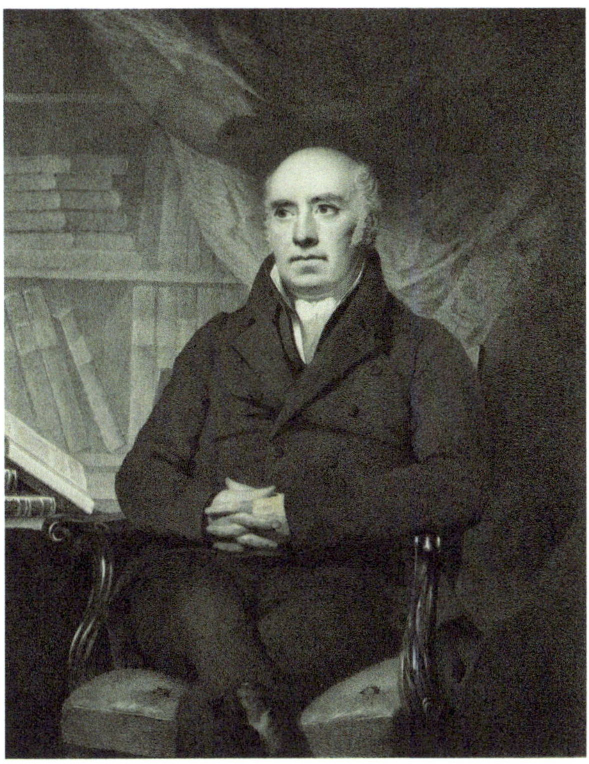

Figure 9.6 Cephas G. Childs after Albert Newsam after Henry Raeburn, *Dugald Stewart*, 1830, lithograph, 30.5×23.1cm, Historical Society of Pennsylvania, Philadelphia

ant, John Syme (1795–1861), who had painted Audubon's father in 1826. Among Audubon's extant paintings are copies after Raeburn's full-length *Mrs. James Hamilton of Kames* (New York Historical Society) and his bust-length *Sir Walter Scott* (Indiana University, Lilly Library). Of more obscure origin is the full-length *Sir Walter Scott* exhibited with three other supposed Raeburn paintings at the Pennsylvania Academy in 1848.[89] The four pictures were loaned by John Gibson (1813–77), a painter and decorator based in Philadelphia, but born in Edinburgh and trained there in the early 1830s by David Ramsay Hay (1798–1866), Walter Scott's protégé and interior designer.[90] It is doubtful that Raeburn painted any of the pictures in the 1848 exhibition. Possibly they were student copies by Hay or Gibson. More likely, they were recent acquisitions by Gibson. As such, they provide tantalising evidence of an American trade in Raeburn copies (or perhaps deliberate forgeries) as early as the 1840s – a clear indication of the artist's perceived value.

As the foregoing discussion has demonstrated, American interest in Raeburn remained strong in the decades after his death, sustained right up to the middle of the nineteenth century. Although he never approached the fame of Reynolds or Lawrence, whose official credentials as presidents of the Royal Academy of Arts bolstered their high standing in the United States, Raeburn's reputation surpassed that of any other British portraitist of his generation. The very few of his paintings that reached American shores prior to the mid-nineteenth century were the objects of close scrutiny and emulation by artists being groomed in the imported artistic traditions of the 'Old World'. On the strength of that handful of works, Raeburn attained a degree of influence that far exceeded what one would expect of a foreign, essentially provincial artist.

Notwithstanding his indisputable merits as a painter, Raeburn's early reception in the United States owed much to his identification with Scotland, raising the question of how differently he might have fared in America had he followed David Wilkie in relocating to London, rather than remaining steadfast in Edinburgh. The staunch manner in which Raeburn cleaved to the land of his birth appeared all the more affecting to a nation of immigrants, many of them also Scottish by birth or descent. As a loyal Scotsman who happened also to be a brilliant painter, Raeburn appealed to a prominent subset of the American elite whose ancestral or intellectual roots lay in Scotland but whose aspirations for the future were intertwined with the still evolving culture of the United States. Raeburn's art figured among myriad Scottish influences that these men and women introduced into American life. Their divided loyalties impressed a distinctly Caledonian mark on the new national culture they were helping to forge.

Notes

1. William Dunlap, *History of the Rise and Progress of the Arts of Design in the United States*, 2 vols, New York, 1969 [1st edn, 1834], I, pp. 395–6; Edinburgh and London 1997–8, p. 12, p. 202.

2. *Letters and Papers of Andrew Robertson, A. M.*, ed. Emily Robertson, London, 1895, p. 9; Dunlap, 1969 (as in note 1), I, p. 397.

3. Megan Holloway Fort, *Archibald and Alexander Robertson and Their Schools, the Columbian Academy of Painting, and the Academy of Painting and Drawing, New York, 1791–1835*, City University of New York, unpublished Ph.D. thesis, 2006, pp. 37–9.

4. Robertson 1895 (as in note 2), pp. 3–5.

5. Ibid., p. 11.

6. Ibid., p. 60; see also p. 41, p. 86, p. 127, p. 134, p. 168.

7. James L. Yarnall and William H. Gerdts, *The National Museum of American Art's Index to American Art Exhibition Catalogues*, 5 vols, 1986, III, p. 2136.

8. 'Review and Register of the Fine Arts,' *The American Monthly Magazine and Critical Review*, I, June 1817, p. 130, from American Periodicals Series Online.

9. Washington Irving, *Letters*, Ralph M. Alderman, Herbert L. Kleinfeld, and Jenifer S. Banks (eds), *The Complete Works of Washington Irving*, Boston, 1978–1982, XXIII, p. 332, p. 333, p. 345, p. 355, pp. 403–10, p. 440.

10. Sir John Carr, *Caledonian Sketches, or, a tour though Scotland in 1807*, New York, 1809, p. 124.

11. 'The Blue-Eyed Lassie' and 'When first I saw my Jeanie's face'; see James Johnson, *The Scots Musical Museum*, 6 vols, Edinburgh, 1787–1803, III, p. 340, 294, and James Gibson and James McKie, *Bibliography of Robert Burns, with Biographical and Bibliographical Notes, and Sketches of Burns Clubs, Monuments and Statues*, Kilmarnock, 1881, p. 144 and appendix p. 198. See also George St Hellman, *Washington Irving, Esquire: Ambassador at Large from the New World to the Old*, London, 1924, pp. 49–51.

12. Mary Balmanno, *Pen and Pencil*, New York, 1858, pp. 174–6.

13. Mary Bartlett Cowdrey, *American Academy of Fine Arts and American Art-Union. Exhibition Record, 1816–1852*, New York, 1953, p. 207.

14. Balmanno 1858 (as in note 12), p. 174. St Hellman, 1924 (as in note 11), p. 52.

15. Wallace Bruce, *In Clover and Heather*, Edinburgh and London, 1896, pp. 126–7; Wallace Bruce, *The Hudson*, Boston, 1881; 'New York's Historic Trees', *New York Times*, 4 May 1902, p. 22.

16. Minutes of 1 February, 5 May, and 5 July 1817, American Academy of Fine Arts microfilm ff. 12, 14–15, 171, New York Historical Society. Allan Cunningham's date of 1 June 1817 is incorrect, *The Lives of the Most Eminent British Painters and Sculptors*, 5 vols, New York, 1834, V, p. 233.

17. Quoted in Cunningham 1834 (as in note 16), V, p. 233.

18. Henry Raeburn to Alexander Robertson, 10 August 1819, American Academy of Fine Arts MSS, vol. 1, case 2, no. 50, New York Historical Society; Mabel C. Weaks, 'Works by Raeburn in America', *Connoisseur*, XCVII, May 1936, p. 276.

19. Ibid. For confirmation of Raeburn's high opinion, see Margaret Hunter Hall, *The Aristocratic Journey: Being the Outspoken Letters of Mrs. Basil Hall Written during a Fourteen Months' Sojourn in America 1827–1828*, New York and London, 1931, p. 22, pp. 31–2. James Grant Wilson (ed.), *Anne Grant, Memoirs of an American Lady*, 2 vols, New York, 1901, II, pp. 243–4. See also Livingston and Peter Van Brugh Livingston Manuscripts, vol. 3, ff. 488–96, New York Public Library, Livingston MSS.

20. As reported by P. V. B. Livingston's grandson, Livingston Bayard, in a letter of 29 January 1934, art reference file, New York Public Library.

21. Peter Van Brugh Livingston to Cornelia van Horne (Mrs Philip) Livingston, 27 July 1819, NYPL, Livingston MSS, vol. 3, f. 534.
22. Ibid.
23. NYPL, Livingston MSS, vol. 3, ff. 482–83.
24. Mackie 1994, Document 19.
25. The quotation is from a letter of 26 February 1893 to James G. Goodwin from Daniel Huntington (1816–1906), president of the National Academy of Design, who claimed to have had 'the account from his [Livingston's] own lips'; see curatorial file, Wadsworth Atheneum, Hartford, Connecticut. I am grateful for the very generous assistance of Erin Monroe in aiding my research at the Wadsworth.
26. NYPL, Livingston MSS, vol. 2, ff. 355–56, 359–60; Ruth Piwonka, *A Portrait of Livingston Manor, 1686–1850*, Germantown, 1986, pp. 126–8, p. 168.
27. NYPL, Livingston MSS, vol. 3, f. 534.
28. Henry Raeburn to Alexander Robertson, 10 August 1819, American Academy of Fine Arts MSS, vol. 1, case 2, no. 50, New York Historical Society.
29. Daniel Huntington to James G. Goodwin, 26 February 1893, curatorial file, Wadsworth Athenaeum, Hartford. See note 25 above.
30. NYPL, Livingston MSS, vol. 3, f. 530; see also vol. ff. 482–3.
31. Peter Van Brugh Livingston to Cornelia van Horne (Mrs Philip) Livingston, 28 December 1818, NYPL, Livingston MSS, vol. 3, ff. 460–68.
32. Peter Van Brugh Livingston to Cornelia van Horne (Mrs Philip) Livingston, 28 December 1818, 16 January 1819, and 25 February 1819, NYPL, Livingston MSS, vol. 3, ff. 469–71, 490.
33. Clare Brandt, *An American Aristocracy: The Livingstons*, Garden City, 1986, pp. 75–6; NYPL, Livingston MSS, vol. 1.
34. NYPL, Livingston MSS, vol. 3, 636; for the conditions of the sale to Maitland, see curatorial file, New York Public Library.
35. Several are mentioned in Weaks, 1936 (as in note 27), p. 277.
36. Minutes of 4 December 1819, American Academy of Fine Arts microfilm, f. 87 and American Academy of Fine Arts Papers, vol. 1, case 2, no. 51, New York Historical Society.
37. 'The Academy of Fine Arts. Volunteers', *New-York Evening Post*, 9 May 1820, p. 2.
38. 'Review of the Seventh Annual Exhibition of the American Academy of Fine Arts', *The New-York Columbian*, 28 May 1821, p. 2 from American Periodicals Series Online.
39. Cowdrey 1953 (as in note 13), p. 293. 'Apollo Exhibition,' *New-York Spectator*, 17 April 1841, p. 2.
40. Connecticut Historical Society, *Historical Documents and Notes. Genesis and Development of the Society and Associated Institutions in the Wadsworth Athenaeum,*

Hartford, 1889, p. 45. Yarnell and Gerdts, 1986 (as in note 7), IV, pp. 2866–7. Charles Henry Hart was mistaken in identifying the Wadsworth portrait as a copy by Sully after Raeburn ('Thomas Sully's Register of Portraits, 1801–1871', *The Pennsylvania Magazine of History and Biography*, 1909, XXXIII, p. 183).

41. American Academy of Fine Arts Papers, vol. 1, case 2, no. 51, New York Historical Society.

42. 'American Painters – and Painting', *The Yankee and Boston Literary Gazette*, July 1829, vol. 2; from American Periodicals Series Online.

43. Alexander Robertson to Henry Raeburn, 10 December 1819. MS. copy, New York Historical Society, American Academy of Fine Arts Papers, vol. 1, case 2, no. 51. See also Fort, 2006 (as in note 3), p. 76.

44. In addition to the works discussed in the text and in the endnotes below, a copy was made by Cornelius Ver Bryck (1813–44), brother-in-law of the artist Daniel Huntington, who studied with Samuel F. B. Morse in 1835. The portrait was also published as a mezzotint in the 1890s by the English-born painter Dawson Dawson-Watson (1864–1939), director of the Hartford Arts Society. See curatorial file, Wadsworth Atheneum.

45. Agate's copy was given to the New York Historical Society by the Ossining Historical Society, courtesy of Mrs Donald Ferguson (1959.58).

46. Edward Biddle and Mantle Fielding, *The Life and Works of Thomas Sully (1783–1872)*, Philadelphia: 1921, p. 214.

47. Monroe H. Fabian, *Mr. Sully, Portrait Painter: The Works of Thomas Sully (1783–1782)*, Washington, DC, 1983, p. 20.

48. Dunlap 1969 (as in note 1), II, p. 135.

49. Ibid., vol. 2, p. 138.

50. A copy attributed to Sully was sold (c. 1880s) with the contents of the Baldwin house, Chestnut Street, Philadelphia, by the New York art dealer J. Purves Carter (with Knoedler, c. 1938). Henry James Brown (1829–84), who studied with Sully in Philadelphia in 1848, painted a copy of Sully's copy (Sweet Briar College, Virginia). Other copies include one given by Mrs. Livingston Cromwell to the New York Historical Society (1960.90) and another purchased from James Lenox by Livingston's friend Henry Cary (1785–1857) and exhibited by him at the Boston Athenaeum in 1850 as *Portrait of an American Gentleman in the Costume of the Fox Club* (curatorial file, Wadsworth Athenaeum; Robert F. Perkins, Jr and William J. Gavin III (eds), *The Boston Athenaeum Art Exhibition Index, 1827–1874*, Boston, 1980, p. 113; Christie's, 16 November 2011, lot 194).

51. Frank H. Goodyear, Jr, 'A History of the Pennsylvania Academy of the Fine Arts, 1805–1976)' in *In This Academy: The Pennsylvania Academy of the Fine Arts 1805–1976*, Philadelphia, 1976, 12.

52. Dunlap, 1969 (as in note 1), II, p. 139. In his original notes, Sully had actually

observed that the pigments in Raeburn's palette were 'applicable to most *male complexions*' (my emphasis), suggesting that further modifications or substitutions would be required in painting females; see Thomas Sully MS. Notebooks, 1809–1871, vol. 1, f. 45, Beinecke Library, Yale University.

53. MS. Notebook of Francis William Edmonds, c. 1835–40, New York Historical Society.

54. Cf. Cunningham 1834 (note 16), vol. 4, p. 186.

55. Fabian 1983 (as in note 47), p. 19. For Sully's account of Lawrence's use of this technique, see his MS. Notebooks, vol. 1, ff. 48, 160, Beinecke Library, Yale University.

56. Helen Darcy Stewart to Philip Tidyman, 6 May 1825, American Philosophical Society, microfilm copy roll no. 35, fr. 178, Archives of American Art.

57. Alexander Broadie (ed.), *The Scottish Enlightenment: An Anthology*, Edinburgh, 1997, p. 275. See also Edinburgh and London 1986, pp. 79–80, pp. 129–30.

58. Mackie 1994 (as in note 24), vol. 1, p. 116.

59. Douglas Catterall, 'The Worlds of John Rose: A Northeastern Scot's Career in the British Atlantic World, c. 1740–1800' in *A Global Clan: Scottish Migrant Networks and Identities since the Eighteenth Century*, ed. Angela McCarthy, International Library of Historical Studies, London and New York, 2006, vol. 36, pp. 67–94; Mabel L. Webber, 'The Bond Family of Hobcaw Plantation, Christ Church Parish', *South Carolina Historical and Genealogical Magazine*, XXV, 1924, pp. 12, 18.

60. John Hammond Moore (ed.), 'The Abiel Abbot Journals: A Yankee Preacher in Charleston Society, 1818–1827', *South Carolina Historical and Genealogical Magazine*, LXVIII, 1867, p. 127; George C. Rogers, *The History of Georgetown County, South Carolina*, Columbia, 1970, p. 298; Webber, 1924 (as in note 59), p. 18; Joseph Ioor Waring, *A History of Medicine in South Carolina, 1670–1825*, Columbia, 1964, pp. 317–18; Benjamin Rush, *A memorial containing travels through life or sundry incidents in the life of Dr. Benjamin Rush*, Philadelphia, 1905, p. 170.

61. Letter of 2 March 1831 to J. K. Kane, copy provided by the Archives of the Pennsylvania Academy of the Fine Arts; James Stuart, *Three Years in North America*, 2 vols, New York, 1833, II, p. 71. James Harold Easterby, *History of the St. Andrew's Society of Charleston, South Carolina, 1729–1929*, Charleston, 1929, p. 78, p. 151; George Jonas Gongaware, *The History of the German Friendly Society of Charleston, South Carolina, 1766–1916*, Richmond, 1935, p. 5, pp. 77–9, pp. 100–3, pp. 105–15, pp. 130–2, p. 172.

62. Indeed, Tidyman returned to Aberdeen at the end of his life and died there on 11 June 1850. See Alexander MacDonald Munro (ed.), *Records of Old Aberdeen*, 2 vols, Aberdeen, 1909, II, p. 50; 'Death of Dr. Philip Tidyman', *Charleston Mercury*, II, July 1850, p. 2.

63. Hall 1931 (as in note 19), p. 214.

64. Paul Wood, 'Introduction: Dugald Stewart and the Invention of "The Scottish Enlightenment"' in Paul Wood (ed.), *The Scottish Enlightenment: Essays in Reinterpretation*, Rochester, 2000, pp. 1–35; Michael O'Brien, *Conjectures of Order: Intellectual Life and the American South, 1810–1860*, 2 vols, Chapel Hill and London, 2004, II, pp. 996–1001.

65. Helen Darcy Stewart to Philip Tidyman, 6 May 1825, American Philosophical Society, roll no. 35, fr. 178, Archives of American Art. *National Gazette* (Philadelphia) 5 September 1825, p. 2.

66. Philip Tidyman to the President and Directors of the Pennsylvania Academy of the Fine Arts, 12 July 1825, Archives of the Pennsylvania Academy of the Fine Arts. I am very grateful to Cheryl Leibold, Archivist of the PAFA, for kindly providing copies of this and other correspondence concerning Tidyman's gift of the Raeburn portrait.

67. Thomas Sully and John Kintzing Kane to Philip Tidyman, 13 August 1825, Archives of the Pennsylvania Academy of the Fine Arts. As the foregoing summary of events makes clear, the portrait was not commissioned by the Pennsylvania Academy (as stated in Edinburgh and London 1986 [as in note 57], p. 79), nor did Raeburn present the academy 'with a replica of his famous portrait of Dugald Stewart' in thanks for his election as an honorary academician (Hart, 1909 [as in note 40], p. 183). I am grateful to Cheryl Leibold, PAFA Archivist, for confirming that the honorary membership actually went to Tidyman.

68. Peter Hastings Falk (ed.), *The Annual Exhibition Record of the Pennsylvania Academy of the Fine Arts, 1807–1870*, Madison, 1988, p. 176; Perkins and Gavin, 1980 (as in note 50), p. 113.

69. Robert Walsh, *Didactics: Social, Literary, and Political*, 2 vols, Philadelphia, 1836, vol. 2, pp. 251–3.

70. Robert Walsh, 'Stewart's Philosophical Essays', *American Review of History and Politics*, I, April 1811, p. 355. See also Mary Frederick Lochemes, *Robert Walsh: His Story*, Washington, DC, 1941, pp. 46–7.

71. William Charvat quoted in Daniel S. Burt (ed.), *The Chronology of American Literature*, New York, 2004, p. 160.

72. Hart 1909 (as in note 40), p. 183. Intriguingly, in 1827 Sully transcribed a lengthy passage from Stewart's *Elements of the Philosophy of the Human Mind* (1792) concerning the difference between copying mechanically and with the aid of 'creative genius' (MS. Notebooks, vol. 1, ff. 61–2).

73. Cunningham 1834 (as in note 16), V, p. 233.

74. See, for example, Catterall, 2006 (as in note 59), passim.

75. *Baltimore Patriot*, 16 November 1822, p. 1.

76. *Charleston Courier*, 16 February 1829, p. 2. See also Anna Wells Rutledge, 'Cogdell and Mills, Charleston Sculptors', *Antiques*, XLI, 1942, p. 192; Sally

Doscher, 'Art Exhibitions in Nineteenth-Century Charleston' and Paul Staiti, 'The 1823 Exhibition of the South Carolina Academy of the Fine Arts: A Paradigm of Charleston Taste?' in David Moltke-Hansen (ed.), *Art in the Lives of South Carolinians: Nineteenth-Century Chapters*, Charleston, 1979.

77. *Charleston Courier*, 11 March 1842, p. 2. *St. Andrew's Society, of the City of Charleston, South Carolina*, Charleston, 1892, p. 130, p. 133.

78. Easterby, 1929 (as in note 61), pp. 112–14, pp. 124–5, p. 151 n. 26; Webber, 1924 (as in note 59), p. 19. Sully's copy of *Dugald Stewart* was for some fifty years confused with Shee's *John Philip Kemble* (mentioned in Tidyman's letter of 2 March 1831 to J. K. Kane, quoted above), which Tidyman bequeathed to the St Andrew's Society. The actual facts were established in 1923 but the misidentification has unfortunately been repeated in Mackie, 1993 (as in note 24), no. 684b.

79. *The Farmer's Cabinet*, 19 June 1845, p. 2.

80. 'Destruction of the Academy of Fine Arts', *North American*, 13 June 1845, p. 2.

81. Robert W. Gibbes, *A Memoir of James de Veaux, of Charleston, S.C.*, Columbia, SC, 1846, p. 17.

82. For example, the '*Portrait of a Gentleman* after Raeburn' by Sully's son-in-law John Neagle (1796–1865), exhibited at the first exhibition of the Artists' Fund Society in 1835 (Falk, 1988 [as in note 68], p. 176) and the reduced-scale copy by the Philadelphia portraitist Edward H. Darley (1828–68), whose brother married Sully's daughter (sold at Bonhams and Butterfield, 1987). A bust-length portrait of an unknown man (Philadelphia Academy of Fine Arts, 1933.10.80) was misidentified as Sully's copy after Raeburn's *Dugald Stewart* in Biddle and Fielding, 1921 (as in note 46), pp. 279–80, no. 1650, and in Mantle Fielding, *Exhibition of American Portraits. Collection of John Frederick Lewis*, Philadelphia, 1934, p. 29, no. 53.

83. I am grateful to Brenda Wetzel of the State Museum of Pennsylvania for her very generous assistance with my research on Mifflin's painting.

84. Anna Wells Rutledge, 'Dunlap Notes', *Art in America*, XXXIX, 1951, p. 45; Cowdrey, 1953 (as in note 13), p. 220; Falk, 1988 (as in note 68), p. 176; Perkins and Gavin, 1980 (as in note 50), p. 113.

85. D. McN. Stauffer, 'Lithographic Portraits of Albert Newsam', *Pennsylvania Magazine of History and Biography*, XXIV, 1900, p. 443. Joseph O. Pyatt, *Memoir of Albert Newsam (Deaf Mute Artist)*, Philadelphia, 1868, p. 54, pp. 90–2.

86. 'Metropolitan Gossipings', *Daily National Intelligencer* (Washington, DC), 18 May 1839, p. 2.

87. *Morning Herald*, 5 December 1838, p. 2. See also pre-1877 Art Exhibition Catalogue Index, Smithsonian American Art Museum. For the provenance of *Lady Belhaven*, see Richard Dorment, *British Painting in the Philadelphia Museum of Art*, Philadelphia, 1986, p. 257 n. 2.

88. John W. Audubon, *Audubon's Western Journal, 1849–1850*, Cleveland, 1906, pp. 24–5.
89. The three other paintings were listed as: *Full length portrait of Sir David Baird; Full length portrait of Sir Ralph Abercrombie*; and *Head of Cupid*, Falk, 1988 [as in note 68], p. 176.
90. For Gibson, see *An Historical Catalogue of the St. Andrew's Society of Philadelphia, with Biographical Sketches of Deceased Members*, 2 vols, Philadelphia, 1907, I, p. 173–5; Edwin T. Freedley, *Philadelphia and Its Manufactures*, Philadelphia, 1859, p. 278: Francis James Dallett, 'John Notman, Architect', *The Princeton University Library Chronicle*, XX, Spring 1959, p. 130, pp. 132–3.

IO

Raeburn and Goya: The Redefinition of Artistic Personality

Sarah Symmons

A recent compilation of painters dedicated to keeping the medium alive in the twenty-first century examined how current art practices learn from the past.[1] Faced with accusations of being conservative, even irrelevant, the contemporary painter will push oil and canvas to the limits of polystyrene resin, dung, blood or glitter on linen, metal or plastic to create illusions on surfaces. In spite of such extremes it is often more prosaic research into the methods of earlier practitioners which obtains the most startling results. Extending a range of references, from Velázquez to Van Gogh, reveals how the magic of painting for the modern artist and spectator can still be an obsession; how the power of paint remains mesmerising. Even the most avant-garde artists cannot resist linking themselves to Old Masters, finding new values in those whose painterly achievements in their own time seemed as unorthodox as those today.

Among the Old Masters transposed into new roles stand Goya and Raeburn, companions in the pantheon of chosen inspirers for the contemporary avant-garde. 'Vitamin P' painters of the present day would not be surprised to learn that their linking of the two in the context of unconventional treatment of the medium, is not the first. The Edwardian period with its enthusiasm for portraiture also explored the work of both artists, while the historiography of French Impressionist portraits claimed not only Whistler and Manet as exponents of the new style, but Goya and Raeburn too. From Whistler to Augustus John, these two relative outsiders from the age of Revolution and Regency became valuable to the revival of portrait painting, a subject which had staled in the salon and academy exhibitions of the nineteenth century.

Raeburn and Goya can be seen as deconstructing the polite portrait standards set by British and French artists in the eighteenth century, by challenging the models offered by seventeenth-century portraiture and wreaking artistic havoc on what their contemporaries believed a portrait was meant to be. They faced tricky eighteenth-century sitters who could turn up late for sittings, demand impracticable details of status and wealth, or refuse to pay. Such patrons found themselves confronted by two bold and original painters for whom a portrait was more about the medium. Goya took risks with size, perspective and surface finish; and Raeburn with lighting, gesture and arrangement. They were both adventurous in their application of colour, and ended up devising portraits as fictions in which narrative and subtext are evoked and play roles beyond the simple requirements of physical appearance and status. Pursuing parallel careers in Edinburgh and Madrid, both emerge as redesigning the conception of what a portrait was. While Raeburn and Goya never met, there are some striking similarities in their respective careers. They both experimented with miniature painting, explored identical influences and developed two distinct and striking personalities as portraitists, which mean that later artists who are influenced by one may also be attracted to the other.

There are even more links between them, which demonstrate how analogous their ambitions were and how they shared methods of developing new portrait techniques, especially at the beginnings of their careers. They came from the artisan class of their respective societies, Raeburn the son of a yarn-boiler and Goya of a gilder. Their early lives are somewhat obscure, with their early works containing little evidence of precocious talent. They seem to have taken similar decisions with regard to vocational travel, an influential marriage and a patron or master who could expedite their ambitions. Like Raeburn, Goya financed himself to go to Italy. Neither had a 'prix de Rome' or scholarship. In Britain this was fairly usual. Even well connected British artists, such as the sculptor John Flaxman, had to support themselves in Italy. In Spain, however, where the Royal Academy in Madrid provided lucrative scholarships, it was unusual to take the risk of travelling without sponsorship, but Goya was twice rejected for academic preferment.[2]

For both Goya and Raeburn, Italy, and especially Rome, seem to have been a turning point in their careers. Goya wrote years later that seeing great works of art in Rome was a formative experience of his early life, and one he never forgot.[3] It was in Italy that he received his first academic recognition, in a history painting competition at the Royal Academy in Parma. Raeburn, too, must have realised that the competitive practice of portraiture in Britain

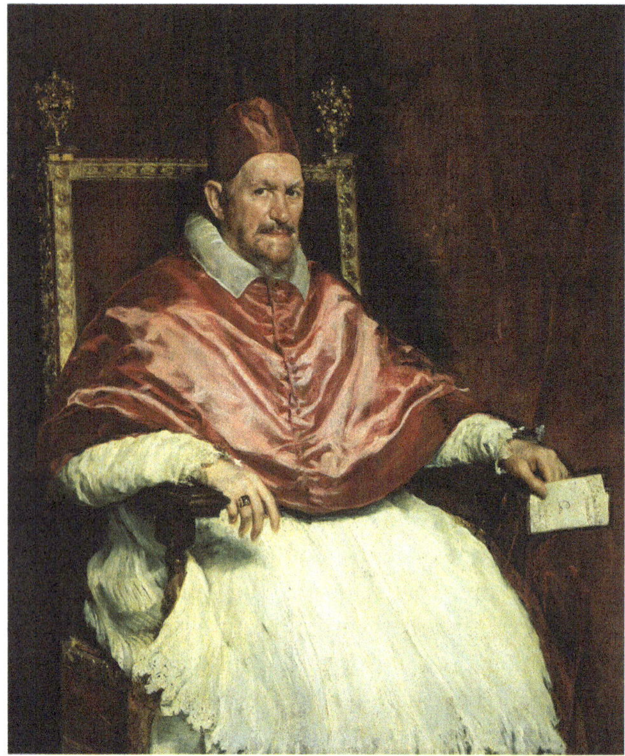

Figure 10.1 Diego Velázquez, *Pope Innocent X*, c. 1650, oil on canvas, 123.2×97.8cm, Galleria Doria Pamphilj, Rome (courtesy of Bridgeman Art Library)

set such high standards that it would be difficult for an outsider to succeed unless he had studied abroad.

Unlike Goya, Raeburn devoted himself exclusively to portraiture from an early age. His declaration that he was a portrait painter on a document prior to his departure to Rome in 1784, is stated a year after Goya made his first influential portrait, that of the prime minister of Spain, the count of Floridablanca.[4] Both artists had aspirations to do other things. Raeburn's early neoclassical studies suggest that he might once briefly have contemplated a career as a history painter. Goya, originally dedicated to becoming a religious artist and graphic designer, decided to diversify and went into portraiture after a serious professional setback at a church in Saragossa.[5]

It was while in Rome that Raeburn discovered one great portrait that was to become a formative influence throughout his career, that of *Pope Innocent X* by Velázquez (Fig. 10.1). Raeburn's fascination with this work not only changed his life as a portraitist, but brought him close to the established painter who may have been something of a mentor for his work, Joshua Reynolds. Reynolds had studied Velázquez's pope some thirty years earlier, while in Rome in 1750–52, and he was later to write that it was 'one of the finest paintings in the world'.[6] Raeburn's admiration for Reynolds is well known, although an undated meeting with James Northcote in Reynolds's London house seems to be the only specific record that the young artist spent time in Reynolds's company.[7]

The influence of Velázquez on British portraiture was a revelation to another Scot, David Wilkie, when he visited Madrid. Wilkie's diary for 29 October 1827 includes the entry: 'Velasquez [sic] . . . may be said to be the origin of what is now doing in England. His feeling they have caught almost without seeing his works; which here seem to anticipate Reynolds, Romney, Raeburn'. And in a letter to Thomas Lawrence written from Spain in November 1827, he added:

> To our English tastes it is unnecessary to advocate the style of Velasquez. I know not if the remark be new, but we appear as if identical with him; and while I am in the two galleries at the Museum [the royal collection in Madrid] half filled with his works, I can almost fancy myself among English pictures, Sir Joshua, Romney and Raeburn, whether from imitation or instinct, seem powerfully imbued with his style and some of our own time, even to our landscape painters, seem to possess the same affinity.[8]

It was Raeburn, however, who was singled out by Wilkie as an artist whose affinity with Velázquez was particularly striking. He wrote that the effect of a single portrait by Velázquez 'produced a similarity both in the natural character and breadth of effect inherent in the portraits of Raeburn and those who have followed him in the same wake'.[9]

Wilkie's emphasis on Raeburn's debt to Velázquez is especially relevant to Raeburn's first major portrait commission after his return from Italy in 1787. The portrait of *Robert Dundas, Lord Arniston* (Fig. 10.2) was painted shortly before the sitter's death and testifies to the effect that the Spanish artist's papal portrait made on the youthful Raeburn. Here is evolved a model which Raeburn was to revisit. What Wilkie called Raeburn's 'square touch', inspired by the Sevillan master's brushwork, is noticeable particularly on the planes of the face, the outlining of the nose and highlight placed over the left nostril. Such broad treatment is complemented by more prosaic references: the slanted pose from left to right in the armchair, the arrangement of the two hands, one dangling with limp fingers, the other curled up, while the chair with its line of carefully-painted gilt studs, the treatment of the crimson

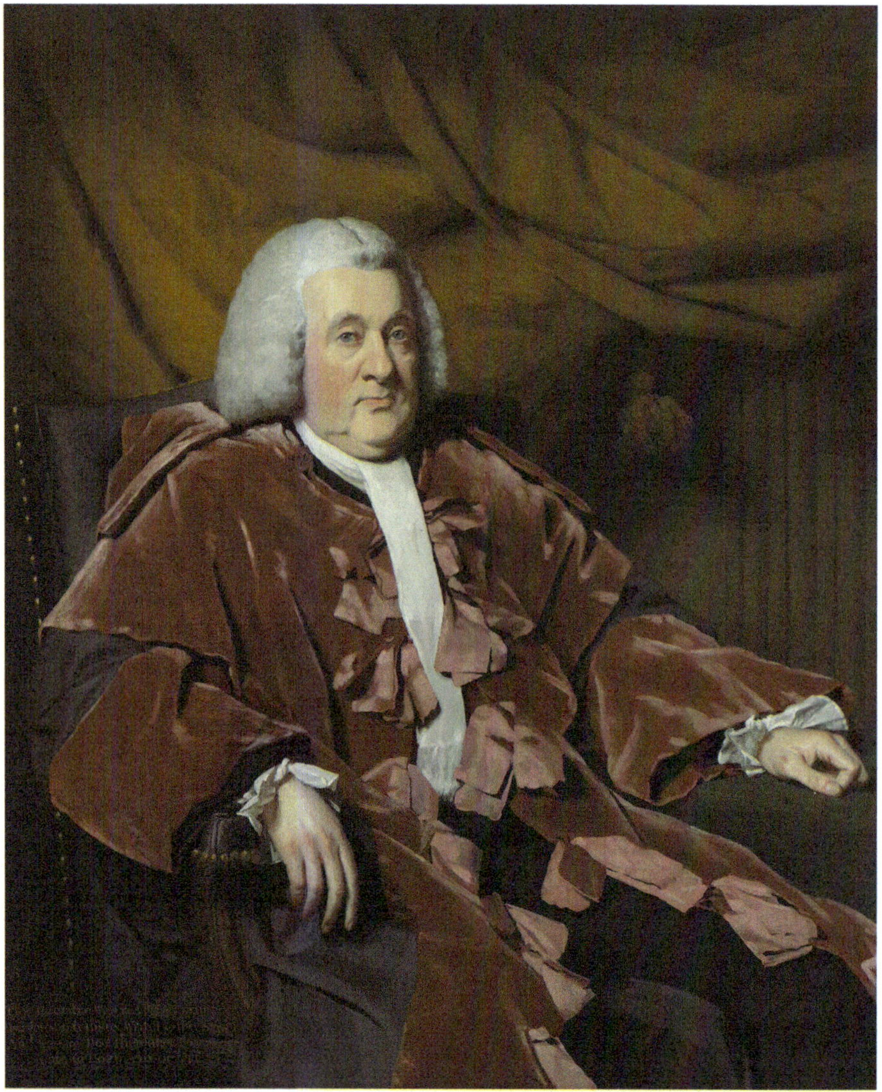

Figure 10.2 Henry Raeburn, *Robert Dundas, Lord Arniston*, 1787, oil on canvas, 121.5×102.5cm, courtesy of the Dundas-Bekker family, Arniston House

drapery and the reddish background curtains, fix the portrait recognisably within the parameters of what Velázquez had achieved in 1650.

In the 1790s Raeburn produced more portraits within the same proto-type, all of them seated half-lengths of Enlightenment men of the University of Edinburgh. John Robison, Adam Ferguson and William Robertson were men of intellect and learning, and the choice of Velázquez as a model for their likenesses seems like a form of artistic strategy as Raeburn absorbed and worked through the influence so that it became an essential ingredient of his style. Goya too was to make a copy of Velázquez's pope and in his portraits of seated intellectuals at desks, executed in the 1790s, depicted amid the clutter of the enlightened statesman or man of affairs, he relies as heavily as Raeburn on lighting, broad brushwork and a glowing tonality that can be found in Velázquez.[10] The intense and introverted expressions of these sitters anchor such portraits to the redefinition of an interior personality, discernable not only in *Lord Arniston* but also in Goya's *Portrait of Don Francisco de Saavedra*, Carlos IV's enlightened Minister of Finance who the Aragonese artist painted in 1798.[11]

Goya turned to the art of Velázquez at a crucial point in his early career. Like Raeburn, who made a study of David and Goliath during his Roman visit, Goya also studied biblical subjects in his Italian notebook, prior to returning to Aragón.[12] Also, like Raeburn, he made an advantageous marriage, so he should have been well placed to succeed. Both men were prepared to gamble when in the early stages of their careers they were struggling to make a living, Goya's greatest gamble being in 1775 when, with a young son and pregnant wife, he left Aragón for the capital.

In eighteenth-century Spain the provinces provided lucrative sources of patronage for local artists. In Britain too, while London remained the principal centre, the provinces could offer a good living, as Gainsborough found in Bath and Ramsay in Edinburgh. Nevertheless, metropolitan centres were also essential for exhibition exposure. After returning from Italy, Raeburn remained in Edinburgh for the rest of his life, but was obliged to travel south, exhibited there and, in 1810, even considered a permanent move to London.[13]

Goya's relocation to Madrid from the provinces was as much of a risky undertaking as his Italian journey. In Saragossa, Aragón, where Goya had set up a local practice after his arrival back from Italy, he had married into an influential artistic family and made many friends. There he was becoming well known. In Madrid, few knew him, apart from the king's painter, Anton Raphael Mengs, the Bohemian artist from Rome, who had become Carlos III's Primer Pintor de Cámara [First Painter to the Court] and who listed Goya as among the most promising young artists of the day.[14]

Like Raeburn, who worked in the applied arts as a goldsmith early in his career, Goya's earliest commissions in Madrid were also in the applied arts, designing for the weavers at the tapestry factory of Santa Barbara. Having left the capital of the region of Aragón where he was born, Saragossa, in January 1775, he became a lowly designer in a large concern. His admiration for Mengs, who was known in Spain not only as a leading neoclassical artist and theorist but also as a major portraitist, was not unlike Raeburn's respect for Reynolds. In the shadow of such lofty idealists, the two young artists obviously felt the need to escape from their association with the applied arts.

In 1776, when Goya had been in Madrid for a year, he was clearly frustrated and planned another risky move: a return to Rome to study with Mengs. His wife was unwilling but persuadable, but the whole project relied on financial support. In a draft letter Goya's respect for the Bohemian artist, as well as his financial need, is made very clear:

> Illustrious and most esteemed friend: I write to trouble you because I have persuaded my wife to change her mind about going to Rome in order to benefit from your favour there. And I ask you for God's sake to speak to His Majesty [Carlos III] on my behalf so that he may give . . . a grant for the maintenance of myself and my family over there, so that I can study with you when you go.[15]

In the event no such grant was ever forthcoming from Carlos III. However, in the same year as Goya considered going to Rome, Don Antonio Ponz, painter and Secretary to the Royal Academy in Madrid, published a letter by Mengs in which the foreigner praised the art of Velázquez.[16] Mengs left for Rome in 1777 and died there in 1779. Goya never saw him again. Perhaps to recover from this disappointment and alleviate the drudgery of designing tapestry cartoons, Goya decided to spend his limited free time making prints after Velázquez's portraits in the Royal Collection. The opinion of Mengs may have had some influence on this decision, and Goya's prints, first published in 1778, the year before Mengs died, were among his earliest major works in graphic design. The whole exercise represented another courageous gamble on the part of the Aragonese painter. It was freelance work in a medium with which Goya was unfamiliar; he faced the challenge of reproducing Velázquez's very personal and well-loved portrait style, and he was competing with professional engravers whose competence in the graphic arts was far in advance of his own.[17]

In Spain, the British enthusiasm for Velázquez, which had increased during the later eighteenth century, was to become part of a revival of native Spanish painting after nearly a century under the Bourbon monarchy when court and church employed foreign artists. The newly enlightened Spanish culture sought in a spirit of reviving nationalism to display and disseminate masterpieces of Spanish painting from the Golden Age, and the demand for copies after Velázquez by British collectors, was welcomed. Antonio Palomino's seminal *Lives of the Eminent Spanish Painters and Sculptors*, which made Velázquez into the hero of the story of Spanish art, was translated and edited into a number of English editions and abridgements.[18] So anxious was

Carlos III to encourage this admiration that he asked for the British monarchy to be made aware that any British artists who wanted to make copies in the Royal Collection would be given accommodation: 'the King . . . authorized me to say, that if the King my master thought fit to send over English artists to copy any of the pictures in his collection, either for engraving or otherwise, he would give them all possible facility and maintain them at free cost, whilst they were so employed.' Richard Cumberland, in Spain in 1780–81, recorded this extraordinary piece of royal generosity.[19] While English artists seem not to have taken much advantage of Carlos III's offer, one Scottish painter, Richard Cooper, made a study of Velázquez, and several Scottish visitors to Spain took advantage of the hospitality of Spanish academicians as regards the promotion of the national style.[20]

In 1781, a Scottish couple, Mary and Thomas Graham, arrived in Madrid and were shown part of the Royal Collection, taken round the Escorial and given a detailed itinerary of the holdings of the Real Academia de San Fernando in Madrid. Mary Graham's Spanish journal itemises the key artworks she saw. Nowadays remembered chiefly as the sitter for one of Gainsborough's most stunning mature portraits and as a victim of tuberculosis, she was taken to Spain and Portugal by her husband in search of a climate more congenial than that of Perthshire. On her journey in 1781 she kept several journals and a sketchbook devoted to recording her Iberian experiences. Mary was especially fascinated by Spanish dress and her drawing and writing reveal her eye for detail. Her drawings additionally show some knowledge of Spanish art.

In the Real Academia in Madrid she admired an early work by Goya. In 1780 Goya had received academic status and membership of the Academy with a *Crucified Christ*, which he subsequently left in the Academy before it was transferred to a Franciscan monastery on the orders of the Count of Floridablanca.[21] The painting was still hanging in the Academy when Mary Graham visited, and she noted in one of her journals: 'a whole length Picture of Our Saviour [,] the Composition of a young Spanish painter of this academy which all thought very well done'.[22] Her comment is intriguing in that she was prepared to admire Goya as well as Velázquez. Goya's *Crucified Christ* is a daring mixture of Mengs and Velázquez in colouring and drawing, which is perhaps why Mary was so struck by it. She would have known how original was the art of Velázquez because one of her closest relatives, her uncle, Sir William Hamilton, owned what was then arguably the best authentic portrait then in British hands, Velázquez's portrait of his half Moorish servant, Juan de Pareja.[23] Mary records that Velázquez was, 'a very famous Spanish painter particularly for portraits'.[24] Even in this context Spanish dress remained her chief source of interest and she marvelled at the hooped skirts of Velázquez's Infantas. She also admired 'a Venus looking at herself in a Glass held by a Cupid where her face appears reflected'.[25] Of Velázquez's other works in the Royal Collection she wrote: 'One need not understand Paintings to admire these as the faces are all so beautiful & the colouring looks so very like the Reality that one cannot pass by them.'[26] Having scrutinised one of the hunting scenes she goes on to describe the portraits of the royal family, some of which had already been copied or were in the process of being copied by Goya: 'a Picture of Don Balthasar Carlos, a child in a riding dress – there is also a picture of an Infanta in an immense hoop and a fine Head of a Pope . . . and a portrait of Philip IV in his youth – All his pictures are very much alike & have a strong resemblance,' she wrote, taken in by the family likeness of the Habsburgs and influenced by the enthusiasm of her Spanish guides.[27] One of these, Bernardo de Yriarte, became the vice-protector of the Royal Academy and the subject of one of Goya's best portraits in 1797. Mary Graham's first view of the painting, categorised then as the most valuable in the Royal Collection, *Las Meninas*, was clearly also disconcerting. 'The Infanta D Margherita de Austria with children & Velazquez's picture of her is much admired by the Spaniards'.[28] Not quite convinced that the figures were dwarves Mary played safe and thought them children, but although she was only an amateur, she knew enough to regard Velázquez's great work as a ' picture' rather than a 'portrait', suggesting that its ranking as a subject picture was already recognisable. This perhaps was not unlike the style of Goya's copies after Velázquez. His first set of prints after the portraits of the Sevillan master were admired by the British Ambassador to Spain, Lord Grantham, who bought eight sets, one of which he presented to Joshua Reynolds.[29] Reynolds's opinion of Goya's prints was very positive and although Goya's friend, the art historian Juan Ceán Bermúdez, was to feel that insufficiently few foreigners knew the art of Velázquez, it was in the eighteenth century that the British were among the first to value the Spanish master's work. In this context it is interesting that Mary Graham was not only the first British woman to admire a work by Goya, but that her family, who were also admirers of Velázquez, were later to commission portraits from Raeburn.[30]

Velázquez's eye for contemporary fashion characterised aspects of Spanish painting, which enchanted many British spectators in the nineteenth century, and this is also a striking feature of the portraiture of Raeburn and Goya. Goya made some sixteen prints after paintings by Velázquez, and the first set, issued and advertised in July 1778, included five equestrian portraits, the full-lengths of Menippus and Aesop and two court dwarves. In December he added two more prints to the set, a copy of *Los Borrachos*, [the Drunkards] and another equestrian of Balthasar Carlos. Goya's prints transform Velázquez's broad and liquid figure paintings and portraits into something immensely delicate in which the light is picked up and becomes all-important. His prints are also extremely lively; far from pedestrian copies, they extend the range of Velázquez's vision, exploring the possibilities of change and innovation. In drapery, jackets, hats and boots the eye is drawn to bold contours and intriguing shadows. Goya's later print of *Las Meninas* also transforms the painting into a personal hierarchy of light and shade in a group composition with the new method of aquatint.

Raeburn too was to use Velázquez as a starting point for a similar revivification of portrait imagery. It is arguable that he might well have seen some of Goya's prints in the Reynolds collection, but there were many more copies of Velázquez circulating in Britain. While *The Archers*, which Raeburn completed c. 1790, has been identified as a Velázquez-inspired portrait composition in terms of colouring and brushwork, the single full-length of *Robert Ferguson of Raith*, in terms of the placing of the legs, feet, gun and dog, appears like a full-blown challenge to Velázquez's portrait of the *Infante Don Fernando* (Fig. 10.3) of which Goya made several engraved copies in the late 1770s and early 1780s.[31] Goya too began his official career as a portrait artist from Velázquez's example. His portrait of the *Count of Floridablanca* of 1783, his first major sitter, was, like Raeburn with *Lord Arniston*, a recreation of many features of the Velázquez portrait style. With subsequent formal portraits, especially state likenesses of Carlos III and his son and heir Carlos IV portrayed as huntsmen, the Velázquez imagery of the Habsburgs is employed by Goya in the most arbitrary way.

The stylistic influence of Velázquez operated as another turning point for both artists. The enlightenment figures who passed through their studios and became their sitters: statesmen, poets, priests and women of fashion, represented a cross section of the society in which the two artists lived and worked. Goya took on the portrait competition in Madrid and dominated it in a short space of time, becoming the major portraitist of the day by the 1780s. Although now regarded as one of the great graphic designers of his age, a modern history painter, religious artist, caricaturist and draughtsman of supreme originality, in his own lifetime Goya's prosperity and public reputation developed mainly through portraiture. It was as a portrait artist that he gave instruction and employment to the foremost copyist of the day, the Valencian, Augustín Esteve, who also became known outside Spain, partly through his outstanding copies of Goya's portraits as well as the Old Masters, his miniatures, and as a major portraitist in his own right.[32] When in June 1814, a deputation arrived in Madrid from the province of Navarra wanting to commission a portrait of the new king Fernando VII, a representative of the Royal Academy told them in a letter 'The most outstanding painters are

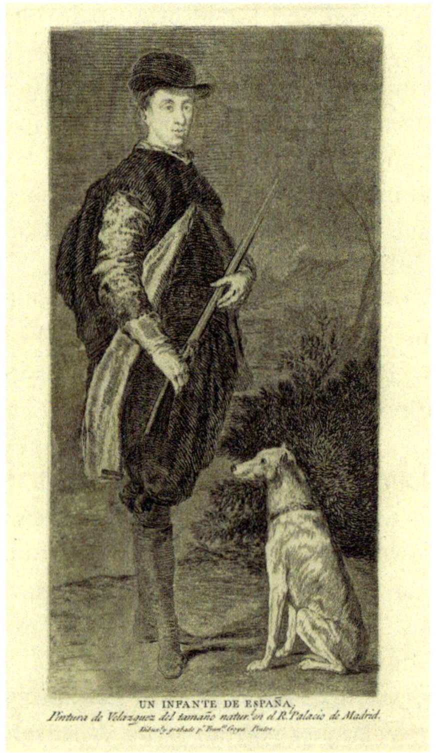

Figure 10.3 Francisco Goya after Diego Velázquez, *The Infante Don Fernando*, 1778, etching and drypoint on paper, 28.2×17cm, Department of Prints and Drawings, The British Museum, London (© Trustees of the British Museum)

Francisco de Goya, from Aragón, recognised as the first, and then Augustin Esteve.'[33]

Just as the deputation from Navarra was unhappy with Goya's half-length portrait of Fernando VII, Raeburn too had problems with his sitters.[34] Both artists experienced variable reactions and both had difficult moments and declines in their portrait reputations. Criticisms veered between brushwork and lighting, which were seen as amateurish, and perspective which could be interpreted as wobbly, even careless. The unpredictable nature of these portraits also, however, became a source of immense liveliness and realism. Raeburn's children, for example, often seem to have problems staying on their feet, rather like Goya's child portraits and images of the Bourbon monarchs.[35] While some may have seen this as a deficiency, it is more likely that such disturbances in the integument of a portrait were deliberate as both artists pursued naturalism to an almost unprecedented degree. In February

1790, after delivering a portrait to King Carlos IV, Goya wrote that the king
was satisfied with the work. 'I am not able to do more than I am doing . . . and
I cannot compromise my nature or talent as some others may.'[36]

Goya's later portraits of the Bourbon monarch Fernando VII, dating
from 1808 to 1815, are not seen as his best works, and even earlier likenesses drew censorship. One of Goya's reluctant sitters actually referred
to his portrait style as 'horrible'.[37] Raeburn attracted similar hostility. In
December 1812, Lord Frederick Campbell offered his full-length portrait
by Raeburn to George Home of Wedderburn and was to express little surprise when the offer was refused.[38] After his death Raeburn had the veracity of his eyesight doubted, while Goya's full-lengths of Fernando VII show
strange positions and arbitrary uses of colour, and have never been redeemed
from the twentieth-century conviction that such features express political
commitment and hidden ironies.[39]

The two artists probably absorbed such daring methods again from their
study of earlier portraiture. It was Velázquez who could make a disabled
child, an ugly man or an overdressed woman into an image so lifelike that
few have ever surpassed the achievement. In exotic and nationalistic portraiture, Velázquez could also be invoked. *Colonel Alastair Ranaldson Macdonell of
Glengarry* (Fig. 10.4), exhibited at the Royal Academy in 1812, sees Raeburn
creating a dramatic piece of history and fiction out of legendary Scottish
costume and trimmings, but the rare full-length with, in this case, the even
rarer half-profile, a challenge which more cautious portraitists tried to avoid,
shows a figure teetering in fabulous costume beside a musket. Here again the
example of daring in full-length likenesses is being interpreted in a manner
not dissimilar to Goya's creations.

The Velázquez portraits, interpreted by Goya, such as the Menippus or
the Habsburg princes in hunting gear, have a similar imaginative range of
expression and inspired some of the artist's most experimental full-lengths.[40]
The way in which Velázquez could transform the weaknesses of a sitter's
deportment into a source of liveliness was never lost on such risk-taking
portraitists whose work did not always satisfy their sitters.

Volume XV of the third edition of the *Encyclopedia Britannica*, published
in Edinburgh in 1797, was to define the portrait as 'the representation of
a person, and especially of a face, done from the life.'[41] The article states
that the chief difference between portraiture and history painting was that
in history painting precise details of personal resemblance were usually disregarded. This was a simplification of Reynolds's definition of the hierar-
chies of painting. The business of portraiture being done from the life was
very much an enlightened ideal and one which both Goya and Raeburn
meticulously carried out. It was also a method cultivated by British artists,

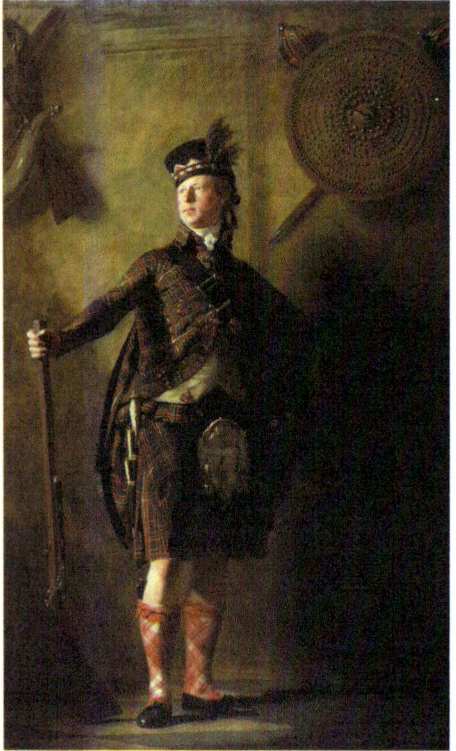

Figure 10.4 Henry Raeburn, *Colonel Alastair Ranaldson Macdonell of Glengarry*, 1812, oil on canvas, 241 × 150cm, Scottish National Gallery, Edinburgh

specifically Reynolds, whose sitter books testify to regular on-site posings. The Revd John Hamilton remembered the long sittings Raeburn exacted and how he tried to amuse the little boy while painting him.[42] In Goya's case no less a witness than the queen consort of Spain herself, Maria Luisa de Borbón, recorded an unforgettable memory of posing for Goya during many exhausting hours, up a ladder and wearing a hat, having been obliged to clear the whole ground floor of the palace while Goya completed her equestrian portrait.[43]

Such fidelity to naturalism may have been another stylistic method gleaned from earlier examples but for Raeburn and Goya it was also an essential part of the process. When a sitter could not pose for as long as was required, as in the case of the Duke of Wellington, Goya used a detailed drawing which fixed the main outlines and obtained an extraordinarily strong impression of personality and movement. Raeburn, according to one witness, obtained similar immediacy by distancing his effects and making sure that a portrait was hung correctly.[44] Other smaller considerations such as accurate portrayals of medals or uniforms were sometimes overlooked. The lively brushwork in the half-length of the Duke of Wellington may not have comforted the sitter's realisation that Goya got the uniform wrong, and Raeburn too was sometimes accused of the same inaccuracies.[45]

For British audiences who crowded into the Royal Academy exhibitions in London the vanity of sitters and the dominance of portraiture became tedious. As early as 1777, the *Morning Chronicle and London Advertiser* reported 'the poverty of the present is . . . apparent . . . from the superabundant numbers of portraits, which, like dominos at a modern masquerade, crowd every corner of the rooms'.[46] Such a commentary was to become a repetitive critique of the Royal Academy in the following century as the commercialisation of art into popular portraiture seemed like a betrayal of the elevated ambitions of Reynolds and the ideals surrounding the founding of the institution.[47] Nevertheless, it was particularly during the last two decades of the eighteenth century, that British portraiture became especially popular in Madrid. For much of the century Spain had been under the artistic domination of the French but the cult of British portraiture grew as enlightened Spaniards visited London and prints after the most famous works were sent to Madrid. The increase in print dealing between Spain and Britain was extensive. Britain had become famous as a centre for new techniques. Mezzotint, for example, with its emphasis on mimicking the effects of brush-strokes, modelling and half tones, was particularly studied by Spaniards who came to London and visited venues such as Boydell's Shakespeare Gallery, where they could see prints as well as paintings. The heroic British style of portraiture was particularly valued in Spain. At the Real Academia de San Fernando in Madrid admiration for Reynolds, Benjamin West, Fuseli and Romney was openly expressed in academic lectures.[48]

Both Raeburn and Goya have been thought to be influenced by Gainsborough. Had Raeburn visited London on his return from Italy it would have been an easy matter for him to have gone to the Gainsborough gallery in Schomberg House, Pall Mall, where Gainsborough's most popular and famous portraits were on view, and which remained accessible long after the artist died in an exhibition maintained by his widow. The Sudbury artist was also much admired in Spain. Ceán Bermúdez wrote praising Gainsborough, together with Reynolds and Romney, as supreme British portraitists in his unpublished manuscript of the history of painting.[49]

Goya owed much of his portrait style of the 1790s and early 1800s to British and French portraitists, as did Raeburn, whose romantic images evolved mainly from a highly original and personal synthesis of styles he had seen in his student years. Both artists established themselves as portrait painters in the late eighteenth century when much had happened to change the status of portrait art and the reproduction of famous sitters.

The sexuality of Raeburn's female portraiture and Goya's powerful images of women turned upon their knowledge of the challenges thrown up by the major European portrait painters of their day, as well as the interest both artists had in jewellery, fabric and clothing, which makes much of their female portraiture driven by fashion. The neoclassical portrait introduced female sitters to a new skill for painting white fabric and came from a mixture of English fashions of the 1780s and French fashion of the Revolution. In 1792, when Henri-Pierre Danloux was domiciled in London, he painted what must have seemed like the most revolutionary female portrait in England, that of Mlle Rosalie Duthé, the former mistress of the Comte d'Artois, and the most famous of the courtesans among the exiled French community.[50] This image of a woman dressed in a simple gown and white scarf *à la citoyenne* epitomised the revolutionary fashions of Paris. When Danloux, somewhat daunted perhaps by the competition of British portraitists in the capital, travelled north in 1796 to work in Edinburgh, Raeburn already possessed accurate information about the new style. Raeburn's wife may have been even more fashion conscious than her husband because her portrait, painted probably before Danloux arrived in Scotland, shows the future Lady Raeburn wearing a white muslin gown and white scarf twisted around her head.[51] Goya too was to keep abreast of the latest fashions in Spain through the sophistication of his wife who was a skilled dressmaker; instructing her husband on the fashion scene in France and England, as several references to her expertise in Goya's letters prove.[52] The Revolution had meant the closure of the French fashion magazines, but the effect of the Revolution on women's dress was extensive and transformed one of Raeburn's most stylish sitters into the archetypical 'citizeness'. Eschewing the ornamentation of hats, high hair and jewellery, *Isabella Macleod, Mrs James Gregory*, painted by Raeburn in 1798 (Fig. 10.5), wears an unrelieved white chemise gown with a white scarf knotted round her neck and shoulders and a plain white scarf on her head, mimicking the antique and austere dress of the virtuous revolutionary.[53]

White muslin dresses had been fashionable in England and France as early as the 1780s. The style was thought to have been introduced into England by Georgiana, Duchess of Devonshire. Later Marie Antoinette gave the chemise gown cult status. The revealing quality of this white transparent gown was always considered daring. Élisabeth Vigée-Lebrun portrayed Marie Antoinette wearing such a gown in 1783 but the portrait was thought indecent and removed from the salon.[54] Nevertheless, the style later became very fashionable and because of the doomed French queen's enthusiasm, was known as the *chemise à la reine*. At the height of the Revolution it was

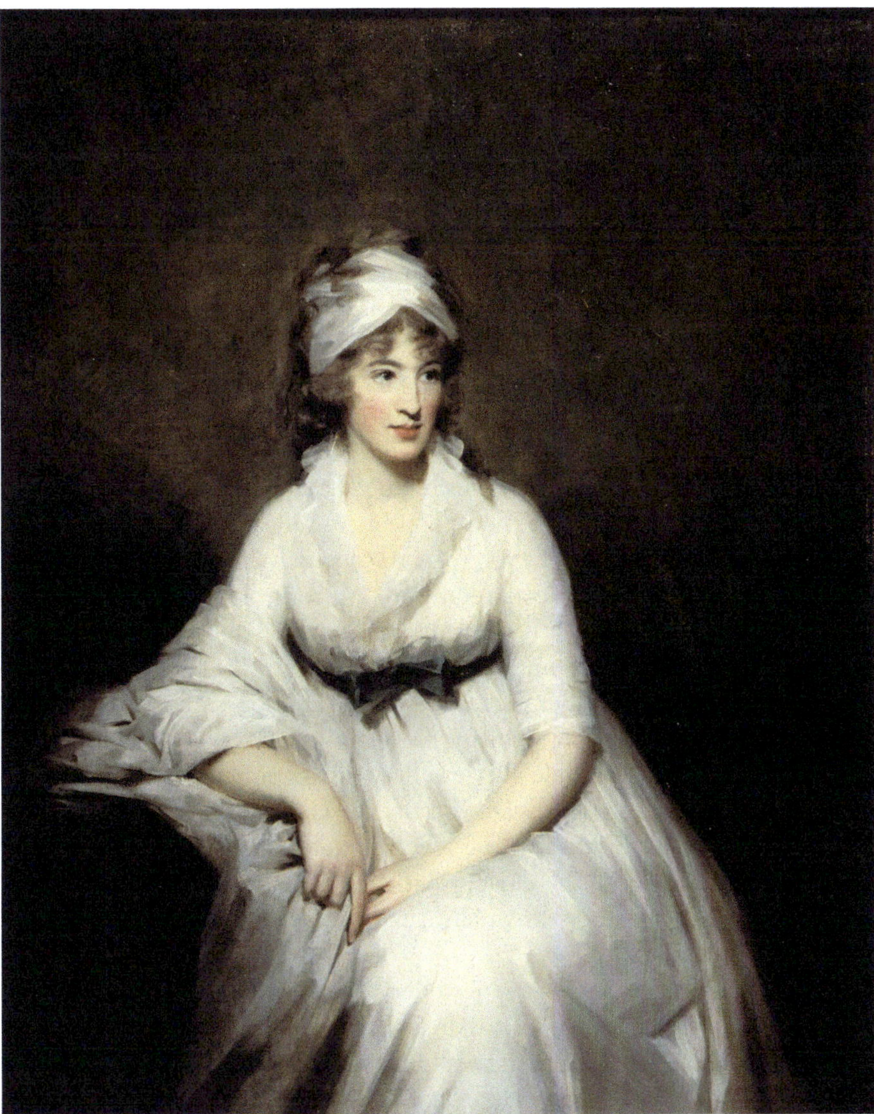

Figure 10.5 Henry Raeburn, *Isabella Macleod, Mrs James Gregory*, late 1790s, oil on canvas, 125×102.2cm, Forbes-Leith Collection, Fyvie Castle, National Trust for Scotland

remarked that women invariably wore white dresses, and French portraits of the period show the white chemise gown with long sleeves and hair usually worn loose or held by a bow or a scarf, and trimmed with a contrasting coloured sash. Later, such details assumed more sinister associations. The white dress and loose hair, unadorned or with a ribbon or kerchief became particularly associated with revolutionary women. Charlotte Corday went to the guillotine in white with a kerchief over her head; Madame Roland, also in a white chemise, wore her hair long and loose. The year before Raeburn's *Macleod* portrait Mary Wollstonecraft sat for her most famous portrait by John Opie, which shows her wearing a white muslin gown with a black kerchief on her head and a red sash.[55]

Although the iconography of the woman dressed in white may have come originally from England, the manner in which Goya and Raeburn adapted it into their female portraits reveals a stronger influence from contemporary French models. The resulting fashion for scarlet on white came from the commemoration of guillotine cuts when red or black ribbons and beads or chokers, scarves or stoles, were worn to memorialise victims. The white dress, scarlet ribbon, choker, stole or sash was a sartorial craze which dominated at parties held in Paris during the Directory. This outfit, intended to make a direct political statement, appears in Goya's first full-length portrait of the *Duchess of Alba* of 1795 (Fig. 10.6) which, like Raeburn's portrait of his wife and Isabella Macleod, retains a stark control of colour. Dressed in white with a broad scarlet sash, scarlet trimming, hair-ribbon and deep-hued coral beads, the duchess points to an inscription: 'A la Duquesa de Alba, Frco de Goya, 1795'. At her feet is a small white dog its back leg bearing another scarlet ribbon. The pointing finger in conjunction with the white dress and the absence of valuable jewellery distinguishes Raeburn's *Isabella Macleod* (Fig. 10.5) and Goya's *Duchess of Alba* (Fig. 10.6) as among the earliest portraits outside France in the revolutionary mode. A later portrait of the *Condesa de Chinchón*, by Goya, positively revels in the taste for natural simplicity with a headdress in which ears of corn are intertwined with the scarf.

As the fashion for expensive jewellery declined in the 1790s, antique-styled ornaments dominated formal dress. Enamels, semi-precious stones and materials like coral were worn in keeping with the neoclassical taste for simplicity and naturalness. The Duchess of Alba wears her hair loose like the little Infanta in Velázquez's *Las Meninas*. Apart from her earrings, her only other jewels are the double-stranded coral beads, a neoclassic armlet, gold on black enamel, bearing the initials TST (Teresa Silva de Toledo), and at her wrist an enamel bracelet, with the initials MTS. With his portraitist's eye and accurate rendering of high fashion Goya may have suggested the new restraint for the duchess's ornaments, or she may herself have wanted to discard the opulent style. Details of the Duchess of Alba's costume relate significantly to French paintings and prints, the tragic monarchy, the revolution and, specifically, to Thermidor, the period which followed the fall of Robespierre and the end of the Terror, from 1794 to 1795.[56]

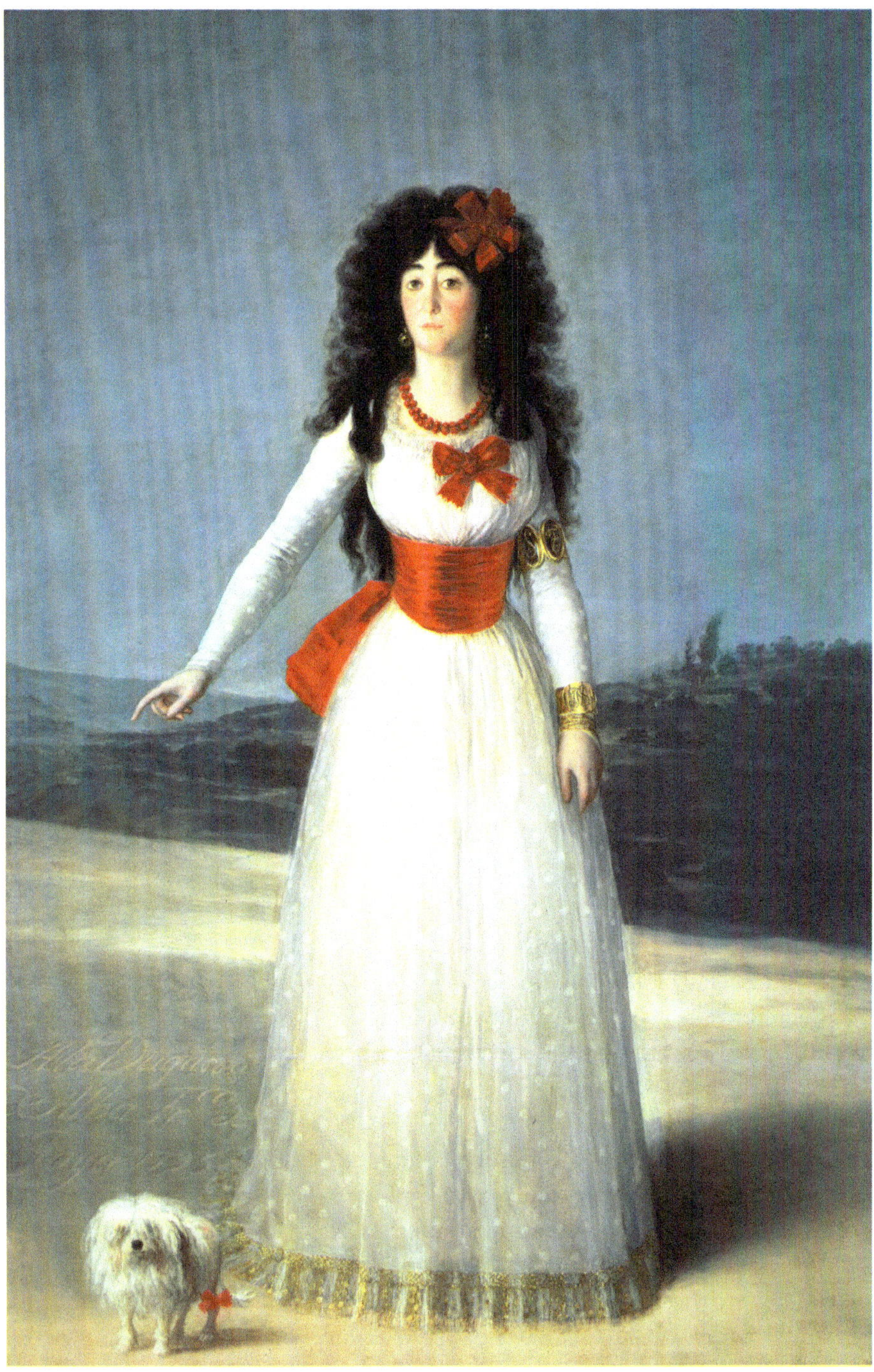

Figure 10.6 Francisco Goya, *The Duchess of Alba*, 1795, oil on canvas, 194×130cm, Alba Collection, Madrid (courtesy of Bridgeman Art Library)

In Britain this style was regarded as daring and in Spain the Duchess of Alba seems to have been among the few of Goya's female sitters to wear it. Raeburn's women patrons too may have requested the new austerity for their depictions and the Scottish artist continued to use the fashion in a number of portraits. He often combined, as Goya had done, the scarlet trimmings with the white chemise. Scarlet and white remained one of Raeburn's chief colour combinations in portraits of women after the turn of the century. His later portraits relied far more on the sexuality of white and scarlet, in depictions such as *Harriet Charlewood, Duchess of Roxburghe, Margaret Macdonald, Mrs Robert Scott Moncrieff* and *Helen Graham, Lady Montgomery*.

The scarlet and white that had dominated dress during the 1790s became even more daring with the quasi-transparent gowns which evoked the image of antique statuary. In Britain the fashion for the transparent chemise in portraits as well as women's dress became subject to ridicule. A verse written by an anonymous English satirist sums up what the British felt about this particular French fashion:

> The Fig-Leaf. A Satirical and Admonitory Poem
> See yonder fashionable Nude advance
> As if just landed from licentious France.
> Where Modesty, Fair woman's glorious pride,
> And virtue's safeguard, has been thrown aside.
> Mark well her lace and other costly whims
> That half conceal and half expose her limbs.
> So fine, so thin the texture, you'd presume
> Her robes were wove in fam'd Arachne's loom
> Behold the drapery! We cannot say
> How gracefully it flows in this our day,
> But. Girted like a bandage round the fair . . .
> Her naked arms too, breast, neck, shoulders bare,
> Do all the same notorious fact declare . . . '[57]

In spite of such censure the fashion remained although Indian muslin was often replaced by satin, silk or even cotton. The strong contrast of scarlet and white with bare arms neck and feet and loose hair lost much of its political stridency and became softer and romantic. The contrasting red and white of women in these outfits, known to have affinities with French politics, remained controversial. It may not have comforted Raeburn to know that David's pupil, Ingres, one of the most fashion-conscious portraitists of the nineteenth century, had exhibited *Madame Pankouke* at the salon in 1811, wearing the white and the scarlet, the same year as Raeburn's *Harriet Frances*

Wynne, Mrs James Hamilton of Kames (Fig. 10.7) was refused by the sitter's family and left unfinished in the painter's studio.[58] Ingres's painting of the white gown and necklace of deep-hued coral is as striking as Goya's some sixteen years earlier, although the dress in a thick satin shows off the sitter's pregnancy. This was also one of the problems of Harriet Frances Wynne's portrait: her pregnancy makes her seem awkward and unwieldy within the tight confines of the white chemise gown.

The juxtaposition of the white and scarlet retained its power to shock even in the 1860s. Whistler's *Symphony in White No. 1: The White Girl* wears her red hair loose and stands on a bearskin with gaping jaws and teeth flecked with red paint, suggesting a violent counterpoint to the white dress and white hangings of the room. Perhaps this was what caused Philippe Burty to write in the *Gazette des Beaux-Arts* in July 1869 that he found Whistler's portrait 'unhealthy and troubling'.[59]

During Raeburn's lifetime none of his images of women appeared among the popular and lucrative editions of prints issued after his portraits, but after the artist's death he was well served throughout the nineteenth century by a number of exhibitions. Whistler could well have seen the famous portrait of Lady Raeburn with her 'greyish chocolate brown' loose coat over her muslin gown, either at the Royal Scottish Academy in 1863 or at the Raeburn exhibition of 1876, also held in Edinburgh, which travelled to the Royal Academy in London the following year. The American artist's fondness for such coats, as well as such subtle colouring, appeared first in his Japanese-styled portraits of the 1860s in which similar garments take the form of dressing gowns or kimonos, which, as has been recently observed, were more allied to western prototypes than to Japan.[60] Whistler's interest in Goya's work has also been seen as a major influence, especially with depictions of female sitters, and the posthumous influences of both artists in terms of portraiture became a major feature of the later Edwardian period.

The revolutionary features of Raeburn and Goya's portraits as fashion statements, their bold, colourful contrasts and striking expressions and gestures drew many later admirers. The major full length of a woman in red and white was picked up by Sargent with *Duchess of Portland*, a portrait which shows another re-adaptation of the Regency period's favourite colour alliance. Significantly, Sargent's passion for Goya was always a major aspect of his earlier work. Even Augustus John, wrestling with the challenge of portraying a woman musician in full performance modelled his *Madame Suggia* on Raeburn's equally stylish portrait of the *Marchioness of Northampton* playing the harp. John's cellist was, as one biographer has put it, not so much a portrait, as a subject picture about the expressive power of art, a notion in tune with much of the avant-garde portraiture of Raeburn's day.[61]

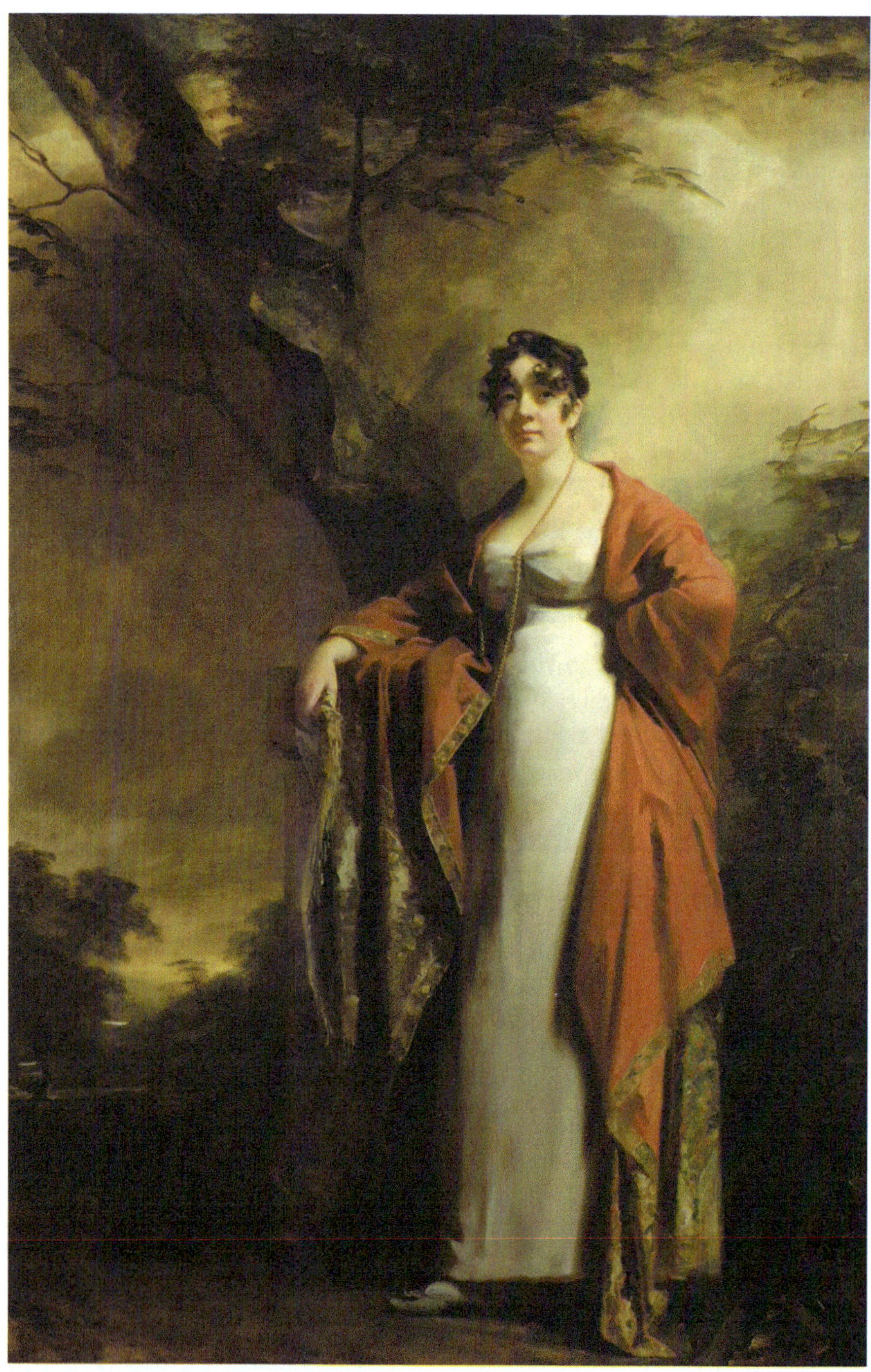

Figure 10.7 Henry Raeburn, *Frances Harriet Wynne, Mrs James Hamilton of Kames*, 1811, oil on canvas, 236.2 × 148.6cm, Scottish National Gallery, Edinburgh

The striking brunette by Raeburn in the flow of musical rapture, dressed in a flowing reddish-brownish wolfskin, rather different from Madam Suggia's satin gown, provided a model of naked arms and absorbed expression and solved John's compositional problems. John's life-long passion for Goya may also have led him to the *Marquesa de Villafranca* of 1804, similarly depicted in the throes of inspiration, with paint brush, palette, naked arms and muslin gown.[62]

In the nineteenth century spectators outside Spain had less opportunity to see Goya's portraits than Raeburn's, although Goya's prints were well known throughout Europe and America. While the Scottish artist never seems to have been out of the public eye, beginning with the memorial retrospective of fifty-eight portraits held in 1824, Goya's first retrospective was held in Madrid in 1900, some seventy-two years after his death. A number of portraits were included in this exhibition, with the *Duchess of Alba* of 1795, the woman in white and scarlet, among the most praised works in the show.[63] British reviewers were quick to see links between Goya's portraits and those of British eighteenth-century portraiture, and Goya's influence on Whistler became a critical trope for foreign writers.

Nineteenth- and twentieth-century admirers of Raeburn and Goya as portraitists shared a fascination with both their personalities and their working methods. Goya's performance as a painter gave rise to some colourful and inaccurate accounts of his working practice. His treatment of the actual medium was seen as brutal and clumsy. His pursuit of naturalism gave rise to dramatic stories, and his art was compared with the poetry of Rimbaud, while his relationship with sitters was said to be problematic, even violent, and his love affairs, specifically with the Duchess of Alba, were notorious.[64] Raeburn established a less melodramatic posthumous reputation, although an anonymous article in *Notes and Queries* at the end of the nineteenth century, told a scandalous story about the Scottish artist's courtship and marriage which is as dramatic as anything pinned on Goya.[65] More interesting is Raeburn's working method, which inspired intimate and detailed accounts and which make it seem as if the writers had themselves been inside Raeburn's studio. Allan Cunningham's *Lives* contains passages about Raeburn's methods which are apparently without any foundation.[66] According to Cunningham he always painted standing, and his fluency and speed came from touches on forehead, chin, nose and mouth. While this could well have been a purely imaginative account on the Scottish critic's part, it may derive from Wilkie's conviction that Raeburn was profoundly influenced by Velázquez and from the texts in English about the Sevillan's working method. Goya too was said to work standing up, and this technique, together with the fluency and distancing of the artist in relation to the sitter, may also derive from a famous passage in Palomino, which related specifically to Velázquez's painting of *Don Adrian Pulido Pareja*:

> he painted it with regular brushes and with thick brushes with long handles that he owned and that he used sometimes in order to paint from a greater distance and more boldly, so that from up close the painting was not intelligible, but from a distance it was a miracle.[67]

Many imaginative methods were posthumously applied to the portrait styles of Goya and Raeburn and brought both to the attention of writers on Impressionism. In 1892, Renoir praised Goya's *Family of Carlos IV*,[68] but it was not until the early twentieth century that similarities between Goya's portraits and those of Manet were seriously analysed.[69] In 1895 and 1900 respectively, R. A. M Stevenson was to see both Velázquez and Raeburn as having stylistic links with Impressionist painters.[70] The influence of Raeburn on the Edwardian period coincides with a period of the Scottish artist's immense popularity in England. The period also coincides with the first English biography of Goya, written by the British painter William Rothenstein, a close friend of Augustus and Gwen John and an enthusiast for Spanish art. This biography concentrated on the difficulties of Goya's struggles in Spain, the Napoleonic invasions and the revival of the Holy Office of the Inquisition under Fernando VII. However, as a portraitist, Rothenstein maintained, Goya was supreme. According to Rothenstein Goya worked from the model in absolute silence, a piece of fiction which may have come from the more Romantic of the artist's posthumous biographers. The difficulties the painter had with his sitters, however, while not always historically accurate, are made much of. While there is little evidence that Goya came to blows with the Duke of Wellington there is a real understanding of the way this highly original artist transformed portraiture.[71] Rothenstein wrote his study under the influence of John Singer Sargent who advised the young man that if he wanted to write about Goya he should go to Madrid and see the works first hand. In many ways Rothenstein's intuiting of Goya's methods was similar to Robert Louis Stevenson's account of Raeburn's realism and instantaneous understanding of his sitters. 'A born painter of portraits', wrote Stevenson. 'He looked at people shrewdly, between the eyes, surprised their manners in their faces, and possessed himself of what was essential in their character before they had been minutes in his studio'.[72]

Although much of Robert Louis Stevenson's writing about Raeburn's portraits is as fictional as Rothenstein writing about Goya, the importance of dramatic expression in portraiture was one way of emphasising the artist's originality. Raeburn's sitters often look nervous or taken unawares. They balance uneasily on their feet, they strike grand gestures which make them seem as if they are about to topple over. Goya pursues a similar agenda with his sitters. It is this improvising from the perceptive process which creates an illusion of speed and life, and which has made these two men into the artistic pointers to a new direction for portraiture in the twenty-first century. For Karen Kilimnik, the American portraitist for whom Raeburn has been a source of new ideas, the Scottish artist represents 'the Modernist sense of mainstream painting'.[73] Goya too made portraits which endured long after their sitters were forgotten, portraits with a sense of elegance, life and that innate incongruity, noticed particularly by the Spanish poet Manuel Machado. On the equestrian portrait that the Queen of Spain worked so hard to help Goya complete, he wrote: 'the dashing tilt of the hat, and the fire in her eyes which has not yet gone . . . this arrogant old lady, this Amazon on a better horse than seems wise'.[74]

Unlike Goya, Raeburn was not a Romantic master obsessed by powerful themes of history, war and injustice, or an ironic observer of social customs, or a satirist of moral disenchantment. However, his portraits, like Goya's, openly tender the primitive and directness of the modern, developing a portraiture which reduplicated and renovated an exhausted genre. Emerging vividly from the microcosms of hats, jewels, fabric, furniture and hairstyles, belonging exclusively to the eighteenth and nineteenth centuries, these images broached the miraculous logic of commodities and fetishes belonging to rank and status, the phantasmagoria of lighting, expression and atmosphere, the enchanting vulnerability of morality within the contexts of power and beauty. Such courageous techniques expanded the limitations of portrait methodology, investing it with an aura of modernity, which contemporary portraitists have used as points of departure. From Freud to Annigoni and Humphrey Ocean, from the film portraits ('screen tests') of Andy Warhol, to the minutiae of personal detail in the work of Richard Billingham and Gillian Wearing, the portrait has come a long way since the eighteenth century. But even these bold experiments can be traced back to the pictorial invention of a few rare professionals whose vision turned the vanity of their models into profound scrutiny.

Notes

1. Valérie Breuvert, Barry Schwabsky et al., *Vitamin P: New Perspectives in Painting*, London, 2002.
2. Goya entered history painting competitions at the Real Academia de San Fernando in Madrid in 1766 and 1767 and on both occasions received no votes from the academic jury.

3. Nigel Glendinning, *Goya and His Critics*, New Haven and London, 1977, p. 31.

4. Edinburgh and London 1997–8, p. 15.

5. Goya had his religious work severely criticised by the commissioners at the Church of El Pilar [Virgin of the Pillar] in 1781. See Sarah Symmons, *Goya: A Life in Letters*, London, 2004, pp. 100–14.

6. Xavier Bray, 'Velázquez and Britain', pp. 92–111 in Dawson Carr et al., *Velázquez*, London, 2006.

7. Mackie 1994, I, p. 92 n. 47.

8. Allan Cunningham, *The Life of Sir David Wilkie*, London, 1843, II, diary entry, p. 113; the letter to Lawrence, p. 472.

9. Quoted in John Burnet, *The Progress of a Painter in the Nineteenth Century*, London, 1854, p. 19.

10. For the copy of Velázquez's Pope attributed to Goya see Nigel Glendinning, 'Goya y el Espíritu de Velázquez', Jesusa Vega (ed.), *Velázquez y Goya: Estudiar a los Maestros*, Zaragoza, 2000, p. 22.

11. Goya's other portraits of seated men of affairs in the 1790s include *Gaspar Melchor de Jovellanos*, 1798 (Madrid, Vizcondesa Irueste), *Bernardo de Iriarte*, 1797 (Strasbourg, Musée des Beaux-Arts, no. 308), *Andres del Peral*, c. 1797–8 (London, National Gallery, no. 1951) and *Ferdinand Guillemardet*, 1798 (Paris, Musée du Louvre, no. M.1.697).

12. El Cuaderno Italiano by Goya (Italian sketchbook) Madrid, Museo del Prado, FA 1732; biblical subjects appear on folios 21, 22, 23, 28, 29, 30, 31, 35.

13. Edinburgh and London 1997–8, p. 11.

14. Glendinning 1977, p. 24.

15. Symmons 2004, pp. 73–4.

16. 'Carta de Don Antonio Rafael Mengs, Primer Pintor de Cámara', published in A Ponz, *Viaje de España*, VI, Madrid, 1776, pp. 64–229.

17. Jesusa Vega, 'Pinturas de Velázquez grabadas por Francisco de Goya, pintor', *Vega*, 2000, p. 56.

18. Antonio Palomino, *Lives of the Eminent Spanish Painters and Sculptors*, Cambridge 1987, pp. x–xi.

19. Quoted by Vega in *Vega*, 2000, p. 59, n. 31.

20. For Richard Cooper see Glendinning in *Vega*, 2000, p. 20.

21. According to the artist in a letter of 1816: Symmons, 2004, pp. 282–3.

22. Mary Graham, Spanish Journal, NLS, Lynedoch MS, no. 3628, f. 32.

23. Bray 2006, p. 95 [see above note 6].

24. Loc. cit. Graham, f. 35ve.

25. Ibid. f. 36.

26. Ibid.

27. Ibid.

28. Ibid. f. 36ve.
29. Nigel Glendinning et al. 'Lord Grantham and the taste for Velázquez: The Electrical Eel of the day', *The Burlington Magazine*, CXLI, 1999, p. 601.
30. The descendants and heirs of Mary Graham and her husband, who became Lord Lynedoch, hung their Raeburns with Mary Graham's portraits by Gainsborough. NLS, Lynedoch Papers, MS 16107, Journal of Mary Graeme, sister of Robert Graham of Redgorton, 1859, fols. 31r–31v.
31. Bray 2006, p. 99.
32. Glendinning 1999, p. 603.
33. Letter from Francisco Ignacio Arrieta to a deputation from Navarra, 16 June 1814, Symmons 2004, p. 278.
34. Sarah Symmons, *Goya: In Pursuit of Patronage*, London, 1988, p. 122.
35. Both artists painted small boys who seem unsteady on their feet and wear skeleton suits, *Manuel Osorio* by Goya, c. 1788 (New York, The Metropolitan Museum of Art, Bache 49.7.41) and Raeburn's *Sir George Sinclair of Ulbster*, c. 1796–7 (The Iveagh Bequest, Kenwood, London).
36. Goya to his friend, Martin Zapater, 20 February 1790, see Symmons 2004, p. 214.
37. Gendinning 1977, pp. 42–3.
38. NAS, Box 17, Bundle 12, letters to George Home of Wedderburn; from Lord Frederick Campbell, 11 December 1812.
39. Glendinning 1977, p. 22.
40. For example, Goya's portrait of the *Duke of San Carlos* 1815 (Saragossa Museum no. 168), which is both a full length and a profile and is highly dependent on Velázquez.
41. *Encyclopedia Britannica*, 3rd edn, Edinburgh, 1797, XV, p. 4006.
42. Raeburn records in Scottish National Portrait Gallery, Edinburgh. Box 1 Scottish IV, Sir Henry Raeburn, Biographical information. Folder 1, Item 2, Extract from the *Autobiography of a Scotch country Gentleman, the Rev. John Hamilton Gray*, edited by his widow, Edinburgh, 1868, pp. 55–7.
43. Glendinning 1977, p. 37.
44. SNPG, Raeburn Folder 7, Item 43, letter from John Buchan recounting Raeburn's advice about hanging a portrait, 20 July 1798, NAS, GD 171/26/35, 'he [Raeburn] is clearly of the opinion the Little Drawing Room is the place for putting up the portrait – He thinks 21 or 22 feet a sufficient distance for it to be view'd at – & also thinks it should be placed 5 feet from the floor.'
45. For the Duke of Wellington's medals see Neil MacLaren, *The National Gallery: The Spanish School*, 2nd edn, rev. by Allan Braham, London, 1970, pp. 16–23. Raeburn also apparently made inaccuracies in uniforms, see Mackie 1994, I, p. 21.
46. *The Morning Chronicle and London Advertiser*, 30 April 1777.

47. By the 1840s this criticism had become more strident among reviewers. See Michaela Giebelhausen, *Painting the Bible*, London, 2006, pp. 33–4.

48. Sarah Symmons, '"A new people and a limited society": British Art and the Spanish Spectator', pp. 101–17 in Christiana Payne and William Vaughan (eds), *English Accents: Interactions with British Art, c. 1776–1855*, London, 2004.

49. J. Ceán Bermúdez, Historia de la Pintura, MS, Archivo de la Real Academia de San Fernando, Madrid, 1824, chapter 39.

50. Lloyd 2005.

51. Ann Edgar, Lady Raeburn, painted early 1790s. Edinburgh and London 1997–8, no. 21, p. 94.

52. Goya's comments on his wife's knowledge of foreign fashions appear in letters dating from 1782. See Sarah Symmons, 'La mujer vestida de blanco: el primer retrato de la duquesa de Alba', *Goya*, Barcelona, 2002, p. 52.

53. This is discussed by Aileen Ribeiro, *Dress and Morality*, Oxford and New York, 2nd edn, 2003, p. 117.

54. Aileen Ribeiro, *Dress in Eighteenth-Century Europe, 1715–1789*, London, 1984, p. 153.

55. NPG, London.

56. Louis Sebastien Mercier, *Nouveau Paris*, 1798, describes balls held in the winter of 1794 when women wore skimpy white dresses with red ribbons. Aileen Ribeiro, *The Art of Dress*, New Haven and London, 1995, pp. 91–2.

57. Oxford, Bodleian Library, Godwyn Pamphlet 2834, 3rd edn, London, c. 1805, pp. 19–21.

58. Edinburgh and London 1997–8, item 45, pp. 148–9.

59. 'The symphony in white, unhealthy and troubling in the sketches of Mr Whistler'. Philippe Burty quoted by Malcolm Warner, 'Portraits of Children: The Pathos of Innocence', Peter Funnell and Malcolm Warner, *Millais: Portraits*, London, 1999, pp. 113–14.

60. Margaret F. MacDonald et al., *Whistler, Women, and Fashion*, New Haven and London, 2003, makes this point about Whistler and Japanese art and fashion, p. 64. For Whistler's dependence on Goya's portraits of women see ibid. pp. 162–3.

61. John apparently had problems with dressing his sitter. Raeburn's marchioness is also compared in style with portraits by Sargent. Andrew Wilton, *The Swagger portrait: Grand Manner in Portraiture in Britain from Van Dyck to Augustus John*, exh. cat., Tate Gallery, London, 1992, item 77, p. 216 and item 49, p. 160. For John's passion for Goya see Michael Holroyd, *Augustus John: The New Biography*, London, 1996, p. 145.

62. *Marquesa de Villafranca*, 1804, Madrid, Museo del Prado, no. 2448. She is shown in the act of painting a portrait of her husband.

63. *Goya 1900: Catálogo ilustrado y studio de la exposición en el Ministerio de instrucción*

pública y bellas artes, 2 vols, Madrid, 2002; on the Duchess of Alba portrait see II, no. 36, p. 78; for Goya's influence on Whistler, see I, p. 296.

64. Glendinning 1977, p. 280.

65. Mackie 1994, I, p. 30.

66. Mackie 1994, I, p. 6. Many reports of Goya's apparent working methods also cannot be substantiated.

67. Palomino, 1987, pp. 151–2.

68. Renoir's comment on *The Family of Carlos IV* is quoted by Glendinning, 1977, p. 281. Goya's links with Impressionism were also emphasised in the 1900 exhibition, see Goya 1900, I, p. 125.

69. By, among others, Aureliano de Beruete, Glendinning, 1977, pp. 132–6.

70. R. A. M. Stevenson writing in Armstrong, 1901, London, and in *Velasquez*, London, 1895, especially chapter 11, sees both artists in this context. In the first chapter of *Velasquez* Stevenson also compared Madrid to Edinburgh as cities, where being a portrait painter was especially difficult.

71. W. Rothenstein, *Goya*, London, 1900, pp. 16–17.

72. Stevenson 1992, p. 32.

73. Breuvert, Schwabsky et al. 2002, p. 174.

74. Glendinning 1977, p. 247.

Part III

Reputation

Raeburn's First Biography: Allan Cunningham's Presentation of the Artist as a Model Scottish Gentleman

Matthew Craske

The death of Henry Raeburn, in the summer of 1823, occurred only a few months after his greatest moment of public recognition. This was the ceremonial dinner organised by the artists of Edinburgh on 12 September 1822 to celebrate his knighthood and appointment as 'Portrait Painter to the King in Scotland'.[1]

By all accounts, the event was a distinctly convivial affair. Raeburn charmed all present with his speech in reply to the plaudits. A review of the event, printed in the *Caledonian Mercury*, concluded that 'as an individual' Raeburn had 'been distinguished by the mildness and gentlemanliness of his manners' and that, beyond his excellence as a painter, these had been the qualities that had endeared him to his 'professional brethren'.[2] The fond impression that Raeburn made at this dinner was to sustain his many mourners. He was remembered not only as the portrait painter who had, for a generation, made record of the Edinburgh elite but also as a fine gentleman of Stockbridge worthy of inclusion in his own pantheon of Scottish worthies. One obituary, in *The Literary Chronicle*, recalled that:

In society, few men were more acceptable than Sir Henry; for he possessed a cheerful disposition, much good sense, and an inexhaustible store of anecdote. In domestic relations, no man could dispense or receive a greater degree of happiness; and those who had the opportunities of seeing him in the midst of his family, will ever relish the recollection of his amiable and endearing qualities.[3]

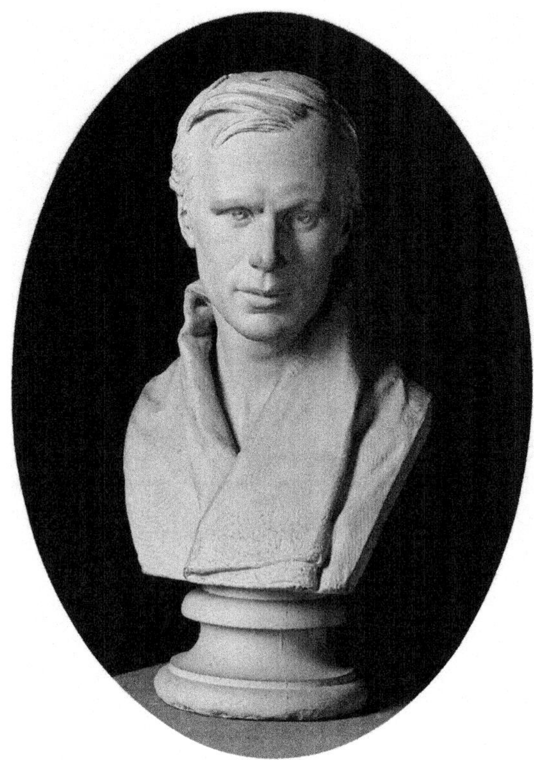

Figure 11.1 Francis Legatt Chantrey, *Allan Cunningham*, plaster bust, height 68cm, Scottish National Portrait Gallery, Edinburgh

Raeburn's capacity to please as a man and artist impressed his contemporaries. The two spheres seemed connected. His 'amiable' nature was widely considered the root of his capacity to see the best in his fellow man; this being the instinctive means by which he satisfied as a portraitist without resort to conscious or artful flattery. The author of the obituary in the *Literary Chronicle* observed that Raeburn had 'possessed a rare faculty of producing an agreeable likeness, and of indicating intellectual expression and dignity of demeanour, wherever they appeared in the original.' Such agreeable aspects of character also pleased one of Raeburn's early biographers, fellow Scotsman, Allan Cunningham (Fig. 11.1). If Cunningham's *Life*, which is the subject of this essay, persuades of anything it is that he was one of those who were charmed by Raeburn, albeit on superficial acquaintance. The following essay sets out to be a critique, rather than an appreciation of, Cunningham's story. Yet, it is questionable whether there is any alternative but to conform to the vision of the model citizen and subject that satisfied in the immediate aftermath of Raeburn's death.

The capacity to be agreeable, which Cunningham and other early biographers considered Raeburn's defining quality, has been noted, but not placed to the fore, in the work of scholars of the last hundred years. The attribute of effortlessness which most impressed Cunningham has not appealed to some who are persuaded of the notion of great art as the product of an intense inward struggle. A review of his portraits, as exhibited at the National Gallery in Edinburgh in 1901, paused to remark:

> It would be absurd to deny Sir Henry Raeburn's immense accomplishment, or his extraordinary facility in fixing at least the superficial characteristics of his sitters, or the brilliance of his execution. To this last, indeed, he sacrificed too much. His touch reveals no sensitiveness to the subtler beauties of form, no impassioned inquiry; with a few blunt rectangular brush marks placed with admirable precision he could convey the general impression of a face and he cared little to enquire further.[4]

Few would now condemn Raeburn for excessive facility or pretend that it is so easy to identify the superficial from the profound in a painted portrait. Yet, even in the context of a more sympathetic estimation, it remains reasonable to question whether there is more to Raeburn than a happy technique. The temptation, therefore, is to look for something beyond, or even beneath, the delightful attributes of character and art that were celebrated by Cunningham and others. However, even if darker and deeper matter could be located and penetrated, there remains the question of whether it is anachronistic even to think in such forensic terms. The challenge of reading Cunningham's biography in the twenty-first century may well be to resist the instinct for subversion of things that can be mistaken for shallow only because they delight in superficiality. Rather, it may, as is argued below, be preferable to attempt to comprehend why Cunningham's contented vision of art and the artist was anticipated to meet the approval of readers. Cunningham's sense of the satisfying experience of immediate sensory impressions, which seems to have been shared by Raeburn, requires sympathetic address because it is representative of an important strand of aesthetic consciousness in early nineteenth-century British culture.[5]

Cunningham's *Life* of Raeburn was published in 1832 as part of a Vasarian series entitled *The Lives of the Most Eminent British Painters, Sculptors and Architects*.[6] It is essential, as this chapter argues, not to consider it in isolation. This is because, as a biographer, Cunningham had certain clear tastes and prejudices which can only be discerned through a wider reading of his *oeuvre*. It is, moreover, important to take into account the broader conventions of the genre of artist's biography in which considerations of 'character' came to be seen as of primary importance. From the 1780s onward, the market for accounts of visual artists in newspapers and magazines had expanded markedly. Extensive obituaries of artists became fashionable, replacing the short death notices that had sufficed earlier in the century. There is no clearer sign of the rising status of the visual artist and of the gradual dissemination of the understanding that the value of a painting or sculpture proceeded from the character of its maker. Competition for readers inevitably led to an escalating demand for convincing, or candid, detail and controversial interpretation of personal motivation or approach. Many late Georgian artists did not wait for their attainments or foibles to be considered and assessed after death. They obliged the press by releasing, in their own lifetimes, the materials necessary for writers to compile accounts of their careers. So it was, for instance, that detailed biographies of the sculptors, John Bacon and Thomas Banks, appeared in the *European Magazine*.[7] Ambitious early nineteenth-century artists tended to live in self-conscious anticipation of the attention of biographers. Diaries or journals were commonly kept, letters preserved, and attention was frequently given to cultivating remarkable attributes of character that would attract anecdote mongers such as J. T. Smith, William Henry Pyne and Henry Angelo.[8]

Henry Raeburn did not fall into this category. He exhibited, as Cunningham testifies, a definite temperament, whilst never being seduced into those eccentricities which marked out a creative figure as 'a character', in the sense of a *dramatis persona*. Raeburn was noted, not least by Cunningham, for a kind of 'modest' charm that allowed him to blend into the fabric of polite Edinburgh society. He was inoffensive, in the old and positive sense of the word. One of Cunningham's highest compliments to Raeburn was that he had never 'permanently offended anyone'.[9] There was, as a consequence of such demure ways, little committed to print concerning Raeburn's life and career until after his death. Cunningham was, thus, obliged to undertake first-hand research. Much of what he wrote was original in content. There were other posthumous biographies. The obituary which is quoted above, from the *Literary Chronicle*, was anonymous. It was printed, either in full or with passages excised, in numerous periodicals.[10] A general appreciation, it contained little by the way of biographical information. It was not just Cunningham who sought to provide something more substantial. A lengthy account of Raeburn's life was produced by Andrew Duncan.[11] Yet, Cunningham's *Life* was far the most frequently quoted by subsequent scholars and remains the most influential. This was largely because of the form in which it was published. Readers came across the *Life* of Raeburn as part of a highly readable series.

Cunningham's appeal, however, was not just owing to his format. He was acknowledged to be a particularly diverting and informative writer. His approach to biography was capably summarised in a review, in *La Belle Assemblée*, of the compilation *Lives* that appeared in 1832. This acknowledged that the author set high standards of evidential research. Such an enthusiasm for the 'truth' was meliorated by an essentially kind and sympathetic nature which was the basis of his broad literary appeal:

> Mr Cunningham has possessed himself of all available information concerning the personal characters and professional pretensions of his subjects, and he has thrown over his narratives an air of truth and kindness and taste and enthusiasm for art, that must recommend them to general favour.[12]

Cunningham's biography of Raeburn was certainly characterised by 'kindness'. The 'air of truth' is a more slippery property, but one which is just as apparent. From the evidence of his published word, Cunningham seems to have imagined that he had cause to like Raeburn. He did not, however, choose to include artists in his series on 'eminent' figures on the simple basis of personal liking. It is clear, for instance, that he held Thomas Lawrence in a certain degree of contempt.[13] Yet, even in his assessment of Lawrence, Cunningham exhibited a talent for good humoured tolerance and a capacity to amuse whilst arriving at shrewd judgements upon character.

Cunningham's sympathy for Raeburn did not promote an appetite for critical investigation. The biography was not, on this account, without certain passages where apologia triumphed over candour. It was in the latter vein that Walter Scott said of Raeburn that he came, with experience, to paint 'for cash'.[14] This was a facet of the painter's career which Cunningham did not want to see. Cunningham knew that Raeburn had substantial business interests outside his painting practice. He seems to have been determined to exonerate his subject of any driving concern for self-enrichment in this capacity. This was probably in order to put aside any suspicions that, in his considerable and profitable dealings as a portrait painter, Raeburn was also motivated by profit. Cunningham, thus, attempted to persuade his readers that Raeburn's positive enthusiasm for going to law in his considerable dealings as a businessman was a sign of canny and endearing intelligence, rather than an excessively litigious nature.[15] No mention was made of Raeburn's short-lived family business in shipping, which precipitated bankruptcy in 1808. It was merely remarked that Raeburn knew a lot about ship building, in the same way as his speculative development of his wife's estate at Stockbridge was attended by a remarkable knowledge of architecture.[16] Hints at blighted financial ambition were, thus, overlooked.[17] Cunningham was not inhibited from bringing to bear his own sense of 'the gentleman' to his biography of artists. This led Raeburn to be described as astute and prosperous but not crudely ambitious or money obsessed. Cunningham's *Life of Raeburn* is a paean to respectability in artistic practice. Whilst it is debatable whether the *Life* is genuinely informative or reliable, it is clearly an interesting contribution to debate concerning how, whether or why an artist ought to be admired for their conformity to the conventional standards of a polite and pleasing demeanour. It is necessarily unclear whether these standards are his own or those of his subject.

In the assessment of the *Life*, therefore, it is as necessary to be aware of the author's personality and biographical profile.[18] Cunningham rose from humble, rustic, beginnings. He had the advantage of a strict religious education. Exceptionally industrious, as well as capable, he elected to prize the latter over the former virtue. Beginning as a mere stonecutter, he found his way into London's premier sculpture workshop, that of Francis Chantrey (Fig. 11.2). His talents in this environment proved to be administrative and social. He became Chantrey's business factotum. As an alternative career as man of letters developed, Cunningham assumed the persona of workshop wit and educated companion to the master. His industry and ambition did not, however, lend him a life-long admiration of raw hard work or scheming careerism. Cunningham was a great believer in natural genius, a quality which he overtly admired in the low-born Chantrey and, covertly, discovered in himself. Having had a punishing and strict religious education, Cunningham developed a humorous contempt for asceticism and over-earnest application. His man of genius was characterised as a figure who took pleasure in fulfilling a desire to create that was born within him. A running theme in his *Lives* was an admiration for conversational wit, a talent for which he himself was noted. No matter from what lowly station an artist arose, his claim to be a gentleman was staked on a capacity to shine in times of leisure. Cunningham was a man of diverse accomplishments and he admired artists whose interests and knowledge were not confined by strict adherence to professional practice. He considered that the man who was required to work so hard as not to aspire to congenial leisure was not a natural genius, to whom attainment ought to come naturally. This meant that, for Cunningham, the genius ought also to have the character of a 'gentleman', this being defined by the capacity to have and enjoy convivial leisure. The great stress that Cunningham placed upon the description of Raeburn's charming conversation was characteristic of his tastes as biographer. John Hoppner, for instance, was also applauded as a figure whose genius was evident in his talents as a conversationalist.[19] Thomas Lawrence, who Cunningham appears to have considered self-consciously and unconvincingly charming, was subtly condemned on these terms.

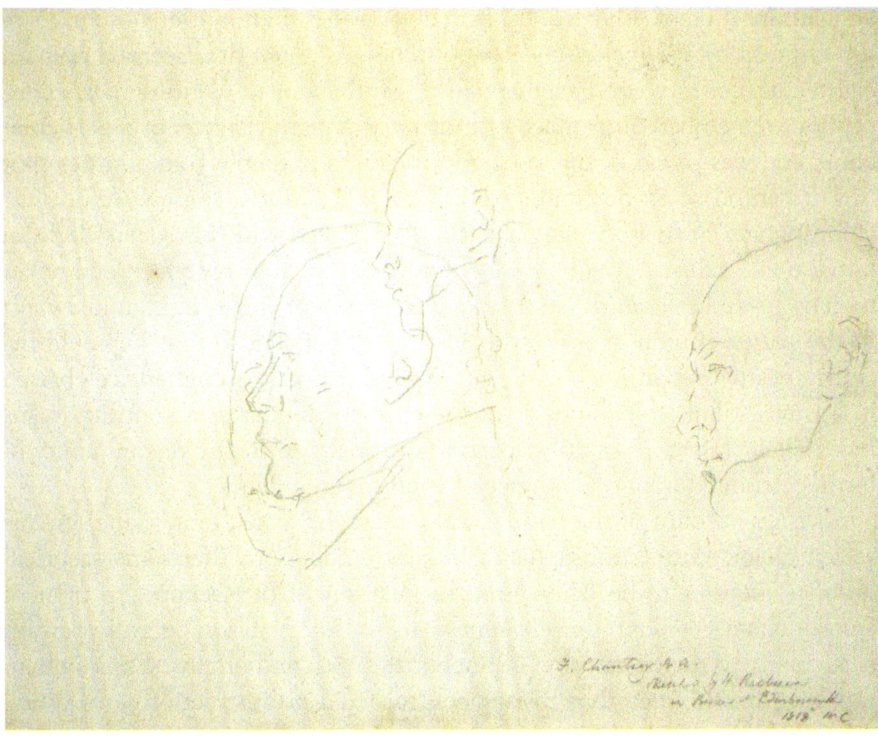

Figure 11.2 Henry Raeburn, *Francis Legatt Chantrey*, 1818, camera lucida drawing
in pencil, 21.4×29.3cm, Scottish National Portrait Gallery, Edinburgh

To state the obvious, Cunningham selected his biographical subjects.
He did not even attempt to form a comprehensive list of major figures, as
had Vasari or Horace Walpole, in charting the rise of a national 'School'.[20]
Many of those who Cunningham elected to celebrate were born outside the
city in which they made their reputation, either in complete rural obscurity
or in the decayed respectability of some provincial town. Few of those he
admired as 'eminent' derived from families of artists that were already situated in London or Edinburgh. He was, then, largely interested in artists who
arrived at their vocation owing to some inner compulsion, as opposed to
the accident of birth. Cunningham categorically did not associate a man's
self-improvement with his development beyond all memory of his humble
beginnings. He became a notable historian of what would now be called
'rustic vernacular culture', rejoicing as much in the traditional legends of
rural England as in those of his native Scotland.[21] An important biographer
of Robert Burns, Cunningham was a great admirer of the man who retained a
strong respect for the specific locality of his birth and the distinctive customs

and culture thereof.[22] His conception of gentility did not, therefore, involve subscription to a universal code of politeness as might be discerned from an eighteenth-century conduct manual. A gentleman, in Cunningham's conception, remembered his place of birth, was a manifestation of a particular clime and was proud of his association with the humble communities that he left behind when he embraced urban respectability. These were not just Cunningham's private values but those he shared with his social circle in London and Edinburgh. His great friend Francis Chantrey was proud never to deny his humble north country origins and went so far as to build a vault in the parish church of his birthplace, near Sheffield, so that he could literally return to home soil.[23] David Wilkie, who Cunningham celebrated in a three-volume biography,[24] expressed such standards of gentility in his *Pitlessie Fair* (1804), a detailed portrait of the artist's humble community of birth, celebrated from the vantage of youthful urban fame.

It is on account of the strong, and remarkably consistent, value systems which characterise Cunningham's literary productions that some sceptical distance requires to be taken from his assessment of Raeburn. In light of Cunningham's concern for self-improvement, such caution ought to pertain particularly to the description of Raeburn's youth and origins. Cunningham was keen on the idea that his subject 'received no instruction' as a young man.[25] He was, as has been acknowledged for over a century, inclined to exaggerate the disadvantages of Raeburn's orphaned childhood to accentuate the understanding that his natural capacities prevailed.[26] It was characteristic of Cunningham's own preoccupation with the facility of talent that he tells his readers that Raeburn was not particularly industrious when training in a goldsmith's shop. Cunningham was a conspicuous patriot, a devotee not just of Scotland but of Britain. He considered the latter to be series of remarkable local cultures from which men of a genius natural to their place of birth arose. He was not a cosmopolitan 'man of taste'. This did not lead him to be dismissive of British artists who trained abroad. Indeed, in his *Life* of Thomas Lawrence, Cunningham criticised George III for undue respect for artists of 'home manufacture' who had not formed their style abroad.[27] Yet, Cunningham himself was heavily inclined to think of the variety of genius as being a spontaneous expression of particular native lands. Thus, it follows that Cunningham predictably described the development of Raeburn's early technique in terms of raw untutored experimentation under the direct influence of the world of human faces around him. He did not look very hard into what Raeburn might have learned in his years in Rome. Equally, he was inclined not to believe that Raeburn, as a figure of exceptional natural gifts, had learned much from working within the supposedly routine Edinburgh portrait practice of David Martin. In general, Cunningham's *Life* describes

Raeburn as a figure true to the countryside of his birth, close to the Water of Leith. This vision of the artist requires to be read in light of the author's preference for gentlemen who did honour to their 'natural' origins.

A man who selected his artists of 'eminence', sometimes giving preference to little known over famous characters,[28] Cunningham is likely to have been aware of his dependence as a biographer upon personal judgement. It was probably for this reason that he put great emphasis on what is now called 'original research', the compilation of a body of 'fact'. He was a commercial writer, but not a routine hack and did not fall prey to the culture of plagiarism that abounded in the magazine press in his lifetime. It is significant, for instance, that when he employed the witness of a rival obituary of Raeburn he took care to place his borrowing within quotation marks.[29] Such scrupulous standards were at the heart of the literary method that was said to convey an 'air of truth'. For this reason, the *Life* of Raeburn centres upon an overt apology for its lack of prosaic factual matter. Its author admitted that he was unable to compensate for his slight personal acquaintance with his subject by process of research. Looking for literary remains, he had approached Raeburn's surviving family and had been disappointed in his efforts to document his practice. It was clear that Cunningham had no access to the kind of archive of correspondence which he later relied upon, and published, in his, much longer, biography of David Wilkie. Having worked as an administrative factotum for the sculptor Francis Chantrey, who kept a detailed ledger, Cunningham seems to have had expectations that he might come across account books listing appointments with sitters.[30] The absence of such records prevented the compilation of an exhaustive list of accurately dated portraits.[31] This remains, because the artist did not send a high proportion of his paintings to exhibition, a problem for scholars. Cunningham is, then, only unjustly criticised for making minor errors of chronology in this biography.

Cunningham described Raeburn as an accomplished socialite, valued in his home city for his winning ways. Yet, if the painter had inclinations to extend his famous conversations in the form of epistolary exchanges there was, at his death, little evidence they were easily accessible. Letters to friends and clients existed, thirty were published by James Greig shortly before the First World War. Cunningham, however, did not attempt to trace such disparate tracks. If copies of outward bound correspondence, or letters received, were kept by Raeburn it is clear that Cunningham was not granted access to them. The understanding that Raeburn left little literary evidence of his own existence, which Cunningham first promulgated, persisted for the rest of the nineteenth century. Before Greig's biography was published in 1911, all accounts of the artist proceeded under the impression that there were no significant manuscript remains. Even a Victorian biography by a blood relative, William Raeburn Andrew's *Life of Sir Henry Raeburn* (1886), was largely devoid of advances in knowledge, beyond Cunningham's narrative, that were consistent with manuscript research. One review of Andrew's *Life* lamented that, for all the writer was a descendant, his account revealed little of 'the inner man'.[32]

Cunningham established the pattern for considering a superficial knowledge of Raeburn no impediment to the appreciation of his art. He found reason not to present his subject to posterity as a fascinating enigma, rather as a figure whose merits transcended pedantic analysis. Raeburn was, to his admirers and detractors alike, a painter who specialised in the wielding of a broad brush which was employed to capture the immediate sensation of character that was lost to detailed and careful study. Cunningham seems to have considered that this bravura method was the signature of a painter whose life and character was best explained in equivalent literary terms. Cunningham noted that Raeburn did not make preparatory drawings, even on the canvas. Thomas Lawrence, the great exponent of brush technique of the London art world, was regarded as timid by comparison. It was recalled that Raeburn

> always painted standing, and never used a stick for resting his hand on; for such was his accuracy of eye, and steadiness of nerve, that he could introduce the most delicate touches, or the most mechanical regularity of line without aid, or any other contrivance than fair off-hand dexterity.[33]

The essential concept in Cunningham's description of Raeburn, in particular with regard to his technical accomplishments, was manliness. He described Raeburn as 'second to none in manliness and vigour of mind'.[34] Cunningham employed standards of manliness that were of his own invention. Yet, it is likely that he was fastening on to a property of character that actually mattered to the painter. The concept of manliness also featured strongly in the biography written by Raeburn's descendant, W. R. Andrew, who had direct family memories at his disposal. Raeburn's original contribution to the technique of painting, in particular as practised in Scotland, was the overt employment of large square-headed bristle brushes, as angular as the most masculine of chins. This became known, through Wilkie's admiring phrasing, as 'the square touch'. For Cunningham, this highly physical brush technique was no less than an expression of manhood. He dwelled on the impressive, athletic, physique of the painter which he accredited to bracing habits of country walking. Indeed, Cunningham described Raeburn's untimely death, in his mid-sixties, as a great surprise to all who were given to believe, from his vigour, that he was invincible. Cunningham was careful to note that Raeburn had died after one of his long rural perambulations. These feats of walking were described as a central love of the painter's life. It was claimed that Raeburn 'loved to make long excursions among the distant glens and romantic woods of his native land and sometimes did not return for weeks'.[35]

The 1820s was a great era of the British sporting life, and it shows in Cunningham's character of Raeburn. The painter's address of the canvas was discussed in terms appropriate to the appreciation of a well-poised pugilist or the steady stance of a fine shot. His mode of painting was considered a matter of masculine confidence and resolution. There are some indications that Cunningham's vision of Raeburn's manly bearing, when in the act of painting, was more than a legend. Walter Scott, when recounting his last sitting for the artist in which he had, for the first time, chatted freely, also recalled a bold, masculine, approach:

> His manly stride backwards as he went to contemplate his work at a proper distance, and when he resolved on the necessary point to be touched, his step forward was magnificent. I see him in my minds eye, with his hand under his chin contemplating his picture, which position always brought to mind of a figure of Jupiter which I have some where seen.[36]

Both Cunningham' and Scott, therefore, recognised Raeburn as a distinctly physical being. It was, according to Cunningham, his physical presence that would be most missed in Edinburgh at his death. Cunningham predicted that 'his tall, handsome, figure, and fine open manly countenance will not be forgotten for many a day in the place that knew him'.[37]

Cunningham's sense of Raeburn's hearty physical presence allowed him to consider the artist as a spontaneous emanation of bracing Scottish nature. Much as Raeburn's mode of painting was understood as a form of athletic feat, the way was open to interpret his work as an attainment of the body as much as of the mind. Raeburn handled his brush with instinct and spontaneous verve, and so it followed that, for Cunningham, he was not the sort of man to spoil the thrill of the moment with undue contemplation or self-analysis. Cunningham considered Raeburn as the manly vessel through which his sitters came to live and breathe on the canvas. Such a figure was a phenomenon of eye and hand and not of the mind, at least in the sense of the latter as the seat of a questioning consciousness. A steady hand, and spontaneous method, was not for Cunningham consistent with a character who found reason to interrogate the moment and his place within the social world. So it is that there is an important connection in Cunningham's biography between the description of his subject's manly technique and his easy conformity to conventional standards of gentility and political decorum.

Having worked for Francis Chantrey, who made much of his living from the production of marble busts, Cunningham was fully aware that portraiture was an art that demanded an easy and agreeable manner. Successful Georgian portraitists tended to see numerous sitters in a day, often for a couple of hours at a time. Although Greig later provided detailed evidence that this is how Raeburn worked, Cunningham simply knew it. He was aware that even these short hours could drag, causing the sitter's social experience to matter. The portrait painter could expect a diverse, if uniformly wealthy, clientele, most of whom could be depended upon to be literate, if not literary. Such a man did not have to be learned. On the contrary, such dusty accomplishments may well have bored clients, or revealed their ignorance. Yet, he did have to be intelligent, diverting, well-informed and capable of tact. In this respect, Cunningham was convinced that, through early education at Heriot's Hospital and a measure of natural good sense and charm, Raeburn had considerable advantages:

> To classical proficiency, indeed, he had at no time ever laid claim, yet his education had been such as enabled him to maintain without reproach an intercourse by letters with some of the first literary men of the age; and his manners had been so well cared for, that he was never found wanting in that gentlemanly decorum and politeness which is not only becoming but necessary in the portrait painter.[38]

Cunningham understood that there were portrait painters who courted and flattered clients and those who were naturally agreeable and amenable. It could be assumed that these distinctions would show through in the tenor of the paintings. He seems to have placed Lawrence in the first category and Raeburn in the second. Whilst Lawrence's performances struck Cunningham as unctuous and insincere, Raeburn conformed to his appreciation of manly adaptability and dexterity. It was observed of Raeburn that 'his colours were of a kind that suited all complexions and the Whig and Tory were alike visitors of his easel'. Cunningham's estimation of Lawrence's avoidance of party was superficially similar, but tinged with negative language.[39] In his *Life* of Hoppner, who had attached himself to the Prince of Wales and the Foxite Whigs, Cunningham recalls Lawrence's conscious policy of remaining above the fray:

> Lawrence, meantime, with a prudence which Hoppner called hypocrisy, was silent in the manner of politics, belonging to neither faction, and so kept his easel ready and his colours in order for all.[40]

Lawrence was one for the ladies and Raeburn, in Cunningham's perception, a man's man. This was a distinction that mattered to Cunningham. He went so far as to state that Raeburn seldom excelled 'in expressing female loveliness'.[41] Although Cunningham found this blindness to feminine wiles admirable, it was largely, as many of Raeburn's surviving portraits testify, indicative of his, rather than the painter's, character. Of all the negative things he had to say of artists, Cunningham was never so severe as in his criticism of Lawrence's attempts to appeal to the ladies. He commented, for instance, that one of Lawrence's earliest accomplishments was to invest the most 'meek and sedate' women of George III's court with the 'lascivious look' of a high-class courtesan.[42] Cunningham's suspicion of any man who seemed to him to be seduced by the theatre of feminine sexual allure could be considered misogynistic. More likely, he was simply hostile to all impressionable flamboyance. He seems to have disliked effete airs and graces, particularly in artists of whom extravagances, still worse eccentricities, might be expected as indicative of 'temperament'. It was a high complement he paid Raeburn when he observed that it was easy to forget, when he was not wielding his brush, that he was a painter. Contempt for calculated artiness was even more evident in Cunningham's accounts of Chantrey, a man who was on friendly terms with Raeburn.[43] From his recollections of the sculptor in the *Quarterly Review* of June 1826, it is easy to imagine that he found in Raeburn a similar, peculiarly British, quality of bluff simplicity:

> England may be justly proud of Chantrey, his works reflect back her image as a mirror; he has formed his taste on no style but that of nature, and no works of any age or country but his own claim back any inspiration which they have lent him. He calls up no shapes from antiquity; he gives us no established visions from the past; the moment he breaths is his; the beauty and manliness which live and move around him are his materials, and he embodies them for the gratification of posterity.[44]

Cunningham, then, was a passionate patriot, as much charmed by the 'roast beef' Englishman as the stolid Scot nourished by the deer of the glens. Britain was representative of their united masculine presence. So magnificent was this age of 'Union' that no previous era commanded nostalgia, no country emulation. Though it passes as generalised bombast, there were specific politics at work here. These had also been present in his account of Raeburn, regarded as a patriot who arrived at his own masterful technique as an encounter with national nature, without recourse to past exemplar or foreign influence. Cunningham was by no means the only critic to find in Raeburn's robust and manly technique the political essence of what it meant to be free and British in the modern era. The 'Character' of the artist printed in the *European Magazine* of November 1823 commented that his free brushwork was a spontaneous expression of British political conditions. The broad brush style of Raeburn and other British artists was ascribed to 'that boldness, and independence of national character resulting from the free and liberal institutions of our country'.[45]

Cunningham's account of Raeburn, like most of his artists' *Lives*, was suffused by a sense of patriotism, which was not devoid of political sentiments. Like the business-like portrait painter, this commercial biographer was sufficiently conscious of the breadth of his market not to reveal party bias in his assessments of artists. However, he was patently well disposed to what might be termed 'establishment' figures. In this respect it is significant to note that Cunningham was a highly sympathetic biographer of David Wilkie, a Scot who was known for his political conservatism. Wilkie had amused the reform-minded Benjamin Haydon and his circle with his timid desire to fit in with the politics that the majority of his landed clients would find acceptable. He had no problems endearing himself with the Duke of York's set, and the brusque Tory, anti-Reform sentiments of the Duke of Wellington. Cunningham, in turn, found no fault in this. In the case of Raeburn, who rose to fame a decade earlier, one can discern in Cunningham's language admiration of an inclination to fit in with social life as he found it. These were the virtues of a conservative, as opposed to a 'radical'. Cunningham's particular admiration fixed on artists who accepted blithely the social world of their country, Scotland or England, and reflected it back upon itself. There could be nothing finer.

Cunningham's attitudes to self-improvement, and what is now thought of as 'rustic vernacular culture', were intimately connected and distinctly political. He was acutely sensitive to the worth of the humble and local man. However, this ought not to be confused with the sentiments of a democrat. Cunningham's political values were fashioned, as were those of Raeburn and Wilkie, in the era of the Revolutionary Wars. Although low born with aspirations to gentility, Cunningham admired the person who kept within the expectations of his social station. Occasionally, he acknowledged, natural genius would cause a man to rise in social stature. However, this was the exceptional circumstance, born of exceptional properties of character that could be identified with 'genius'. It was, categorically, not to be considered part of the equal 'rights of man', that all should be fully involved in the political community and province of refined culture. Cunningham's personal politics are no where clearer than his assessment of the meaning of Wilkie's *Village Politicians* (1806). Although Wilkie himself did not make a political meaning obvious, Cunningham had no doubt of his purpose. The *Village*

Politicians was, he claimed, a satire upon the era of the French Revolution when previously contented rustics were caught in the ferment of unjustified expectation that their opinions mattered in the wider political community. Cunningham describes the politics of the Revolution as an unfortunate 'yeast' that fostered the pretensions of the people to rise up throughout the rest of Europe.[46] These were the interpretive values of a Tory, which pervade Cunningham's estimation of Raeburn. The portrait painter rose to fame during the 1790s, in the era of the Revolutionary Wars, and Cunningham leaves his readers in no doubt that he had no disconcerting commonality with the Continental freethinker, or libertine. Insularity was a virtue for Cunningham, in so far as the hearth and home harboured the best influences. He presented his subject as a domestic paragon, the very antithesis of a cosmopolitan creative rebel. It was recalled that Raeburn:

> did the honours of a handsome house and elegant table with all the grace of a highbred gentleman. His practice never kept him from his place in church on Sunday and in days of trouble he was a zealous volunteer.[47]

Cunningham, therefore, presented Raeburn as an exemplary British gentleman: churchgoing, domestically steadfast, a proud Scot, yet committed, to the extent of taking up arms, to the Union and loyal to his King and Country. These virtues were considered to proceed from a man who understood the distinction between the merits of intellectual curiosity and the pitfalls of an overzealous engagement with the world of ideas. In particular, he was cautious of those ideas of a political nature that might get in the way of the appreciation of his country as it appeared before him. In this respect also Cunningham's familiarity with Chantrey is of relevance. Born near Sheffield, of lowly social origins, the sculptor began his career in the 'radical' circle of Horne Tooke.[48] Nevertheless, ambition and success quickly fostered within him a knack for finding favour with the landed establishment, both Whig and Tory. The key to this process was, as it seems to have been for Raeburn, the adoption of a conspicuously 'manly' self-image. As his surviving letters show, Chantrey cultivated the persona of a bluff Hogarthian 'true Briton', prone to express himself in amusing terse, yet intelligent, statements. Such a man was disarmingly free of the sort of extravagancies of character that could make an artist an uncomfortable figure in what, for a social and political conservative, passed for good company.[49] Chantrey, indeed, was sufficiently suspicious of the application of ideas to his sculpture that he avoided the employment of allegory throughout his career. For his part, Raeburn never attempted a history painting and was no less hailed by Cunningham on this account. Cunningham positively admired Raeburn's contentment with the ambition to reflect, rather than reform, his home community. For what was there to be reformed? Cunningham's *Life* of Raeburn is, then, one of the many literary sources that is sidelined on the way to the acceptance of John Barrell's argument that 'civic humanist' ideals were predominant in the 'political theory' and culture of the visual arts from 'Reynolds to Hazlitt'.[50] Cunningham, and one suspects Raeburn, had no pretence of respect for the notion that a great artist can be defined by his capacity to communicate profound, morally reforming, ideas.

Cunningham made an observant connection, which art historians could profitably revive, between the satisfactory spontaneity of Raeburn's technique and his success with investing his subjects with a relaxed demeanour that conjures a satisfying impression of familiarity. For Cunningham the pleasing nature of Raeburn's portraits was indicative of his skilful command of inoffensive chitchat. Such talents were consistent with Raeburn's capacity to discern and penetrate that illusive phenomenon, the establishment. It was not in the creative or business interests of a man who sought to put wealthy people at their ease to assume the character of an intense critic of the social and political world. In his several lives of British portrait painters, Cunningham addressed, consciously or otherwise, the long tradition of despising artists of this sort as flatterers whose practice was limited to the skilful production of a seeming 'likeness', as opposed to demanding encounters with the world of ideas. At times he could see the validity of such criticism. He did not spare the rod, for instance, in his description of Richard Cosway, who rose to fame in the dissolute Carlton House circle. Cosway was said to have risen to fame as a painter of miniatures 'amid all this waste and vanity'.[51] Yet, Cunningham understood that the portrait painter did not simply profit from vanity. Raeburn was, indeed, his great example of how this need not be the case. He was, for instance, categorical in congratulating Raeburn for attaining satisfactory, and pleasing, likenesses; considering it no indignity for a man with pretensions to creative genius to base his reputation upon such delightful mimicry and illusion. He was insistent that Raeburn's immediate gifts as a mimic of surface appearances was no impediment to an instinctive grasp of deeper matters of character. It was remembered that 'such was the intuition with which he penetrated at once to the mind, that the first sitting rarely came to a close without his having seized strongly upon the character and disposition of the individual'.[52]

As a writer of artists' *Lives*, therefore, Cunningham was conscious of the claim of the portraitist to be a species of biographer, one who attained his ends more through 'intuition' than research. He was careful to point out that Raeburn had not been the kind of portraitist to give no attention to the intellectual greatness of his sitters. It was this, Cunningham claimed, that caused him to create a sort of pantheon of those in Scottish society who were most worthy of fame. Here again, the biographer mistook his own for his subject's scruples. Whilst Raeburn did manage to paint many of the most famous characters to pass through Edinburgh in his times, it was also the case that his brush was employed on anybody who could pay. Indeed, Raeburn painted, in Greig's estimation, well over a thousand portraits in his career, most of which were not known to Cunningham and are not of cultural luminaries.

It was probably on account of the critical supposition that a portraitist was likely to be an insincere flatterer that Cunningham makes frequent reference to Raeburn's honesty. So it was that the writer presented his character as someone who understood how to please, without diverting from a manly sense of the truth which was deemed necessary to art. He presented such honesty as a matter of instinct and temperament; remembering Raeburn as a man who effortlessly pleased the world with his art because it brought him simple enjoyment:

> He was happy and charmed, he often said, with the work of the day, and described portrait painting as the most delightful thing in the world, in as much as everybody came to him with their happiest moods and pleasantest faces and went away happy to see that they looked so well on the canvas.[53]

It was this sense of enjoyment that, in Cunningham's estimation, allowed Raeburn to express successfully his facility without straying into the territory of the facile flatterer which he discovered in the character of Lawrence. The connection that Cunningham drew between Raeburn's effortlessness and the enjoyable sensation of looking at his work also pertained to a suspicion of the romantic myth of the painter as a figure who required to suffer for his art. At pains to point out that Raeburn enjoyed his profession, Cunningham considered him a stranger to the midnight toils of the garret. Cunningham was careful to note that his subject kept strict professional hours, which he described as a 'regular system of labour'. He recalled that Raeburn 'remained in his painting room until a little after five o'clock, then he walked home and dined at six'. He was lost in admiration of an anecdote concerning how, when he had a dinner appointment in town, Raeburn simply put down his brushes, entered a changing room, and appeared a few minutes later in dress 'worthy of the first company'.[54]

To gain a full appreciation of Cunningham's fundamental point in noting these regular habits, one only requires to compare his comments on Raeburn's 'regular system' with certain passages in his *Life* of James Barry, a figure who openly disdained the dependence of the British art market upon portraiture. Cunningham set out clear reasons why Barry found himself an outsider to the academic, religious and political establishment. It was with a certain amount of bemused incomprehension that Cunningham noted of Barry that he was, from his youth, determined to endure self-imposed privations for his art. Revealing a Protestant suspicion of embracing pain for its own sake, Cunningham associated Barry's self-destructive rebelliousness, the traits which rendered him an outsider, less with his republican sympathies than with his Catholicism. It was recalled that 'even in these early days he exhibited a spirit intractable and capricious, and declared his love for those ascetic and self-denying habits which assume the name of virtues in the legends of the Roman church'.[55] Such a painter could be expected to dwell upon his art at the expense of sleep, whilst the Protestant Raeburn was comfortably tucked up in bed. Indeed, Cunningham noted, without overt admiration, that Barry tended to work into the night.

With all his references to regular hours, domestic rectitude, and charming attendance to customer needs, Cunningham is likely to have been aware of the danger that his *Life* of Raeburn could be easily mistaken for a tribute to the model Protestant bourgeois. This was how some later nineteenth-century commentators classified the artist. Raeburn, indeed, may well have learned more from his early years working in an Edinburgh goldsmith's shop than Cunningham cared to notice. The basic description of Raeburn's practice – the grand business premises, pleasing productions and easy way with the clients – were entirely consistent with the priorities of a successful, upmarket, retailer. It may not, therefore, have been just a 'kind' disposition which prevented Cunningham from making reference to Raeburn's disastrous underwriting of his family's maritime trading and shipping business. It is now clear, owing to Stephen Lloyd's research as published in this volume, how the artist became bankrupt through these dealings. This suggests that his quest for wealth was not satisfied by his considerable and lucrative 'art' practice. Cunningham, nevertheless, liked to believe that Raeburn was above concerning himself with the management of money. He found reason to explain the absence of business records, which he encountered when researching the painter's life, as evidence of contempt for the small concerns of the ledger. He stated that Raeburn had an 'invincible repugnance to keeping either the lists of his portraits, or any account of his earnings. He, perhaps, enjoyed life too much to be very eager about fame or money.'

One of the factors that most risked the recognition of Raeburn as a businessman was his strong connection with the city. Raeburn, however, was as much a figure of Stockbridge, then a genteel and semi-rural suburb, as the centre of Edinburgh. The way was open, therefore, for the painter to being interpreted as a character of the country as well as the city. Cunningham did his best to accentuate the countryman:

> Though his painting-rooms were in George Street, his dwelling-house was at St Bernard's, near Stock Bridge – a romantic place. The steep banks were finely wooded, the garden grounds varied and beautiful; and all the seclusion of the country could be enjoyed without remoteness.[56]

Again, this preference for the countryman may well derive from Cunningham's admiration for Francis Chantrey who identified himself as a gentleman by cultivating the accomplishments of a field sportsman. Such healthy diversions excused a man the reputation of a puny shopkeeper, most at home in the confines of his urban premises. Cunningham, as we have already noted, stressed Raeburn's manly liking for his home landscape of Stockbridge and the great open spaces of Scotland:

> We can easily imagine that a walk on the banks of the river with his wife, or looking at the flowers of his garden, or sketching the landscape to introduce into the backgrounds of his pictures, might be much more to his taste than the Ready Reckoner [book of accounts]. Indeed, he acknowledged that in his wandering during the morning and evening, he saw clouds, and skies and landscapes which he brooded upon, and fixed in his imagination, where they remained until transferred to canvas.[57]

When noting the painter's love of walking through, and drawing, the landscape, Cunningham invited the viewers of his portraits to see more to his backgrounds than the formulae of the studio. Thus, he countered any simplistic assumption that the fashionable portrait painter was defined by the bounds of a town premises and commercial practice.

It seems likely, in conclusion, that Cunningham reacted to his inability to know Raeburn through a process of documentation by characterising him as a kind of Scottish 'gentleman' which he could admire. So it is that Cunningham's account of Raeburn probably reveals as much about the social identity of the author as his subject. Whilst it is necessary to acknowledge this process of character elision, it remains difficult to analyse its mechanics. The writer of the most lengthy and well-considered obituary of Raeburn, a figure who had few biographical notices during his lifetime, Cunningham exerted a strong influence over how his subject was subsequently understood. His vision of Raeburn's art as a matter of technique and intuition is difficult to resist, not least because the painter's social identity remains, for all the subsequent compilation of biographical matter, so difficult to ascertain. This last circumstance is, it must be said, not owing to Cunningham's failings. It is remarkable, on reading Cunningham in detail, how many leads he provides that have not been followed up by recent scholars. He points to numerous matters of social involvement – volunteer service, religious observance, and 'scientific' interest – which do not appear to have stimulated curiosity. Moreover, the substantial passages concerning the building of 'Raeburnville', and the painter's alternative career as an architect, have not been met with resolute enquiry. Raeburn becomes, in socio-historical terms, a more interesting figure when one takes into account that his contribution to polite Edinburgh society was more extensive than the provision of a painted record of its inhabitants.

The advantage of looking again at Cunningham's *Life* may, therefore, be that it hints at profitable fresh ways of approaching the painter's place in 'society'. At present, scholarship of this sort is not advanced. More than twenty years ago, Duncan Macmillan, in his survey *Scottish Art, 1460–1990*, advanced a new socio-historical approach to this painter. He suggested that Raeburn required to be comprehended within a tradition of 'empirical' enquiry that was distinctive to the Scottish Enlightenment, in specific the philosophical works of the circle of Thomas Reid.[58] Whilst interesting, Macmillan's determination to discover an intellectual context for Raeburn's painting style was entirely associative. Nothing was demonstrated of concrete influence, and the description of social context amounts, as a consequence, to little more than a matter of zeitgeist. This type of approach was taken further seven years later in an essay by Nicholas Phillipson on Raeburn's place in the 'Scottish Enlightenment'.[59] Once again, the tenor of this essay was that of the provision of a broad contextual framework. A loose sense of intellectual environment was provided but little in the way of fresh understanding of Raeburn's particular social identity. One is left with the impression that appreciation of the 'Scottish Enlightenment' had much improved over the previous twenty years, but that knowledge of the painter's particular presence in his society was little advanced. It remains, for instance, a puzzle why scholars still have to resort to generalities concerning Raeburn's 'empiricism', when we know from Cunningham of his personal interest in 'scientific' contraptions and botanical learning, which caused him to become a member of the Royal Society of Edinburgh.[60] Moreover, it is difficult to explain why the specific use of language employed by the first biographers to describe Raeburn's gentility featured so little in Phillipson's account of the painter's 'manners, morals and character'.

Macmillan and Phillipson's accounts of Raeburn can reasonably be regarded as attempts to move from a vague sense of the artist's place in Edinburgh society to a scholarly appreciation of his Scottishness. Indeed, the 1980s and 1990s were a time when a rising tide of Scottish nationalism demanded a 'Scottish art' of the eighteenth and early nineteenth centuries and the preferred method was to generate some sense of Edinburgh's distinctive contribution to the pan-European spirit of 'Enlightenment'. Cunningham never mentions this 'Enlightenment', although some of his commentaries on Raeburn are open to interpretation as descriptions of some of its characteristics. His vision of what made Scotland distinct resided far more in the intellectual territory of Walter Scott and the location, if not invention, of distinctive local tradition. Cunningham created a Raeburn who was the son of a particular soil. His was the account of a proud Scot, who was claiming Raeburn as one of his ancestral kin. However, his vision of what it was to be a Scot is not fully reflected in recent analysis of Raeburn's Scottishness. Cunningham was a resolute supporter of the Union and his political outlook may not, as a consequence, be particularly amenable to those who seek to define what was distinctively Scottish about Raeburn's art. Yet, in light of the strong possibility that he had a comprehension of Raeburn's place in the Scottish establishment that was based on genuine sympathy of mind, it may be desirable to look more closely at what he has to say on these matters.

The final passages of Cunningham's *Life* suggest that it would be desirable in the future to bring together the portraits of eminent Scotsmen made by Raeburn to form a gallery in homage to the attainments of the country and age. These were times when phrenology was in fashion and the shape of the head and proportions of the face were considered revelatory, not least of natural and national distinctions between men. It followed that a collection of portraits of high-achieving Scotsmen would amount to no less than a physical description of what rendered the nation remarkable. Cunningham's concluding prompt to posterity was eventually taken seriously when in 1876 an exhibition of Raeburn's portraits, largely of the famous men of Edinburgh, was organised at the Royal Scottish Academy.[61] In the same vein, a volume of photographs after Raeburn's works was commissioned in 1876 by the Edinburgh publisher Andrew Eliot, with a forward by Dr John Brown. The illustrations were selected in such a manner as to indicate that the artist's prime achievement was to record the physical essence of the Scottish establishment at times of peculiar national attainment: examples included portraits of Henry Mackenzie, David Baird, Francis Cockburn, Lord Eldin, and Dugald Stewart. One reviewer of this book expressed clearly the understanding that Raeburn recorded the pleasant evening of natural Scottish separateness, prior to complete submission to the culture of the Union:

> The mention of these names, and they are but a few of the men distinguished in their day in Scottish life, reveals the busy professional career of the painter. To Scotsmen the Raeburn Gallery has a special interest. Although England and Scotland had long been united under one crown and legislature, the union was far from complete in literary and professional and social life, when Raeburn drew

his historical portraits. Not till the days of the Regency, and the Reform Bill, and the railroads, did the fusion of the two nations really begin. In art it was yet far from complete . . .[62]

This account of the artist is perceptive. He was, by and large, a figure of the Revolutionary and Napoleonic wars, when the 'fusion of the two nations' did 'really begin'. Raeburn spent the majority of his life in Edinburgh, and was demonstrably often blissfully unaware of the London art world. He was, nevertheless, a component of an establishment, at once proudly Scottish and resolutely loyal to Crown and Union, that was loosing its cultural distinction from its London equivalents. It is clear that Cunningham, a biographer of Robert Burns, but who willingly spent the majority of his life in London, was a sympathetic reviewer because he shared a basic cultural and political outlook as a proud Scot and loyal Briton. It was not without significance, therefore, that, for all Cunningham described Raeburn as a paragon of Scottish refinement, he elected to have this account bound into a series of biographies of 'British' artists.

Notes

1. I have seen, in early nineteenth-century sources, numerous versions of the title that Raeburn was given. Another was 'Limner and Painter to the King in Scotland' or 'His Majesty's Painter for Scotland' (*The Caledonian Mercury*, 19 July 1823).

2. *The Caledonian Mercury*, 3 October 1822. This account was extensively reprinted in the London press, appearing, for instance, in *The Morning Post*, 9 October 1822.

3. *The Literary Chronicle*, 26 July 1823.

4. *The Atheneaum*, 28 September 1901, p. 420.

5. Raeburn has long been thought to have anticipated some aspects of Impressionism. This sense of his importance was articulated in Walter Armstrong's account of the artist of 1901. I would of course discourage such largely unhistorical approaches. However, it is probably worth considering that there was something in Raeburn's technique which appealed to those later Scottish artists who were influenced by Impressionism and combined it with the characteristic 'square brush' approach of the early nineteenth-century master.

6. Cunningham appears to have become interested in the format of the Vasarian series when he revised Matthew Pilkington's *A General Dictionary of Painters*, which he published in two volumes in 1824. Pilkington was a purposefully arid writer, who believed that Vasari and other biographers of the Italian 'Renaissance' abounded in frivolous stories. Cunningham clearly did not take

his literary style from Pilkington but was probably influenced by his predecessor's admirable scruple with regard to discerning 'fact' from evidence.

7. I here refer to the *Life of Bacon*, which appeared in the *European Magazine* for August 1790, pp. 83–4. This was a shortened version of a *Life* supplied to the *British Magazine* on the completion of the monument to Chatham at Guildhall in 1782.

8. I have selected these names as the most remarkable publishers of anecdotes relating to the visual arts in the 1820s and early 1830s. Pyne's work is exemplified by *Old Wine and Walnuts or After Dinner Chit Chat* (1823). J. T. Smith is best remembered for *Nollekens and his Times* of 1828. Henry Angelo published his *Reminiscences of Henry Angelo* in 1830.

9. Cunningham 1829–33, V, p. 208.

10. I am unsure which journal or magazine printed the master copy of the text that appeared in the *Literary Chronicle*. I suspect it was the *European Magazine* (LXXXIV, pp. 435–7) because this periodical had an excellent record of covering the lives of artists. I have found many variants of this text, some full length, others with parts excised.

11. Duncan 1824.

12. *The Belle Assemblée*, 1 April 1832.

13. For hostile responses to Lawrence see Cunningham 1829–33, VI. pp. 168–9, 174, 185, 208.

14. As recorded by Greig 1911, p. xxviii.

15. Cunningham 1829–33, V, p. 229.

16. Ibid. p. 229.

17. I am aware that this passage may make it seem as if there are clear suggestions of Raeburn over reaching himself in the desire for enrichment. The case for this, such as it is, remains in infancy. I cannot agree with Duncan Macmillan who, in his survey of 'Scottish Art' of 1990, which is discussed below, suggests that Raeburn's bankruptcy was owing simply to his unfortunate involvement in his brother-in-law's affairs. Since he published these opinions, a bare bones account of these financial matters was produced by David Mackie in the documentation section of the catalogue for the last major exhibition of the artist's work in 1997–8. This makes it clear that Raeburn's personal involvement went far deeper than Macmillan suggests. The circumstances of this are documented in more detail by Stephen Lloyd in his chapter for this volume.

18. The text below is gleaned from David Hogg's *The Life of Allan Cunningham: with selections from his works and correspondence*, London, 1875.

19. Cf. the *Life* of Hoppner, Cunningham 1829–33, V, p. 271.

20. Horace Walpole, *Some Anecdotes of Painting in England*, first published 1762.

21. Cunningham published *Traditional Tales of the English and Scottish Peasantry* in 1822.

22. Cunningham published *The Life of Robert Burns* in 1836. His own interest in the language of Scotland was enduring. He published *Songs: Chiefly in the Rural Language of Scotland* in 1813.
23. See an account of Chantrey's death and funeral in *The London Saturday Journal*, 1842, p. 93.
24. Cunningham 1843.
25. Cunningham 1829–33, V, p. 207.
26. James Greig, who published *Sir Henry Raeburn R.A: His Life and Works* in 1911, was much inclined to question the legends of the painter's youth provided by Cunningham.
27. Cunningham 1829–33, VI, p. 172.
28. Cunningham included figures such as William Owen and George Harlow who were not particularly famous in their own lifetimes.
29. Cunningham 1829–33, V. p. 238.
30. Ibid. p. 218. Cunningham notes that the painter's disregard for book keeping was 'very disadvantageous to the biographers'.
31. Greig 1911 (p. 51) later revealed that Raeburn had kept an account book. This suggests that Cunningham was not given access to family papers by the surviving family. Henry Raeburn junior deplored prurient interest in his father after death. He is known, for instance, to have denied access to his father's body for the taking of the death mask. It seems likely that there were personal papers which the family elected to destroy. That there was no body of papers for William Raeburn Andrew to utilise in the 1880s suggest that this process happened soon after death.
32. As appeared in *The Athenaeum*, 14 August 1886, p. 212.
33. Cunningham 1829–33, V, p. 217.
34. Ibid., V. p. 239.
35. Ibid., V. p. 235.
36. Greig 1911, p. xxxvii.
37. Ibid., V. p. 239.
38. Ibid., V. p. 204.
39. Ibid., V. p. 224.
40. Ibid., V. p. 248.
41. Ibid., V. p. 240.
42. As appears in the *Life* of Hoppner, ibid., V. p. 297.
43. Chantrey and Raeburn were on friendly terms from at least 1814. In 1818 they drew each other with the aid of Chantrey's preferred camera lucida. These two drawings are in the collection of the SNPG.
44. I refer here to a quote from this article, which appeared in an account of Chantrey in the *London Saturday Journal*, 19 February 1842, p. 92.
45. *The European Magazine*, November 1823, LXXXIV, p. 436.

46. Cunningham 1843, I, p. 112.

47. Cunningham 1829–33, V, p. 239.

48. For an account of these early years consult *The London Saturday Journal*, May, 1842, p. 235.

49. I refer here to the character produced by George Jones in his *Francis Chantrey R.A. Recollections of his Life, Practice and Opinions*, London, 1849.

50. John Barrell, *The Political Theory of Painting from Reynolds to Hazlitt*, New Haven and London, 1986.

51. Cunningham 1829–33, V. p. 7.

52. Ibid., p. 217.

53. Ibid., V, p. 218.

54. Ibid., V. p. 217.

55. Ibid., II, p. 63.

56. Ibid., V, p. 219.

57. Ibid.

58. Macmillan 1990, pp. 154 –7.

59. Phillipson in Edinburgh and London 1997–8.

60. Cunningham 1829–33, V, p. 233.

61. As reviewed in *The Art Journal*, November 1876, p. 349. There was also an interesting review in *The Glasgow Herald*, 5 October 1876.

62. *The Leisure Hour*, 4 March 1876.

12

'Synonymous with manly portraits': Re-evaluating Raeburn's Women

Jordan Mearns

This chapter focuses on Raeburn's portraits of women, which have hitherto been unfairly eclipsed in art historical scholarship in favour of his portraits of Enlightenment men – leading members of Scotland's intelligentsia. It will not subject Raeburn's female portraiture to the type of formal analysis already such a defining feature of the literature, but will instead sketch a historiography charting the secondary position they have come to occupy in accounts of Raeburn's portrait output. The unflagging interest displayed towards Raeburn's male portrayals is typically proportional to the prestige of the sitter depicted, but is also deeply rooted in the conviction that Raeburn's male portraits have a greater capacity to faithfully delineate national character, and a sense of the sitter's intellectual qualities. The keen interest in Raeburn's 'characterful' male portraiture has been exacerbated by the primacy of physiognomy used as a guiding critical yardstick in nineteenth- and twentieth-century evaluations of the artist's output. This essay will underline the persistence of such tropes in the literature, which has a clear sense of continuity from the first accounts of the artist in the nineteenth century through the early twentieth century and perpetuated in recent scholarship. Raeburn's portraits of Enlightenment worthies have been implicated in nationalistic readings of his output. Portraits of prestigious scholars have been seized upon to furnish legitimising artistic and intellectual traditions for Scotland; these categories in turn have often been conflated. Portraits of members of Scotland's intellectual elite have been construed as

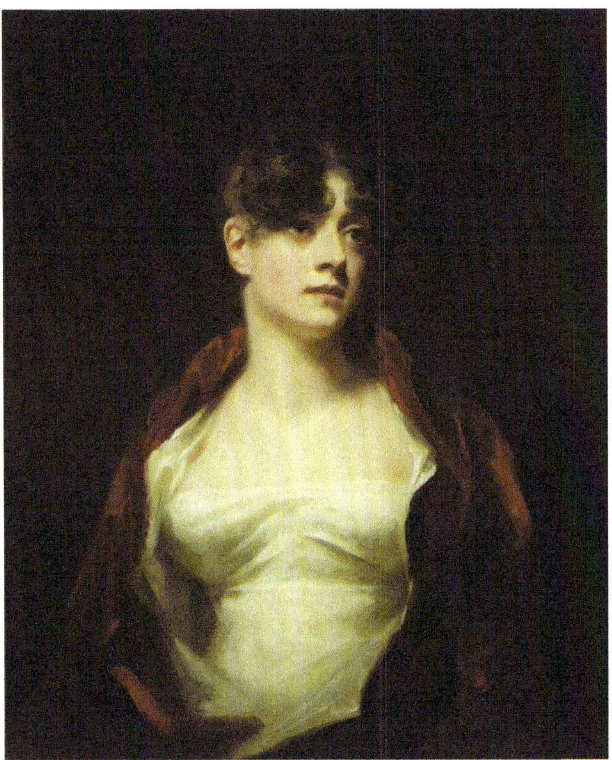

Figure 12.1 Henry Raeburn, *Margaret Macdonald, Mrs Robert Scott Moncrieff*, c. 1814, oil on canvas, 74.9×62.2cm, Scottish National Gallery, Edinburgh

proof of an ideological affinity between artist and sitter even where there is no evidence to justify such claims.[1] This chapter will also examine the critical inequality that exists between evaluations of Raeburn's portraits of young women which, when compared with those of more mature sitters, have been subject to less connoisseurship and art historical scrutiny.

Leaving aside the canonical full length tartan portraits *Sir John Sinclair of Ulbster, Francis MacNab* (Fig. 7.2) and *Colonel Alastair Ranaldson Macdonell of Glengarry* (Fig. 10.4), two other works have come to dominate accounts of the art of Henry Raeburn: the contentious sporting picture of *The Revd Robert Walker ('The Skating Minister')* (Fig. 1.4) and the perennially seductive *Margaret Macdonald, Mrs Robert Scott Moncrieff* (Fig. 12.1). The treatment of both portraits in the existing art historical literature exposes many of the significant flaws that mar Raeburn scholarship. Stephen Lloyd challenged art historical orthodoxy when he argued in a 2005 article that a more likely candidate for the authorship of *The Skating Minister*, an established icon of

Scottish art, might be the French émigré artist Henri-Pierre Danloux.[2] Lloyd's proposed re-attribution stirred up a furore among Scottish art historians, inspiring a riposte by Duncan Thomson seeking to endorse the status quo and an animated debate among press columnists.[3] The ensuing defence of the original attribution by Thomson highlighted the methodological reliance on traditional connoisseurship, which has hitherto dominated Raeburn scholarship.[4] Although the portrait's authorship has little direct bearing on this chapter, the strident nationalism that tinctured the fallout from Lloyd's re-attribution should be noted, as it runs like a vein through much existing writing on the artist, hinting at the prevailing conception of Raeburn as a peculiarly 'national' artist and, as I will argue, fuelling the eclipse of Raeburn's female portraiture.

The fact that Raeburn left no sitter-books – and only an episodic, business-like paper trail to posterity – has encouraged art historians to toil over the formation of a stylistic chronology of some one thousand canvases. The urge to divide Raeburn's works into neat chronological phases – before Rome, post-Rome or early, mature and late works has precluded more searching thematic or contextual analysis. The paucity of historical evidence relating to the artist's stylistic development and influences has, however, encouraged greater evils, which continue to bedevil Raeburn studies. The lack of nuanced information relating to Raeburn's stylistic development, during formative sojourns, briefly in London and then in Rome, has allowed the myth of the artist's Scottish stylistic exceptionalism to go unchecked, colouring accounts of the artist from the mid-nineteenth century to the present day.

Many of Raeburn's portraits of women, however, attest to the artist's readiness to engage with fashionable London portrait practice, but the prevailing tendency in the writings of recent Raeburn specialists is to downplay any such influence.[5] A glance at Raeburn's *Lady Gordon-Cumming* (Fig. 12.2), however, should be enough in itself to put paid to the notion that Raeburn operated in self-imposed isolation from the influence of his metropolitan contemporaries. *Lady Gordon-Cumming*, exhibited at the Royal Academy in 1817, is an essay in the racy mannerism and heightened sensuality of Thomas Lawrence's female portraiture and is a direct stylistic quotation of Lawrence's *Mrs Wolff* (Fig. 12.3), exhibited two years earlier in 1815. The artist himself, in a rare surviving insight into his opinion of his own work, opined that the portrait was 'by much the best and handsomest female picture I have yet painted . . .'.[6] Although Raeburn's pride in this portrait is flagged by Duncan Thomson, he frames it as an aberration in the artist's output and continues to emphasise Raeburn's geographical and, by extension, supposed artistic 'remoteness from the mainstream'.[7] Raeburn however, arguably envisioned the portrait to act as an advertisement of his awareness

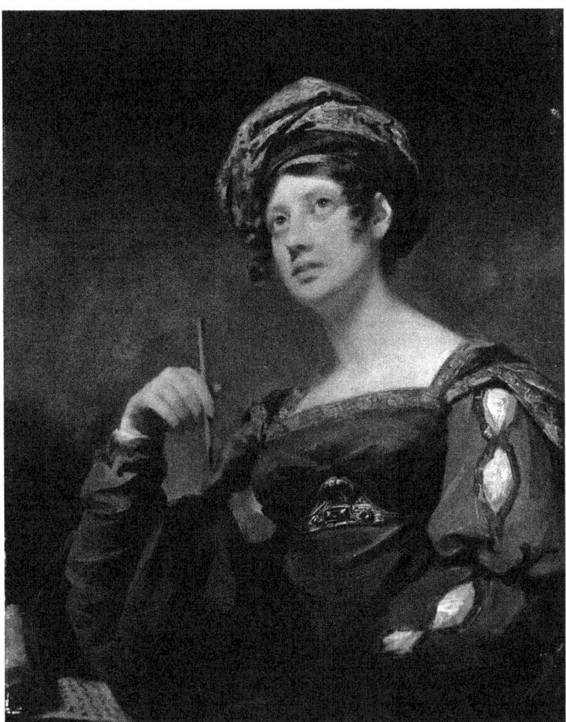

Figure 12.2 Henry Raeburn, *Eliza Mary Campbell, Lady Gordon-Cumming*,
exh. RA 1817, oil on canvas, 76×63.5cm, formerly in the collection of Sir
Felix Cassel in 1951, current location unknown (courtesy of the Witt Library,
Courtauld Institute of Art, London)

of modish London portrait practice: it is amongst the handful of portraits of
women he sent to be exhibited at the Royal Academy.[8] Although, admit-
tedly the artists occupy different poles in terms of technique – Lawrence's
minutely descriptive drawing versus Raeburn's direct, generalising and
broadly painted approach – the Scottish artist's indebtedness to Lawrence
and his high-keyed bravura style is clear in his later female portraits. Lloyd's
call for the reattribution of *The Revd Robert Walker* (*'The Skating Minister'*)
also has implications for the stylistic cross-fertilisation often apparent, but
rarely accepted in Raeburn's female portraiture. Lloyd makes the claim that
Raeburn's *Isabella McLeod, Mrs James Gregory* (c. 1798; Fig. 10.5), a portrait
as stylistically anomalous as *The Skating Minister* (Fig. 1.4), but with a water-
tight attribution to Raeburn, may serve as an instance of the artist taking his
lead from the polished softness and restricted harmonious palette of Danloux.
Duncan Macmillan has gone further in distancing Raeburn from the influence of London-based portraitists. In the chapter on Raeburn entitled 'The

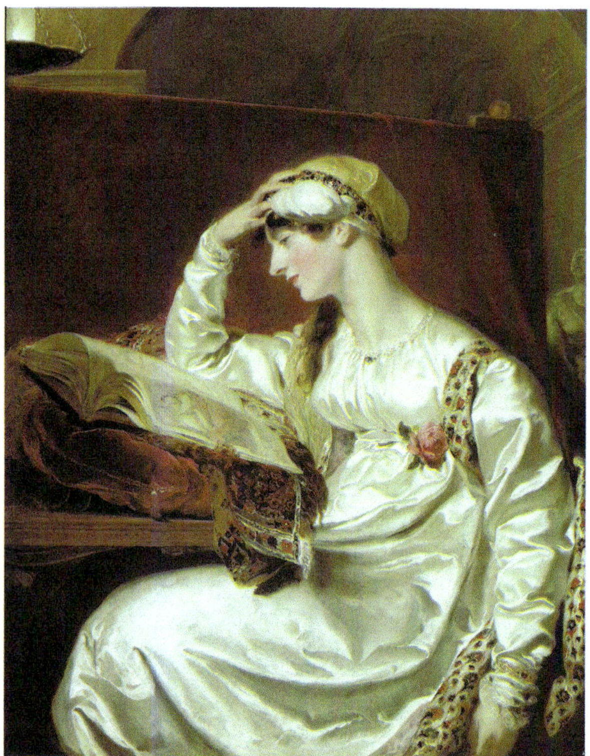

Figure 12.3 Thomas Lawrence, *Isabella Hutchinson, Mrs Jens Wolff*, 1803–15, oil on canvas, 128.2 × 102cm, Mr and Mrs W. W. Kimball Collection, The Art Institute of Chicago (photography © The Art Institute of Chicago)

Portraiture of Common Sense', from the catalogue of his 1986–7 exhibition *Painting in Scotland*, Macmillan has suggested forcefully that the writings of Thomas Reid, especially his work on perception, guided Raeburn's approach to portraiture. Aside from imparting intellectual *cachet* to Raeburn's *oeuvre*, this purported Scottish intellectual influence on Raeburn's style allows Macmillan to ignore the clear affinities between his work and that of artists, including John Hoppner, who worked south of the border.

Mrs Scott Moncrieff (Fig. 12.1), the artist's totemic 'beauty portrait', on the other hand, has been invoked in almost every work on the art of Raeburn and has appeared in almost every exhibition. The portrait, though, has engendered almost no more critical comment than that the sitter is particularly beautiful. *Mrs Scott Moncrieff* is a singularly sensual depiction of femininity, the bitumen-darkened background throws the sitter into high relief, and a strangely gaping cloak emphasises the sitter's improbably high and splayed breasts. Perhaps *Mrs Scott Moncreiff's* beauty has been seized upon with such enthusiasm as many commentators find depictions of beauty otherwise lacking in Raeburn's portrait output, unlike Lawrence who has long been associated with portrayals of beautiful women. So closely trained has the focus been on Raeburn's male portraits that he has gained the epithet 'synonymous with manly portraits,' in turn substantive analysis of his portraits of women is absent in major accounts of his work.[9] Although they inhabit only a secondary role in accounts of the artist's output, Raeburn's portraits of women occupied a conspicuous position in the demand for British portraits during the era of Joseph Duveen, the most prominent transatlantic dealer active during the early decades of the twentieth century. In his study *The Economics of Taste: The Rise and Fall of Picture Prices 1760–1960* (1961), Gerald Reitlinger notes 'the code of the English portrait market has always been chivalrous; women and children first' and in relation to Raeburn that 'it was [. . .] American competition which kept Scottish lairdry on such an exhalted plane'[10] The prices achieved by Raeburn canvases at auction also fascinated one of Raeburn's biographers James Greig, who worked for the London art trade, and who notes with apparent satisfaction that Raeburn's full-length portrait, *Mrs Robertson Williamson*, broke saleroom records for the price realised for a painting of any school when bought by Joseph Duveen in 1910.[11] Greig also predicts, clearly aware of the market for full-length female portraits in the USA, that although bought by Duveen the painting was likely to 'add to the parade of wealth on the other side of the Atlantic'.[12]

The clear disjunction between the cool reticence of British art historians towards Raeburn's female portraits and the thriving market for them among American collectors, suggests a historiographical root in Scottish art history for the liminal position they occupy. The Scottish tendency to appropriate Raeburn's portraiture as a legitimising national historical document is encapsulated by W. Blaikie Murdoch, who writes in *Art Treasures of Edinburgh* (1924), 'Raeburn was a master historian, conferring eternal life on a grand period in Scotland. Whence to his compatriots, his works must ever have an interest above that which they hold for other people'.[13] As Blaikie Murdoch plainly states in a Scottish context, the prestige of Raeburn's male sitters has often outweighed these portraits' importance as art objects, whilst significantly diminishing the relevance of his portraits of women. Furthermore, the focus on Raeburn's male worthies mirrors contemporary cultural and political imperatives. The rise of interest in Raeburn's portraiture in the early twentieth century coincides with the birth of the phrase 'Scottish Enlightenment' and attendant scholarly interest in the phenomenon as a whole.[14] More recently reviews of the 1997 exhibition forged a contrived association between Raeburn's supposed Scottish qualities and the devolution issue, suggesting that Raeburn's critical fortunes were and are still inextricably linked to the tides of national political issues.

Allan Cunningham's chapter on Raeburn in his *The Lives of Eminent British Painters, Sculptors and Artists* (1829–33) is the first major biographical account of Raeburn and his art. Despite its factual unreliability, Cunningham's *Life* has been crucial in establishing the tone and agenda of subsequent literature relating to the artist, particularly in privileging male portraits. Cunningham offers a justification for the pre-eminence accorded to portraits of men in assessments of the artist's portrait output. He writes:

> To the great body of mankind the worth of a portrait consists in its faithful delineation, mental and bodily, of some person whom fame or history cares about; and they will turn carelessly away from the painting of one of whom they have never heard: in short it is only the heads of distinguished men, or of women more than usually lovely, that they regard at all.[15]

According to Cunningham, the biography of the (male) sitter takes precedence over the visual qualities of the portrait as art object, unless the sitter happens to be a beautiful woman. The totemic *Mrs Scott Moncrieff* neatly exemplifies this phenomenon. Her biography is a remarkably grey area, the portrait hung discreetly in an Edinburgh dining room until its owner, the sitter's husband, died in 1854 leaving the portrait to the Royal Scottish Academy, from whence it was transferred to the National Gallery in 1910. This paradigm is constantly repeated in the nineteenth and early twentieth century reception of Raeburn's female portraiture, where quite unlike their male counterparts, female portraits are primarily valued as beauty pieces, divorced from the identity of their sitters. In her discussion of the female self-portrait, Felicity Edholm succinctly delineates the differing qualities sought in portraits of men and women. She particularly elaborates on the centrality of beauty as opposed to biography as a vital criterion for portraits of women, mirroring Cunningham's early nineteenth-century narrative. Edholm argues that the varied semiotic possibilities offered by the status and achievements of men has allowed male portraiture to visualise and valorise its sitters in a way unfeasible in portraits of women, where physical attractiveness consequently becomes of heightened import. She explains,

> Behind many portraits [. . .] is an assumption of a biography, a known or knowable story, for men in particular a story of potential when young and achievement when middle aged. Women's lives and faces cannot tell the same story [. . .] in terms of representation; it is beauty when young, and the loss of beauty when old.[16]

The model Edholm describes is nicely illustrated by the reception of Raeburn's portraiture, where his portraits of women have either been deemed to have failed in the delineation of female beauty or otherwise have been lumped under the rubric of beauty without any critical or contextual analysis. Cunningham's narrative clearly conforms to Edholm's standpoint; his biography continues to explain that 'he painted all the eminent men of his time and nation; and a gallery of the illustrious heads of a most brilliant period might almost be completed from his works alone'.[17] Cunningham anticipates a feature of many studies relating to the artist in foregrounding his portraits of figures of the Scottish Enlightenment, manifest in ensembles such as the University of Edinburgh's 'Raeburn Room' (Fig. 1.3) and in exhibition form by 'James Hutton and Some of his Friends'.[18] Cunningham's Scottish background also provides a motive for his role in the creation and veneration of a gallery of national worthies, imparting a strongly nationalist nuance to his narrative. In his *Lives* Cunningham does much to reclaim other Scottish painters, including George Jamesone, from obscurity. The author's close association with senior members of the British artistic establishment including the sculptor Francis Chantrey lends credence and an authoritative air to his account, helping to explain the faith put in it. Elsewhere, relating specifically to Raeburn's portraits of women Cunningham agrees with an unnamed correspondent 'in whose judgement I [Cunningham] put much trust', who opines that Raeburn

> seldom excelled in the soft graces of style and sentiment suitable to ladies [. . .] in representing beauty he always appeared to me to fail fearfully; his style of colouring, and his indefinite outline, caught neither the roses and lilies, nor the contour of youth and loveliness.[19]

The fact that Cunningham sees little beauty in Raeburn's female portraits, for him among their most important desiderata, justifies his largely dismissive attitude toward them.

The prejudice against Raeburn's female portraits evinced in the above excerpts from the nineteenth and early twentieth centuries manifests itself in the major exhibition of Raeburn portraits held at the Royal Scottish Academy in 1876. Despite the fact that the exhibition displayed a broad cross section of Raeburn's artistic output, 325 portraits in total, the hang displayed a clear penchant for Raeburn's portraits of men; 244 male portraits, compared to only 74 portraits of women were featured in the exhibition. The accompanying catalogue also adhered to the formula proposed by Cunningham earlier in the century by stressing the significance of Raeburn's portraits of prominent men. The catalogue's author enthused: 'Men of the highest position – stars in our firmament of recent Scottish history – were brought before the spectators to the delight of all and the instruction of many'.[20] The author further maintained that, 'In his portraits of men in particular, he gives the characteristic expression in a simple but effective, decided and impressive manner'.[21] Raeburn's portraits of men are not only accorded pre-eminence in sheer numbers but his painterly style, itself connotative of masculinity, becomes a gendered anthropomorphism: 'his style was manly and vigorous, well calculated for the representation of the marked physiognomies of his countrymen, at a period when many distinguished characters stood prominently before the public'.[22]

Robert Louis Stevenson penned a lengthy review of the 1876 exhibition, published in essay form as 'Some Portraits by Raeburn' in 1881. The historiographical significance of this essay is immeasurable, lying chiefly in the illumination of the reception of Raeburn's portraiture to a nineteenth-century audience, and in providing an historical contextualisation for the routine privileging of Raeburn's portraits of men. In the essay, Stevenson is predictably disparaging of Raeburn's portraits of women:

> Although young ladies in Great Britain are all that can be desired of them, I would fain hope they are not quite so much of that as Raeburn would have us believe [. . .] Raeburn's young women, to be frank, are by no means of the same order of merit [as his men]. In all these pretty faces you miss character, you miss fire, you miss that spice of the devil which is worth all the prettiness in the world; and what is worst of all you miss sex.[23]

Elsewhere, Stevenson does grudgingly suggest a small series of 'beauty portraits' in Raeburn's *oeuvre*, noting as an aside, 'no one of course could be insensible to the presence of *Miss Janet Suttie* or *Mrs Campbell of Possil*. When things are as pretty as that, criticism is out of season'.[24] Stevenson's appraisal of Raeburn's female portraits demonstrates, in Anne Bermingham's words, the 'connoisseur's tendency to exercise aesthetic judgment over art and femininity [. . .] a power ultimately tied up with the establishment of masculine subjectivity through the fetishization of women'.[25] In the same vein as the author of the 1876 exhibition catalogue, Stevenson claims that Raeburn's male portraits, especially those of key enlightenment figures, function as a quasi-biography of the sitter. Clearly influenced by the contemporary popularity of physiognomy as a critical idiom he writes:

> Each of his portraits is not only 'a piece of history' but a piece of biography into the bargain. It is devoutly to be wished that all biography were equally amusing, and carried its own credentials equally on its face. These portraits are racier

than many anecdotes, and more complete than many a volume of sententious memoirs. You can see whether you get a stronger and clearer idea of Robertson the historian from Raeburn's palette or Dugald Stewart's woolly and evasive periods.[26]

Stevenson ostensibly believes that Raeburn's painted face outperforms Stewart's written account of the historian. Stevenson's assumption that the character of Raeburn's sitters is legible in their faces is in line with the position of high importance occupied by physiognomy in art history and connoisseurship during the late nineteenth century. In the context of nineteenth-century art criticism Elizabeth Rigby, Lady Eastlake, elucidates the authority invested in physiognomy. She writes,

> It is only in the highest masters of the art of portrait-painting that we can find those intricate shades and grades – those crossings and blending of character, in which, upon close examination, the physiognomical identity of the individual is found to lie.[27]

Notwithstanding the formal qualities of the portraits themselves, the incorporation of physiognomy as a critical apparatus in studies relating to Raeburn, has influenced the reception of his portraits of women.

As adopted by Scottish art historians, notably in the writings of James Caw (a vociferous advocate for the existence of a distinct Scottish school of art) in his work *Scottish Painting Past and Present 1620–1908* (1908), the language of physiognomy is additionally imbued with an extraordinary nationalist slant. His nationalist art historical agenda becomes apparent when he states 'painting being a universal language, evinces of national character,' predating the Pevsnerian mantra 'there is the spirit of an age, and there is national character' by almost fifty years.[28] Caw writes,

> a very individualistic people themselves, the Scots possess an inherent curiosity as regards character. The history of Scotland has often been individualised, as it were, in a very striking way, in the persons of the chief actors in its great events.[29]

In the case of Raeburn's career, the 'great event' was the Enlightenment, and its 'chief actors' its exclusively male literati. It is worth noting that many of Raeburn's commentators, including Caw, and later Edward Pinnington, who employ physiognomy as a critical tool, cite the distinctive physiognomies of Raeburn's male sitters, as telling both of their supposed intellectual characters *and* their national identity. That Raeburn's male portraits have been interpreted as constituting a faithful delineation of a supposedly finite and coherent Scottish national identity is evinced by Pinnington who claims: 'That his subjects are types is due to the decision of the Scottish character which they represent, and in nowise to his art. [. . .] His sitters might be racial types, but he merged the typical aspect in the individual'.[30] Mary Cowling proffers a convincing explanation for the interrelation of nationality and physiognomy in her study, *The Artist as Anthropologist* (1989), arguing that during the course of the nineteenth century anthropology and the study of anatomy were routinely conflated with physiognomy in much published discourse.[31]

Crucially, in traditional accounts, Scottish national identity is couched chiefly in terms of male figures 'the more obvious symbols of Scottish national identity are masculine and invite easy confirmation of the view that representations of Scottish national identity privilege the masculine'.[32] The focus on men as dominant purveyors of national identity, in evidence throughout Scottish art historical studies, has in turn diminished both the historical and art historical importance of Raeburn's female portraits. Raeburn's portraits of women have instead literally been taken at face value, judged either to have succeeded or failed in the delineation of beauty. Elsewhere in his account, Caw instils character itself with a gendered bias claiming that 'approaching portraiture chiefly through character, it is not surprising perhaps that Scottish painters have been more successful in painting men than women'.[33] Caw equates the artistic depiction of character in portraiture squarely with men; an investigation into the work of prominent physiognomists reveals that this gendered bias is ingrained in the discipline itself.

Tellingly, the language of physiognomy has a distinctive Scottish heredity in some of its leading exponents such as Alexander Walker.[34] Walker examined women in terms of the 'science' of physiognomy; his tomes on female beauty offer heredity for the strong gendered bias found in James Caw's approach to Raeburn's portraits. Walker argues:

> I have in my work on beauty, shown that beauty of the mental or thinking system is less proper to woman than to man – is less feminine than beauty of the vital or nutritive system; and that it is not the mental, but the vital system, which is, and ought to be, most developed in woman. Still less is it cerebral or intellectual, considered apart from mere sensitive beauty, which ought to characterize her.[35]

Walker's thesis parallels trends in mid-eighteenth- to early nineteenth-century medical and scientific literature, in which a huge degree of physiological and psychological difference between men and women was assumed.

According to Walker women's faces are incapable of satisfactorily expressing the type of character so prized in Raeburn's male portraits, perhaps laying the groundwork for Caw's narrative. Walker offers a pseudo-physiological framework for Caw's art historical bias, strenuously avowing:

> In woman the countenance is more rounded, as well as more abundantly furnished with that cellular and fatty tissue, which fills all the chasms, effaces all the angles and unites all the parts by the gentlest transitions. At the same time, the muscles are feebler [. . .] The result of all this is that the muscles do not profoundly modify the face, which consequently has not so much of permanent character as that of man, and which permits us more difficulty to discover [. . .] her character and various feelings.[36]

Walker's account offers a background for the greater interest accorded to Raeburn's portraits of male sitters in the nineteenth century, where beauty of 'the mental or thinking system' was in evidence, unlike 'the mere sensitive beauty' desirable, but too often found to be lacking in his portraits of women. In an essay of 1930 which looks at Raeburn portraits in American collections, Alfred M. Frankfurter in a description of Raeburn's *Mrs Irvine Boswell* (Fig. 12.4), datable c. 1815, echoes the model offered by Walker:

> Here it is pure artistic supremacy that carries the picture, for the subject is too young to display any marked intellectual or psychological characteristics. There is but one factor: a beautiful woman, resplendent in the glory of youth and sex.[37]

Collins Baker, in his cursory summary of Raeburn's career in *British Painting* (1933), also notes in a similar vein that as regards his 'women portraits, Raeburn frequently makes contact with the naïve simplicity and genuine human qualities of his sitters. Not that he goes deep into their psychology: in women portraiture he hardly ever penetrates beyond passivity'.[38]

In an attempt to account for the perceived weakness of Raeburn's portraits of young women, Stevenson goes on to equate the encounter between Raeburn and the female sitter as a highly sexualized and embarrassing encounter, 'to say the truth either Raeburn was timid with young and pretty sitters; or he had stupefied himself with sentimentalities'. Conversely, with older women Stevenson conjectures, 'he could look into their eyes without trouble; and was not withheld, by any bashful sentimentalism, from recognizing what he saw there and unsparingly putting it down upon the canvas'.[39] In an interesting echo of Stevenson's essay A. Cassandra Albinson, writing in the catalogue accompanying the recent Thomas Lawrence exhibition (2010), counterpoints Lawrence's racy private life and reputed risqué relationships

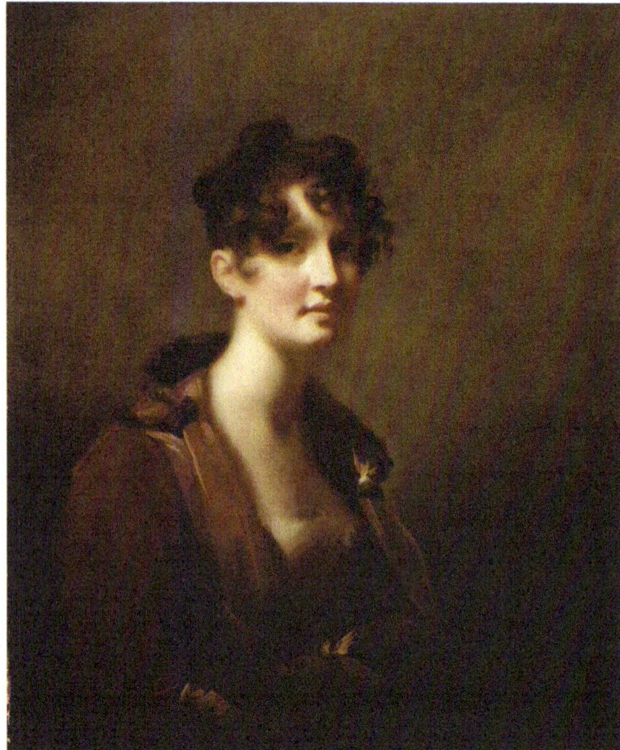

Figure 12.4 Henry Raeburn, *Margaret Christie, Mrs James Irvine Boswell*, c. 1815–20, oil on canvas, 76.2×63.5cm, bequest of Eleanor Clay Ford, Detroit Institute of Arts (courtesy of Bridgeman Art Library)

with 'The other leading portraitists of Lawrence's day – William Beechey, John Hoppner and Henry Raeburn – [who] all constructed lives of studied domestic probity deliberately at odds with the sensual interpersonal dimensions of portraiture'.[40] The fact that Raeburn drew upon Lawrence's portrait of *Mrs Wolff* (Fig. 12.3), a woman with whom Lawrence supposedly had a scandalous sexual relationship, however, as a key source of inspiration problematises Albinson's biographical extrapolation. Raeburn also depicted women in a highly sensual manner, germanely *Mrs Scott Moncrieff* (Fig. 12.1), despite his vaunted 'domestic probity', suggesting that the celebration of sensuality in female portraiture and an artist's biography have little tangible correlation.

The current reception of Raeburn's portraits of women is a product of the critical literature of the late nineteenth and twentieth centuries, which still figures highly: tropes that regularly surface in the nineteenth century linger on in modern scholarship. Although the writers discussed above focused attention on Raeburn's female portraits, they did so at a high price, by contributing to the veneration of a small canon of highly prized female portraits. Female beauty, as a key consideration in Raeburn's portraiture, has remained largely intact, most recently evidenced in the Edinburgh and London exhibition (1997–8). The entry for Raeburn's portrait of *Charles Hay, Lord Newton*, describes the portrait as 'one of Raeburn's greatest achievements' continuing, 'Part of that achievement is the startling agreement between the personality and outward appearance of the man as Raeburn has portrayed him, and how he was perceived and described by contemporaries'.[41] In the same catalogue *Mrs Scott Moncrieff*, Raeburn's most famous female portrait is described as 'a portrait where the subject's appearance and personality are generalised to the point of stereotype'.[42]

In her essay *An Enquiry Concerning the Principles of Taste, and of the Origin of our Ideas of Beauty, &c.* (1785), Frances Reynolds, the sister of Sir Joshua, offers an insight into the relationship between age and beauty. In her tract Reynolds argues that beauty is inseparable from both nature, and truth; and thus that beauty should conform to immutable principles. According to Reynolds, beauty for different ages should reflect the moral attributes characteristic of that age, thus:

> As the strongest proof that the moral sense is the governing principle of beauty, we may remark, that the human form, from infancy to old age, has its particular beauty annexed to it from the virtue or affection that nature gives it, and which it exhibits in the countenance. The negative virtue, innocence, is the beauty of the child. The more formed virtues, benevolence, generosity, compassion, &c. are the virtues of youth, and its beauty. The fixed and determined virtues, justice, temperance, fortitude, &c. compose the beauty of manhood. The philosophic and religious cast of countenance is the beauty of old age.[43]

Dibdin follows Reynolds's model in choosing selective examples to illustrate 'the Seven Ages of Woman', which create 'a gallery of the female sex of the better classes as it existed in Scotland before and after the beginning of the nineteenth century'.[44] Dibdin goes on to state that 'Neither age nor sex made a difference; the flower like charm of youth, the lust vigour and beauty of early maturity, the strength and force of full manhood, the dignity of later years, and the pathetic beauty of age'.[45] However, from this list it is Raeburn's portraits of mature female sitters that have received the highest praise.[46]

Chroniclers of Raeburn's art have singled out for particular praise portraits including that of the artist's wife *Lady Raeburn*, *Mrs James Campbell* and the elderly *Mrs Malcolm* (Fig. 12.5). Although largely disparaging of Raeburn's portraits of young women, R. L. Stevenson concedes that 'on the whole, it is

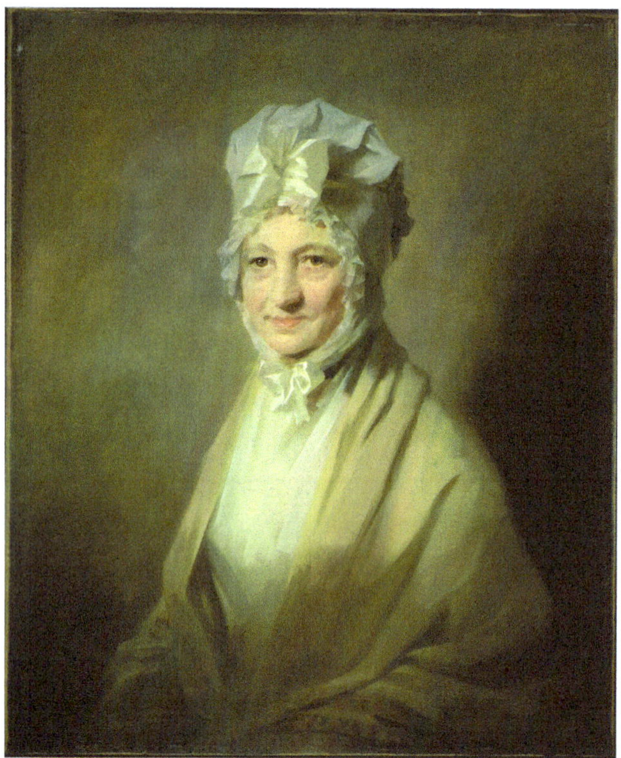

Figure 12.5 Henry Raeburn, *Mrs Malcolm*, c. 1820, oil on canvas, 75.9×63.5cm, Samuel Courtauld Trust, Courtauld Gallery, London

only with women of a certain age that he can be said to have succeeded, in at all the same sense as we say he succeeded with men'.[47] Later, Pinnington, who similarly enthuses about Raeburn's 'representations of beauty in age' when discussing *Mrs James Campbell of Ballimore*, rhapsodises 'it is impossible to look at it without feeling something akin to the pulsing enthusiasm of the rapt painter, and without recognizing the absolute rightness of his work'.[48]

Characteristically, at the exhibition of thirty Raeburn portraits held at the French Gallery in London in 1911, many of the reviewers made unfavourable comparisons between Raeburn's male and female portraiture. Among the chorus of voices was Sir Claude Phillips, who wrote, 'almost invariably in a Raeburn exhibition the portraits of men overshadow those of the women; for the Scottish artist was above all a painter of men and boys'.[49] However, among the lineup was Raeburn's portrait of the elderly *Mrs Malcolm*, which engrossed the attention of the exhibition's reviewers rather than the portraits of young women (Fig. 1.2). A reviewer in the *Pall Mall Gazette* comments

'Sir Henry Raeburn seldom dealt in beauty, except the beauty of old age, in which character has left its imprint'.[50] A correspondent writing for *The Glasgow Herald* enthused 'The old lady, wearing a dainty white mutch and a cashmere shawl, has her image thinly floated on to the canvas with what it would hardly be an exaggeration to call a spiritual tenderness of apprehension'.[51] A third critic in the *Observer* notes of the picture 'superb again is his portrait of Mrs Malcolm. Here age has left upon the sympathetic benevolent face, framed by a frilled cap, its lines and marks which make the pictorial task akin to that of painting a man's face'.[52]

In the chapter on Raeburn in their book *Scottish Painters at Home and Abroad 1700–1900*, David and Francina Irwin attest to the continuing popularity of Raeburn's portraits of older women. They claim

> He succeeded best where features were pronounced and modelling could be deep and sculptured. With age, the differences between male and female faces diminish, and women's faces begin to show the underlying bone structures more clearly. His style was not suited to delineating the less formed features of a young and pretty face.[53]

Interestingly, like the *Observer* review quoted above, the Irwins draw a parallel between the faces of elderly women and those of men. In her consideration of portraiture during the eighteenth century in Scotland Stana Nenadic examines portraits of elderly women as a distinct category. Situating them in the context of the Scottish Enlightenment she claims: 'there was a distinct genre of portraits of mature and sensible bourgeois women connected to the Enlightenment by association, if not directly by virtue of their own intellectual ability'.[54] Nenadic's comment does not necessarily apply to the portraits under discussion here as their sitters were not universally connected to the Enlightenment. Nenadic picks up on examples painted by Allan Ramsay, chiefly his *Mrs Adam* (1757). There are also clear affinities between many of Ramsay and Raeburn's depictions of old women. Raeburn's *Jean Gray* (c. 1792–5), for example, is highly redolent of Ramsay's *Mrs Adam*. While it is outside the focus of Nenadic's account to provide any credible indication of a relationship between Ramsay and Raeburn's portraits of older women, one instance exists: Raeburn's copy, datable c. 1810, after Allan Ramsay's *Anne Cockburn, Lady Inglis*, painted c. 1747 (Fig. 12.6).[55]

Writing in 1911, James Greig mistakenly opined that this portrait depicted Raeburn's wife and dated from his period in Rome, showing the influence of Nicolas de Largillière; 'the only probable explanation of this curious pastiche is, that Raeburn may have visited the French Academy at Rome, and been impressed by some of the work there'.[56] In his 1925 account Rimbault Dibdin

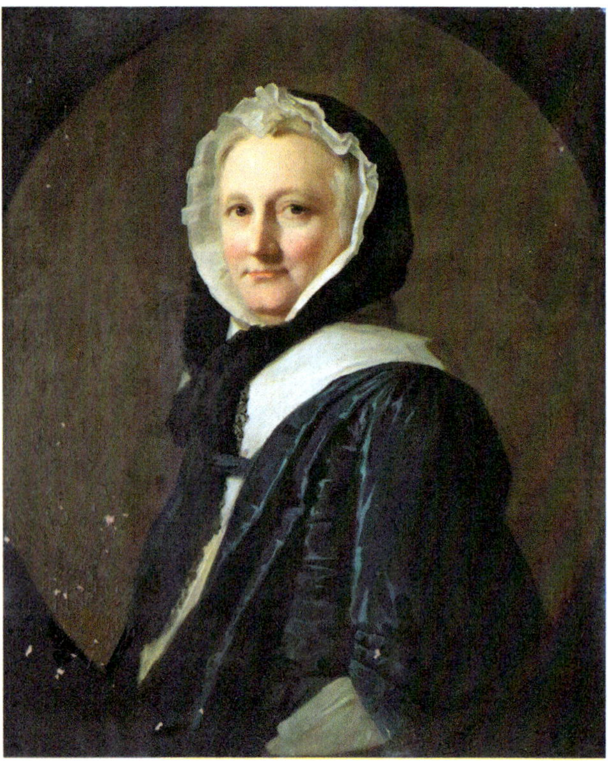

Figure 12.6 Henry Raeburn after Allan Ramsay, *Anne Cockburn, Lady Inglis*, c. 1810 (after original datable c. 1747), oil on canvas, 76.2×63.5cm, Sotheby's, New Bond Street, London, 23 November 2006, lot 60, Private Collection (courtesy of Sotheby's)

unquestioningly accepts Greig's hypothesis. Raeburn's copy of Ramsay's portrait not only provides a concrete example of his awareness of Ramsay's depictions of aged sitters, his copy is by no means a verbatim facsimile of the original, and is therefore telling of his approach to the depiction of mature female sitters. Raeburn both copies and interprets; his depiction is less meticulous and unflinching than Ramsay's original. The costume in Raeburn's copy is somewhat simplified in that he omits the intricacies of embroidery in the sitter's dark silks, and generalises the pattern of the lace trimmings. More pertinently, Raeburn bathes *Lady Inglis* in a softer more diffuse light which renders her features less harshly; the dramatic modelling and play of light with which Ramsay depicts the sitter, are less unforgiving in Raeburn's copy. Raeburn also considerably softens the modelling of the sitter's jaw-line therefore de-emphasising the double chin, which Ramsay picks out.

Although Raeburn's portraits of mature women have inspired proportionally more praise from critics and art historians than his portraits of young women, this should not blind us to the fact that his frank depictions of elderly female sitters are not unique in British art. Striking examples of presentments of female maturity occur in the *oeuvres* of many of his English contemporaries, although there is little scope to fully consider the depiction of elderly women in the outputs of his contemporaries a few examples will suffice for the purpose of this chapter. James Lonsdale's *Mrs Linley* (c. 1815–20) offers an image of a forthright woman past middle age, John Singleton Copley's *Mrs Seymour Fort*, exhibited at the Royal Academy in 1778, and John Opie's *The Artist's Mother* (c. 1791) are other germane examples. Raeburn's portraits of elderly female sitters continue to occupy a privileged position in accounts of his portrait output, supplying the lack of character found in his portraits of young women.

A thorough examination of Raeburn's portraits of women is not merely overdue, it is crucial in overcoming many of the lingering bugbears of Raeburn scholarship. Raeburn's portraits of women, perhaps more clearly than those of men, evince Raeburn's awareness of London artists. Raeburn seems to have employed a greater degree of stylistic variety in his female portraiture in comparison with the more convention-bound portraits of academics and professionals that dominate accounts of his output. Clear instances of Raeburn drawing inspiration from artists such as Reynolds, Hoppner and Lawrence are evident in his portraits of women; while they occupy such a secondary role, Raeburn's engagement with fashionable practice can safely be swept under the carpet. More importantly though, the nationalism of existing art historical accounts of the artist that has sought to distance Raeburn from the British artistic mainstream has also diminished the attention devoted to his female portraits, especially of young women. His portraits of older women have garnered a more positive engagement only by being likened to presentments of 'characterful' men.

Notes

1. Duncan Macmillan's chapter on Raeburn in *Painting in Scotland: The Golden Age* (Edinburgh and London, 1986–7, pp. 74–136) most forcefully proposes a link between the work of Thomas Reid on perception and Raeburn's painterly style. In so doing Macmillan effectively sidesteps more likely sources of formal inspiration, the work of Raeburn's contemporaries in London for example, with which the artist would have been familiar both through the exposure to the portraits themselves and through prints after them.
2. Lloyd 2005.

3. One journalist – in a magniloquently sensational article – went so far as to liken Lloyd's devastating findings to 'saying Burns did not write *Tam o' Shanter* or suggesting Sean Connery is Albanian', *The Sunday Herald*, 20 August 2005.

4. Thomson 2007.

5. Many of Raeburn's commentators, including Duncan Thomson, David Mackie and Duncan Macmillan, are keen to underplay outside influence on Raeburn's painterly style, the lack of clear information relating to his formative studies exacerbating the situation. These scholars therefore construe Raeburn as a kind of self-taught genius or maverick practitioner, peculiar to Scotland.

6. Transcript of letter, Greig Archive, SNPG.

7. Edinburgh and London 1997–8, p. 27.

8. Algernon Graves's list of 53 Raeburn portraits exhibited at the Royal Academy lists six portraits of women: 1792 *Portrait of a Lady* (no. 351), 1814 *Portrait of a Lady* (no. 153), 1817 *Lady Cumming Gordon* (no. 84), 1818 *Portrait of a Lady* (no. 293), 1821 *Portrait of a Lady* (no. 420), and 1823 *Portraits of a Lady and Child* (no. 200).

9. Collins Baker 1933, p. 163.

10. Gerald Reitlinger, *The Economics of Taste: The Rise and Fall of Picture Prices 1760–1960*, London 1961, pp. 192–4.

11. Greig devoted a whole chapter to the fluctuating prices fetched by Raeburn portraits at auction, while Brotchie included a list of 'leading Raeburn prices' at the conclusion of his monograph on the artist. *Mrs Robertson Williamson* was sold on 19 May 1911 at Christie's for 22,300 guineas. The same painting was sold again in 1926, when it was bought by Knoedler for £24,675, but by 1957 in a depressed market the portrait raised only £5,000. It is now in the Columbus Museum of Art, Ohio.

12. Greig 1911, p. liv.

13. W. Blaikie Murdoch, *Art Treasures of Edinburgh*, Edinburgh, 1924, p. cvi.

14. See 'Introduction' in M. A. Stewart (ed.), *Studies in the Philosophy of the Scottish Enlightenment*, Oxford, 1990, pp. 1–3.

15. Cunningham 1829–33, V, p. 222.

16. Felictiy Edholm, 'Beyond the Mirror: Women's Self-Portraits', in Francis Bonner, Lizbeth Goodman, Richard Allen, Linda James and Catherine King (eds), *Imagining Women: Cultural Representations and Gender*, Cambridge, 1995, pp. 159–60.

17. Cunningham 1829–33, V, p. 222.

18. The 'Raeburn Room' or Senate Hall at the University of Edinburgh contains Raeburn's portraits of *William Robertson*, *Adam Ferguson*, *John Robison* and *John Playfair*, all professors and Enlightenment figures associated with the university.

19. Cunningham 1829–33, V, p. 222.

20. Edinburgh 1876, p. 21.

21. Ibid.

22. Ibid. The longevity of the curatorial penchant for Raeburn's male portraits is evidenced by the 1997–8 exhibition in Edinburgh and London. There the ratio of male to female portraits in oils remained almost unaltered, when compared with the 1876 show: thirty-four male portraits were exhibited compared with fourteen of women. There were eight portraits of teenagers and younger children, including six of boys and two groups including girls. Also selected were three group portraits of adults, two of which depicted married couples.

23. Stevenson 1992, p. 36.

24. Ibid.

25. Ann Bermingham, 'Elegant Females and Gentleman Connoisseurs', in *The Consumption of Culture 1600–1800: Image, Object, Text*, Ann Bermingham and John Brewer (eds), London and New York, p. 502.

26. Stevenson 1992, p. 32.

27. Quoted in Sharonna Pearl, *About Faces: Physiognomy in Nineteenth Century Britain*, Cambridge, MA, 2010, p. 101.

28. Caw 1908, p. 486; Nikolaus Pevsner, *The Englishness of English Art*, London, 1956, p. 16.

29. Caw 1908, p. 473.

30. Pinnington 1904, pp. 209–13.

31. Mary Cowling, *The Artist as Anthropologist: the representation of type and character in Victorian art*, Cambridge, 1989, pp. 54–86.

32. Ester Breitenbach and Lynn Abrams, 'Gender and Scottish identity', in *Gender in Scottish History since 1700*, Lynn Abrams, Eleanor Gordon, Deborah Simonton and Eileen Janes Yeo (eds), Edinburgh, 2006, p. 22.

33. Caw 1908, p. 475.

34. Alexander Walker was most famous for his best-selling works linking physiology and aesthetics, *Physiognomy, founded on Physiology* (1834), *Beauty, illustrated chiefly by an analysis and classification of Beauty in Women* (1836), and *Women Physiologically Considered* (1839).

35. Alexander Walker, *Woman Physiologically Considered, as to Mind, Morals, Marriage, Matrimonial Slavery, Infidelity and Divorce, with an Appendix containing Notes and Additions* (1840), p. 247.

36. Alexander Walker, *Beauty illustrated . . .*, I, p. 39.

37. Alfred M. Frankenfurter, 'Paintings by Raeburn in America', *Antiquarian*, XIV, January 1930, p. 35.

38. Collins Baker 1933, p. 163.

39. Stevenson 1992, pp. 36–7.

40. A. Cassandra Albinson, Peter Funnell and Lucy Peltz (eds), *Thomas Lawrence: Regency Power and Brilliance*, exh. cat., Yale Center for British Art, New Haven, and National Portrait Gallery, London; New Haven and London, 2010, p. 30.

41. Edinburgh and London 1997–8, p. 146.
42. Loc. cit., p. 164.
43. Frances Reynolds, *An Enquiry Concerning the Principles of Taste, and of the Origin of our Ideas of Beauty, &c.*, London, 1785, p. 34.
44. Dibdin 1925, p. 146.
45. Ibid., p. 148.
46. In their accounts of female portraits Stevenson, Armstrong, Caw, Pinnington, Greig and Dibdin all cite portraits of older women as among his finest.
47. Stevenson 1992, p. 36.
48. Pinnington 1904, p. 170.
49. London 1911, unpaginated.
50. Ibid., unpaginated.
51. Ibid., unpaginated.
52. Ibid., unpaginated.
53. Irwin and Irwin 1975, p. 157.
54. Stana Nenadic, 'Enlightenment Scotland and the popular passion for portraits', *Journal for Eighteenth Century Studies*, XXI, no. 2, 1998, pp. 175–92, quotation from p. 188.
55. The Ramsay portrait of *Lady Inglis* is in the SNG, Edinburgh, acc. no. NG 2152, cf. NGS 1997, p. 96.
56. Greig 1911, p. xxiv.

13

Raeburn and France

Olivier Meslay

Few British painters enjoy a reputation in France as well defined and as unreserved as that of Raeburn. Might it be that his Scottish nationality and the memory of 'the Auld Alliance' grant him special treatment? Allan Ramsay, David Wilkie and the Scottish Colourists do not share such a reputation. It is necessary to look for this French admiration in terms of other criteria, such as frankness, bravura and painterly technique. The support for Raeburn is relatively recent. References in art reviews were relatively slow in coming and he therefore remained unknown to the French public until the end of the nineteenth century.

The only contemporary reference to Raeburn, even if he is not quoted by name but by a recognisable painting, the double portrait of *Sir John and Lady Clerk of Penicuik* (Fig. 7.4), was made by Henri-Pierre Danloux (1753–1809) in his diary. He is the same artist now thought to be responsible for *The Skating Minister* (Fig. 1.4).[1] On 1 August 1792, Danloux, then in London, wrote:

> I am going to visit the Shakespeare galleries with abbot du Luchet . . . Mr du Luchet, who is no art connoisseur at all, was happy to see some charm in several of the paintings, but was mostly struck by the portrait of a man and a lady made by an Edinburgh artist. The effect represented is indeed rather unusual; the sun is supposed to be behind the man's head, he is lit by the reflection of the light on his wife's head and on her blue clothing.

This comment was not published until 1910 by the Baron de Portalis in his monograph on Danloux.[2] Danloux was later, following his various extended visits to Scotland, to be strongly influenced in his portraiture by the example of Raeburn.

Only one published travel account mentioned Raeburn during his lifetime. In *Voyage d'un Français en Angleterre pendant les années 1810 et 1811* by

Louis Simond, the author mentions the artist whilst reporting on the annual exhibition of the society of associated artists held in Edinburgh:

> Just like London, Edinburgh has an annual exhibition, but it is proportionally better. Mr Raeburn is a first-class painter, a portraitist (it goes without saying), but I saw such action portraits made by him which show that he could easily be a history painter. He made some child portraits in particular whose grace equalled those executed by Sir Joshua Reynolds and whose colours were much better.[3]

It is only at the beginning of the 1870s that the first studies on Raeburn started to appear in specialised French publications. The first one was written by Théophile Thoré, also known as Thoré-Burger, in his *Histoire des peintres de toutes les écoles*, which he wrote under the name William Burger.[4] It was there that he dedicated a short, one-page study to the Scottish artist. The study was evidently drawn from reading Allan Cunningham's *Lives of the Most Eminent British Painters, Sculptors and Architects*, which Thoré quoted.[5] He recalled however that he had referred to the artist and his portraits of *Francis MacNab*, known as 'The Macnab' (Fig. 7.2), and of *Henry Raeburn Inglis* ('*Boy and Rabbit*') (Fig. 7.6) in his account of the famous *Treasures of Art* exhibition in Manchester.[6] He saw *Henry Raeburn Inglis* ('*Boy and Rabbit*') again at the international exhibition in London in 1862. The following remark is of interest in order to gauge Raeburn's burgeoning international reputation. Burger writes:

> It was during the 1862 exhibition that foreigners were able to judge Raeburn and his clear-cut style, slightly inspired by Reynolds and Lawrence. One of the most remarkable works was a portrait of his son riding a grey pony, belonging to the National Gallery of Scotland, and several other portraits, very simple in their composition and very true colour-wise.

Burger then gave a short biography of the artist before concluding:

> The list of portraits executed by Raeburn is very long indeed. To the names of the noble Scotsmen already given, one must add Walter Scott, of whom he painted two full-length portraits, Dugald Stewart, Francis Jeffrey, Henry Mackenzie, John Rennie, etc. He also made a beautiful portrait of the sculptor Chantrey. Northcote, who was a very difficult character, and Wilkie, who was so skilful, both admired Sir Henry Raeburn's talent very much. Allan Cunningham dedicated forty pages to his biography, and all the English writers praised his broad and bold style, his precise lines and the rich colours used by

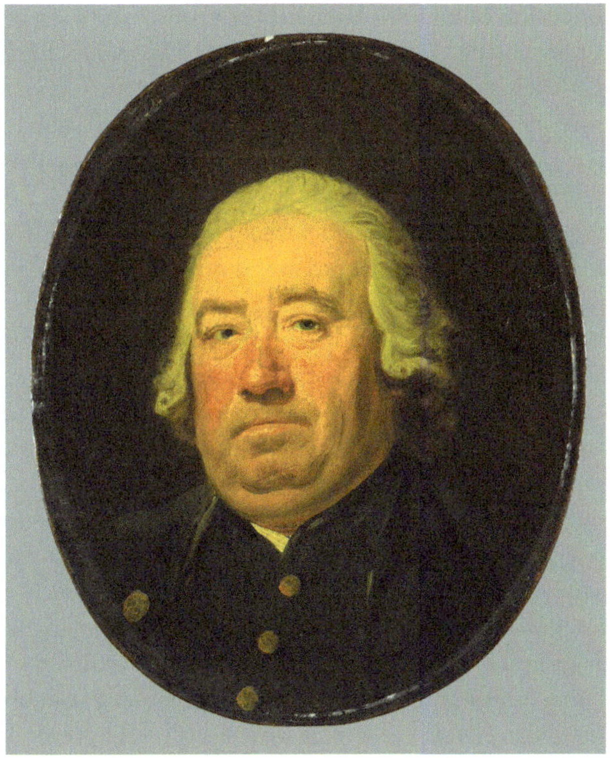

Figure 13.1 British School, *A Greenwich Pensioner*, c. 1800, oil on canvas, 72.4×63.5cm, Musée du Louvre, Paris (courtesy of Réunion des musées nationaux)

this painter, who also had much influence on the development of the arts in Scotland.

This article marked the beginning of Raeburn's critical fortune in France. Burger's authority in French artistic circles truly opened doors to the artist's reputation. It grew during the following years paradoxically thanks to a painting, now in the Louvre, which was at that time attributed to Raeburn, but whose authorship is now widely thought to have no connection to Edinburgh's premier portrait painter. This painting, *A Greenwich Pensioner* (Fig. 13.1), was first sold in Paris in 1873 in a sale said to be that of the Marquis de la Rochebousseau, a fictitious name.[7] Henri Perrier mentioned the work in the *Gazette des Beaux-Arts* for 1873.[8] He rehearsed Raeburn's biography before describing the picture: 'The impasto is very beautiful, the tones really exceptionally fine, it is strongly executed, and has a distinction that one only rarely sees'. Five years later, the same painting reappeared in the sale of the collection of Laurent Richard (1811–86) and is again mentioned by Alfred Lostalot in the *Gazette des Beaux-Arts*: 'we should happily mention the portrait by Raeburn [. . .] which was engraved in the Gazette, a generous and wholesome picture whose aspect is most delightful'.[9] The painting did not sell until 28 May 1886 when it was bought directly by the Louvre.[10] It was therefore with this picture, soon after downgraded to the British School, that Raeburn's reputation in France can said to have started.[11]

It is interesting to read and analyse the qualities lent to both the artist and the painting prior to its arrival in the Louvre collections. They are a true leitmotif of the way late nineteenth-century French connoisseurs were analysing Raeburn's art. The words most used were 'robuste', 'sain', 'franc' and 'sincère'. Ernest Chesneau, in his monograph on the British School, included a few paragraphs on Raeburn, illustrated with the *Portrait of an Invalid* that had just entered the Louvre collections. In the course of this description we can also enjoy a long series of clichés on the coarseness of the subject:

> This last study is a very delicate interpretation made with such spirit as is rare everywhere and especially in the English School. This well-groomed English sailor with his neat outfit, retaining under his skin rendered red by the sun of far-away seas and drunken nights, the fresh complexion of Saxon blood is considered a masterpiece. His eye containing some sleep, his shiny nose, his mouth and its implied taste for tobacco and gin are extraordinarily expressive; there are very few painters who have been able to convey with such fluidity the transitions from darkness to halftone to light. Raeburn lived in Edinburgh, away from the clamour of London, and has not yet gained the reputation his immense talent, I should nearly say his genius, should give him in the esteem of art-lovers.[12]

He added at the end of his biographical note on the artist that although

> well-regarded in England, Raeburn's portraits are not as esteemed as they deserve to be. They are admired for their breadth, their character, their individuality, a feeling of truthfulness, but they are given no consideration as artworks. I do not share this point of view.[13]

At the end of his book Chesneau lists four paintings by Raeburn and adds that none of the London public galleries show any of this 'excellent artist's' work. The four pictures listed are: *Portrait of the Son of the Artist on a Grey Pony* (SNG, Edinburgh), *Portrait of the Artist* (H. Raeburn Esq. [now SNG]), *Portrait of Lord Eldin* (Sir W. Gibson Craig [now SNPG]), and *Portrait of McDonald of Saint Martin* (Highland and Agricultural Society of Scotland).

French interest in Raeburn took hold during the last two decades of the nineteenth century. The French eagerly followed British exhibitions and publications about the artist. In 1886, an article by Amédée Pigeon reported on the publication of the monograph by William Raeburn Andrew about his great-grandfather only a few months after it came out.[14] The most remarkable French effort to know and understand Raeburn was the quick translation made of the monograph by Walter Armstrong, following its publication in England in 1901, which was immediately translated into French and published the following year by Hachette.[15] It was also in 1901 that the Louvre purchased what was then thought to be a Raeburn portrait, of a woman said to be Hannah More (1745–1833), a fine picture catalogued by Armstrong. Three years later in 1904 the Louvre bought another portrait, then also considered to be by Raeburn, a weaker picture representing *Mrs Allan Maconochie of Meadowbank*,[16] which has since been de-attributed. It was only in 1908 that a real masterpiece by Raeburn entered the collections: the portrait of *Captain Hay of Lawfield and Spott* (d. 1844) (Fig. 13.2). A whole article was dedicated to the painting[17] by Paul Leprieur in *Revue de l'Art* in 1909. The text started with a tribute to Raeburn, who was still noted for his special touch 'made first and foremost of naturalness and frank spontaneity, of robust simplicity emanating from his native country where he spent his whole life'.[18]

This purchase was made rather quickly at Agnew's in London in 1908. The funds used came from a donation made by an eccentric Frenchman, Paul Bareiller, who had bequeathed half of his fortune to the Konprinz of Germany (who refused it) and the other half to the National Museums of France. In his article, Paul Leprieur placed the portrait on the same level as the double portrait by Thomas Lawrence (1769–1830) representing *Mr and Mrs Angerstein*:[19]

> One can sense the decorative qualities this painting will take in the gallery once it has definitely been set up opposite the Angerstein Family painted by Lawrence, the main work of the English section. Its dimensions as well as its colours will make it its worthy counterpart.

Leprieur also drew a parallel between Raeburn's painting and *General Fournier-Sarlovèze* by Gros. Thus Raeburn's work went straight into the pantheon of master portraits in the Louvre's collection, a status it continues to maintain. In the same article in the *Revue de l'art*, Leprieur listed two Raeburn portraits in a private collection in Paris, unveiling a new taste among French collectors. The first picture was in the Camille Groult collection. It was the portrait of *Major James Lee Harvey* in the uniform of the Gordon Highlanders.[20]

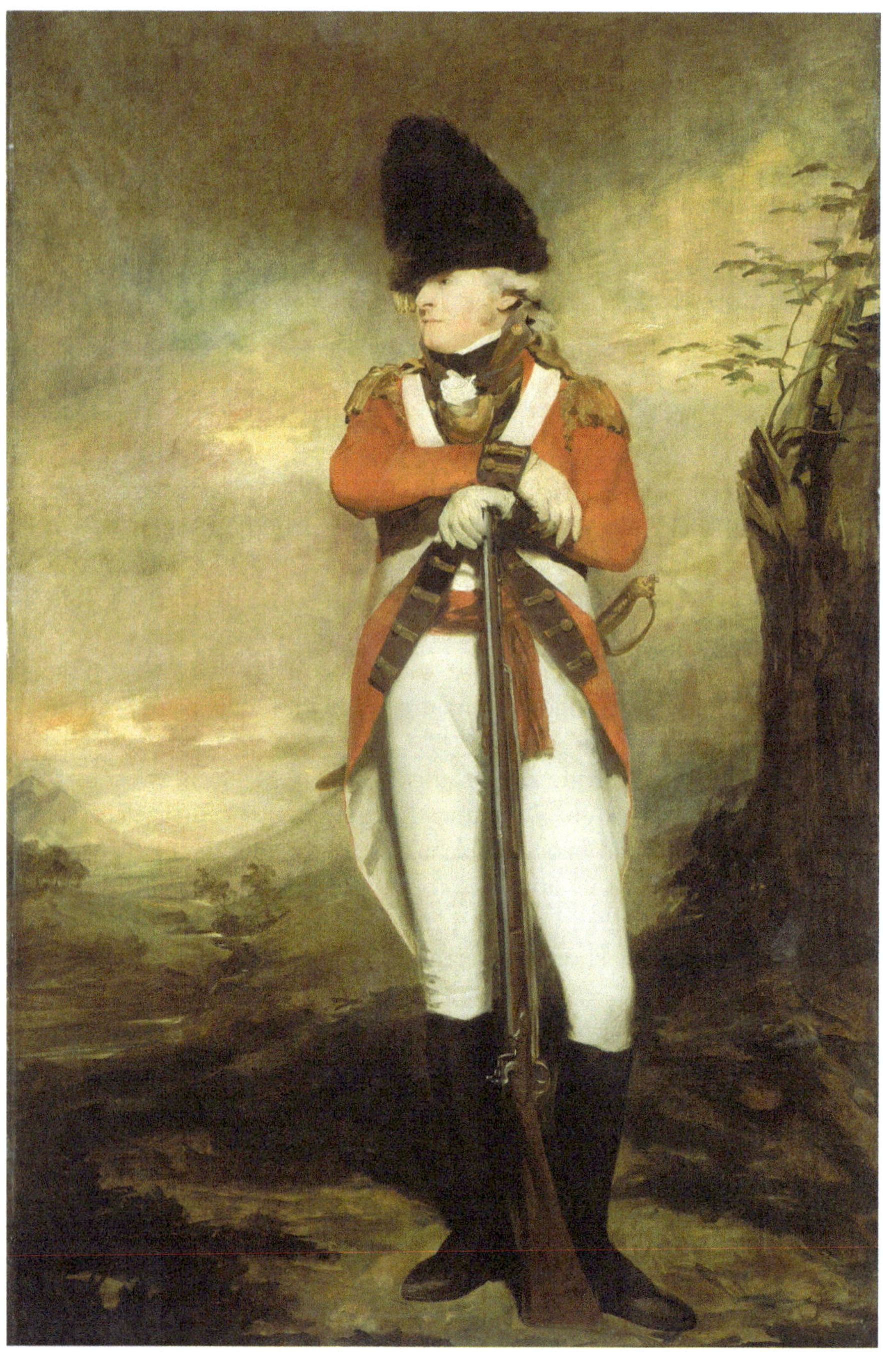

Figure 13.2 Henry Raeburn, *Captain Hay of Lawfield and Spott*, c. 1795–1800, oil on canvas, 240×151cm, Musée du Louvre, Paris (courtesy of Réunion des musées nationaux)

The second painting was a portrait said to be of *Mrs James Campbell*,[21] which had just been presented at the exhibition of *One Hundred Female Portraits*.

Among Raeburn collectors in France, Maurice Kahn (c. 1840–1906) owned a large number of works, probably the largest number owned by a private collector outside Scotland at this time. A banker from Frankfurt, Kahn lived at 49 allée d'Iéna in a private mansion built by Ernest Sanson adjoining that of his brother Rodolphe Kahn (1844/5–1905). In less than thirty years, Maurice Kahn had built up a remarkable collection of pictures, *objets d'art* and sculptures thanks to his taste, and the fortune he had made trading diamonds and gold from South Africa, but also thanks to the advice of Wilhelm von Bode (1845–1928), the famous German art historian and director of the Berlin Museums. When Kahn died, the Duveen and Gimpel brothers bought most of the collection and sent it to the United States. Among the treasures acquired, there was an impressive collection of works by Raeburn. There were no less than eight paintings by or attributed to the artist.[22]

Amongst the works sold in Paris on 9 June 1911 were the portrait of *Mrs Campbell*,[23] that of *Jane Anne Catherine Fraser*,[24] *Mrs Hunter*,[25] the portraits of *James Cruikshank*,[26] of *J. A. Macdonnel Bonar*,[27] of the young *James Hepburn*,[28] and of *William Fraser junior of Reelig*.[29] There was a near perfect balance between portraits of women, men and children. The collection was of the highest quality. The best example now in a public collection is the portrait of *James Cruikshank* (Fig. 13.3), at The Frick Collection in New York. Nearly all the Raeburn portraits from the Maurice Kahn collection came from one art dealer: Charles Sedelmeyer (1837–1925). Many of Raeburn's works came into France through him and it was also thanks to his agency that a large part of the British art collections present in France were constituted.[30]

A search for Raeburn's pictures listed in the numerous Sedelmeyer catalogues gives more than forty paintings. However, this large number includes pictures that have since been de-attributed. In spite of this, it was a spectacular gathering of works. It is not possible here to put together a complete list of those paintings as they were not all accurately described and not always reproduced. One can nevertheless make a representative anthology. In order to assemble this selection, only the pictures catalogued and published by James Greig in his catalogue raisonné published in 1911, are discussed.[31] The paintings already referred to above in the Maurice Kahn sale will not be mentioned again.

Charles Sedelmeyer was at his most active for about twenty years, during which time he offered a remarkable body of paintings, which he presented for sale in a very modern manner through catalogues richly illustrated with photographs. The first Raeburn painting to appear in the Sedelmeyer sale

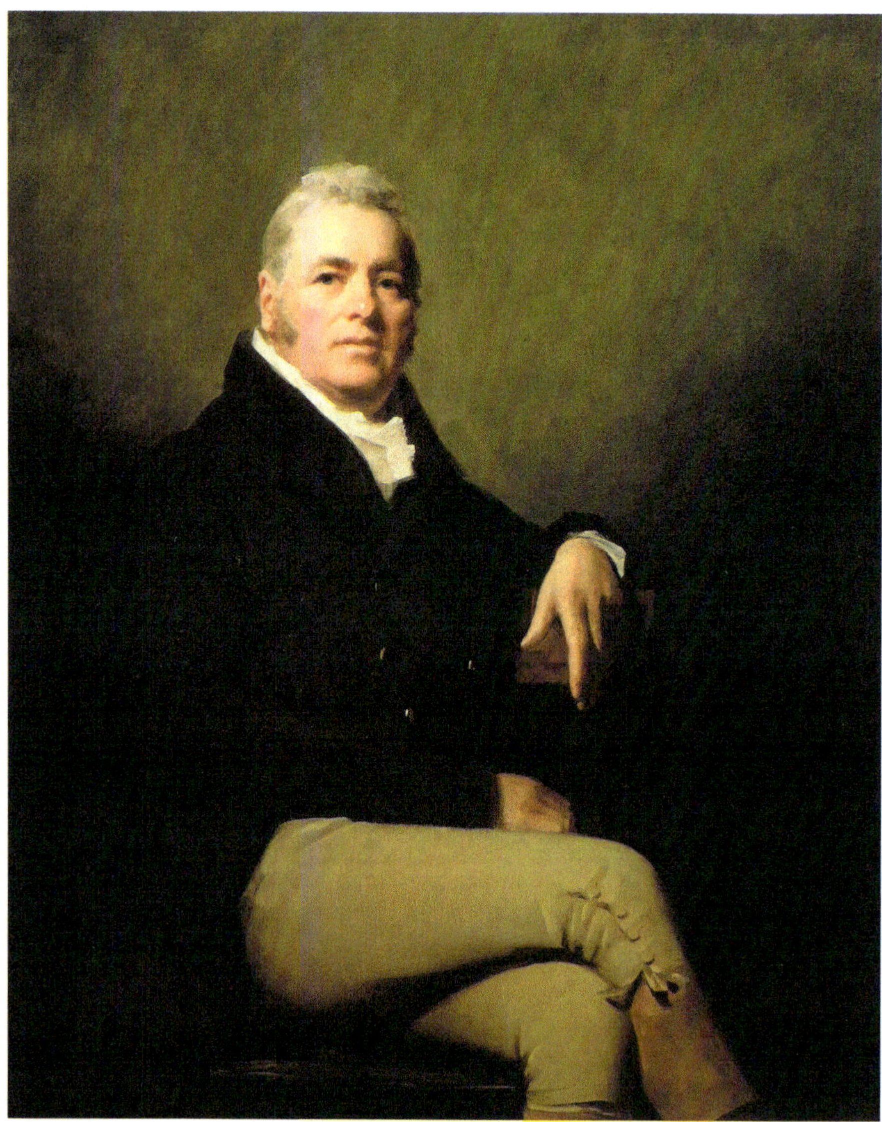

Figure 13.3 Henry Raeburn, *James Cruikshank*, c. 1805–8, oil on canvas,
127×101.6cm, The Frick Collection, New York

catalogues was the portrait of *The Revd Lucius O'Beirne* in 1896.[32] In 1899,
he presented the portrait of *Miss Ann Cunningham Graham of Gartmore*.[33]
Three years later, in 1902, it was followed by the portraits of *Miss Somerset*,[34]
of *Mrs White of Howden*,[35] and that of *Colonel Robert Macdonald*.[36] In 1905
the dealer presented the portrait of *Mrs Douglas of Brighton*.[37] In 1906 he
offered that of *Sir William Napier*;[38] in 1907, the portraits of *Lady Ramsey*,[39]

of *Mrs Pattison, née Margaret Moncrieff*,[40] of *Colonel Ramsey and his wife*,[41] and of *J. Murray and his brother*.[42] In 1911, it was the portrait of *Mrs Hart*,[43] that of *Mrs James Monteith, née Miss Margaret Thompson of Camphill*[44] and that of *J. Patterson Esq.*[45] In 1913, there were the portraits of *Mrs Craigie Halkett*,[46] of *Mrs Elizabeth Ann Stewart Richardson*[47] and of *John Home*;[48] the latter was to reappear in several French sales before returning to Scotland in a 2004 sale at Bonham's, Edinburgh.[49] The First World War stopped this influx of Scottish paintings, which were set to be hung on the tall walls of Parisian town houses. One can easily see from the list made above that the French fondness for Raeburn was no small matter. It must also be borne in mind that all the main French art dealers sold Raeburn paintings, even though they did so with less consistency and on a smaller scale than Charles Sedelmeyer.

Among the Raeburn pictures which do not appear to have been sold by Sedelmeyer but can nonetheless be found in sales or in French private collections, there were the following works: in the M. L. A Gaboriaud sale,[50] there was, along with paintings from Sedelmeyer, a portrait of a young woman with a dog catalogued by Armstrong.[51] One finds the presumed portrait of the *Duke of Bedford* in the Léon Gauchez collection,[52] or the portrait of *General Campbell* in the Marczell Nemes collection.[53] No more portraits by Raeburn seem to have been imported after the First World War. The major part of the artist's work in France today therefore entered the country between 1880 and 1914. Raeburn specialists must study the large body of work mentioned in part in this essay if they want to rediscover a whole area of the master's work. All these paintings, dispersed amongst French collections, have often been resold since; slowly, sale after sale, the finest ones have come back to Britain.

Of those works that remained in France, a number entered French public collections. Already discussed are the pictures bought by the Louvre at the end of the nineteenth century, which have since been de-attributed. Also listed is the fine portrait of *Captain Hay of Lawfield and Spott*. Three other paintings have joined the collections since 1908. In 1943, Mme Albert Eugène Lemonnier, née Rosa Ellen Augusta Whaley (1864–1943), gifted a small male portrait. Little is known today about the donor and the portrait itself (Fig. 13.4).[54] Slightly more is known about a painting bequeathed by Mme Pierre Lebaudy (1871–1962)[55] to the Louvre in 1962. It came from the collection of Sir Cecil Miles, before passing through Sedelmeyer and the Duveen brothers.[56] The painting, entitled portrait of *Nancy Graham* ('Innocence') (Fig. 13.5),[57] almost appears to be the companion piece to Raeburn's reception work at the Royal Academy, *Henry Raeburn Inglis* ('Boy and Rabbit') (Fig. 7.6). It is the outstanding example in France of Raeburn's

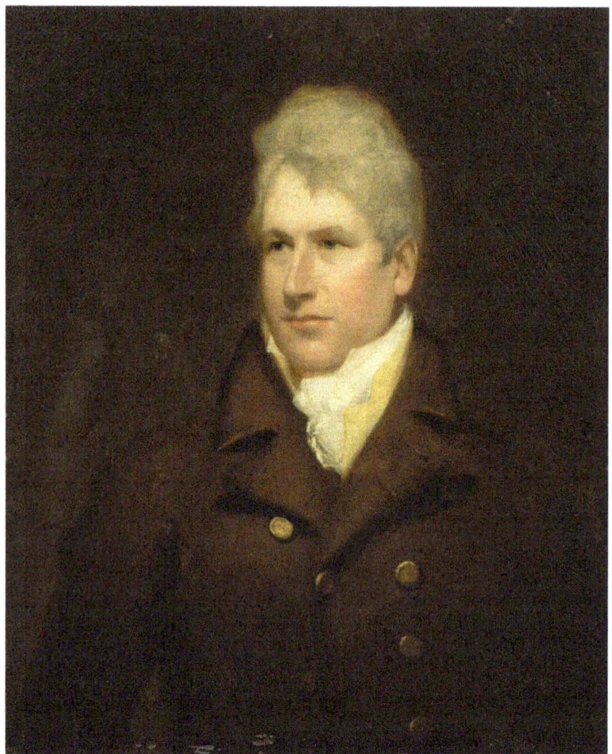

Figure 13.4 Henry Raeburn, *An Unknown Man*, c. 1800–10, 76×63cm, Musée du Louvre, Paris (courtesy of Réunion des musées nationaux)

more sentimental work, belying the idea that he was first and foremost a portraitist of men and the military. The donor, the widow of a wealthy sugar manufacturer, had put together a fine art collection from which she bequeathed several pieces, many of them to the Department of Objets d'Art at the Louvre.

The most recent Raeburn acquisition by the Louvre was made in 1995: it is the portrait of *Major James Lee Harvey* (Fig. 13.6),[58] from the collection of Camille Groult (1837–1908), which Leprieur had praised in his article about the purchase of the portrait of *Captain Hay of Lawfield and Spott* (Fig. 13.2) in 1908. The Groult collection was the largest collection of British art ever constituted in France, and most likely the finest one outside an Anglo-Saxon country. It included dozens of high-quality works; the Turner collection (to cite just one name) was outstanding. The collector himself was an eccentric whose taste was both excellent and original. For a while he had thought of creating a museum of British art in the château of Bagatelle, in place of the

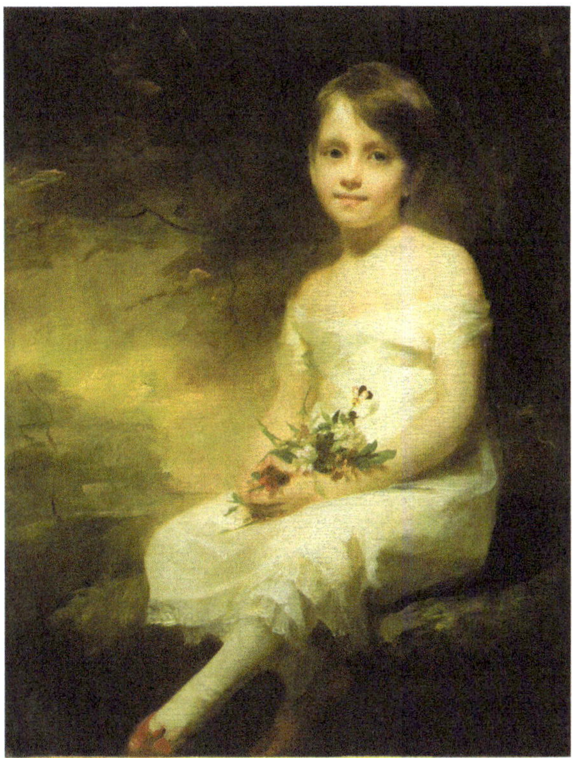

Figure 13.5 Henry Raeburn, *Nancy Graham ('Innocence')*, c. 1815, 91×71cm, Musée du Louvre, Paris (courtesy of Réunion des musées nationaux)

Wallace Collection. The museum only lasted for a year and the works came back to his large *hôtel particulier* in the rue Malakoff. His Raeburn painting is of remarkable quality, much in keeping with the other works of his collection. It is however slightly surprising that Camille Groult did not buy any more works by Raeburn despite amassing examples by Reynolds, Lawrence and Turner. The Louvre collection is therefore of high quality and three of the works are amongst Raeburn's best work. There are no Raeburns however anywhere else in French public collections. Two portraits, one in Bayonne (representing an *Unknown Elderly Man*)[59] and another in Béziers (portrait of *Fredérick Ellerman*)[60] are attributed to him mistakenly.

This virtual absence of Raeburn from regional collections is rather surprising, as one would have expected to find there numerous pictures that came to France at the beginning of the twentieth century, just as Lawrence or Reynolds can be found, if only infrequently, all over the country. It appears that due to Raeburn's late arrival into the pantheon of British portraitists,

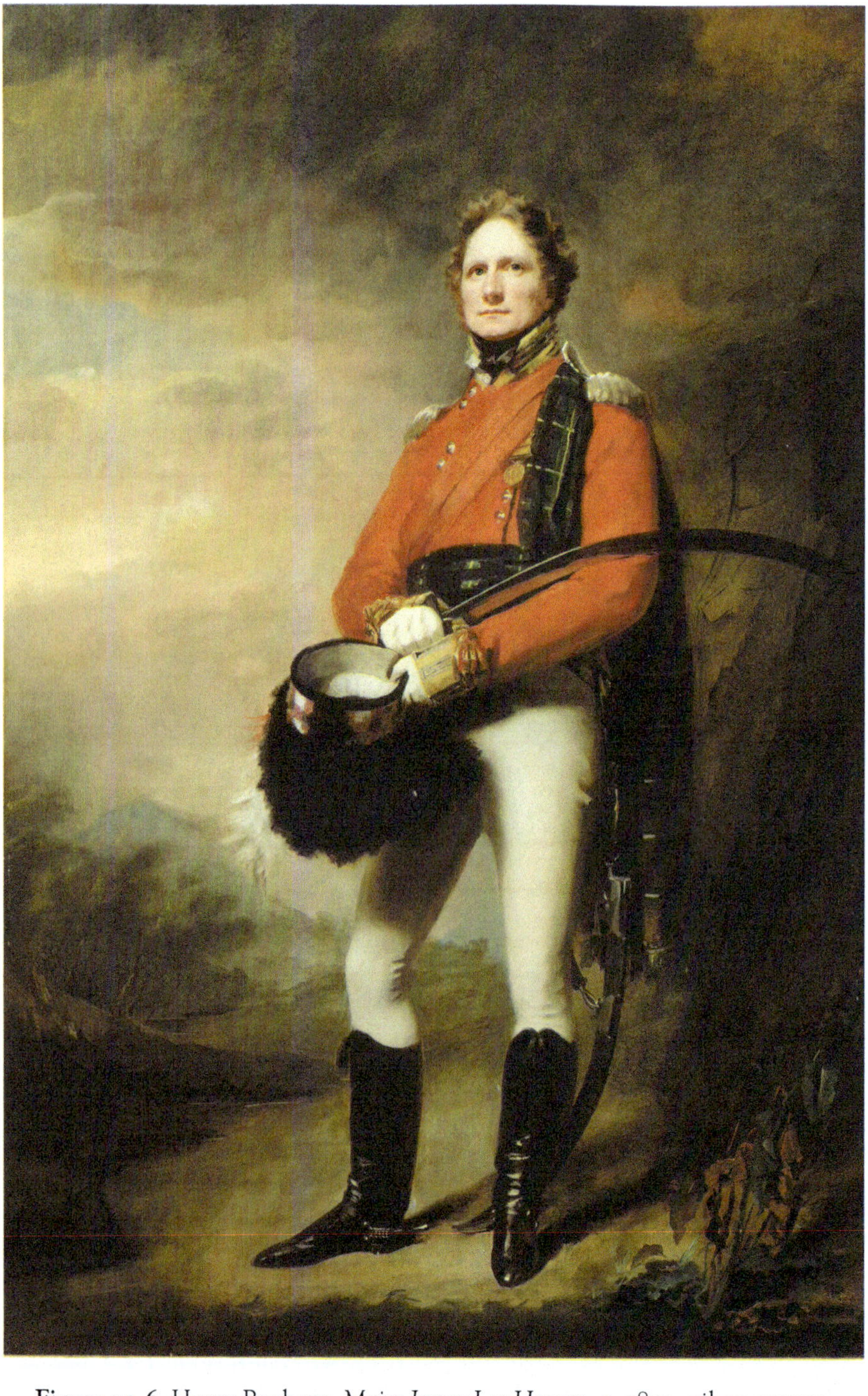

Figure 13.6 Henry Raeburn, *Major James Lee Harvey*, c. 1820, oil on canvas, 238×153cm, Musée du Louvre, Paris (courtesy of Réunion des musées nationaux)

he was only mentioned from the end of the nineteenth century, thus affecting his reputation. Reynolds, Lawrence and the landscapist Constable, for instance, were famous in France during their lifetimes – enjoying a profile not shared by Raeburn.

Despite this rather late recognition, Raeburn's reputation is now, and has been for over a century, that of an exceptional artist. It is difficult to precisely analyse the reasons that led to this, but a look at French *amateurs* of British art seems to indicate that he is most likely admired for his touch. Remarks made about his spontaneity and his frankness often indicate a true admiration for the swiftness of his brush and his 'brave' (*veta brava* is the term used for Spanish paintings) way of painting. Not only does he show aspects of eighteenth-century art, but also and especially a certain way of defying prudence that recalls Manet. Away from the aristocratic elegance of an artist like Lawrence, Raeburn shows a kind of solid naturalness. All these qualities made Raeburn an object of fascination for the French public and explain why they have given him this particular place in their pantheon of British artists.

Notes

1. Lloyd 2005.
2. Baron Roger Portalis, *Henry Pierre Danloux et son journal*, Paris, 1910.
3. Louis Simond, *Voyage d'un Français en Angleterre pendant les années 1810 et 1811*, Paris, 1816, p. 62.
4. William Burger, *Histoire des peintres de toutes les écoles, Ecole anglaise*, Paris, 1871, pp. 12–13 of the appendix.
5. Cunningham 1829–33.
6. Théophile-Thoré, *Trésors d'art exposés à Manchester en 1857 et provenant des collections royales, des collections publiques et des collections particulières de la Grande-Bretagne*, by W. Burger, Paris, 1857.
7. Fictitious name, in fact a sale organised by the dealer Léon Gauchez, Paris, 5–8 May 1873, no. 45 (Raeburn, *Portrait d'un invalide de l'hospice de la Marine, à Greenwich*).
8. Henri Perrier, 'De Hugo van der Goes à John Constable', *Gazette des Beaux-Arts*, VII, 1873, p. 254.
9. Alfred Lostalot, 'La collection Richard', *Gazette des Beaux-Arts*, XVII, 1878, T. XVII, p. 460.
10. Laurent-Richard, Paris, his estate sale, Paris, 28 May 1886, lot 41 (id.).
11. The downgrading took place during the 1890s.
12. Ernest Chesneau, *La peinture anglaise*, Paris, c. 1882, pp. 65–6.
13. Ernest Chesneau, op. cit. p. 66, end of the note started on p. 65.

14. Amédée Pigeon, 'Le mouvement des Arts en Angleterre', *Gazette des Beaux-Arts*, XXXIV, 1886, pp. 492–9.

15. Walter Armstrong, *Sir Henry Raeburn: avec une introduction par R. A. M Stevenson et un catalogue biographique et descriptif par J. L. Caw*, traduit par B. H. Gausseron, Paris, 1902.

16. Musée du Louvre, RF 1511.

17. Coll. Arthur Sanderson, Edinburgh; his sale, Christie's London, 3 July 1908; Agnew's, London; acquired in 1908, on the arrears of the Paul Auguste François Bareiller bequest, oil on canvas, 240×151cm, Musée du Louvre, RF 1729.

18. Paul Leprieur, 'Le portrait du capitaine Hay of Spot par Raeburn, au musée du Louvre', *La Revue de l'Art*, XXVI, 1909, p. 19.

19. Musée du Louvre, RF 1028.

20. Leprieur 1909, p. 21; it can be compared with a fine similar portrait in the Groult collection.

21. Portrait of *Mrs James Campbell* from the collection of R. Patrick Thomson Esq., oil on canvas, 76×63cm; exhibited in Paris in 1909 in the exhibition of *Cent Portraits de Femmes des écoles anglaise et française*, Salle du Jeu de Paume, Paris, 1909, no. 33. Probably the portrait in Kahn's collection, see below note 23.

22. Vente de la collection M. Maurice Kahn, *Catalogue des tableaux anciens . . .*, Galerie Georges Petit, Paris, 19 June 1911.

23. Ibid., lot 44 ; Vente la collection la marquise de Ganay, Paris, Galerie Georges Petit, 18–20 May 1922, lot 58, oil on canvas, 74×62cm.

24. Ibid. (Kahn sale), lot 41 (the painting was in the Affleck Fraser collection in London in 1897). See Walter Armstrong, *Sir Henry Raeburn*, Paris, 1902 p. 88 (repr.); Greig 1911, p. 8 (repr.) and p. 46, oil on canvas, 75×62cm.

25. Ibid. (Kahn sale). This was previously in the Douglas family until 1905, then with Sedelmeyer; sold since on 21 May 1941 in Paris, Drouot, Me Ader, lot 18; sale, Drouot, Paris, 27 March 1987, lot 16; sale, Christie's, New York, 2 June 1988, lot 107; sale, Christie's, New York, 11 January 1991, lot 35, oil on canvas, 90×69cm.

26. Ibid. (Kahn sale), lot 43; previously with Sedelmeyer, see *Illustrated Catalogue of the Ninth Series of 100 Paintings by Old Masters of the Dutch, Flemish, Italian, French, and English Schools, being a portion of the Sedelmeyer Gallery which contains about 1500 original Pictures by ancient and modern Artists*, Paris, 1905, no. 88, p. 110 (repr.) p. 111; Edinburgh and London 1997–8, p. 22, oil on canvas, 127×101cm; The Frick Collection, New York, acc. 1911.1.94. My grateful thanks to Claire Pratte for her research on these two pictures.

27. Ibid. (Kahn sale), lot 42; previously in the Sedelmeyer collection, see ibid. (*Illustrated Catalogue* [. . .] *of the Sedelmeyer Gallery . . .*), no. 89, p. 110 (repr.) p. 111.

28. Ibid. (Kahn sale), lot 46; oil on canvas, 72×60cm.

29. Ibid. (Kahn sale), lot 47; oil on canvas, 73×63cm, previously Affleck Fraser Collection, London, 1897.

30. Olivier Meslay, 'Collectionner Constable, une longue habitude française', *Constable: Le choix de Lucian Freud*, Paris, 2002, p. 55; Olivier Meslay, 'Romney in France', in *Transactions of the Romney Society*, IX , 2004, p. 23.

31. Greig 1911.

32. Ibid., p. 55, 88×68cm; now in Gemäldegalerie, Dresden.

33. Ibid., p. 34, repr.

34. Ibid., p. 60.

35. Ibid., p. 62.

36. Ibid., p. 51, 121×101cm.

37. Ibid., p. 61.

38. Ibid., p. 55, 228×142cm.

39. Ibid., p. 57, 75×62cm.

40. Ibid., p. 53, 125×100cm.

41. Ibid., p. 57, 125×100cm.

42. Ibid., p. 54, 123×98cm.

43. Ibid., p. 48. This picture was described as painted c. 1810.

44. Ibid., p. 54. This picture was described as painted c. 1820.

45. Ibid., p. 55, 127×76cm.

46. Ibid., p. 47, 76×61cm.

47. Ibid., p. 58.

48. Ibid., p. 48. 91×68cm.

49. Bonham's, Edinburgh, 20 August 2004, lot 1087.

50. Galerie Charpentier, Paris, 17 May 1950. There was also in this sale a Raeburn from the Sedelmeyer sale of 1913, no. 87, *Lady Holland*.

51. Armstrong et al., op. cit., 1902, p. 106, 90×70cm.

52. Greig 1911, op. cit., p. 38, 126 x100cm.

53. Greig 1911, op. cit., p. 40, 123 x105cm; Marczell Nemes sale, Paris, 18 June 1913.

54. RF 1943.11, T. H. 76×63cm.

55. Mme Pierre Lebaudy, née Marie-Marguerite Luzarche d'Azay.

56. Getty Research Institute, Duveen papers, box 270, file 30, it appears that it was sold to Mme Lebaudy in 1928.

57. Coll. Cecil Miles, his sale, Christie's London, 13 May 1899, no. 70; Galerie Sedelmeyer, Paris; Duveen Brothers, 1928; Mme Pierre Lebaudy; bequeathed by her to the Musée du Louvre in 1962; oil on canvas, 91 × 71cm; Musée du Louvre, RF 1962–15.

58. *Major James Lee Harvey*, oil on canvas, 238×147cm; Gift from the Société des Amis du Louvre, 1995, RF 1995–9. Olivier Meslay, 'Le portrait du major Lee Harvey en uniforme de Gordon Highlander par Sir Henry Raeburn',

Revue du Louvre, 1995, no. 4, pp. 16–17; Olivier Meslay, *Le major James Lee Harvey par Henry Raeburn*, *Le tableau du mois no. 17*, Musée du Louvre, Paris, July 1995.

59. *Unknown elderly Man*, oil on canvas, 67×50cm, Inv. 1018.
60. *Fréderick Ellerman*, oil on canvas, 75×63cm, Musée des Beaux-Arts, Béziers.

14

Raeburn and the Revival of Mezzotint Portraiture, 1890–1930

David Alexander

At the end of the nineteenth century there was a revival in Britain of portrait engraving in mezzotint. Many contemporary portraits were engraved but there was also a demand for mezzotints of eighteenth-century portraits of the kind which were being promoted by dealers such as Joseph Duveen and Agnews. Among the principal painters whose work was engraved was Henry Raeburn. Between about 1890 and 1930 some seventy mezzotints, initially in black and white but later frequently printed in colour, were issued by leading London publishers. One particular feature of this phenomenon was that many of the plates after Raeburn were of his female sitters, none of which had been engraved during his lifetime.

There was little demand beyond the small circle of portrait collectors for prints of eighteenth-century portraiture during the early part of the nineteenth century.[1] The first sign of a revival of interest was following the exhibition of 1867 when some of the finest paintings by Joshua Reynolds were shown, and the veteran engraver Samuel Cousins was persuaded to come out of retirement to engrave some of the most striking portraits.[2] These were bought for display by people who did not necessarily think of themselves as print collectors. At the same time print collectors began to search out the most attractive of the mezzotints engraved at the time that these pictures were painted, and the prints were catalogued by John Chaloner Smith.[3]

Paintings by Raeburn were included in various exhibitions, starting with the Old Masters exhibition at Burlington House in 1877, and it was then that several of his most arresting female portraits were seen on public view for the first time. Reynolds had become known, right from the beginning of his career in the 1750s, through mezzotints made of his portraits of women, but it was a singular fact that not one of Raeburn's portraits of women was engraved as a single print during his lifetime. The first one to be published was a mezzotint by Thomas Gooch Appleton (1854–1924) of *Mrs Scott Moncrieff*, issued in 1887. This picture was one of the first of Raeburn's pictures to be known to the public, since it had been given to the Royal Scottish Academy in 1854. Two exact contemporaries of Appleton's, John Cother Webb (1855–1927), and Joseph Bishop Pratt (1854–1910) also engraved plates after Raeburn. Appleton, who made his name through his plates of subject pictures, notably after Edwin Landseer, showed a plate of Raeburn's portrait of *Henry Raeburn Inglis ('Boy and Rabbit')*, Raeburn's Royal Academy diploma picture, at the Academy in 1903.

These engravers belonged to the school of commercial engravers who used mixed methods to produce plates that were issued by publishers. Although from the late 1840s the newly formed Printsellers' Association had made public the numbers of proof impressions taken from plates, the numbers of ordinary prints could still be very high.[4] By 1887 a different tradition of more artistic printmaking was re-asserting itself. The 'Etching Revival', associated with Whistler and his associates, is the best-known aspect of this. Less known today are the engravers trained at the Bushey School of Art, founded by the Bavarian-born artist Herbert von Herkomer (1849–1914), who was a printmaker of great versatility as well as a celebrated painter.[5] Pure mezzotint, rather than the mixed methods used by more commercial engravers, was one of the techniques which interested Herkomer and one that he encouraged his pupils to take up.[6] He recommended mezzotint engraving as a way for young artists to make money until they had established themselves as painters. Many of his students showed mezzotint plates at the Royal Academy, which had relaxed the earlier rules limiting the exhibition of prints. There were also exhibitions held by dealers. In 1905 Thomas Agnew, the important firm of London picture and print dealers, who had started their business in Manchester, held an exhibition of *Modern Mezzotints by the principal living engravers*, which included seven mezzotints after Raeburn's female portraits by Appleton, Webb, Pratt, as well as two Bushey graduates, Harry Scott Bridgwater (1864–1946) and Ernest Stamp (1869–1942). Stamp showed a plate of *Mrs Urquhart*, a picture that had become well known as it had been presented to Glasgow by the sitter's daughter-in-law in 1900. This picture was one of those which was engraved several times between 1904 and 1933; in the eighteenth century plates were rarely engraved more than once, since impressions continued to be produced from the plate. The limited number impressions of the twentieth-century editions made it commercially viable for another engraver to produce a new plate once the original one was sold out.

The huge popularity of eighteenth-century portraits, skilfully transferred from their aristocratic owners in Britain by Joseph Duveen, Agnew and other

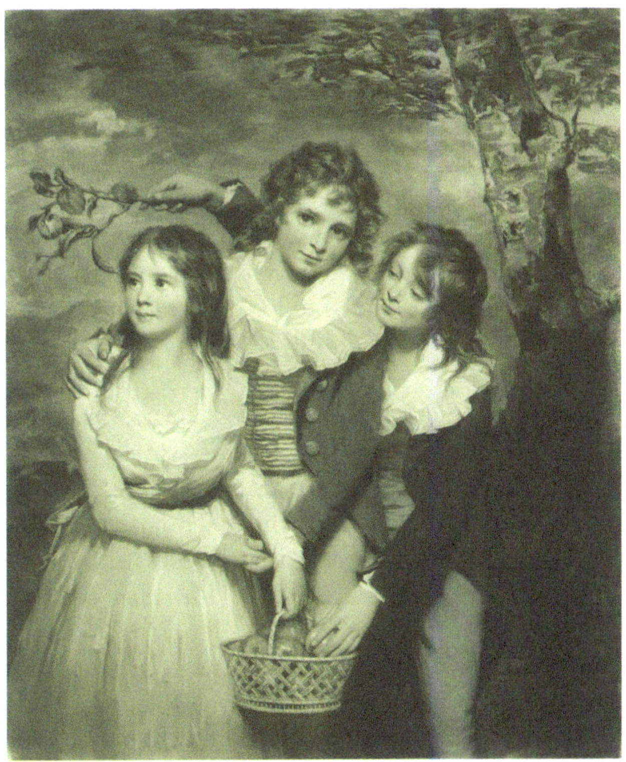

Figure 14.1 Norman Hirst after Henry Raeburn, *The Patterson Children*, 1913, mezzotint, published by Thomas Agnew (Collection of David Alexander)

dealers, to American millionaires, drew public attention to these pictures.[7] Print publishers realised that there was a market, particularly in the United States, for prints of these paintings. Dealers throughout North America, for example W. Scott Thurber in Chicago, stocked and promoted British mezzotints, which found their way onto the walls of many middle-class homes. The international exhibitions at which some of the mezzotints were shown, such as that at St Louis in 1904, also made them better known. Norman Hirst, who was one of the engravers who gained a medal at St Louis, engraved plates of *Lady Hamilton* after Romney for Leggatt Brothers in 1903 and of Lawrence's portrait of *Emily Anderson ('Pinkie')* for Agnew in 1908. Hirst, together with another Bushey graduate, Elizabeth Gulland, was among the few contemporary mezzotinters to have been praised by Cyril Davenport in his widely-read book, *Mezzotints*, published in 1904. Hirst's prints of Raeburn's *Lady Maitland* (1906), after the picture acquired by J. Pierpont Morgan, and *The Patterson Children* (1913) (Fig. 14.1), both published by Agnew, are marvellous renderings, worthy to be placed alongside all but the finest of eighteenth-century mezzotints. The price of these earlier prints, particularly of female full-lengths, rose to extraordinary levels, and in comparison newly engraved mezzotints costing between four and twelve guineas seemed inexpensive. The prints were regularly advertised in periodicals which had an Anglo-American readership, notably *The Connoisseur*, founded in 1901. Shortly before the First World War some of the mezzotints, for example those by Ernest Stamp, began to be issued in colours, but the more traditional engravers such as Hirst tended to look askance at colour. The war did not totally interrupt the production of these mezzotints, partly because the American market was largely unaffected until the United States entered the war in 1917. Frost & Reed, for example, issued a mezzotint of Raeburn's *Mrs Gregory* by Eugene Tily in 1916.

The immediate post-war prosperity saw new engravers begin to compete with the established ones. Thus the painter Thomas Hamilton Crawford (1860–1948), who must have learned mezzotint while studying under Herkomer at Bushey, engraved a plate of *Lady Helen Hall* which was published by H. C. Dickins, the firm started in 1887 by Henry Collingwood Dickins, in 1923, by which time Crawford was in his sixties. The same publishers, who set up an American branch at 665 Fifth Avenue in the 1920s, were also the principal publisher of plates by Henry Macbeth, who as a young man had added 'Raeburn' to his surname in order to prevent him being confused with his older brother Robert. This was prescient because between 1918 and 1926 he engraved a dozen or so colour-printed plates after Raeburn. The first was that of *The MacNab*, published by John Dewar & Son in 1918; this was followed by a plate of *Mrs Finlay*, published by Arthur Greatorex in 1921, but after that plate the engraver seems to have published through Dickins, who published in the same year plates of the archer *Dr Nathaniel Spens*, which had originally been engraved in line in 1796 by John Beugo (Fig. 2.5), and *Sir John Sinclair*, 'Agricultural Sir John', which had never been engraved. His plates were generally of a uniform size, approximately 26 by 16 inches, one exception being the Raeburn *Self-portrait* that was 15 by 12 inches. Those published by Dickins bore the name of the plate printer H. E. Carling, which was only fair since much of their appeal lay in the colour. Macbeth-Raeburn was proud of the fact that the plates were wholly printed in colours, without the final re-touching by hand which was usual with such mezzotints. These were expensive plates: that of *Miss Carmichael*, published in an edition of 300 by Colnaghi, cost eight guineas.

The Wall Street Crash of 1929 and the subsequent Great Depression put a sudden end to the market for mezzotints of eighteenth-century portraits, as well as of other kinds of prints. There was also something of a reaction against the backward looking and romanticising attitude which they represented. Their almost total loss of value must have turned many purchasers against them, and because a number of the plates had been slip-shod and sentimental, all the products of this revival were generally condemned as being beneath notice. One of the last to be promoted was a plate in colour of *Mrs Urquhart* by Ellen Jowett, which was issued in an edition of 200 colour printed impressions at the large price of twelve guineas in 1933. The only prints to have remained in demand after that were Macbeth-Raeburn's plates. An impression of *The MacNab*, issued in 1918, made no less than £35 at auction in 1935. Such prints were not only very decorative but carried an appeal to those wishing to be associated with Scotland, and Macbeth-Raeburn continued to engrave plates after Raeburn until his death in 1947.

Few of the engravers were ever written up in periodicals such as the *Print Collectors' Quarterly*, or even listed in catalogues raisonnés of masters' work. Consequently relatively few of the prints were ever acquired by public institutions, even by gift. By 1925 the British Museum had only about forty-five mezzotints by the engravers listed below; there were, for example, none of Macbeth-Raeburn's plates, though the artist later gave examples of his work, including proofs, to the Victoria and Albert Museum and to the British Museum. The general oblivion is undeserved, in part because the prints include some very fine work, and in part because they are a reflection of contemporary taste. In the context of this chapter, they provide evidence of Raeburn's reputation and, with the emphasis on the painter's female sitters, show the wider appreciation of his work as a whole, which had been made possible as a result of exhibitions including his work and by the entry into public collections of some of his finest pictures of women.

Mezzotints After Henry Raeburn, 1887–1947

As these engravers have been so little regarded information about them is not readily available, and therefore some of what has been garnered by the present writer is included here. The prints seldom carry the names of the sitter or painter, but are generally signed in pencil by the engraver, with the blind stamp of the Printsellers' Association in the left-hand margin. The published registers of the Association give the number of proofs (generally described as 'Artist's Proofs') of some of the earlier prints. The dimensions of the engraved area in inches are given in brackets. Because so few of these prints are in public collections it has not been possible to describe some of those traced only through auction records. The British Museum collection of these prints was considerably increased in 2010 by the acquisition of examples from the collection of the Hon. Christopher Lennox-Boyd. Details of prints in the British Museum are available from the online collection catalogue on their website.[8]

Appleton, Thomas Gooch (1854–1924)

Appleton, son of William and Pauline Appleton, was born on 20 July 1854 and was baptised in St Michael's Church, Liverpool, 13 August 1854. He moved to London.

1. *Mrs Scott Moncrieff*, pub. by P. &. D. Colnaghi, 1 Oct. 1887.

Banner, Hugh Harmwood (1865–1941)

Banner was the son of Alexander Banner, who taught at Glasgow School of Art, where his son trained. He was a versatile artist and mezzotint engraving was only a side-line.

2. *Sir Walter Scott*, pub. F. J. Dennis, London, and Schwartz's Sons & Co., New York, printed in colours, 1916 (BM).

Bridgwater, Henry Scott (1864–1946)

Bridgwater, painter and engraver and artist, began to exhibit at the Royal Academy in 1889, from Bushey; most of his prints were after contemporary painters.

3. *Lady Carmichael*, pub. T. Agnew & Sons, and P. & D. Colnaghi, 1903, 300 proofs (16×14in) (BM).

4. *Mrs Home Drummond*, pub. P. & D. Colnaghi, 1903, 350 proofs (19×15in).

5. *Mrs Lee Acton*

6. *Sir Walter Scott*, exh. RA 1923.

7. *Mrs William Urquhart*, pub. Alfred Bell & Co., 1923, after the picture presented to Glasgow Art Gallery in 1900; 300 impressions printed in colours (14×11in) (Fig. 14.2).

Chapman, John Watkins (1832–c. 1903)

Genre painter who exhibited at the Royal Academy 1880–1903 and who engraved at the end of his career.

8. *Mary Smith*, wife of James Smith of Jordanhill, pub. Shepherd Bros & Boussod Valadon & Co., 1890, 175 proofs, £5 (21×17in).

Clouston, Robert Stewart (1857–1911)

Clouston was born in Scotland but moved south as a young man and exhibited at the Royal Academy 1888–1904. An authority on old furniture as well as an artist, he died on a visit to Australia.

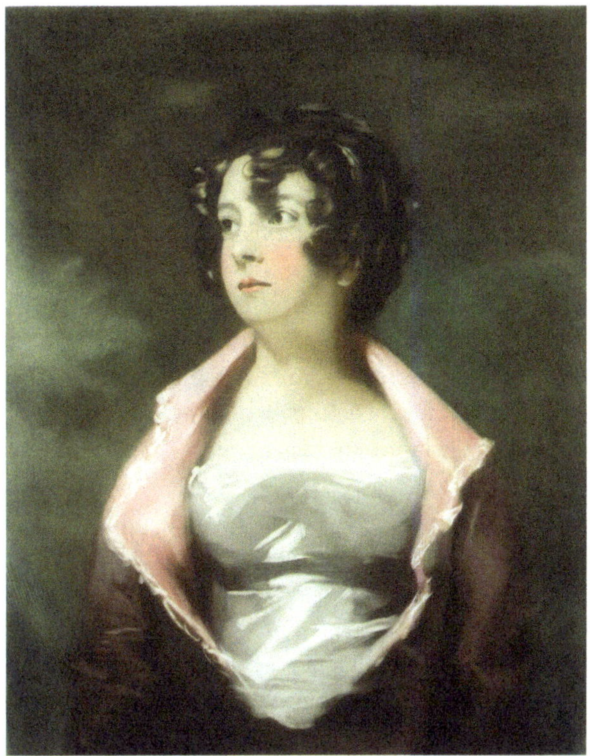

Figure 14.2 Henry Scott Bridgwater after Henry Raeburn, *Mrs Urquhart*, 1923, mezzotint, printed in colour, published by Alfred Bell & Co., one of 300 impressions, sold at 6 guineas each (Collection of David Alexander)

9. *'Janet'*, pub. Archibald Ramsden, 1898, 100 proofs, £3.3s (22×17in).
10. *Mrs Scott Moncrieff*
11. *Miss Suttie*, pub. Arthur Tooth, 1893, 100 proofs, £5 (21×17in); after the picture now in Cincinnati Art Museum.

Cormack, Minnie (1862–1919 or later)

Minnie Cormack, née Everett, was born in Skibereen, Cork, and was a pupil of T. G. Appleton. She engraved *Lady Nugent* after Lawrence, pub. Agnew, 1890, and exhibited two portrait mezzotints after contemporary painters at the RA in 1892–3 but later she seems to have worked principally as a miniature painter. She exhibited at the RA for the last time from Salcombe in 1919.
12. *Mrs Scott Moncrieff*, pub. Fine Art Society, 1911, 300 proofs, £4.4s (13×11in).

Cox, Walter Alfred (b. 1862)

Artist and engraver who trained under Jean Ballin.

13. *Mrs Lauzun*, pub. H. Graves, 1908, 350 proofs, £3.3s, exh. RA 1910; after the picture bequeathed to the National Gallery, London (now at Tate Britain, London), by Henrietta Lauzun in 1900.

Crawford, Thomas Hamilton (1860–1948)

Crawford, born in Glasgow, was a pupil of Herkomer at Bushey. He made his name as an artist, exhibiting pictures from 1891 at the Royal Academy, but also exhibited mezzotints, including seven at the Paris Salon 1911–28. His output of mezzotints increased after the First World War. Most of his plates were published by H. C. Dickins, who employed H. E. Carling as their printer. Crawford's final plate may be one after Gainsborough published by Dickins in 1930.

14. *Lady Helen Hall*, pub. H. C. Dickens, 1923; exhibited RA 1923 (BM).
15. *Henry Raeburn Inglis ('Boy and Rabbit')*, pub. Alfred Bell, 1 Dec. 1913 (BM).

Greenhead, Henry T. (1849–1926)

Greenhead was one of the older engravers involved in the revival of mezzotint. He exhibited mezzotint portrait prints at the Royal Academy from 1896 to 1910. His prints were issued by leading publishers such as Dickinson & Foster of Bond Street.

16. *Miss Ross*

Gulland, Elizabeth (c. 1865–1934)

Gulland, born in Edinburgh, was a pupil of Herkomer's at Bushey, where she lived for many years. She exhibited at the Royal Scottish Academy from 1887–1910. She was among the first to produce plates for colour printing, some of which she did herself. She continued to engrave into the late 1920s: her plate of *Mrs Curwen* after Romney was issued in 1926 by H. C. Dickins, and printed by H. T. Cox of Bushey.

17. *Mrs Irvine Boswell*
18. *Miss De Vismes*, published H. C. Dickins, 1911, 250 proofs in colour, £5.5s (13×9in) (BM).
19. *Mrs Scott Moncrieff*, print exh. RA 1910.
20. *The Hon. Mrs Spiers*, after the picture belonging to the Marquess of Zetland.
21. *Lady Stewart of Physgill*
22. *Mrs William Urquhart*, pub. Dickins, 1911, 250 proofs, £5.5s (13×9in).

23. *The Hon. Mrs Wharton*, after the picture belonging to the Marquess of Zetland.
'A *Lady*', pub. H. C. Dickins, 1911, 250 proofs, £3.3s (9×7in). [This may be one of the undescribed prints above and is therefore not numbered.]

Henderson, William (c. 1866–c. 1926)
24. *Flora*, published Thos. McLean, 1905, 150 proofs, £5.5s; unspecified number of prints, £1.1s (15×12in).
25. *Mrs Urquhart*, pub. T. McLean.

Hester, R. Wallace (1866–1923)
Artist and engraver, son of the engraver Edward Hester; he exhibited at the RA 1897–1904.
26. *Mrs Murchison*, pub. A. Tooth, 1904, 250 proofs, £6.6s (20×15in).
27. *Mrs Bell*, pub. by Henry Graves, 100 proofs at £3.3s; unspecified number of prints sold at £1.1s in 1903.

Hirst, Norman (1862–1956)
Hirst, artist and engraver, was, next to Frank Short, probably the most accomplished mezzotint engraver at work in the early twentieth century. He was at Bushey between 1885 and 1895, after which he continued to use the printing studio there of H. T. Cox. He exhibited at the RA until 1929, though his last reproductive print was sent in 1922. He became A.R.E. in 1931. As well as employing mezzotint for portrait prints he also used it for landscape work, producing plates after Constable as well as his own landscapes. His executors burned most of the prints left in his studio on the grounds that they were valueless.
28. *Mrs Irvine Boswell*, pub. T. Agnew, 1906, 350 proofs, £6.6s (17×14in); print exh. RA 1906 (BM); after the picture now in the Detroit Institute of Art.
29. *Lady Maitland*, pub. T. Agnew, 1907 350 proofs, £8.8s (18×14in); print exh. RA 1907 (BM); after the picture in the hands of Agnew's in 1905, acquired by J. Pierpont Morgan, and now in The Metropolitan Museum of Art, New York.
30. *The Patterson Children*, pub. T. Agnew, 1913 (16×14in) (Fig. 14.1).

Hogg, Arthur (1872–1949)
Mezzotint engraver who worked closely with Thomas Ross & Sons, the copper plate printers who also published plates.
31. *Robert and Ronald Ferguson ('The Archers')*, pub. Frost & Reed, 1928 (BM).
32. *Seated young woman* (BM 2010,7081.4367, as after Raeburn).

James, Clifford R.
33. *Mrs Urquhart*, c. 1920 (BM).

James, George P.
34. *Sir John and Lady Clerk of Penicuik*
35. *Mrs Macrae*

Jowett, Ellen (b. 1874)
Ellen Jowett's first plates appeared just before the 1914–18 War, when she was based in Manchester. Her mezzotints were primarily after earlier painters, for example Lawrence.
36. *Henry Raeburn Inglis ('Boy and Rabbit')*, pub. Frost & Reed, 1923.
37. *Mrs Urquhart*, pub. Frost & Reed, 1933; 200 proofs at £12.12s; advertised in the *Connoisseur*, XCII, October 1933, p. 386.

Macbeth-Raeburn, Henry (1860–1947)
This artist was the son of Norman Macbeth RSA and after attending Edinburgh University and studying at Jullians Studio and elsewhere, he set up as a portrait painter in London. He had been baptised 'Henry Raeburn Macbeth' but in order to distinguish himself from his older brother Robert, also an artist, he called himself 'Henry Macbeth-Raeburn'. He visited Spain as an artist in 1889, but his career changed direction after he took up engraving in 1890. He became A.R.E. in 1894 (R.E. in 1920). His first mezzotint after Raeburn was of the painter's *Self-portrait*, published in 1908. He became well known through the large mezzotints, printed in colours, which he produced after the 1914–18 War, the majority of which were after Raeburn. He became ARA in 1922 and RA in 1933. He continued to engrave plates after Raeburn after the print market collapsed in 1929. His second wife Marjorie (née Bacon) engraved and exhibited at the RA plates of *Lord Newton* and *John Lock*, both after Raeburn, as late as 1956 and 1958. The British Museum has many of his prints and he presented some proof impressions to the Victoria and Albert Museum.
38. *Lady Belhaven*, after the picture acquired by the Hon. T. S. Astor in 1920.
39. *Miss Eleanor Carmichael*, pub. Colnaghi.
40. *Lady Carnegie*, pub. H. C. Dickens, 1925, exhibited RA 1941 (BM).
41. *Sir John and Lady Clerk of Penicuik*, pub. H. C. Dickins, 1 June 1923, print exh. RSA 1923 (BM) (Fig. 14.3).
42. *The Drummond Children*, print exh. RA 1939.
43. *Mrs Alexander Finlay*, pub. Arthur Greatorex, Sept. 1921 (26×16in) (BM; VAM).

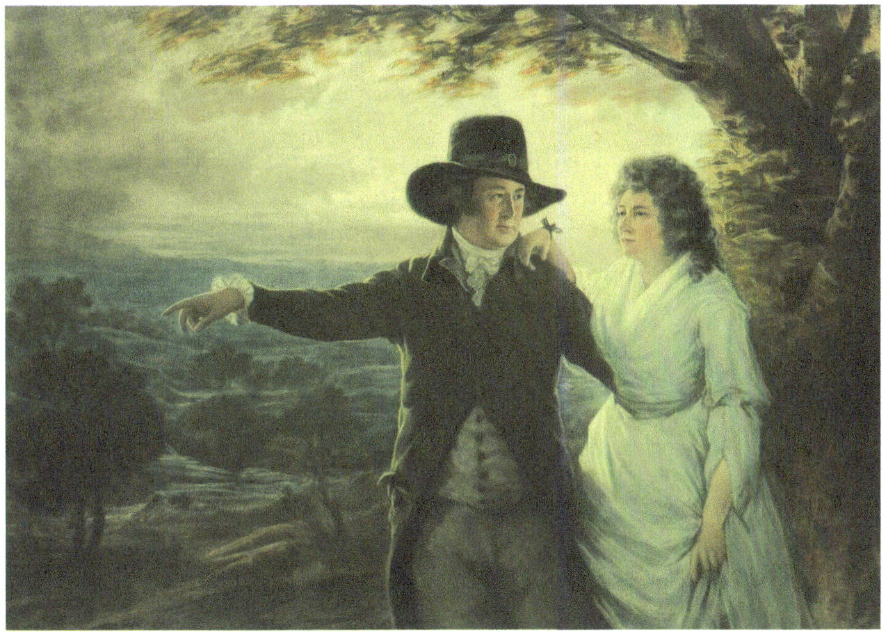

Figure 14.3 Henry Macbeth-Raeburn after Henry Raeburn, *Sir John and Lady Clerk of Penicuik,* 1923, mezzotint, published by H. C. Dickens (Collection of David Alexander)

44. *John Earl of Hopetoun,* exh. RA 1939.

45. *Col. Alastair Macdonnell,* pub. H. C. Dickins, 1922 (25×16in) (BM; VAM).

46. *Col. Hay McDowell* (26×16in) (BM; VAM).

47. *Sir George Mackenzie of Coul* (25×16in) (VAM).

48. *The MacGregor,* exh. RA 1947.

49. *Francis MacNab ('The MacNab'),* pub. John Dewar & Sons, 1918 (BM).

50. *Mrs Malcolm* (BM).

51. *Lady Montgomerie,* exh. RA 1940.

52. *Henry Raeburn (Self-portrait),* pub. Goupil & Co., 1908, 125 proofs, £3.3s (15×12in) (BM; VAM).

53. *Miss Mary Ruck,* pub. Lawrence & Bullen, 1904 (BM).

54. *Sir John Sinclair of Ulbster,* pub. H. C. Dickins, 1921 (26×16in), exh. RSA 1923 (BM; VAM).

55. *Dr Nathaniel Spens of Craigsanquhar,* pub. H. C. Dickins, 1921 (26×16in), exh. RSA 1923, and RA 1943; ill. *Connoisseur,* Aug. 1922 (BM; VAM).

56. *Thomas Telford*, pub. H. C. Dickins, 1935 (BM); after the picture at the Lady Lever Art Gallery, Port Sunlight.

McCulloch, George

McCulloch seems to be identifiable with the Scottish landscape painter who appears in Whistler's correspondence in 1897 when he had to take a print publisher to court for not paying him for a commissioned mezzotint plate.
57. *Henry Raeburn Inglis ('Boy and Rabbit')*

Milner, Miss Elizabeth Eleanor (1862–1953)

Milner, artist and engraver, was daughter of the vicar of Elton, Stockton-on-Tees (of which her brother Harry was rector 1902–36). She attended various art schools, and worked as a painter as well as engraver, remaining in Bushey for some years, at least until 1907, the year she sent the last of some eleven mezzotints to the Society of Women Artists. One of her final plates was of Lawrence's *Master Lambton*, published by Frost & Reed in 1930.
58. *Mrs Bell*, pub. by the Fine Art Society, 300 proofs in colour, £4.4s, 1911 (13×10in).
59. *Mrs Ferguson of Raith and two of her children*
60. *General Sir Ronald Ferguson*
61. *Henry Raeburn Inglis ('Boy and Rabbit')*, pub. Frost & Reed, 1928 (BMst).

Norman, H.

62. *Lady Carmichael*, pub. Alfred Bell, 1911, 300 proofs in colours (12×10in).
63. *Mrs Home Drummond*, pub. Alfred Bell, 1911, 300 proofs in colours (12×10in).

Pratt, Joseph Bishop (1854–1910)

Pratt was born in St Pancras, London, and in the late 1860s was a pupil of David Lucas, the interpreter of John Constable, for five years. He exhibited at the Royal Academy from 1874. He worked initially as a mixed method engraver of contemporary pictures but worked in pure mezzotint later in his career, starting to engrave portraits after earlier painters in the mid-1890s. His output was very large and at the time of his death he was considered to be the leading reproductive mezzotint engraver.
64. *Mrs Gregory*, after the picture exhibited regularly from 1872, pub. T. Agnew, 1898, 225 proofs at £8.8s, 100 other proofs, £5.5s (18×14in) (BM).
65. *Miss Ross*, pub. T. Agnew & Sons, 1904, 275 proofs, £10.10s (18×15 in) (BM) (Fig. 14.4).

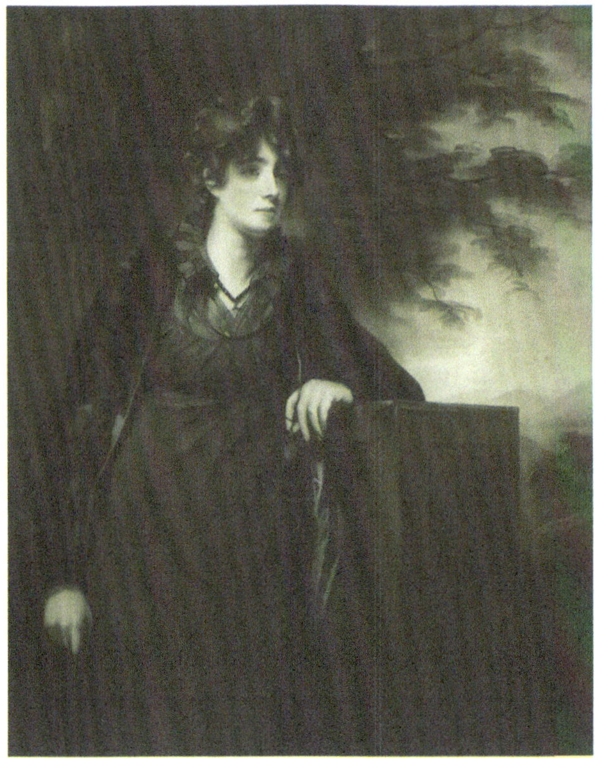

Figure 14.4 Joseph Bishop Pratt after Henry Raeburn, *Miss Ross*, 1904, mezzotint, published by Thomas Agnew (Collection of David Alexander)

Sedcole, Herbert (b. 1864)

Sedcole, son of James W. Sedcole, studied under J. B. Pratt, and exhibited between 1889 and 1931.

66. *Mrs Lauzun*, pub. Alfred Bell, 1911, 300 proofs in colours, £3.3s (15×12in); after the picture earlier engraved by Walter Cox (qv).

Skrimshire, Alfred J. (1872–1927)

67. *Francis MacNab ('The MacNab')*, pub. Arthur Greatorex, 1929 (BM).

Stamp, Ernest (1869–1942)

Stamp was born in Sowerby Bridge, Yorkshire; he studied under Herkomer and became known as a painter and engraver. He exhibited from Bushey at the Royal Academy from 1892 and from Northampton in 1898. Recognition came early with election as A.R.E. in 1894. He lived in Hampstead for much of his career.

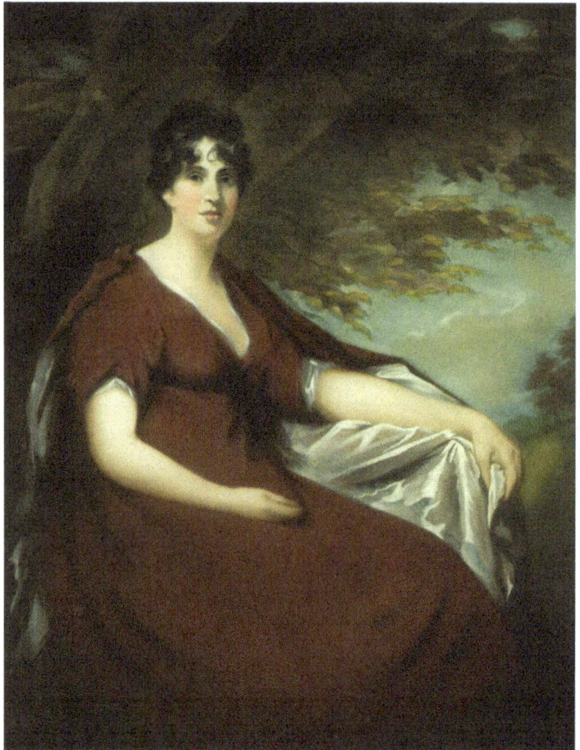

Figure 14.5 Ernest Stamp after Henry Raeburn, *Mrs Hay of Spott*, 1912, mezzotint, printed in colours, published by H. Drake (Collection of David Alexander)

68. *Mrs Hay of Spot*, pub. H. Drake, Leadenhall St, 1912, printed in colours (18×14in) (Fig. 14.5).
69. *Mrs Stewart of Physgill*, pub. L. H. Lefevre, 1903, after the picture in the hands of Messrs. Duveen around this time; 300 proofs, £6.6s (24×16in).
70. *Mrs Urquhart*, pub. Gooden & Fox, 1904, 200 proofs, £6.6s (19×15in).

Sternberg, Frank (1858–1927)

Sternberg, artist and engraver, who may possibly have been born in Prussia. Was based in Leeds for part of his life. He studied at Bushey under Herkomer and exhibited at the Royal Academy from 1885 to 1904.
71. *Lady and child*

Stewart, Robert Wright (c. 1885–c. 1950)

Stewart, who came from Dysart, Fife, studied at the Royal College of Art. He was elected A.R.E. in 1911, and made etchings of Scottish scenes, of

which there are some in the Victoria and Albert Museum. He made his name as a landscape painter, exhibiting at the RA and elsewhere from London addresses between 1909 and 1940, and retiring to Dysart, from which he sent pictures to the RSA in the late 1940s.
72. *Mrs Bell*

Tily, Eugene James (1870–1937)

Tily was born at Walkern, Herts. He gained a gold medal at the St Louis exhibition in 1904. His final exhibit at the RA, sent from Sutton in 1913, was *The Empty Saddle* after James Beadle.
73. *Mrs Gregory*, pub. Frost & Reed, 1916 (BM).

Webb, John Cother (1855–1927)

Webb, born in Torquay, began to engrave reproductive prints at an early age. His first exhibit was *The Hot Breakfast* after Edwin Landseer, which he sent to the Royal Academy in 1875 from the house of Thomas Landseer, who appears to have been his master.
74. *Mrs Anderson of Inchyra*, pub. Gooden & Fox, 1904, who may then have owned the picture; 200 artist's proofs, £6.6s each (19×14 in) (Fig. 14.6).
75. *Henry Raeburn Inglis ('Boy and Rabbit')*, after the picture pub. by Dowdeswell & Dowdeswell, 1902 (18×14in), exh. RA 1903.

Wilson, Sydney Ernest (b. 1869)

Wilson was a pupil of J. B. Pratt. He was a prolific engraver, almost exclusively after eighteenth-century paintings. He exhibited at the RA from Harpenden from 1910 to 1913. His mezzotints were considered to be rather inferior but they were popular and a catalogue of them was produced in 1911 by Vicars Brothers, his principal publisher.
76. *Mrs Bell*

Notes

1. This essay follows my work on the mezzotints after Raeburn done during his lifetime. I am grateful to Stephen Lloyd for his invitation to contribute to the exhibition and accompanying catalogue (Edinburgh 2006) and for encouraging me to pursue the present study.
2. Alfred Whitman, *Samuel Cousins*, London, 1904.
3. Chaloner Smith 1878–84.
4. The Printsellers' Association published lists of the engravings registered by them in various formats up to 1912.
5. For Herkomer see the contemporary study by A. L. Baldry, *Herbert von Herkomer,*

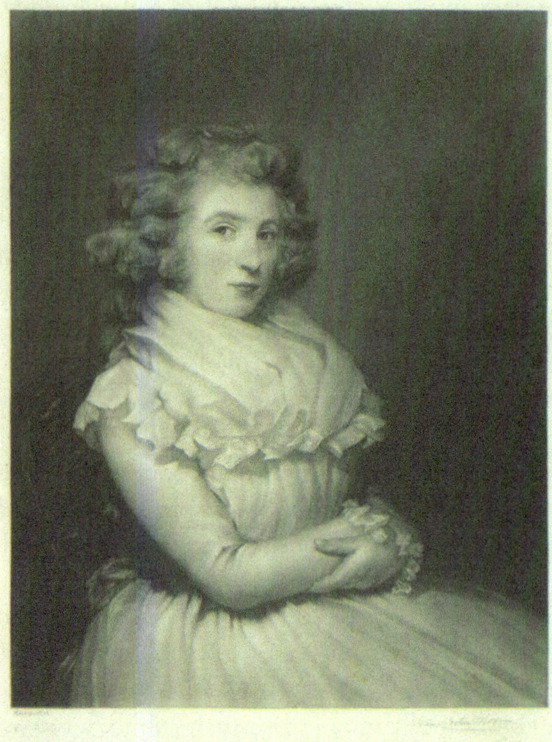

Figure 14.6 John Cother Webb after Henry Raeburn, *Mrs Anderson of Inchyra*, 1904, mezzotint, published by Gooden & Fox (Collection of David Alexander)

London, 1901, and the recent work of Lee MacCormick Edwards, who contributed the entry on him to the *Oxford Dictionary of National Biography*.

6. Herkomer was working in mezzotint by 1880, sending *Grandfather's Pet* to the Dudley Gallery in that year, and *Sheridan*, after Reynolds, to the RA in 1881.

7. S. N. Behrman, *Duveen* (New York, 1952), is the classic account of the great dealer, and was enhanced by the illustrations in the edition produced by George Rainbird Ltd for Hamish Hamilton (London, 1972). Raeburn was a second division artist as far as Duveen was concerned but among the artist's pictures handled by his firm were *Master William Blair*, sold to Henry E. Huntington for the (Huntington Library, San Marino, CA) and *William Scott-Elliot*, sold to Jules S. Bache (The Metropolitan Museum of Art, New York).

8. This is very much a preliminary list and the author would be grateful to receive amendments and additions.

Select Bibliography

J. H. L. A. 1876 J. H. L. A., 'Some Old Scottish Celebrities: a Walk through the Raeburn Exhibition', *London Society: an illustrated Magazine of light and amusing Literature for The Hours of Relaxation*, XXX, 1876, pp. 426–31

ANDREW 1886 Andrew, William Raeburn, *Life of Sir Henry Raeburn, R.A. with Portraits and Appendix*, London: W. H. Allen and Co., and Edinburgh: John Menzies & Co., 1886

ARMSTRONG, CAW AND STEVENSON 1901 Armstrong, Sir Walter, *Sir Henry Raeburn*, with an Introduction by R. A. M. Stevenson and a Biographical and Descriptive Catalogue by J. L. Caw, London: William Heinemann and New York: Dodd, Mead & Company, 1901 (French edn, Paris, 1902)

BAKER 1933 Baker, C. H. Collins, *British Painting*, London: Medici Society, 1933

BROTCHIE 1924 Brotchie, T. C. F., *Henry Raeburn 1756–1823*, London: Cassell & Co. Ltd, 1924

BROWN 1875 Brown, John, *Portraits by Sir Henry Raeburn, Photographs by Thomas Annan, with Biographical Sketches*, Edinburgh: printed for private circulation, 1875

CAW 1908 Caw, James L., *Scottish Painting Past and Present 1620–1908*, Edinburgh: T. C. and E. C. Jack, 1908 (reprinted, 1975)

CAW 1909 Caw, James L., *Raeburn: Masterpieces in Colour*, Edinburgh: O. Schulze & Co., 1909

CHALONER SMITH 1878–84 Chaloner Smith, John, *British Mezzotinto Portraits: being a Descriptive Catalogue of these Engravings from the Introduction of the Art to the early part of the present Century*, 6 vols, London, 1878–84

CLOUSTON 1907 Clouston, R. S, *Sir Henry Raeburn*, London: George Newnes Limited and New York: Frederick Warne & Co., 1907

CUNNINGHAM 1829–33 Cunningham, Allan, 'Raeburn', *The Lives of the most Eminent British Painters, Sculptors and Architects*, 6 vols, London; John Murray, 1829–33 [Life of Raeburn, V (1832), pp. 204–41]

CUNNINGHAM 1843 Cunningham, Allan, *The Life of David Wilkie; with his journals, tours and critical remarks of works of art; and a selection from his correspondence*, 3 vols, London: John Murray, 1843

CURSITER 1949 Cursiter, Stanley, *Scottish Art to the Close of the Nineteenth Century*, London: George G. Harrap and Co. Ltd, 1949

DIBDIN 1925 Dibdin, E. Rimbault, *Raeburn*, London: Philip Allan & Co., 1925

DUNCAN 1824 Duncan, Andrew, *A Tribute of Regard to the Memory of Sir Henry Raeburn, R.A. Portrait Painter to the King for Scotland: read at the forty-second anniversary meeting of the Harveian Society of Edinburgh*, Edinburgh, 1824

EDINBURGH 1824 *Catalogue of Portrait by the late Sir Henry Raeburn, R.A. now exhibiting in No.32, York Place [Edinburgh]*, 1824

EDINBURGH 1850 *List of Portraits painted by the late Sir Henry Raeburn, R.A., exhibited in the College of Edinburgh during the Meeting of the British Association*, Edinburgh, 1850

EDINBURGH 1876 *Exhibition of the Works of Sir Henry Raeburn, R.A. in the Royal Academy*, National Galleries, exh. cat., Edinburgh, 1876

EDINBURGH 1883 *Works of Old Masters & Scottish National Portraits*, exh. cat., Board of Manufactures, Edinburgh, 1883

EDINBURGH 1884 *Scottish National Portraits*, exh. cat., Board of Manufactures, Edinburgh, 1884

EDINBURGH 1901 *Pictures by Sir Henry Raeburn and other Deceased Painters of the Scottish School*, exh. cat., National Gallery of Scotland, Edinburgh, 1901

EDINBURGH 1951 *Exhibition of Raeburns and 18th Century Silver*, exh. cat., The National Trust for Scotland, Charlotte Square, Edinburgh, 1951

EDINBURGH 1956 *Raeburn Bi-Centenary Exhibition*, exh. cat., National Gallery of Scotland, Edinburgh, 1956

EDINBURGH 2006 *Henry Raeburn and his Printmakers*, by David Alexander with contributions from Viccy Coltman and Stephen Lloyd, exh. cat., The University of Edinburgh and the National Galleries of Scotland, Edinburgh, 2006

EDINBURGH and LONDON 1986–7 *Painting in Scotland: the Golden Age*, by Duncan Macmillan, exh. cat., Talbot Rice Art Centre, University of Edinburgh and Tate Gallery, London (Oxford: Phaidon Press), 1986–7

EDINBURGH and LONDON 1997–8 *Raeburn: the Art of Sir Henry Raeburn 1756–1823*, Duncan Thomson (ed.), exh. cat., Scottish National Portrait Gallery, Edinburgh and National Portrait Gallery, London, 1997–8 [including, Nicholas Phillipson, 'Manners, Morals and Characters: Henry Raeburn and the Scottish Enlightenment', pp. 29–38; John Dick, 'Raeburn's Methods and Materials', pp. 39–45; and David Mackie, 'Documentation', pp. 201–13]

EUROPEAN MAGAZINE 1823 Anon., 'Character of the late Sir Henry Raeburn, R.A.', *The European Magazine and London Review*, LXXXIV, November 1823, pp. 435–7

FORBES 1998 Forbes, Duncan, 'Raeburn, the Reviewers and the Referendum' [a review of Edinburgh and London 1997–8], *History Workshop Journal*, XLV, Spring 1998, pp. 223–6

GREIG 1911 Greig, James, *Sir Henry Raeburn, R.A.: his Life and Works with a Catalogue of his Pictures*, London: The Connoisseur (Otto Limited), 1911

HARRIS 1966 Harris, Rose, *Raeburn*, 'The Masters' series, XLVI, London: Purnell & Sons Ltd (Knowledge Publications), 1966

HENLEY 1890 Henley, William Ernest, *Sir Henry Raeburn: a Selection from his Portraits reproduced in Photogravure by T. and R. Annan with Introduction and Notes*, Edinburgh: T. and A. Constable for the Royal Association for Promotion of the Fine Arts in Scotland, 1890

IRWIN 1973 Irwin, Francina, 'Early Raeburn Reconsidered', *The Burlington Magazine*, CXC, April 1973, pp. 239–44

IRWIN and IRWIN 1975 Irwin, David and Irwin, Francina, *Scottish Painters at Home and Abroad 1700–1900*, London: Faber and Faber Ltd, 1975

KERR 1982 Kerr, Andrew, *A History of Ann Street*, Edinburgh: printed for private circulation, 1982

KIDSON 1997 Kidson, Alex, 'Raeburn: Edinburgh and London' [a review of Edinburgh and London 1997–8], *The Burlington Magazine*, CXXXIX, no. 1136, pp. 808–10

LLOYD 2003 Lloyd, Stephen, '"A very chowder-headed person", Raeburn's portraits of Scott', *Abbotsford and Sir Walter Scott: The Image and the Influence*, Iain Gordon Brown (ed.), Edinburgh: Society of Antiquaries of Scotland, 2003, pp. 98–114

LLOYD 2005 Lloyd, Stephen, '"Elegant and graceful attitudes": the painter of the "Skating Minister"', *The Burlington Magazine*, CXLVII, no. 1228, July 2005, pp. 474–86

LONDON 1877 *Catalogue of the Works of the late Sir Henry Raeburn, R.A., recently exhibited in the Royal Academy, National Galleries, Edinburgh, and Burlington House, which (by order of the Raeburn family) will be sold by auction*, Christie, Manson and Woods, London, 7 May 1877

LONDON 1911 *Pictures by Sir Henry Raeburn R.A.*, exh. cat., The French Gallery, Pall Mall, London, 1911

LONDON 1939 *Scottish Art*, exh. cat., Royal Academy of Arts, London, 1939

LONDON 1997 'Raeburn (Sir Henry) Collection of family papers relating to Raeburn's bankruptcy of 1808 . . . ', Sale of Books, Manuscripts, Photographs, Atlases and Maps, Phillips, New Bond Street, London, 13 November 1997, lot 350 [purchased in 1997 by the National Library of Scotland, Edinburgh, Acc. 11479]

McKAY 1906 McKay, William D., *The Scottish School of Painting*, London: Duckworth, 1906

MACKIE 1994 Mackie, David, 'Raeburn, Life and Art', unpublished Ph.D. thesis, 6 vols, University of Edinburgh, 1994

MACMILLAN 2000 Macmillan, Duncan, *Scottish Art 1460–2000*, Edinburgh: Mainstream, 2000 [1st edn 1990]

MACMILLAN 1996–7 Macmillan, Duncan, 'Oil Portraits and Portrait Galleries', *The Carlyle Society Papers*, new series, X, 1996–7

MILES 1973–4 Miles, Hamish, 'Raeburn's Portraits of the 4th Earl of Hopetoun', *Scottish Art Review*, XIV, no. 2, 1973, pp. 30–6 and 'Postscript to Raeburn's portraits of the 4th Earl of Hopetoun', ibid., XIV, no. 3, 1974, p. 28

MORRISON 1843 Morrison, John, 'Reminiscences of Sir Walter Scott, The Ettrick Shepherd, Sir Henry Raeburn, &c, &c. – No. II', *Tait's Edinburgh Magazine*, X, 1843, pp. 780–83

MURRAY and SCOTT 1824 [Murray, Hugh and Scott, Sir Walter], 'Sir Henry Raeburn, R.A.' [Obituary], *The Annual Biography and Obituary for 1823*, VII, London, 1824, pp. 378–91

NENADIC 2010 Nenadic, Stana (ed.), *Scots in London in the Eighteenth Century*, Lewisburg: Bucknell University Press, 2010

NGS 1997 *The National Gallery of Scotland: Concise Catalogue of Paintings*, Edinburgh: National Galleries of Scotland 1997

O'DONOGHUE and HAKE 1908–25 O'Donoghue, Freeman and Hake, Henry M., *Catalogue of Engraved British Portraits preserved in the Department of Prints and Drawings in the British Museum*, 6 vols, London, 1908–25

PINNINGTON 1904 Pinnington, Edward, *Sir Henry Raeburn R.A.*, London, 1904

ROBERTSON 1897 Robertson, Emily (ed.), *Letters and Papers of Andrew Robertson, A. M., born, 1777, died 184, miniature painter to his late Royal Highness the Duke of Sussex; also a treatise on the Art by his eldest brother Archibald Robertson, born 1765, died 1835, of New York*, London: Spottiswoode, 1897

SANDERSON 1925 Sanderson, Kenneth, 'Engravings after Raeburn', *Print Collectors' Quarterly*, XII, 1925, pp. 128–55

SMAILES 1990 Smailes, Helen E., *The Concise Catalogue of the Scottish National Portrait Gallery*, Edinburgh: National Galleries of Scotland, 1990

SMAILES 2009 Smailes, Helen E., '"Uno Sfortunato Scultore Scozzese chiamato Campbell": the Correspondence of Thomas Campbell (1791–1858) and his Banking Maecenas, Gilbert Innes of Stow (1751–1832)', *Walpole Society*, LXXI, 2009, pp. 217–323

SODEN 2006 Soden, Joanna, 'The Raeburn Studio Revived', *Scottish Society of Art Historians Bulletin*, Autumn / Winter 2006, pp. 4–5

STEVENSON 1992 Stevenson, Robert Louis, 'Some Portraits by Raeburn' (from *Virginibus Puerisque*, 1881), *R. L. Stevenson: Essays and Poems*, Claire Harman (ed.), London: J. M. Dent Ltd, 1992, pp. 31–7

STEVENSON 1998 Stevenson, Lesley A., 'The technique of Sir Henry Raeburn examined in the context of late-eighteenth century British portraiture', *Painting Techniques, History, Materials and Studio Practice (The International Institute for Conservation: Contributions to the Dublin Congress, 7–11 September 1998)*, Ashok Roy and Perry Smith (eds), London, 1998, pp. 194–9

THOMSON 1994 Thomson, Duncan, *Sir Henry Raeburn 1756–1823*, Scottish Masters Series, XXI, Edinburgh: National Galleries of Scotland, 1994

THOMSON 2007 Thomson, Duncan. 'Raeburn revisited: the "Skating Minster"', *The Burlington Magazine*, CXLIX, no. 1248, March 2007, pp. 185–90

Notes on the Contributors

DAVID ALEXANDER is Honorary Keeper of British Prints at the Fitzwilliam Museum, University of Cambridge, and has contributed to many publications on eighteenth-century prints. His publications include *Affecting Moments: Prints of English Literature made in the Age of Romantic Sensibility* (York, 1993), and *Richard Newton and English Caricature in the 1790s* (Manchester, 1998). He wrote the main essay in the catalogue for the exhibition, *Henry Raeburn and his Printmakers*, held at the University of Edinburgh in 2006. He has recently compiled a catalogue of the prints of George Vertue and is currently working on a *Dictionary of British and Irish Engravers 1714–1830*.

ROBYN ASLESON is an independent art historian based in Washington, DC, specialising in British art of the eighteenth and nineteenth centuries. She has a particular interest in Anglo-American crosscurrents in art, patronage, and collecting. Her publications include *A Passion for Performance: Sarah Siddons and Her Portraitists* (Getty, 1999), *British Paintings at The Huntington* (New Haven, 2001); *Great British Paintings from American Collections* (New Haven, 2002); *Notorious Muse: The Actress in British Art and Culture, 1776–1812* (New Haven, 2003). She is currently researching the critical reputation and technical influence of Thomas Lawrence in nineteenth-century America.

PHILIPPE BORDES is Professor in the Department of History of Art at the Université Lumière – Lyon 2. He was founding director of the Musée de la Révolution française (Vizille) from 1984 to 1996. He has taught in several universities in Europe and the United States (Montpellier, UCLA, University College London, Paris Ouest). From 2007 to 2010, he was director of the department of studies and research at the Institut national d'histoire de l'art in Paris. The author of numerous articles and books on the art of the French Revolution and Empire, he recently published *Représenter la Révolution* (Lyon, 2010). His current projects include a history of representations of the family in modern Europe and a critical edition of the letters of Jacques-Louis David.

VICCY COLTMAN is a Senior Lecturer and Head of History of Art at the University of Edinburgh. She is the author of *Fabricating the Antique: Neoclassicism in Britain, 1760–1800* (Chicago, 2006) and *Classical Sculpture and the Culture of Collecting in Britain since 1760* (Oxford, 2009). An edited volume *Making Sense of Greek Art* is forthcoming with Exeter University Press. She has been the recipient of various research fellowships, notably in the United States and is currently working on a new book project devoted to the representation of Scots and Scotland in metropolitan, cosmopolitan and imperial contexts, from 1745 to 1832.

MATTHEW CRASKE is a Reader in Art History at Oxford Brookes. He has published a number of books and articles on eighteenth-century Western art, including most recently *The Silent Rhetoric of the Body: A history of monumental sculpture and commemorative art in England, 1720–1770* (New Haven, 2007). Although specialising in British sculpture, he has written on design, architecture, and painting in the period from the Restoration to the accession of Queen Victoria.

GODFREY EVANS is Principal Curator of European Applied Art at the National Museums Scotland, Edinburgh. He was awarded his Ph.D. on Alexander, 10th Duke of Hamilton, as patron and collector in 2009 and has recently published articles on the 10th Duke's restoration and enlargement of Hamilton Palace in the *Review of Scottish Culture* (2009), and the 11th Duke and Duchess of Hamilton and France in the *Journal of the Scottish Society for Art History* (2009–10). Dr Evans is a director of the Virtual Hamilton Palace Trust and is currently supervising aspects of the Hamilton collection with the history of art department at the University of Glasgow.

STEPHEN LLOYD is Curator of the Derby Collection at Knowsley Hall on Merseyside. He was previously Senior Curator at the Scottish National Portrait Gallery (1993–2009) and President of ICOM's Committee for Museums and Collections of Fine Arts (2004–10). He received his D.Phil. on the Regency artists Richard and Maria Cosway, about whom he organised an exhibition at the National Portrait Galleries in Edinburgh and London in 1995–6; he is completing monographs on both artists. A specialist in the history and collecting of portrait miniatures, in 2008–9 he co-curated with

Kim Sloan an exhibition held at the Scottish National Portrait Gallery and the British Museum, *The Intimate Portrait: Drawings, pastels and miniatures from Ramsay to Lawrence.*

JORDAN MEARNS is a Ph.D. candidate in History of Art at the University of Edinburgh. His research centres on the role of Scottish art in the formation of a notional British school of art, its reception in metropolitan exhibition culture and particularly in the treatment of Scottish subject matter by non-Scottish artists. He has previously been a graduate curatorial intern at The Frick Collection, New York, and recently worked as an exhibition research assistant at the National Galleries of Scotland, preparing a touring exhibition on the depiction of golf in art.

OLIVIER MESLAY is Associate Director of Curatorial Affairs at the Dallas Museum of Art. Until 2006, he was in charge of British, Spanish and American art in the Painting Department at the Louvre, where the exhibitions he curated include: *D'outre Manche, British Art in French Public Collections*; *Constable, selected by Lucian Freud*; *British art in the collections of the Académie française*; and *William Hogarth*. He has published extensively on British art and France.

STANA NENADIC is Senior Lecturer in Social History at the University of Edinburgh and a Commissioner of the Royal Commission on the Ancient and Historical Monuments of Scotland. Her research is mainly concerned with the middle classes and elites in Britain in the eighteenth and nineteenth centuries. She is also interested in material culture. She is the author of *Lairds and Luxury: the Highland Gentry in Eighteenth-century Scotland* (Edinburgh, 2007) and editor of a recent volume of essays titled *Scots in London in the Eighteenth Century* (Lewisburg, 2010). Her current project is concerned with professionals in London and Edinburgh, 1750–1800.

HELEN E. SMAILES has been Senior Curator of British Art at the National Gallery of Scotland since 1993 and an Honorary Fellow in History of Art at the University of Edinburgh, since 2005. Her research interests include British eighteenth- and nineteenth-century narrative painting, Scottish nineteenth-century figure and portrait sculpture, plaster casts and early art education in Britain. A recognised authority on the Scottish sculptor Thomas Campbell, she published a critical edition of his correspondence with his first patron Gilbert Innes of Stow in *The Walpole Society* (2009). She is currently engaged on a critical catalogue of the Scottish National Gallery's collection of over five hundred Scottish paintings.

SARAH SYMMONS is a former Reader in Art History at the University of Essex. She has established an international reputation as the author of six books on Spanish art and British eighteenth- and nineteenth-century sculpture, which have received many awards. Her latest book *Goya: a life in letters* (London, 2004) is the definitive English edition of Goya's writings. She contributed to *English Accents* (Aldershot, 2004), a study of Spanish attitudes to eighteenth-century British art, and to *Spanish Art in Britain and Ireland 1750–1920* (Woodbridge, 2010). She has organised exhibitions on British Romantic Art and on the sculptor John Flaxman; a biography of the Honourable Mary Graham is in preparation.

NICHOLAS TROMANS has taught at Kingston University, London, since 2005. He has specialised in nineteenth-century British painting, with a particular interest in the popular experience of art in this period. His most recent books are *David Wilkie: The People's Painter* (Edinburgh, 2007), *The Lure of the East: British Orientalist Painting* (as editor, London, 2008), *Hope: The Life and Times of a Victorian Icon* (Compton, 2011) and *Richard Dadd: The Artist and the Asylum* (London, 2011). He is now writing a book about pictures in domestic interiors.

Index

EU Authorised Representative:

Easy Access System Europe Mustamäe tee 50, 10621 Tallinn, Estonia

gpsr.requests@easproject.com

Printed and bound by CPI Group (UK) Ltd, Croydon, CR0 4YY

13/03/2026

02070943-0001